THE MAKING OF SELIM

THE MAKING OF SELIM

Succession, Legitimacy, and Memory in the Early Modern Ottoman World

H. Erdem Çıpa

Indiana University Press
Bloomington and Indianapolis

This book is a publication of

Indiana University Press
Office of Scholarly Publishing
Herman B Wells Library 350
1320 East 10th Street
Bloomington, Indiana 47405 USA

iupress.indiana.edu

The paper used in this publication meets the minimum requirements of the American National Standard for Information Sciences—Permanence of Paper for Printed Library Materials, ANSI Z39.48-1992.

Manufactured in the United States of America

Library of Congress Cataloging-in-Publication Data

Names: Çıpa, H. Erdem, author.
Title: The making of Selim : succession, legitimacy, and memory in the early modern Ottoman world / H. Erdem Çıpa.
Description: Bloomington : Indiana University Press, 2017. | Includes bibliographical references and index.
Identifiers: LCCN 2016037588 (print) | LCCN 2016050318 (ebook) | ISBN 9780253024237 (cloth : alk. paper) | ISBN 9780253024282 (pbk. : alk. paper) | ISBN 9780253024350 (ebook)
Subjects: LCSH: Selim I, Sultan of the Turks, 1470-1520. | Turkey—History—Selim I, 1512-1520.
Classification: LCC DR504 .C56 2017 (print) | LCC DR504 (ebook) | DDC 956/.015—dc23
LC record available at https://lccn.loc.gov/2016037588

1 2 3 4 5 21 20 19 18 17

To Christiane—haklısın, evimiz saraydır . . .

Contents

Acknowledgments *ix*
Note on Transliteration *xiii*

Introduction *1*

Part 1. The Making of a Sultan

1 Politics of Succession: Selīm's Path to the Throne *29*

2 Politics of Factions *62*

Part 2. The Creation of Selīm's Composite Image

Part 2. Introduction: A Historiographical Survey *111*

3 Selīm, the Legitimate Ruler *132*

4 Selīm, the Idealized Ruler *176*

5 Selīm, the Divinely Ordained Ruler *210*

Conclusion *251*

Notes *257*
Bibliography *367*
Index *413*

Acknowledgments

I REMAIN INDEBTED to various institutions and many friends, colleagues, and family members, who all generously helped me in more ways than one over the years that this study was in the making. It is a great pleasure to finally thank them for all their support, encouragement, guidance, and criticism, without which this book would not have come to fruition.

Research for this study was conducted with the assistance of the Center for Middle Eastern Studies at Harvard University; the Arthur Lehman Scholarship for dissertation research; the Joukowsky Family Foundation grant of the American Research Institute in Turkey; Indiana University's College Arts and Humanities Institute research travel grant; and the Research Center for Anatolian Civilizations at Koç University, Istanbul. I would also like to thank these organizations at the University of Michigan, Ann Arbor: the College of Literature, Science, and the Arts; the Islamic Studies Program; the Office of Research; and the ADVANCE Faculty Summer Writing Grants Program. I have been lucky to hold joint appointments in two academic units, and thus my sincere thanks go to the Department of History and the Department of Near Eastern Studies for welcoming me into an intellectually stimulating and nurturing environment. Both departments provided the financial support necessary to complete the final phases of research, copyediting, and indexing for this book.

I conducted the greater part of my research in Istanbul. I am grateful for the assistance provided by the archivists, librarians, and staff at the Ottoman Archives of the Prime Ministry, the Süleymaniye Library, the Istanbul University Central Library, and the Topkapı Palace Museum. I thank the staff at the Topkapı Palace Museum Archives as well as the former director of the archives, Ülkü Altındağ, and the current director, Sevgi Ağca. I am particularly grateful to Gülendam

Nakipoğlu and Zeynep Çelik-Atbaş at the Topkapı Palace Museum Library. I also extend my heartfelt thanks to my dear friend and photographer extraordinaire Hadiye Cangökçe for providing the digital image reproduced on the cover of this book. Last but not least, I thank Muhittin Eren and Salih Aguş of Eren Kitap for helping me locate even the rarest scholarly books.

Throughout the research and writing process, I was fortunate that friends and colleagues agreed to read parts or all of the text at various stages of completion. They offered invaluable advice, insightful comments, and constructive criticism. They saved me from numerous pitfalls and helped me correct several mistakes. Cemal Kafadar has been a true mentor and constant inspiration since the moment I became his advisee—a long, long time ago. Over the years, Yücel Demirel and the late Şinasi Tekin taught me the intricacies of Ottoman Turkish. I could not have dealt with the narrative material in Persian without Wheeler Thackston, who introduced me to that language and its poetry during my graduate years. Emine Fetvacı and Christiane Gruber shared their expertise in all things art historical, while Mariya Kiprovska and Grigor Boykov generously helped me with all things Rumelian. Kaya Şahin read the complete manuscript and provided thoughtful commentary and constructive criticism. In addition, I benefited immensely from the scholarly guidance and critical insight provided by my senior colleagues in Ann Arbor. Kathryn Babayan and Val Kivelson, my "official" mentors, offered their friendship along with their academic expertise and helped me to think about my project within a larger theoretical and comparative framework. My "unofficial" mentor, Gottfried Hagen, generously shared his seemingly endless knowledge of early modern Ottoman history and historiography. Gary Beckman, Kathleen Canning, Katherine French, and Raymond van Dam participated in my manuscript workshop and were joined by Jane Hathaway and Douglas Howard in helping me sprint toward the finish line. I discussed various aspects of this study with and received helpful feedback from many other individuals. I extend my thanks to

Nuri Akbayar, Yiğit Akın, Helga Anetshofer, Sabri Ateş, Evrim Binbaş, Günhan Börekçi, Giancarlo Casale, Murat Dağlı, Suraiya Faroqhi, Cornell Fleischer, Şükrü Ilıcak, Ahmet T. Karamustafa, Hakan Karateke, Alexander Knysh, Cihan Yüksel Muslu, Can Nacar, Gülru Necipoğlu, Leslie Peirce, Ahmet Tunç Şen, Baki Tezcan, Nabil al-Tikriti, and the two anonymous reviewers for Indiana University Press. I would like to express my gratitude for their suggestions and improvements that I incorporated and my apologies for those I resisted. Any faults or weaknesses that remain in this study are entirely my own.

I am also thankful to those who assisted in the production of this book. I owe a great debt of gratitude to Robert Sloan, former editor in chief at Indiana University Press, who supported the project from its inception. Gary Dunham, director of the Press, and Janice E. Frisch, assistant editor, prepared the book for publication in an exceptionally smooth manner. Janet Rauscher copyedited the original manuscript with her typically meticulous touch. It is also thanks to her that this book has an index. Once at the Press, the text benefited from the editing skills and suggestions of Gretchen Otto and Alison Rainey as well. Last but not least, I would like to thank Rachel Trudell-Jones for the beautiful maps she produced.

No words of appreciation can express my gratitude to my family in Istanbul. I am eternally grateful to my parents, Sabiha and Erdinç Çıpa; my sister, Şebnem Belgin; and my uncle Ergin Tınaz for having made their unconditional love felt from across the ocean. Whip smart, strong willed, and absolutely adorable, my little niece, Melek is still too young to realize how much dancing, playing, and just being with her invigorated me throughout the writing process.

Last but certainly not least, I wish to dedicate this book to Christiane Gruber, my much better half and partner in crime, co-çapulcu and squirrel whisperer, who has embraced me with love and encouragement—and patience—since the moment we met at the Topkapı Palace Museum Library more than a decade ago. With her serene strength, she was a constant source of support throughout the gestation of this book. She read every single line, even the boring parts. She helped me clarify my arguments for the non-Ottomanist reader. She made critical observations and always-helpful suggestions about my writing. I owe my peace and sanity to her soothing presence as well as to our winged, finned, and rooted progeny at home.

Note on Transliteration

For the sake of consistency, all Arabic, Persian, and Ottoman Turkish titles of historical works, the names of their authors, and original quotations have been transliterated. Ottoman Turkish, Arabic, and Persian words have been transliterated according to the *International Journal of Middle East Studies* system, with the exception that, in Ottoman-Turkish words, *ḫ* has been used for خ and *h* for ه. Persian words follow the Arabic transliteration system, but their slight variations in pronunciation have been taken into consideration. The titles of historical works were transliterated in accordance with the language of composition.

All personal names and technical terms were also fully transliterated. For the sake of convenience and legibility, however, words that appear in English dictionaries (for example, *sultan, pasha,* and *kadi*) have been Anglicized unless they appear as part of an individual's name. Place names have been given in their modern and commonly accepted Anglicized forms (for example, Bosnia, not Bosna).

Names of individuals are followed by their year of death (d.), regnal years (r.), or, for authors, the years during which their literary activities flourished (fl.) if their dates of death are unknown. When dates of death or activity have not been fully established, several dates or a range of dates (ca.) are given. Unless otherwise specified, dates follow the Gregorian calendar.

THE MAKING OF SELIM

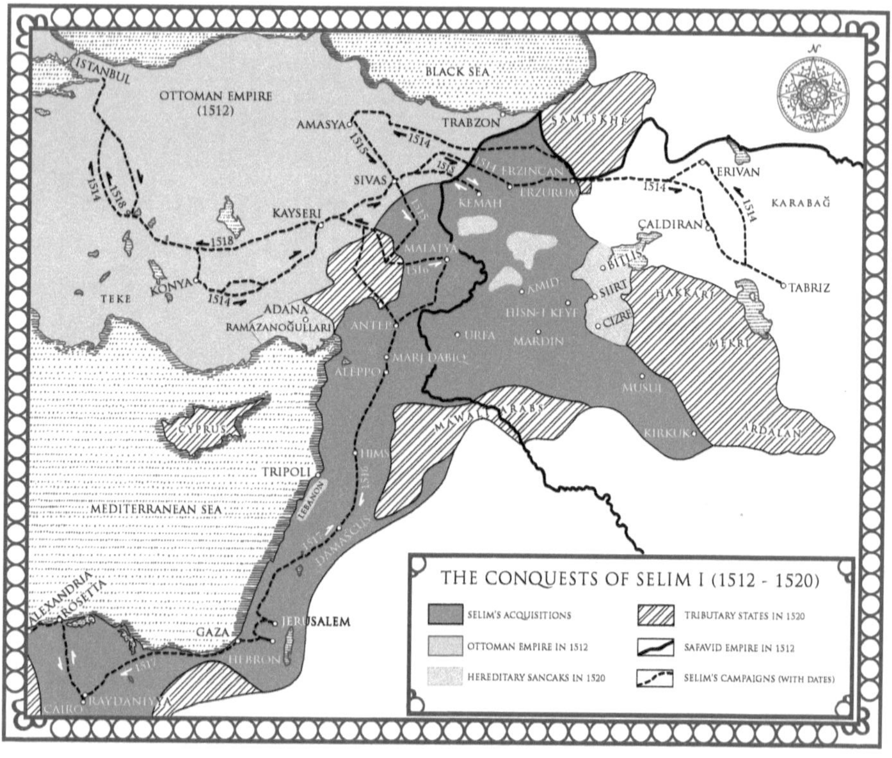

Map 0.1. The Conquests of Selīm I, 1512–1520. Map by Rachel Trudell-Jones. Based on "Map XX," in Donald Edgar Pitcher, *An Historical Geography of the Ottoman Empire from Earliest Times to the End of the Sixteenth Century* (Leiden: Brill, 1972).

Introduction

On SEPTEMBER 22, 1520, Selīm I died of a boil.[1] The reign of the conqueror of eastern Anatolia, Syria, and Egypt thus ended not with a bang but with a whimper. For a monarch who had established the Ottomans' incontrovertible domination in the Islamic world and styled himself "Master of the Auspicious Conjunction" (*ṣāḥib-ḳırān*) and "Shadow of God" (*ẓıll-Allāh*), this was undoubtedly an incongruous fate. Chroniclers of the Ottoman tradition narrate proudly that Selīm, while still a prince, had defeated the "infidel" (*kāfir*) Georgians, crushed the armies of the "heretical" (*mülḥid, zındīḳ*) Safavids in 1514, and brought Mamluk history to a close three years later. In addition to applauding Selīm for his expansionist strategies and effective military expeditions, both of which doubled the geographical extent of the Ottoman realm, authors also praise him for having been the first Ottoman ruler to use the title "Servitor of the Two Sacred Cities (that is, Mecca and Medina)" (*ḫādimü'l-ḥarameyn*), thus giving further credence during his reign to Ottoman claims of preeminence in the lands of Islamdom. In numerous contemporary accounts he is hailed as the ever-victorious combatant sultan, the ultimate "Warrior of Faith" (*ġāzī*), "Messiah" (*mehdī*), and "Renewer of the Faith" (*müceddid*). Resolute but just, Selīm was considered the ideal Muslim ruler personified.

When addressing the circumstances of Selīm's death, however, some of the same chroniclers also allude to the controversial nature of his ascendance to the Ottoman throne. Reminding their readers that he was a valiant but violent prince who forcibly deposed his father, Bāyezīd II (r. 1481–1512), the legitimate ruling sultan, they remark in a discernibly didactic tone—and not without a certain degree of irony—that Selīm "migrated from the Abode of Annihilation [that is, this world] to the Abode of Eternity [that is, the other world] at the spot where he had fought his father."[2] Some go further and insinuate that the deposed Bāyezīd's death—on his way to mandatory retirement—was caused, or at least expedited, by his ambitious son.[3] Noting the frequency with which Selīm executed his viziers, several chroniclers also remark that rival members of the Ottoman military ruling elite cursed one another by wishing for their opponents to be granted high offices by Selīm;[4] others provide gory details of the fate awaiting those unfortunate enough to be on the receiving end of Selīm's wrath.[5] One such account recalls Selīm so enraged that he not only ordered an Ottoman statesman to be decapitated but also kicked the severed head of the deceased multiple times when it was brought to him by the royal guards.[6]

The myriad images of Selīm I projected by Ottoman historiography oscillate between hero and villain. Such ambiguity is likewise reflected in the dubious meaning of his posthumously acquired epithet. Ottoman chronicles remember Selīm's forefathers with honorific titles such as "Warrior of Faith" (*Ġāzī*), "Lord" (*Ḫüdāvendigār*), "Thunderbolt" (*Yıldırım*), "Conqueror" (*Fātiḥ*), "Saint" (*Velī*), and "Devout" (*Ṣofu*).[7] In European sources, Selīm's own son Süleymān I (r. 1520–1566) is frequently dubbed "the Magnificent," while in Ottoman chronicles he is praised as "the Lawgiver" (*Ḳānūnī*). Due to his controversial rise to the Ottoman throne and his iron-fisted style of rule, however, Selīm is less laudably remembered as "the Grim" (*Yāvuz*).[8]

Despite the absence of any definitive textual evidence that "yāvuz" was used for Selīm I during his time, in all modern Turkish scholarship the appellation is employed uncritically as descriptive praise, even a complimentary nickname.[9] In reality, like some other members of the House of ʿOs̱mān, Selīm appears to have acquired his title only posthumously.[10] In fact, to the best of my knowledge, the earliest usage of "yāvuz" as Selīm's epithet is recorded in an anonymous work composed by a veteran janissary nearly a century after Selīm's death, during the reign of Aḥmed I (r. 1603–1617).[11] Furthermore, the only reference explaining how Selīm came to be known as "yāvuz" is included in a mid-nineteenth-century copy of an anonymous chronicle. Written by an author with a discernibly critical attitude toward Selīm, this apocryphal tale portrays him as the insolent governor-general of Anatolia (*Anaṭolı beglerbegi*) who did not contribute even one asper (*aḳçe*) to the imperial treasury (*mīrī*) during his ten-year gubernatorial tenure. The anonymous author further notes that, when notified of his son's truancy, Bāyezīd II reportedly stated, "That is how that boy became grim (*yāvuz*)."[12]

The Reign of Selīm I

There is no doubt that Selīm acquired his unseemly epithet due to his brutal efficiency in enacting affairs of the state. It seems that Selīm resembled his grandfather Meḥmed II ("the Conqueror," r. 1444–1446 and 1451–1481), insomuch as his reign was marked by a ruthless strategy of territorial expansion. Unlike his own father, Bāyezīd II, whose reign can be characterized as one of prolonged consolidation, Selīm almost doubled the geographical extent of the Empire during his short reign of eight years.[13] His triumph against the Safavids at the Battle of Çaldıran in 1514, together with the fatal blow he inflicted on the principality of Dulkadir in 1515, brought eastern and southeastern Anatolia under unquestionable Ottoman control; his victories against the Mamluks in 1516 and 1517 added Syria, Palestine, Egypt, and the Hijaz to the Ottoman domain. Selīm's territorial gains—and the unprecedented revenue sources his empire commanded after the annexation of Egypt—without a doubt planted the seed for the Ottoman imperial grandeur typically associated with the reign of his son, Süleymān I.[14] This fact is acknowledged by numerous Ottoman authors, but perhaps none have expressed it as explicitly as did the renowned statesman and litterateur Luṭfī Pasha (d. 1563). Luṭfī Pasha, who had been at the pinnacle of the Ottoman imperial administrative hierarchy as Süleymān's grand vizier (1539–1541), emphasized the significance of Selīm's reign for the achievements of the Süleymānic age by stating in his dynastic history, entitled *Tevārīḫ-i āl-i ʿOs̱mān* (Chronicles of the House of ʿOs̱mān), that "Sulṭān Selīm faced the troubles of this world, cleared its thorns and thistles, and transformed it into an orchard [while] Sulṭān Süleymān received and possessed the fruits of that orchard without any trouble or hardship."[15]

Chronicles of the Ottoman dynasty are in agreement that Süleymān was the heir presumptive throughout Selīm's reign. There even exists a tradition that the "thorns and thistles" that Selīm cleared included three of his own sons, who were executed in 1514—on the eve of the expedition against the Safavids—in order to secure Süleymān's unchallenged accession in the event that Selīm should die while campaigning against Shāh Ismāʿīl (r. 1501–1524).[16] European sources also allude to the great lengths to which Selīm went to clear Süleymān's path to the throne. In fact, the account of the renowned French polymath Guillaume Postel (d. 1581) appears to confirm the Ottoman tradition regarding Selīm's execution of his three sons. Postel, who served as interpreter to Jean de la Forêt (d. 1537), the first official French ambassador to the Ottoman court (1534–1537), relates that, in an effort to assess the loyalty of his sons, Selīm announced to them that he was contemplating retirement from the sultanate and asked which of them wished to replace him. In Postel's words, "Those who were so bold as to respond died. . . . Sultan Süleymān, admonished by his mother, who understood the Prince [that is, Selīm], refused all, and said he was his father's slave, and not his son, and that even after his death he could assume that responsibility only with the greatest distress."[17] Some (possibly apocryphal) sources even mention that Selīm refrained from consorting with women so as not to jeopardize Süleymān's future sultanate by fathering additional sons.[18] Although it is impossible to ascertain whether Selīm's (ultimately successful) strategy of securing Süleymān's sultanate involved violence against his other sons, the fact that Süleymān was the only prince whom Selīm appointed to a gubernatorial seat indicates that he had been groomed for the Ottoman throne throughout his father's reign. Selīm's policy of privileging Süleymān not only secured the sultanate for the latter—thereby preventing an internecine war among his potential heirs—but also precluded any challenge to Selīm during his own reign.

Although Süleymān "the Magnificent" and his reign have been the preferred subjects of inquiry in the field of Ottoman history,[19] recent scholarship hints at the importance of Selīm's role in determining the political, religious, and cultural agenda of the Ottoman enterprise throughout the sixteenth century.[20] Duly highlighted in this context are the expansion of Ottoman territories at the expense of the Ottomans' Safavid and Mamluk neighbors; the articulation of a political theology identifying the Ottomans as the preeminent Sunnī rulers in Islamdom;[21] the formulation of Ottoman claims of universal sovereignty vis-à-vis the Habsburgs, the Safavids, and the Mamluks; and the construction of a truly imperial polity with a sophisticated, routinized administrative and bureaucratic apparatus. Without a doubt, Selīm played a pioneering role in all of these arenas.

Contemporary historical narratives praise Selīm as the foremost warrior-sultan. They also unanimously emphasize the Ottomans' military superiority as compared to the Safavids and the Mamluks, highlighting the unprecedented extent to which Selīm harnessed the potential of gunpowder technologies against his Muslim rivals.[22] Although they disagree on the total number of soldiers in the imperial armies of the three Islamic polities, these narratives consistently report that at the Battle of Çaldıran (August 23, 1514), Selīm deployed five hundred field cannons and twelve thousand janissary musketeers against Shāh Ismāʿīl, who had neither muskets nor cannons.[23] Moreover, at Marj Dabik (August 24, 1516) and Ridaniyya (January 22, 1517), Selīm's troops faced Mamluk armies who were at the early stages of embracing gunpowder technologies but nevertheless were no match for the (many more) Ottoman cannons.[24] As a result of Selīm's victory against the Safavids in 1514, the Ottomans extended their rule over eastern and southeastern Anatolia.[25] With the conquest of the Dulkadirid domains in 1515, Selīm secured a military itinerary against his next target, the Mamluks of Egypt. The defeats that Qānṣūh al-Ghawrī (r. 1501–1516) and Ṭūmānbāy (r. 1516–1517) suffered at Selīm's hands in 1516 and 1517, respectively, brought Syria, Palestine, Egypt, and the holy cities of Mecca and Medina under Ottoman sovereignty.[26] Taking full advantage of the unquestionable supremacy of his armies over those of his rivals, Selīm followed an unrelenting policy of territorial expansion, establishing Ottoman preeminence in the Abode of Islam (*dār al-Islām*).[27]

The establishment of Ottoman domination in Islamdom required more than military might, however. Selīm also needed to articulate a coherent theological response to the politico-ideological challenges represented by the Safavids and the Mamluks. To that end, he sought the espousal of the Ottoman religious establishment, and numerous scholars of religion (*ʿulemā*) were pleased to oblige.[28] Additionally, the campaign against the Safavids was sanctioned specifically by the legal opinions (*fetvā*) of two distinguished religious scholars, Mevlānā Nūreddīn Ḥamza Ṣarugürz (d. 1521) and Kemālpaşazāde (İbn Kemāl, d. 1534), both of whom opined that Shāh Ismāʿīl and his followers were "unbelievers and heretics" (*kāfir ve mülḥid*) and that it was incumbent on the "Sultan of Islam" (*Sulṭān-ı İslām*) to eradicate them.[29] It was with the backing of religious decrees like these that Selīm ordered the systematic massacre of tens of thousands of Shāh Ismāʿīl's Anatolian sympathizers before embarking on the Çaldıran campaign.[30] Before he died, Selīm asked for the renewal of legal opinions sanctioning war against the Safavids, which further suggests that he identified Shāh Ismāʿīl as his primary target.[31]

For the Sunnī Ottomans, who styled themselves as the defenders of "true religion," establishing the legality of war against the Shīʿite Safavids does not appear to have constituted much of a challenge. In fact, Kemālpaşazāde, who was appointed to the highest office in the Ottoman religious hierarchy, serving Süleymān I as chief jurisconsult (*şeyḫü'l-islām*) between 1526 and 1534, analogized the war against Shāh Ismāʿīl and his followers to that waged against non-Muslim enemies of Islam (*cihād*).[32] The Mamluks, however, were Sunnī Muslims who, at the time, served as guardians of the "Two Sacred Cities (that is, Mecca and Medina)." Because Islamic law considered as permissible "only a war having an ultimate religious purpose, that is, to enforce the sacred law (*sharīʿa*) or to check transgression against it," Selīm's military strategy against the Mamluks was canonically questionable at best.[33] Once again, though, members of the Ottoman religious establishment provided the legal justification Selīm needed. Based on reports suggesting that the Mamluks were colluding with the Safavids,[34] religious scholars declared that "those who aid heretics are themselves heretics" (*mülḥidlere muʿāvenet itmeleriyle mülḥid ḥükminde olurlar*). Thus, the *ʿulemā* voiced their full support of Selīm's hardline policy of religious conformity.[35]

Both the frequency and the scale of Selīm's remarkable military endeavors required rigorous control and regulation of manpower, deployment of increasingly large financial resources, and improved management of imperial revenue sources.[36] Since the inception of the Ottoman polity, the single largest source of military manpower—the provincial cavalry (*tīmārlı sipāhī*, or *timariot*)—was sustained by the assignment of nonhereditary prebends (*tīmār*) in exchange for obligatory military service.[37] In the beginning of the sixteenth century, when the pulse of Shāh Ismāʿīl's politico-religious movement was being thoroughly felt in Anatolia, Ottoman subjects who joined the Safavid cause included not only nomads, tribesmen, and townsfolk but also, and most prominently, disgruntled *tīmār*-holders.[38] To achieve tighter control over provincial, especially Anatolian, cavalrymen, Selīm followed some of his grandfather Meḥmed II's centralizing strategies.[39] He imposed strict regulations regarding the obligations of *timariots*;[40] he assigned Anatolian fiefs to cavalrymen whom he transferred from the Balkan provinces;[41] and, in the eastern provinces of the Empire, he granted privileges such as freehold rights and internal autonomy to several Kurdish tribal leaders in order to secure their loyalty and cooperation in his struggle against the Safavids.[42] Through such measures, Selīm not only significantly undermined age-old networks of local allegiances but also demonstrated that he was the principal, if not the sole, source of political power and sustenance in his realm.[43]

Even following these crucial steps toward the co-optation and/or assimilation of local power holders, Selīm still faced the challenge of establishing definitive control over eastern and southeastern Anatolia, greater Syria, and Egypt. In addition to representing a geographical shift in the center of gravity for the Ottomans, these acquisitions also signified a demographic—and hence cultural—shift. To begin with, the near doubling of the empire's territories resulted in a proportionate rise in the number of Ottoman subjects. As conqueror of the Arab heartlands of the postcaliphal Islamic world, Selīm also became the first Ottoman monarch to rule over a predominantly Muslim population. Over time, this significant development resulted in fuller implementation of traditional Islamic practices and institutions from the Arab provinces in Ottoman administrative, bureaucratic, and religious establishments.[44]

For their political dominance to endure in the newly acquired territories, the Ottomans faced the choice of either creating a new bureaucratic-administrative apparatus or incorporating into their own structure existing mechanisms created by earlier, mostly Islamic, polities. They ended up doing a little of both. The integration of centuries-old institutions, laws, regulations, and customs, established by previous Muslim states, into the Ottoman legal, bureaucratic, and administrative machinery would "require a careful work of harmonization and adaptation on the part of the Ottomans."[45] Selīm did not live long enough to accomplish it, however. In fact, the Ottoman administrative reorganization of and significant degree of control over the Mamluks of Egypt and the finances of the province were instituted during the reign of Selīm's son Süleymān I after a new Egyptian law and tax code had been prepared by grand vizier İbrāhīm Pasha (d. 1536).[46] While bureaucratic-administrative consolidation in the newly acquired territories ultimately was achieved during the Süleymānic age, there is little doubt that the foundations of a sustainable Ottoman administration were laid during Selīm's reign. In addition to instituting the financial commissariat-general of the newly conquered Safavid and Mamluk territories (*ʿArab ve ʿAcem defterdārlıġı*), Selīm ordered the preparation of cadastral surveys (*taḥrīr*) for greater Syria in order to register revenue sources, record the status of all arable land—that is, freehold (*mülk*), pious endowment (*vakıf*), or eligible for distribution as a prebend (*tīmār*)—and initiate construction and repair work on infrastructural projects, such as irrigation systems.[47] In Egypt, he not only completed land surveys and registered the status of all agricultural property in court records but also established a court system in which all four schools of religio-legal thought (*mez̲heb*) were represented.[48]

Territorial expansion into Arab lands and an augmented institutional infrastructure supporting an integrated bureaucratic-administrative apparatus constituted essential components of the Ottoman process of empire building.[49] Yet the establishment of a truly imperial legal, bureaucratic, and administrative system also depended on learned men, educated in the art of statecraft. The conquests of vast regions led to a drastic increase in the demand for such individuals. Consequently, Selīm's reign corresponded to the early stages of the emergence of a new class of bureaucrats, administrators, and secretaries as well as a parallel expansion in the ranks of the Ottoman religious establishment. Numerous leading figures who served at various levels of the military-administrative structure of the Ottoman polity during the Süleymānic age entered Ottoman service or rose to prominence during Selīm's reign.[50] In addition to serving as bureaucrats, administrators, and secretaries, many of these functionaries also composed works of literature, history, or advice. They thus contributed to another aspect of empire building: the written articulation of a religio-ideological paradigm that could be deployed against rival polities. The literary-historical production of this new class of learned men added a powerful weapon to the rhetorical and ideological arsenal of Ottoman sultans and erudite members of the military ruling elite.

On a religious level, contemporary Ottoman historiography depicts Selīm as the foremost champion of the Sunnī faith. His struggles against the "infidel" (*kāfir*) Georgians and the "heretical" (*mülḥid*, *zındīḳ*) Ḳızılbaş during his princedom are praised in numerous chronicles. These historical narratives identify Selīm as the valiant warrior prince destined to rule the Empire, retrospectively legitimizing his controversial rise to the throne. They also depict him as the only one of Bāyezīd II's sons who could meet the military challenges posed by Shāh Ismāʿīl, his disciples (*mürīd*), and his subjects.[51] Undoubtedly the most successful Islamic ruler of his age, Selīm thus emerges from these chronicles as the ultimate triumphant Sunnī monarch and the defender of religious orthodoxy against the "heretical" Shīʿism propagated by the Safavids and their Ḳızılbaş adherents.

Ottoman victories in Marj Dabik and Ridaniyya not only ended Mamluk rule in Egypt but also made Selīm the "Servitor of the Two Sacred Cities" and the protector of the Muslim faithful traveling to perform the annual pilgrimage (*ḥajj*).[52] Coupled with his victory against Shāh Ismāʿīl, the Safavid ruler who fashioned himself as a monarch ruling on behalf of the messianic Hidden Imām of Twelver Shīʿism,[53] Selīm's conquest of Arab lands definitively sealed the political, ideological, and religious identification of the Ottomans with Sunnī Islam. Such conquests also established geographical boundaries that were as political as they were confessional.[54]

By the end of Selīm's reign, the foundations of an intense political, cultural, and ideological competition were established along the Habsburg-Ottoman-Safavid axis. Over the course of the sixteenth century, the Sunnī Ottomans would compete with the Shīʿite Safavids over the definition of Islamic orthodoxy and the leadership of the community of Muslims (*umma*),[55] whereas rival claims of universal sovereignty would constitute the principal theme of the Ottomans' conflict with the Habsburgs. Selīm's conquest of Egypt, moreover, conferred on the Ottomans control of parts of the Red Sea coast and the Arabian Peninsula, leading to another competition with the Portuguese over supremacy in the Indian Ocean and ultimately to what Andrew Hess called "the beginning of the sixteenth-century world war."[56] In fact, as Giancarlo Casale insightfully argues, Selīm's takeover of the Mamluk domains "set his successors on a collision course with the Portuguese for control of the Indian Ocean," catalyzing the parallel development of Portuguese and Ottoman competitive claims to universal sovereignty on a global scale.[57]

Selīm's self-fashioning as "Master of the Auspicious Conjunction" (*ṣāḥib-ḳırān*) and as the "Shadow of God" (*ẓıll-Allāh*) who is "succored by God" (*mu'ayyad min Allāh*) in the Persian prologue to the Law Code of Niğbolu (*Ḳānūnnāme-i Nigbolu*) must be analyzed within the context of this interimperial competition.[58] As Cornell Fleischer notes, *ẓıll-Allāh* represents "a perfectly normal arrogation of an important standard element of caliphal titulature by Muslim rulers of the post-Mongol era," whereas the phrase *mu'ayyad min Allāh* signified direct divine support for the individual claimant and thus was used to refer to a ruler who was never defeated in battle.[59] It stands to reason that both terms were included in the prologue to an authoritative document penned in 1517, immediately after Selīm's victories against the Mamluks added southeastern Anatolia, Syria, Palestine, and Egypt to the Ottoman domains and thus brought the three holy cities of Mecca, Medina, and Jerusalem under Ottoman control. Triumphant against both the Safavids and the Mamluks, Selīm was indeed a monarch "succored by God" who was never defeated in battle during his sultanate.[60] Without a doubt, his claim to be the divinely appointed "Shadow of God" carried legitimate weight within Islamdom.

Whereas those first two elements in Selīm's royal titulature constituted sources of legitimacy for a claim to regional preeminence (limited to the Abode of Islam), the third signified a transcendental claim to ecumenical sovereignty. Although pre-Islamic Iranian in origin, the title *ṣāḥib-ḳırān* acquired prominence during the early modern era.[61] With the post-Mongol nomadic emperor Tīmūr (r. 1370–1405), who successfully combined "the Turko-Mongolian conception of authority based on charisma (*qut*) rather than birthright . . . with Perso-Islamic notions of divinely bestowed kingly glory (*farr*), good fortune (*daulat*, *bakht*), and manifest destiny (*maqdūr*),"[62] this honorific epithet acquired explicit connotations of universal sovereignty and came to signify "the world conqueror whose advent was indicated by appropriate celestial events and astrological signs,"[63] specifically the great conjunction of Saturn and Jupiter. By fashioning himself as "Master of the Auspicious Conjunction," Selīm highlighted his military charisma and articulated a claim to the universal sovereignty of a world conqueror.[64] In addition, he transcended the regional limitations of an Ottoman dynastic claim as a source of legitimacy for sovereignty. Selīm's utilization of *ṣāḥib-ḳırān* in his official titulature thus not only denoted a politico-ideological challenge addressed to the rivals of the House of ʿOs̱mān in Christiandom and Islamdom but also expressed Ottoman awareness of the messianic and apocalyptic expectations and ideological paradigms prevalent in the Mediterranean and Eurasian cultural zones in the sixteenth century and leading up to the Muslim millennium.[65]

Selīm as an Early Modern Eurasian Ruler

In a posthumously published essay, Joseph Fletcher makes the case for what he calls "integrative history," which seeks to highlight interconnections and horizontal continuities stretching across Eurasia during the early modern period.[66] In addition to the growth of population, the emergence of regional urban centers, the rise of city-based commercial classes, the increase in rural unrest, the decline in nomadism, and the prominence of revivalist religious movements, Fletcher describes a trend that transcended all of these phenomena: a faster pace of historical change, a "quickening tempo," across the Eurasian landmass.[67] His aggregate sketch depicts an early modern Eurasia of which the Ottoman Empire was both geographically and culturally an integral part.[68]

Focusing on themes such as imperial ideology, identity, legitimacy, space, the production of literary-historical texts, and the articulation of universalist political theologies, recent scholarship on Ottoman history has identified Ottoman early modernity as part of a larger European and/or Mediterranean phenomenon, and some studies have widened the scope of this comparative framework.[69] Despite prioritizing the interconnections between the Ottomans and their European counterparts, Cemal Kafadar has highlighted "shared discourses" and "shared rhythms" beyond the Mediterranean basin and recognized the simultaneous emergence of new literary forms, architectural expressions, imperial identity, and sites of sociability as threads that were woven throughout early modern Eurasia.[70] Most recently, Kaya Şahin's analysis of the life and oeuvre of Celālzāde Muṣṭafā (d. 1567), a prominent bureaucrat and man of letters of the Süleymānic age, positioned the sixteenth-century Ottoman variant of empire building firmly and persuasively within the early modern Eurasian context.[71] Guided by the general historical-geographical framework articulated by Joseph Fletcher, the present study similarly aims to build on the scholarly literature that has characterized the sixteenth- and seventeenth-century Ottoman experience as early modern, as Eurasian, or as both.

The contextualization of sixteenth-century Ottoman realities within the early modern Eurasian milieu is certainly not meant to deny the valuable contributions of scholars who have emphasized the kinship between the Ottomans (ca. 1300–1922), the Safavids (1501–1722), and the Mughals (1526–1857). After all, all three were military-agrarian polities of the gunpowder era with predominantly, though by no means exclusively, Muslim populations ruled by Muslim dynasts.[72] Located in the eastern part of the Eurasian landmass, all three were connected by a common religio-ideological paradigm inspired primarily by Islam.[73] Their most essential attribute was not military-agrarian, gunpowder-harnessing, or Islamic, however. The Ottomans, along with their Safavid and Mughal counterparts, were first and foremost imperial entities; as such, they shared equally imperial destinies with their contemporaries on the western part of Eurasia.[74] As highlighted by Sanjay Subrahmanyam, the Ottomans, the Mughals, and the Habsburgs were equally familiar with the challenges of territorial expansion, bureaucratization, legal codification, and efficient tax collection.[75] Their "connected histories" stretched across the early modern Eurasian cultural zone, intricately linking them together via the articulation of ideas on universal sovereignty and expressions of millenarian and messianic expectations.[76]

If the sixteenth-century Ottoman polity indeed constituted the crucial geographical and cultural link between the eastern and western parts of Eurasia, Selīm's reign represented the historical moment when the Ottomans secured their position as principal protagonists within that geotemporal framework. For these reasons, this study interprets Selīm's achievements as a momentous leap toward the complete integration of the Ottoman Empire into the early modern Eurasian political-cultural zone and its "quickening tempo." It also recognizes the significance of Selīm's effective strategy of geographical expansion, the prestige he acquired as the preeminent Sunnī ruler in Islamdom, and his status as an undefeated warrior-king. Together, these characteristics were legitimate grounds for a claim of universal sovereignty within that particular historical context.

And yet, in Ottoman historiography, the legitimacy of Selīm's ascendance to the throne has been mired in controversy. Beginning with the inception of the military-political enterprise, the Ottomans practiced a competitive form of succession that Cemal Kafadar has called "unigeniture." This custom involved a contentious process in which one of the deceased sovereign's male relatives eliminated all other rival pretenders to the throne in order to assume control of the entire empire.[77] In contradistinction to the common Turco-Mongol practice of dividing the realm among members of the ruling family after the death of a sovereign, unigeniture prevented fragmentation of Ottoman domains and ensured their preservation for future generations of sultans.[78] Darwinian in nature, competitive unigeniture also legitimized succession by combat, which—although perfectly in accordance with the fundamental ideology of an expansionist military polity—led to devastating fratricidal wars during the fifteenth and sixteenth centuries.[79]

Selīm secured his sultanate as a result of such internecine wrangling. To establish his uncontested authority as the sole ruler of the Ottoman realm, he executed two brothers and seven nephews in 1513.

A year earlier, he had become the first and only member of the Ottoman dynasty to have forcibly deposed, and almost certainly poisoned, a legitimate ruling sultan, his father, Bāyezīd II.[80] Because fratricide had already been an integral part of Ottoman succession politics, reaching the throne over the dead bodies of actual or potential rival members of the dynastic family was an established practice by the time Selīm ascended to the sultanate. The forcible deposition of a reigning sultan, however, was an entirely different matter. Coupled with Selīm's notorious penchant for violence, this unprecedented act was so contentious that it ultimately led to his reputation as "the Grim" (*Yāvuz*).

Previous Scholarship

To date, no scholarly monograph on Selīm I exists in any language other than Turkish, and Turkish-language studies remain wanting at best. Euro-American literature, however, addresses the impact of Selīm's reign on particular historical developments, especially on the relationship between the Ottomans and the Safavids and on the history of postconquest Egypt.[81] The unique aspects of Selīm's succession and the creation of his posthumous image have received only scant scholarly attention, despite the remarkable implications of these aspects for the Ottoman Empire and the early modern Eurasian world around it.[82]

In the case of modern Turkish scholarship, this dearth bears crucial testimony to the success of the sixteenth- and seventeenth-century Ottoman historiographical tradition in posthumously exonerating this controversial monarch.[83] Produced in a politico-religious landscape shaped first by the predominantly secular, nationalist ideology of the early Republic, then by the official state doctrine of "Turkish-Islamic Synthesis," and more recently by the rise of the Sunnī-Turkish variant of political Islam and a concomitant sentiment of neo-Ottomanism, this modern-era scholarship hails Selīm's reign, along with that of his son Süleymān, as part of an idealized Ottoman "golden age."[84] In such works, Selīm is represented as foremost among the ever-victorious ancestors of the citizens of the Republic of Turkey, who established Sunnī-Turkish domination over three continents.[85] As works of *histoire événementielle*, these studies provide a valuable political-historical narrative of Selīm's reign, especially of his military achievements. With a few notable exceptions, however, they assume a rather defensive, apologetic, and/or selectively merciful tone when discussing the controversial moments of Selīm's life and reign, including the death of his father, his ascent to the throne, and the systematic massacre of thousands of the Empire's Anatolian Ḳızılbaş subjects.[86] More significantly, from a historiographical vantage point, they espouse an expository approach to source materials without providing an analysis of the differences between various narrative accounts and archival documents. Finally, they neither assess the relative credibility and/or historicity of various alternative statements nor address questions about the varied political, social, and cultural contexts within which these Ottoman sources were penned.[87]

Structure, Sources, and Interpretive Framework

The present study reevaluates the unprecedented nature of Selīm's ascendance to the Ottoman throne and analyzes the historiographical processes that resulted in the "mythification" of his persona over the course of the sixteenth and seventeenth centuries.[88] In doing so, it addresses the interrelated processes of empire building and history writing in order to highlight the crucial role of historiography in articulating specific political arguments, expressing ideological viewpoints, and shaping imperial identities in the early modern Ottoman context. This study not only emphasizes that history writing as a political and cultural activity contributed to the formation of the Ottoman imperial enterprise but also demonstrates that the posthumous idealization of Selīm in Ottoman historiography was part of a larger development: the construction of an ideal image of Muslim sovereignty within an early modern Eurasian setting.

This book employs a two-pronged approach to addressing the dialectical interplay between the past itself and the past as it is remembered—what Jan Assmann calls "history proper" and "mnemohistory," respectively.[89] This study is divided into two parts in order to explore both the historical circumstances of Selīm's rise to prominence and the development of the textual iconography of his persona and rulership. Whereas the "historical" part of this book uses a prosopographical approach to examine Selīm I's rise to the Ottoman throne via the contributions of various military and political factions, the "mnemohistorical" part uses a source-critical approach to analyze the posthumous "mythification" of this monarch via the historiographical contributions of numerous Ottoman authors over the course of the sixteenth and seventeenth centuries.

Ottoman succession struggles were almost always marginalized in Ottoman historiography because they exposed the weaknesses of the Ottoman order as well as the dividing lines that separated various factions. Moreover, modern studies tend to ignore such struggles because they defy the myth of a smooth-functioning, orderly Ottoman state. Selīm's case represents a particularly thorny problem because he succeeded to the throne by rebelling against his own father—an act of defiance that was considered illegitimate by his contemporaries. Part 1 begins with an overview of the processes that brought Selīm to power and aims to present this complicated story in a holistic manner for the first time. To that end, it brings together various contemporaneous Ottoman perspectives on Selīm's success(ion), as exemplified by a wide array of mostly Ottoman archival and narrative sources.

The great majority of sixteenth-century Ottoman chronicles focus primarily on the sultan or the imperial capital as the locus of political power. In addition to addressing historical developments from the vantage point of the imperial center, these narratives tend to portray—and at times even reflect—the political and ideological sentiments of the power holders in Istanbul. Most chronicles pay little or no attention to the power dynamics between the sultan and various politico-military factions, particularly those located on the periphery. In juxtaposition, archival documents—such as imperial decrees (*ḥükm*), letters (*mektūb, kāġıd*), petitions (*ʿarż*), and spy reports—serve as a corrective to the sultan- and Istanbul-centered narrative provided by Ottoman chronicles. Diverse, eclectic, and poised to be read in a variety of ways, these materials documented the unfolding of contemporary events nearly instantaneously, before certain details were forgotten, neglected, ignored, or edited out—and thus silenced by later narrators, either intentionally or unintentionally. Although—or maybe because—they were penned for the sultan and members of his administration, these little-studied archival documents also reveal the dynamics of the power struggle among the sultan, his statesmen, his agents, and his rivals before the voices of the losers were suppressed by the winners. By bringing archival sources to the fore, Part 1 provides a nuanced and polyphonous narrative that places particular emphasis on the significant role played by military and political figures and factions situated in the Rumelian territories of the Ottoman realm in tipping the scales in Selīm's favor.

Based on both archival and narrative sources, Chapter 1 aims primarily to provide a coherent story. Intended to offer a meaningful frame of reference for the unfolding of events that culminated in Selīm's accession to the throne, it also traces the intertwined trajectories of four dynastic protagonists—Bāyezīd II (r. 1481–1512), the ruling sultan, and his sons, princes Aḥmed (d. 1513), Ḳorḳud (d. 1513), and Selīm—and explores the ever-shifting loyalties of the military and political factions that supported these royal protagonists. Chapter 1 further pinpoints the controversial aspects of this succession struggle by identifying specific events of questionable legitimacy, including Selīm's departure from his gubernatorial seat in Trabzon, his collaboration with the Crimean Tatars, the military clash between his forces and the royal army commanded by his father, the circumstances surrounding his ultimate accession to the Ottoman throne, Bāyezīd II's suspicious death, and the manner in which Selīm eliminated remaining members of the dynasty who posed an actual or potential threat to his sultanate.

Chapter 2 builds on this historical sketch to address broader issues in early modern Ottoman history. Exploring the perennial tension between the centrifugal tendencies of frontier lords (*uc begi*) and the centripetal policies of Ottoman rulers throughout the early history of the Empire, this chapter examines the nearly constant (re)negotiation of power relations among various historical actors. In particular, it highlights the crucial role played by peripheral sociopolitical and military groups, whose power bases were located in the Balkan provinces, in elevating Selīm to the throne. This chapter also addresses the international dimensions of this otherwise domestic dynastic struggle, the interrelations between various politically significant factions within the Ottoman military ruling elite, and the quandary posed by an Ottoman prince who deposed a ruling sultan. Chapter 2 further serves to explore Ottoman chroniclers' ongoing concerns regarding the legitimacy of Selīm's rule by underlining the contentious military and rhetorical strategies he used as well as the political and ideological ramifications of his exploits. Moreover, it relates a more textured story about the Ottoman monarchy. Presenting the Ottoman political process as one of negotiation, this chapter neither emphasizes the Ottoman sultan's absolute autocratic rule nor highlights his inability to control the entire domain. By focusing on military and political actors thought to be peripheral to Ottoman imperial politics, Chapter 2 aims to provide a more dynamic and inclusive understanding of the interplay between power and politics in the early Ottoman context.

On the basis of the foundation laid in Part 1, Part 2 addresses the Ottoman historiographical tradition and begins with a prologue that provides a survey of the development of Ottoman history writing from the beginning of the fifteenth century to the end of the sixteenth century. The analysis in Part 2 takes its cue from the work of two scholars in particular. First and foremost is Peter Burke's pioneering work on the role played by literary and visual representations in shaping the image of royal personas—such as Charles V (Holy Roman Emperor, r. 1519–1556) and Louis XIV (King of France and Navarre,

r. 1643–1715)—for contemporary audiences as well as for posterity.[90] In accordance with Burke's maxim that "all history involves representation, and all representations are part of history," Part 2 studies textual representations of Selīm not as "unproblematic 'reflections' of the reality" of his age but as constantly refracted and at times consciously manipulated images created by authors at specific times and with noticeably presentist agendas.[91] Thus, not unlike Burke's study of the place of Louis XIV in the "collective imagination" of his contemporaries, Part 2 of this work is concerned not so much with Selīm the man or Selīm the sultan as with the manufacturing of his image.[92] In terms of methodology, it also follows Burke's work on representations of Charles V by focusing on the posthumous "mythification" of Selīm rather than on the contemporary "fabrication" of his image. In fact, my analysis of the formation of Selīm's textual representation in Part 2 illustrates Burke's definition of the "slippery term" myth:

> In the first place, a myth may be described as a story of marvellous or extraordinary events in which the protagonists are larger than life and endowed with superhuman qualities, whether they are heroes or villains. Indeed these protagonists represent, embody or symbolize values, making abstract ideas concrete and so more memorable. In the second place, from a structural point of view, a myth may be viewed as a story composed of schemata, in other words recurrent or prefabricated elements which wander or float from one story or one protagonist to another. In the third place, from a functional point of view, a myth may be regarded as a story about the past, the purpose of which is to legitimate a situation or an institution in the present.[93]

Ever mindful of the ceaseless engagement between the past and a given present, my analysis in Part 2 is also informed by Jan Assmann's concept of "mnemohistory," which refers to the investigation of the history of cultural memory.[94] This section explores Selīm's place in the ongoing work of Ottoman historians' "reconstructive imagination," which was triggered by the dramatic and traumatic nature of his ascendance to the throne.[95] Essentially intertextual, the chapters comprising Part 2 analyze how the composite image of Selīm was constructed and reconstructed in historical texts over the course of the sixteenth and seventeenth centuries. The result of all this reconfiguration was a hegemonic, highly edited metanarrative that chronicles a legitimately appointed, posthumously idealized, and divinely ordained Ottoman monarch. As mnemohistorical essays, these chapters do not attempt to unearth a definitive factual, historical persona for Selīm I from the numerous complex, interrelated historiographical strata. Instead, they identify many alternative, complementary, and at times conflicting discourses for which the varied representations of Selīm functioned as expressions of equally diverse political, ideological, and religious viewpoints. In other words, instead of providing a definitive portrait of Selīm, these chapters take the reader through a gallery of portraits of this controversial monarch, unveiling the multiplicity of characters and attributes affixed to him. At the same time, they uncover the political expectations and cultural ideals of early modern Ottoman authors.

As such, Part 2 offers an investigation not of Selīm but of memories of Selīm. These memories were articulated by sixteenth- and seventeenth-century Ottoman authors who were not passive transmitters of factual information but active participants in the process of meaning-making through time. The literary-historical texts they composed were what Pierre Nora calls *lieux de mémoire*, "places" where memories of Selīm converged, condensed, and clashed while remaining "in permanent evolution, open to the dialectic of remembering and forgetting, unconscious of its successive deformations, vulnerable to manipulation and appropriation, susceptible to being long dormant and periodically revived." Contra Nora, however, this study does not regard memory and history as "in fundamental opposition" but rather emphasizes their interdependence.[96]

Aware of the pitfalls of document fetishism and its linguistic counterpart, this study neither silently accepts an authoritative documentary paradigm imposed by a vulgar positivism that leaves little or no room for historical imagination nor surrenders to the onslaught of the kind of poststructuralism that suggests a rupture between verbal signs and material referents, thus denying the very possibility of historical knowledge.[97] Guided by the writings of Gabrielle Spiegel and Frank Ankersmit, it instead seeks a "middle ground" or a "*juste milieu* between the extravagances of the literary approach to historical writing and the narrow-mindedness of empiricists."[98] Thus, while acknowledging the linguistic character of even the most instrumental language preserved and reproduced in archival records and historical narratives, this study also aims to analyze the development of an intricate reciprocal relationship between extant historical sources and the historical reality they claim to reflect. Specifically, it argues that the complex interrelations among various parameters of historical writing formed the contours of Selīm's posthumous textual iconography. Perpetually in flux, these parameters include but are not limited to the context of production (both chronological and spatial), the sociology of authorship, and the relations of patronage, all of which are constitutive elements of what Spiegel calls the "social logic of the text."[99]

In particular, Part 2 explores three main strands of memory that together culminated in the composite textual iconography of Selīm as a legitimate, idealized, and divinely ordained Ottoman sultan. In this context, Chapter 3 provides a thorough comparative examination of the variant narrative renderings in Ottoman historiography of certain critical events that transformed an unruly prince into a legitimate monarch. This chapter focuses primarily, though by no means exclusively, on a corpus of Ottoman literary and historical narratives that, because of their thematic consistency, may be conveniently classified as *Selīmnāmes* (*Vitas* of Selīm). It argues that this corpus of texts should be considered a conscientious—and ultimately successful—project of early modern Ottoman revisionist historiography aimed at rehabilitating Selīm's image. Lastly, by emphasizing the significance of these narratives as vehicles for the expression of internally coherent political and ideological positions, this chapter addresses the varied intellectual and political motivations of their authors, in light of their target audiences and actual or hoped-for patrons.

In Chapter 4, the focus shifts away from historical narratives whose most immediate objective was to legitimize Selīm's accession to the Ottoman throne by clearing his name of any wrongdoing. The great majority of the textual sources analyzed in this chapter belong to a genre generally called "advice literature" (*naṣīḥatnāme*), which was a corpus of political treatises that were comparable to the "mirrors for princes" (*Fürstenspiegel*) genre in the European context but that often addressed a wider audience than the sultan and the leading members of his ruling elite. Written (to varying degrees) with presentist concerns in mind, these sources have a discernible tendency to contrast a corrupt present with an idealized past. They praise the "good old days" in which Selīm is depicted, in revisionist terms, as one of the paradigmatic rulers of a mythical Ottoman golden age. Thus, the *naṣīḥatnāme* literature crafts a panoply of images of Selīm while also reflecting the particularities of the historical context within which these representations emerged.

Chapter 5 addresses the development of a more popular image of Selīm I as an Ottoman monarch bearing otherworldly, saintly, prophetic, and even messianic qualities. Building on the analyses, undertaken in the previous chapters, of different genres of Ottoman historical writing, Chapter 5 highlights the intellectual history behind historical texts that were composed at a time when millennial, apocalyptic, and messianic sentiments prevailed throughout Eurasia; when claims to universal sovereignty were expressed as fundamental elements of competing imperial ideologies produced at the Ottoman and the Habsburg courts; and when the Sunnī-Shīʿī rift crystallized, even fossilized, into rival political theologies reflecting the ideological framework within which the Ottoman and Safavid ruling elites operated.

Taken as a whole, this book aims to contribute to the study of the history and historiography of the early modern Ottoman enterprise in four specific ways. First, it provides a revisionist analysis of the controversial succession struggle between Selīm I and other dynastic protagonists. It also engages in conversation with two scholarly works by Dimitris Kastritsis and Şerafettin Turan on the internecine struggles between the sons of Bāyezīd I (r. 1389–1402) and between those of Süleymān I (r. 1520–1566), respectively. In so doing, it fills a historiographical lacuna in the study of Ottoman sociopolitical history during the so-called "Classical Age."[100] Second, this book emphasizes the significance not of the janissaries located in Istanbul but of the social, military, and political groups whose power bases were located in the Balkan provinces. It considers the political and military leaders situated on the Ottoman borderlands not simply as docile or complacent servants to the all-powerful sultan but instead as independent agents with their own interests and agendas. Depicting a dynamic political process based on constant negotiation rather than one dominated by mere clientelism and patronage, it thus diverges from the state-oriented approach that permeates the field of Ottoman studies. Instead, this study demonstrates that, even in a period when the Ottoman polity was assumed to have been highly centralized, the outcomes of succession struggles were largely determined by military-political actors located in the so-called periphery. Third, via an analysis of the historiographical "mythification" of Selīm, this book explores the development of several genres of Ottoman historical writing over the course of the sixteenth and seventeenth centuries. It aims to map the intellectual landscape of Ottoman authors who composed literary, historical, and political texts during a period when the Empire underwent significant transformations in all spheres. In doing so, this study sheds light on the varied, and at times conflicting, preoccupations of Ottoman authors as well as on the crafting of historical knowledge and memory through textual production in the early modern Ottoman context. Finally, through the lens of Selīm's story, this book aims to contribute to larger scholarly debates about sovereignty, royal authority, and political theology. It explores the making of an idealized representation of an early modern Sunnī-Muslim monarch imagined as a universal conqueror and messianic redeemer of the faith. As such, it engages emerging scholarship on the formulation of rival imperial identities in the early modern Eurasian context, when the Ottomans competed with the Habsburgs in Europe and the Safavids in the East over claims to universal sovereignty and the definition of Islamic orthodoxy.

PART 1
THE MAKING OF A SULTAN

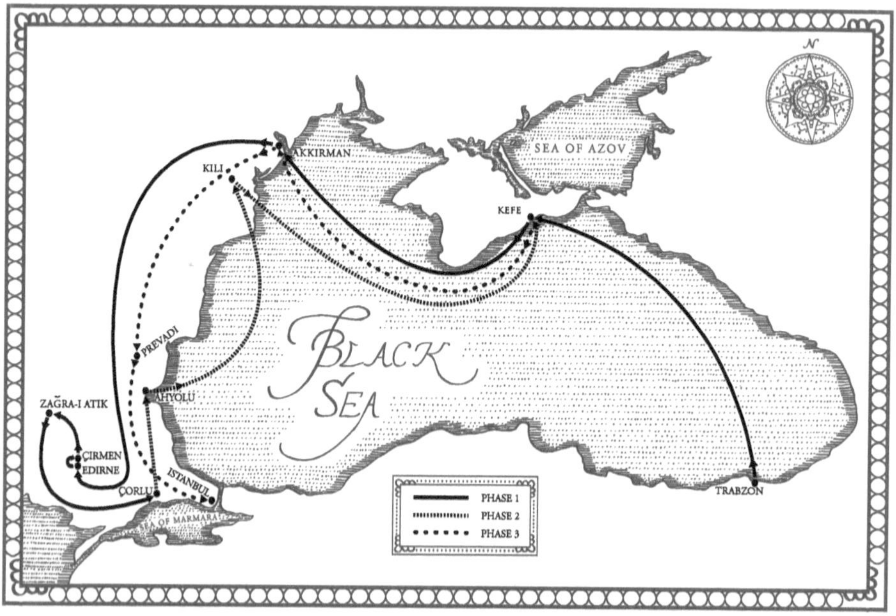

Map 1.1. Selīm's Itinerary during the Succession Struggle. Phase 1: From the Princely Governorate of Trabzon to the Battle of Çorlu (October 1510 – July 1511); Phase 2: Escape from Çorlu to Kefe (August 1511); Phase 3: From Kefe to the Throne (April 1512). Map by Rachel Trudell-Jones.

1 Politics of Succession: Selīm's Path to the Throne

Muradiye, sabrın acı meyvası[1]

Ottoman succession practices have been aptly labeled "succession of the fittest."[2] The terms the Ottomans used to denote successor (*ḫalef*), conflict (*iḫtilāf*), and opposition (*muḫālefet*) share a common Arabic root, indicating that they were certainly conscious of the inherent potential for crisis that all successions represent.[3] The Darwinian nature of their succession practices was further accentuated by the fact that no ascriptive or routine principle regulated succession to the Ottoman throne on anything more than a temporary basis until the codification of primogeniture in the last quarter of the nineteenth century.[4] Hence, Anthony Dolphin Alderson's frank assessment is apt: "Far from there being any theory of primogeniture . . . the law of succession may well be described as a 'free-for-all,' in which the strongest of the sons inherited the throne, while the others . . . suffered death."[5]

The absence of a predetermined system of imperial succession did not mean that the Ottoman practice of dynastic succession was haphazard. On the contrary, the Ottomans followed certain principles, some upheld by earlier Turco-Mongolian polities, in an exceptionally deliberate fashion. First, in accordance with the premodern Turco-Mongolian political tradition, the entire imperial territory was considered the patrimony of the dynastic family. Second, each and every male member of the House of ʿOs̱mān was considered the beneficiary of divine grace and therefore was theoretically eligible, and equally legitimate, to rule.[6] This was why, as Halil İnalcık notes, earlier Turkish rulers of tribal empires in Central Asia attributed their sovereignty to a sacred source of authority and their own personal fortune (*ḳut*).[7] Within the Ottoman context, this notion of personal fortune, along with its connotations of innate charisma and divine mandate to rule, corresponded to the concept of *devlet*.[8] The intricate correlation between possessing personal fortune and attaining the sultanate was signified semantically as well; the word "state" in Arabic, Persian, and Turkish evolved from the Arabic word *dawla*, the connotations of which include "change or turn of fortune."[9] Third, that all male members of the House of ʿOs̱mān possessed innate charisma and personal fortune did not mean that they possessed them equally. Rather, the Ottoman practice of battling for succession was based on the assumption that at any given time only one male member of the dynasty was invested with the divine mandate to rule the entire imperial realm.

Within a political-theoretical framework restricted by these parameters, the Ottomans persistently pursued a competitive form of a succession practice that Cemal Kafadar has called "unigeniture."[10] Competitive unigeniture was essentially a zero-sum game and entailed a contentious process by which one of the deceased sovereign's male relatives eliminated all other rival pretenders for the throne in order to assume control of the entire empire.[11] Although the Ottomans practiced it consistently ab initio, unigeniture was systematized as a method of succession only when Meḥmed II declared in his code of law (*ḳānūnnāme*) that "it is appropriate for whichever of my sons attains the sultanate with divine assistance to kill his brothers for the sake of the world order (*niẓām-ı ʿālem*)."[12] The destructive nature of competitive unigeniture was experienced both before and after the codification of fratricide, as evidenced by the fatal competitions of the fifteenth and sixteenth centuries between the sons of Bāyezīd I, Meḥmed II, Bāyezīd II, and Süleymān I.[13] In 1574, when Murād III acceded to the throne, he executed all five of his younger brothers; in 1595, his son Meḥmed III, on his own accession, executed nineteen.[14]

The devastating effects of fratricidal wars notwithstanding, the practice of unigeniture in the form of "succession by combat"—by which the Ottoman monarch was principally defined as a conqueror—fell perfectly in line with the fundamental ideology of an expansionist military polity.[15] Despite the Ottomans' strict adherence to unigeniture, their succession practices were akin to those of other, earlier Turco-Mongolian polities of the steppes. As Joseph Fletcher argues, the Ottomans were also sedentary heirs to the Inner Asian tribal custom called "tanistry," which prescribed, usually via murder or war, the transition of supreme rule of the empire to the most competent member of the ruling family.[16] To ensure the enthronement of the most suitable candidate, the Ottomans practiced both customs; in this context, unigeniture enabled them to successfully combine an overarching and time-honored Turco-Mongolian tribal principle with their aversion to a predetermined system of imperial succession and with a special emphasis on fortune (*devlet*). Thus, until the introduction in the seventeenth century of a preference for seniority, battles for succession were waged—both literally and figuratively—as battles of fortune.[17]

In an effort to prove that he indeed possessed the exclusive divine mandate to rule, each claimant to the Ottoman throne had to demonstrate that his fortune was superior to the fortunes of his rivals. This competitive endeavor was such an integral part of Ottoman political culture that there existed an idiomatic expression to denote the mutual testing of fortune (*devlet ṣınaşmak*).[18] The ultimate proof of an individual's fortune was embodied in his success on the battlefield. When it came to Ottoman successions, nothing succeeded like success, which was recognized as the ultimate expression of divine favor, emanating from the same sacred source as charismatic authority.[19] That was why, per Halil İnalcık, "when Bāyezīd II and Selīm, Süleymān the Lawgiver and Muṣṭafā confronted each other in battle, they believed that they were subject not to their own will, but to the will of an incorporeal power, the will of God and the state." It is for these reasons that, in large part, they accepted the outcome of dynastic struggles by entrusting their fates to God (*tevekkül*).[20]

Bāyezīd II's fate was to die under suspicious circumstances on the way to his mandatory retirement in Dimetoka (Didymotichon,

Greece); Selīm's fate was to rule the Empire as its ninth sultan. One cannot help but wonder whether the deposed sultan indeed accepted this unfortunate turn of events as divine judgment. There is absolutely no doubt, however, that each of the claimants to Bāyezīd's throne worked diligently to manipulate God's will by securing the political and military assistance of various factions at the imperial capital and in the provinces of the Empire. There is also no doubt that among Bāyezīd's princes, Selīm was the most successful at this manipulation.

Based on a wide array of (primarily Ottoman) archival and narrative sources, this chapter addresses the rise to power of Selīm I. It traces the complicated trajectories of four dynastic protagonists and examines the shifting loyalties of the military and political factions that supported them, thus building a coherent story of—and a meaningful frame of reference for—the events that culminated in Selīm's accession to the Ottoman throne on April 24, 1512. Bāyezīd II, the legitimate ruling sultan at the time, and his sons, Princes Aḥmed, Ḳorḳud, and Selīm, are the principal actors in this political drama.

Whereas the later chapters of this book focus on the historiography on Selīm I and the posthumous construction of his image, the present discussion is strictly historical in nature. It draws from sources that include but are not limited to imperial decrees (*ḥükm*), letters (*mektūb, kāġıd*), petitions (*ʿarż*), spy reports, copybooks of correspondence (*münşeʾāt*), general histories of the Ottoman dynasty (*tevārīḫ-i āl-i ʿOs̱mān*) by known and anonymous authors, a corpus of literary-historical narratives commonly referred to as *Selīmnāme*s (*Vita*s of Selīm), and, last but not least, Venetian *relazioni*. The précis of events provided in the following pages is based on these textual sources, whose authors display a variety of attitudes and agendas.[21]

Succession Politics: The Provincial Factor

Let us begin at the very beginning. Bāyezīd II had eight sons, five of whom preceded him to the grave.[22] With the notion of unigeniture dictating Ottoman succession practices since the inception of the polity and with the competitive nature of that concept, which was explicitly revealed by Meḥmed II's codification of fratricide in the last quarter of the fifteenth century, the stage for the struggle between Bāyezīd's remaining sons was set long before violence erupted in 1511.[23] Because securing the imperial capital on the death of an Ottoman ruler was of paramount importance for contenders to the throne, the dissension between Bāyezīd's princes manifested initially as an incessant struggle over the provinces; each contender sought to outmaneuver his rivals by scoring a gubernatorial appointment to the province nearest to Istanbul. With gubernatorial seats in the Balkan provinces denied to Ottoman princes since the civil war following the Battle of Ankara in 1402, this struggle was initially confined to Anatolia.[24]

Ḳorḳud's career as governor (*sancaḳ begi*), for example, began with an appointment to the western province of Saruhan in 1491.[25] After Bāyezīd II denied his request to be posted in the northwestern town of Bergama, in 1502 Ḳorḳud was appointed to the southwestern province of Teke, with the province of Hamid added to his domain in 1503.[26] Although this appendage more than doubled Ḳorḳud's annual income, there was little doubt that the prince was being kept at arm's length from the seat of imperial power. A few years later, Ḳorḳud had a falling-out with grand vizier Ḫādım ʿAlī Pasha (d. 1511), the most prominent supporter of his older brother Aḥmed, over hunting grounds (*şikāristān*) and ports (*iskele, līmān*) located within the borders of his province.[27] This appears to have been the proverbial straw that broke the camel's back; on May 18, 1509, shortly after his disagreement with the grand vizier, Ḳorḳud sailed to Egypt.[28] Having failed to secure the military support of the Mamluk ruler Qānṣūh al-Ghawrī (r. 1501–1516) in his quest for the Ottoman throne, however, Ḳorḳud had no choice but request to be reinstated to his former governorate.[29] Ḳorḳud's letters of apology, addressed to Bāyezīd II and Ḫādım ʿAlī Pasha—as well as a treatise he composed to explain that he came to Egypt not to defy his father's orders but to go to Mecca to perform the pilgrimage—apparently had the desired effect.[30] Once back in the

Ottoman realm, however, Ḳorḳud resumed his bid for an appointment closer to Istanbul, petitioning to be transferred to the province of Aydın.[31] Judging by the desperate tone of a letter he sent to his sister in 1511, Ḳorḳud's request fell on deaf ears. In this letter, he complains of being treated as an outcast, left to suffer in his current province.[32] Moreover, inaccurate intelligence concerning his father's decision to grant Manisa to his rival brother Selīm appears to have increased Ḳorḳud's desperation. Anxious to overtake his adversary, Ḳorḳud left his province and set out for Manisa.[33] The consequences of Ḳorḳud's choice to leave his gubernatorial seat were more momentous than he could have anticipated; to no small extent, it sparked the Safavid-instigated Şāhḳulu rebellion the same year.

Conversely, Ḳorḳud's older brother Aḥmed had been appointed to the prestigious province of Amasya in 1481, as soon as his father had ascended to the Ottoman throne. He was not, however, absolutely free of anxiety. Although his brothers governed distant provinces, Aḥmed became increasingly concerned about keeping his path to the imperial capital clear as Bāyezīd II's days were coming to a close. Thus, he kept a vigilant eye on Ḳorḳud's movements in western Anatolia and also observed Selīm's activities closely, intervening immediately in 1509, when the latter requested for his son Süleymān the governorship of Şebinkarahisar (Şebḫāne Ḳaraḥiṣārı).[34] Because Aḥmed was unwilling to accept the appointment of his principal rival's son to a neighboring province, Bāyezīd II decided to appoint Süleymān to Bolu. When Aḥmed reportedly stated that "the province of Bolu is [on] the path from Amasya to the capital" and refused to accept this appointment as well, Bāyezīd finally assigned Süleymān to Kefe (Theodosia, Ukraine) on August 6, 1509.[35] Because the governorships of Bolu, Çorum, and Osmancık were later assigned to Princes ʿAlāʾeddīn (d. 1513), Süleymān (d. 1513), and ʿOs̱mān (d. 1513), respectively, Aḥmed succeeded in gaining absolute control of the path to Istanbul through the appointments of his sons.[36] What Aḥmed could not foresee, however, was that Süleymān's appointment to Kefe would open the gates of Rumelia for Selīm, an advantage he fully exploited during the final phase of the succession struggle.

Although it is impossible to ascertain the exact date when the rift between Bāyezīd II and his youngest son, Selīm emerged, a clear indication of discord could be seen as early as 1487, when the latter was appointed to the farthest princely governorate—Trabzon, on the Black Sea coast.[37] Despite being a distinct sign of Selīm's unpopularity at Bāyezīd's court, this appointment proved to be a blessing in disguise. To begin with, the proximity of Selīm's province to the realm of Shāh Ismāʿīl (r. 1501–1524) brought him into direct contact with the Safavids, who constituted a serious threat to the Ottoman polity. Although the danger posed by the Turcoman followers of the Shāh in southern Anatolia was clearly demonstrated by the Şāhḳulu revolt in 1511, alarm bells had begun ringing earlier and had resulted in the exile of Shīʿī sympathizers to the newly conquered Peloponnesian maritime stations of Moton and Koron.[38] In fact, according to the sixteenth-century Ottoman historian Kemālpaşazāde, one of the factors leading to Ḳorḳud's assignment to Teke in 1502 was the need for a "majestic and strong commander" to control the unruly population of the region comprising Shāh Ismāʿīl's adherents.[39] A more immediate threat emerged in 1507, when Shāh Ismāʿīl violated Ottoman sovereignty by invading the Dulkadir emirate, crossing over Ottoman lands and enrolling in his army Turcomans who were Ottoman subjects.[40] Bāyezīd II did not trust Ismāʿīl, whose letter of apology referred to the aging sultan as his "illustrious and noble father,"[41] and kept Anatolian soldiers on alert against a possible Safavid invasion, rounding up probable supporters of the Shāh in the Anatolian provinces. Still, the Ottoman sultan chose a policy of nonconfrontation.[42]

Unlike his father, Selīm did not hesitate to antagonize Shāh Ismāʿīl. Safavid complaints concerning Selīm's aggressive military policy reached Bāyezīd's court as early as 1505.[43] Two years later, when Ismāʿīl sent his brother with three thousand soldiers to pillage and plunder Selīm's province, the latter retaliated by raiding Safavid territories, defeating the troops, and confiscating their arms and armaments.[44] An envoy sent by Shāh Ismāʿīl to Bāyezīd II complained about Selīm's attack and asked for the restitution of Safavid weapons captured by the prince.[45] Although Bāyezīd ignored this request, he sent the Safavid ambassador back with precious gifts and messages of friendship.[46] The uneasy relationship between the Ottomans and Safavids was tested again in 1510, when Shāh Ismāʿīl gathered his troops to attack Selīm, who had taken the region of Erzincan. As with previous military contentions in eastern Anatolia, reconciliation was achieved through Bāyezīd II's nonconfrontational diplomatic strategy.[47]

Given Bāyezīd's cautious policy of nonviolence toward the Safavids, it is not surprising that Selīm's uncompromising attitude and belligerent actions during the first decade of the sixteenth century were construed by members of the pro-Aḥmed faction at the Ottoman court as a form of insubordination.[48] Despite being scolded by his father, Selīm continued to maintain a strategy of aggression against the Ottomans' eastern neighbors.[49] Of great significance in that respect were Selīm's well-organized forays into Georgian territories in 1508; more than ten thousand Georgians reportedly fell captive (*esīr*) to the forces of the prince during these raids.[50] According to Kemālpaşazāde, Bāyezīd's response to his son's success against the "unbelievers" (*kefere*) conveyed mixed messages: the Ottoman sultan welcomed Selīm's success by awarding him royal presents and regal favors but emphatically stated that the "multiplication of enemies was unacceptable."[51]

Counter to Bāyezīd II's unwillingness to take action against Shāh Ismāʿīl, Selīm's relentless call for a more forceful international policy must have been uplifting for common people and soldiers alike, as it meant safety for the former and the opportunity for gainful participation in military expeditions for the latter. Indeed, while the promise of an active military policy helped him garner the favor of the military classes, whose wealth and promotions depended on successful campaigns, Selīm's effective retaliatory measures against the incursions of Safavid forces into the Ottoman realm and his successful raids into Georgia apparently led to increasing popular support. If one is to believe the Ottoman historian and statesman Celālzāde Muṣṭafā (d. 1567), Selīm's expeditions against the Safavids and Georgians strengthened his reputation as *the* champion of faith against "heretics" and "infidels" and contributed to the emergence of songs chanted at social gatherings that praised the prince as the preeminent sovereign of the time.[52]

There is no doubt that Selīm's antagonistic approach toward the Georgians and the Safavids, along with his open criticism of Bāyezīd's inactivity, made him unpopular at the Ottoman court.[53] Moreover, for members of the Ottoman ruling elite belonging to the pro-Aḥmed camp, his enthusiasm for revitalizing Ottoman imperial policy signified a clear break from the status quo, which they were hoping to preserve (along with their offices) by bringing Aḥmed to power. Aḥmed's supporters did everything they could to convince Bāyezīd that Selīm's actions bordered on insubordination, and the latter's unequivocal accusation that the ruling monarch's inactivity was the primary cause of chaos in the Anatolian provinces solidified Bāyezīd's antagonism toward his son.[54] Already the most powerful member of the pro-Aḥmed faction, Bāyezīd increasingly disapproved of Selīm's military endeavors and began to refuse the majority of Selīm's demands in order to secure Aḥmed's sultanate.

Crossing Over: Selīm in the Crimea

It is noteworthy that Bāyezīd II granted all of Aḥmed's wishes and none of Selīm's until the latter's son Süleymān was finally assigned to the governorship of Kefe on August 6, 1509.[55] Paradoxically, although Bāyezīd succeeded in handing over control of strategic Anatolian provinces to his eldest son, he also enabled Selīm to capture the Ottoman throne via a forced detour through Rumelia.[56]

Selīm's intention to leave Trabzon was no secret to the sultan.[57] When Süleymān was due for an appointment to a gubernatorial province, therefore, Selīm shrewdly requested for his son Anatolian provinces that were unnervingly close to those controlled by Aḥmed or by one of Aḥmed's sons, knowing full well that the sultan, in an effort to prevent Süleymān (and, by extension, Selīm) from blocking Aḥmed's path to Istanbul, would decline. Selīm's clever maneuvering proved effective when Bāyezīd was forced to grant Süleymān the distant Rumelian governorate of Kefe, enabling Selīm to cross over to the Crimea and garner the support of military commanders stationed in the Balkan provinces. With the arrival from Istanbul of his father's statement that he intended to abdicate in favor of Prince Aḥmed, Selīm decided to embark on the second phase of his march to the sultanate and followed the Black Sea route to Kefe in October 1510.[58]

Once in Kefe, Selīm continued to insist on being granted a Rumelian province, stating that his aim was to "fight the infidels" in the westernmost provinces of the Empire.[59] Already alarmed by the unruly prince's presence in the Balkan provinces, members of the pro-Aḥmed faction responded that such an appointment was "against sultanic law." They tried to persuade the sultan that granting Selīm's wishes would only lead to further chaos, and they urged Bāyezīd II to order the prince to return to his province.[60] The sultan did not need much convincing. In fact, as soon as Selīm crossed over to the Crimea, Bāyezīd seems to have ordered the governors of Kili (Kilia, Ukraine) and Akkirman (Cetatea Alba/Bielgorod, Ukraine) to watch all roads and prevent Rumelian soldiers from joining Selīm's following.[61] He also ordered his son back to Trabzon. According to the Ottoman chronicler Ṣolaḳzāde Meḥmed Hemdemī Çelebi (d. 1657), the sultan had responded negatively to Selīm's previous request for permission to organize "raids into the Circassian province," first by ordering him to "go back to [his] place" and then by sending him "reprimanding letters" inquiring whether he intended to become a "partner in the sultanate."[62] When scolding proved ineffective, Bāyezīd chose a course of action that he hoped would induce less resistance: he sent the respected religious scholar and statesman Mevlānā Nūreddīn Ṣarugürz (d. 1521) as his envoy to Selīm's camp on October 29, 1510.[63] Selīm's response only escalated tensions. According to a letter penned by Mevlānā Nūreddīn, Selīm told the envoy that he would not accept

Bāyezīd's orders to return to Trabzon "even if Gabriel descended from the sky and the Messenger [that is, the Prophet Muḥammad] wished it." Referring to Ḳorḳud's Egyptian experience, Selīm also emphasized that, unlike his brother, he would neither return after setting out for a destination nor change his mind.[64]

Selīm was not the only person that Mevlānā Ṣarugürz visited during his mission. He also delivered a letter from Bāyezīd II to Mengli Girāy (d. 1515), the Khan of Crimea, asking for his assistance in convincing the prince to return to his province; correspondence between the two rulers suggests that the Khan obliged. Although the Crimean ruler claimed that, as the Ottoman sultan's "sincere servant," he warned the unruly prince that he did not approve of "orders contrary to the will of the sultan," there are numerous indications that his deeds betrayed his words.[65] Whereas archival documents refer to soldiers sent by the Khan to increase Selīm's military strength,[66] reports sent to the imperial capital by Bāyezīd's agents also mention three hundred soldiers of Saʿādet Girāy (d. 1538), the Khan's younger son, among Selīm's three-thousand-strong troops.[67]

Shift in Succession Politics: Selīm in Rumelia

The unfolding of the negotiation process from that point onward indicates that Selīm had no intention of returning to Anatolia. Announcing that he would not accept any province of lesser value than that given to Aḥmed, Selīm rejected Bāyezīd's offer of the southwestern Anatolian province of Menteşe and requested Silistre (Silistra, Bulgaria) instead.[68] Selīm's insistence on a province in the Balkans is indicative of his primary aim: attaining political power by approaching the imperial capital via Thrace, where the Ottoman ruler had been residing since the devastating earthquake of 1509.

Bāyezīd's efforts to keep Selīm at a safe distance from the seat of the sultanate proved ineffective, as the latter did not linger for long in Kefe. As soon as Bāyezīd's envoy left, Selīm also departed from Kefe, arriving on the northwestern coast of the Black Sea, probably near Akkirman, on June 1, 1511.[69] Although Ottoman archival and narrative sources do not mention the exact dates corresponding to each stop (*menzil*) along Selīm's itinerary in the Rumelian provinces, the fact that his expedition came to an end on August 3, 1511, indicates that the prince had only two months to organize his Rumelian troops before confronting his father at Çorlu.[70] This speedy organization of forces strongly suggests that Selīm initiated contact with Rumelian commanders well before his arrival in the Balkan provinces. Two lists of supporters who joined Selīm in Rumelia recorded these commanders under the heading "These are the ones who welcomed Selīm since Aḳkirman" (*Aḳkirmandan berü istiḳbāle gelenler bunlardur*), implying that these figures had expected Selīm's arrival in their provinces and once again indicating that he had secured military assistance well in advance.[71]

Selīm's westward movement appears to have been progressively militaristic in nature. According to reports sent to Bāyezīd II by numerous agents, by the time Selīm reached Akkirman, his fleet included one hundred ships as well as seven boats,[72] and his troops numbered around three thousand[73] (including members of his own retinue[74] along with three hundred soldiers of Saʿādet Girāy).[75] Another report by a commander loyal to Bāyezīd reveals that the addition to Selīm's forces of one thousand soldiers, sent by the Crimean Khan, increased his military strength even further.[76] That many more joined Selīm in Rumelia is indicated not only by various spy reports that Bāyezīd's agents composed but also by numerous petitions that Selīm's supporters sent to him after his accession to the Ottoman throne. These petitions demanded the rewards that were promised to the supporters in return for their military backing during the succession struggle.[77]

The inhabitants of Akkirman refused to allow Selīm to enter the city, and those of Kili responded to the arrival of the four boats he sent with cannon fire.[78] Evidently, support for Selīm's military was not shared by the urban population of the region. Needless to say, the lack of a warm welcome by commoners changed nothing for Selīm, who continued his southward march.[79] Despite his explicit promise that he would not cross the Danube,[80] Selīm appears to have been closing in on Edirne while waiting for Bāyezīd's reply, which he anticipated would be negative; Selīm used this negotiation process as a means to stall his father from committing to a more active military policy. The to and fro of envoys, who conveyed Selīm's impractical requests (that is, provinces in the Balkans) and his various implausible explanations for his maneuvers (for example, the sole purpose of his troubles being his desire to kiss his father's hand),[81] had the desired effect: by the time Bāyezīd II decided to send Ḥasan Pasha (d. 1514), a prominent commander and the governor-general of Rumelia, to confront his son's forces, Selīm had already reached Edirne.

The dispatch of Ḥasan Pasha can be interpreted as Bāyezīd's acknowledgment of the possibility of a military confrontation. There is also little doubt that the pasha's return to Edirne was interpreted by many as a sign of the strength of Selīm's army—and perhaps even as an indication that he would be the one to succeed his father.[82] Certainly aware of the meaning of, and the grave danger posed by, the presence of his son's troops in the close vicinity of Edirne, Bāyezīd II decided to respond proactively, moving his army toward his son's encampment.[83] At a moment when a military clash seemed unavoidable, Nūreddīn Ṣarugürz was sent, once again, as an envoy to Selīm to establish a truce. Although Ottoman sources disagree as to how this attempt at diplomacy originated and who requested the conciliation, they unanimously record that Ṣarugürz was successful in his mission. Despite Bāyezīd's earlier refusal to grant Selīm a governorship in Rumelia, he now allowed his son to choose between Semendire (Smederevo, Serbia), Bosnia, and Mora (Peloponnesos, Greece).[84] The unruly prince gladly accepted the first option. According to Saʿdeddīn and Muṣṭafā ʿĀlī, Bāyezīd was so pleased with Selīm's conciliatory attitude that he added Vidin (Vidin, Bulgaria) and Alacahisar (Kruševac, Serbia) to his son's lands.[85] Selīm thus avoided immediate war with his father and gained the Rumelian province he so long sought. Most pleasing to Selīm, no doubt, was the sultan's written pledge (*ʿahdnāme*) that he would not abdicate in favor of any prince.[86]

Indeed, it was only after this assurance that Selīm (pretended to) set out toward his new governorship.

There is no reason to believe that Bāyezīd ever intended to keep his promise. His written intention that he would not abdicate (implicitly, in favor of Aḥmed) and his quick departure toward Istanbul as soon as Selīm agreed to the terms of the truce strongly suggest that the sultan consented to the appointment of Selīm to Semendire only as a strategy of appeasement intended to keep the latter away from the imperial capital. Despite Bāyezīd's best efforts to secure the sultanate for his eldest son, his policy of pacification appears to have incurred Aḥmed's resentment. In a letter of complaint written in an aggressive tone, Aḥmed stated that the grant of these three provinces effectively signified the bestowal of the sultanate on his principal rival, who now lacked only the other two symbols of sovereignty (that is, the pronouncement of Friday sermons and the minting of coins in Selīm's name). He therefore threatened to occupy Anatolia and kill everyone who disobeyed him.[87] Undoubtedly aware of his brother's intimidation tactics as well as his father's real intentions—and possibly on the advice of his supporters—Selīm delayed his departure for Semendire.[88] His insistence on staying near Edirne appears to have been motivated by two factors: a desire to monitor his father's actions from an acceptable distance and the need for more time for potential supporters to join him in his quest. Bāyezīd II reacted to his son's procrastination by ordering him to set out for Semendire immediately. His order was in part due to Selīm's success in attracting many disgruntled soldiers, commanders, and "numerous sons of notables" to his camp.[89] The sultan must have also considered the possibility that his own soldiers could change sides. Although Selīm attempted to continue delaying his departure, using the ongoing Şāhḳulu rebellion as an excuse, his father insisted that he leave for Semendire as soon as possible, on the grounds that the protection of that city was critical.[90] Following the advice of his Rumelian commanders, Selīm seems to have taken his time in obeying his father's orders, first moving westward to Çirmen (Ormenio, Greece) but later changing his course northward toward Zağra-i Atik/Zağra Eskisi (Stara Zagora, Bulgaria), possibly hoping to attract more warriors to his side under the premise of organizing raids.[91] According to some sources, Selīm may have also used this opportunity to observe his father's troops by approaching them in disguise; perhaps he attracted some of the sultan's soldiers by offering them double pay before facing his father's troops near Çorlu.[92]

The Şāhḳulu Rebellion and Its Impact

By the time Bāyezīd and Selīm confronted each other in Rumelia, the Ḳızılbaş uprising led by a certain Şāhḳulu had been wreaking havoc in Anatolia for more than three months. This revolt triggered the final military phase of the succession struggle; it also strengthened Selīm's claim to the sultanate by revealing the shortcomings of his rivals. For these reasons, the Şāhḳulu rebellion deserves consideration prior to a discussion of Selīm's final face-off with his father.

Şāhḳulu (lit. "Slave of the Shāh") was a Ḳızılbaş sheikh who led a popular revolt that originated in the southwestern Anatolian province of Teke and wreaked havoc throughout Anatolia between early March and late July 1511. The extent of the defeat and devastation inflicted by Şāhḳulu's forces on Ottoman imperial armies and subjects indicates that the success of the insurgency was not accidental. In terms of its broader historical context, the emergence of Şāhḳulu as the leader of an army that included the Ḳızılbaş adherents of Shāh Ismāʿīl, peasants, tribesmen, and disgruntled provincial cavalrymen (*sipāhī*) can be explained primarily, though not exclusively, by the volatile combination of two major factors. The first was the centralizing strategies of Ottoman monarchs, due to which provincial cavalrymen hailing from old Turco-Muslim families lost their nonhereditary prebends (*tīmār*) to government officials, members of their retinues, or other, Christian-born cavalrymen.[93] The second, more immediate factor was the increasing influence of Shāh Ismāʿīl's politico-religious movement in Anatolia.

In fact, the roots of the strong influence that Şāhḳulu exerted on Ottoman subjects in the province of Teke began with his father, Ḥasan

Ḫalīfe, who had served Sheikh Ḥaydar (d. 1488), Shāh Ismāʿīl's father, and had become his representative (*ḫalīfe*) charged with proselytizing the population of that province.[94] The reputations of Şāhḳulu and his father as spiritual leaders apparently reached Bāyezīd II, who reportedly sent an annual allowance of six or seven thousand aspers (*aḳçe*) for their blessing.[95] There is also strong evidence that Şāhḳulu's representatives helped spread the sheikh's reputation and influence beyond Anatolia by carrying his letters (*kāğıd*) to numerous locations in the Balkan provinces of the Empire, such as Serez (Serres, Greece), Selanik (Thessaloniki, Greece), Zağra Yenicesi (Nova Zagora, Bulgaria), Filibe (Plovdiv, Bulgaria), and Sofya (Sofia, Bulgaria).[96] Although the content of these letters is unknown, the fact that Şāhḳulu's representatives communicated the sheikh's message to his actual or potential supporters in Rumelia only one year before his uprising in Anatolia suggests a plot for a broader uprising across the Empire. Whatever Şāhḳulu's initial design may have been, the geographical scope of his rebellion remained limited to the Anatolian provinces.

The earliest indications of a revolt appeared in the first months of 1511, when the Ottoman throne seemed about to change hands. According to the celebrated Ottoman statesman and historian Muṣṭafā ʿĀlī (d. 1600), when a rumor about Bāyezīd II's intention to abdicate in favor of Prince Aḥmed began to spread, all three princes announced their rightful claim to the Ottoman throne.[97] Because securing the imperial capital was the first step to becoming sultan, all three immediately mobilized their supporters and moved closer to Istanbul. Ḳorḳud and Aḥmed left their provinces and arrived at Manisa and Ankara, respectively, while Selīm was already in Kefe. In March 1511, shortly before Ḳorḳud left his province in haste, twenty unruly agents of Şāhḳulu were captured, but the rebel leader managed to escape.[98] Şāhḳulu apparently suffered little from this setback, as he emerged in charge of many more followers as soon as Ḳorḳud left for Manisa. Spreading the rumor that Korḳud's sudden departure from Teke was a sign of the sultan's death, Şāhḳulu asserted that the realm was available; he possibly intended to utilize this opportunity to seize the whole country.[99] While the *kadi* of Antalya reported that Şāhḳulu's followers had propagated a message about the rebel leader's divinity and prophethood,[100] other reports sent to the imperial capital stated that he had claimed to be the Messiah (*mehdī*).[101] When combined with the absence of Ḳorḳud's gubernatorial authority, Şāhḳulu's propaganda strategies apparently had a significant impact on Ottoman subjects in the province, attracting to his cause disgruntled timariots (*sipāhī*) and villagers (*ḳurā ḫalḳı*) alike.[102]

Although Şāhḳulu's minor victories against Ottoman forces near Antalya contributed to his reputation among Ottoman subjects, the actions of his agents and followers instigated a quick response from the imperial capital.[103] On reports of violent and sacrilegious acts such as pillage, plunder, murder, rape, and public burnings of Qur'āns,[104] Bāyezīd II immediately ordered Ḳaragöz Pasha (d. 1511), the governor-general of Anatolia (*Anaṭolı beglerbegi*), to suppress the rebellion. Despite the destitute condition of most of his followers and with the help of well-trained members of the provincial cavalry forces who had changed sides during earlier skirmishes between the rebels and Ḳorḳud's representatives, Şāhḳulu managed to defeat first the auxiliary troops sent by Ḳaragöz Pasha near Burdur and then the troops commanded by the governor-general himself at Kütahya.[105] Anticipating the dire situation in which Ḳaragöz Pasha would find himself, Bāyezīd had already ordered both Ḳorḳud and Aḥmed to assist the governor-general. That neither prince was at his provincial seat at that time, however, cost Ḳaragöz Pasha his life; captured by the rebels, the governor-general was impaled, and his body burned, outside the citadel of Kütahya on April 22, 1511.[106] The news of the defeat suffered by Ḳorḳud's forces on their way to Manisa[107] combined with reports of the increasing influence of Ḳızılbaş agents on members of the Ottoman dynasty, including Aḥmed's son Murād (d. 1521)[108] and Bāyezīd II's son Şehinşāh (d. 1511),[109] led to shock in the imperial capital and thus to grand vizier Ḫādım ʿAlī Pasha's appointment as commander-in-chief against Şāhḳulu.[110]

The assignment of ʿAlī Pasha to this mission carried a dual significance. The designation of the highest-ranking Ottoman official to the task of suppressing Şāhḳulu's rebellion was an acknowledgment of the gravity of the situation by Bāyezīd II's court, and the crossing over to Anatolia of the most prominent member of the pro-Aḥmed faction further signaled the beginning of the final phase of the succession struggle. In charge of a significant force, ʿAlī Pasha was ordered not only to totally annihilate the rebels but also to be in mutual correspondence and consultation (*müşāvere*) with Prince Aḥmed at all times.[111] Aḥmed was ordered to do the same, making it more than likely that the grand vizier was also charged with bringing the prince back to Istanbul to be appointed the new sultan on the successful suppression of the Şāhḳulu rebellion.[112] Despite the high number and superior quality of his troops, ʿAlī Pasha's campaign ended in utter disappointment and precluded the execution of Bāyezīd's plan to abdicate in Aḥmed's favor. ʿAlī Pasha's failure to acknowledge the severity of the situation—his attribution of Şāhḳulu's success solely to the deficiencies of the governor-general of Anatolia, his decision to delay the final attack on the rebel forces, and his insistence on underutilizing Aḥmed's forces with the intention of keeping the prince out of harm's way—resulted in the initial escape of Şāhḳulu and his followers.[113] Forced to confront Şāhḳulu's forces near Sivas without adequate preparation and possibly also betrayed by some of his own soldiers during this final skirmish, ʿAlī Pasha fell on July 2, 1511.[114] ʿAlī Pasha's death certainly denoted a victory for Şāhḳulu and his followers, who continued the eastward march to their Shāh after the confrontation with the imperial army, laying waste to eastern Anatolian provinces along the way. Despite various inconclusive reports, however, there is strong evidence that Şāhḳulu did not survive the battle to enjoy his success.[115] The fact that his name is not mentioned among those who managed to reach Shāh Ismāʿīl's court further confirms that the rebel leader died during his final encounter with the Ottoman forces.[116]

Although Şāhḳulu's rebellion changed little in terms of the relationship between Bāyezīd II and Shāh Ismāʿīl, its impact on the ongoing succession struggle between the Ottoman princes was immense.

To begin with, the actions of both Ḳorḳud and Aḥmed before and during the rebellion stripped them of any claim to effectiveness as prospective rulers.[117] Although Ḳorḳud had already been considered the academic type by many and was criticized for his choice to leave for Egypt in 1509, his exploits after his return from Mamluk lands, especially his untimely departure from his gubernatorial province, proved to be even more problematic and were considered the immediate reason for the outbreak of the Şāhḳulu rebellion. One can argue that Ḳorḳud's culpability, however limited it may have been at the beginning of one of the most devastating revolts the Empire had ever experienced, tainted him in the eyes of many and gave his brothers' supporters justification for their criticisms of his eligibility for rulership.

In the case of Prince Aḥmed, the damage was even more severe. Aḥmed was already suspected of being a Ḳızılbaş sympathizer due to the influence of Shāh Ismāʿīl's representatives at his gubernatorial court in Amasya,[118] and his claim to legitimacy as the prospective ruler of the Sunnī Ottoman polity was further weakened when his son Murād reportedly joined the ranks of the Ḳızılbaş.[119] But the most significant Ḳızılbaş-related issue that cost Aḥmed dearly in political terms appears to have been his ineffectiveness during the Şāhḳulu episode. Although initially successful in taking the necessary precautions to block the escape routes of Şāhḳulu and his followers, Aḥmed played a minor role during much of the campaign.[120] Although the underutilization of his forces may have been the result of ʿAlī Pasha's efforts to keep him safe, it may also have been part of a strategy to provide the heir-apparent with the opportunity to communicate directly with soldiers and receive their approval for his imminent sultanate. Whatever the logic behind Aḥmed's limited involvement in the suppression of the Şāhḳulu rebellion, several Ottoman chronicles describe the prince's attempt to secure the support of imperial forces during this campaign as well as his utter failure to do so. These sources report that the "soldiers and janissaries" (*sipāh ve yeñiçeri*) explicitly and definitively rejected Aḥmed's claim to the sultanate by refusing to take an oath of allegiance (*bīʿat*) on the grounds that Bāyezīd II was still alive.[121] This rejection of the soldiers was a serious blow to Aḥmed's hopes of succession, but the worst was yet to come. When ʿAlī Pasha died during a skirmish against Şāhḳulu, Aḥmed lost not only his most important political ally at the Ottoman court but also his reputation as a viable candidate for the throne. Criticizing the tardiness of Aḥmed's troops in responding to ʿAlī Pasha's call for help, soldiers held him responsible for the grand vizier's demise and accused him of "cowardice" (*ḫavf*) and "softness" (*tenperver*), two qualities perceived as inappropriate for a prospective Ottoman sultan.[122] According to various Ottoman sources, the janissaries' ultimate hatred (*teneffür*) of the heir-apparent resulted from Aḥmed's premature attempt to impose an oath of allegiance on the soldiers and his general ineptitude during the Şāhḳulu rebellion.[123]

What hurt Ḳorḳud and Aḥmed politically benefited their brother Selīm, who played the Ḳızılbaş card successfully. Unlike Ḳorḳud, whose departure from Antalya ignited Şāhḳulu's rebellion, and Aḥmed, a suspected Ḳızılbaş sympathizer whose ineffectiveness during the revolt proved fatal for an Ottoman grand vizier, Selīm had earned a reputation as a champion of the true faith during his governorship of Trabzon. Thus, a popular movement instigated by the agents of the Safavid ruler, whom Selīm considered his biggest enemy, ironically endowed him with a sense of legitimacy vis-à-vis his rival brothers. It also allowed him the time he so desperately needed to organize his movement in the Balkan provinces before confronting his father's forces at Çorlu, which was one of the most controversial military encounters in Ottoman history.

The Battle of Çorlu and Its Aftermath

In the last days of July 1511, the news of Bāyezīd II's departure for the imperial capital, along with the plausible rumor that the sultan intended to leave his throne to Prince Aḥmed, reached Selīm's camp near Zağra.[124] Although the Ottoman chronicler Ṣolaḳzāde goes further—stating that some of Selīm's "friends" at the imperial court had urged him to act quickly, before the sultan reached Istanbul—Venetian sources explain Bāyezīd's departure as a response to another rumor: that Selīm planned to move on to Istanbul to seize the imperial treasury.[125] Although it is impossible to ascertain who acted first, there is no doubt that Selīm immediately set out for Edirne, where he freed prisoners and "shamelessly" appointed superintendents to proclaim his rule.[126] As soon as the city was secured, he moved on to Istanbul, caught up with his father's forces near Çorlu, and sent Şarābdār Muṣṭafā Çelebi to inquire as to why the sultan was acting against their previous agreement. There is no indication that the envoy was received by the sultan. Instead, Bāyezīd's viziers advised him to attack immediately and unexpectedly, arguing that Selīm had not yet been joined by all of his followers and that those who were already with the prince had not had the chance to rest properly.[127] In an attempt to persuade the sultan, some high-ranking members of his retinue even pointed at Selīm's considerable troops, claiming that the unruly prince's intention was not to visit his father but to kill him with the "sword of hatred."[128]

Contemporary and near-contemporary Ottoman historiography provides only a murky account of the unfolding of events at Çorlu.[129] It is impossible to ascertain, for example, who was responsible for the initial assault. Because any political-military endeavor aimed at overthrowing a ruling sultan was by definition illegitimate, almost all chronicles of the Ottoman tradition make every effort to prove that it was not Selīm who initiated the conflict. Some even argue, albeit unpersuasively, that he gave explicit orders to his soldiers not to engage the enemy.[130] Considering that Selīm systematically gathered military supporters throughout his journey from Trabzon to the Balkan provinces via Kefe, there is no doubt that he expected to confront his father's troops at some point.[131] If he was at all reluctant to fight them at Çorlu, it was probably due to the military advantage that Bāyezīd's forces enjoyed. In particular, they had more troops, were better organized, and had access to field cannons.[132]

Despite lengthy diplomatic maneuvers intended to keep Selīm at a safe distance, Bāyezīd II must have foreseen that the final confrontation would be a military one. The very fact that he did not grant an audience to Şarābdār Muṣṭafā Çelebi, the last envoy sent by his son, indicates that he probably predicted a military showdown by the time both sides had reached Çorlu. Although most historical narratives of the Ottoman tradition hold the sultan responsible for launching the attack on Selīm's forces, they disagree on the extent of the influence exerted by members of the pro-Aḥmed faction at his court. While some argue that Bāyezīd personally ordered the attack,[133] others claim that it was his "wicked" viziers who intentionally misinterpreted the sultan's words of caution and ordered the assault themselves.[134] Regardless of who was responsible for initiating the battle, there is no doubt that it was Selīm's insistence on following his father's troops closely that made a military clash inescapable and ultimately resulted in a crushing defeat for the prince on July 28, 1511.[135] With the help of Ferhād Beg (d. after 1560), who later held the office of the vizierate, and probably also with the help of those Rumelian commanders who were in Bāyezīd's army but sympathized with the prince's cause (and thus prevented the sultan from following his successful offensive with a sustained assault), Selīm barely escaped death. He arrived at Ahyolu (Pomorie, Bulgaria) on August 3, 1511, and crossed over by boat, once again, to Kefe. Nearly three thousand of his supporters reached the same destination over land.[136]

That only a limited number of soldiers reached Selīm's camp at Ahyolu is generally attributed to the devastating defeat his forces had suffered: the majority of his sympathizers had been killed. Although this assumption is largely accurate, archival sources indicate that a rather significant number of soldiers and commanders elected not to join Selīm's retinue. Whereas some were persuaded by Bāyezīd's commanders not to follow the prince to the Crimea, others chose to retreat and regroup closer to their power bases, waiting for a more opportune time to reunite with the unruly prince.[137] Archival sources also suggest that many soldiers were imprisoned, and many others simply could not reach Ahyolu before Selīm's departure.[138] Regardless of the reasons why Selīm had only a few thousand soldiers at his camp, the severe blow his army had suffered apparently triggered a significant shift in strategy. Although some anonymous chroniclers relate that Selīm returned to Rumelia as soon as he secured additional funds (*ḫazīne*) from Deve Kemāl Agha, the warden of the castle of Kefe,[139] other chronicles include lengthy passages that describe Selīm refusing Mengli Girāy's (*Tatar Ḫān*) offer of military assistance as well as his daughter's hand in marriage,[140] primarily because he did not want to become indebted to the Crimean ruler.[141] The letter that Selīm sent to his father after the battle in an attempt to explain his actions leading up to the confrontation at Çorlu is likewise worth noting due to its obedient tone.[142]

Contrary to Selâhattin Tansel's argument, there is no plausible reason to assume that Bāyezīd II's disapproving attitude toward Selīm changed simply because he received an apologetic letter from his rebellious son.[143] Nor can the fact that Bāyezīd acted against his viziers' advice and allowed Selīm to govern his Rumelian provinces in absentia, while he resided in Kefe, be construed as a sign of shifting favor.[144] If Bāyezīd pursued a seemingly gracious policy toward Selīm, it must have been, once again, a calculated strategy to keep him at a safe distance at a critical moment in time. Both Selâhattin Tansel and Çağatay Uluçay also argue that Bāyezīd II was forced to summon Prince Aḥmed to Istanbul despite the latter having fallen from grace due his insistent and insubordinate behavior.[145] Bāyezīd II's subsequent actions not only suggest that the direction of his political trajectory remained unchanged but also clarify why he needed Selīm as far from the imperial capital as possible. According to one narrative source, when Bāyezīd received the sad news of the deaths of Prince Şehinşāh and of grand vizier ʿAlī Pasha, prominent statesmen belonging to the pro-Aḥmed faction abused the sultan's vulnerable emotional state and persuaded him to summon Prince Aḥmed to Istanbul.[146] According to another chronicle, Bāyezīd did not need any persuasion; he took the initiative by summoning the "pillars of the state" himself.[147] Despite grand vizier Hersekzāde Aḥmed Pasha's (d. 1516) words of caution, moreover, the Ottoman sultan appears to have asked the Rumelian commanders and the remaining statesmen for their oaths of allegiance at the same time that he sent financial commissary-general (*defterdār*) Ḳāsım Çelebi to invite Prince Aḥmed to Istanbul.[148]

Sultan's Servants Speak Out: The Janissary Coup

By the time Ḳāsım Çelebi reached Aḥmed's camp at Üsküdar, the latter had already sent his adviser Yularḳaṣdı Sinān Pasha (d. 1514) to the imperial capital to finalize arrangements for his accession to the Ottoman throne. Although Sinān Pasha's arrival prompted an adverse reaction from the janissaries and the Rumelian troops, the worst was yet to come.[149] First, they proclaimed that they would neither accept as sultan nor obey anyone except Prince Selīm.[150] After they were informed that prominent members of the pro-Aḥmed faction likened them to dogs, chaos broke out. The janissaries first left letters of warning on the doors of second vizier Muṣṭafā Pasha (d. 1513), chief military judge (*ḳāḍīʿasker*) Müʾeyyedzāde ʿAbdürraḥmān Efendi (d. 1516), governor-general (*emīrü'l-ümerā* or *mīrmīrān*) Ḥasan Pasha (d. 1514), and chief chancellor (*nişāncı*) Tācīzāde Caʿfer Çelebi (d. 1515) in reaction to insulting words reportedly uttered by these figures.[151] When these warnings were ignored and preparations to welcome Prince Aḥmed continued, however, five thousand soldiers expressed their resentment by attacking the residences of several statesmen with known pro-Aḥmed inclinations.[152] Although the insults of the pro-Aḥmed faction may have initiated the janissaries' violent behavior, it would be safe to assume that the underlying reason for it was their staunch support of Selīm. In fact, according to an anonymous account, these attacks were the result of an explicit agreement that the janissaries had reached with him.[153] Unable to capture these statesmen, the insurgents asked to be forgiven for their unruly behavior and demanded that Müʾeyyedzāde ʿAbdürraḥmān Efendi, Muṣṭafā Pasha, Ḥasan Pasha, Tācīzāde Caʿfer Çelebi, Mīrim Çelebi (d. 1524), and

Āḫī Çelebi (d. 1524) be expelled from the city.[154] They also threatened to cause further devastation if Prince Aḥmed did not return whence he came.[155] Although Bāyezīd dismissed all of the aforementioned statesmen (with the possible exception of Muṣṭafā Pasha), the troops followed and once again threatened Yūlārḳaṣdı Sinān Pasha on his way to Prince Aḥmed's camp on the other side of the Bosphorus.[156]

With his bid for the sultanate in Istanbul in jeopardy, Aḥmed had no other option but to transform Anatolia into his power base. To this end, he not only summoned leaders of tribal groups of seminomads but also took the liberty of appointing his men to key Anatolian provinces.[157] By the time Bāyezīd II put into effect appointments negotiated with the janissaries who supported Selīm, Aḥmed's son ʿAlāʾeddīn was pillaging and plundering numerous villages in Anatolia. A potentially more devastating struggle ensued when Aḥmed attacked the city of Konya. He had already made repeated demands to be granted the province of Karaman, but Bāyezīd had rejected them on the grounds that Konya was the gubernatorial seat of Prince Meḥmed (d. 1512), the son of the deceased Prince Şehinşāh. Still, Aḥmed proceeded to capture the city and began issuing orders as the sole and independent ruler of the Ottoman realm in Anatolia. Aḥmed's attack and conquest of the gubernatorial seat of an appointed prince gave Selīm's supporters the opportunity to argue that the former had committed acts of "rebellion and insubordination" (*ʿiṣyān-ü-ṭuġyān*).[158] As far as Selīm's supporters were concerned, Aḥmed's violent takeover of Konya and his ineffective measures against a new wave of rebellions led by Nūr ʿAlī Ḫalīfe (d. 1512), a representative of Shāh Ismāʿīl, together with Ḳorḳud's initiation of hostile measures against his older brother, not only delegitimized the claims of these two contenders for the Ottoman throne but also confirmed the urgent need to reestablish law and order by bringing a strong military figure to the sultanate.[159]

At this juncture, the janissaries intensified their pressure on Bāyezīd II. Forcefully expressing their dissatisfaction with the sultan's ineffectiveness, they communicated to Bāyezīd directly that they needed a "true" ruler and asked that it be Selīm.[160] Archival evidence also indicates that the janissaries were in constant communication with the prince, informing him of the recent additions of significant political personalities to his camp and even providing him with advice on securing the support of Rumelian commanders.[161] The janissaries' perseverance, coupled with increasing factional support for Selīm at the imperial capital, apparently forced the sultan to grant the pro-Selīm faction their wishes. Hoping that an appointment to the office of commander in chief (*serdār*) of the imperial troops would appease Selīm and his supporters, Bāyezīd II issued an order to that effect on March 27, 1512.[162] Although Selīm was thus granted control of the imperial army, he apparently exercised caution before setting out for Istanbul; he invited certain Rumelian commanders as well as the chief officer of the janissaries, Ferhād Agha, to join him.[163] That Ferhād Agha decided to stay in Istanbul to ensure that the janissaries would keep their promise suggests that Selīm's appointment was not yet universally accepted.[164]

Moreover, this critical phase corresponds to the arrival to Istanbul on March 30, 1512, of Prince Ḳorḳud, who hoped to turn the tide to his advantage. Selīm was aware that his brother was well respected by the janissaries, whom he had treated generously while awaiting their father's succession to the throne in 1481. Although Ḳorḳud resided among the janissaries and attempted to gain their favor by promising to distribute great sums of money to his potential supporters, he ultimately failed to win them over to his side.[165] When Bāyezīd II expressed his displeasure on receiving the news of Ḳorḳud's unsanctioned arrival in Istanbul, the janissaries explicitly stated that they sided with Selīm but promised Ḳorḳud that he would not be harmed.[166] Unable to persuade either party, Ḳorḳud joined the janissaries in awaiting his younger brother's imminent arrival.[167]

Selīm's Accession to the Throne

Although sources generally agree that Selīm arrived in Yenibahçe, within the city walls, before proceeding to the imperial palace, historical narratives vary on how he was proclaimed the new Ottoman sultan on April 24, 1512.[168] Some sources claim that Selīm spent only one night in Yenibahçe and that Bāyezīd II willingly abdicated in favor of his son.[169] Whereas certain sources suggest that Bāyezīd's decision to abdicate was instigated by his personal observation that the janissary troops already accepted Selīm as their new sultan, others argue that Selīm arrived at his father's court to demand the sultanate only after he received the full backing of the imperial troops while still in Yenibahçe.[170] Regardless of these differences, contemporaneous and near-contemporaneous narrative sources of the Ottoman tradition note that Selīm was forced to reside in Yenibahçe for more than a week, indicating an extended negotiation process rather than a quick and simple abdication.[171]

Numerous factors confirm a lengthy discussion. First, the longevity of the conflict between Bāyezīd II and Selīm leaves no plausible reason that the former would leave his throne to the latter without a battle. That Bāyezīd invited Selīm to the imperial capital not with the intention of abdicating in his favor but to grant him the office of commander in chief of the imperial forces to be sent against Prince Aḥmed also suggests that the Ottoman sultan remained hopeful that he could maintain his throne long enough to grant it to his oldest son. Certain historical narratives constantly allude to the unrelenting presence of janissaries in the company of Prince Selīm, and several Ottoman chroniclers acknowledge explicitly the forcible nature of Selīm I's succession to the throne.[172] Whereas Muḥyīüddīn Çelebi states that Bāyezīd never intended to abdicate in favor of Selīm, Muṣṭafā ʿĀlī argues that the sultan did so because he could not find a way to fend off his youngest son.[173] Some anonymous accounts also claim that Selīm's supporters threatened Bāyezīd's viziers with death. All of these sources, moreover, argue that Bāyezīd consented to Selīm's demands only after being told that his son's supporters were ready for a violent takeover if he did not relinquish the sultanate voluntarily.[174] In fact, Muṣṭafā ʿĀlī notes that Bāyezīd II tried to convince his son to accept the title of commander in chief (*serdār*) in charge of the troops to be sent against Shāh Ismāʿīl. His offer fell on deaf ears, however, because Selīm responded that he would be no different than the other viziers if he were to accept this proposal and that it would be impossible to confront the Safavid enemy "without the sultanate."[175] Thus facing the risk of a violent coup, Bāyezīd II was forced to accept the demands of the janissaries, who had long complained that they needed a strong sultan, and so abdicated in favor of Selīm, the prince-turned-sultan.[176]

The "Suspicious" Death of Bāyezīd II

As noted previously, most sixteenth-century Ottoman historians go to great lengths to clear Selīm I's name of any wrongdoing that could render his sultanate illegitimate. Some even go so far as to argue that Selīm did not intend to overthrow his father by force but rather was "obliged" (*żārūrī*) to come to the imperial capital due to pressure from the janissaries.[177] Considering the fact that Bāyezīd II, Prince Aḥmed, and Prince Ḳorḳud would constitute a constant political threat as long as they were alive, it seems obvious that Selīm's troubles did not end with his accession to the Ottoman throne. In fact, succession was nothing but the necessary, though by no means sufficient, condition for the rulership of the Empire, with the elimination of all actual and potential rivals perceived as an absolute necessity. Although not universally accepted as a preferred path, the practice of fratricide had been well established by the time Selīm came to power.[178] The elimination of a retired sultan, however, was utterly unprecedented—hence the special care with which contemporary Ottoman chroniclers broach Bāyezīd's suspicious death on his way to mandatory retirement in Dimetoka (Didymotichon, Greece).

Whereas some narrative sources suggest that Selīm tried to convince his father to remain in Istanbul,[179] others make no mention of such an attempt and depict him as an obedient son who responded positively to his father's wish to retire from worldly affairs and the sultanate.[180] A certain Yūsuf b. ʿAbdullāh argues, however, that it was Selīm who sent his father instead to Edirne to retire.[181] There is nothing surprising about Selīm's reluctance to send his father to a Balkan province or Bāyezīd II's eagerness to undertake such a journey. Taking up residence in Dimetoka would enable the retired sultan to escape the close surveillance Selīm could, and undoubtedly would, establish in the imperial capital. More importantly, residing in Rumelia would allow Bāyezīd to employ the very political and military power base that brought Selīm to power, a risk all too familiar to the new sultan. Seen in this light, Selīm's decision to send two prominent statesmen, Yūnus Pasha and Ḳāsım Pasha, as well as representatives from various janissary regiments on the journey with his father can be interpreted as an attempt to minimize the threat his father's retirement could pose to his sultanate.[182] Extending surveillance beyond the imperial capital proved to be unnecessary, however, when Bāyezīd died on May 26, 1512, shortly after his departure from Istanbul.

The curious timing of Bāyezīd II's death has long been a matter of controversy.[183] Although various European and a few Ottoman sources argue that Bāyezīd was poisoned on Selīm's orders, the great majority of works comprising the Ottoman historiographical tradition do not include any such reference.[184] But the fact that most Ottoman chronicles refer to the incident only very briefly while the tone of some others is extremely defensive does not mean that they entirely lacked implicit criticism.[185] In this regard, one can point to various chronicles that refer to Bāyezīd II's advice to Selīm I shortly before his departure to Dimetoka; the retiring sultan told the latter that he should not "shed anyone's blood unjustifiably."[186] Considering that Bāyezīd's death occurred immediately after he dispensed this advice, the statements in such narratives can be read as implicit criticism of Selīm's deeds through a vague reference to Bāyezīd's premonition of his own demise.

The potential involvement of Selīm in his father's death would harm the legitimacy of his already problematic rise to the Ottoman throne, as reflected in the chroniclers' cautious attitude toward the matter. Modern Turkish historians writing about this controversial episode display similar anxieties. In an effort to make a case for the legitimacy of Selīm's sultanate, contemporary historians such as

Selâhattin Tansel, Çağatay Uluçay, Ahmet Uğur, and Feridun Emecen expend great efforts to prove his innocence. Although providing one of the most detailed narratives of the succession struggle, including that of Selīm's elimination of his rival brothers and their sons, Uluçay emerges as the most implicitly defensive of all, as he does not even refer to Bāyezīd II's death. Whereas Uğur briefly states that the retired sultan's death was caused by his old age and illness,[187] Tansel admits that Bāyezīd's death was "suspicious" but still argues that there was no reason why Selīm would kill his own father.[188] But of course there was an excellent reason: only a dead Bāyezīd could not reclaim Selīm's throne.

The Elimination of Remaining Rivals

Even with Bāyezīd gone, Selīm worried about securing his sultanate. His most significant rival, Prince Aḥmed, was already acting as the sole and independent ruler of the Ottoman realm in Anatolia, demanding men and monies from various provinces.[189] Archival sources also suggest that Aḥmed utilized the forces under the command of his son ʿAlāʾeddīn. These forces included prominent members of the Turco-Muslim military elite, such as Ḏulḳadiroğlu, Ramażānoğlu, Ṭurġudoğlu, Reyḥānoğlu, and Mıdıḳoğlu, who were in charge of tribal groups of seminomads.[190] In addition to various other distinguished commanders, such as Şehsüvāroğlu, Ḳaraoğlu Aḥmed Beg, and Tāceddīn Beg, who supported his quest, Aḥmed appears to have sought and temporarily secured the assistance of commanders from the provinces of Taşili and Karaman.[191]

Despite the impressive array of military figures at his camp, the support Aḥmed enjoyed proved to be short-lived. The capture of Bursa and the subsequent impositions of Prince ʿAlāʾeddīn stirred a violent reaction from the inhabitants of the city, and the turmoil caused by Aḥmed's supporters in Eskişehir and the Menteşe province decreased his chances of receiving further popular support.[192] The news of Bāyezīd's death as well as Selīm's intention to cross over to Anatolia apparently also had an adverse effect on Aḥmed's actual and potential military supporters. Yet, according to a letter included in a copybook of correspondence (*münşe'āt*), Aḥmed was confident enough to demand the Anatolian provinces as his share of the inheritance and as a precondition for the establishment of peace throughout the Empire.[193] Although no record of Selīm's response (if there was any) to this particular request survives, the fact that he finally called for his son Süleymān to secure the imperial city while he crossed over to Anatolia clearly indicates a decision to act on the threat posed by Aḥmed and his supporters.[194]

With his options significantly limited due to this new development, Aḥmed apparently contemplated seeking asylum in Safavid or Mamluk lands, which led to serious disagreements among his supporters and therefore ceased to be a viable option.[195] Aḥmed then demanded Karaman as his share of the realm, only to be refused by Selīm once again.[196] The tension that had long been escalating due to this bargaining process between Aḥmed and Selīm reached a new threshold when the former captured Amasya in November 1512. Selīm responded by executing Muṣṭafā Pasha, whom he suspected of supporting Aḥmed, and, on December 16, 1512, all the remaining sons of his deceased brothers (that is, Prince Maḥmūd's sons Mūsā, Orḫān, and Emīr; Prince ʿĀlemşāh's son ʿOs̱mān; and Prince Şehinşāh's son Meḥmed), who had taken refuge in Bursa. We are told that Selīm acted with the intention of restoring the "order of the universe."[197]

İdrīs-i Bidlīsī (d. 1520) notes that, on being scolded by Selīm, some disgruntled janissaries murmured that there were eleven legitimate "inheritors of the realm" (*vāris̱ā-ye mulk*) who could potentially rule the Empire instead of Selīm. Selīm's awareness that every male member of the House of ʿOs̱mān, if left breathing, constituted a potential threat to his sultanate explains the urgency with which the princes were executed.[198] With most of his potential rivals thus eliminated, Selīm turned his full attention to his remaining brothers. Suspicious of Ḳorḳud's request of Midilli (Lesbos, Greece) and then of the provinces of Teke and Alanya (ʿAlāʾiye) and wary of his reluctance to disperse the troops under his command, Selīm was apparently busy preparing a justifiable excuse to eliminate his brother.[199] When Ḳorḳud responded eagerly to false invitations to the sultanate via numerous letters from authors impersonating Ḳorḳud's fictional supporters, Selīm finally entrapped his rival and, now armed with an enhanced legal justification, ordered his execution in March 1513.[200]

Selīm employed a similar strategy to persuade his most significant rival, Prince Aḥmed, that he had enough military support to secure the sultanate.[201] Devastated when some of his men defected and other supporters proved to be fictitious, on April 15, 1513, Aḥmed lost the battle on the plain of Yenişehir, near Bursa, and was eventually executed after being captured near Izmit (Iznikmīd).[202] With his principal opponent finally eliminated, Selīm concluded this lengthy succession struggle by ordering the execution of Prince Aḥmed's son ʿOs̱mān and Prince Murād's son Muṣṭafā on May 14, 1513.[203] With three battles and nine executions since leaving Trabzon as prince, Selīm thus established his uncontested authority as sultan.[204]

Conclusion

It is noteworthy that whereas some sources refer to Selīm's departure from his province of Trabzon simply as "migration" (*göç*),[205] others use terms such as "coming out" (*ḫurūc*)[206] or "emergence" (*ẓuhūr*).[207] These terms are also used in premodern Islamic sources to refer to a political bid. A failed *ḫurūc* or *ẓuhūr*, of course, is nothing more than a revolt, and both terms are used in that sense as well.

Selīm's choices led him to the plain of Çorlu to face his father's forces in a bloody skirmish that culminated in Bāyezīd II's forced deposition from the Ottoman throne; there is thus little doubt that his venture had the characteristics of a *ḫurūc* or *ẓuhūr* rather than those of a *göç*. Evidence from Ottoman archives as well as from Venetian narrative sources certainly suggests so. Although both contemporaneous and later Ottoman narrative sources clearly describe the unfolding of events as such, their accounts are colored by an effort to clear Selīm's name of any illegitimate act against Bāyezīd, the rightful ruler of the Empire, because such an act would in essence render Selīm's own sultanate illegitimate. In line with these Ottoman sources and most certainly possessing a similarly defensive tone, modern Turkish historiography on the saga exhibits a tendency to depict Selīm's struggle not as part of a long-standing and carefully planned endeavor but as the result of external conditions that developed independently of his imperial ambitions. Composed in an effort to exonerate Selīm, Ottoman historical narratives read as a roster of seemingly contradictory events rather than as a cohesive account outlining the unambiguous trajectory of an increasingly volatile succession struggle that Selīm had no intention of losing.

As a result, modern Turkish scholarship on sixteenth-century Ottoman history downplays or even silences the forceful nature of Selīm's takeover. It is not surprising, therefore, that such contemporary scholarly works do not include an analysis of the post-Kefe phase of Selīm's enterprise, when the unruly prince successfully secured the assistance of the Crimean Khan and, most importantly, attracted to his side the Rumelian commanders and soldiers who played a pivotal role in helping him to realize his imperial dream. By focusing on a wide array of primarily Ottoman archival and narrative sources—including but not limited to imperial decrees, letters, petitions, spy reports, copybooks of correspondence, general histories of the Ottoman dynasty, *Selīmnāmes*, and Venetian *relazioni*—the next chapter aims to provide a clearer picture of Selīm's struggle by further identifying those political and military factions comprising his power base.

2 Politics of Factions

> So little value is attached to high birth in the Turkish realm. I saw also, in other places, descendants of the imperial families of the Cantacuzeni and Palaeologi, whose position among the Turks was lower than that of Dionysius at Corinth. For the Turks do not measure even their own people by any other rule than that of personal merit. The only exception is the House of Othman; in this case, and in this case only, does birth confer distinction.[1]

ON DECEMBER 2, 1503, Andrea Gritti (d. 1538) presented before the Venetian Senate one of the earliest surviving examples of a Turkish *relazione*. The document evaluated Bāyezīd II's sons' chances of succession in the following manner:

> Aḥmed has always been stationed in the province (*sancaḳ*) of Amasya, where he leads a life of leisure. They say that he has a regal presence, and an amiable nature, but he is not generally considered to have a good understanding of affairs of state. He defers to the council of his advisers, and above all wants to live free of work or worldly cares, hoping to succeed his father in nature of being the eldest born son.
>
> Ḳorḳud is small in stature, and completely devoted to the study of philosophy. He composes works of Islamic theology, and lives in Manisa. He is convinced of one day being sultan, hoping that his father will favor him over the others because of his piety. Because of this, and because of his feelings of filial loyalty, he has for now renounced any role in government in order to leave his father, as long as he lives, in complete control.
>
> Selīm is of medium build, but very fit and agile, with a small black face and two big mustaches. He is considered to be more ferocious and cunning than his brothers, and his eyes betray a cruel

> streak. He is extremely generous, and at the same time a warmonger, and thanks to these two qualities he has made great strides, such that there are some who say that he will be the one to succeed his father. They reason that the janissaries, whose favor is decisive in determining the succession, will not want Aḥmed, who cares only for his own pleasures, or Ḳorḳud, who spends all his time with books, but this [Selīm], who will maintain the empire wisely, and conquer new lands, and through his generosity will build new and valorous armies, giving them all of his favor and grace.
>
> The Sultan, for his part, wants Aḥmed, who is temperate and quiet, to succeed him, since he fears—according to what [Hersekzāde] Aḥmed Pasha told me one day—the excessive ferocity of Selīm. And this would also be the best outcome for Your Serenity [that is, the Venetian government] and for all the Christian rulers, because, besides the fact that Aḥmed has a peaceful character, the trouble that he will face from his brothers and their partisans will be such that he will always be preoccupied with fighting them.[2]

Best known today for Titian's famous portrait of him as the Doge of Venice, Gritti (r. 1523–1538) was perhaps the most prominent Venetian with close ties to the Ottoman court at the beginning of the sixteenth century.[3] Having spent much of his early life in Istanbul, Gritti served his city-state during his stay in the Ottoman capital by overseeing Venetian commercial and political interests as well as contributing to political intelligence through reports to the Senate. Although Gritti was imprisoned on charges of espionage during the conflict between Venice and the Ottoman Empire (1499–1503), his exceptionally close ties to members of the Ottoman court apparently saved his life, and his appointment as the Venetian negotiator of the peace treaty with Bāyezīd II gave him the opportunity to observe the sultan and his viziers at work.[4] Gritti seems to have used this opportunity effectively, composing a vivid portrayal of Ottoman statesmen and of Bāyezīd's probable intentions regarding Ottoman relations with Venice.[5] His personal connections with leading members of the Ottoman ruling elite, including the sultan and his grand vizier

Hersekzāde Aḥmed Pasha (d. 1516), also enabled him to identify the contenders for Bāyezīd's throne and to forecast the outcome of the succession struggle eight years before its final phase was triggered by the Safavid-instigated rebellion of Şāhḳulu in the southern Anatolian province of Teke.[6]

Gritti's *relazione* is a relatively normative historical narrative in terms of its Istanbul-centered outlook and its emphasis on the decisive role of the janissaries in determining Ottoman succession.[7] In fact, approximately one month before Selīm I's accession to the Ottoman throne, Andrea Foscolo, a Venetian envoy to the imperial capital, also emphasized the definitive influence exerted by the janissaries and the officials of the Porte in determining the outcome of political power struggles in general and of the internecine strife among Bāyezīd's sons in particular. He wrote that "they are the ones who dominate and rule the country."[8] The fact that both Gritti and Foscolo resided in Istanbul for a considerable amount of time can serve as a partial explanation for their knowledge of, and emphasis on, political actors located in the imperial capital. That a janissary revolt indeed turned the tide in favor of Selīm and ultimately sealed his sultanate confirms that these prominent Venetians were justified in recognizing the power of the Ottoman military ruling elite in Istanbul. As will be demonstrated in this chapter, however, Gritti and Foscolo's inaccurate evaluations, based on their personal observations, of the complex interrelations among holders of political power led to an incomplete analysis of the historical episode in question. Thus, they ignored the extent of the politico-military support Selīm enjoyed in the Balkan provinces of the Empire.

Similarly, the analysis provided by several modern historians of the power struggle during the last years of Bāyezīd II's reign is flawed in a number of ways. For example, in relating the last phase of the succession struggle as perceived by the agents of a European nation, Sydney Nettleton Fisher accounts for the factions supporting each Ottoman prince by stating that "Bāyezīd and his viziers preferred Aḥmed, the poets and the theologians supported Ḳorḳud, but the soldiers chose Selīm."[9] As appealing as these clear-cut categorizations might seem, various factors render them problematic. To begin with, Fisher's claim fails to go beyond the simplistic interpretations of his Venetian sources; it also betrays a lack of understanding of the structure of the Ottoman administration. Because all members of the Ottoman ruling elite, including the sultan and his viziers, were essentially members of a military class (*ʿaskerī*), Fisher's use of the generic term "soldiers" is too nonspecific to be of any analytical value. His classification gives an inaccurate impression of mutual exclusivity among the sociopolitical groups supporting each prince, and his argument lacks historicity because it refers to the factions in static terms without taking into account the shifts in allegiance that occurred over the course of the struggle for the Ottoman throne.

Turkish historians Çağatay Uluçay and Selâhattin Tansel use strikingly similar—and at times equally vague and misleading—terminology in addressing the question of factionalism during the internecine strife between Bāyezīd's three sons. Despite their extensive use of Ottoman archival and narrative sources to undergo a detailed exploration of the sequence of events, both historians' analyses suffer significantly because of the nonspecific vocabulary they use to refer to the politico-military factions supporting each prince. Uluçay, for example, refers to Aḥmed's supporters as "the statesmen" (*devlet adamları*), Selīm's as "the army" (*ordu*), and Ḳorḳud's simply as "many" (*birçokları*).[10] Tansel, however, mentions the ruling sultan, his viziers, and "the commoners" (*halk tabakası*) among Aḥmed's supporters and refers to the followers of Ḳorḳud vaguely as "some of the statesmen" (*devlet erkanından bazıları*) and "a faction of the janissaries" (*yeniçerilerden bir kısmı*).[11] Although all three scholars name several prominent members of the Ottoman military ruling elite as members of the pro-Aḥmed faction, they fail to identify the precise factions that brought Selīm to power.[12] By failing to delineate the origins and relations of political power, modern historiographers also fail to recognize the significance of non-janissaries in Selīm's successful bid for the Ottoman throne.

The primary aim of this chapter is to rectify the Istanbul- and janissary-centered arguments prevalent in Ottoman studies by demonstrating that political support for Selīm crossed social and military classes and thus that the outcome of the succession struggle was decided by the degree of support Selīm enjoyed in the "periphery" (that is, the Balkan provinces of the Empire) as much as by the backing of politico-military factions at the imperial "center" (that is, Istanbul). Based on a variety of (mostly Ottoman) narrative and archival sources—including but not limited to general histories of the Ottoman dynasty (*tevārīḫ-i āl-i ʿOs̱mān*), anonymous chronicles, literary-historical narratives specifically focusing on Selīm and his reign (*Selīmnāme*), imperial decrees (*ḥükm*), letters (*mektūb*), petitions (*ʿarż*), spy reports, and Venetian *relazioni*—the discussion that follows concentrates on each contender for Bāyezīd II's throne and explores the politico-military alliances they employed with varying degrees of success. The primary empirical basis of this prosopographical analysis consists of two undated, single-page archival documents listing the names of military commanders whose power bases were located in Rumelia and a salary register (*mevācib defteri*) dated 1512 that includes the names of members of Selīm's royal retinue immediately after his accession to the throne.

This chapter also addresses the larger question of Ottoman patrimonialism. The received wisdom of modern scholarship is that the essentially feudal political structure of the Ottoman polity during its formative period (that is, between the inception of the Ottoman enterprise around 1300 and the conquest of Constantinople in 1453) was transformed into a patrimonial one, whereby the vassals or allies of a suzerain became the slaves or clients of a patriarch, during the reign of Meḥmed II (r. 1444–1446 and 1451–1481) and was ultimately perfected by Süleymān I (r. 1520–1566).[13] Although this transformation may have indeed been the intended goal of the centralizing efforts of all Ottoman rulers, an exploration of succession struggles preceding and including the one that brought Selīm I to power indicates that this portrayal is grossly oversimplified. In fact, an analysis of factional politics during Selīm's struggle for the Ottoman throne suggests that the Ottoman polity in the first quarter of the sixteenth century was not a patrimonial empire in which all political power emanated from the sultan, located at the apex of a pyramid-like political structure. On the contrary, within the context of the never-ending process of centralization, relations of relative power between military-political factions and various members of the Ottoman dynasty changed continuously, as alliances shifted constantly. Even if patrimonialism constituted one of the dominant features of the relationship between the Ottoman monarch and the members of his ruling elite, the fact that it was constantly tested, fissured, fractured, renegotiated, and rebuilt begs the question of whether the Ottoman polity ever epitomized the patrimonial empire imagined by most modern scholars.[14]

Selīm's rise to the sultanate exemplifies this dynamic process. For example, although the janissaries sympathized with Selīm as early as 1503 (per Andrea Gritti's *relazione*), they fought as part of Bāyezīd II's army against Selīm at Çorlu (August 1511) and negotiated with Selīm's rival brother Ḳorḳud in their barracks in Istanbul (March 1512) before they assisted Selīm's efforts to depose his father (April 1512). Although their final act of siding with Selīm represented a concrete fissure in the theoretically patrimonial relationship between the now-deposed sultan and his slave-servants, it did not automatically establish unconditional boundaries with their new master. On the contrary, references in several chronicles reveal the symbolic negotiation process by which parameters of this new political relationship between Selīm and the janissaries were decided.[15] Writing during the last decade of the sixteenth century, Muṣṭafā Cenābī (d. 1590) relates that before Selīm's accession the janissaries stood on both sides of the entrance to the imperial palace and crossed their rifles, swords, and javelins, expecting the new sultan to pass under their weapons in accordance with what they called an "ancient custom" (*ʿādet-i ḳadīme*). This act would, at least symbolically, render him "submissive" (*rām ideler*). Cognizant of the fact that such an act would be construed as a "sign of defeat" (*maġlūbluḳ ʿalāmeti*), Selīm refused and acceded to the throne after slipping into the palace secretly.[16] One of Cenābī's contemporaries, historian-bureaucrat Selānikī Muṣṭafā Efendi (d. 1600), relates the unfolding of a similar process at the time of Selīm II's (r. 1566–1574) accession in 1566. Selānikī tells his readers that when Süleymān I died in Szigetvár while campaigning in southwestern Hungary, grand vizier Sokullu Meḥmed Pasha (d. 1579) invited Prince Selīm to the army camp to assume control of the imperial army and take over his father's household. Selīm refused, however, when one of his advisors remarked that the grand vizier had an ulterior motive: "to dominate the ruler" (*murādları ḥākimi maḥkūm idinmekdür*). It is especially remarkable that another advisor referred to the old saying that "no [member of the] House of ʿOs̱mān ascends to the throne without passing under the swords of the household troops first (*āl-i ʿOs̱mān salṭanat taḥtına geçmez mādem ki ḳuluñ ḳılıcı altından geçmeye*)," but he noted that because Selīm II's accession was uncontested, the axiom did not apply. Unlike Selīm II's accession, Selīm I's was nothing if not contested, which explains why, according to several anonymous chroniclers, Selīm established new rules of engagement as soon as he acceded to the throne; he ordered the execution of a janissary officer (*üsküflü yeñiçeri*) by hanging and a member of the regular cavalry corps of the Porte (*ʿulūfeci*) by the sword, but only after he inquired as to whether the janissaries "accepted" his sultanate (*ḳabūl ider misüz*).[17]

The accession of a new monarch was the moment when the cards that had been dealt during the reign of the previous Ottoman sultan were reshuffled. This process allowed for factional permeability for rank-and-file soldiers and high-ranking statesmen alike, regardless of their factional identity *before* the accession of the new sultan. Within the context of Selīm I's rise to power, for example, this reshuffling led to the incorporation into the new sultan's retinue of numerous soldiers who previously had been associated with rival members of the Ottoman dynasty or had belonged to the entourages of statesmen with known or suspected pro-Aḥmed stances.[18] As previously stated, this process of reconstitution was not limited to rank-and-file soldiers; it encompassed high-ranking statesmen as well. Indeed, those employed at Selīm's court included such prominent members of the pro-Aḥmed faction as Müʾeyyedzāde ʿAbdürraḥmān Efendi (d. 1516), Tācīzāde Caʿfer Çelebi (d. 1515), Hersekoğlu Aḥmed Pasha (d. 1516), and Yūnus Pasha (d. 1517), some of whom furthered their careers during the reign of their new master.

By the time Selīm made his political bid, dynastic struggles had become ordinary phenomena, but they had involved battling princes and their respective factions only *after* the death of a sultan.[19] Selīm's ascent to the Ottoman throne is thus highly significant, as it marked a first in Ottoman history: the overthrow of a legitimate Ottoman ruler by one of his sons. That Selīm deposed his father is meaningful in itself because it undermines the validity of the claim that the sixteenth-century Ottoman polity embodied a patrimonial empire. On the contrary, Selīm's successful bid for his father's throne signified a challenge to the basic assumption of patrimonialism: the (at the least, conceptual) continuity between the sultan, his household, and his dominion. The janissaries' espousal of Selīm's cause not only constituted a rupture in the presumed continuity between the sultan and his household but also led to Bāyezīd II's complete loss of control over his dominion.

The dominion of an Ottoman sultan was not limited to the imperial capital, however. As will be emphasized below, numerous politically significant social groups and military factions resided in the Anatolian and Rumelian provinces of the Ottoman realm. For ruling sultans, the centrifugal tendencies of these groups and factions constituted a challenge; for royal contenders, their manpower presented an opportunity. Their effective mobilization during succession struggles could empower a new sultan, and the enthronement of a new monarch could allow them to renegotiate their positions vis-à-vis the imperial center. The analysis below focuses on the many politico-military factions located both at the imperial center and in the peripheral provinces. The various factions supporting each prince are addressed separately in order to demonstrate how alliances between these groups and the contenders for the throne shifted over the course of the succession struggle.

The Pro-Aḥmed Faction: Defenders of the Status Quo

Shortly before his death in 1481, Meḥmed II may have contemplated killing his son Bāyezīd because of the abundance of the latter's sons;[20] like many of his contemporaries, the Conqueror may have considered the potential for political turmoil following Bāyezīd's death. Although he certainly could not have foreseen that five of his grandsons would precede their father to the grave before they could make any bid for political power, the launch of a brutal succession struggle among Princes Aḥmed, Ḳorḳud, and Selīm proved that his hunch was correct.[21]

Ottoman and non-Ottoman sources agree that Aḥmed, the oldest surviving son of Bāyezīd, was the most formidable contender for the throne when the ailing ruler began to lose his grip on the sultanate. The authority of Aḥmed's most significant ally, however, was questioned before the final phase of the succession struggle. Bāyezīd's international policies vis-à-vis the Mamluks and the newly emerging Safavids were considered ineffective by his moderate critics; his more radical opponents regarded them as acts of treason against Ottoman soldiers, whom Bāyezīd left unprotected against the attacks of enemy armies.[22] Various Ottoman chroniclers also castigated Bāyezīd for playing an increasingly insignificant role in decision-making processes regarding affairs of the state and for allowing prominent but undeserving viziers to exert undue influence on the administration of the realm.[23]

Although the frequent references in the *Selīmnāme*s and anonymous chronicles to Ottoman viziers as "mischief-makers" (*müfsid*) are in part due to problems the Empire faced in the domestic and international arenas during the final years of Bāyezīd's reign, this negative terminology was also a reflection of the chroniclers' anti-Aḥmed attitude. In fact, numerous viziers at the Porte who openly aligned themselves with Aḥmed and supported Bāyezīd's pro-Aḥmed inclination gained infamous partisan epithets such as "Aḥmedī," "Aḥmedlü," or even "Bāyezīdī." Ottoman chroniclers frequently referred to these statesmen collectively as "grandees belonging to Aḥmed's faction" or as "subjects of Aḥmed."[24] There is nothing unique about using the name of a contender for the throne to identify a failed political faction, especially because the historians who recorded the succession struggle had the luxury of retrospective knowledge. That the supporters of a legitimate Ottoman monarch were reduced to a mere political collective is noteworthy, however, because their categorization constitutes an implicit statement about the perceived illegitimacy of Bāyezīd's attempt to bring Aḥmed to power. Similarly, that Ottoman chroniclers never refer to Selīm and his supporters as "Selīmī" must be considered an indication of the unquestioned legitimacy he acquired *after* becoming the sole ruler of the Ottoman realm.[25]

As the foremost member of the pro-Aḥmed faction, Bāyezīd II received special attention from the chroniclers. He is depicted as the ruling dynast whose legitimacy was questioned due to his advanced age and deteriorating health, both of which led to the increasing influence of his statesmen. Yet, at the same time, he is given credit as a decisive sultan, announcing his preference for his oldest son early in the succession struggle.[26] That he never endorsed the candidacy of either one of his other two sons and maintained his support for Aḥmed as long as the latter's sultanate remained a viable option also suggests his staunch endorsement of his eldest son.

Although it is impossible to determine the exact reasons for Bāyezīd's unyielding support for Aḥmed, Ottoman and non-Ottoman sources mention a variety of possible factors. Some of these factors—for example, Bāyezīd's emphasis on the abundance of Aḥmed's children,[27] his appreciation of Aḥmed's temperate nature coupled with his fear of Selīm's excessive ferocity,[28] and the influence of the sultan's statesmen who preferred the status quo and were especially enjoying their recently attained power and privilege—are more plausible than others.[29] Although all of these considerations may have led to Bāyezīd's overt endorsement of Aḥmed, the support that the latter enjoyed from prominent members of the Ottoman military ruling elite at the Porte must have been the most significant factor. First, Aḥmed was generally regarded as someone who lacked leadership qualities and deferred to his advisers for important decisions.[30] Indeed, he enjoyed the support of statesmen who were accustomed to positions of power and authority during his father's reign, and he benefited from the constant presence of his servants in Istanbul.[31] The extent of his connections to holders of power at the imperial capital is impressive, especially in comparison to the failure of his two rival brothers to garner political backing at the Porte.

Within this context, grand vizier Ḫādım ʿAlī Pasha (d. 1511) emerges as the leading member of the pro-Aḥmed faction at the Ottoman court. ʿAlī Pasha's appropriation of fiefs within the borders of Ḳorḳud's province[32] and his presentation of Selīm's activities in the Balkan provinces as acts of insubordination and rebellion[33] are only two examples of the grand vizier's numerous attempts to weaken Aḥmed's adversaries. His later efforts, however, were apparently more focused on providing military support *for* Aḥmed rather than on placing obstacles *against* Aḥmed's rivals. The grand vizier's collaboration with Bāyezīd II during the Şāhḳulu rebellion is especially significant in this regard. Although ultimately aborted due to the revolt of the janissaries in Istanbul, ʿAlī Pasha's dual mission of suppressing the Safavid-instigated popular rebellion and bringing Aḥmed to the imperial capital was especially noteworthy in that it signaled the beginning of the final phase of the succession struggle, which Bāyezīd seems to have hoped to conclude by appointing Aḥmed to the sultanate.[34]

Chronicles of the Ottoman tradition generally do not mention individual members of political factions by name. Instead, they tend to define them descriptively as a group (for example, "Aḥmedlü," "Aḥmedī," and "grandees belonging to Aḥmed's faction"). But they do include specific references to some key historical figures in their narratives of certain events. One such episode is the janissary revolt that took the form of attacks on the residences of statesmen with known pro-Aḥmed inclinations. Although the lists of those harassed given by most chronicles include second vizier Muṣṭafā Pasha (d. 1512), chief military judge (*ḳāḍīʿasker*) Müʾeyyedzāde ʿAbdürraḥmān Efendi (d. 1516), Rumelian governor-general (*mīrmīrān*) Ḥasan Pasha (d. 1511), and chancellor (*nişāncı*) Tācīzāde Caʿfer Çelebi (d. 1515), some narratives also refer to grand vizier Hersekoğlu Aḥmed Pasha (d. 1516) and Yūnus Pasha (d. 1517).[35]

Muṣṭafā Pasha, ʿAbdürraḥmān Efendi, Ḥasan Pasha, and Caʿfer Çelebi are mentioned in practically all general histories of the Ottoman Empire, but references to Hersekoğlu Aḥmed Pasha and Yūnus Pasha are found exclusively in anonymous chronicles.[36] The apparent correlation between the type of historical account (that is, general history or anonymous chronicle) and the names included in the pro-Aḥmed faction strongly suggests that the curious exclusion of Aḥmed Pasha and Yūnus Pasha from general histories was not accidental. In fact, a comparison of the later careers of these two figures with those of other members of the pro-Aḥmed faction indicates quite the contrary, illustrating that the Ottoman dynasts worked diligently to preserve their elites, even at times of political strife.

Curiously enough, with the exception of Muṣṭafā Pasha, all of these prominent statesmen continued their political careers during the reign of Selīm I despite having supported Selīm's archrival Aḥmed during the succession struggle.[37] While Müʾeyyedzāde ʿAbdürraḥmān Efendi served as military judge of Rumelia until his retirement in 1514,[38] Tācīzāde Caʿfer Çelebi held the offices of chancellor (*nişāncı*) and chief military judge (*ḳāḍīʿasker*) of Anatolia.[39] The lives of some of these figures later took turns for the worse;[40] Hersekoğlu Aḥmed Pasha and Yūnus Pasha emerge as the only members of the pro-Aḥmed faction who furthered their careers under Selīm by serving in the highest possible position: grand vizier.[41] Seen in this light, the exclusion of the names of these two individuals from the list of pro-Aḥmed statesmen whose residences were attacked by the janissaries can be interpreted as an attempt by the authors of general histories to clear the names of those closest to Selīm (and currently in office) from the stain of their earlier anti-Selīm stance. Archival documents on this particular episode of the succession struggle add the names Mīrim Çelebi (Maḥmūd Efendi, d. 1524) and Āḫī Çelebi (Meḥmed Efendi, d. 1524) to the list of statesmen whom the janissaries demanded be expelled from Istanbul.[42] That the former had been one of Bāyezīd II's teachers and the latter had served both Bāyezīd and Selīm as chief physician indicates that membership in the pro-Aḥmed faction, which the janissaries perceived as a political threat, was not limited strictly to "men of the sword" (*seyfiyye*).[43]

Although Aḥmed's most prominent supporters were located at his father's court in Istanbul, pro-Aḥmed inclinations extended beyond high-ranking statesmen at the imperial capital. Especially after the janissaries' anti-Aḥmed sentiments took the form of an uprising against his allies, the prince appears to have sought and temporarily secured the military assistance of commanders from several Anatolian provinces.[44] In addition to recruiting regular troops from the province of Karaman (*Ḳaraman ʿaskeri*),[45] Aḥmed formed alliances with nomadic groups like the Varsaḳ and Ṭurġud,[46] and the forces under the command of his son (and ally) ʿAlāʾüddīn included such prominent members of the Turco-Muslim military elite as Ḏulḳadiroğlu, Ramażānoğlu, Ṭurġudoğlu, Reyḥānoğlu, and Mıdıḳoğlu, who were in charge of tribal groups of seminomads.[47] Various other distinguished commanders—including Şehsüvāroğlu, Ḳaraoğlu Aḥmed Beg,[48] and Tāceddīn Beg[49]—also supported Aḥmed in his quest, attesting to the remarkable extent of the network of politico-military power that the Ottoman prince managed to garner in Anatolia.

This military support was at least partially due to an ingenious recruitment strategy. Throughout contemporary archival and narrative sources, numerous references to a cluster called *yevmlüler* or *yevmlü ṭāʾifesi* ("day-wage men") among Aḥmed's supporters indicate that the prince recruited tax-paying subjects (*reʿāyā*) in return for daily wages—quite possibly a first in Ottoman history.[50] Aḥmed's strategy capitalized on the fact that military campaigns and succession struggles constituted rare moments of opportunity for tax-paying subjects, especially those who were Muslim-born, because the otherwise rigid boundaries between the *reʿāyā* and the social stratum composed of warriors became temporarily permeable; tax-paying subjects of the Empire joined the ranks of regularly paid troops in large numbers, attempting to achieve upward social mobility by becoming members of the prince's regularly paid troops.[51]

Despite his clever recruitment strategies, several factors may have rendered Aḥmed's cooperation with Anatolian commanders and their troops ephemeral. Judging from the immediate negative effect of the news concerning Sultan Bāyezīd's death, the Karamanian commanders apparently realized that his passing would reduce them to supporters of a rebellious prince rather than of an appointed heir apparent and would thus jeopardize any legitimacy they could claim for their actions.[52] There is also little doubt that the news of Selīm's intention to cross over to Anatolia contributed to their reluctance, especially because it forced Aḥmed to consider seeking asylum in Safavid or Mamluk lands.[53] Altogether, considerable disagreement among the Karamanian commanders about which path to follow may have compelled them to reconsider the viability of Aḥmed's cause.[54]

The Pro-Ḳorḳud Faction

Compared to his older brother, Ḳorḳud benefited little, if at all, from the political support of the "men of the sword." As a scholar, he was held in high esteem;[55] he was also respected by the janissaries, whom he had treated generously while awaiting his father's succession to the throne in 1481.[56] However, his lack of male offspring and, more importantly, his perceived incompetence on the battlefield made him unfit to rule in the eyes of many, including his father.[57] Unable to secure within the Ottoman realm the backing necessary to counter his brothers' bid for the sultanate, Ḳorḳud turned his attention to allies outside the Empire, particularly to the Mamluk ruler Qānṣūh al-Ghawrī (r. 1501–1516).[58]

Ottoman princes who held gubernatorial seats were strictly prohibited from abandoning their assigned provinces without the authorization of the ruling monarch; nonetheless, Ḳorḳud departed for Egypt. His move was not unprecedented: his uncle, Cem (d. 1495), had also traveled to Egypt to gain safety from, and support against, his own brother, Bāyezīd, during the period of internecine strife following the death of Meḥmed II.[59] What made Ḳorḳud's case unique, however, was the scholarly sophistication with which he defended himself against accusations of the unlawful dereliction of duties. By 1508, Ḳorḳud had already composed a work in Arabic entitled *Daʿwat al-nafs al-ṭāliḥa ilā al-aʿmāl al-ṣāliḥa* (The Erring Soul's Summons to Virtuous Works), asking to be released from his princely duties and candidacy for the Ottoman throne—perhaps he knew that he had little chance of succeeding his father and that he would be executed by whichever brother did ascend to the throne.[60] Later, in another autobiographical treatise, he justified his sudden departure for Egypt with reference to the fulfillment of his religious duty to perform pilgrimage (*ḥacc*).[61] Although nothing is known about Bāyezīd's reception of this work, the curious timing of Ḳorḳud's departure must have alarmed the sultan as to the motives of his son, and justifiably so. The fact that Ḳorḳud left his province the month after that year's pilgrimage ritual had ended shows that he was motivated by the political affairs of this world rather than a desire to set out on a spiritual journey to the heart of Islam.

Although the purpose of Ḳorḳud's sojourn cannot have been purely religious, there is also no definitive evidence that he was "the primary Ottoman agent behind early cooperative Mamluk-Ottoman actions in the Indian Ocean against the Portuguese," as Nabil Al-Tikriti contends.[62] At a time when Ḳorḳud's relationship with his brother Aḥmed was already strained and his falling-out with grand vizier Ḫādım ʿAlī Pasha (over the appropriation of fiefs within the borders of his province) once again indicated the limits of his political authority,[63] departure for Egypt could only mean that he hoped for the assistance of the Mamluk court and that he regarded Qānṣūh al-Ghawrī as an ally in the imminent succession struggle.[64] Despite the warm reception he received, however, Ḳorḳud was unable to secure the military support of the Mamluk ruler, possibly due to a letter of warning from Bāyezīd II.[65] Realizing that his efforts were in vain, Ḳorḳud sent letters of apology to his father and the grand vizier, along with the aforementioned treatise, so that he could once again enjoy the advantage of following the unfolding of events from his (former) province.[66] After his request for reinstatement was granted, Ḳorḳud returned to Antalya[67] only to resume his efforts to receive an appointment closer to Istanbul. He petitioned for the governorship of the province of Aydın, which included Menemen, the location of his private properties (*mülk evler*).[68] When his request fell on deaf ears, Ḳorḳud set out for Manisa, and later for Istanbul, to persuade the janissaries at the imperial capital to support his political bid.[69] Although there is no reason to accept Kemālpaşazāde's assumption that Ḳorḳud lacked the motivation to voice his claim for the Ottoman throne, the timing of his arrival in Istanbul strongly suggests that the encouragement of some members of the pro-Aḥmed faction played an important role in his decision to do so.[70] Various near-contemporary sources note that Ḳorḳud was invited to Istanbul by those who regarded him as their last chance for continuation of the status quo after Aḥmed had left the vicinity of Istanbul and just before Selīm set out for the imperial capital following his appointment to commander in chief (*serdār*) of the imperial troops.[71] That Ferhād Agha, the janissary commander, decided to stay in Istanbul to ensure that the janissaries would keep their promise to Selīm suggests not only that the latter's appointment as the commander of imperial forces to be sent against Aḥmed was not yet universally accepted but also that Ḳorḳud might have thought that he indeed had a chance, however slight, to turn the tide in his favor.[72]

Once he arrived at the imperial capital, Ḳorḳud realized that the respect of the janissaries would not necessarily translate into political endorsement. Despite his attempts to gain the support of the troops by residing among the janissaries[73] and by promising to distribute great sums of money to his potential supporters,[74] Ḳorḳud failed; the janissaries explicitly stated their endorsement of Selīm. But as a sign of the great respect they had for the scholarly prince, who likely had hoped to benefit from their regard, they promised Ḳorḳud that he would not be harmed after Selīm's ascension to the throne.[75] Nevertheless, once Selīm secured the sultanate, Ḳorḳud was among those executed.

The Pro-Selīm Faction: Janissaries, Pashas, Tatars, and Rumelian Champions

Selīm succeeded impressively where both Aḥmed and Ḳorḳud had failed miserably: he was able to mobilize the janissaries to block Bāyezīd II's plan to appoint his eldest son to the throne. The janissaries not only attacked the residences of all prominent statesmen with known pro-Aḥmed tendencies but also threatened the ruling sultan himself. Their acts clearly revealed their aversion to Bāyezīd and his policies at this particularly critical juncture, and their explicit espousal of Selīm has been singled out by both contemporary and modern historians of the Ottoman Empire as the principal factor that paved Selīm's way to the sultanate.[76] There is no doubt that the janissaries' fierce struggle in the final phase of the internecine strife was a decisive factor in forcing Bāyezīd to abdicate in Selīm's favor. It is the principal argument of this study, however, that this common perception is flawed, as it ignores other bases of political and military power that ultimately enabled Selīm to ascend to the throne.

Most modern historians assume that Selīm had no supporters at his father's court. Selīm did not suffer from a shortage of information about the developments at Bāyezīd's court, however, indicating that he benefited from the assistance of numerous agents who were close enough to the central locus of political power to provide valuable information.[77] Moreover, despite the identification by historians of several viziers who were members of the pro-Aḥmed faction, there are clues to suggest that support for Selīm was not limited to rank-and-file soldiers but most likely included higher-ranking Ottoman officials as well. According to the seventeenth-century chronicler Ṣolaḳzāde Meḥmed Hemdemī (d. 1658), for example, it was Selīm's unidentified "friends at the imperial court" who urged the prince to act quickly and reach Istanbul before the sultan could bring Aḥmed to power.[78] Writing in the second quarter of the sixteenth century, a certain Mevlāna ʿĪsā referred even more specifically to Selīm's supporters at the imperial capital as "the pashas," suggesting that the unruly prince enjoyed the backing of high-ranking officials in Istanbul.[79] Seen in this light, Saʿdeddīn Efendi's (d. 1599) references to Bālī Pasha, Ferhād Pasha, and Aḥmed Pasha as well as Celālzāde Muṣṭafā's (d. 1567) mention of Pīrī Meḥmed Pasha, Yūnus Agha, and Ḳāsım Pasha as part of the pro-Selīm faction is extremely significant.[80]

Another oft-neglected aspect of Selīm's struggle for the throne is its international dimension. Islamic polities neighboring the Ottoman realm had an immense impact on the unfolding of the succession struggle between Bāyezīd's sons. As mentioned earlier in this chapter, Aḥmed, for example, appears to have seriously contemplated seeking asylum in Mamluk or Safavid realms after it became evident that he would be defeated by Selīm.[81] Ḳorḳud went one step further, of course, pursuing Mamluk support during a period of self-exile in Egypt in 1509.[82] Although both princes eventually failed to attain any significant backing from Muslim polities to the east and southeast, Selīm succeeded in garnering the valuable support of a political entity to the north, the Crimean Khanate. Curiously, Ottoman chroniclers are extremely reticent—and at times absolutely silent—about the details of Selīm's stay in the Crimea. The majority of anonymous chronicles and *Selīmnāme*s do not mention the military support provided by the Crimean Khan Mengli Girāy (r. 1466, 1469–1475, 1478–1515) within their discussions of Selīm's itinerary.[83] Several others argue—defensively—that Selīm did *not* accept either the Khan's offer of military assistance or the Khan's daughter in marriage[84] primarily because he did not want to become indebted to the Tatars.[85] In light of the fact that relations between the Crimean Tatars and the Ottomans oscillated between enmity and friendship, the chroniclers' attempts to silence, or at least downplay, the role played by Selīm's Crimean connection is unsurprising.[86] Correspondence between Bāyezīd II and

Mengli Girāy indicates, however, that the Ottoman sultan was not only aware of the potential collaboration between his unruly son and the Khan but considered it perilous enough to ask for the Khan's assistance in convincing Selīm to return to his province. Although the Khan appeased the Ottoman ruler by diplomatically promising that he would abide by his wishes (he is said to have warned Selīm, stating forcefully that, as the Ottoman sultan's "sincere servant," he did not approve of "orders contrary to the will of the sultan"),[87] his deeds appear to have contradicted his words. Indeed, there is strong evidence that the soldiers sent by the Crimean Khan increased Selīm's military strength significantly. Whereas prominent commander Bālī Beg's dispatch mentions that one thousand Ḳazaḳ soldiers sent by the Khan joined Selīm's forces,[88] reports sent to Bāyezīd by his agents refer to three hundred soldiers of Saʿādet Girāy, the younger son of the Khan, among Selīm's three-thousand-strong troops.[89]

In addition to the archival evidence of Crimean support for Selīm's bid, there are rare but explicit references in several narrative sources that break the silence, or lack the defensiveness, of Ottoman chroniclers. Unsurprisingly, the most unambiguous reference is found in a non-Ottoman source: a seventeenth-century Greek chronicle, which explicitly states that Selīm "arranged a pact with the Tatar lord" and "gathered a large army with the aid he received."[90] According to the anonymous author of this chronicle, it was thanks to the valuable military contribution of the Khan that Selīm's armies included "Turks and Tatars, horsemen and foot soldiers."[91] More unexpected is the lengthy section in Celālzāde Muṣṭafā's *Meʾāsir-i Selīm Ḫānī* that relates the context within which Selīm accepted Mengli Girāy's help. Celālzāde presents Selīm's agreement to the Khan's proposal of military assistance not as a choice but as the result of a failed negotiation process. According to Celālzāde, Selīm was asked by the Khan's older son, Muḥammed Girāy, to match an offer made by Aḥmed in an attempt to block Selīm's passage to Rumelia; the offer included the control of various strategic fortifications as well as a deed of ownership (*mülknāme*) of numerous villages in the province of Kefe.[92] When Selīm blatantly refused the proposal, Muḥammed Girāy gathered his troops to attack Selīm's forces.[93] Acknowledging Selīm as the probable winner of the succession struggle, Mengli Girāy sent his younger son to notify the Ottoman prince of the danger posed by Muḥammed Girāy. Although Celālzāde's narrative lacks any explicit reference to the troops in Selīm's company, the flow of the narrative implies that Selīm's forces included Crimean soldiers on their way to Akkirman.[94]

For Selīm, the Crimea carried deep significance. First and foremost, as the location of his son Süleymān's gubernatorial seat, it functioned as a safe haven. It thus served as the Rumelian point of departure for his military endeavors; it also functioned as a place of refuge where he could regroup if and when necessary, such as after the defeat at Çorlu. Perhaps most importantly, the Crimea was the source of the valuable military assistance he received from the Khan of the Tatars. Although it is difficult to ascertain the extent to which Mengli Girāy's military support affected the final outcome of the succession struggle, there is little doubt that the alliance between Selīm and the Khan provided initial momentum that enabled the former to attract to his side a key faction within the Ottoman military ruling elite: the Rumelian commanders.[95]

Selīm's Men in Rumelia

Contemporary Ottoman and European narrative sources relate the unfolding of events from the vantage point of the Ottoman imperial center. They focus almost exclusively on the janissaries as the decisive politico-military faction that determined the outcome of the succession struggle, and their accounts lack a detailed analysis of Selīm's activities once he crossed over to Rumelia. Most sources suggest that the sole reason for Selīm's choice of Kefe as the Rumelian point of departure for Istanbul was the inaccessibility of an Anatolian route; they do not consider his intention of gathering supporters from the Balkans to his camp. Thus, these sources do not properly explore the significance of Selīm's Crimean connection or assess the value of the Rumelian provinces, the location of an immense pool of potential military supporters.

Contrary to what most Ottoman chroniclers suggest, Selīm's Rumelian aspirations appear to have been long-standing. Although the assignment of governorships to Ottoman princes as a form of political and administrative apprenticeship dated to the reign of Murād I (r. 1362–1389), this practice was discontinued after the stability (if not the unity) of the Ottoman polity was challenged by the internecine strife between Bāyezīd I's sons (1402–1413), the rebellion of Sheikh Bedreddīn (d. 1416), and the revolt of Prince Muṣṭafā.[96] Subsequently realizing that the presence of large numbers of troops on active military duty in the Balkan provinces not only contributed to the inherent volatility of succession struggles but also constituted the backbone of social rebellions, Ottoman monarchs after the first quarter of the fifteenth century no longer granted Rumelian provinces as princely governorates. This logic behind the limitation of princely governorships to Anatolian provinces was exactly the reason that Selīm requested a gubernatorial assignment in Rumelia. The fact that he regarded the Balkan provinces as his political and military power base well before departing from his gubernatorial seat in Trabzon can be inferred not only from his demand for a transfer to a Rumelian province as early as 1510[97] but also from his insistence on receiving the province of Silistre even after Bāyezīd granted him the Anatolian province of Menteşe.[98] Although Selīm's Crimean connection (via his son Süleymān and the Tatar Khan) may have provided him with a Rumelian stronghold and some degree of military support for a planned expedition to Istanbul, the question of how the dissident prince realized his ultimate goal of securing the sultanate remains. One explanation of Selīm's ability to build a base of power in Rumelia is his success in securing the assistance of a key faction within the Ottoman military ruling elite: commanders and governors stationed in the Balkan provinces (*Rūmili begleri*). Despite Bāyezīd's specific orders to the governors of Kili and Akkirman to watch all roads and prevent Rumelian soldiers from joining Selīm,[99] the troops under these commanders appear to have served as a substantial source of manpower for the ambitious prince; in the Crimea, Selīm had three thousand soldiers under his command, and when he faced his father at Çorlu, his army is reported to have been about thirty thousand strong.[100]

Despite their silence about Selīm's lengthy stay in Rumelia between his departure from Trabzon and his arrival at Çorlu, various Ottoman sources allude to the political weight of the Rumelian commanders, who helped seal the sultanate for this contender to the throne. For example, within his discussion of Bāyezīd II's attempts to secure the sultanate for Aḥmed during the Şāhḳulu episode, İsḥaḳ Çelebi (d. 1537) states repeatedly that the sultan summoned "the governors of Rumelia" (*Rūmili sancağı begleri*) to Edirne because he was aware that "the sultanate of Sulṭān Aḥmed depended on their acceptance."[101] As soon as Bāyezīd announced his intention to abdicate in favor of Aḥmed and finally set out for Istanbul, some of these commanders changed sides and joined Selīm in his pursuit of the sultan, increasing the number of Selīm's soldiers significantly.[102] In fact, one of these Rumelian warlords was responsible for the provisioning of Selīm's troops on their way back to Kefe in the immediate aftermath of the defeat they suffered at Çorlu.[103] Unsurprisingly, when Selīm finally secured the Ottoman throne, the Rumelian commanders who were summoned to Istanbul to conclude the succession process accepted him enthusiastically as their new sultan and swore oaths of allegiance.[104]

Similarly, Celālzāde Muṣṭafā refers to Selīm's extensive troops gathered from the Balkan provinces, including numerous "champions of Rumelia" (*Rūmili dilāverleri*);[105] he also mentions the summoning of Rumelian commanders to Bāyezīd's court. His account differs from İsḥaḳ Çelebi's, however. Following the common trope of criticizing the evil advisors of a monarch instead of the monarch himself, Celālzāde Muṣṭafā states that it was those who composed the pro-Aḥmed faction in the Ottoman court, and not Bāyezīd, who brought "all of the commanders of Rumelia as well as the victorious soldiers" to the audience of the sultan and ultimately succeeded in triggering Bāyezīd's decision to set out for the imperial capital.[106] Although Celālzāde also tells his readers that "all of the commanders-in-chief of Rumelia" who were gathered at Bāyezīd's court in Edirne agreed to bring Aḥmed to the throne, he does not refer to any commanders who switched sides before the sultan departed for Istanbul.[107]

In addition to providing the seal of approval for newly appointed Ottoman rulers, Rumelian commanders seem to have performed a conciliatory function in times of contention. For example, just before the conflict at Çorlu between the forces of Selīm and the imperial troops under the command of Bāyezīd II, Rumelian commanders requested an amicable solution to prevent a military clash but failed due to the persuasive powers of seditious viziers at the Ottoman court.[108] The conciliatory attitude of "the governors of Rumelian provinces" was primarily a result of their pro-Selīm stance and was vitiated by their intentional delay in arriving at Bāyezīd's court, most likely because they feared that their presence could be used to seal Aḥmed's sultanate.[109]

Although the Rumelian commanders ultimately failed to avoid a military confrontation, various archival documents suggest that they served Selīm in a different capacity after the Çorlu episode. A petition addressed to Selīm and signed by a certain Ḳara Ḥüseyin Agha refers to at least three other military figures who assisted the defeated prince in his escape.[110] Another such petition includes a reference to a commander named Maḥmūd Beg, described as the son of Yaḥşī Beg, who rescued one of Selīm's supporters from execution.[111] Perhaps the most significant of these documents, which was composed by one of Bāyezīd II's officers, mentions several commanders by name, including Baltaoğlu Pīrī, Rüstem, and Ḳāsım, whose names also appear in the list of Selīm's supporters who joined him in Akkirman.[112]

In addition to naming several Rumelian commanders who cast their lot with Selīm in Rumelia, the latter document is especially noteworthy because it lists subdivisional commanders of provincial cavalry companies (*sūbāşı*), senior officers (*aġa*), raiders (*aḳıncı*), low-ranking officers of raiders (*dūvıca*), and sons of notables (*begzāde*) among Selīm's military supporters.[113] Whereas the mention of *sūbāşıs* and *aġas* indicates the extent of assistance Selīm received from Ottoman officials, the references to *aḳıncıs* and *dūvıcas* highlight the prince's success in attracting troops of raiders stationed in the Balkan provinces.[114] Given Selīm's notoriously warlike nature, it is unsurprising that considerable support for his cause originated from the frontier regions of the Empire, where the socioeconomic welfare of the low-ranking members of the military classes depended, at least partially, on the amount of booty acquired during raiding expeditions.[115] Selīm attracted warriors with the premise of organizing raids throughout his stay in the Balkan provinces.[116] His conscious and effective recruitment strategy is documented in frequent archival references to considerable numbers of raiders, raider officers, and rank-and-file soldiers among his supporters.[117]

Recruiting Men of Merit: The Curious Case of *Merdümzādes*

Narrative evidence suggests that Selīm had tested this recruitment strategy long before he ever set foot on Rumelian soil. *Meʾāṣir-i Selīm Ḫānī*, a historical text in the *Selīmnāme* genre composed by Celālzāde Muṣṭafā Çelebi (d. 1567), includes the apocryphal account of a speech delivered by Selīm before he embarked on an expedition into Georgian lands (*Gürcistān*). Addressed to "some of the notable and courageous warriors coming from Anatolia, Rūm, and Ḳaraman," Selīm's speech (or, rather, Celālzāde Muṣṭafā's rendering thereof) focuses primarily on Bāyezīd II's failure to appoint qualified statesmen to the upper echelons of the imperial administration.[118] Considering that Celālzāde composed *Meʾāṣir* sometime between his retirement from Süleymān I's chancellorship (*nişāncı*) in 1557 and his death in 1567, one can surmise that the author's account of the speech reflects his concerns about state appointments during Süleymān's reign rather than an entirely accurate representation of Selīm's mindset at the time of the Georgian expedition. Its presentist agenda notwithstanding, as a segment of a narrative penned by a prolific historian and prominent statesman who lived during the reigns of both Selīm I and Süleymān I, *Meʾā̱sir* offers a rendering of Selīm's address that is especially valuable for its categorization of the pro-Selīm faction located within the borders of the Empire:

> The meritless ones, the plunderers, and those who covet wealth and possessions at my father's threshold idolize presents and worship them. They are addicted to calamities. I heard that, since my great ancestors disregarded the promotion of *merdümzāde*s and brave and distinguished champions and celebrated heroes who had been serving our threshold for ages, [since] they always favored *ḳul*s and did not appoint anyone other than *ḳul*s to high offices, brave members of the people of our province and country were inclined toward joining the Ḳızılbaş and attending their threshold. That is why I chose to raid (*aḳın*) the Georgian lands and that is why I summoned you. My benevolent gaze is upon your kind. Since the days of our grandfathers the advice given to us has been that our true servants at our threshold are our companions who faithfully risk their lives to accompany us in battle and to serve us. Exalted offices and valuable fiefs belong to them. If the praised and exalted God bestows the sultanate upon me, my benevolent gaze will be upon *merdümzāde*s. The grace of my kindness is upon brave and distinguished champions who deal out blows with their swords. Our *ḳul*s are our true servants and it is necessary to promote those among them who are pious and virtuous Muslims. Promoting incapable, miserly and lowly ones just because they are *ḳul*s, however, is unbecoming of a sultan. It is not permissible to neglect *merdümzāde*s. God willing, that is my firm intention.[119]

As mentioned above, any analysis of the content of Selīm's speech needs to take into consideration the Janus-like character of Celālzāde Muṣṭafā's account. Not unlike other historical texts, Celālzāde's narrative relates the events of the past but is anchored in the present and has the immediate future in view. As such, it speaks to the concerns of two epochs and quite possibly of two historical personas. It thus needs to be interpreted with two separate but intricately interrelated temporal contexts in mind. The first is the era in which Celālzāde composed his *Meʾās̱ir*, the last decade of Süleymān I's reign, when a critical historical consciousness of "decline" began to emerge in Ottoman learned circles. Indubitably, the most lucid expression of this consciousness was generated by "advice literature" (*naṣīḥatnāme*), a genre of literary-historical writing that proliferated from the middle of the sixteenth century onward. Because this particular temporal context will be discussed in Chapter 4, the analysis here focuses on the second temporal context, the period of time during which Selīm, then governor of Trabzon, organized raids (*aḳın*) into Georgia. Examined from the vantage point of this second temporal context, Celālzāde's account sheds light not only on the strategies Selīm used to recruit warriors for an expedition against his foreign enemies in 1508 but also on the social composition of his domestic supporters during his bid for the Ottoman throne three years later.

Selīm's address, as rendered by Celālzāde, is laced with acerbic criticism of Bāyezīd II's strategy of assigning high offices only to those members of the Ottoman military ruling elite of *devşirme* origin (*ḳul ṭāʾifesi*). Perfectly in line with a variety of *ḳul*-critical sentiments, which were voiced in Ottoman works of advice and other historical narratives from the mid-fifteenth century onward, its principal argument is that a pro-*ḳul* recruitment strategy bore detrimental consequences for the House of ʿOs̱mān, both at home and abroad.[120] Domestically, this exclusivist policy led to the monopoly of high offices by unqualified and corrupt statesmen. As signaled by the mention of Ottoman subjects who joined the Ḳızılbaş, the strategy also affected the precarious power balance between the Ottomans and the Safavids, tipping the scales in favor of the latter. Celālzāde's account is certainly noteworthy for addressing these concerns, frequently mentioned in Ottoman historiography throughout the sixteenth century, but the significance of the speech for the purposes of this study is that it reveals that Selīm, then on the verge of an extensive struggle for the throne, targeted specific social groups of a military character that had been marginalized by his father.

The atypical terminology that Celālzāde employs to name Selīm's target audience is also historically significant. Celālzāde's allusions to Ottoman subjects engaged in military service for the Empire as "champions" or "heroes" reflect the predictably vague vocabulary of his contemporaries.[121] The only exception is *merdümzāde*, an obscure word used by the author to identify Selīm's intended audience.[122] Although the term eludes a definitive translation, the fact that it denoted a polite, civilized, and worthy man in its original Persian form (*mardum*) suggests that Celālzāde used it in a general sense to refer, however vaguely, to the descendants of prominent men.[123] That similar terms, such as *kişizāde* and *vezīrzāde,* were used by the most erudite of the author's contemporaries to refer to actual or potential members of the Ottoman ruling elite (and to emphasize these individuals' honorable descent) supports this interpretation.[124] Despite the linguistic challenge that the term obviously poses, the social category it signifies is exceptionally significant. For any meaningful analysis of Celālzāde's terminology, however, a few questions require satisfactory answers: Who were the *merdümzāde*s? What was the basis for the distinction between a *merdümzāde* and a *ḳul*? Were these two categories mutually exclusive? Did this differentiation have ethnic, linguistic, or religious dimensions?

Fortunately, the answers to some of these questions can be found in other sections of Celālzāde Muṣṭafā's narrative. To begin with, the general tenor of Selīm's speech suggests that *merdümzāde*s belonged to a social category whose members were marginalized by Bāyezīd II's pro-*ḳul* policies. Indeed, at first glance, *merdümzāde*s and *ḳul*s appear to be mutually exclusive social groups;[125] two additional references in *Meʾās̱ir*, however, not only nuance this impression but also provide further clues about the qualities that distinguish a *merdümzāde*. In the first instance, the term is used in a critique of the statesmen whom Bāyezīd II had appointed to high office, especially to the vizierate:

> Until the reign of Sulṭān Bāyezīd Ḫān . . . the households (*ḳapu*) of all celebrated rulers at the exalted threshold of the Ottoman dynasty

> were not closed but open . . . The pillars of the state and the notables of the sultanate were the *merdümzādes* of the time, who were servants cultivated with complete knowledge and virtue and genuine Muslims who were pure of belief, free from bigotry, merciful, and pious. Those who lacked these qualities would not become viziers to the sultan. [Even] if a *merdümzāde* was not of noble descent (*aṣīl*), [but was] a slave who had been fed in [the sultan's] sublime threshold, nourished with teaching, and cultivated with virtue and knowledge, he, too, would be granted that exalted office, provided he be absolutely worthy and deserving.[126]

In the Ottoman context, the term *ḳapu* ("door," "gate") referred to the immediate entourage or the household (as in *ḳapu ḫalḳı*) of any member of the military ruling elite, including the sultan.[127] Thus, *Meʾās̱ir*'s reference to the openness of the royal households of Ottoman rulers before Bāyezīd II is to be taken as an argument in favor of a more "democratic" system of recruitment based on merit and qualification, which would give Ottoman statesmen of varied backgrounds the opportunity for upward professional, social, and political mobility. In fact, the statement that the office of the vizierate should be granted to *merdümzādes* regardless of whether they were of noble descent (*aṣīl*) or of palace-educated slave background suggests that Celālzāde simultaneously imagined two categorical distinctions. The first, horizontal distinction was based on pedigree, which could be defined by an individual's ethnic, social, or religious identity; noble descent; *devşirme* origin; or even the duration of his tenure in Islam.[128] The second, vertical distinction was based on merit and qualification. It was in respect to this distinction that Celālzāde defined the social category of *merdümzāde*, which included Ottoman subjects of diverse backgrounds, even *ḳuls*, as long as they were "absolutely worthy and deserving."

That said, perhaps the most striking feature of this passage is that it refers to noble descent (*aṣīl*) as a preferable quality for a *merdümzāde*. The significance of this aspect of Celālzāde's categorization is further illuminated in another section of *Meʾās̱ir*, in which the author criticizes (unidentified) Ottoman sultans for their exclusive preference of *ḳul*s and expresses abhorrence for unqualified office holders:

> When the precious gaze of those who possessed the sultanate and administered the affairs of the caliphate at the exalted threshold was exclusively directed upon *ḳuls*, [when] *merdümzāde*s of personal merit and ancestral distinction as well as janissaries (*ocāḳ erleri*) were deprived of appointments to high-offices, [when] premium fiefs were not granted to valiant heroes but were assigned to unpatriotic, lowly, miserly, ignorant, and effeminate ones, real champions despaired and everyone suffered.[129]

This excerpt is especially noteworthy in that it provides clues to the social milieu of those whom the author classifies as *merdümzādes*. Within the temporal context of *Meʾās̱ir*'s composition, the mention of both personal merit (*ḥaseb*) and ancestral distinction (*neseb*) as qualities of a deserving *merdümzāde* undoubtedly underlines Celālzāde's preference for qualified, worthy, meritorious statesmen to be assigned to high offices of the imperial administration. Within the historical context of Selīm's bid for the sultanate, however, this characterization points not vaguely to an unidentified mélange of meritorious men but specifically to a variety of military figures with actual or potential access to *ʿaskerī* status. These figures included noble families of frontier lords whose members had served the Ottoman Empire from its earliest stages.

Perhaps the most compelling espousal of such an interpretation comes from *Cāmiʿü'l-meknūnāt*, a chronicle composed during the first half of Süleymān I's reign by a mystically inclined deputy judge named Mevlānā ʿĪsā.[130] That this versified historical narrative was penned at least two decades before *Meʾās̱ir* and that it is, to the best of my knowledge, the only other Ottoman source that mentions the term *merdümzāde* in the context of Selīm's bid for the throne suggests that Mevlānā ʿĪsā may have been the one who originally coined this obscure expression. Even if Celālzāde Muṣṭafā borrowed it from

Mevlānā ʿĪsā, the two authors seem to have used it somewhat differently; whereas the former mentioned it in a general sense and within the context of a speech that Selīm reportedly addressed to an unidentified group of military figures in Anatolia, the latter employed it in a specific instance, to refer to the warriors and commanders that Selīm gathered in Rumelia.[131]

References in Ottoman sources indicate that a noteworthy segment of Selīm's supporters belonged to a social stratum composed of *begzādes*, or sons of notables, whom Selīm may have identified as a principal component of his power base at the very outset of the succession struggle. Scarce hints in reports penned by Bāyezīd's informants notwithstanding, the identities of individual members of the pro-Selīm faction have heretofore remained in obscurity.[132] Ottoman chronicles likewise provide little help in this regard. In most narratives, the princely factions, particularly the one that brought Selīm to power, are described in extremely vague terms. Such accounts unanimously refrain from disclosing the identities of Selīm's supporters, perhaps avoiding the implicit suggestion that the conqueror of Arab lands and of Persia was just another unruly prince fighting for his father's throne. In fact, in most historical narratives of the Ottoman tradition, Selīm's quest is presented as a struggle with a divinely predetermined outcome, not as an attempt to attain the sultanate via seditiously mundane means.

Raider Commanders and Their Lineages

The calculated silence of Ottoman chronicles is, however, shattered by an undated, single-page document.[133] This previously unstudied archival record comprises a list of the names of military commanders who came with Selīm from Kefe (Feodosia, Ukraine) as well as those who joined him from Akkirman (Bilhorod-Dnistrovskyi, Ukraine) onward. As such, it is the only known comprehensive list of members of the pro-Selīm faction in the Rumelian provinces around 1511;[134] but, the dearth of concrete corroborating documentary or narrative evidence (in the form of specific references to the military figures mentioned therein) poses significant challenges to a definitive prosopographic analysis. One obvious challenge concerns the intended audience of the document. It seems that his was an immediate and contemporary audience with firsthand knowledge of the identities of individual commanders. As I have discussed previously, the identity of some commanders can be established conclusively, whereas it has proven impossible to ascertain that of others.[135] In the case of some, a lack of individual personal information is, curiously, combined with an abundance of references to their ancestors or relatives. In addition, a cursory glance at the family trees of these figures sheds some light, however indirectly, on the political stances of specific commanders. Even the tentative identification of thirty-six commanders who cast their lot with Selīm during the initial phase of his bid for the Ottoman throne reveals the reach of the networks of political and military power that contributed to the rise of the dissident prince in Rumelia. As will be demonstrated later in this chapter, the most important characteristic common to the majority of these military figures is a well-established base of political and military power in the Balkan provinces of the Empire.

First and foremost, with the possible exception of three commanders, the military leaders mentioned in the list of Selīm's supporters held important offices in Rumelia.[136] A careful consideration of the descriptive, patronymic identifications of these figures suggests that several of them were affiliated with individuals of varying political significance situated at the imperial palace.[137] Some were Ottoman governors or their descendants.[138] Whereas a few of these officeholders were descendants or relatives of statesmen of *devşirme* background,[139] the use of the titular term *voyvoda* in the case of several other individuals indicates that they served the Empire as governors, provincial revenue collectors, or commanders of local cavalry subdivisions or of troops of raiders (*aḳıncı*) and thus played a key role in the westward expansion of the Ottoman polity in the Balkans.[140] At least two of these commanders appear to have been descendants of rulers of petty dynasties, which were established in Anatolia and posed a significant challenge to the centralizing efforts of the Ottoman state during the first quarter of the fifteenth century, particularly within the context of the civil war that ensued after the Battle of Ankara in 1402.[141] One of these figures, Minnetoğlu Ḳazġān Beg, was in all likelihood a descendant of Minnet Beg, the leader of Tatars who were exiled to Rumelia by Meḥmed I, who perceived them as a threat to the reestablishment of Ottoman sovereignty over Anatolia.[142] Despite the danger they may have posed to Ottoman centralization efforts in Anatolia, once transferred to Rumelia, Minnet Beg and his Tatar followers, along with their descendants, appear to have served the Ottoman polity as troops of raiders for generations to come.[143] Similarly, İsfendiyāroğlu Celīl Çelebi's lineage can be traced to İsfendiyār Beg (d. 1439), the eponymous founder of the Turco-Muslim emirate situated in the province of Sinop on the Black Sea coast of Anatolia; the latter's close connections to figures with known anti-Ottoman and/or anti-centralization sentiments during the formative years of the Ottoman enterprise rendered his relationship with Ottoman rulers uneasy at best.[144]

Especially noteworthy are the commanders who descended from or were related to early Ottoman families of wardens of frontiers (*uc begi*) and pre-Ottoman (or late Byzantine) noble lineages active in the Balkan provinces. Based on patronymic evidence, at least nine commanders on the list can be placed in this category, representing the single largest contingent of figures with a common geographical, military, and political background.[145] Within the context of Selīm's rise to power, these individuals were particularly important as prominent commanders with well-established bases of political and military power in the Rumelian provinces of the Empire. Their patronymic appellations indicate that they were descendants or associates of renowned lineages of frontier lords—including Malḳoçoğlu, Gümlioğlu, Ḳarlıoğlu, Ṭuraḫānoğlu, and Mīḫāloğlu—who contributed as *aḳıncı* commanders to the expansionist policies of the Ottoman enterprise during its formative phase.

One of the most celebrated noble families of the early Ottoman period, whose members played a central role in Ottoman expansion in the Balkans from the reign of Bāyezīd I on, was the Malḳoçoğlu.[146] The eponymous founder of this notable lineage, Malḳoç Muṣṭafā Beg (d. after 1402), one of Bāyezīd I's trusted commanders, was captured by Tīmūr's forces at the Battle of Ankara in 1402.[147] His descendants, especially his son Malḳoçoğlu Bālī Beg and his grandsons ʿAlī and ʿAlī Ṭur figure prominently in Ottoman chronicles as triumphant *aḳıncı* commanders and competent governors.[148] In fact, Uruç Beg refers to Bālī Pasha as governor (*sancaḳbegi*) of Akkirman and as organizer of a major raiding expedition in 1498, for which his son ʿAlī Beg is mentioned among the participating commanders.[149] Although Malḳoçoğlu Ṭur ʿAlī Beg can be singled out as the commander Selīm I sent against his brother and archrival Aḥmed, perhaps the most striking common attribute of the Malḳoçoğlu brothers is that they both fought and died for Selīm at the Battle of Çaldıran in 1514.[150] Given the fate of these Malḳoçoğlus, it is only fitting that a certain "Üveys *voyvoda* of Malḳoçoğlu," an *aḳıncı* commander affiliated with them, is listed among Selīm's supporters in the Balkans as early as 1511.[151]

Two prominent commanders mentioned among Selīm's Rumelian allies are identified in terms of their relation to Yaḥyā Pasha (d. 1507). Initially a commander of raiders during the reign of Meḥmed II, Yaḥyā Pasha not only served Bāyezīd II as governor, governor-general, and vizier but also joined the royal family as his son-in-law.[152] The fact that Ottoman historical tradition refers to his descendants as "sons of Yaḥyā Pasha" (*Yaḥyā Paşazāde*) attests to his preeminent status as commander, statesman, and member of the extended Ottoman royal family. In addition to a certain Rüstem Beg, who is identified as a "relative (*ḫışm*) of Yaḥyā Pasha," the list of Selīm's Rumelian supporters includes the name of the foremost frontier warrior of Yaḥyā Pasha's lineage, namely his son Meḥmed Pasha (d. 1551).[153] Partly Ottoman by blood, Meḥmed Pasha continued his ancestors' legacy of frontier warfare. Tasked with *aḳıncı* regiments, he organized raiding expeditions into regions as far as Moravia and Bavaria in 1529. Well before he challenged Christian commanders in central Europe, however, he apparently played a leading role in the succession struggle between

Bāyezīd II's sons. The monies allocated to Meḥmed Pasha far exceeded the funds assigned to any other commander, suggesting that, as early as 1511, he was in charge of a sizeable army, certainly the largest contingent in support of Selīm.[154]

The names of most of these noble families arise in earlier periods of Ottoman history, implying that they were supporters of several dissident princes. As such, these supporters continued a long-established trend of constantly renegotiating their positions vis-à-vis the increasingly centralized imperial authority; this evidence can also be considered an indication of the resentment felt by members of these families toward the ongoing process of centralization. As a case in point, two members of the Gümlioğlu family are mentioned in the list of Selīm's supporters in Rumelia.[155] References in early chronicles as well as in archival documents suggest that the eponymous ancestor of this family was a frontier lord of renown. ʿĀşıḳpaşazāde and Neşrī mention the name of a certain Gümlioğlu, along with prominent *aḳıncı* commanders Ṭuraḫān Beg and Evrenos Beg, within the context of the rebellion of Bāyezīd I's (r. 1389–1402) son Muṣṭafā ("Düzme" or "False," d. 1422?) against Murād II (r. 1421–1444 and 1446–1451).[156] Although initially a supporter of Muṣṭafā, Gümlioğlu seems to have followed Ṭuraḫān Beg and Evrenos Beg in joining Murād, thus contributing to the demise of Muṣṭafā.[157]

Flexible loyalties apparently served the Gümlioğlu family well. Although Murād II continued to doubt the fidelity of frontier lords,[158] his grant of freehold properties was followed by similar grants made by Meḥmed II and Bāyezīd II.[159] Whereas an anonymous narrative of Murād II's military endeavors refers to a certain Gümlioğlu as governor of Sarāc-ili (near Timok, Serbia), another Gümlioğlu served the Ottoman state as governor of Severin (Szörény, Hungary).[160] The list of Selīm's Rumelian allies includes the names of two members of this lineage: Gümlioğlu Muṣṭafā Beg and Gümlioğlu İskender Beg. Thanks to numerous references in tax registers (*taḥrīr defteri*) composed during the reigns of Selīm I and Süleymān I, both men can be identified conclusively. Whereas Muṣṭafā Beg died at the Battle of Çaldıran in

1514, İskender Beg appears to have enjoyed the support of successive Ottoman rulers.[161] Of particular significance in this context is a cadastral register (*taḥrīr defteri*) compiled during the reign of Selīm I, which confirms not only that Meḥmed II had granted numerous villages in Zağra Eskisi to Gümlioğlu's sons Ṣāltıḳ Beg and İskender Beg but also that their freehold (*mülk*) status was acknowledged first by Bāyezīd II and then by Selīm himself.[162] The practice of granting villages to descendants of Gümlioğlu both as freehold property and as pious endowment (*vaḳıf*) grew significantly over time, indicating that members of this prominent family of frontier lords successfully negotiated their positions vis-à-vis successive Ottoman monarchs. Among these frontier lords, Selīm must have felt particularly indebted to Gümlioğlu due to the latter's military contributions during his bid for the Ottoman throne.

The Ḳarlıoğlu family presents a strikingly similar case. The family's patronymic can be traced to Carlo Tocco (d. 1429),[163] and the lands under their rule, called "Ḳarlı-ili," are recorded in historical narratives from the end of the fourteenth century.[164] Carlo Tocco seems to have entered the scene of Ottoman history in 1413. During the interregnum period following Bāyezīd I's defeat at the hands of Tīmūr at the Battle of Ankara, Tocco supported Mūsā (d. 1413), one of four remaining Ottoman princes fighting for supremacy, who had defeated his brother Süleymān Çelebi (d. 1411) and claimed legitimacy as the Ottoman ruler in the Balkans. When Meḥmed I (r. 1413–1421) eliminated Mūsā and reunited Ottoman lands on both sides of the Straits, Tocco became his vassal. As part of an agreement to secure Tocco's support for the Ottomans, he was required to send his illegitimate sons to Istanbul. From 1423 on, as Murād II's vassal, he held the title Despot of Ioannina and Arta. In 1430, on the conquest of Selanik (Thessaloniki, Greece) and Yanya (Ioannina, Greece) by Ottoman forces under the command of Sinān Pasha (d. after 1442), the Ottomans began to rule Ḳarlı-ili directly; Carlo Tocco II (d. 1448) was the first of the hereditary governors belonging to his family.[165]

Although numerous references to members of this family can be found in contemporary Ottoman chronicles, the definitive identifying evidence on Ḳarlıoğlu İskender Beg, whose name is mentioned among Selīm's Rumelian supporters, comes from an endowment deed (*vaḳfiye*) dated 1496.[166] In this document, he is called "İskender Çelebi," one of the five sons of the eponymous founder of the town of Karlova (Karlovo, Bulgaria) and the patron of its mosque. He fashioned himself as "the great *emīr*, the master of the sword and of the pen, the tutor ʿAlī Beg, son of Ḳarlı" (*amīru'l-kabīr ṣāḥibu's-sayf va'l-ḳalam lala ʿAlī Beg bin Ḳarlı*).[167] Ḳarlıoğlu ʿAlī Beg's claim to preeminence appears to have been justified. Archival evidence indicates that his mastery of the sword was rewarded by both Meḥmed II and Bāyezīd II, and his status as one of the prominent commanders (*ümerāʾ*) of Bāyezīd was acknowledged during the reign of Murād IV (r. 1623–1640).[168] Yet, for ʿAlī Beg, acknowledgment of his status as a "master of the pen" appears to have been just as important: whereas the endowment deed of 1496 makes a laconic reference to his tutorship, the dedicatory inscription (*kitābe*) of the Karlova mosque, dated 1485, reveals the identity of his disciple as Cem Sulṭān (d. 1495), Meḥmed II's son and Bāyezīd II's archrival for the throne.[169]

Ḳarlıoğlu ʿAlī Beg's association with Cem Sulṭān is worthy of note on several counts. His appointment to the tutorship of an Ottoman prince is indicative of his distinguished standing among the high-ranking officials at Meḥmed II's court.[170] If ʿAlī Beg, "the European" (*Frenk ʿAlī Beg*) mentioned by Aḥmed Şikārī (d. ca. 1512) as Cem's trusted steward (*ketḫüdā*), is indeed the same person as Ḳarlıoğlu ʿAlī Beg, he may have played an even more important role during the struggle for the Ottoman throne between Meḥmed II's sons.[171] Despite his relationship with Cem, however, ʿAlī Beg apparently suffered little when his master lost the battle for the throne. During the reign of Bāyezīd II, ʿAlī Beg not only successfully completed the construction of his mosque in Karlova but also secured full proprietorship of his estates in the region.[172] ʿAlī Beg's descendants and relatives appear to have continued both aspects of his legacy, as patrons of architecture and as trustees (*mütevelli*) and superintendents (*nāẓır*) of the family endowment;[173] they also consistently served the Ottoman state as commanders and provincial administrators in Rumelia.[174] Some of them did both. For example, ʿAlī Beg's second son, Meḥmed Beg, was patron of the Burmalı mosque complex in Üsküp (Skopje, Macedonia) and the governor (*sancaḳ begi*) of Vulçitrin (Vučitrn, Kosova) during the reign of Selīm I.[175] He also was married to one of Bāyezīd II's daughters.[176]

The marriage of Meḥmed Beg into the Ottoman royal household did not ensure the allegiance of the entire Ḳarlıoğlu clan to Bāyezīd II. Fluctuating loyalties are suggested by the fact that one of his younger brothers was aligned with Selīm well before the latter's accession to the throne and continued to serve the Ottoman state during the reign of Süleymān I.[177] Although the list of Selīm's Rumelian supporters refers to Ḳarlıoğlu İskender Beg as among the military leaders who joined the troops of the unruly prince in Kefe, a budgetary register prepared during the early years of Süleymān I's reign mentions him as commander of the tax-exempt auxiliary troops (*müsellemān*) of Ḳırḳkilīsā (Kırklareli, Turkey).[178] Collectively, archival evidence suggests that both an anti-Bāyezīd stance and a preference for an expansionist military policy ran in the Ḳarlıoğlus' blood: whereas Ḳarlıoğlu ʿAlī Beg served Cem Sulṭān—Bāyezīd II's archrival—Ḳarlıoğlu İskender Beg sided with Selīm, who successfully deposed him.

The list of Selīm's Rumelian allies also includes Ṭuraḫānoğlu Ḫıżır Beg and İdrīs Beg, son of ʿÖmer Beg. They were both of yet another lineage of notable frontier lords whose members were active throughout the fifteenth century as *aḳıncı* commanders in the Morea.[179] The exceptional contribution of the descendants of Ṭuraḫān Beg (d. 1456) to the westward expansion of the Ottoman realm cannot be overemphasized. Indeed, they were so significant that one of the two principal wings of the Rumelian *aḳıncı* forces was named after this family (*Ṭuraḫānlu*).[180] Considered the eponymous founder of this family of *aḳıncı* leaders, Ṭuraḫān Beg himself seems to have been heir to a tradition established by his father, Paşa Yigit Beg (d. 1413), the celebrated conqueror of Üsküb (Skopje, Macedonia).[181] Extending his father's legacy, Ṭuraḫān Beg conquered Thessaly and became the warden of its marches (*uc begi*). His own sons, Aḥmed and ʿÖmer (d. 1489?), as well as his grandsons, Ḥasan and İdrīs, controlled extensive estates around Yeñīşehr-i Fenār (Larissa, Greece). Collectively, they contributed to the development of their provinces through architectural patronage, engaged in successful frontier warfare in service of the Ottoman polity, and held gubernatorial seats.[182]

Ṭuraḫānoğlu ʿÖmer Beg seems to have been exceptionally effective as an *aḳıncı* commander in the Balkans, but the information available on his sons does not prompt a definitive conclusion regarding their military prowess. Although Babinger states that Ṭuraḫānoğlu Ḥasan Beg was active as an *aḳıncı* commander in 1554, Ṭuraḫānoğlu İdrīs Beg may have been more a scholar than a military leader. There is, however, no reason to believe that the Ṭuraḫānoğlus lost their significance as *aḳıncı* leaders by the beginning of the sixteenth century.[183] In fact, the very mention of both Ṭuraḫānoğlu Ḫıżır Beg and Ṭuraḫānoğlu İdrīs Beg among Selīm's Rumelian allies in 1511 gives the opposite impression, suggesting that several members of this lineage extended the legacy of their illustrious ancestor and supported an ambitious prince's bid to power against his father and brothers.[184]

Perhaps the most significant of the *aḳıncı* families whose members cast their lot with Selīm in Rumelia is the Mīḫāloğlu, a lineage of frontier lords so prominent that the "right wing" of the Rumelian *aḳıncı* forces was named after them.[185] The origins of the Mīḫāloğlu family date to the earliest years of the Ottoman dynasty.[186] Their eponymous ancestor, commonly referred to as "Mikhalis the Beardless" (*Köse Mīḫāl*) by Ottoman tradition, was a Bithynian Christian and the Byzantine headman of the village of Ḥarmanḳaya; he converted to Islam and took the name ʿAbdullāh.[187] Subsequently known as Ġāzī Mīḫāl, he accompanied ʿO͟smān Beg (r. ?–1324?)—and, later, ʿO͟smān's son Orḫān Beg (r. 1324–1362)—on numerous raids and military expeditions. Especially active as lords of the marches in command of raiders (*akıncı*) along the ever-shifting Ottoman frontier in the Balkans, Mīḫāl's descendants contributed to the westward expansion of the Ottoman polity. They were rewarded with large estates in Rumelia, which they held as hereditary fiefs.[188] Some of these holdings were located around Edirne, the Ottoman capital before the conquest of Constantinople, while others were situated in present-day Bulgaria.[189] Although the Mīḫāloğlu family's holdings located near Edirne certainly were substantial, the fact that the two major branches of the family were called *İḫtimānlı* (of İḫtimān) and *Pilevneli* (of Pleven) suggests that their estates in western and northern Bulgaria were especially significant for the later development of this mini-dynasty.[190]

Possibly the earliest reference to İḫtimān is included in Enverī's *Düstūrnāme*, a versified dynastic history completed in 1465.[191] The Mīḫāloğlu family's holdings in and around the town clearly inspired the designation of a major branch of the family as "sons of İḫtimān" (*İḫtimānoġulları*). Moreover, the identification of the other major offshoot of the family as *Pilevneli* clearly indicates that the distinction was made to identify the power bases of the respective wings of the greater Mīḫāloğlu family. At least two descendants of the İḫtimān branch are named among Selīm's Rumelian supporters: İḫtimānoğlu Ḳāsım Beg and İḫtimānoğlu Meḥmed Beg;[192] both can be identified easily. References to Ḳāsım Beg's (d. 1532) service in the Ottoman army place him among the most prominent *akıncı* commanders of the Moldavian campaign of 1498; he also served in Süleymān I's Hungarian campaign of 1532.[193] The longevity of Meḥmed Beg's service in the Ottoman army seems to have resembled that of Ḳāsım Beg. His name is first mentioned in the context of Selīm I's army during his campaign against the Safavids in 1514, when he was commander of the *akıncı* forces. In 1521, during the siege and subsequent conquest of Belgrade under Süleymān I, he served in the same capacity, leading his troops into Transylvania and Bosnia. The number of *akıncıs* under his command during the Hungarian and German campaigns of 1530 and 1532, respectively, exceeded fifty thousand, underscoring his prominence as a military leader.[194] Why members of the *İḫtimānlı* branch of the Mīḫāloġlus supported Selīm's bid for the sultanate but members of the *Pilevneli* branch did not remains an open question.[195]

As can be gleaned from extant evidence, the most recurrent common denominator among commanders who supported Selīm's bid for the sultanate was the possession of political or military power bases in Rumelia. With only a few exceptions, these figures served the Ottoman state in various capacities: as provincial tax collectors, governors, lords of the marches, and, most notably, commanders of troops of raiders. The fact that the single largest contingent among Selīm's allies included members of the Malḳoçoġlu, Gümlioġlu, Ḳarlıoġlu, Ṭuraḫānoġlu, and İḫtimānoġlu families indicates that *aḳıncı* commanders of noble descent were pivotal actors in Ottoman dramas of succession as late as the first quarter of the sixteenth century—well after Meḥmed II's unrivaled legitimacy as the long-awaited Conqueror of Constantinople had enabled him to eliminate the possibility of an individual from any of these lineages claiming the sultanate.

Battling of Fortunes: Succession Struggles and Frontier Lords

The anxiety of Ottoman monarchs about the possible usurpation of their sovereignty by families of lords of the marches predated Meḥmed II's reign. Such fears are suggested by an anonymous Greek chronicler's narrative of a dream experienced by Meḥmed's father, Murād II:

> They say that Murād had a dream one night, which he then related and the Turks believed it to be prophetic: he saw a man dressed in white garments, like a prophet, who took the ring that his son was wearing on his middle finger and transferred it to the second finger; then he took it off and put it on the third; after he had passed the ring to all five fingers, he threw it away and he vanished. Murād summoned his hodjas and diviners and asked them to interpret this dream for him. They said: "Undoubtedly, the meaning is that only five kings from your line will reign; then another dynasty will take over the kingdom." Because of this dream it was decided that no members of the old, noble families, i.e., the Ṭuraḫānoġlu, the

> Mīḫāloġlu, or the Evrenos, would be appointed governor generals (*beglerbeg*) or viziers and that they should be restricted to the office of the standard-bearer of the *aḳıncı*, i.e., the horsemen who owe military service and receive no salary when they form the vanguard during campaigns. There is another family of this kind, called Malḳoçoġlu. These standard-bearers are under the command of the governor general. All these families had hoped to reign but, because of Murād's dream, they were deprived of their former considerable authority.[196]

Judging from the momentous policy changes put into effect in the dream's immediate aftermath, this prophetic vision must have felt like a nightmare rather than something from a sweet slumber. The "old, noble families" mentioned by the anonymous author were descendants of such charismatic frontier warlords as Ṭuraḫān Beg, Mīḫāl Beg, Evrenos Beg, and Malḳoç Beg. Potentially, these families could have established their own dynasties and carved out autonomous areas of influence. Murād's fear of losing his unconditional sovereignty over Rumelia thus was warranted—especially as he could not have foreseen that his son, Meḥmed, would soon render his fears meaningless by initiating the most drastic phase of the (nonlinear) process of centralization since his conquest of Constantinople.[197]

Meḥmed II's strategies, by which he gradually and systematically curbed the autonomy of families of frontier lords, were multidimensional. Some of them were symbolic but unambiguous in conveying the message of Meḥmed's "imperial project." His adoption of new titulature, such as "the ruler of the two seas and the two continents," not only firmly established the unquestionable and absolute authority of the House of ʿOs̱mān over the entirety of the Ottoman realm but also heralded dynastic claims of universal sovereignty. His choice to abandon certain *ġāzī*/frontier traditions that had been observed by all previous Ottoman rulers found its most public expression in his refusal to stand up at the sound of martial music (*mehter*). Through such symbolic acts, Meḥmed not only fashioned himself as an emperor for whom being a frontier warrior was no longer the primary component of a complex political identity but also unmistakably presented himself as the overlord of all frontier lords, for whom *ġāzī*-hood was the principal source of legitimacy and charisma.[198]

Meḥmed II's more pragmatic centralizing strategies proved exceptionally detrimental to the military, political, and economic power of frontier lords. One such strategy was the incorporation of the *aḳıncı* troops into the centralized imperial army, which transformed the relatively independent soldiers of fortune of the past into agents of the highly centralized imperial structure of the future.[199] Raids now required the sanction of the sultan in Istanbul, undermining the economic autonomy both of raiders and of their commanders, whose prosperity depended primarily on spoils of war. It also undercut their political independence. Frontier lords, once semiautonomous comrades of ʿOs̱mān Beg who governed the regions they conquered as appanages (*yurtluḳ*), retained their hereditary command of the *aḳıncı* troops but had limited regional power as governors (*sancaḳbegi*) appointed directly by the ruling Ottoman monarch and only for short periods of time.[200] To prevent prominent lords of the marches from residing in provinces that included their hereditary domains and thus establishing military and political strongholds, Ottoman rulers, especially from Meḥmed II on, followed a strict policy of frequent rotation of gubernatorial appointments.[201] Perhaps the most effective of Meḥmed II's policies intended to curtail the power of frontier lords was the confiscation of their privately owned estates and the subsequent transformation of these estates into imperial fiefs (*tīmār*).[202] Although Bāyezīd II reversed this (particularly resented) policy and reprivatized previously confiscated family endowments, the Conqueror's strategies marked a new threshold in the centralization of the Ottoman polity, one that, as Mariya Kiprovska has noted, ultimately led to "the assimilation of the representatives of the frontier culture into the centralized structures of the growing Empire."[203]

The distinguished families of frontier warlords such as Ṭuraḫānoğulları, Mīḫāloğulları, and Malḳoçoğulları were ultimately subjugated by ʿOs̱mānoğulları. Although they ceased to experiment with the idea of establishing their own dynasties, their capacity to serve as alternative focuses of military and political power was not entirely obliterated; the succession struggle that brought Selīm I to power is certainly a case in point. Moreover, despite the fact that troops of raiders virtually disappeared from Ottoman warfare in the first half of the seventeenth century,[204] contemporary observers seem to have believed that members of certain *akıncı* families were worthy of the sultanate as late as the last years of Süleymān I's reign. Narrative evidence of such an assessment is found in a *relazione* penned by the Venetian *bailo* Daniele Barbarigo, who, as Zeynep Yürekli states, evaluated "worst-case scenarios for the future of the Ottoman throne in 1564"[205] with the following words:

> Should the Ottoman sultans have no male offspring, many people want to have members of eight noble families succeed, four of them in Greece [referring here to the Balkans] and four in Anatolia. The four in Greece are *Micali* [Mihallı, that is, Mīḫāloğlu], *Ersecli* [Hersekli], *Eurenesli* [Evrenezli, that is, Evrenosoğlu] and *Egiachiali* [Yaḥyālı]; but these are not as much in consideration as the ones in Anatolia, which include *Cheselamatli* [Ḳızıl Aḥmedli, that is, İsfendiyāroğlu/Cāndāroğlu], *Diercanli* [Ṭurḥānlı?], *Durcadurli* [Ḏulḳadirli], of which there are many in Persia; the fourth of them, who have the greatest pretension, are *Ramadanli* [Ramażānoğlu], who used to be called *Spendial* [İsfendiyār] in old times.[206]

At first glance, Barbarigo's account seems burdened by two factual errors. First, the Ṭuraḫānoğlus (*Diercanli*) were based in Rumelia, not in Anatolia; second, the descendants of İsfendiyār (*Spendial*) were the Ḳızıl Aḥmedli (*Cheselamatli*), not the Ramażānoğlu (*Ramadanli*).[207] There is also no concrete, corroborative, historical evidence that the notable families mentioned in Barbarigo's *relazione* were indeed perceived by Ottoman subjects as viable alternatives to the House of ʿOs̱mān. In fact, by the time Barbarigo was able to observe the attitudes of Ottoman subjects, the descendants of these families had been integrated into the juggernaut of a highly centralized imperial structure. That the members of these families were presumably not regarded as prospective rulers of the Ottoman realm, however, does not mean that Barbarigo's depiction was simply the wishful projection of an agent of *La Serenissima*. In fact, his report is illuminating on several counts. For instance, it speaks to the resilience of *aḳıncı* families as politically active and publicly recognized entities who could be imagined as worthy of the sultanate (should their rule become necessary) by Ottoman subjects and by European observers alike.

Just as significantly, Barbarigo's *relazione* forecasts the direction of recent scholarship on lineages of notable families. Whereas earlier work on the Ottoman Empire generally considered lords of the marches akin to agents of the House of ʿOs̱mān, whose raison d'être was loyal service—as conquerors and as administrators—to the highly centralized imperial polity, recent scholarship has explored them as "minidynasties" who governed the Balkan provinces as de facto rulers during the formative years of the Ottoman state.[208] New studies—wary of the tacit anachronisms that result from retrospective analyses of fourteenth-, fifteenth-, and even early-sixteenth-century realities (from the vantage point of, say, the Süleymānic age)—opt for an evaluation anchored in the contemporary historical context within which these renowned lineages operated. As a result of this novel approach, distinguished lineages of *aḳıncı* commanders are no longer viewed simply as a dependent social group devoted to frontier warfare on behalf of the House of ʿOs̱mān but as sociopolitical entities with their own courts, pious endowments (*vaḳıf*), and vast hereditary fiefs. They were protectors of poets who had mystical inclinations and whose verses carried overtones of defiance against members of the Ottoman dynasty.[209] These lords created towns and erected mosques, madrasas, dervish lodges, and shrines, and their centrifugal tendencies stood in stark contrast to the centripetal urges of Ottoman monarchs. Their architectural patronage is no longer regarded as a charitable endeavor undertaken in service of the Ottoman dynasty but as a distinct expression of rival political claims, the overtones of which changed with time and in response to the ever-shifting balance of power between the families and the House of ʿOs̱mān.[210] Additionally, these lords had sizable troops of raiders under their command, and (if Selīm's bid for the sultanate is any indication) they were not afraid to lead these raiders into battle against a legitimate ruling sultan. In fact, succession struggles like the one between Bāyezīd II's sons provided them with the perfect opportunity to express their political claims, make their own bids as kingmakers, and renegotiate their positions vis-à-vis the new Ottoman monarch they empowered.[211]

The enhancement of the frontier lords' bargaining power during periods of dynastic transition—particularly contested ones—was a foremost consequence of Ottoman succession practices; the succession struggle between Bāyezīd II's sons presented all power brokers with the opportunity to participate in the formation of a new regime and thereby improve their own lot. In this particular race of open succession, these power brokers included the janissaries in Istanbul and, most notably, the Rumelian commanders, most of whom were associated with families of frontier lords.

Conclusion

The significance of Selīm's rise to power is not limited to its theoretical repercussions regarding the structure of the Ottoman polity. Although the crystallization of the loyalty of the janissaries and prominent statesmen proved to be a prolonged process, Selīm enjoyed the allegiance of a particular military-political faction throughout the succession struggle. Unlike the slave-servants and the household of Bāyezīd II situated at the imperial center, members of this military-political faction were located on the periphery and were associated primarily with notable families of frontier lords (*uc begi*) and their Rumelian troops.

The fact that these Rumelian power brokers played a pivotal role in bringing Selīm to power is of paramount importance. It highlights the resilience of the *akıncı* families that survived as politically influential entities well into the first half of the sixteenth century despite the centralizing efforts of Ottoman monarchs—

including, most notably, Meḥmed II, the quintessential centralizing emperor. The military strength and political weight of these notable Rumelian families not only serves as a reminder that centralization was a perennially incomplete process but also challenges the notion that the sixteenth-century Ottoman state was the epitome of a patrimonial empire. As demonstrated earlier in this chapter, the political relationship between Bāyezīd II and the noble lineages of *aḳıncı* commanders (including, but not limited to, Malḳoçoğlu, Gümlioğlu, Ḳarlıoğlu, Ṭuraḫānoğlu, and Mīḫāloğlu) was not one between a patriarch and his slaves or clients; it was one between a suzerain and his vassals or allies. In fact, the battle of fortunes between Bāyezīd II's sons presented the noble lineages in Rumelia with one last opportunity to reenact their role in earlier periods of dynastic transition by making their own bid as kingmakers and thereby accepting the suzerainty of a new dynastic lord. As such, the same Rumelian notable families who gave Murād II premonitory nightmares enabled his great-grandson Selīm to realize his own dream of rulership.

PART 2

The Creation of Selīm's Composite Image

Part 2 Introduction: A Historiographical Survey

> When eating spinach in the royal tent our compassionate sultan asked me, "I wonder if the historian would write in the chronicle the fact that I am eating spinach as well." This most humble slave [i.e., I] responded respectfully, stating "my sultan's royal wish with this joke must surely be that it should be written." Thus I recorded this incident here.[1]

This curious episode concerning the Ottoman ruler Muṣṭafā II (r. 1695–1703), which adorns the pages of Silāḥdār Meḥmed Agha's (d. 1723) *Nuṣretnāme*, has intrigued generations of scholars of the Ottoman Empire. Fascinated by this anecdote, Rifaʾat Abou-El-Haj argued that the sultan's concern for recording such trivial details as eating spinach reveals "the vanity of a self-conscious exhibitionistic person whose chief preoccupation is himself."[2] To Cemal Kafadar, Muṣṭafā II's behavior suggested that "the boundaries between his private self and public personality" had lost their clarity.[3] Although the sultan's mental condition is an interesting subject in its own right, the most fascinating aspect of this episode is not that it provides insight into the disposition of this late-seventeenth-century Ottoman monarch but that it highlights the historiographical impact of the other, rather unassuming, protagonist of the story: the chronicler.

In an effort to create for posterity an official imperial memory of his patron's reign, Silāḥdār Meḥmed Agha not only provided the usual *histoire événementielle* of Muṣṭafā II's reign but also reported curious incidents laden with symbolic meaning and historical significance. One such episode is that of a Greek Orthodox priest whose dream vision included the Prophet Muḥammad (d. 632) and Muṣṭafā II's father, Meḥmed IV (r. 1648–1687). When the Prophet invited the priest to convert to Islam, Meḥmed IV told the priest that during his son's reign "many an enemy domain will be conquered and recovered." Another intriguing occurrence mentioned in the chronicle was the miraculous discovery—in the sultan's own treasury!—of the invincible sword that David used to slay Goliath.[4]

There is no reason to doubt Abou-El-Haj's assertion that Silāḥdār Meḥmed Agha's chronicle, written at the behest of Muṣṭafā II following his accession to the Ottoman throne, was part of this sultan's "self-conscious image-manipulation."[5] Although the sultan may well have been the determined initiator of this image-making process, the success of that process depended largely on the aptitude of his chronicler. After all, it was the chronicler who attributed divine sanction to the sultan's enterprises by composing the narrative of the priest's conversion dream featuring the Prophet Muḥammad. It was also the chronicler who recounted the discovery of David's sword as a harbinger of the militarily successful reign that awaited Muṣṭafā II. Last but not least, it was the chronicler who told his audience about the spinach the sultan had had for dinner and thus created a royal persona characterized, among other qualities, by thriftiness and humility. In the end, it was the chronicler's authorial choice that transformed the process of image manipulation that was initiated by the self-conscious sultan into the successful creation of official imperial memory, in the form of an authoritative historical narrative in the Ottoman tradition. Thanks to the concerted efforts of the sultan and his court chronicler, this historiographical tradition now includes a reference to a thing as mundane as, and a vegetable as bland as, spinach.

Court-Sponsored Historiography during the Reign of Bāyezīd II

We do not know whether Selīm I's diet included spinach. What we do know is that he did not employ a court chronicler. In fact, no Ottoman monarch permanently retained the services of an official chronicler until the late 1690s, when Muṣṭafā Naʿīmā (d. 1716) was appointed as the first imperial annalist (*vaḳʿanüvīs*).[6] That the practice of royal sponsorship of historical works had a long history by that time, however, is indicated by the fact that even the earliest extant text of Ottoman history, Aḥmedī's (d. 1413) *İskendernāme*, was composed under the patronage of a member of the Ottoman dynasty.[7] Yet the received wisdom in the field of Ottoman studies considers the unprecedented proliferation of historical works in the late fifteenth century a watershed.[8] Beginning with Halil İnalcık, several Ottomanists have posited Bāyezīd II's active patronage of historians as a major factor that contributed to this surge in historiographical production.[9] Some have even hailed Bāyezīd's reign as the beginning of the "golden age of historical writing" and emphasized the sultan's vision and sponsorship of literary activity as the principal factor that ushered in a new era in Ottoman historiography.[10] Most recent scholarship seems to agree with İnalcık's view that in the aftermath of the Ottoman conquests of Kili (Kilia, Ukraine) and Akkirman (Cetatea Alba/Bielgorod, Ukraine) in 1484, Bāyezīd initiated a historiographical project to highlight his military achievements against the "infidels," thereby formulating a new ideology to express "the consciousness of having established a universal Muslim empire in competition for supremacy with the Mamluk and Persian states."[11] But a point of criticism was recently raised by Murat Cem Mengüç, who disagrees with İnalcık's state- and sultan-centered approach to early Ottoman historiographical production. Mengüç points out that Bāyezīd extended his patronage to prominent historians İdrīs-i Bidlīsī (d. 1520), Rūḥī (fl. 1511), and Kemālpaşazāde (d. 1534) only during the last decade of his reign and not immediately after 1484. Reminding his readers of the rise to prominence in the 1470s of comprehensive popular Ottoman histories commonly called the *Anonymous Chronicles* of the House of ʿOs̱mān,[12] Mengüç argues that the emergence of a new historical self-consciousness during the reign of Bāyezīd II "may have been a collective act of the Ottoman educated class" as much as it was the result of sultanic initiative.[13]

Mengüç's valid critique is not intended to mitigate the fact that the formulation of a new ideological framework for the Ottoman enterprise was a decisive factor in the intensification of Ottoman historical production during the end of the fifteenth and the beginning of the sixteenth centuries. There is ample textual evidence in the chronicles composed or completed during the reign of Bāyezīd to suggest that the sultan had intended, even insisted, that these works address a wider Turkish-speaking public—beyond the immediate circle of Ottoman learned men. In the introductory sections of their histories, Rūḥī, İdrīs-i Bidlīsī, Kemālpaşazāde, and Neşrī (d. ca. 1520) explain the "reason of composition" (*sebeb-i teʾlīf*) for each of their individual chronicles, with explicit references to the sultan's request that these works be histories worthy of the House of ʿOs̱mān, addressing the learned and commoners alike (*ḫavāṣṣ-u-ʿavāmm*). With the exception of Bidlīsī, who composed his *Hasht bihisht* (Eight Paradises) in Persian, and Ḳaramānī Meḥmed Pasha, who penned his *Tawārīkh al-salāṭīn al-ʿUthmāniyya* (Histories of Ottoman Sultans) in Arabic, these histories were written in Turkish. Rūḥī, for example, states that he set out "to collect the histories in Turkish which are circulating in the Ottoman dominions . . . [and to compose] a compilation written in a language for everybody's profit." Similarly, Neşrī expresses his concern that works "on [Ottoman dynastic] history still remain scattered, especially in Turkish." Finally, Kemālpaşazāde's statement that the sultan commissioned him to compose a history "in a clear style in Turkish" indicates that the principal audience Bāyezīd—or at least some of his historians—had in mind was not limited to the learned men in the upper echelons of the Ottoman ruling elite but may have extended to his literate Turkish-speaking subjects.[14] Thus, there is little doubt that Bāyezīd II's patronage of several prominent historians was intended to promote the development of a specific kind of dynastic history that was narrated from the vantage point of the imperial center rather than from the perspectives of "gazis, gazi-dervishes, and their followers or clients [who] laid competitive claim to the glorious deeds of the past in the name of themselves, their kin, their patron, or their solidarity group."[15] Addressed to a Turkish-speaking audience of varied sociopolitical backgrounds, this historiography bestowed on the

House of ʿOsmān a prominent place in world history wherein the Ottoman monarchs were portrayed primarily as "the most honorable of sultans" (*eşref-i selāṭīn*) rather than depicted more modestly, as warriors of faith (*ġāzī*) on the frontiers of the Islamic world.[16]

This does not mean that Bāyezīd's project replaced early Ottoman chroniclers' emphasis on the *ġāzī* ethos with an exclusive claim to the Ottomans' preeminence in Islamdom. If anything, the Ottomans' prestige, emanating from their status as *ġāzī*s fighting on behalf of the Islamic faith, was enhanced by the assertion that they were the foremost *ġāzī*s in the Islamic world. This royal initiative also did not succeed in establishing a monolithic, homogeneous, and state-centered historiographical tradition uncritical of the Ottoman enterprise. As Cemal Kafadar observes, it was precisely at the historical juncture represented by Bāyezīd II's reign, "in a context that was ready to hear those voices, when Bāyezīd was searching for the right dose of appeasement after his father's harsh centralism," that numerous critical chronicles were composed, adding to the already complex and interrelated textual network of "competing or at least mutually incompatible accounts representing different politico-ideological positions."[17] As the following chapters will demonstrate, this multiplicity of voices continued to be a dominant feature of Ottoman history writing in later periods as well.

That a range of political and ideological viewpoints was expressed by numerous authors does not, however, diminish the significance of Bāyezīd's initiative. On the contrary, this royal project, although limited in scope and success, signified the beginning of a novel approach to historical writing, whereby Ottoman rulers commissioned dynastic histories to propagate a particular ideological vision and dynastic image, addressed not only to their learned servants but possibly also to their commoner subjects. The royal image that Bāyezid intended to publicize through these historical works was that of a monarch who legitimately eliminated the challenge posed by his younger brother Cem (d. 1495) after the death of their father, Meḥmed II; restored the privileges of those harmed by the Conqueror's centralizing policies, which included the confiscation of more than one thousand estates that were previously held as freeholds or endowments; and proved himself a competent warrior-sultan triumphant against the "infidels." Moreover, at a historical juncture when the Ottomans were in direct competition with the Mamluks, the representation of Ottoman monarchs as "the most honorable of sultans"—a novel claim to Ottoman leadership throughout the Islamic world—carried particularly poignant overtones for audiences both within and beyond the borders of the Ottoman Empire.[18]

Experimenting with Official Historiography: Ottoman *Şehnāmeci*s and the *Shāhnāma* Genre

Dynastic histories composed by Rūḥī, İdrīs-i Bidlīsī, Kemālpaşazāde, and Neşrī—along with the histories of the House of ʿOs̱mān penned by other learned Ottoman authors—constituted the textual foundations of numerous later chronicles. Likewise, there is little doubt that Bāyezīd II's methodical patronage of historians for the articulation of specific imperial politico-ideological viewpoints had a significant impact on Ottoman historiography of later periods. The same cannot be said, however, about what has been regarded as the first Ottoman experiment in official historiography: the establishment of the "permanent and salaried" post of court historiographer (*şehnāmeci*, that is, *şehnāme*- or *shāhnāma*-writer) by Süleymān I in the 1550s.[19]

As indicated by the brief survey of early Ottoman historiography in the preceding section, Ottoman literati hailing from a variety of sociopolitical milieus expressed their equally varied politico-ideological viewpoints through an impressive corpus of historical works from the early fifteenth century onward. The resulting historiographical output was composed in verse and in prose, in a range of languages, and in a variety of literary-historical genres. That popular Turkish epics and the Islamic religio-heroic literature (*menāḳıb*) were among the sources of inspiration for Ottoman authors can be gleaned from the title of the earliest Ottoman historical narrative, the dynastic history entitled *Menāḳıb-ı āl-i ʿOs̱mān* (Tales of the House of ʿOs̱mān), composed in prose by a certain Yaḫşı Faḳīh (fl. 1413).[20] Similarly, the significance of the *ġāzī* ethos is discernable in the oldest extant annalistic account of the Ottoman dynasty: Aḥmedī's (d. 1413) versified epic poem, *Tevārīḫ-i mülūk-i āl-i ʿO̱smān ve ġazv-ı īşān bā-küffār* (Histories of the Rulers of the House of ʿO̱smān and Their Raids against the Infidels), which covers the period from Ertuġrul (d. 1281) to Emīr Süleymān (d. 1411).[21] In addition to these dynastic narratives, Ottoman authors also penned universal histories. In fact, even Aḥmedī's *Tevārīḫ* is not a stand-alone dynastic chronicle per se but the final chapter of a world-historical account included in the author's *İskendernāme* (Book of Alexander).[22] Although later chroniclers emphasized Ottoman prominence in Islamic lands by referring to members of the House of ʿO̱smān as "the most honorable of sultans" or by praising them as universal monarchs (*ṣāḥib-ḳırān*), most of these early accounts identify them as triumphant yet humble warriors of faith (*ġāzī*) fighting "on the path of God" (*fī sebīlillāh*) on the frontiers of the Islamic world. Thus, it comes as no surprise that the military achievements of Ottoman rulers (and their allies) were also celebrated in treatises of conquest (*fetḥnāme*) and heroic narratives of military exploits (*ġazavātnāme*).[23] In addition to dynastic and universal histories as well as accounts dealing with specific military-political events, Ottoman historiography included narratives of the reigns of individual sultans; Ṭursun Beg's (d. after 1499) *Tārīḫ-i ebū'l-fetḥ* (History of the Conqueror), which covers the reign of Meḥmed II in its entirety, is among the earliest such texts.[24]

Although these historical writings appear in different genres and in a variety of languages, cover periods of various lengths, and focus variously on the reign of a single sultan or on the entire history of the Ottoman enterprise, they all share a common principal emphasis: the military achievements of members of the House of ʿO̱smān. Thus, the versatile literary-epic genre of *Shāhnāma* (Book of Kings) presented itself as the ideal literary-historical vehicle for memorializing the military achievements of Ottoman dynasts for contemporary and future audiences. The designation of the term *şehnāmeci* to refer to Süleymān I's court historiographer is a testament not only to the sultan's consciousness of this fact but also to the influence of Persianate literary traditions on the development of Ottoman court literature and historiography.[25]

Shāhnāma (Book of Kings) is the revered Persian poet Firdawsī's (Abu'l-Ḳāsim al-Ṭūsī, d. 1020) monumental, versified epic masterpiece recounting the history of Iran from its mythical beginnings to the Islamic conquests of the seventh century. As an idealized account of the heroic deeds of the mythical and historical kings of Iran, *Shāhnāma* appears to have been particularly popular within the Ottoman context among both the illiterate commoners throughout the imperial realm and the learned men at the royal court. Pertev Naili Boratav and Mehmet Fuat Köprülü have recognized the popularity of "professional story-tellers of the urban milieu," whom the Ottomans called *meddāḥ* ("panegyrist"), *ḳıṣṣaḫān* (literally, story-reader), or *şehnāmeḫān* (literally, *şehnāme*-reader) and whose repertoire of orally performed texts included themes derived from the historical-legendary narratives of champions of Islam (for example, *Ḥamzanāme*), the Anatolian-Turkish religious-heroic literature (for example, *Baṭṭālnāme*, *Dānişmendnāme*, and *Ṣaltuḳnāme*), and, most notably, Firdawsī's *Shāhnāma.*[26] Recent studies (following Boratav and Köprülü) have acknowledged the established tradition of orally reciting *Shāhnāma* tales for the entertainment of Ottoman subjects in public spaces but focus on such performances in court settings. Halil İnalcık mentions that histories, campaign narratives (*ġazavātnāme*), and religious epics (*menāḳıbnāme*) also were read aloud at the Ottoman court by history readers (*tārīḫḫān*), storytellers (*ḳıṣṣaḫān*), and *şehnāme* reciters (*şehnāmeḫān*), continuing a tradition established by Seljukid sultans and Turcoman *begs* of Anatolian principalities.[27] Noting the interchangeable Ottoman usage of the terms *şehnāmeḫān*, *şehnāmegūy* (*şehnāme* performer), and *şehnāmeci* (*şehnāme* maker or writer) to refer to the official court historian, Emine Fetvacı further emphasizes the importance of group readings or oral performances of texts.[28]

The Ottoman imperial treasury's impressive collection of luxury copies of *Shāhnāma* in the original Persian alone is a testament to the admiration the Ottoman sultans had for Firdawsī's work and for its production as lavishly illustrated manuscripts. That *Shāhnāma* was translated into Turkish several times on imperial orders and that these *Şehnāme-i Türkī* are still part of the manuscript collections of the Topkapı Palace Museum Library further attests to the royal esteem Firdawsī's poem and its various renderings enjoyed at the Ottoman court.[29] The enthusiastic reception of *Shāhnāma* in the medieval and early-modern Turco-Persian world and beyond can be explained by many factors: that the principal protagonists of *Shāhnāma* are primordial kings and legendary heroes (from the mythical Kayumars to the historical Sassanian monarchs), that Firdawsī's poetry articulates profound dimensions of the human experience (romance, moral struggles, death, suffering, and so on), and that the narrative is a fascinating amalgam of pre-Islamic traditions, oral literature, lore, and history.[30] In addition to the immense literary prestige of the work, the more specific appeal of the *Shāhnāma* tradition among the Seljuks of Rum, the Turco-Muslim polities of Anatolia, and, finally, the Ottomans may have been the result of several interrelated factors. First, one of the principal narrative plots of *Shāhnāma* revolves around the epic feud between the Iranians and Turanians (the former associated with Persians, the latter with ethnic Turks).[31] As a theme, the legendary rivalry between Iranians and Turanians echoed the actual conflict between the Safavids and the Ottomans throughout the sixteenth century with one notable difference: whereas the Turanians lost the legendary battle, the Ottomans proved themselves the winners in the historical one.[32] Second, Firdawsī's account offers lessons in morality as well as models of conduct for rulers and thus functions as a "mirror for princes."[33] This factor must have rendered the *Shāhnāma* especially relevant for Ottoman monarchs. Third, and far more significantly for the purposes of this study, *Shāhnāma* describes the martial exploits of legendary Iranian kings and heroes, bestowing this narrative with an immense expressive power that could be harnessed not only for literary purposes but also for political, ideological, and dynastic ones.

The development in Ottoman literature of an "imitative *şehnāme* genre" from the fifteenth century onward indicates that the Ottomans were well aware of the expressive potential of this versatile genre.[34] That they considered it not simply a means of timeless literary-cultural expression but also an instrument by which to communicate a specific politico-ideological message in a particular historical context is evident in the way they departed from the Persian prototype: whereas Firdawsī's *Shāhnāma* in part recounts legendary events that occurred only in the imagination of the poet, Ottoman *Şehnāme*s relate contemporary or near-contemporary achievements of Ottoman monarchs in panegyric language. For example, the earliest such *şehnāme*-style works, Kāshifī's versified *Ghazānāma-yi Rūm* and Muʿālī's *Ḫünkārnāme*, were composed in praise of the reigning sultan Meḥmed II's military achievements.[35] As Halil İnalcık and Christine Woodhead point out, the beginnings of this style of literary-historical writing were partially due to the arrival of Persian poets at Meḥmed II's new imperial capital, Istanbul. Meḥmed's court also welcomed Turkish-speaking "Rūmī" poets such as Şehdī, suggesting that the presence of a miscellany of writers in Ottoman courtly circles was part of the larger phenomenon of the sultan's policy of cultural patronage.[36] Whereas some writers, including Laṭīfī (d. 1582), the author of a biographical dictionary of poets, mention Meḥmed's strategy of literary patronage matter-of-factly and note that "thirty poets were granted salaries and yearly pensions [by the Conqueror] who were putting in rhyme his history or writing poems in his praise,"[37] others used poetry to express their resentment of the sultan's advancement of outsiders:

> If you wish to stand in high honor on the Sultan's threshold,
> You must be a Jew (*Yahūd*), or a Frank (*Frenk*), or a Persian (*ʿAcem*);
> You must choose the name Ḳābīlī, Habīlī, Ḥāmidī,
> And behave like a Zorzi (*Żūrzī*); show no knowledge.[38]

Ottoman authors continued to compose *şehnāme*-style narratives of specific military campaigns, of the reigns of individual sultans, or of general histories of the Ottoman dynasty in later periods.[39] But Süleymān I's establishment of the post of court historiographer around 1555 marked the beginning of a new era of court-sponsored production of literary-historical works with a politico-ideological agenda. The timing of the establishment of the office of *şehnāmeci* strongly suggests that Süleymān I, like his grandfather, envisioned this corpus of works as a conduit for the dissemination of a particular imperial vision and royal image at a critical juncture: when his own prestige was approaching its nadir. Süleymān was no longer the triumphant warrior-sultan of the 1520s and 1530s who had achieved impressive victories against his rivals. In the West, Ottoman engagements with the Habsburgs (primarily over Hungary) between 1536 and 1547 had ended with the signing of a truce by Süleymān, Ferdinand I (King of Hungary, r. 1526–1564), and Charles V (Holy Roman Emperor, r. 1519–1556). In the East, the Amasya settlement of 1555 between Süleymān and Shāh Tahmāsb (r. 1524–1576) signified the belated recognition that neither the Ottomans nor the Safavids could realize their ambitious expansionist and imperialist projects.[40] Taken together, these peace agreements not only denoted a stalemate between the Ottomans and their principal enemies but also compelled Süleymān to acknowledge the limits of his imperialist ambitions and to forgo any aspirations of universal monarchy he may have had earlier in his reign, especially because he faced political challenges from within his own family.[41] To secure his position on the throne and to establish his unquestioned authority during the last decade of his reign, Süleymān ordered the executions of his sons Muṣṭafā and Bāyezīd in 1553 and 1561, respectively. The fact that these acts tarnished Süleymān's reputation significantly is suggested by numerous elegies composed by contemporary poets who decried Prince Muṣṭafā's execution and explicitly criticized the sultan for ordering it.[42] In addition to revealing the popularity of Süleymān's sons, such lamentations also indicate that, in the early 1550s, the creation of a favorable royal image became a necessity for the aging sultan. It was thus apparently no coincidence that Süleymān appointed ʿĀrifī (also Fetḥullāh Çelebi or ʿĀrif, d. 1562) to the post of *şehnāmeci* at that particular historical juncture.

Despite Cornell Fleischer's observation that the establishment of the office of *şehnāmeci* was "the first attempt by the dynasty to assert direct control of the literary expression of historical ideology and imperial image," however, the historiographical output of this office had practically no impact on contemporaneous or later Ottoman historiography.[43] Between ʿĀrifī's appointment as the first *şehnāmeci* in the mid-1550s and the disappearance of the office in the early years of the seventeenth century, a total of five official historiographers composed about fifteen literary-historical narratives of the contemporary or near-contemporary history of the House of ʿOs̱mān.[44] There is also no compelling indication that the corpus of literary-historical works created under the supervision of the *şehnāmeci* was intended for a broad audience beyond the imperial palace. On the contrary, that most *şehnāme* works were produced as unique and exquisitely illuminated presentation copies; that such court historiographers as ʿĀrifī, Eflāṭūn (d. 1569), and Seyyid Loḳmān (d. after 1596) worked in large formats; and that most of these manuscripts were kept in the inner treasury and the sultan's privy chamber at the imperial court all suggest that they were primarily, although by no means exclusively, literary and cultural artifacts. That access to these works was restricted to the sultan and his royal household serves to explain in part why, with the notable exception of prominent bureaucrat and litterateur Muṣṭafā ʿĀlī (d. 1600), no Ottoman author seems to have consulted a *şehnāme* as his source.[45]

The limited dissemination of these works and the apparent lack of contemporary interest in using *şehnāme* texts as sources for Ottoman history writing do not, however, mean that this court-supported historiography lacked political significance. First and foremost, the fact that a particular manuscript may have indeed "addressed *only* the inner court circle of the Topkapı Palace, including the slave pages educated in the sultan's private household as the future ruling elite, and the members of the dynasty on whom the perpetuation of the dynasty depended," does not mean that this "restricted audience" was numerically insignificant.[46] On the contrary, despite the established practice of imperial seclusion, the Ottoman imperial palace was "necessarily a heavily populated space."[47] The fact that the "courtly community also borrowed books from the treasury or the smaller libraries scattered throughout the palace for their own use"[48] suggests that such books may have enjoyed a wide potential readership.[49] Furthermore, although the circulation of some of the lavishly illustrated manuscripts may have been necessarily limited,[50] the creation of a permanent post for a salaried official to oversee the production of lavishly illustrated manuscripts—with texts that exhibit a significant degree of literary sophistication—was itself a political act, as it established a network of artistic patronage, at the center of which was the Ottoman sultan, the foremost patron and employer of a great number of artists, scribes, calligraphers, bookbinders, and many other craftsmen.[51] Additionally, the sultan, the epicenter of this network, was not just the passive recipient of the finished manuscript. Although both the production process and the content of a *şehnāme* was supervised primarily by high-ranking members of the sultan's entourage, evidence suggests that the sultan also participated actively, examining its quality as well as its content, approving works in progress, and reviewing samples of verse submitted for his approval.[52] In addition to ensuring the creation of an objet d'art of the highest caliber, worthy of the Ottoman dynasty, this process also guaranteed that the finished product would promulgate the intended political message of its ultimate patron, the Ottoman sultan.

The principal politico-ideological message conveyed by ʿĀrifī's *Shāhnāma-ye āl-e ʿOs̱mān*, for example, was that Süleymān I personified a saintly, divinely ordained, ideal monarch.[53] Part of a larger dynastic literary project that Sinem Eryılmaz has called "Süleymān-centric sacred history writing," ʿĀrifī's work, together with that of his successor Eflāṭūn, portrays Süleymān as "the second person in history (both sacred and human) after the Islamic prophet Muḥammed who combined perfectly in himself the qualities of a political and spiritual leader."[54] Similar messages of political significance resonated in later *şehnāme* works. The representation of the House of ʿOs̱mān as the seal of all dynasties and the portrayal of Ottoman monarchs as divinely preordained rulers of unrivalled stature constitute the primary visual and verbal arguments of several works completed during the reign of Murād III (r. 1574–1595).[55] One of these works, *Ṭomār-ı hümāyūn* (Imperial Scroll), which Baki Tezcan has wittily described as "arguably the longest piece of Ottoman history writing," was begun by ʿĀrifī, continued by Eflāṭūn and Seyyid Loḳmān, and possibly updated until the early years of Meḥmed III's reign.[56] Stretching 102 feet in length and 2.6 feet in width, the Imperial Scroll is a universal history in the form of an annotated genealogy, wherein the Ottoman dynasty is depicted as the apogee of a divinely ordained cosmic plan.[57] The same message constitutes the main politico-ideological thrust of *Zübdetü't-tevārīḫ* (Quintessence of Histories), which includes the revised and updated contents of the *Ṭomār-ı hümāyūn* in book form.[58] Portraying Ottoman monarchs as descendants of the Old Testament prophet and leader Noah (via Moses, the Prophet Muḥammad, and Süleymān I), *Zübdetü't-tevārīḫ* represents Murād III as "having the double duties of prophet and worldly ruler."[59] In the face of contemporary criticisms leveled at Murād III for destabilizing the grand vizierate and weakening the positions of members of the judicial elite, the shared message conveyed by *Ṭomār* and *Zübdet* was undoubtedly intended to buttress the sultan's image as well as his absolutist ambitions.[60] The sheer size and the not-so-user-friendly shape of the *Ṭomār* alone reveal that this enigmatic royal document was not meant to be consulted frequently or by many, but its (revised and updated) contents were presented as *Zübdetü't-tevārīḫ* to Sultan Murād III, the chief black eunuch Meḥmed Agha (d. 1591), the grand vizier Siyavuş Pasha (d. 1601), and the sultan's tutor Ḫoca Saʿdeddīn Efendi (d. 1599).[61] Although *şehnāme* works in general were not intended to address a wide audience, the identities of the three individuals to whom copies of *Zübdetü't-tevārīḫ* were presented suggests that Murād III indeed targeted readers beyond his dignitaries. Given that the grand vizier, the chief black eunuch, and the royal tutor were pivotal figures in the military-administrative structure of the Empire, in the palace household, and in the intellectual elite, respectively, it is highly likely that the sultan intended for the carefully crafted textual and visual project of *Zübdet* to be circulated within these interconnected networks. Unlike earlier products of court historiography, which were accessible to a rather limited audience of readers at the imperial court, *Zübdet* thus could have served as a more effective vehicle for what Baki Tezcan calls "the propagandist voice of the court."[62] There is evidence that copies of *Zübdetü't-tevārīḫ* indeed circulated beyond their original owners,[63] but there is no indication that the politico-ideological message of the work, or that of any other *şehnāme*, generated a response from contemporary Ottoman readers.[64]

Baki Tezcan reads this silence as the Ottoman intelligentsia's implicit yet fateful criticism of Murād III's use of court historiography to endorse his contested version of "royal absolutism." Tezcan evidently considers court historiography to be primarily a tool for political propaganda, and he contends that both the disappearance of the post of *şehnāmeci* within a few years of Murād's death and "the fate of the works produced by court historiographers should be interpreted as signs of a royal failure to dictate a certain understanding of Ottoman history to the intellectual elite [who had their own] legalist agenda."[65] Christine Woodhead provides a more nuanced reading, remarking that "silence may equal criticism, or simply lack of interest."[66] Approaching the subject primarily from a literary perspective, Woodhead describes the multiplicity of "contemporary readings" of *şehnāme* works, emphasizes the issues of artistic production and patronage, and insightfully states that "*şehname*s were literary and cultural artefacts first, and vehicles for sultanic propaganda second, though a clear distinction is not always evident nor, probably, intended."[67] Woodhead observes that illustrated manuscripts crafted under the supervision of the royal *şehnāmeci*, especially those manuscripts created during the reign of the sedentary Murād III, could be interpreted as "demonstrable responses" to the growing corpus of works of advice in this period.[68] As for the demise of the post of *şehnāmeci* in the early years of the seventeenth century, she argues—contra Tezcan—that it makes more sense "to regard the *şehnāmecilik* not as a failure which was actively rejected by a certain group but more generally a casualty of the political, economic and social changes at the end of the sixteenth century."[69] Among these changes, Woodhead highlights two in particular: the lack of interest that Ottoman rulers Meḥmed III (r. 1595–1603) and Aḥmed I (r. 1603–1617) had in the literary output of the court historiographer and the increasingly close association of the *şehnāmeci*'s secondary task—keeping an official daybook—with the job of members of the secretarial class (*kātib*), which ultimately rendered his office obsolete.[70] To these factors Emine Fetvacı adds a shift in aesthetic preferences at the Ottoman court—and at the courts of their Safavid and Mughal contemporaries—and observes that at the turn of the seventeenth century the Ottomans moved away from illustrated histories and focused instead on the art of album-making.[71] Reminding her readers that the illustrated official histories "represent only one moment in the long and varied history of Ottoman art," Fetvacı stresses the need to understand the artistic products of the Ottomans not as timeless artifacts but as historically specific products "anchored in the social and political contexts of their makers and audiences." She concludes that "the illustrated history was produced during a certain period to meet specific needs and to cater to new audiences, and its disappearance signals the declining importance of its function and changing notions of the book."[72] Unlike Tezcan, Fetvacı and Woodhead refuse to sacrifice the literal and the cultural for the political. Thus, rather than considering court historiography "a royal failure to dictate a certain understanding of Ottoman history to the intellectual elite," they convincingly argue that the post of *şehnāmeci* outlived its usefulness as a result of specific and interconnected institutional, social, cultural, and aesthetic changes that occurred toward the end of the sixteenth century. Chief among these factors appears to have been the increasingly obvious inappropriateness of a literary genre with an emphasis on chivalry to eulogize the progressively sedentary sultans at a time of military-political troubles.

Post-Süleymānic Sultans and the *Shāhnāma* Genre

Unlike the *ġāzī*-sultans who led their armies in battle during the formative years of the Ottoman enterprise, the majority of Ottoman monarchs after Süleymān I entrusted the leadership of imperial armies to their grand viziers or other high-ranking statesmen.[73] Based on a simplistic reading of Ottoman works of advice (*naṣīḥatnāme*) composed during the sixteenth and seventeenth centuries, several modern scholars have interpreted the Ottoman sultans' military inactivity and progressive seclusion from public view as the consequence of worldly preferences. Citing the court-bound upbringing and inadequate education of Ottoman princes, the increasing influence of women, eunuchs, and royal tutors in the affairs of the state, and the prevalence of palace intrigues as primary causes of Ottoman "decline," these scholars have referred to the irresistible allure of the pleasures of courtly life as an explanation for the military inertia and incompetence of sultans of the post-Süleymānic era.[74] Recent analyses demonstrate, however, that this phenomenon, namely the physical absence of sultans from military expeditions, was the result of various interrelated factors.[75]

To begin with, Ottoman monarchs who came to power following the conquests of Selīm and Süleymān inherited such an expansive empire that any military campaign beyond its borders required the sultan's lengthy absence from the imperial capital, which could jeopardize his sultanate. The ever-increasing distances between the imperial capital and various frontiers had rendered the protection of the imperial borders an increasingly significant physical and financial challenge by the middle of the sixteenth century. That the technological and cost-related constraints on—and the physical, environmental, and motivational limits of—early modern Ottoman warfare resulted over time in more stalemates or losses and proportionally fewer victories on the battlefield may also have been among the factors that led to the increasing reluctance of Ottoman sultans to lead imperial armies in campaigns.[76] Last but certainly not least, the military inertia of the post-Süleymānic monarchs may be attributed to the changing nature of Ottoman rulership and the establishment of an increasingly procedural relationship between the sultan and his officials.[77] In fact, by the early sixteenth century Ottoman monarchs had already delegated most everyday affairs of the state to high-ranking officials. By the late sixteenth century, Hakan Karateke observes, a new kind of rulership "whereby the practice of imperial seclusion now widened to include the sultan's military activities" was already in the making.[78] As a result, toward the end of the sixteenth century, Ottoman political theory and discourse identified the sultan primarily as a figure legitimizing a military-administrative structure otherwise managed by the grand vizier.[79]

Whatever underlying factors might have existed, that neither Selīm II (r. 1566–1574) nor Murād III (r. 1574–1595) participated in a military expedition marked a stark contrast between these sultans and their immediate ancestors, Selīm I (r. 1512–1520) and Süleymān I (r. 1520–1566), who were arguably the most militarily active and mobile monarchs in Islamic history. Süleymān personally led a total of thirteen campaigns, including two naval expeditions (to Corfu and Rhodes), and traveled as far as Tabriz and Baghdad to the east and Vienna to the west. Over the course of his forty-six-year reign, he spent more than ten years away from Istanbul, and he died in Szigetvár, while campaigning in Hungary. By contrast, Murād III never left the imperial capital; during the last years of his reign, he never ventured from his palace. In fact, he is the only Ottoman monarch who failed—for more than two years—to make the customary public appearance for Friday prayers at an imperial mosque.[80] As a "stay-at-home sultan who clashed drastically with the military-heroic imagery that had until then defined the sovereign's public persona," Murād III was difficult to eulogize via the traditional genres of Ottoman historiography, especially through the *Shāhnāma* paradigm.[81] The emergence of this new type of sultan necessitated a new interpretative framework for his textual and visual iconography.[82] It is therefore no coincidence that illustrated manuscripts produced at the court of Murād III emphasize the dynastic identity of the sultan rather than his military exploits. Created under the supervision of royal *şehnāmeci* Loḳmān, works such as *Hünernāme* (Book of Skills), *Zübdetü't-tevārīḫ* (Quintessence of Histories), and *Ḳıyāfetü'l-insāniyye fī şemā'ilü'l-'Os̱māniyye* (Human Physiognomy and the Disposition of the Ottomans) could not, and did not, legitimize Murād's sultanate with reference to his successes on the battlefield. Instead, they collectively highlighted the sultan's genealogy and his innate moral qualities as the fundamental sources of legitimacy for the rightful Ottoman monarch, ruling by divine grace.[83]

Copyediting a Sultan: Selīm in Ottoman Historiography

Despite its versatility as a style of literary-historical writing with the expressive potential to articulate specific political and ideological viewpoints, the *Shāhnāma* genre, with its military-heroic emphasis, was particularly unsuitable for portraying the increasingly sedentary Ottoman sultans of the post-Süleymānic era.[84] Conversely, one cannot imagine a narrative genre better suited to recounting the reign of a sultan like Selīm I, whose military prowess on the battlefields of Çaldıran (1514), Marj Dabik (1516), and Ridaniyya (1517) doubled the geographical extent of the Ottoman realm and thereby established the preeminence of the Ottoman polity vis-à-vis other Islamic empires. Selīm spent nearly half of his eight-year reign on campaign, making even Süleymān look sedentary.[85] Due to his unequalled military mobility, Selīm was remembered by none other than Muṣṭafā Na'īmā (d. 1716), the Empire's first official annalist (*vaḳ'anüvīs*), as "seldom sedentary" (*ḳalīlü'l-ḳarār*) even nearly two centuries after his death.[86] Whereas Selīm's military ability as the warrior-sultan par excellence made the immortalization of his reign through *Shāhnāma*-style narratives a decided possibility, his controversial rise to the Ottoman throne and his infamous proclivity to violence made the restoration of his reputation a necessary imperative.

As the next three chapters will demonstrate, Selīm's dramatic ascendance to the Ottoman throne coupled with his propensity to rule by fear triggered the "reconstructive imagination" of contemporary and later Ottoman authors.[87] Over the course of the sixteenth and seventeenth centuries, Ottoman authors hailing from diverse socioeconomic, ethnic, and religious backgrounds composed literary-historical works in a variety of genres; in these works they articulated a plethora of politico-ideological viewpoints and addressed a range of presentist concerns. In so doing, they simultaneously constructed and reconstructed a highly polished composite image of Selīm as a legitimately appointed, posthumously idealized, and divinely ordained Ottoman monarch. The organization of the following chapters reflects the triple-helical structure of the narrative (re)imagination of Selīm along a chronological axis.

Memories of Selīm remained "in permanent evolution, open to the dialectic of remembering and forgetting, unconscious of [their] successive deformations, vulnerable to manipulation and appropriation, susceptible to being long dormant and periodically revived."[88] As a consequence, each chapter focuses primarily, although not exclusively, on one of the three principal strands of memory that culminated in the composite textual iconography of Selīm as a legitimate, idealized, and divinely ordained Ottoman sultan. Chapter 3 addresses the issue of legitimacy. As mentioned earlier, Selīm's attributes as a combatant sultan rendered him the ideal protagonist for a *Shāhnāma*-style literary-historical narrative. It is therefore apropos that several works in the *Shāhnāma* genre focusing on Selīm's life and reign were presented to his son Süleymān. Over the course of the sixteenth and early seventeenth centuries, nearly two dozen such narratives were composed to relate significant historical events that transpired during Selīm's sultanate, with specific emphasis on his military successes. As demonstrated in Chapter 3, this corpus of literary-historical works, generally called *Selīmnāmes*, served to clear Selīm's name from any wrongdoing, legitimize his controversial actions, and, by extension, further emphasize the legitimacy of his descendants for contemporary and future audiences.

The remarkable success of this conscientious project of early modern Ottoman revisionist historiography constitutes the principal theme of Chapter 4, which addresses the posthumous idealization of Selīm's memory in Ottoman historiography, with particular emphasis on Selīm's portrayal as the foremost sultan of a mythical Ottoman "Golden Age" in Ottoman advice (*naṣīḥatnāme*) literature. Penned by learned men of diverse backgrounds between the later years of Süleymān I's reign and the beginning of the eighteenth century, these political-historical treatises address various contemporary challenges faced by the Ottoman state and society. They also propose a plethora of remedies, some more realistic than others. Several of these works condemn particular statesmen; some even criticize a ruling sultan. Despite their authors' disparate, and at times conflicting, political and ideological viewpoints, however, Ottoman advice works collectively contributed significantly to the idealization of Selīm's image for posterity.

The period when literary, historical, and political writings of Ottoman learned men—especially those who authored *Selīmnāmes* and *naṣīḥatnāmes*—contributed to the "mythification" of Selīm as a legitimate and ideal ruler was also a time when Ottoman notions of sovereignty changed within the larger context of Eurasia; it was a time in which millennial, apocalyptic, and messianic sentiments prevailed. The development of Selīm's image as a monarch bearing otherworldly, saintly, prophetic, and even messianic qualities was a consequence of these interrelated political, ideological, and religious developments. Building on the analyses provided in the previous chapters, Chapter 5 discusses the development of this third strand of memory regarding Selīm's divinely ordained rulership, with reference to the rival political theologies that reflect the ideological framework within which the Ottoman, Safavid, and Habsburg ruling elites operated.

3 Selīm, the Legitimate Ruler

> [Selīm] delighted in blood, whether it were of animals slain in the chase, to which he was passionately addicted, or that of his enemies on the battle-field; and the bloodless slaughter by the bow-string, which is the privilege of the progeny of Othmān, was hardly sufficiently exciting for this sanguinary tyrant, whose fierce blazing eyes and choleric complexion well accorded with his violent nature. He watched from an adjoining room the ghastly scene, when the mutes strangled his five orphan nephews, and the resolute resistance of the eldest and the piteous entreaties of the little ones could not move him from his cruel purpose.[1]

OTTOMAN HISTORIOGRAPHY on Selīm I and his reign is saturated with anecdotes relating, in gruesome detail, the violence the sultan inflicted on those around him. To mention but one contemporary account, Ḥaydar Çelebi's journal (*rūznāme*) of the Safavid and Mamluk expeditions narrates that Selīm dismissed his viziers Hersekzāde Aḥmed Pasha (d. 1516) and Dūḳaginzāde Aḥmed Pasha (d. 1514) during the Çaldıran campaign and humiliated them by pulling their tents down on their heads before personally stabbing the latter and ordering his decapitation; that he physically assaulted viziers Hersekzāde Aḥmed Pasha and Pīrī Meḥmed Pasha (d. 1523) on various occasions and hit another vizier, Muṣṭafā Pasha (d. 1513), multiple times with a bow; and that he oversaw the summary execution of vizier İskender Pasha (d. 1515) and chancellor Tācīzāde Caʿfer Çelebi (d. 1515) during a meeting of the imperial council. Ḥaydar Çelebi also notes that Selīm's wrath was so severe that he not only ordered the decapitation of his grand vizier Yūnus Pasha (d. 1517) on the way back to Istanbul but also carried his severed head for three days, thus denying the deceased a proper Muslim burial.[2] Episodes revealing Selīm's fascination with summary executions do not end there. An anonymous contemporary author depicts Selīm as so enraged that he first ordered Hemdem Pasha (d. 1514) to be decapitated and then kicked the unfortunate governor-general's severed head with his heels.[3]

In light of the anecdotes related in Ḥaydar Çelebi's journal, it is no surprise that of the six men who served Selīm as grand vizier, only one, Pīrī Meḥmed Pasha (d. 1533), survived his master.[4] References in Ottoman chronicles indicate that Pīrī Pasha owed his survival to his exceptional standing among bureaucrats and statesmen of his age. For example, Celālzāde Muṣṭafā (d. 1567) and Muṣṭafā ʿĀlī (d. 1600), prominent men of letters and prolific masters of Ottoman epistolary prose (*inşāʾ*) historical writing, praise Pīrī Pasha as the epitome of excellence in statecraft and service to the Empire.[5] In fact, in an unnerving anecdote composed on the authority of Celālzāde Muṣṭafā, Muṣṭafā ʿĀlī emphasizes Pīrī Pasha's indispensability as a servant of the House of ʿOs̱mān:

> The late Pīrī Pasha always remained alone and without a companion in the post of vizierate; and those appointed vizier were executed within a month's time. During the reign of the late Sultan Selīm [executions] reached such a [high] level that statesmen cursed one another by saying "May you become vizier to Selīm." Those appointed to the ministry would bring their last will and testament tucked in their chest; and every time they went in to an audience with the sultan and came back out, they would rejoice as if they had been born again. It is related that one day Pīrī Pasha expressed his fear by saying to the lands-conquering ruler [that is, Selīm], "If you are going to kill me in the end under some pretext, it would be appropriate if you were to release me [from life] promptly." The ruler of the world laughed much and stated jokingly and with innuendo: "This is also my intention; and to render you lifeless and to raze you to the ground is what my heart and mind desire. However, there is no man who can take your place and there exists no person who can properly perform the duties of the vizier. Otherwise, to fulfill your desire is an easy task."[6]

Similar references in numerous historical narratives composed throughout the sixteenth century suggest that Muṣṭafā ʿĀlī's striking remark—that rival members of the Ottoman military ruling elite cursed one another by wishing for their opponents to be granted high offices by Selīm—is as plausible as Pīrī Pasha's fears were warranted. That three of Pīrī Pasha's five predecessors had been executed by sultanic order suggests that few, if any, were indispensable in Selīm's eyes.

Selīm's violence extended to members of his own family as well. As highlighted in Chapter 1, despite its status as a canonically sanctioned policy since its codification by Meḥmed II in the last quarter of the fifteenth century, dynastic fratricide remained a controversial subject well into the beginning of the nineteenth century.[7] Thus, when Selīm executed his two rival brothers, Aḥmed and Ḳorḳud, along with his seven nephews, the notion that this act was a necessary evil perpetrated for the restoration of universal order (*niẓām-ı ʿālem*) carried significant weight.[8] Recognition of the execution of (actual or potential) rivals as a legitimate course of action did not preclude the simultaneous prevalence of antifratricide sentiments, however. To diffuse the air of mourning after the execution of Prince Aḥmed, Selīm is said to have ordered the distribution of seventy thousand aspers (*aḳçe*) and the meat of one thousand slaughtered sheep to the inhabitants of Bursa, repeating a gesture he had made after ordering the strangulation of Ḳorḳud.[9] There is also evidence to suggest that Selīm expedited the execution of the popular scholar-prince Ḳorḳud due to fear that delaying the matter could result in a janissary reaction.[10]

Ottoman chroniclers spared no effort in diminishing Selīm's responsibility for his brothers' demise. They portrayed him not as a fratricidal monarch but as a mournful brother. The following poignant anecdote, included in Ṣolaḳzāde Meḥmed Hemdemī Çelebi's (d. 1657) *Tārīḫ-i āl-i ʿOs̱mān*, provides a case in point. Reportedly occurring in the immediate aftermath of the decisive battle between Selīm and his most significant—and last remaining—adversary, Prince Aḥmed, on the plain of Yenişehir (April 15, 1513), the historic confrontation described in this passage sealed Selīm's sultanate while heralding Aḥmed's demise:

> It is related that when Sinān Agha arrived in the presence of the late prince [that is, Aḥmed] for the latter's removal [that is, execution], Sultan Aḥmed, who had on his finger a ring the value of which equaled the tribute of the province of Rūm, took it off and handed over that precious gem to Sinān Agha, and said: "We have nothing else befitting the Pādişāh; may he show benevolence and forgive us." It is told by the aforementioned Sinān Agha that when that peerless ring reached the prosperous Excellency of the Pādişāh [Selīm], he was taken over by weeping, involuntarily held his waist cloth over his blessed face and cried bitterly.[11]

According to Ṣolaḳzāde, although Selīm acknowledged the necessity of maintaining "the order of the universe" (*niẓām-ı ʿālem*) in conformity with "the traditions of the House of ʿO̲smān" (*ḳavāʿid-i āl-i ʿO̲smān*), he nevertheless decried the means through which that order had to be achieved.[12] Another chronicler portrays a Selīm so distraught that he cursed his ancestors who had canonized that uniquely Ottoman practice of fratricide, wishing that they be "remote from God's mercy in this world and the next."[13] Selīm's mood after the execution of Ḳorḳud is depicted in a similar fashion. Ottoman sources relate that, when informed by his executioner about the imminence of his doom, Ḳorḳud requested one more hour, during which he composed a versified letter addressed to Selīm, who reportedly wept on reading it.[14]

Taken together, these narratives construct the image of a grief-stricken sultan overwhelmed by feelings of loss and affection for his deceased brothers and crushed under the heavy burden of ensuring the unity of the Ottoman realm. Reading such narratives, one almost forgets that it was Selīm himself who ordered these royal executions.[15] These accounts also include subtle hints intended to justify Selīm's actions. For instance, Ṣolaḳzāde refers to the value of Aḥmed's ring, a common topos in Ottoman historiography, suggesting the much-criticized worldliness of the prince. Although it is almost a pity to subject such dramatic narratives to historical criticism, a careful evaluation of numerous other chronicles of the Ottoman tradition reveals that the relationship between Selīm and his brothers was less than amicable. Indeed, in the versified *Selīmnāme* of Şükrī-i Bidlīsī (d. after 1530), one catches a glimpse of the mutual animosity between Prince Aḥmed and Selīm when the former reportedly states, "I do not love them and they do not love me."[16] The same narrative sources suggest that Selīm was not a man prone to tears, even when his own father died.

The Death of a Sultan

On May 26, 1512, one month after he was forcibly deposed by his son Selīm, Bāyezīd II died on his way to mandatory retirement in Dimetoka. Contemporaneous European observers reporting from within the Ottoman establishment did not doubt Selīm's involvement in this inauspicious turn of events. Giovanni Antonio Menavino (fl. 1519), a Genoese who served Bāyezīd II and Selīm I as a page at the imperial palace and was a member of Bāyezīd's entourage on what became the deposed monarch's last journey, stated that the ailing sultan was poisoned by his Jewish physician "Ustarabi."[17] Theodoro Spandugino, whose familial relations extended to Bāyezīd's grand viziers Mesīḥ Pasha (d. 1501) and Hersekzāde Aḥmed Pasha (d. 1516), presumed that the sultan was poisoned on Selīm's orders.[18] Donado da Lezze (d. 1526), a prominent Venetian resident of Istanbul, similarly stated that Selīm had decided to kill his father and alluded to the fact that Bāyezīd's presence in Dimetoka would constitute a significant risk for Selīm at a time when he had yet to confront his rival brothers.[19] The Jewish rabbi and doctor Domenico Hierosolimitano (d. 1622), who served Murād III (r. 1574–1595) as his court physician for an unspecified period during the last quarter of the sixteenth century, bluntly noted that Selīm "slaughtered his father in order to reign."[20] Writing at the beginning of the seventeenth century, Richard Knolles (d. 1610) also related that Selīm "resolved most viper-like to kill his father" and realized the potential of poison to achieve "his damnable device" with the help of "Hamon the false Jew."[21] These and similar references were incorporated into the narratives of the majority of European historians in later periods, suggesting that this particular strand of memory—holding Selīm directly responsible for his father's death—proved remarkably durable in European historiography concerning the House of ʿOs̱mān.

Ottoman historiographical tradition exhibits the opposite tendency: references to Selīm's direct or indirect involvement in Bāyezīd's death are nearly nonexistent. Almost all Ottoman chronicles mention the incident briefly but refrain from elaborating on its circumstances. The rare narratives that relate the manner in which the sultan died are defensive in tone, obscure in language, or, frequently, both. Ottoman authors were not unaware of testimonies that held Selīm responsible for his father's death, however; two narrative accounts, Şükrī-i Bidlīsī's (d. after 1530) *Selīmnāme* and Hezārfen Ḥüseyin Efendi's (d. 1679) *Tenḳīḥü't-tevārīḫ*, refer to the deceased sultan as a "martyr" (*şehīd*), an allusion that has been interpreted as implying that Bāyezīd did not die of natural causes.[22] These particular pieces of textual evidence are inconclusive at best, however, primarily because Şükrī's account is a eulogy of Selīm that was presented to his son and heir Süleymān—certainly not the kind of work that would implicate its principal protagonist in the murder of his own father—whereas Hezārfen's *Tenḳīḥ* is a chronicle in which Selīm is remembered in unequivocally laudatory terms.[23] Furthermore, it can be argued that the term *şehīd* served as an expression of respect for deceased Ottoman sultans, who, as warriors of faith par excellence, by definition fought and eventually died as martyrs "on the path of God" (*fī sebīlillāh*). In this sense, the term would be particularly appropriate for Bāyezīd II, who was hailed by his contemporaries as "saintly" (*velī*) and "devout" (*ṣofu*) due to his personal piety and his reverence for the Ottoman religious establishment.[24]

In addition to these rather inconclusive references, several Ottoman narrative sources implicitly allude to Selīm's responsibility for his father's death. Noteworthy in this regard are reports of Bāyezīd II's advice to Selīm I before his departure to Dimetoka, urging the latter to not "shed anyone's blood unjustifiably."[25] In light of the fact that Bāyezīd died soon after he dispensed this sage advice, one can surmise that references of this sort—made through vague allusions to Bāyezīd's presentiment of his own death—probably were intended as implicit criticism of Selīm's violent deeds.

Selīm's acts of violence almost certainly included the poisoning of his father. In addition to the European accounts, rare Ottoman texts relate Bāyezīd's suffering during the last hours of his life. The most noteworthy among these is Keşfī Meḥmed Çelebi's (d. 1524) statement that "one morning the sultan's . . . rose-cheeked face turned pale-yellow like a water lily due to excess bile, . . . his head and torso shivered like a willow, his body caught fire and burned due to fever, numerous cold sores appeared on his lips, and he lost his mind due to immense vertigo and headache."[26] Counter to most Ottoman authors' silence concerning the circumstances of Bāyezīd's death, Keşfī's meticulous (yet intentionally vague) description of the suspiciously quick deterioration of the sultan's health suggests symptoms of poisoning.

The explicit attribution of Bāyezīd II's death to poisoning appears to have been a late sixteenth- and seventeenth-century phenomenon. Writing in the late 1580s, Muṣṭafā Cenābī (d. 1590) depicted Bāyezīd as a pious Muslim preparing for the noon prayer. He states that it was at this time that "they" put poison in the water with which Bāyezīd performed his ablutions, leading to the sultan's demise. We are told that, after losing the hairs on his beard, Bāyezīd died on the way back to Istanbul.[27] Undoubtedly intended to emphasize the piety of this devout Muslim monarch as well as the gravity of the injustice inflicted on him, this brief, poignant anecdote was reiterated with minor modifications by two chroniclers who used Cenābī's work as their source.[28] Cenābī's *Tārīḫ* is a testament to the fact that, at the turn of the seventeenth century, a recollection of Bāyezīd's death by poison survived in the collective memory of several Ottoman authors.

Although the majority of these authors penned their chronicles in Arabic,[29] explicit references to Selīm's patricide by poison were also included in historical works composed in Ottoman Turkish, the preferred language of the predominantly Turcophone Ottoman military ruling elite and intelligentsia. Whereas Evliyā Çelebi (d. after 1682) reported cautiously that "some [say that Bāyezīd II] died due to being poisoned," Peçevī İbrāhīm Efendi (d. 1650) stated unequivocally that Selīm "poisoned his father Sultan Bāyezīd."[30]

The primary reason why contemporary Ottoman authors edited the memory of Selīm's potential or actual involvement in his father's death concerned the legitimacy of Selīm's succession. As Nabil al-Tikriti has insightfully noted, "Dysfunctional as such a psychologically imbalanced, inter-married, and internally murderous family [the Ottoman dynasty] may seem to some, its individual actors appear to have been acting according to a well-defined—if ambiguously recorded—set of systemic imperatives."[31] Indeed, by the time Selīm made his bid for the sultanate, fratricidal conflicts between Ottoman princes after the death of a sultan had become commonplace. As early as 1389, Bāyezīd I (r. 1389–1402) had secured his sultanate by executing his brother, Yaʿḳūb Çelebi. The protracted civil war that followed what has been called the "Timurid débâcle" was fought between Bāyezīd's own sons; after eleven years of internecine strife, Meḥmed I (r. 1413–1421) was the last prince standing.[32] Meḥmed's great-grandson Bāyezīd II spent nearly half of his reign worrying about the possibility of a coup headed by his brother Cem (d. 1495). Yet there was a qualitative difference between the dynastic struggles that preceded the sixteenth century and the one involving Bāyezīd II's sons: whereas previous battles for the throne were fought *after* the death of the sultan, the greater part of the succession struggle between Aḥmed, Korḳud, and Selīm transpired while Bāyezīd II was alive. Because Ottoman sultans ruled for life, Selīm's ascent to the throne by way of deposing his father was by definition illegitimate. Even the suspicion of Selīm's involvement in his father's death constituted a grave insult added to an already illicit injury. And none of the aforementioned systemic imperatives could justify the violent overthrow and murder of a legitimately ruling member of the House of ʿOs̱mān. The suppression of any memory of the suspicious circumstances surrounding Bāyezīd's death therefore must be evaluated as an attempt on the part of Ottoman authors to defend the legitimacy of Selīm's rise to the sultanate. In fact, by hushing the ethically questionable methods by which Selīm secured his sovereignty, these authors paved the way for the rehabilitation of his royal image.

Rehabilitating Selīm: *Selīmnāme* Literature

In light of these references to acts of violence and cruelty, it is nothing short of a miracle that the inauspicious connotations of *yāvuz*, Selīm's posthumously acquired epithet, over time were replaced with more laudable overtones.[33] Selīm's remarkable achievements on the battlefield certainly contributed to the creation of the memory of a praiseworthy warrior-sultan during whose reign the Ottoman polity rose to preeminence in Islamdom. Without a justificatory memory of his controversial ascendance to the throne, however, Selīm's sultanate would have been remembered as nothing but the fruit of a poisonous tree. The suppression of the memory of Selīm's violent overthrow of his father and the creation of an alternative, acceptable memory was in itself a miraculous enterprise, one that involved a historiographical process that required the active participation of a great number of Ottoman historians.[34]

Of particular importance in this context is a corpus of literary-historical narratives that, because of their thematic consistency, may be classified conveniently as *Selīmnāme*s (Book of Selīm, or Vita of Selīm).[35] *Selīmnāme* works extant in manuscript form include İsḥaḳ b. İbrāhīm's (d. 1537) *İsḥaḳnāme* (Book of İsḥaḳ), ʿAlī b. Muḥammad al-Laḫmī's *al-Durru'l-muṣān fī sīratu'l-muẓaffar Selīm Ḫān* (Protected Pearls: Victorious Life of Selīm Khan), Muḥammed Edāʾī's (d. 1521) *Shāhnāma-ye Salīm Ḫānī* (Shāhnāma of Selīm Khan), Kebir b. Üveys Ḳāḍīzāde's *Ġazāvāt-e Sulṭān Salīm* (Military Exploits of Sultan Selīm), Muḥyī's *Selīmnāme*, İdrīs-i Bidlīsī's (d. 1520) *Salīmshāhnāma*,[36] Şīrī's

Tārīḫ-i Fetḥ-i Mışr (History of the Conquest of Egypt), Keşfī's (d. 1524) *Tārīḫ-i Sulṭān Selīm Ḫān* (History of Sultan Selīm Khan), Sucūdī's *Selīmnāme*, Şükrī-i Bidlīsī's (d. after 1530) *Fütuḥāt-ı Selīmiyye* (Conquests of Selīm), Saʿdī b. ʿAbdü'l-müteʿāl's *Selīmnāme*, Celālzāde Muṣṭafā Çelebi's (Ḳoca Nişāncı, d. 1567) *Meʾāṡīr-i Selīm Ḫānī* (Illustrious Acts of Selīm Khan), Saʿdeddīn's (d. 1599) *Selīmnāme*, Çerkesler Kātibi Yūsuf's *Selīmnāme*, ʿAzmīzāde Muṣṭafā's (d. 1622) *Selīmnāme*, Cevrī İbrāhīm Çelebi's (d. 1654) *Selīmnāme*, an anonymous *Selīmnāme* covering the years 1511–1518, and an anonymous *Tārīḫ-i Sulṭān Selīm Ḫān* (History of Sultan Selīm Khan) covering the years 1499–1520.[37]

Like earlier examples of Ottoman *şehnāme*-style works composed from the reign of Meḥmed II (r. 1444–1446 and 1451–1481) on, *Selīmnāmes* were inspired by Firdawsī's (d. 1020) versified epic masterpiece, *Shāhnāma* (Book of Kings). When adapting this versatile literary-epic genre to the Ottoman context, however, most *Selīmnāme* authors, like their *şehnāme*-composing predecessors, departed from the Persianate prototype in significant ways. The most obvious feature of Ottoman adaptations of this genre is that their subject matter is historical rather than mythical; that is, whereas Firdawsī's *Shāhnāma* relates the martial exploits of the legendary kings and heroes of Iran, Ottoman *Selīmnāmes* eulogize the military feats of a historical protagonist, Selīm I, who, much like the epic heroes of Iran, achieved almost legendary status as a warrior-sultan.

Some of the other adaptive strategies deployed by Ottoman authors were linguistic. The most significant among these was the rise to prominence of Turkish, which had become the preferred literary language by the sixteenth century, in tandem with the emergence of a cultural consciousness among members of the Ottoman military-bureaucratic elite who considered their cultural identity different from, and undoubtedly superior to, that of the Arabs or the Persians. As Cemal Kafadar notes, this consciousness was propagated by Ottoman statesmen, bureaucrats, and intellectuals, the majority of whom were situated, both geographically and culturally, in "the lands of Rum." These individuals "spoke Turkish (preferably a refined kind of Turkish, but not necessarily as their mother tongue) and acquired their social identity within or in some proximity to urban settings, professions, institutions, education and cultural preferences."[38] As a result, throughout the sixteenth century and thereafter, Ottoman historiographical production was marked by an overwhelming preference for Ottoman Turkish over Persian.

This linguistic preference extended to *Selīmnāmes* as well; with the exception of Muḥammed Edā'ī's (d. 1521) *Shāhnāma-ye Salīm Ḫānī*, İdrīs-i Bidlīsī's (d. 1520) *Salīmshāhnāma*, and Ḳāḍīzāde's *Ġazāvāt-e Sulṭān Salīm*, which were written in the prestigious linguistic medium of the original *Shāhnāma*, Ottoman *Selīmnāmes* were composed almost exclusively in Ottoman Turkish.[39] A preference for prose over verse was equally tangible. In fact, of the eighteen *Selīmnāmes* with extant manuscripts, only five—those penned by Edā'ī, Şükrī-i Bidlīsī (d. after 1530), Şīrī (d. after 1545?), ʿAzmīzāde Muṣṭafā, and Cevrī İbrāhīm Çelebi (d. 1654)—were versified works.[40] The remaining narratives were rendered in a highly sophisticated Ottoman-Turkish epistolary prose (*inşā'*), with versified segments scattered throughout the text.[41]

As this brief survey indicates, scholarly attempts to classify *Selīmnāmes* as a corpus of literary *or* historical narratives are rather futile.[42] Whereas some of these narratives are situated closer to the literary end of the textual spectrum, others are located nearer to the historical. Even within the same narrative, sections with a discernable literary flavor coexist with those of more rigorous historical scholarship. In this regard, Celia Kerslake's remarks about the value of Celālzāde Muṣṭafā's (d. 1567) *Me'āṣir-i Selīm Ḫānī* as a historical source are also applicable to all other *Selīmnāmes*: "Large sections of [*Me'āṣir*] are predominantly rhetorical, and deficient or inaccurate in factual detail. Other sections, however, contain significant historical material, some of which is not found in other sources."[43] In addition, Jane Hathaway's statement that *Selīmnāmes* are "not historical chronicles in the conventional sense but hagiographies" is likewise accurate.[44] That said, these narratives are not devoid of historical value. On the contrary, even when evaluated from the vantage point of a conventional positivist approach, the "mixed quality" of *Selīmnāme*s as literary *and* historical narratives renders them exceptionally valuable both historically and historiographically.[45]

Contexts of Composition

While acknowledging the influence of a text's linguistic characteristics on its effectiveness in articulating a specific politico-ideological viewpoint, this chapter focuses on the historiographical process by which *Selīmnāme*s contributed to the making of a legitimate image for their pugnacious protagonist. For this reason, factors such as context of composition, authorship, intended audience, and patronage must be taken into account.[46] *Selīmnāme*s were not produced during the reign of a particular sultan but were written over the course of the sixteenth and seventeenth centuries, with dates of completion for the earliest manuscripts corresponding to the reign of Selīm I (r. 1512–1520) and the latest to that of Murād IV (r. 1623–1640).[47] A closer look at the chronology of composition of these narratives reveals that they were created in distinct waves. Quite a few *Selīmnāme*s were composed, at least partially, during Selīm's reign.[48] In fact, the earliest *Selīmnāme* is known to have been penned by İsḥaḳ Çelebi (d. 1537) sometime between 1512 and 1514.[49] İdrīs-i Bidlīsī, Edāʾī, Keşfī, Muḥyī, Sucūdī, al-Laḫmī, Ḳāḍīzāde, and Şīrī completed theirs a few years later, between 1517 and Selīm's death in 1520.[50] It is noteworthy that the first major wave of *Selīmnāme* production, with the exception of İsḥaḳ Çelebi's work, aligned precisely with the immediate aftermath of a three-year period marked by decisive Ottoman victories: first against the Safavids at Çaldıran (August 23, 1514) and then against the Mamluks at Marj Dabik (August 24, 1516) and Ridaniyya (January 22, 1517). At this juncture, Selīm must have appeared to many an Ottoman author as a *Shāhnāma* hero come to life. That some of these works were addressed not to Selīm but to his son Süleymān was the result of his early death: Selīm enjoyed the sultanate for only eight years before he passed away unexpectedly—of an infected boil—in 1520, leaving barely enough time for the commission, composition, and presentation of historical works dedicated to him during his lifetime.[51]

The timing of the second wave of *Selīmnāme* production is equally noteworthy. The three works composed in this peculiar phase are based on Şükrī-i Bidlīsī's versified *Selīmnāme*, which, as its author remarks, was itself written twice.[52] In 1620, Çerkesler Kātibi Yūsuf produced a prose version of this work, which was followed by the re-versification of Şükrī-i Bidlīsī's *Selīmnāme* by ʿAzmīzāde Muṣṭafā and Cevrī İbrāhīm Çelebi in 1622 and 1627, respectively.[53] The quick succession of these *Selīmnāme*s mirrored the rapid succession of Sultans ʿOs̱mān II (r. 1618–1622), Muṣṭafā I (r. 1622–1623), and Murād IV (r. 1623–1640) in what was one of the most turbulent periods in the history of the House of ʿOs̱mān. The deposition and subsequent assassination of ʿOs̱mān II by the janissaries was followed by the re-enthronement of ʿOs̱mān's insane uncle, Muṣṭafā I. Forced to abdicate after four months, Muṣṭafā was succeeded by Murād IV.[54] There is little doubt that the military assertiveness of ʿOs̱mān II—one of the few post-Süleymānic sultans to lead his armies personally—and the decisive role played by the janissaries in the succession politics at this time were reminiscent of Selīm's warlike character and his controversial rise to power.[55] Textual evidence for such an interpretation is provided by Tūġī Çelebi, who penned a contemporary account of ʿOs̱mān II's deposition and execution by the janissaries. By way of comparison, the author notes that "such cruelty did not occur" (*bu cefālar olmadı*) even at the time of Selīm's forcible overthrow of his father, Bāyezīd II.[56]

Celālzāde's *Meʾās̱ir* and Ebū'l-fażl Meḥmed's rendering of *Salīmshāhnāma*, which was written by his father, İdrīs-i Bidlīsī, do not belong to either of the aforementioned waves of composition. Rather, they were composed in the mid-1560s, at another critical juncture in the history of the Ottoman dynasty. Ebū'l-fażl Meḥmed (d. 1579) states that he was ordered by Süleymān I to complete his father's work but does not specify the date of this sultanic order. The fact that Ebū'l-fażl completed his work in 1567 suggests that during the last few years of his own reign, Süleymān ordered the reincarnation of a narrative highlighting his father's achievements. It is noteworthy that Celālzāde's *Meʾāṣir* was completed in the mid-1560s as well. That these works' near-concurrent composition was simply a coincidence is highly unlikely, as even a quick glance at the unfolding of events during the later years of Süleymān I's reign certainly suggests otherwise. Marked by a lengthy lull in sultanic campaigns before the Hungarian expedition of 1566, this period was colored by dynastic tension and strife, first between the aging Süleymān and his popular sons Muṣṭafā (d. 1553) and Bāyezīd (d. 1562) and then between Bāyezīd and his brother Selīm (later Selīm II, r. 1566–1574).[57] Thus, Celālzāde Muṣṭafā's decision to begin composing his *Meʾāṣir* in the early 1560s—concurrent with Süleymān's order to Ebū'l-fażl Meḥmed—appears in no small degree related to the power struggles between Süleymān's sons as well as to the resurgence of tropes easily associated with Selīm I.[58]

Patrons, Informants, and Audiences

Intricately linked to contexts of composition are questions of patronage and audience. Christine Woodhead accurately describes the *Selīmnāme* literature as a revisionist historiographical project supported by Selīm's son Süleymān I in order to clear his father's name and thus further emphasize his own legitimacy.[59] There is indeed consensus among modern scholars that *Selīmnāmes*—regardless of whether they were produced before, during, or after Süleymān's reign—played a significant role in exonerating Selīm from the ruthlessness denoted by his epithet, *yāvuz*. Woodhead's more specific claim that "early in his reign Süleymān *commissioned* a series of works aiming to restore the reputation of his father Selīm" remains unsubstantiated, however.[60] Ebū'l-fażl Meḥmed's remark that he collated and completed his father's *Salīmshāhnāma* on Süleymān I's order constitutes narrative evidence that at least one *Selīmnāme* was indeed the result of sultanic initiative.[61] However, the fact that *Salīmshāhnāma* was ultimately presented to Süleymān I's son Selīm II (d. 1566–1574) suggests that the work was completed during the later years of Süleymān's sultanate and not "early in his reign." For reasons enumerated above, it makes perfect sense that Ebū'l-fażl Meḥmed was requested to collect his father's writings on Selīm I during the later years of the reign of his son Süleymān. There is also both archival and narrative evidence indicating that at least one other *Selīmnāme*—the versified work of Şükrī-i Bidlīsī (d. after 1530), composed in Ottoman Turkish—was presented to Süleymān in 1530.[62] Leaving aside for the moment whether ten years into a reign can be considered "early," it is noteworthy that the work was presented to Süleymān via his grand vizier İbrāhīm Pasha (d. 1536), who was also a prominent patron of the arts.[63] Although it is certainly likely that several other *Selīmnāme*s were presented to Süleymān, to the best of my knowledge there is no evidence that he actually commissioned any of those works.[64]

As this brief survey indicates, most *Selīmnāme*s, although not necessarily commissioned specifically by Ottoman sultans, were penned by poets and historians seeking patronage or reward. These authors presented their texts to royal persons and other high-ranking members of the military-administrative elite. Whereas some of these writers were members of the Ottoman ruling elite themselves, others were men of letters of varying prominence who had personal connections with those in power. Thus, they were not apolitical figures. On the contrary, *Selīmnāme* authors, not unlike historians in other eras, used their literary-historical narratives to express and strengthen a variety of politico-ideological perspectives that they (or their patrons) held.

Before moving on to an analysis of these narratives, the connection between patronage and authorship must be identified. Regarding the question of patronage, it is noteworthy that İsḥaḳ Çelebi, who composed his *Selīmnāme* in the wake of Selīm's accession, sought the sultan's sponsorship and possibly attained the status of a royal gentleman-in-waiting (*muṣāḥib*) as a result of his literary labors.[65] Whereas Ḳāḍīzāde notes that he produced his *Ġazāvāt-e Sulṭān Salīm* with the encouragement of a certain Seyyid Emir Ṣadreddīn Meḥmed,

Edā᾿ī identifies his patron as a chief military judge (*ḳāḍīʿasker efendi*) by the name of Muḥammed. And while the honorific title of the individual who urged Ḳāḍīzāde to compose his work indicates that he claimed familial descent from the line of the Prophet Muḥammad, circumstantial evidence reveals that Edā᾿ī's patron was Fenārizāde Meḥmed Şāh Çelebi (d. 1523), who hailed from a prominent family of jurists and judges and introduced the author-poet to Selīm's court. That Meḥmed Şāh Çelebi was appointed chief military judge during the Mamluk expeditions (1517) and later served as chief military judge of Rumelia (1518–1521) is testament to Selīm's confidence in this scholar-statesman.[66] Sucūdī's connections were equally impressive and most notably included Pīrī Meḥmed Pasha (d. 1532), who served both Selīm and Süleymān as grand vizier continuously between the years 1517 and 1523.[67] Having joined Pīrī Pasha's retinue at an early age, Sucūdī apparently served him as secretary (*dīvān kātibi*) before holding the office of secretary of the royal guards (*silāḥdār kātibi*) during the later years of Selīm's reign. Additionally, the specific and detailed information he provides on Selīm's military campaigns against the Safavids and the Mamluks strongly suggests that Sucūdī participated in these expeditions.[68]

Pīrī Meḥmed Pasha was Celālzāde Muṣṭafā's patron as well. In fact, that various parts of *Me᾿āṣīr*'s narrative depend on Pīrī Meḥmed's statements indicates that the grand vizier was Celālzāde's foremost informant. With the knowledge that Selīm had consulted the same Pīrī Pasha when he decided to send forged letters of support to Aḥmed to justify his eldest brother's execution, it becomes obvious that both Sūcūdī and Celālzāde were connected to the pro-Selīm faction via the grand vizier's patronage.[69] Whereas Sucūdī's and Celālzāde Muṣṭafā's association with Pīrī Meḥmed Pasha may have situated them in close proximity to the pro-Selīm faction, Keşfī appears to have been at its center since Selīm's days of princely governorship. Having joined Selīm's retinue in Trabzon, Keşfī served the sultan first as secretary of the imperial council (*kātib-i dīvānī*), then as confidential secretary (*sır kātibi*) during the Safavid and Mamluk expeditions, and finally, from 1519 on, as financial commissary general of Anatolia (*Anaṭolı defterdārı*) until relieved of this duty in 1521. But although Keşfī was close to Selīm, his early academic relationship with such a known pro-Aḥmed figure as Tācīzāde Caʿfer indicates that such connections were not necessarily exclusive.[70] In fact, the case of Şīrī ʿAlī, the author-poet who composed *Tārīḫ-i fetḥ-i Mıṣr* (History of the Conquest of Egypt), demonstrates that even relatives of known pro-Aḥmed figures composed *Selīmnāmes*. Şīrī's position as the son of Hersekzāde Aḥmed Pasha (d. 1517), a staunch supporter of Prince Aḥmed at Bāyezīd II's court, indeed appears to have had an impact on the tenor of his account of Selīm's rise to the sultanate: *Tārīḫ-i fetḥ-i Mıṣr* is the only narrative in this genre that refers to Selīm's political ambitions by explicitly noting that "the throne was [Selīm's] uttermost desire."[71] Similarly, Keşfī's connection to Caʿfer Çelebi may explain why his is the only *Selīmnāme* describing Bāyezīd II's death in a manner that suggests poisoning as its cause.[72]

In comparison, Şükrī-i Bidlīsī's *Selīmnāme* is unusual, as it was commissioned neither by the sultan nor by any of the members of his royal household in Istanbul. The work owed its existence to the support of two patrons—who were also Şükrī's principal informants—with connections to the lands of the semiautonomous Turcoman emirate of Dulkadir.[73] Selīm decided to annex the emirate's territories, which had long constituted a buffer zone between the Ottoman and Mamluk realms. However, when Dulkadirid ruler ʿAlāʾ al-dawla (d. 1515) refused to assist him during his march against Shāh Ismāʿīl in 1514, on his return from Çaldıran, Selīm sent governor-general Ḫādım Sinān Pasha (d. 1517) and Şehsüvāroğlu ʿAlī Beg (d. 1522) against ʿAlāʾ al-dawla. The latter was defeated and killed, and his severed head was sent to his Mamluk allies in Cairo as an uncanny warning gift.[74] Having thus annexed the Dulkadirid territories in 1515, Selīm appointed Şehsüvāroğlu ʿAlī Beg, ʿAlāʾ al-dawla's nephew and rival, to the governorship of this new Ottoman province. ʿAlī Beg distinguished himself as a valiant commander during Selīm's Egyptian campaign. Despite the significant role he played in the Ottoman suppression of Janbirdī al-Ghazālī's (d. 1521) rebellion in former Mamluk lands following Süleymān I's accession, he was nevertheless executed soon thereafter due to his centrifugal political tendencies.[75]

In explaining his *Selīmnāme*'s reason for composition (*sebeb-i te'līf*), Şükrī identifies as his patron and informant ʿAlī Beg, who encouraged him to relate Selīm's heroic exploits in a work composed in the style of Aḥmedī's (d. 1413) *İskendernāme*.[76] The first version of the text, completed in 1521, was indeed based on ʿAlī Beg's account. ʿAlī Beg's execution in 1522, however, left Şükrī without a sponsor, and the author-poet decided to seek the patronage of the new governor (*sancaḳ begi*) of the province of Dulkadir, Ḳoçi b. Ḫalīl Beg. Once Şükrī presented his *Selīmnāme*, Ḳoçi Beg asked him to revise his text, remarking that his account included many mistakes (*sehvüñ çoḳ durur*), as it was based on the account of Şehsüvāroğlu ʿAlī Beg, who knew only what others had told him (*ṭaşradan diñlerdi*). In contrast, Ḳoçi Beg benefited from direct access to Selīm, as his gatekeeper (*ḳapucıbaşı*). Thus, the second version of *Selīmnāme*, completed in 1524, was based on his account.[77]

From a historiographical standpoint, Şükrī's *Selīmnāme* is a unique work because it exists in two versions. Şükrī composed both versions with the same aim: to create a legitimate memory of Selīm for contemporary and future audiences. Yet the two versions reflect the perspectives of two different patrons with rival sociopolitical backgrounds and competing claims to authenticity.[78] Whereas the 1521 version of Şükrī's *Selīmnāme* was based on the account of Şehsüvāroğlu ʿAlī Beg, who was a member of an Anatolian-Turcoman dynasty, the 1524 version reflects the narrative of Ḳoçi b. Ḫalīl Beg, whose ancestors, by the patron-informant's own account, had served the House of ʿOs̱mān as janissary commanders (*yeñiçeri aġası*) for generations.[79] Although both versions were created by an author-poet in collaboration with a patron-informant, the "final" version of each work—and, along with it, the acceptably polished memory of Selīm—that was ultimately presented to Süleymān I in 1530 was based on Ḳoçi Beg's account. As a result, the textual representation of Selīm that reached Süleymān was the one sponsored not by an ally-turned-governor-turned-rebel but by a loyal servant of the House of ʿOs̱mān.[80]

The patrons, informants, and intended audience of most *Selīmnāme*s belonged to the highest echelons of the Ottoman military-administrative structure, but some of these narratives appear to have been written with humbler audiences in mind. A case in point is Çerkesler Kātibi Yūsuf's prose version of Şükrī-i Bidlīsī's *Selīmnāme,* composed in 1620 so that "the common people can take delight in [*Selīmnāme*'s] prose."[81] We do not know whether Yūsuf's rendering in prose indeed reached "the common people." What is evident, however, is that Ḫoca Saʿdeddīn Efendi's (d. 1599) *Selīmnāme* enjoyed remarkable popularity by the middle of the seventeenth century and, according to Kātib Çelebi (d. 1657), "changed hands frequently,"[82] thereby contributing to the rehabilitation of Selīm's image in the eyes of many an Ottoman subject.

Textual Interdependency and Historiographical Factions

The already blurry distinction between patron and informant becomes even murkier within the complicated matrix of textual interdependency among *Selīmnāme* texts. İsḥaḳ Çelebi's *Selīmnāme*, for example, served as a source for many later historians, including other *Selīmnāme* authors.[83] İdrīs-i Bidlīsī's *Salīmshāhnāma* appears to have had a similar historiographical impact. In fact, Edāʾī acknowledges İdrīs-i Bidlīsī's work as a source of inspiration for the compilation of his own account.[84] Despite his statement that *Meʾās̱ir* is based on what he heard from "the knowledgeable ones" (*erbāb-ı ıṭṭılāʿ*) and on what he himself witnessed (*müşāhede*),[85] Celālzāde Muṣṭafā similarly identifies İdrīs-i Bidlīsī, Edāʾī, and the prominent chronicler and jurisconsult Kemālpaşazāde as his sources.[86] In the same vein, Saʿdeddīn quotes Kemālpaşazāde directly, relating the story of the dervish who foretold the birth of Selīm and claimed that the little prince would grow up to defeat as many rulers as the number of moles (*ḫāl*) on his body.[87] Saʿdeddīn's primary informant, however, was his father, the famous Ḥasan Cān b. Ḥāfız Muḥammed Iṣfahānī, who was among the men of letters Selīm brought to Istanbul after the capture of Tabriz.[88] Saᶜdeddīn specifically states that he documented the events as witnessed and the correct information as remembered by his late father. That Ḥasan Cān had direct access not only to the sultan himself but also to all Ottoman statesmen and bureaucrats of high status during the six years he spent in the service of Selīm—as his intimate friend and boon companion (*nedīm*)—establishes Saᶜdeddīn's *Selīmnāme* as one of the most important historical sources on the (near-)contemporary perception of Selīm I and his reign.

What is even more significant for the purposes of this study is that Saᶜdeddīn also mentions Bālī Pasha and Ferhād Pasha as his father's—and, by proxy, his—informants. That both of these commanders openly sided with Selīm during the succession struggle and were present at Çorlu clearly identifies them as members of the pro-Selīm faction. Ferhād Pasha was the commander who single-handedly saved Selīm's life during the Çorlu episode, distinguishing him as Selīm's most prominent associate.[89] Both he and Bālī Pasha supported Selīm's bid all along. Moreover, perhaps the most obvious textual evidence of a pro-Selīm stance comes from Celālzāde's *Meʾās̱ir*, wherein the author characterizes those who supported Aḥmed by joining Bāyezīd II as *Aḥmedī* and *Bāyezīdī*, thereby reducing even the ruling sultan and his royal entourage to a mere political faction. These appellations effectively strip them of their unquestioned legitimacy.[90]

This said, *Selīmnāme*s did not lack any criticism of Selīm, however implicit such criticism may have been. In Celālzāde's otherwise pro-Selīm account, for example, three prominent personalities are praisefully identified: Pīrī Pasha, former *defterdār* and Selīm's grand vizier; Ḳāsım Pasha, also former *defterdār* and tutor (*lala*) of Süleymān I; and Tācīzāde Caᶜfer Çelebi, renowned chief clerk (*münşī*) and chief chancellor (*nişāncı*), who served both Bāyezīd II and Selīm I.[91] The mention of the first two figures is nothing out of the ordinary, as both Pīrī Pasha and Ḳāsım Pasha were respected members of Selīm's immediate circle of statesmen. Tācīzāde Caʿfer, however, was a prominent scholar and a notable supporter of Selīm's rival brother Aḥmed. By Celālzāde's own account, Tācīzāde Caʿfer was executed because he had unwisely insulted Selīm by referring to him as a "dog" (*seg*) in the aftermath of the Battle of Çorlu.[92] Seen in this light, the mere inclusion of Tācīzāde Caʿfer's name among praised individuals may be interpreted as implicit criticism of Selīm's proclivity to resort to summary executions of statesmen and scholars alike.

Selīm's deeds appear to have been criticized by his contemporaries as well. Deploying a trope common in literary-historical accounts of the Islamic tradition, some of these—per force implicit—criticisms appear to have been pandered as advice and expressed not by the voice of the chronicler but as remarks attributed to a historical persona. The difference between Edāʾī's and Keşfī's renderings of Bāyezīd II's address to Selīm after the latter's accession offers a fascinating example. Before Bāyezīd "gave [Selīm] the sultanate of the land of Rūm" (*dād sulṭānī-yi mulk-i Rūm*), Edāʾī remarks, the former urged the latter to rule with justice (*ʿadl*), to follow the laws of his ancestors (*ḳānūn-i acdād*), to protect the Empire's tax-paying subjects (*raʿāyā*), to accept the primacy of the sharia (*sharʿ*), to prevent sedition (*fitna*), and to hold in high esteem "not properties, armies, possessions, or soldiers" (*mulkat-u-ganj-u-māl-u-sipāh*) but the "Creator of the World" (*ḫudā-ye jehān*).[93] Similarly, Keşfī's account launches with a to-do list for the new sultan: Bāyezīd advises Selīm to protect the reputation of the dynasty, to follow his exalted ancestors, and to prevent oppression, as the great Ottoman sultans before him did. The later part of the retired sultan's counsel assumes a rather cautionary tone, however, and concludes with a list of caveats, advising Selīm not to convert his subjects' religion (*diyānet*) into murder (*cināyet*), oppress his subjects, cause harm to his soldiers, or yield to lust.[94] The fact that this roster of prohibitions echoes some of the criticisms leveled at Selīm during his sultanate strongly suggests that Keşfī assumed the deceased sultan's voice in order to safely articulate contemporary disapproval of his protagonist.

Fashioning Legitimacy: The Rise of Selīm in *Selīmnāme* Literature

Despite sharing a common protagonist, *Selīmnāme* narratives evidently do not compose a homogeneous corpus. They exhibit great variety in terms of their dates of composition, authorship, patronage, and target audiences. They are composed in all three major languages of the Islamic world but predominantly in an ornate Ottoman Turkish epistolary prose (*inşāʾ*), which was related to the language of the Ottoman court, called *mülemmaʿ*.[95] They belong to various points on the literary versus historical scale. And, last but not least, these narratives are quite diverse in terms of their coverage.

In accordance with the military-epic focus of Firdawsī's *Shāhnāma*, almost all *Selīmnāme*s pay particular attention to Selīm's conquests and describe his victories at Çaldıran (1514), Marj Dabik (1516), and Ridaniyya (1517) in vivid detail. In fact, two of these narratives, those penned by Ḳāḍīzāde and al-Laḫmī, are *ġazavātnāme*-style accounts focusing exclusively on Selīm's three major campaigns against the Safavids and the Mamluks.[96] Primarily emphasizing Selīm's military achievements, most other *Selīmnāme*s cover the entirety of his reign.[97] Whereas some of these narratives commence with Selīm's accession to the throne in 1512, others also address the dynastic struggle for succession before that date.[98] In fact, one such narrative, İsḥaḳ Çelebi's *Selīmnāme*, covers only the three-year period between the major Istanbul earthquake of 1509 and Selīm's accession. As such, it is the only *Selīmnāme* without reference to Selīm's victories against the Safavids and the Mamluks. It is also the only *Selīmnāme* that narrates the dynastic struggle between Bāyezīd II and his sons in its entirety, rendering it an exceptionally important source on the topic.

In the eyes of Ottoman authors, what rendered Selīm particularly mythifiable—not to mention a perfect vessel for the expression of a variety of politico-ideological viewpoints—were his military victories against rival Muslim empires abroad and his iron-fisted rule at home. Although all *Selīmnāme* narratives offer valuable insights on Selīm's international and domestic policies, the principal issue that required the rewriting of Selīm's story was his controversial rise to the Ottoman throne.[99] Consequently, the remainder of this chapter focuses on the narrative strategies through which *Selīmnāme*s contributed to the creation of a legitimate image for their protagonist within the context of the dynastic struggle between Bāyezīd II and his sons.[100]

As previously noted, *Selīmnāme* authors deployed various narrative strategies when addressing the conditions of Selīm's rise to power. For several authors, omission appears to have proven an effective strategy. For example, whereas ʿAlī b. Muḥammad al-Laḫmī and Kebir b. Üveys Ḳāḍīzāde do not even mention the dynastic struggle between Selīm, his father, and his brothers Aḥmed and Ḳorḳud, Sucūdī refers to that episode by stating briefly—and no doubt intentionally vaguely—that Selīm "annihilated all of those in opposition and those who made a bid for the sultanate and caliphate in a short time, in a pleasing manner, and in the best way."[101] In keeping with the authors of most other *Shāhnāma*-style narratives, these three writers selected Selīm's major expeditions against the Safavids and the Mamluks as their exclusive focus, emphasizing their protagonist's victorious and heroic deeds as a sultan. It is nevertheless striking that they ignore Selīm's successful raids into Georgia and his battles against Safavid forces during his princely governorship of Trabzon. Why would these authors sacrifice the narrative of a period of successful warfare against "infidels" (that is, Georgians) and "heretics" (that is, Safavids) when its inclusion would only strengthen their overarching argument: that Selīm I was the preeminent champion of "true" (that is, Sunnī) Islam? Was this curious omission a means of avoiding reference to the unpleasant memory of the Battle of Çorlu, which Selīm fought against Bāyezīd II?

Although the silence shared by these three narratives precludes any satisfactory answer to these questions, the *Selīmnāme*s penned by İsḥaḳ Çelebi, İdrīs-i Bidlīsī, Edāʾī, Keşfī Meḥmed Çelebi, Şīrī, Saʿdī b. ʿAbdü'l-müteʿāl, Şükrī-i Bidlīsī, Celālzāde Muṣṭafā Çelebi, and Saʿdeddīn offer valuable clues in their selective coverage and meticulous editing of several contentious episodes that paved Selīm's path to the Ottoman throne. These episodes include but are not limited to Selīm's departure from his gubernatorial seat in Trabzon and the Crimean phase of his venture; his activities in the Rumelian provinces that led to the military confrontation at Çorlu; the circumstances of his ultimate accession to the throne; the death of Bāyezīd II; and the executions of his rival brothers as well as of his seven nephews.[102] The manner in which these episodes are related in these nine *Selīmnāme*s constitutes the basis for the comparative textual analysis undertaken in the following pages, which also will address questions of authorial agency and textual interdependency.

Selīm on the Move: From Trabzon to the Crimea

Let us begin at the beginning, both historically and historiographically, by addressing Selīm's collaboration with the Crimean Tatars, as addressed in İsḥaḳ b. İbrāhīm's (d. 1537) *Selīmnāme*. As the earliest *Shāhnāma*-style composition about Selīm devoted exclusively to the succession struggle between Bāyezīd II's sons, İsḥaḳ's account is the only *Selīmnāme* that does not include a narrative of Selīm I's military victories against Shāh Ismāʿīl, Qānṣūh al-Ghawrī (r. 1501–1516), and Ṭūmānbāy (r. 1516–1517). Because İsḥaḳ Çelebi's account set the tone for numerous later historical narratives and wielded an unmistakable influence on Ottoman historical writing for decades to come, it is justifiably regarded as the cornerstone of any historiographical discussion of Selīm I's rise to power.

An erudite member of the religious-scholarly establishment (*ʿulemāʾ*), İsḥaḳ was respected for his valuable contributions to Ottoman literature, both in verse and in prose.[103] Ottoman biographical dictionaries note that İsḥaḳ was one of three individuals selected by the "pillars of the state" (*erkān-ı devlet*) to serve Selīm as companions in conversation (*muṣāḥib*) when the sultan was in Syria during the Egyptian expedition. These sources also relate that all three, in an effort to demonstrate that they were companions worthy of a world conqueror, and contrary to all established customs and protocol, attended Selīm's audience armed to the teeth; barely avoided the sharp edge of Selīm's sword; and were immediately sent back whence they came.[104] Despite being widely blamed for this unfortunate turn of events, İsḥaḳ Çelebi does not seem to have given up hope of attaining Selīm's grace. On the contrary, there is evidence to suggest that İsḥaḳ Çelebi wanted to seize Selīm I's succession as an opportunity to jump-start his career by becoming a gentleman-in-waiting (*muṣāḥib*) to the new sultan.[105] In fact, the existence of his *Selīmnāme*, a literary-historical account that celebrates Selīm's military achievements, can be considered tangible proof of such an assertion. If this was indeed his intention, why, then, did İsḥaḳ Çelebi compose a narrative treating events that almost exclusively precede Selīm's succession? Although the curtailed chronological coverage of the *Selīmnāme* may be partially explained by İsḥaḳ Çelebi's tacit—and hurried—intention of memorializing Selīm's accession as quickly as he could, there is no doubt that İsḥaḳ also anticipated the historiographical need to tackle the thorny issue of Selīm's controversial rise to the sultanate. As the following textual analysis demonstrates, İsḥaḳ's *Selīmnāme* proved to be a remarkably successful historiographical attempt at editing Selīm's image for contemporary and future audiences.

Regarding Selīm's departure from his gubernatorial seat, İsḥaḳ Çelebi begins his account with laudatory remarks concerning Selīm's expeditions against the Georgians and the Safavids during his governorship of Trabzon, praising the prince's bravery in confrontations with "infidels" and "heretics."[106] When juxtaposed with Bāyezīd's expression of his dissatisfaction with Selīm's raids into Safavid lands, İsḥaḳ's emphasis on the danger posed by the Safavids due to their influence over the Turcomans of Anatolia is undoubtedly intended as an implicit criticism of the aging sultan's treatment of his youngest son.[107] Moreover, by depicting Selīm's request for a governorship in the Balkans and his subsequent journey to Kefe as a response to Bāyezīd's reprimand, İsḥaḳ not only justifies Selīm's leaving his province but also avoids any accusation of rebellion that could be leveled at him.[108] İsḥaḳ's explanation of Selīm's choice of Kefe as his destination is also significant. By simply referring to Kefe as the *sancaḳ* of

Selīm's son, Süleymān, the author categorically omits any mention of Menglī Girāy (r. 1466, 1469–1475, 1478–1515), the Crimean Khan, whose contribution to Selīm's bid for the sultanate was established fact by the time this *Selīmnāme* was composed.

There can be little doubt that İsḥaḳ's omission of any reference to the Crimean Khan was deliberate, as it enabled the author to depict Selīm as an affectionate father who missed his son rather than as a rebellious contender who sought military assistance from a supposedly faithful—yet politically inferior—ally of the Ottoman polity against a legitimate Ottoman sultan.[109] Although İdrīs-i Bidlīsī, Keşfī, Şīrī, and Edāʾī imitate İsḥaḳ's authorial choice, several other *Selīmnāme* authors nevertheless describe the extent of Selīm's association with the Crimean Khan.[110]

One of these authors is Saʿdī b. ʿAbdü'l-müteʿāl, who composed his *Selīmnāme* during the reign of Süleymān I, probably sometime between 1525 and 1536.[111] With the exception of his name, nothing is known about Saʿdī's identity—although, on the basis of his father's name, several modern scholars have assumed that he was the son of a convert, probably born in Rumelia.[112] His possible Rumelian origins may partially explain his emphasis on Selīm's stay in the Balkan provinces. Moreover, Saʿdī wrote during the reign of a sultan who requested and received auxiliary troops of significant number from the Crimean Tatars, which may explain his curiously comfortable tone in describing the communication between Selīm and Menglī Girāy.[113] In fact, Saʿdī is the only *Selīmnāme* author who openly states that Selīm was glad that Bāyezīd declined his previous requests of provinces in Anatolia, as this would give him the opportunity to demand the *sancaḳ* of Kefe, the grant of which would fit well with his plans of crossing to Rumelia.[114] When his request was granted, Saʿdī maintains, Selīm immediately composed a letter to his father, seeking permission to cross over to Kefe in order to see for himself whether the province was appropriate for his son Süleymān. He did not wait for the sultan's response, however, before preparing his retinue and setting out for the Crimea.[115] As soon as Selīm arrived at his destination, he sent gifts to Menglī Girāy, as the latter's realm was on the path to Rumelia.[116] When notified that his presents were well received at the Tatar court, Selīm then invited the Khan to Kefe. Menglī Girāy responded immediately in the affirmative and volunteered to guide the Ottoman prince through his realm. Although Saʿdī does not refer to any specific military assistance that Menglī Girāy may have provided, the flow of his narrative and his remarks about Selīm's preparations for a military expedition certainly hint at close collaboration between the Khan and the prince.[117]

Şükrī-i Bidlīsī and Celālzāde Muṣṭafā further reveal the extent of the military alliance between Selīm and Menglī Girāy. In fact, Celālzāde's account includes a lengthy section on Selīm's stay in the Crimea. On realizing that Bāyezīd's viziers intended to bring his brother Aḥmed to the Ottoman throne, Celālzāde states, Selīm decided to set out for Kefe,[118] where he met with Menglī Girāy, who had always been on friendly terms with Bāyezīd II.[119] That Menglī Girāy had also had peaceful relations with earlier Ottoman sultans is suggested by his letter to the Ottoman court stating that "we shall be a friend of the friend of the Pādişāh, as well as the enemy of His enemy."[120] When notified of Selīm's move toward the Crimea, however, Aḥmed immediately sent to the Khan an envoy carrying a letter that promised a deed of private ownership (*mülknāme*) of numerous villages as well as control of some key fortifications in return for his help in blocking Selīm's passage to Rumelia.[121] Although the Khan refrained from accepting Aḥmed's proposal, his older son and heir, Muḥammed Girāy (r. 1514–1523), wanted to make the best of this opportunity and asked Selīm to match Aḥmed's offer. According to Celālzāde, Selīm found the proposal unacceptable and responded resolutely that "rulers take countries; they do not give them away to anyone."[122] His demands rejected, Muḥammed Girāy decided to gather his troops to attack Selīm's forces.[123] Menglī Girāy, though, acknowledged Selīm as the probable winner of the succession struggle and sent his younger son, Saʿādet Girāy, to notify him of the danger posed by Muḥammed Girāy.

Following the Khan's advice, Selīm was "compelled" (*bi'ż-żarūrī*) to cross to Akkirman, at which time he wrote a letter to his father asking for permission to meet with him.[124]

Whereas Celālzāde depicts Saᶜādet Girāy merely as a messenger sent to Selīm to communicate the Khan's caveat and to guide the prince on his way toward Akkirman, Şükrī-i Bidlīsī portrays him as the Tatar prince who actively joined forces with Selīm in his struggle for power.[125] The author states that Selīm crossed over to Kefe so that he could meet with his father and observe the attitudes of Bāyezīd's viziers, possibly with the hope of persuading them to support his bid for the sultanate.[126] Şükrī's account of the negotiations between Selīm and Menglī Girāy is strikingly similar to that provided by Celālzāde and concludes with the prince's rejection of the Khan's offer of military help.[127] Şükrī's otherwise defensive attitude does not, however, prevent him from noting later that Saᶜādet Girāy joined Selīm's troops.[128]

Saᶜdeddīn Efendi mentions Selīm's meeting with Menglī Girāy (*Tātār Ḫān*) as well. In the second anecdote of his *Selīmnāme*, Saᶜdeddīn relates that the two met on the Crimean frontier in the immediate aftermath of the "crushing defeat" (*hezīmet*) the prince suffered against his father at Çorlu. Menglī Girāy consoled Selīm by telling him "not to grieve for having been routed and because of the leaning of viziers and commanders toward Prince Aḥmed" and proposed to help the defeated prince by placing "the Tatar army" under his command so that he could "attain possession of [his] inheritance with overwhelming force."[129] Selīm, however, rejected the Khan's offer of military assistance, stating that he had not approached his father to depose him but to request additional troops in order to fight the rebellious groups within and outside the Ottoman realm who were running rampant due to the weakness of the sultan and the negligence of military notables.[130] Emphasizing Selīm's unwillingness to accept the assistance of the Crimean Khan, Saᶜdeddīn states that the prince also rejected the hand of the Khan's daughter in marriage.[131] It is at this point in the narrative that Saʿdeddīn expresses clear anti-Tatar sentiments, as verbalized through Selīm:

> Even if we covet sovereignty, how can we choose to be propped up by the Khan? And how can one enjoy such a sultanate? Especially, is it not apparent that it is a mistake to expose the protected domains conquered by our ancestors to be trampled upon by the flood-like and plundering Tatars? Even if the sultanate is demanded, it is possible to attain it with divine assistance and without [the aid of the Tatars]. There is no need for Tatar help.[132]

This brief survey of the representation of the Crimean phase of Selīm's bid for the sultanate suggests that several *Selīmnāme* authors acknowledge Selīm's association with Menglī Girāy but keep the prince at a safe distance from any allegation of military cooperation with the Tatar Khan. In fact, their collective argument is simple: Selīm did not collaborate with the Crimean Khan, period. Whereas the cautious tone assumed by Saʿdī b. ʿAbdü'l-müteʿāl, Şükrī-i Bidlīsī, and Celālzāde Muṣṭafā reflects the conventional attitude toward the Crimean Khanate of the majority of sixteenth- and seventeenth-century Ottoman authors, Saʿdeddīn Efendi's *Selīmnāme* stands alone in its strikingly anti-Tatar attitude. This discursive discrepancy begs the question why.[133]

The answer involves Saʿdeddīn Efendi's target audience and the historical context of his composition. Saʿdeddīn Efendi's *Selīmnāme* was a popular work, and circumstantial textual evidence suggests that the author composed it for multiple audiences with similar literary preferences. In the introduction to his work, Saʿdeddīn states vaguely that he intended the text as "a memorandum for posterity" (*yād-dāşt içün*) and "a souvenir on the pages of time" (*ṣaḥīfe-i rūzgārda yādigār*), suggesting that he indeed had a wide readership in mind.[134] There is no doubt, however, that the popularity of Saʿdeddīn's *Selīmnāme* was the result of its uniqueness in both form and content. Unlike any other *Selīmnāme*, his account is structured thematically rather than diachronically: it consists of a preface (*muḳaddime*) and twelve anecdotes (*ḥikāyet*) that offer fascinating historical and hagiographic vignettes from the life of Selīm I. In addition to praising the royal protagonist as the "renewer of religion" (*müceddid*), Saʿdeddīn portrays Selīm as a divinely ordained sultan with superpowers who delves into the realm of meditation (*murāḳabe ʿālemi*), communicates with the saints of the other world (*ricāl-i ġayb*) and the "rightly guided" caliphs (*rāşidūn*), and foretells the future.[135] Although otherworldly saints, caliphal ghosts, and dream narratives are certainly appealing topics for any readership in any historical era, the fact that they were transmitted via the medium of easily comprehensible brief anecdotes hints at an intended audience with simpler literary tastes (and shorter attention spans). Although this audience may have included various segments of Ottoman society with diverse levels of literacy, related evidence suggests that Saʿdeddīn's immediate addressee was probably Meḥmed III (r. 1595–1603).[136]

Saʿdeddīn served as the tutor of Meḥmed III's father Murād III and had close relationships with both sultans. Murād III was known to have been "favorably inclined towards history and the accounts of rare and strange events," with a particular interest in occult sciences and astronomy.[137] In addition to sharing his father's mystical inclinations, Meḥmed III is also remembered for his penchant for short stories with morals that were written in simple Ottoman Turkish—qualities likewise found in Saʿdeddīn's *Selīmnāme*.[138] Because Meḥmed III was among the few post-Süleymānic sultans to participate in a military campaign, Saʿdeddīn's choice of Selīm, the warrior-sultan par excellence, as his protagonist does not seem to have been arbitrary. Archival evidence reveals that Meḥmed III was interested in the history of Selīm's reign. This interest is indicated by his request of a manuscript entitled *Kitāb-ı tevārīḫ-i Sulṭān Selīm* (The Book of the Chronicles of Sultan Selīm) when he stayed at the Davud Pasha Palace in 1603.[139] It is impossible to ascertain whether Saʿdeddīn Efendi knew of Meḥmed III's interest in Selīm; it is possible that, as the royal tutor, he may have been the one who cultivated that interest in the first place. Be that as it may, the experienced statesman certainly had his own reasons for praising this bellicose sultan. Especially after the reign of a particularly sedentary sultan like Murād III, many Ottoman statesmen opined that the sultan's participation in military campaigns would lead to victories that had long eluded Ottoman armies.[140] As one of the two prominent figures who convinced Meḥmed to lead the imperial army in the Egri campaign of 1596, Saʿdeddīn must have thought similarly.[141] If a historical narrative was indeed the textual conduit through which Saʿdeddīn decided to remind Meḥmed III of his military responsibilities, he could not have imagined a royal exemplum more appropriate than Selīm I.[142]

Saʿdeddīn's account of Selīm's activities in the Crimea must be interpreted in light of these considerations as well as in relation to the Egri campaign. One can even imagine a frustrated Saʿdeddīn penning the words "plundering Tatars" (*Tātār-ı yaġmā-kār*) within the context of what Carl Max Kortepeter has aptly called "the intrigues and the counterintrigues of the year 1596."[143] The dizzying sequence of events to which Kortepeter refers was the outcome of the intricate interplay between the dynastic politics of the Crimean Khanate and the factional politics at the court of the Khan's overlord, Ottoman ruler Meḥmed III. The developments in question also were related specifically to the performances of Ġāzī Girāy II (r. 1588–1596, 1597–1607) and his brother Feth̲ Girāy during the fateful battle between the Ottomans and the combined forces of the Habsburg-Transylvanian army on the Plain of Mezö Kerésztés (Ott. Haç Ovası) from October 24 to 26, 1596. Although Ġāzī Girāy refused to go on campaign in person, Feth̲ Girāy assisted the Ottomans valiantly. Consequently, Ġāzī Girāy was deposed and Feth̲ Girāy was appointed Khan of the Crimean Tatars. Reinstated to the Khanate after only a few months, Ġāzī Girāy ordered the execution of Feth̲ Girāy and all of his sons, a turn of events that undoubtedly reminded contemporary Ottomans of Selīm's execution of two brothers and seven nephews as well as of Meḥmed III's execution of nineteen brothers.[144]

The protagonists of this political drama were members of the Crimean Tatar dynasty, whose fate was determined, to a significant degree, at the Ottoman court.[145] H̬oca Saʿdeddīn Efendi, the royal tutor, was a prominent member of the political faction that guided Meḥmed III's political decisions.[146] In fact, Çiġālazāde Sinān Pasha, the grand vizier who appointed Feth Girāy to the Khanate, was Saʿdeddīn Efendi's protégé. One can thus assume that the sentiments Saʿdeddīn expressed in his *Selīmnāme* mirrored his political stance in the context of "the intrigues and the counterintrigues of the year 1596." More specifically, Saʿdeddīn's anti-Tatar attitude can be interpreted primarily as a reaction to the violent turn of dynastic events in the Crimea, which led to the demise of the candidate Saʿdeddīn had supported. Furthermore, the reinstatement of a formerly insubordinate Khan may have obliged Saʿdeddīn to emphasize that the protagonist of his *Selīmnāme* did not rise to the sultanate thanks to an unruly and uncontrollable horde of "plundering Tatars."

When compared to Saʿdeddīn's account, earlier *Selīmnāme*s depict Selīm's association with the Crimean Tatars with remarkable subtlety. Whereas İsḥaḳ Çelebi, İdrīs-i Bidlīsī, Keşfī, and Edāʾī ignore the subject altogether, Saʿdī, Celālzāde Muṣṭafā, and Şükrī-i Bidlīsī acknowledge the relationship between Selīm and the Khan, albeit defensively. This division between two groups of authors is revealing in itself. The authors in the first group penned their *Selīmnāme*s during the reign of their protagonist, at a time when the recent memory of the Crimean contribution to Selīm's bid for the throne could imply that the new sultan and the Khan were of comparable status.[147] The authors in the second group, however, composed their works during the reign of Süleymān, at a time when the absolute overlordship of the Ottoman sultan had been firmly established. Finally, the fact that no *Selīmnāme* writer described the significant extent of the military collaboration between Selīm and the Crimean Khan is understandable, as having done so would have suggested that the vassals of the Ottoman polity were sultan-makers, perhaps even co-equals.

A Poisonous Tree: The Battle at Çorlu

Most *Selīmnāme* narratives obscure the military nature of Selīm's Rumelian endeavors to such a degree that one catches the first glimpse of the rebellious prince's troops on the plain of Çorlu, facing the imperial army under the command of Bāyezīd II, without any clue as to how—let alone why—tens of thousands of soldiers congregated on Selīm's side in the first place.[148]

İsḥaḳ Çelebi, Edāʾī, Keşfī, Sucūdī, and Saʿdeddīn remain silent about Selīm's activities after he crossed over to Rumelia, whereas Saʿdī remarks in one sentence that the prince was welcomed around Edirne.[149] Similarly, Celālzāde merely mentions the presence of the "champions of Rumelia" (*Rūmili dilāverleri*) in Selīm's army on the battlefield at Çorlu.[150] Rare references to the gathering of soldiers in the accounts of İdrīs-i Bidlīsī and Şükrī-i Bidlīsī do not reveal much, either. İdrīs-i Bidlīsī depicts Selīm as the passive beneficiary of a gathering of troops in two instances: when "three thousand" join him during his march from the Danube to Edirne and when numerous commanders and soldiers enlist in his army for an expedition against Hungary.[151] Whereas İdrīs-i Bidlīsī does not provide any information as to why soldiers joined Selīm's forces during the first episode, he states that the reason behind the enthusiastic participation of commanders and soldiers during the second episode was their desire to demonstrate their bravery on the battlefield. Moreover, in an effort to clear Selīm's name from the charge of gathering troops against his father, the author emphasizes that the Hungarian expedition was not an enterprise that Selīm initiated but a mission he was instructed to complete at the behest of Bāyezīd II. Unlike İdrīs-i Bidlīsī, Şükrī-i Bidlīsī depicts Selīm not as the princely servant following the sultan's orders but as the active warrior-prince organizing military raids into Hungary. In addition to giving Selīm credit for the initiative, Şükrī-i Bidlīsī also applauds Selīm's success in gathering troops by stating that his call for "Holy War" (*ġazā*) was met with such enthusiasm that "the army the visionary [prince] gathered pleased even the angels in the heavens."[152]

We do not know whether the army that "pleased even the angels" was the same army that Bāyezīd II faced at Çorlu eight months before he lost his throne to his rebellious son. What we do know, however, is that *Selīmnāme* authors handled this momentous battle between the legitimate sultan and the unruly prince with a discernably defensive tone, either by categorically omitting any mention of the military confrontation or by assigning the blame for the initiation of the bloody skirmish to everyone except Selīm.[153]

Sucūdī dodges the subject by referring to Selīm as the "Master of the Auspicious Conjunction of the Age" (*ṣāḥib-ḳırān-ı ʿaṣrī*)[154] who rose to the sultanate in the "soundest way" (*ṭarīḳ-i eslem birle*).[155] İsḥaḳ Çelebi emphasizes Selīm's good intentions in approaching his father's camp and accuses Bāyezīd's viziers of convincing the sultan of the necessity of a military clash[156] before placing the onus on the sultan for giving the order to attack.[157] Similarly, İdrīs-i Bidlīsī, Şīrī, and Saʿdī deny any military intentions Selīm may have harbored and accuse Bāyezīd's viziers of persuading the sultan to attack his son's troops.[158] Şükrī-i Bidlīsī blames Bāyezīd as well; he identifies the sultan's condescending attitude vis-à-vis the humble and respectful attitude of his son as the principal cause of the battle. Whereas several other Ottoman chronicles repeat this particular trope, Şükrī's account is original in that it refers to the physical narrowness of the plain where the two armies met as the ultimate factor that ignited the skirmish.[159]

Other *Selīmnāme*s are similarly colored by a discourse that shields Selīm from any accusation of transgression against his father. Yet none of the other authors display this imperative as blatantly as do Celālzāde and Saʿdeddīn. Both the content and tone of Celālzāde's introduction indicate that the author's primary objective was to legitimize Selīm I's accession to the Ottoman throne by clearing his name from any wrongdoing against the rightful Ottoman ruler.[160] To achieve this goal, Celālzāde ventures into a discussion of the Çorlu episode. After stating that the chroniclers who accused Selīm of "insubordination and rebellion" (*ʿiṣyān ve ṭuġyān*) did so because of their "deficient intelligence" (*ʿuḳūl-ı ḳāṣıra*), he argues that the sole purpose of Selīm's attempts to meet with Bāyezīd was not to wage war against him or even to convince him to abdicate in his favor but to see his father's face and kiss his hand, as would be expected from a respectful son.[161] Although he emphasizes that Selīm did not intend or even imagine any military confrontation with his father, Celālzade nevertheless refers to Selīm's extensive troops without giving any reason as to why the prince approached his father with fifty thousand soldiers gathered from the Balkan provinces.[162] If Selīm had any intention of attacking his father, Celālzāde argues, he would have succeeded easily with the help of the "champions of Rumelia" (*Rūmili dilāverleri*) and the janissaries (*yeñiçeri*), especially because those in Bāyezīd's own retinue (*ḳapu ḫalḳı*) had crossed over to Anatolia to suppress Şāhkulu's rebellion.[163] The author then deploys the common displacing trope of "evil advisors" and focuses on the consistent efforts of Bāyezīd's viziers to convince the sultan that his son's intention was to secure the Ottoman throne.[164] To that end, Celālzāde states that those who composed the pro-Aḥmed faction in the Ottoman court went so far as to bring "all of the commanders of Rumelia as well as the victorious soldiers" to the audience of the sultan, ultimately triggering Bāyezīd's decision to set out for the imperial capital.[165] On the way to Istanbul, writes Celālzāde, when the imperial army reached a steep hill near Çorlu, the seditious viziers approached the sultan once more, pointed out Selīm's extensive troops in pursuit, and finally convinced Bāyezīd of the necessity of defeating the unruly prince. Faced with the assault of the imperial troops acting on Bāyezīd's orders, Selīm proved unwilling to aggravate the situation, according to Celālzāde. Instead, he departed for Kefe, boarding the ships waiting for him at the port of Ahyolu.[166]

What follows is a vivid narrative of the crushing defeat Selīm's troops suffered at the hands of the imperial army. Still, Celālzāde maintains that the rumors initiated by Bāyezīd's viziers—to the effect that "Sulṭān Selīm was defeated and ran away"—did not reflect the truth,[167] emphasizing once again that it was not Selīm but Bāyezīd's viziers who were responsible for this unfortunate turn of events.[168] This motif resurfaces at a later point in *Me'āṣīr*, in which the author revisits the Çorlu episode and argues that it was the "ignorant ones" (*nādānlar*) in Bāyezīd's entourage who initiated the skirmish by pointing at Selīm's army of thirty thousand soldiers.[169] These individuals, we are told, deliberately misinterpreted the sultan's wish that Selīm be protected from peril. Providing another creative example of reverse logic, Celālzāde also argues that Selīm could not have initiated the military confrontation, as he would have succeeded in defeating Bāyezīd's troops had he in fact engaged his father.[170] Celālzāde presents the fact that none of Selīm's famous soldiers "of Persian royal descent" died on the battlefield as the ultimate proof that it was not Selīm who instigated the battle.[171]

Celālzāde's *Meʾās̱ir* is an unusual text in its organization as well as in its narrative content. Most historical narratives in the Ottoman tradition commence with an eloquent praise of the patron to whom the work is dedicated, explain the reason for the work's composition (*sebeb-i teʾlīf*), and state the specific occasion at which the final product is to be presented (for example, royal succession, military expedition, or princely circumcision). By referring to Süleymān I's patronage, Celālzāde follows this customary practice. Yet *Meʾās̱ir* diverges from most historical narratives in the content of its introduction, wherein Celālzāde discusses the validity and accuracy of various interpretations of a specific historical event—Selīm's battle with Bāyezīd II—only to reject them all as politically motivated fabrications. Considering that the same episode constitutes the subject of one of *Meʾās̱ir*'s later chapters, Celālzāde's introduction reads like an apologetic manifesto.

As curious as Celālzāde's obsession with the Battle of Çorlu may seem at first glance, a consideration of the context of *Meʾās̱ir*'s composition suggests that the author's emphasis on this event was not solely due to his pro-Selīm stance. There is nothing unexpected about Celālzāde's partiality, as he had entered Ottoman service as a secretary of the imperial council (*dīvān kātibi*) in 1516, during the reign of Selīm I.[172] There is no doubt, however, that both the content and tone of *Meʾās̱ir* also were influenced by the dynastic strife that marked the later years of the reign of Süleymān I, Celālzāde's master throughout much of his imperial service. Süleymān had already executed one rebellious son, Muṣṭafā, in 1553.[173] In the early 1560s he was preoccupied with the conflict between his remaining two sons: Prince Selīm, who, after Süleymān's death, ascended to the Ottoman throne as Selīm II (r. 1566–1574), and Prince Bāyezīd, whose open rebellion paved the path to his ultimate execution in 1562.[174] In light of the noticeable sense of urgency in *Me'āṣīr*'s introduction, Celālzāde appears to have been equally preoccupied with themes pertaining to dynastic power struggles. In fact, as noted by Kaya Şahin, "[an] old and ailing sultan, his warring sons, the throne in the balance, tensions between a Bāyezīd and a Selīm" were tropes germane not only to the unfolding of events around the time of *Me'āṣīr*'s composition but also to the succession struggle through which Selīm I attained the sultanate.[175]

Writing during the last years of the sixteenth century, Sa'deddīn shares Celālzāde's sentiments. He mentions the Battle of Çorlu no fewer than four times in the first two episodes (*ḥikāyet*) of his *Selīmnāme*. In the first episode, Sa'deddīn describes a conversation that he witnessed between his father, Ḥasan Cān, and Bālī Pasha, the retired governor-general and Selīm's trusted commander. Quoting Bālī Pasha's statements concerning the confrontation between Selīm and Bāyezīd II, Sa'deddīn accuses the sultan's viziers of inciting the battle and states that Selīm came to Thrace to visit his father in order to discuss the upheavals of the time (that is, Şāhkulu's rebellion). Based on Bālī Pasha's eyewitness account, the second *ḥikāyet* begins by referring to the Battle of Çorlu as a crushing defeat (*hezīmet*), relates the previously analyzed dialogue between Selīm and Menglī Girāy (*Tātār Ḫān*), and, finally, accuses the "pillars of the state" (*erkān-ı devlet*) of causing the confrontation at Çorlu. In both episodes, the blame is placed on the "wicked" viziers and "corrupt" courtiers in Bāyezīd's entourage, while the cause of the skirmish is attributed either to an order of attack issued by Bāyezīd or to a fight between one of Selīm's soldiers and those in Bāyezīd's army.[176]

Selīm's Accession to the Throne

In addition to clearing Selīm's name in the Battle of Çorlu by shifting the blame to the viziers of the aging and ailing sultan, *Selīmnāme* authors also emphasize the consensual nature of Bāyezīd's abdication from the Ottoman throne.[177]

İsḥaḳ Çelebi, the author of the earliest *Selīmnāme*, barely mentions the janissary rebellion directed against members of the pro-Aḥmed faction before Selīm's ascension to the throne.[178] Furthermore, by depicting the janissary reaction as an anti-Aḥmed movement rather than as a pro-Selīm one, the author avoids creating a causal link between janissary unrest and Selīm's political bid.[179] İsḥaḳ Çelebi also portrays Bāyezīd as an estranged father who, like his janissaries, was alienated from Aḥmed.[180] Through such leitmotifs, he prepares his narrative foundation to present Bāyezīd's deposition as a voluntary abdication rather than as a forcible dethronement.[181]

Keşfī reaches the same conclusion by beginning with the description of Bāyezīd's final days. The image Keşfī provides is of an elderly and ill Bāyezīd who is aware that "the scribe of death rolled up the scroll of his life."[182] Keşfī's Bāyezīd is a sagacious sultan who auspiciously realizes the necessity of bringing to power "a strong lion from his brave bloodline" not only to defeat domestic and foreign enemies but also to be accepted wholeheartedly by all Ottoman subjects (*reʿāyā*).[183] The author's emphasis on popular consensus permeates his narrative. Keşfī relates that Bāyezīd convened the imperial assembly, distributed gifts to the viziers, janissaries, and imperial servants, and asked the opinions of those present.[184] Once Bāyezīd received the approval of members of the imperial council, Keşfī states, he pronounced Selīm "royal heir apparent and deputy sultan" and "handed over the throne of sovereignty and the administration of the realm." Succession was achieved not by force but by Bāyezīd's own action and volition.[185]

Like Keşfī, İdrīs-i Bidlīsī and Şükrī-i Bidlīsī emphasize the voluntary nature of Bāyezīd's abdication. There is some variation in their retelling of the events leading up to that point, however. İdrīs-i Bidlīsī, for example, mentions that the janissaries attacked the residences of pro-Aḥmed statesmen before noting that Bāyezīd was persuaded by Selīm's supporters to bestow the sultanate on the prince. Here, İdrīs-i

Bidlīsī implicitly acknowledges the causal link between the janissaries' actions and Selīm's rise to power.[186] Şükrī-i Bidlīsī, on the other hand, makes no mention of the revolt of the janissaries and instead refers only to their disapproval of Prince Aḥmed.[187] By presenting Bāyezīd's decision to abdicate in Selīm's favor as the result of his consultation with Prince Ḳorḳud, Şükrī also extends Bāyezīd's approval to one of the other two contenders to the Ottoman throne.[188]

Similarly, Edāʾī and Celālzāde relate the circumstances of Selīm's succession in impressive detail. Edāʾī, for example, begins his narrative by referring to the rebellion of Şāhḳulu and the death of ʿAlī Pasha during his fight against the insurgents.[189] Aḥmed's failure to confront the rebels and avenge the loss of ʿAlī Pasha, Edāʾī states, resulted in the janissaries' realization that Aḥmed was not worthy of the "throne and crown" (*taḫt-u-tāj*).[190] According to Edāʾī, although Bāyezīd initially considered Aḥmed worthy of rulership, he later observed that Selīm was supported by soldiers (*sepāhī*), janissaries (*yañichari*), townsfolk (*shahrī*), commoners, and notables (*ḫāṣṣ-u-ʿavāmm*).[191] A group of prominent statesmen who opposed Selīm, however, asked Aḥmed to come to Istanbul as soon as possible.[192] When Bāyezīd summoned these same trusted statesmen for consultation, Edāʾī argues, he realized that their opinions were seditious (*fitna*) and remained silent about abdicating in favor of one of his sons. In the evening of the same day, the streets of Istanbul witnessed pro-Selīm demonstrations by the janissaries. To further emphasize the popularity Selīm enjoyed among Ottoman subjects, Edāʾī notes that, in every corner, people shouted, "Sulṭān Selīm is the ruler of the world!"[193] Aware of the danger posed by a potential pro-Aḥmed coup at the imperial palace, the janissaries reached an agreement with "the pillars of the state" (*arkān-e dawlat*) to bring "the sultan of the nation" (*sulṭān-e millat*) to the Ottoman throne.[194] In keeping with the demands of the janissaries, Bāyezīd II (*ṣāḥib-sarīr*) ordered the composition of a letter informing Selīm that the sultanate had been bestowed on him.[195] On the auspicious date determined by the "philosophers of the land of Rūm" (*ḥakīmān-e Rūmī*),[196] Edāʾī states, Bāyezīd summoned his son, kissed his face, and granted him the sultanate in accordance with the order he had received from the "other world" (*ġayb*); the use of the latter trope emphasizes that Selīm's sultanate was divinely mandated.[197]

Although Edāʾī acknowledges the role played by the janissaries, he nevertheless depicts Bāyezīd's decision to abdicate as a voluntary choice. In this regard, Celālzāde's account differs significantly. In a lengthy section colored by bitter anti-Aḥmed rhetoric, Celālzāde compares the "effeminate" (*muḫanneṣ*) qualities of Aḥmed with Selīm's virile endeavors against the "heretical" Safavids.[198] Because the janissaries regarded the actions of those intent on bringing Aḥmed to the Ottoman throne as a "great sin" (*ulu günāh*),[199] Celālzāde explains, they attacked the houses of pro-Aḥmed notables, including the prince's tutor (*lala*) Yularḳaṣdı Sinān Pasha (d. 1514). Celālzāde records the janissaries harassing Sinān Pasha while emphasizing that Aḥmed was not welcome in the imperial capital, as his failure to suppress the Şāhḳulu rebellion despite the support of his "infinite" troops indicated that he was not worthy of the sultanate.[200] Once notified by his *lala* about the janissaries' position, Celālzāde reports, Aḥmed decided to set out for Karaman to become the independent ruler of the Anatolian provinces (*müstakil pādişāh ola*).[201] Aḥmed's supporters at Bāyezīd's court enacted a dual strategy. On the one hand, they acknowledged the fact that their alliance with Bāyezīd fell short of bringing their candidate to the Ottoman throne and therefore followed the sultan's orders to invite Selīm to Istanbul.[202] On the other hand, they secretly sent letters to Ḳorḳud, inviting him to the imperial capital to seek the support of the janissaries, whose backing had already proven decisive in the ultimate outcome of the succession struggle.[203] Their anti-Selīm strategy failed again, however, because the janissaries respected Ḳorḳud as a scholarly figure but rejected him as a viable candidate for the Ottoman throne due to his "unmilitary nature."[204]

Unwilling to concede, the viziers in the pro-Aḥmed faction resorted to one last tactic to delay Selīm's accession—or to get rid of him (*defʿ*) altogether; they convinced Bāyezīd to send Selīm as commander-in-chief (*ser-ʿasker*) against unidentified rebellious groups still active in the Anatolian provinces.[205] When the imperial decree (*emr-i ḫāḳānī*) was presented by the viziers, Celālzāde states, Selīm notified the troops that he had accepted his father's orders. "Some eloquent warriors" responded by stating that they would obey the imperial decree only if Selīm were granted the sultanate.[206] In response, the sultan first asserted that, because he was still healthy, he would not give up the sultanate.[207] When his viziers, in fear for their lives and with tears filling their eyes, hesitated to convey Bāyezīd's message to the janissaries and begged him to reconsider, the sultan, too, cried and abdicated "under duress" (*bi'ż-żarūrī*) in Selīm's favor.[208]

It is noteworthy that Saʿdī's narrative explicitly states that the janissaries intended to kill Yularḳaṣdı Sinān Pasha and therefore highlights the violent nature of the janissary rebellion.[209] As in his discussion of the correspondence between Selīm and the Crimean Khan Menglī Girāy, Saʿdī thus addressed a theme that all other *Selīmnāme* writers carefully avoided, implicitly referring to the forceful nature of Selīm's succession. Perhaps even more striking in its implications for the legitimacy of Selīm's accession is Şīrī's double-edged depiction of Bāyezīd's abdication. Şīrī notes that the sultan voluntarily renounced (*ferāġat*) his sultanate on the advice of his statesmen and because he "recognized on [Selīm's] face the radiance of fortune (*fer-i devlet*)." However, he also quotes Selīm admitting his guilt over the Battle of Çorlu and asking for his father's forgiveness: "I know my sin, my Khan, show benevolence; forgive my crime, my Sultan, show benevolence."[210] Thus, Şīrī's account is noteworthy as the only *Selīmnāme* in which Selīm himself admits to the illegitimacy of his bid for the sultanate. As such, *Tārīḫ-i fetḥ-i Mıṣr* reminds its readers that even literary-historical narratives penned with the ultimate aim of shielding Selīm from criticism may provide clues as to why he was criticized at all. Considering that Şīrī was the son of Bāyezīd II's pro-Aḥmed grand vizier Hersekzāde Aḥmed Pasha, this versified literary-historical account further highlights the intricate relationship between the identity and position of an author and the degree of criticism he may have been willing to level against Selīm.

The Removal of Rivals

Selīmnāmes vary significantly in their discussions of Bāyezīd's death and of the elimination of the remaining Ottoman princes. İsḥaḳ Çelebi's account, for example, lacks references to the demise of Selīm's rivals; the author creates absolutely no narrative link between Bāyezīd's death and Selīm's succession. The defeat and subsequent execution of Aḥmed is only implied, and allusions to the executions of Ḳorḳud and the remaining grandsons of Bāyezīd are entirely omitted. By stating that Selīm accepted the oath of allegiance of Ottoman princes in various Anatolian provinces, İsḥaḳ implies that Selīm left his nephews alive.[211] Similarly, Sucūdī omits references to Bāyezīd's death, whereas İdrīs-i Bidlīsī, Edāʾī, Saʿdī, Şīrī, Şükrī-i Bidlīsī, and Celālzāde mention the incident only very briefly, identifying "divine decree" as its ultimate cause.[212]

A striking exception in this regard is the account of Keşfī, which includes a vivid description of the rapid and unexpected deterioration of Bāyezīd's condition before the deposed sultan's death. Especially noteworthy is Keşfī's description of Bāyezīd's complexion changing significantly as he suffered from high fever and body shakes and became insane before the imperial physicians could do anything to save his life.[213] As discussed at the onset of this chapter, Keşfī's account attests to rumors that Selīm poisoned his own father. His detailed narrative of the deterioration of Bāyezīd's health may be attributed to his early connection with chancellor Tācīzāde Caʿfer Çelebi, a pro-Aḥmed figure executed on Selīm's orders in 1515.[214]

In *Selīmnāmes*, the deaths of Selīm's remaining rivals are handled with great caution. Whereas some authors ignore the subject altogether, others cover it ingeniously, without mentioning the names of the executed princes.[215] Keşfī, for example, does not mention the capture and subsequent executions of Princes Ḳorḳud (March 1513) and Aḥmed (April 1514), although his cryptic statement that Selīm "completed the deeds and ended the lives of those who engage in quarrel and opposition" suggests that the new sultan eradicated the challenge posed by his brothers via the well-established practice of fratricide.[216] Like Keşfī, Sucūdī undoubtedly alludes to Aḥmed and Ḳorḳud when he notes that Selīm "expanded the canons of royal justice, spread the laws of Ottoman equity, [and] annihilated all of those in opposition and those who made a bid for the sultanate and caliphate in a short time, in a pleasing manner and in the best way."[217] Similarly, and even more subtly, Edāʾī refers to Selīm's thorough application of the law of fratricide by stating that "those who desired the crown" (*ḫāhanda-ye tāj*) lost their "heads, lands, and possessions" (*sar-u-mulk-u-mālesh*) and reached their goal of the sultanate only "under the ground" (*zīr-e zamīn*).[218] Much more explicitly, Şīrī states that Selīm "annihilated all royal sons," including his nephews.[219]

The authors who enumerate the names of the executed princes happen to be those who provide a justification for Selīm's practice of fratricide.[220] While İdrīs-i Bidlīsī, Saʿdī, Şīrī, Şükrī-i Bidlīsī, and Celālzāde express grief for these members of the House of ʿOs̱mān, they also highlight the regrettable necessity of eliminating potential contenders for the Ottoman throne in order to (re)establish the "order of the universe" (*niẓām-ı ʿālem*) and to prevent "sedition" (*fitne*).[221] In fact, İdrīs-i Bidlīsī justifies Selīm's acts by referring to an incident in which disgruntled janissaries stated that there were eleven alternative members of the Ottoman dynasty who would willingly rule the Empire.[222] Because all male members of the House of ʿOs̱mān were legitimate heirs to the sultanate, each and every prince was by definition a contender for the throne. Such a threat was obviously not one that any Ottoman sultan, but especially a sultan like Selīm, would be willing to tolerate.

Despite the fact that fratricide was a well-established and legitimate practice by the time Selīm came to the throne, the execution of Ottoman princes remained controversial. This controversy in turn explains why *Selīmnāme* authors did their best—by ignoring the princely executions, reinterpreting their circumstances, or justifying the wrath that Selīm inflicted on his brothers and nephews on his succession—to clear their protagonist's name from any transgression vis-à-vis his actual and potential rivals. In the end, all of the deceased were members of the royal House of ʿOs̱mān. The "reconstructive imagination" of *Selīmnāme* authors, however, authenticated Selīm as the only Ottoman prince predestined to rule the entire realm. These writers thus cleared the historiographical path that led to his subsequent idealization as the foremost Ottoman sultan.

4 Selīm, the Idealized Ruler

> ʿAbd-al-Malik b. Marwān asked Salm b. Yazīd al-Fahmī, "Which was the best of the times you have lived in and which rulers were the most perfect?" He replied, "I have seen no ruler who did not have both critics and eulogists. And time has always raised up some people and put down others. All men criticize their time because it wears out the new and makes the young old and decrepit, and everything in it comes to an end except hope."[1]

> There is no just sultan left in the world, and no Perfect Man (*insān-ı kāmil*). There is no Master of the Auspicious Conjunction (*ṣāḥib-ḳırān*) left, no brave champion, and no courageous Pādişāh. The whole zeal and burden of the land and the sea, of the West and the East, of eighteen thousand worlds, and of all Mankind, of the Beginning and the End, and of all those who follow God's law, and of all Muslims rests solely on my sultan's sacred being. The zeal of Islam and the companionship of faith are on my blessed sultan's neck like a sublime necklace and a divine collar made of light. The universe of secrets is absolutely vacant. If your sacred being is not within the universe of faith, God's caliph and the caliph of the Messenger of God will perish. God forbid, this people intend to destroy the foundation of the beautiful Islam and the basis of faith.[2]

For many an Ottoman subject, the early years of the sixteenth century were troubled times—and a certain ʿAlī b. ʿAbdülkerīm Ḫalīfe was one such pessimistic subject. In an undated petition (*ʿarż*) addressed to Selīm I in the wake of his controversial accession to the throne, ʿAlī Ḫalīfe not only expressed his personal grievances but also provided an exposé of political problems, bureaucratic malfeasances, social ills, and religious perils that, in his opinion, were destroying the foundations of the Ottoman polity and society. In a hortative tone, ʿAlī Ḫalīfe explains that the scores of infidels, oppressors, heretics, and rebels running rampant in the realm during the reign of Bāyezīd II were ruining the pure faith of Ottoman subjects. The judges (*ḳāḍī*), their representatives (*nāʾib*), and the police prefects (*subaşı*) were "corrupted sodomites," and wine was consumed in such great quantities that there were no grapes left to eat in most parts of the Ottoman realm. "Judges drink [wine], *subaşı*s drink, commanders drink, viziers drink, religious scholars drink, ignorant ones drink, animals drink, humans drink . . . the poor ones drink, the old ones drink, the young ones drink, boys drink, husbands drink, and, as we have sometimes become aware, even wives drink," ʿAlī Ḫalīfe complained bitterly, asking Selīm whether the royal treasury would be empty "if there were no taverns, no taxes imposed on taverns, if this filthy wine is not drunk." In his opinion, all taverns (*meyḫāne*) should be shut down. He wrote of an immoral world "filled with innovation (*bidʿat*), corruption (*ḍalālet*), rebellion (*ʿiṣyān*), ingratitude (*küfrān*), and insubordination (*ṭuġyān*)," in which "everyone was so committed to drinking, adultery, sodomy, usury that they said that these abominable acts were sins but did not actually consider them sinful."

ʿAlī Ḫalīfe associated these signs of moral decay with policies followed by previous sultans. For instance, he criticized Bāyezīd II for favoring the religious scholars (*ʿulemāʾ*) in Istanbul and Edirne, as if "the religious scholars, righteous people (*ṣuleḥāʾ*), the poor and the destitute" in other parts of the Ottoman realm were not worthy of his attention. Pillars of the state during Bāyezīd's reign concerned themselves with accumulating personal wealth; bribery became the norm, and the state imposed unreasonably high levies on peasants who held little or no land (*bennāk resmi*). Due to the exorbitant exactions demanded by judges, imams, müezzins, and various other officials, it became impossible, for example, for the poor to marry. Excessive taxes on inheritance caused "orphans [to] suffer from hunger and [to] die weeping." The divide between the rich officials and the poor subjects was such that "one dies of satiety, one dies of starvation."

Although the moral and socioeconomic troubles he enumerated were certainly significant, for ʿAlī Ḫalīfe, the principal battle to be waged was in the sphere of religion. There was no shortage of people who pretended to belong to the Prophet's lineage (*müteseyyid*) or claimed to be spiritual leaders (*müteşeyyiḫ*), but there were no worshippers in the mosques of some urban neighborhoods, some villages did not even have mosques, and some mosques were left in ruins. The majority of Anatolians had become followers of Shāh Ismāʿīl (*Erdevīlī*, r. 1501–1524). ʿAlī Ḫalīfe warned Selīm against "those who deny the Word of God, disbelieve the Religion of God, destroy the Law of God" and also against the "heretics" who "destroyed mosques and pulpits, cut open the bellies of dogs and shoved Qurʾāns and books in dogs' bellies, hanged and attached [Qurʾāns] on the necks of dogs, dragged [them on the ground], placed them under their feet, and crushed them into pieces under their soles." Yet ʿAlī Ḫalīfe's confidence in Selīm was unconditional, as the latter was "the discoverer of the Book of God, the conqueror of the Law of God, the confidant of the Messenger of God, the companion of the Beloved of God." For a concerned subject like ʿAlī Ḫalīfe, Selīm was the hoped-for redeemer, the ideal sultan who could right the wrongs of his predecessors.[3]

A few years before ʿAlī Ḫalīfe addressed his admonitory petition to Selīm, similar anxieties pertaining to moral, religious, administrative, and political affairs were expressed in a lengthy treatise entitled *Daʿwat al-nafs al-ṭāliḥa ilā al-aʿmāl al-ṣāliḥa* (An Erring Soul's Summons to Virtuous Works).[4] Composed in 1508 by Selīm's brother Ḳorḳud (d. 1513) for the reigning Bāyezīd II (r. 1481–1512), *Daʿwat* served as a textual conduit through which the scholarly prince expressed, first and foremost, his desire to be excused from governmental duties and to resign from candidacy for the Ottoman throne. Ḳorḳud's reasoning was simple: given the impossibility of enforcing the revealed principles of Holy Law (*sharīʿa*) within the specific context of the Ottoman realm—in which secular, imperial legal conventions (*ʿurf*) reigned supreme—it was virtually impossible for him to be both an effective ruler (*amīr*) and a righteous believer (*muʾmin*). His examination of the state of affairs at the beginning of the sixteenth century, however, resulted in nothing short of a blistering critique of numerous Ottoman institutions and practices.

Ḳorḳud condemned judges for exacting illegal fees, adjudicating *sharīʿa* cases by *ʿurf* procedures, and accepting stipends from the state, whose communal treasury (*bayt al-māl*) included both licit (*ḥalāl*) and illicit (*ḥarām*) funds. He considered the janissaries, as well as members of military units of *devşirme* origin at the imperial palace, to be disorderly and violent, "as were their infidel fathers." Palace gatekeepers (*bawwābān*) committed acts of injustice in the provinces; other officials abused the imperial communication system (*barīd*), violated the rights of tax-paying subjects (*raʿāya*), and seized animals belonging to these subjects. Courtly profligacy harmed imperial subjects by siphoning off precious metals from circulation. The state's failure to enforce religious social standards resulted in neglect of prayers, lax performance of ritual ablutions, and widespread ignorance about even the most basic requirements of the law throughout the realm. Sufis with latitudinarian tendencies influenced military administrators (*wulāt*) as well as members of the ulema and led to their moral decrepitude. Even the practice of *ghazā*, once a pillar of religious legitimacy for the Ottoman state, lost its legality, as it now involved attacks on other Muslim entities and unlawful apportionment of spoils of war. Thus, as a believing Muslim concerned about his salvation, Ḳorḳud must have felt that he had no choice but to withdraw from political governance. Although the *Daʿwat* served as a vehicle for the articulation of the devout prince's otherworldly considerations, the timing of its composition suggests that Ḳorḳud had earthly trepidations as well. While he may indeed have designed this treatise "to buttress his image as an ethical candidate who would rule according to *sharīʿa* norms if given the opportunity,"[5] he must have also realized that either Aḥmed (d. 1513) or Selīm would eventually attain the sultanate and most likely execute him, in compliance with the long-standing Ottoman dynastic practice of fratricide. Thus, when Ḳorḳud was composing *Daʿwat*, survival instinct, pure and simple, was probably at least as operative as his concern for salvation.

The expression of specific grievances by Ottoman princes in their correspondence with the ruling sultan and other prominent statesmen was nothing out of the ordinary. In fact, Selīm himself was the author of several petitions in which he criticized Bāyezīd II's viziers for the oppression of poor subjects in the Anatolian provinces and blamed these statesmen for neglecting their principal duty of "warding off the pertinacious sedition and mischief affecting Muslims."[6] Although the composition of a sophisticated, thematically coherent critique of numerous Ottoman institutions and practices, written by an exceptionally erudite member of the ruling house, was quite unusual, if not unique, Ḳorḳud's treatise and ʿAlī Ḫalīfe's petition had a number of characteristics in common. To begin with, both were essentially personal documents that do not appear to have circulated widely. As a petition addressed to Selīm, ʿAlī Ḫalīfe's piece was intended for the sultan's eyes only; Ḳorḳud's *Daʿwat* is not mentioned in any other major historical work.[7] The two documents are also comparable in that they address similar types of imperial abuses, utilize a *sharīʿa*- and orthopraxis-minded religious framework, include conventional tropes concerning the requirements of ideal Muslim monarchs, and even issue similar warnings about the otherworldly fate that awaits Ottoman sultans who fail to rule in strict accordance with divine law. Although neither Ḳorḳud's treatise nor ʿAlī Ḫalīfe's petition can be assumed to reflect objective Ottoman realities at the beginning of the sixteenth century, the observations and criticisms voiced by their authors were certainly "part of the common stock of Islamic juridical lore on worldly government."[8] Perhaps more importantly for the purposes of this study, these criticisms signify an intellectual link with a corpus of political treatises, namely the *naṣīḥatnāme* literature, an impressive genre that flourished in the Ottoman realm during the sixteenth and seventeenth centuries and, as will be argued below, constituted an integral part of the historiographical process that culminated in the creation of a legitimate and idealized image of Selīm I.

Naṣīḥatnāme Literature: Preliminary Notes

Although this genre of Ottoman historical writing defies any simplistic and uncritical appellation, the works that it comprises have been variously identified as decline treatises,[9] mirrors for princes/kings,[10] literature of reform,[11] political advice literature,[12] advice to princes,[13] and advice for kings.[14] Some of these works were indeed considered by their authors as "a mirror that shows the world" (*āyīne-i cihān-nümā*),[15] but the use of the terms "treatise" (*risāle*) and "book of advice" (*naṣīḥatnāme*) as the most frequent self-designations indicates that their Ottoman authors considered the primary function of these works to be the provision of counsel. In order to best reflect their authorial choice, I have retained the term *naṣīḥatnāme* throughout this study.

The previous chapter highlighted the palpable influence of Persianate discourse on Ottoman literary and political culture with reference not only to the popularity of the *Shāhnāma* as a literary-historical genre of writing but also to the adoption of Persian symbols of imperial rule and regal vocabulary in the titulature of Ottoman sultans from the fifteenth century onward.[16] Similarly, the Ottoman variety of the *naṣīḥatnāme* genre, though rooted in the advice literature produced in central Eurasia and Asia Minor, was particularly indebted, both formally and conceptually, to certain works written in Persian in the eleventh century and translated into Ottoman Turkish by the fifteenth. Kay-Kāʾūs ibn Iskandar's *Ḳābūsnāma*, Niẓām al-Mulk's (d. 1092) *Siyāsatnāma*, and al-Ghazālī's (d. 1111) *Kitāb naṣīḥat al-mulūk* served as models for Ottoman *naṣīḥatnāme* authors, further attesting to the significant impact of Persian works of advice on the related Ottoman corpus of political-literary writing.

With the exception of the few treatises penned in the fourteenth and fifteenth centuries, the proliferation of a distinctly Ottoman advice literature is a sixteenth- and seventeenth-century phenomenon.[17]

The relatively late production of specifically Ottoman works of advice cannot be explained by the delayed maturation of Ottoman Turkish, which had been employed as a sophisticated medium of literary expression from the fifteenth century onward. Rather, what impelled the Ottoman composition of works of advice was the emergence of a historical consciousness of "decline" in Ottoman learned circles from the middle of the sixteenth century on. Indubitably, the *naṣīḥatnāme* genre provides the most lucid expression of that consciousness.[18]

Works of advice featured prominently as a dynastic project not only for the House of ʿOs̱mān but for Safavid and Mughal rulers as well.[19] The fundamental concern of Ottoman works of advice was the same as that of their earlier Persianate models: the establishment and maintenance of dynastic sovereignty legitimated by unconditional adherence to justice and equity (*ʿadālet*). The most lucid expression of this notion was embodied in Ḳınālızāde ʿAlī Çelebi's (d. 1572) depiction of "the circle of equity" (*dāʾire-i ʿadālet*):[20]

> There can be no royal authority without the military
> There can be no military without wealth
> The subjects produce the wealth
> Justice preserves the subjects' loyalty to the sovereign
> Justice requires harmony in the world
> The world is a garden, its walls are the state
> The Holy Law (*sharīʿa*) orders the state
> There is no support for the *sharīʿa* except through royal authority[21]

In addition to being a work that highlights the complex interrelation between ethics and politics, Ḳınālızāde ʿAlī Çelebi's *Aḫlaḳ-ı ʿalāʾī* (Sublime Ethics) represents the "theoretical foundations of the compartmentalized social order" addressed by Ottoman *naṣīḥatnāme* authors.[22] Although even a partial examination of the Ottoman *naṣīḥatnāme* literature is well beyond the scope of this chapter, a few remarks can be offered.[23] Most works belonging to this corpus were penned by both known and unknown authors after Selīm's lifetime, and they exhibit immense variety in terms of chronology, content, authorship, and target audience. Composed between the later years of Süleymān I's (r. 1520–1566) reign and the beginning of the eighteenth century, these works address a plethora of challenges and crises faced by the Ottoman state and society within the context of ever-changing historical circumstances during a particularly transformative period of Ottoman history. In an age when the maintenance of increasingly larger armies strained the Empire's fiscal structure, Süleymān I's grand vizier Luṭfī Pasha (d. 1563) stated bluntly that "soldiers should be few but good . . . fifteen thousand paid soldiers are too many soldiers" and remarked that "paying fifteen thousand people from year to year is indeed an act of heroism."[24] Writing in 1596, just before Meḥmed III's (r. 1595–1603) Egri campaign, Ḥasan Kāfī el-Aḳḥiṣārī (d. 1616) commented on the sedition and destruction afflicting "the order of the world" (*ʿālemüñ niẓāmında fesād ve bozġunluḳ*) and highlighted the technological inferiority of Ottoman armies vis-à-vis their enemies and the lack of discipline among Ottoman soldiers as principal causes of the frequent setbacks suffered on the battlefield.[25] Some *naṣīḥatnāme* authors ascribed primary responsibility for all of the ills afflicting the Ottoman state and society to the sultan's slave-servants (*ḳul*). Whereas Ḥasan Kāfī el-Aḳḥiṣārī assigned the blame for the "oppression and tyranny" (*ẓulüm ve taʿaddī*) that imperial subjects suffered in the Anatolian provinces to the janissaries (*ḫünkār ḳulı*) stationed there,[26] Muṣṭafā ʿĀlī (d. 1600) went so far as to declare the pivotal Ottoman institution called *devşirme* ("gathering")—through which Christian-born subjects of the Empire entered the Ottoman military-administrative structure and became the sultan's slave-servants—to be "at variance with the Divine Law" (*şerʿe muġāyır*).[27] At a time when the imperial administration was dominated to a significant degree by high-ranking members of the Ottoman military ruling elite of *devşirme* origin (*ḳul ṭāʾifesi*) and when the janissaries exerted increasing influence on the affairs of the state, Luṭfī Pasha argued that grand viziers should control the janissaries via the appointment of "prudent and restraining" commanders.[28] Highlighting forty years of incessant warfare, onerous taxation, corrupt judges, unqualified office holders, and the devastation caused by the constantly campaigning Ottoman armies as among the causes of the disorder afflicting the subjects of the Empire, Veysī (d. 1628), a prolific poet and prose writer who composed quite a peculiar treatise entitled *Ḫābnāme* (Book of Dream) in 1608, complained about unruly and disobedient "slave-servants" (*ḳul*) of the Ottoman dynasty by using Aḥmed I (r. 1603–1617) as his mouthpiece: "If the *ḳul*, my *ḳul*, does not submit to me and obey my orders, how can I protect the *reʿāyā* with the sword of justice and equity, and control and govern the realm?"[29] The fact that Sultan ʿOs̱mān II (r. 1618–1622) was deposed and executed by the janissaries a little more than a decade after the composition of the *Ḫābnāme* suggests that Veysī's complaints were indeed justified.[30]

In their works, *naṣīḥatnāme* authors proposed remedies as well. Although they were unanimous in their emphasis on justice and equity (*ʿadālet*) as a precondition for the (re)establishment of universal order (*niẓām-ı ʿālem*), they differed in their suggestions for how this could be achieved. Assuming the role of the biblical king Solomon's trusted advisor Asaph, Luṭfī Pasha not only called for exclusively merit-based appointments of qualified statesmen to the grand vizierate but also stressed the need for strict measures to prevent the infiltration of the ranks of the military ruling elite by tax-paying subjects (*reʿāyā*).[31] As a countermeasure against the corruption he observed in the highest echelons of the administrative-bureaucratic apparatus, prominent bureaucrat and prolific intellectual Muṣṭafā ʿĀlī suggested that high-ranking positions be granted as hereditary offices to qualified persons for their lifetime.[32] Some of Muṣṭafā ʿĀlī's suggestions were exceptionally specific, such as banning the use of gold in gold thread (so that it does not vanish "without a trace like the zephyr").[33]

Naṣīḥatnāme authors were learned men of diverse socio-cultural backgrounds (for example, freeborn Muslim, *devşirme*, and so on), most of whom had served the Ottoman polity as statesmen, administrators, bureaucrats, or scholars (or, as in most cases, a combination thereof), possessed varied skill sets, and benefited or suffered from different life experiences. No doubt influenced by these factors, they expressed disparate, and at times conflicting, political and ideological viewpoints, not to mention specific presentist agendas.[34] Some had personal axes to grind as well. Divorced by the sultan's sister and dismissed by the sultan himself, Süleymān I's grand vizier Luṭfī Pasha stated that he composed his *Āṣafnāme* in retirement, safe from the "wickedness" of womankind and the deceit of hypocrites.[35] Ḥasan Kāfī el-Aḳḥiṣārī and Veysī, two advice authors who proposed adherence to Holy Law (*sharīʿa*) as the principal remedy for all contemporary ills, were members of the religious establishment. Veysī, who asked Ottoman sultans and their viziers to appoint only qualified judges, was a judge himself, and Ḥasan Kāfī el-Aḳḥiṣārī, who emphatically noted that "scholars of religion do not commit fraud or treason," was a member of the Ottoman *ʿulemāʾ*.[36] Muṣṭafā ʿĀlī, a freeborn Muslim frustrated by (what he perceived as) a lack of recognition of his qualifications and a parallel lack of promotion to high office, complained about the abuses of the slave-servants (*ḳul*). He wrote that all problems resulted from "the wickedness of the viziers and the unawareness of the land-conquering sultan" and so urged Murād III (r. 1574–1595) to apply meritocratic principles to any and all appointments to administrative-bureaucratic offices.[37] Conversely, the anonymous author who complained about "innovations" (*bidʿat*) that culminated in the weakening of the janissary corps and loathed the freeborn Muslim "Turks-Murks" (*Türk Mürk*) who joined the ranks of the janissaries contrary to established laws and practices was himself a veteran janissary of *devşirme* origin.[38]

Much like their authors, the intended audiences for Ottoman works of advice also varied, ranging from a single person (for example, their patron or the sultan) to an entire group of people (for example, educated scribes, bureaucrats, or viziers). Whereas Pál Fodor claims that "most of the works at issue were really intended for the sultans," Douglas Howard accurately observes that "the advice for kings genre gained currency during this period of bureaucratic eclipse" and argues that the genre's "primary audience was not the sultan but the educated group of scribes and bureaucrats who staffed the great

Ottoman administrative offices and who identified themselves with an idealized sultanic absolutism whose actual force depended heavily on them."[39] As will be emphasized below, there is no doubt that any analysis of works of advice and their politico-ideological framework needs to take into account a spectrum of audiences, from the sultan to the scribe.

Despite the many differences among them, each of the texts that compose this corpus captures the Ottoman zeitgeist of its specific period. Most significantly for the purposes of this study, in the process of addressing contemporary troubles afflicting the Ottoman state and society, they praise Selīm as a combatant sultan, a discerning administrator, an egalitarian dispenser of taxes, a provider of peace, a keeper of state secrets, and a ruler who valued the company of, and consulted with, learned men. In these texts, Selīm is hailed as a *ḳānūn*-conscious monarch as well as a meritocratic sultan. Collectively, sixteenth- and seventeenth-century works belonging to the Ottoman *naṣīḥatnāme* literature memorialize Selīm as the foremost Ottoman sultan, superior to all other members of the House of ʿOs̱mān, including even Meḥmed "the Conqueror" and Süleymān "the Lawgiver." Taken together, they contributed, consciously or unconsciously, to the creation of the myth of an Ottoman "Golden Age" and to the imagination of a mythified Selīm as its foremost sultan.

Unlike scholars who have considered the reign of Süleymān I (r. 1520–1566) to be the Ottoman "Golden Age," Cornell Fleischer and Cemal Kafadar refrain from using the term to refer to any particular period of Ottoman history, except when framed by emphatically placed quotation marks.[40] Whereas Fleischer notes that the existence of Ḳorḳud's *Daʿwat* "challenges the notion that a fifteenth- or sixteenth-century Golden Age ever existed"[41] and argues that "the progressive shift in the locus of the Golden Age, and the brevity of its duration, show that it was more a literary than an objective reality,"[42] Kafadar states unequivocally that "the whole notion of a 'golden age' seems alien to the Ottoman intellectual tradition."[43] Nonetheless, both scholars also point to the *naṣīḥatnāme* literature as the principal origin of the conceptualization of a rather idealized Ottoman "classical" era and suggest that the practices of that period were regarded by many an intellectual as a remedy against the ills ruining the Ottoman state and society.[44] A minor difference notwithstanding, they even provide a specific time frame.[45] Whereas Kafadar suggests that "it refers back to a specific time period from the middle of the 15th to that of the 16th century, in other words *from* the reign of Meḥmed II *to* that of Süleymān I," Fleischer claims that this era was "identified with the reign of *either* Meḥmed II *or* Süleymān I, depending upon the author."[46] As will be demonstrated later, a comparative look at the references to Ottoman monarchs in works of the *naṣīḥatnāme* literature suggests that, if there was indeed an idealized reign of an equally idealized Ottoman sultan, Selīm I would have been the most suitable candidate for the honor.

An Ideal Sultan: Selīm in *Naṣīḥatnāme* Literature

Not all works of advice contributed equally to the creation of Selīm's idealized image. In fact, some do not mention Selīm at all.[47] Unless a sultan happened to be his patron, most *naṣīḥatnāme* authors did not mention Ottoman monarchs. Nevertheless, Luṭfī Pasha's (d. 1563) *Āṣafnāme*,[48] Muṣṭafā ʿĀlī's (d. 1600) *Nuṣḥatü's-selāṭīn*,[49] Koçi Beg's (d. ca. 1650) *Risāle*,[50] *Ḳānūnnāme-i Sulṭānī li ʿAzīz Efendi*,[51] Hezārfen Ḥüseyin Efendi's (d. 1679) *Telḫīṣü'l-beyān fī ḳavānīn-i āl-i ʿOs̱mān*,[52] and the anonymous *Ḥırzü'l-mülūk*,[53] *Ḳavānīn-i yeñiçeriyān*,[54] *Kitāb-ı müstetāb*,[55] and *Kitāb meṣāliḥü'l-Müslimīn ve menāfiʿü'l-müʾminīn*[56] are well-known works of advice that aimed to provide their readers with a recipe for returning the Ottoman state and society to its proverbial "good old days." These texts, which are central to this study, refer to the reign of Selīm as an exemplary period when "classical" and unadulterated Ottoman institutions, traditions, and laws reigned supreme. By emphasizing certain specific achievements and attributes of Selīm, the authors of these works also appear to have contributed to the making of his image as an ideal—or, rather, idealized—Ottoman monarch.

Selīm as Fearsome Ruler

That Ottoman works of advice typically highlight the praiseworthy facets of Selīm's persona does not mean that they are unconditionally silent about some of the less charming aspects of his character. Whereas some reveal that Selīm regarded fear as an indispensable tool for the maintenance of law and order throughout the Empire as well as within the imperial court, others address his proclivity for ordering summary executions of statesmen, servants, and subjects alike. Albeit at times implicitly critical, treatises of the *naṣīḥatnāme* literature generally tend to interpret Selīm's wrathful character and frequent recourse to violence as an integral part of the sultan's bid to maintain universal order (*niẓām-ı ʿālem*) at any cost.

One such treatise, *Ḳavānīn-i yeñiçeriyān* (Laws of the Janissaries), suggests that even Selīm's own son, the future Süleymān "the Magnificent," was not immune to the sultan's wrath. This work was composed by an anonymous veteran janissary during the reign of Aḥmed I (r. 1606–1617) in the immediate aftermath of the most significant wave of the Celālī uprisings that wreaked havoc in Anatolia between 1595 and 1609.[57] *Ḳavānīn* addresses the laws, regulations, and customs that governed the janissary establishment, which was part of the larger *ḳul* system that encompassed all of the sultan's slave-servants who entered the Ottoman military-administrative structure via the method of recruitment called *devşirme*. Written in an era when the abandonment of the long-standing practice of the levy of Christian children (and the conscription of Muslim-born "intruders" in their place) led to the gradual disintegration of the traditional hierarchy of the janissary corps, *Ḳavānīn* calls for the restoration of time-honored conventions (*ḳānūn*) and a recruitment system based on merit. The anonymous author praises Selīm both for respecting established traditions and for applying a merit-based method of recruitment.

To explain why the servants who tended the gardens in the second courtyard of the Topkapı Palace (*ḳulle bāġçesinüñ oġlanları*) were paid the same daily salary—two silver aspers (*aḳçe*)—as the more prestigious servants of the sultan's private gardens (*ḫāṣbāġçe oġlanları*), an anecdote in *Ḳavānīn-i yeñiçeriyān* alleges that the origins of that convention date to Süleymān's princehood. The anonymous author relates that, in a moment of "wrathfulness" (*ġażabla*), Selīm ordered his son Süleymān to be killed by the commander of the imperial guard (*būstāncıbāşı*), who silently (and wisely) disobeyed the sultan's orders by hiding the prince, disguised as a royal servant, in the palace courtyard. Later, when Selīm's anger gave way to regret, the guard revealed that Süleymān was still alive. We are told that when Süleymān ascended to the throne he increased the daily salary of servants of the second courtyard by half an asper—in remembrance of and gratitude for the many days he spent there.[58]

In light of a tradition that Selīm had three of his sons executed in order to clear Süleymān's path to the Ottoman throne,[59] this curious anecdote is particularly significant in that it illustrates the magnitude of the sultan's rage, which reportedly was often directed at members of his family and immediate entourage. Thus, that Selīm's frequent recourse to summary executions constituted the principal cause for criticism by his contemporaries (most of whom were justifiably too frightened to express their thoughts on the matter) is not surprising. In *Nuṣḥatü's-selāṭīn* (Counsel for Sultans), the prominent bureaucrat and intellectual Muṣṭafā ʿĀlī (d. 1600) unambiguously expresses this point, stating that critics "found it better to keep silent and to obey, thinking that the ferocious lion was looking for a caracal, that the man-eating king of the beasts was waiting for an opportunity to flare up in a rage [as] it so happened that at that time most of the viziers had been destroyed by the sultan's wrath."[60] Considering that Selīm notoriously executed his viziers, it is more than likely that Luṭfī Pasha also had Selīm in mind when he warned Ottoman rulers against the summary execution of high-ranking statesmen.[61]

Several historical accounts of the Ottoman tradition nevertheless include references to certain exceptionally courageous statesmen who stood up to Selīm. Although not part of the *naṣīḥatnāme* literature, Ṭaşköprīzāde Aḥmed Efendi's (d. 1561) biographical dictionary, entitled *Al-Şaḳāʾiḳ al-nuʿmāniyya fī ʿulamā al-dawlat al-ʿOs̱māniyya* (The Crimson Peonies: Religious Scholars of the Ottoman State), is of great significance in that it corroborates the common perception of Selīm's fearsome nature as expressed by several contemporary Ottoman chroniclers and *naṣīḥatnāme* authors. In Ṭaşköprīzāde's work, Selīm and his chief jurisconsult (*şeyḫü'l-islām*) Zenbīlli ʿAlī Efendi (d. 1526) are the protagonists of two episodes in which the former is implicitly criticized for quickly and arbitrarily resorting to capital punishment for a relatively minor crime while the latter is praised for prudently saving the lives of a great many people. In the first episode, ʿAlī Efendi's intervention is reported to have stayed the execution of 150 servants of the imperial treasury; in the second, the chief jurisconsult is praised for having saved four hundred Ottoman subjects who had been sentenced to death by Selīm for disobeying an imperial ban on the silk trade.[62] The second anecdote is among the most commonly cited episodes that contrast the arbitrary nature of Selīm's violent methods with the acts of justice of his son Süleymān in the immediate aftermath of the latter's accession to the throne.[63] The first episode mentioned above is reported in a *naṣīḥatnāme* entitled *Ḥırzü'l-mülūk* (Amulet of Rulers) as well. Although it is difficult to ascertain whether the anonymous author of *Ḥırzü'l-mülūk* used Ṭaşköprīzāde's biographical dictionary as a source, both works utilized an earlier historical source or relied on popular oral accounts. It is noteworthy that the criticism against Selīm is less implicit in *Ḥırzü'l-mülūk*, quite possibly due to the anonymity of its author: Zenbīlli ʿAlī Efendi is reported to have accused the sultan of "unjustly killing Muslims solely for one's own pleasure," and Selīm is portrayed as a "wrathful" (*ġażūb*) sultan who decreed "the execution of a great many servants for a minor sin."[64]

Ottoman works of advice refer to numerous other incidents of the sultan's wrath being directed at many an unfortunate servant or subject. The anonymous author of *Ḳavānīn-i yeñiçeriyān*, for example, reports that Selīm considered executing a great number of janissaries due to their insubordination in the aftermath of the Battle of

Çaldıran; he was convinced otherwise only after "learned and virtuous men" (*ʿulemāʾ ve fużalāʾ*) remarked that their execution would lead to greater chaos.[65] Koçi Beg, the renowned Ottoman bureaucrat and intellectual who presented his reform treatises to Sultans Murād IV (r. 1623–1640) and İbrāhīm I (r. 1640–1648), also mentions that Selīm threatened to execute a wealthy merchant, along with several of his viziers and his finance minister (*defterdār*), when the merchant petitioned for his son to be recruited to the sultan's retinue as reimbursement of a hefty sum he had loaned the Ottoman ruler during the Egyptian expedition. The only reason why Selīm did not execute all of the parties involved, Koçi Beg tells his readers, is that he wanted to avoid rumors that he "coveted the possessions of a greedy merchant and thus killed him with an excuse, and also murdered a couple of innocent viziers and a finance minister."[66]

It is noteworthy, however, that some *naṣīḥatnāme* authors interpreted even Selīm's penchant for excessive punishment in a somewhat favorable light. The sultan's tendency toward wrathfulness was in some instances "regarded as most beneficial for religion and state," as an "enraged" (*ḫışm-nāk*) sultan would instill fear in the hearts of his grand viziers, who would thus refrain from making mistakes while handling affairs of the state.[67] At times, quick dismissals and summary executions of commanders and viziers were explicitly considered "acceptable method and reasonable behavior" (*ṭarz-ı maḳbūl ve vażʿ-ı maʿḳūl*), indicating that at least some advice authors, who may have "identified themselves with an idealized sultanic absolutism whose actual force depended heavily on them," construed Selīm's acts of violence as an essential aspect of royal enforcement of imperial policy.[68]

Selīm as Keeper of Secrets

There is little doubt that Selīm used fear as a versatile tool to teach members of his court a lesson, and, as Selīm's grand vizier, Pīrī Meḥmed Pasha (d. 1533) was the unfortunate target of the sultan's expressions of ruthlessness more frequently than other statesmen. A remarkable episode reported in the anonymous *naṣīḥatnāme* entitled

Kitāb-ı müstetāb (The Pleasant Book), written around 1620 and most likely presented to ʿOs̱mān II (r. 1618–1622), provides a detailed account and thus deserves to be cited in full:

> His Excellency, the Pādişāh [Selīm I], had a dwarf boon companion [*cüce nedīm*] he liked. Pīrī Pasha wrote a brief note to that companion and insisted: "My son, the day before yesterday, when I was admitted to the sultan's court, His prosperous Excellency, the Pādişāh, ordered preparations to be made for a military expedition. However, whether the expedition would be in the direction of Anatolia or Rumelia did not become known. So that it would not be attributed to my stupidity, I am embarrassed to ask or to petition [the sultan about this matter]. Now, do me a favor, as a duty of a son, at a moment of the prosperous sultan's cheerfulness, make an effort to learn his noble wish as to the direction of the expedition." When the unfortunate dwarf, deceived by the grand vizier's note and compliments, asked the late sultan about affairs pertaining to the expedition, the late sultan, startled, addressed the dwarf, saying: "Tell me immediately, who told you about the affairs related to the expedition?" When the dwarf, going out of his mind, said "By God, my Pādişāh, your servant Pīrī Pasha sent a note to this servant of yours, since he was scared and embarrassed to petition our felicitous Pādişāh. The order belongs to my Pādişāh," the late sultan stated, "Since you are my boon companion, what if, solely as a joke, I say that my expedition is toward Rumelia, or, I say it is toward Anatolia even though it is toward Rumelia, and you, thinking you received sound information, tell the grand vizier, who then proceeds to make the wrong preparations in accordance with your word? Now, do people like you get involved in issues pertaining to the Exalted State (*Devlet-i ʿĀliye*) and the affairs of the sultanate?" [Selīm] immediately ordered the dwarf's head to be cut off. Then, as ordered, the dwarf's head was placed on a tray, bundled in a wrapper, sealed, and sent along with an imperial decree addressed to Pīrī Pasha, stating: "Oh, Black Turk! I had only one companion, and you considered him too much for me. Now I am sending you his head. If you wish to inquire about my expedition, it is toward Persia

(*ʿAcem seferidir*). Consider the requirements and make the necessary preparations. Otherwise, I will do the same to your head." When Pīrī Pasha received the bundle with the note and realized what went on, he went out of his mind. Thus, except for the grand vizier, no one should be privy to the affairs pertaining to the sultanate.[69]

This narrative highlights the notion that Selīm may have used fear as a moralizing pedagogical device and demonstrates its petrifying effects on his grand vizier. More importantly, the didactic statement at the end of the anecdote leaves little doubt that the anonymous author's primary intention was to emphasize the significance of protecting state secrets at all costs—a theme addressed by several other *naṣīḥatnāme* authors, who praised Selīm's caution in this regard.

A case in point is Süleymān's scholarly grand vizier and brother-in-law Luṭfī Pasha, who hailed Selīm as the foremost Ottoman sultan not only in his *Āṣafnāme* (Book of Asaph) but also in his dynastic history entitled *Tevārīḫ-i āl-i ʿO̱smān* (Chronicles of the House of ʿO̱smān). The themes addressed in *Āṣafnāme* testify to Luṭfī Pasha's acute awareness of the challenges faced by the Ottoman polity in the process of empire building in the aftermath of the conquests of Selīm and Süleymān. Writing in the mid-1550s, Luṭfī Pasha expressed his concerns regarding the increasing imbalance between revenues and expenditures, the infiltration of the ranks of the military ruling elite by tax-paying subjects (*reʿāyā*), the promotion of unqualified statesmen to high offices, the abandonment of an unconditional adherence to dynastic laws (*ḳānūn*), and the relaxation of practices that once rendered state secrets accessible only to an exceptionally limited number of statesmen.[70]

Luṭfī Pasha considered the administration of the Empire to be the business of the sultan and his grand vizier. Discernibly preoccupied with keeping state secrets contained at the highest echelon of political power, he applauds Selīm in this context. In the first instance, Selīm is commended somewhat circuitously via a worthy surrogate: his own grand vizier Pīrī Meḥmed Pasha. After emphatically stating that "not only outsiders, but even other viziers should not be privy to the [state] secrets shared between the grand vizier and the sultan," Luṭfī Pasha tells his audience that Pīrī Pasha petitioned Selīm to dismiss vizier Mesīḥ Pasha for curiously inquiring about the grand vizier's conversation with the sultan the previous day.[71] Luṭfī Pasha's praise for Selīm is not limited to his appointment of trustworthy and discreet statesmen to high office alone. The section of *Āṣafnāme* in which Luṭfī Pasha describes the hierarchy of various administrative offices includes a brief but instructive anecdote illustrating Selīm's emphasis on the degree of access to state secrets as a principal factor in determining the pecking order of Ottoman officials:

> One day during the reign of the late Sulṭān Selīm a herald (*çāvuş*) and a scribe (*kātib*) quarreled. When the matter was brought to the attention of His Excellency Sulṭān Selīm Ḫān, he decreed: The scribe is to be given precedence. The scribe serves the secrets of the sultanate; the herald serves the external affairs [of the sultanate].[72]

This story was repeated frequently by later *naṣīḥatnāme* authors.[73] In fact, the significance of Selīm's attentiveness to state secrets was highlighted in the late seventeenth century by Hezārfen Ḥüseyin Efendi, who addressed the same theme in his *Telḫīṣü'l-beyān fī ḳavānīn-i āl-i ʿOs̱mān* (A Memorandum on the Laws of the House of ʿOs̱mān):

> During the reign of His Excellency, the Pādişāh whose sins are forgiven, Sulṭān Selīm the indefatigable (*ġayūr*), there were solid regulations and exalted rules concerning the conducts of the sultanate such that no one was cognizant of their truths except for the grand vizier, the chancellor (*nişāncı*), and the scribe of the imperial council (*dīvān kātibi*). The secrets of the sultanate and the conditions of the caliphate were extremely guarded and protected.[74]

The harmonious partnership between just rulers and their highest-ranking advisors as a precondition to that polity's success and legitimacy is certainly a common trope in Islamic (political) literature. The fact that *naṣīḥatnāme* authors followed such literary conventions to various degrees does not, however, mean that their accounts lacked historically bound, presentist agendas. For example, when Luṭfī Pasha, the anonymous author of *Kitāb-ı müstetāb*, or Hezārfen Ḥüseyin wrote about the keeping of state secrets they were not merely making abstract points about the necessity of restrictions regarding access to confidential information; they also were addressing specific audiences, which probably included Süleymān I, ʿOs̱mān II, and Meḥmed IV (r. 1648–1687), respectively. As such, it is plausible to assume that, for these political commentators, Selīm served as the perfect model for emulation. In turn, this practice of regal comparison served to enhance his idealized image for posterity: an Ottoman monarch who paid close attention to the safeguarding of state secrets and emphasized the maintenance of the traditional administrative hierarchy as defined by time-honored customs and, most importantly, Ottoman dynastic law (*ḳānūn*).

Selīm as *Ḳānūn*-Conscious Monarch

As Cornell Fleischer insightfully notes, for Ottoman intellectuals and statesmen, *ḳānūn* was "at once a symbol of the Ottoman commitment to justice, a corpus of secular legislation, and accepted customary practice."[75] Especially in the late sixteenth century, the concept of *ḳānūn*, both as legislation and as practice,[76] appears to have become a preoccupation of Ottoman historians and political commentators who were particularly concerned with the crisis they perceived in the state of the Empire. Among these intellectuals were the authors of Ottoman works of advice who identified disregard for *ḳānūn* as one of the principal factors that led to the troubles afflicting the Ottoman state and society. Tracing the origins of this disregard to the later years of Süleymān I's reign, *naṣīḥatnāme* authors also depicted his father, Selīm I, as a *ḳānūn*-conscious monarch.

Luṭfī Pasha's *Āṣafnāme*, which has been regarded as among the best examples of advice literature in the sixteenth-century Ottoman context, is quite a representative work in this regard.[77] Composed in an era of remarkable literary activity and in an intellectual atmosphere characterized by what has been called "*ḳānūn*-consciousness,"[78] *Āṣafnāme* has also been considered the precursor of a literature of reformism marked by a sense of "*ḳānūn*-mindedness."[79] As previously mentioned, Luṭfī Pasha served Süleymān I as grand vizier between 1539 and 1541 and was briefly at the pinnacle of an administrative hierarchy established, supported, and legitimized by Ottoman dynastic law. Furthermore, each and every stage of Luṭfī Pasha's career, from the time he entered Bāyezīd II's royal household as a *devşirme* conscript up to and including his dismissal from the grand vizierate, had been instituted in accordance with *ḳānūn*. The preponderance in his work of a sense of both *ḳānūn*-consciousness and *ḳānūn*-mindedness thus is not surprising. In fact, Luṭfī Pasha states in the introduction to his *Āṣafnāme* that he composed the treatise as a keepsake for the grand viziers who would come after him, because (from the time of the bestowal of the high office by the sultan) he witnessed certain "manners, conducts, and dynastic laws concerning the imperial council that were in a wretched state and contrary to those [he] had observed earlier." In a premonitory tone, he then seeks refuge in the only "sultan without vizier," emphasizing, once again, the preeminence of dynastic laws as the bedrock of the Ottoman state: "May God, from Whom we seek aid, and in Whom we trust, secure the laws and foundations of the House of ʿOs̱mān from the fear and peril of fate and the evil eye of the foe."[80] It is with this conviction that Luṭfī Pasha enumerates contemporary woes (some mentioned by Selīm's own brother Ḳorḳud and a certain ʿAlī Ḫalīfe several decades earlier),[81] instructs the sultan in correct conduct, describes the qualities required of a grand vizier, and gives counsel to both on their duties concerning military expeditions, the maintenance of the imperial treasury, and the just treatment of tax-paying subjects.[82] The overall tenor of *Āṣafnāme* indicates that Luṭfī Pasha perceived contemporary troubles as a consequence of straying from the path indicated by the laws, decrees, and practices established by earlier Ottoman sultans. As a competent monarch and a vigilant executor of Ottoman dynastic law (*ḳānūn*), Selīm appears to be the only ruler among these sultans deserving of the grand vizier's praise.[83]

Writing in 1581, Muṣṭafā ʿĀlī, the preeminent bureaucrat, littérateur, and intellectual of the Süleymānic age, appears to have been as *ḳānūn*-conscious as Luṭfī Pasha.[84] Opening his monumental *Nuṣḥatü's-selāṭīn* with the assessment that "all good and evil events of this time . . . spring entirely from the wickedness of the viziers and from the unawareness of the land-conquering sultan,"[85] ʿĀlī incisively details the ills affecting Ottoman state and society during the last quarter of the sixteenth century. He especially warns his readers against disturbances caused by the disregard of dynastic laws (*ḳavānīn*).[86] Despite hailing Ottoman dynastic law as the foundation of a highly sophisticated imperial structure,[87] ʿĀlī, like Luṭfī Pasha before him, also sees the welfare of the state—and not a blind obedience to *ḳānūn*—as the utmost priority of Ottoman monarchs. Thus, when emphasizing the need for merit-based appointments at all levels of the administrative hierarchy, he particularly praises Selīm for granting high offices to deserving and wise men, even when doing so required the sultan to act in a manner contrary to established traditions and "the old law" (*ḳānūn-ı ḳadīm*).[88] Similarly, the anonymous author of *Ḥırzü'l-mülūk* commends Selīm for his swift execution of any decision beneficial to "Religion and State" (*dīn-ü-devlet*), regardless of whether it contradicts "Ottoman law" (*ḳānūn-ı ʿOs̱mānī*).[89] He even applauds the absolutist mindset of the sultan by approvingly reporting his statement that "whatever the great sultans do becomes law."[90] This commendation was probably a reaction to the conservative interpretation of the concept of *ḳānūn* as a legal instrument to quash the demands for sociopolitical change that were advocated by some of his contemporaries.[91]

Although the decreeing of laws was certainly one of the many privileges of Ottoman monarchs, other works in the *naṣīḥatnāme* genre suggest that not all royal decrees were unquestionably accepted, especially when they were the pronouncements made by sultans whose absolutist agendas weakened other power wielders in the imperial administration. *Ḳavānīn-i yeñiçeriyān* is one such work. Composed during the reign of Aḥmed I (r. 1603–1617) by an anonymous author who served the Empire as a janissary and scribe for more than two decades, *Ḳavānīn* is an invaluable source not only for the history of the janissary corps but also for the cumulative popular memory of members of that pivotal Ottoman institution.[92] One of the anecdotes narrated in the work involves Sultan Murād III (r. 1574–1595), who, on the occasion of his son's circumcision, disregarded established rules concerning the recruitment of janissaries through the practice of *devşirme* and allowed new converts to Islam to be enrolled in the janissary corps, regardless of their urban backgrounds and unruly behavior.[93] Unlike the author of *Ḥırzü'l-mülūk*, who welcomed Selīm's statement about the establishment of laws by Ottoman rulers, the veteran janissary who penned *Ḳavānīn-i yeñiçeriyān* explicitly criticizes Murād III's decision to violate long-standing regulations, brusquely stating, "I did [it and] it became law."[94]

As these examples demonstrate, Ottoman *naṣīḥatnāme* writers not only were conscious of the importance of the concept of law for the ideal administration of the Empire but also accepted, within limits, the sultan's absolutist privilege to decree laws as legitimate and normative.[95] Still, these authors do not appear to have considered all dynastic laws categorically beyond reproach. Although the nature and extent of the consensus about specific codes of law depended on their content, rectitude, and legitimacy, the requirements and the welfare of the Ottoman state appear to have been the ultimate criteria for acceptance. Thus, *naṣīḥatnāme* authors praise laws that they consider beneficial for the Ottoman state and criticize those they deem detrimental. It is therefore no coincidence that Murād III's choice to bend long-standing rules concerning the recruitment of janissaries is criticized as a violation while Selīm's decision to disregard established traditions regarding the recruitment of statesmen is hailed as ideal.[96]

Selīm as Meritocratic Ruler

In Ottoman *naṣīḥatnāme* literature, Selīm is represented as a *ḳānūn*-conscious monarch, ever-mindful of the laws of the House of ʿOs̱mān yet in constant pursuit of ways to strengthen the Empire—making him, in the eyes of several authors, the ideal Ottoman ruler. In this regard, Selīm's meritocratic approach to any and all appointments appears to have been his most praiseworthy attribute as an Ottoman monarch.

The anonymous author of *Ḳavānīn-i yeñiçeriyān*, for example, emphasizes Selīm's absolutely meritocratic policy by relating an episode concerning appointments to the rank of chief drill sergeant (*taʿlīmḫānecibaşı*). In the relevant passage, the author explains that Selīm insisted the office be given to any qualified individual, regardless of whether he was a member of the janissary corps or not, even when the individual in question hailed from the lands ruled by the Ottomans' archrivals in the east:

> The drill-sergeants do not know this. Now this rank belongs to qualified ones. [The drill-sergeant] may be accepted from outside, as long as [he is] qualified. At the time of *Yāvuz* Sulṭān Selīm a man came from Persia (*ʿAcem diyārı*) and surpassed all marksmen in the corps. When the sultan asked him what his wish was, he requested the rank of the chief drill sergeant. When the sultan granted [his wish] and issued an imperial decree [to that effect], the janissaries refused to accept it for some time, contending that "this is a rank [to be given to someone from] among us; we will not allow it to be granted to others." The sultan decreed again, "This rank certainly belongs to those qualified and I granted it. If anyone among them is superior to [the current holder of the rank] he will [be the chief drill sergeant]." Since no one from among them proved himself superior, they consented whether they liked it or not.[97]

Although this anecdote reveals that some *naṣīḥatnāme* authors applauded Selīm's hands-on approach to rulership and the merit-based employment policy he applied even to lesser offices, the consequences of his meritocratic approach to appointments of high-ranking bureaucrats and statesmen are highlighted much more frequently. In this context, no other person features more prominently than Pīrī Meḥmed Pasha, who, when serving as a provincial judge, was appointed first to the directorship of finances (*defterdār*) and later to the grand vizierate—despite established traditions requiring a palace education for that high office. Pīrī Pasha's case is mentioned in several works of advice, within discussions on acceptable exceptions to the strict observance of dynastic laws.

In an effort to portray Selīm as a righteous sultan who granted high offices to deserving statesmen, Luṭfī Pasha also draws attention to Pīrī Pasha's "intelligence and comprehension" (*aḳl-ü-idrāk*) as well as to his protection of state secrets.[98] Similarly, the anonymous author of *Ḥırzü'l-mülūk* uses Pīrī Pasha's unusual career path as a case in point and applauds Selīm's choice of this worthy statesman as his grand vizier, despite the fact that he had not been educated in the imperial palace. Merit is the primary criterion here for the appointment of statesmen and bureaucrats.[99] Additionally, Muṣṭafā ʿĀlī emphasizes Pīrī Pasha's exceptional qualifications several times in his *Nuṣḥatü's-selāṭīn*.[100] He singles out Selīm's grand vizier, commends the sultan for sagaciously recognizing the perfect mind of the former judge of Kütahya during a royal hunt near the imperial capital, and underscores the harmony between Selīm's ideas and Pīrī Pasha's loyal service, which led to unequalled successes. It is also in this context, when referring to the principles the sultan reportedly laid out for the recruitment of statesmen, that ʿĀlī reserves his ultimate praise for Selīm as the foremost Ottoman monarch:

> [Also] because of the expanse of the empire an increase in the number of statesmen was obviously a necessity for Religion and State (*dīn-ü-devlet*). Therefore [the Sultan] had ordered Pīrī Pasha: "I herewith authorize you to recruit the viziers and statesmen. In selecting them I empower you to screen everybody in my glorious capital down to the porters that carry loads on their backs. Do not

> let the thought influence you that that was not a proper, dignified thing to do. Most of all, do not follow the road of favoritism by being accessible to interventions. And if you find a wise and experienced person, even among that trade, I shall accept him as my representative; my noble glance shall only see the essence, I shall not say '[No,] this one comes from outside (i.e., has not been educated in the Palace),' and shall in every respect refuse to pay attention to his outward circumstances." This his zeal was the cause that he raised the honor of the Empire higher than under his great ancestors, and adding the noble title of Servitor of the two Sacred Cities (*ḫādimü'l-ḥarameyn*) to his illustrious *ḫuṭbe* he surpassed all the other sultans in rank.[101]

The causal link created by Muṣṭafā ʿĀlī between Selīm's meritocratic approach to all appointments in the Empire and his standing as the foremost Ottoman sultan echoes the sentiments of several other authors writing in the late sixteenth and early seventeenth centuries. Most of these writers were freeborn Muslim madrasa graduates who entered the Ottoman ruling elite as scribes or secretaries and hoped to rise to prominence in the ranks of the Ottoman imperial administrative-bureaucratic structure. Each writer's degree of success in achieving his professional or political goals depended on his own efforts and personal merit as much as his professional connections and patronage networks. As Muslim-born individuals, they most notably competed against members of the Ottoman military ruling elite of *devşirme* origin (*ḳul ṭāʾifesi*). Thus, they voiced their most potent criticisms against Ottoman monarchs who employed a pro-*ḳul* recruitment strategy, which significantly restricted opportunities for freeborn Muslims to be promoted to bureaucratic and administrative high offices. As in the case of Muṣṭafā ʿĀlī, or the previously mentioned Celālzāde Muṣṭafā (d. 1567), an argument for meritocratic recruitment, appointment, or promotion was often code for an anti-*ḳul* sentiment.[102]

Seen in this light, the mention of Pīrī Pasha as the epitome of the meritorious statesman was not accidental. That Pīrī Pasha survived

Selīm's reign constituted a remarkable success story in itself. Far more important for authors like Muṣṭafā ʿĀlī or Celālzāde Muṣṭafā, however, seems to have been what Pīrī Pasha represented: a provincial judge turned *defterdār* turned grand vizier, who hailed from the humble background of a Turkish-speaking freeborn Muslim but was promoted to the highest office in the Ottoman imperial military-administrative structure based on meritocratic principles alone. In a period of rapid and tumultuous transformation of the institutional structure of the Empire, these authors, along with several other *naṣīḥatnāme* writers, witnessed the increasing bureaucratization of the imperial government and the professionalization of the bureaucratic establishment, especially when compared to the late fifteenth and the early sixteenth centuries.[103] To their disfavor, these intellectuals also saw an increasing number of commoners with economic power incorporated into the ranks of the Ottoman political elite.[104] Unable, and quite possibly unwilling, to comprehend the magnitude and direction of the changes in both administrative practice and individual career patterns, many of these authors appear to have retrospectively idealized the merit-based employment policies of Selīm I, who ruled the Empire before the onset of an era of institutional and bureaucratic change.

Selīm as Yardstick: Meḥmed II and Süleymān I in Comparative Perspective

The exclusively merit-based recruitment of Ottoman statesmen was by no means the only reason why *naṣīḥatnāme* authors deemed Selīm superior to other sultans of the House of ʿOsmān, although it was the most significant one. As one would expect, he is most frequently compared to Meḥmed II and Süleymān I, the two monarchs whose names are typically associated with an Ottoman "Golden Age"—if there ever was one.[105]

The sections of advice works in which Selīm is compared explicitly to Meḥmed II or Süleymān I indeed corroborate Muṣṭafā ʿĀlī's argument about Selīm's superiority to both. For example, the third chapter of *Nuṣḥatü's-selāṭīn* includes ʿĀlī's most acrimonious critique of the corruption that plagued all levels of the imperial administrative hierarchy. Here, Selīm's name appears only once, within the author's vivid description of the detrimental effects of disproportionate impositions of the levy of army provisions (*nüzül*) and extraordinary taxes (*ʿavārıż*):

> The poor are moaning under the hardships of destitution while such rich blockheads thrive in pomp and power. While the burden of frustration weighs heavily on the weak, it is clear in many respects that the excess of world-enjoyment of the rich is counter to perfect wisdom and circumspect policy. Among these the merchants of Cairo, Damascus, and Aleppo have each one purse filled with several thousand gold coins and the unlimited ability of gaining twenty and thirty thousand gold pieces every year. Moreover, their daily expenditures never reach one florin; it is ridiculous to think that they spend a gold piece on their daily supplies. How come that the levy (*nüzül*) of the poor people of an [entire] *sancaḳ* is not imposed on each one of them, in which way some order could be brought into the affairs of the people (*reʿāyā*)? In particular, the felicitous Sultan Meḥmed Ḫān, the conqueror of Istanbul, used either to take several thousand gold pieces as a loan from Stingy Ḥamīd, the rich man of that time, or, asking him to assist the champions for the Faith, imposed on the above-mentioned a payment of several purses (*kīse*) of florins at once. Likewise, Sultan Selīm Ḫān, the conqueror of Egypt . . . has often at the time of his reign imposed substantial payments (*küllīce salġun*) on similar rich men and has demanded [from them] bag after bag of gold pieces, saying that it was more meritorious and better to support the war of the Faith than to waste [one's money] on [the construction of] arches and galleries. . . . It is truly regrettable that His Majesty, the honorable and felicitous Sultan [Murād III] . . . does not show alertness and vigilance in this respect.[106]

In addition to revealing Muṣṭafā ʿĀlī's unambiguous abhorrence of wealthy merchants in Arab lands, who accumulate "profit and capital during the justice-guided reign of the Sultan" but do not "perform any service to the army of Islam" or "every now and then assist the public treasury (*beytü'l-māl*),"[107] this section of *Nuṣḥatü's-selāṭīn* also serves to advise Murād III to follow the examples of Meḥmed II and Selīm I. Although the mention of "the Conqueror" as the earliest precedent is certainly noteworthy, ʿĀlī emphasizes Selīm as the superior champion of the faith by—allegedly—citing him verbatim. Muṣṭafā ʿĀlī also applauds Selīm for appreciating the value and company of learned men[108] and even likens him to Alexander the Great, who "appointed Plato as his representative and always had priceless consultations with Aristotle,"[109] and King Solomon, who "enjoyed the honor of consulting with Loḳmān and Āṣaf."[110] More importantly, he portrays Selīm as a ruler following the perfect example of the Prophet Muḥammad, whose habit of "turning to the first four caliphs (*çār-yār-ı ʿuẓmā*) in worldly affairs and of requesting the aid of his pure companions (*aṣḥāb-ı bā-ṣafā*) in matters of the community clearly had the purpose of educating his noble adherents and of teaching the illustrious sultans to employ learned men in their service."[111] ʿĀlī further emphasizes Selīm's acknowledgment of men of learning as a principal pillar of the state by mentioning his reign as part of an era in which the Ottoman *medrese* system produced great scholars.[112]

This very point—Selīm's appreciation for learned men—is among the frequently highlighted parallels between the styles of rulership of Meḥmed II and Selīm. Composed during the reign of Murād III by a learned holder of a fief (*dirlik*), *Ḥırzü'l-mülūk* also employs this comparative method. The anonymous author depicts both Meḥmed and Selīm as rulers who conferred with worthy members of the Ottoman elite, whether these were "Men of Learning" (*ʿilmiyye*) or "Men of the Sword" (*seyfiyye*). Whereas Meḥmed is said to have constantly interacted (*muʿāşeret*) with scholarly, righteous, virtuous, and wise men (*ʿulemā ve ṣuleḥā ve fużalā ve ʿuḳalā*), Selīm is depicted as always consulting (*müşāvere*) with his viziers.[113] Another point of similarity between Selīm and Meḥmed mentioned in *Ḥırzü'l-mülūk* is that apparently neither sultan had any patience for incompetent or scheming statesmen: whereas Meḥmed dismissed and at times even executed commanders and viziers exhibiting dereliction of their duties, Selīm immediately rendered viziers "food for sword" (*ṭuʿme-i şimşīr*) if they expressed a desire to cater to their own interests instead of those of the Ottoman state and its subjects.[114] Last but not least, *Ḥırzü'l-mülūk*'s author places Selīm on par with Meḥmed in terms of his absolutist approach to governance, emphasizing the former's insistence on granting high offices to worthy and deserving individuals even when doing so constituted a break with the seemingly timeless Ottoman imperial legal tradition (*ḳānūn-ı ʿOs̱mānī*).[115]

In *naṣīḥatnāme* literature, comparisons between Selīm and Süleymān are much more common. In *Ḥırzü'l-mülūk*, for example, Süleymān is portrayed as foolishly alienating numerous prebends by assigning them as freehold (*temlīk*) to conniving grand viziers. In contrast, Selīm's strict observance of the state's overlordship (*mīrī*) over revenue sources is emphasized with a reference to his refusal to grant his exemplary grand vizier Pīrī Meḥmed Pasha a village as freehold, noting that "sultans need soldiers and lands."[116] Composed by a learned fief holder from the chronological vantage point of a later financial crisis, *Ḥırzü'l-mülūk* undoubtedly serves a presentist agenda. Yet it is noteworthy that a similar attitude toward Selīm's superior attributes is discernable in Luṭfī Pasha's writings as well. The anecdote about the quarrel between the herald and the scribe as related in *Āṣafnāme* is a case in point.[117] As argued earlier, the episode served to underscore Selīm's attentiveness to the safeguarding of state secrets as well as his vigilance regarding the maintenance of the traditional administrative hierarchy. There is, however, little doubt that the same episode was also used by the author to implicitly criticize other Ottoman rulers, including his former master Süleymān, who failed in both regards. In fact, Luṭfī Pasha appears to have used Selīm as a yardstick against which Süleymān is measured.[118] Through the recurrent mention of Pīrī Pasha's virtues, the author portrays Selīm as a meritocratic sultan who granted high offices to qualified statesmen. But Luṭfī Pasha mentions only two of Süleymān's contemporaries, grand vizier

İbrāhīm Pasha (d. 1536) and the finance minister (*defterdār*) İskender Çelebi (d. 1534), who both became notoriously wealthy while in office and enjoyed the unwarranted favor of the sultan. Breaking with tradition, Süleymān "personally visited their palaces and gardens."[119] Although both figures ultimately, and in Luṭfī Pasha's opinion deservedly, incurred the sultan's wrath and were executed, *Āṣafnāme*'s reference to the royal esteem they once enjoyed can be interpreted as an implicit criticism of Süleymān's inability to select righteous men for high office and of his failure to curb their excesses. The general tenor of *Āṣafnāme*'s references further attests to Luṭfī Pasha's disapproval of Süleymān's preferential treatment of certain statesmen and disregard for the established norms concerning the traditional boundaries between Ottoman monarchs and their servants.

Comparisons between Selīm and Süleymān, inherently in favor of the former, do not end here. Luṭfī Pasha seems to suggest that, unlike Selīm, who imposed an extraordinary levy (*ʿavārıż*) on tax-paying subjects only once during his reign, Süleymān enforced such levies more frequently, causing undue distress for Ottoman subjects.[120] Perhaps even more importantly, when commenting on the imperial treasury, the author declares that at the time of Süleymān's accession the state's revenues (*īrād*) equaled its expenditures (*maṣraf*)—suggesting that Selīm left behind a balanced budget.[121] Luṭfī Pasha states, however, that when he was appointed to the grand vizierate in 1539, the treasury was in disarray and deficient—implying that Süleymān failed to manage it efficaciously, at least until Luṭfī Pasha came along.[122]

Like Muṣṭafā ʿĀlī, Luṭfī Pasha seems to have considered Selīm superior not only to Süleymān but to all previous Ottoman rulers as well. The most explicit (albeit quite formulaic) expression of this view is found in *Āṣafnāme*, in which Selīm is described as "the most honorable one among sultans in intelligence and comprehension as well as in justice and benevolence, the *ṣāḥib-ḳırān* who reached the happiness of becoming the Servitor of the two Sacred Cities (*ḫādimü'l-ḥarameyn*) and attained the status of the Prince of Egypt (*ʿazīz-i Mıṣr*)."[123] In Luṭfī Pasha's other well-known historical work, *Tevārīḫ-i āl-i ʿOs̱mān*

(Chronicles of the House of ʿOs̱mān), the claim for Selīm's preeminence becomes more specific.[124] Here, Selīm is called the "Lord of the Age" (*server-i devrān*)[125] and identified as the most distinguished "Renewer of the Faith" (*müceddid*) produced by the House of ʿOs̱mān, the historical significance of which will be addressed in Chapter 5.[126]

Conclusion: The Making of an Idealized Selīm

"The ideal prince is a timeless necessity," wrote Bernard Guenée, before remarking that the specific characteristics attributed to that ideal prince are products of the age during which his venerated representation is constructed.[127] As demonstrated in this chapter, in an effort to present an exemplary monarch to be emulated in combatting contemporary troubles afflicting the Empire, Ottoman *naṣīḥatnāme* authors frequently praised Selīm as a warrior-sultan who defeated both the Safavids and the Mamluks; a discerning administrator, well informed about the needs of the state and capable of addressing them; an egalitarian disposer of taxes, who requested that rich merchants make financial contributions to the state's military efforts that were proportional to their wealth; a balancer of books, during whose reign state revenues well surpassed expenditures; and a ruler, who, like Alexander the Great and the Prophet Muḥammad, valued consultation with learned men. While some of these are conventional plaudits also accorded to other Ottoman rulers, Selīm held a privileged standing among *naṣīḥatnāme* authors. Although the theme-based survey in this chapter makes Selīm's idealized image appear timeless, the making of that image was a historically contingent process. In fact, the principal focus of the *naṣīḥatnāme* writer was the present, not the idealized past, and the construction of an idealized memory of Selīm was more an unintended consequence than the result of a calculated and meticulously executed plan.

There are several reasons why a controversial historical character such as Selīm was hailed as the foremost Ottoman monarch, whose reign is remembered as an era governed by justice and equity. The first concerns the historical context within which this specific genre of Ottoman writing flourished. Unlike the *Selīmnāme* literature, which culminated in the creation of a legitimate image for Selīm, Ottoman advice literature lent itself as a versatile template to Ottoman statesmen, bureaucrats, and scholars of varied social backgrounds, who, in the face of contemporary crises, apparently shared a consciousness of "decline" after the middle of the sixteenth century.[128] As witnesses to rapid transformations in all spheres of life, Ottoman intellectuals used works of advice to articulate their assessments of contemporary challenges to the Ottoman state and society. They did so by contrasting their own "corrupt" times with an increasingly idealized past. This intellectual process not only culminated in the conceptualization of a rather paradigmatic but imprecise Ottoman "classical" era but also led to the selective recollection of choice achievements of past Ottoman monarchs, among whom Selīm appears to have been accorded supreme status as primus inter pares. With a discernible tendency to contrast an iniquitous present with an idyllic past, most *naṣīḥatnāme* authors located the origins of several controversial institutional developments during the reign of Süleymān I, thus evoking Selīm's reign as the last era when unadulterated, "classical" Ottoman institutions still reigned supreme.[129]

Specific dimensions of Selīm's idealized composite image were anchored firmly in the historical context in which Ottoman authors produced their works of advice. It is no coincidence that the two works of advice in which Selīm is praised for frequently consulting with learned scholars and capable statesmen (*müşāvere*) were composed by Muṣṭafā ʿĀlī and an anonymous fief holder quite possibly at exactly the same time and, most notably, during the reign of Murād III, who was heavily criticized by his contemporaries for his absolutist ambitions and agenda. Those who emphasized Selīm's *ḳānūn*-consciousness and meritocratic strategies likewise wrote during the second half of the sixteenth century, in an age when the process of early modern empire building required the expansion of the imperial military, administrative, and bureaucratic structure. This process necessitated the integration of increasingly large numbers of individuals into the juggernaut of a highly centralized imperial apparatus. Scribes, bureaucrats, judges, and soldiers were recruited through traditional methods and according to venerated customs and regulations. At the same time, the changing balance of power between the Ottoman polity and its most immediate rivals, the Safavid and the Habsburg Empires, resulted in a stalemate, especially from the second half of Süleymān I's reign on. Wars now lasted longer; decisive victories became rarer. With limited, if any, geographical expansion, revenues fluctuated or decreased; fiscal problems became entangled with military ones. Desperate times called for desperate measures, and some of the established norms and standards that had regulated the recruitment and promotion of those employed throughout the Empire's administrative-bureaucratic structure were abandoned, while new methods and practices, including those pejoratively called innovations (*bidʿat*), were introduced. It was against this backdrop that authors like Luṭfī Pasha, Muṣṭafā ʿĀlī, and the anonymous janissary-turned-scribe who composed *Ḳavānīn-i yeñiçeriyān* praised Selīm as a *ḳānūn*-consciousness and meritocratic sultan. It was also this tumultuous time of transformation that led to the *naṣīḥatnāme* authors' collective idealization of Selīm as the foremost Ottoman sultan, paving the way for other Ottoman writers to wax poetic about his divinely ordained attributes.

5 Selīm, the Divinely Ordained Ruler

Shortly before the Battle of Ridaniyya (January 22, 1517), in a letter addressed to the Mamluk sultan Ṭūmānbāy (r. 1516–1517), Selīm claimed to have received glad tidings of his fate from a sacred source: "It has been revealed to me that I shall become the possessor of the East and West, like Alexander the Great. [. . .] You are a Mamluk, who is bought and sold, you are not fit to govern. I am a king (*malik*), descended through twenty generations of kings."[1] The principal thrust of Selīm's message is the superiority of his noble dynastic lineage over Ṭūmānbāy's indentured pedigree. Because Selīm was the ninth ruler of the House of ʿOs̱mān, the letter's reference to "twenty generations of kings" was undoubtedly intended to stress the longevity of the Ottoman lineage as well as the prominence of Selīm's pre-Ottoman ancestors of Oghuz-Turkish origin.

Less than a year later, Selīm fashioned himself quite differently in the Persian prologue to *Ḳānūnnāme-i Nigbolu* (Law Code of Niğbolu). Composed following the annexation of Egypt, this official document alludes to Selīm's sacrality by referring to the Ottoman conqueror of the Arab lands as "Master of the Auspicious Conjunction" (*ṣāḥib-ḳırān*) and "Shadow of God" (*ẓıll-Allāh*) who is "Succored by God" (*muʾayyad min Allāh*).[2] The iconography deployed in this legal code reveals a significant shift in Selīm's royal self-representation. In his letter to Ṭūmānbāy, Selīm had expressed his claim of superiority vis-à-vis one ruler, the Mamluk sultan; in the prologue to *Ḳānūnnāme*, however, he combined a claim to ecumenical sovereignty—as *ṣāḥib-ḳırān*—with an emphasis on his divinely decreed superiority over all Muslim monarchs—as *ẓıll-Allāh* and *muʾayyad min Allāh*. This sudden surge in Selīm's hubris, and the concomitant increase in the number of direct references to the sacred nature of his sovereignty, was by no means accidental. In fact, one can safely posit that the foremost factor that contributed to the differences between these two texts, which were composed only one year apart, was the context of composition for each document: Selīm's correspondence predated the Ottoman conquest of Egypt, whereas his legal code was prepared in its immediate aftermath.

Although the constitutive elements of Selīm's royal titulature highlighted his unequalled status as the preeminent Sunnī Muslim monarch and universal sovereign, such lofty claims were not unique in sixteenth-century Eurasia. Rather, Selīm belonged to a larger fraternity of early modern Eurasian rulers who articulated competing claims to universal sovereignty through rival political theologies.[3] Selīm's victory against Shāh Ismāʿīl and his conquest of Arab lands set the stage for two interrelated competitions that forged the dynamics between several Eurasian empires throughout the sixteenth century, culminating in Ottoman rivalries with the Habsburgs (over universal monarchy and territorial expansion), the Safavids (over "true Islam" and territorial expansion), and the Portuguese (over supremacy in the Indian Ocean and universal sovereignty). Selīm's military achievements constituted a definitive step toward the integration of the Ottoman polity into the Eurasian political-cultural arena, thus making Ottoman history one of the "connected histories" of early modern empires that stretched across the Eurasian landmass.[4]

Connected Histories, Interrelated Concepts: Millenarianism, Messianism, and the Ever-Approaching Apocalypse

The histories of early modern Eurasian empires were "not separate and comparable, but connected," notes Sanjay Subrahmanyam, highlighting the interconnectedness and permeability of cultural zones from the Iberian Peninsula to India and beyond.[5] Although Subrahmanyam acknowledges the significance of the flow of precious metals, military technologies, mercenaries, and bureaucratic and intellectual elites in the formation of an interconnected Eurasia, he places particular emphasis on the circulation of ideas and concepts. His analysis of the rival claims to universal sovereignty expressed—and competing political theologies articulated—by the Portuguese, Habsburgs, Ottomans, Safavids, and Mughals highlights the prevalence of millenarian and messianic sentiments as well as of apocalyptic expectations throughout Eurasia during the early modern era.

Scholarship on the circulation of such thought around the Mediterranean basin in the fifteenth and sixteenth centuries not only substantiates Subrahmanyam's argument but also indicates that similar ideas were shared by individuals across political borders, social classes, religious groups, and gender lines. A puritanical Dominican friar in Renaissance Florence who called for Christian renewal and universal peace and an Ottoman author who composed a religious-cosmographical work of apocalyptical tenor were connected through a millenarian and apocalyptic conjuncture as were a miller and "heresiarch" from Montereale, Italy, and a female seer and prophetic dreamer in Philip II's (r. 1581–1598) Spain.[6] In the fifteenth and sixteenth centuries, Ottoman politico-religious thought was likewise informed by millenarian and ecumenical religio-ideological currents then prevalent around the Mediterranean basin.

Sixteenth-century Ottoman political theology certainly developed in dialogue with the imperial ideologies of Christian polities in the western Mediterranean, but it was more akin to its Islamic counterparts in Safavid Iran and Mughal India—contexts that have been masterfully studied by Kathryn Babayan and Azfar Moin, respectively. In addition to exploring the process through which the disciples of the Safavid sheikhs were transformed into the subjects of Safavid shahs, Babayan highlights the waning messianic dimensions of Safavid rulers' religio-political self-fashioning over the course of the sixteenth century.[7] Her conceptualization of the early modern millenarian worldview as "part of a wider cultural system spanning the realms of the Ottomans, the Safavids, and the Mughals" is taken up by Moin, whose study of the Mughal mode of sacred kingship throughout the sixteenth and the early seventeenth centuries emphasizes the interconnectedness of the Safavid and Mughal politico-cultural realms through "a common pattern of monarchy based upon Sufi and millennial motifs."[8] Adroitly arguing for a comparative study of early modern Muslim empires, Babayan and Moin position sixteenth-century Safavid and Mughal emperors firmly within an early modern Eurasian milieu—a cultural context marked by millenarian, messianic, and apocalyptic sentiments.

The significance of the millenarian religio-ideological worldview and the intricate relationship between sovereignty and (claims to) sacrality in early modern Eurasia have been explored by scholars of Ottoman history as well. Thanks to the seminal contributions of Barbara Flemming, Stéphane Yerasimos, Laban Kaptein, and Cornell Fleischer, there exists a critical and expanding scholarly corpus that addresses millenarianism, messianism, and apocalyptic sentiments in the fifteenth- and sixteenth-century Ottoman context.[9] Yerasimos, for example, focuses on Ottoman apocalyptic narratives centering on Constantinople.[10] Highlighting the significance of the exchange of apocalyptic tropes between Byzantine and Islamic traditions in the emergence of Ottoman variants of apocalyptic thought, Yerasimos notes that the fall of Constantinople featured prominently in these religious and intellectual traditions as one of the Portents of the End. To demonstrate that Constantinople constituted the spatial hinge connecting Byzantine/Christian and Ottoman/Islamic variants of apocalyptic thought, Yerasimos pays particular attention to the oeuvre of an Ottoman mystic named Yazıcıoğlu Aḥmed Bī-cān (d. after 1465), whose cosmographical work *Dürr-i meknūn* (The Hidden Pearl) includes a legendary account of the foundation of Constantinople wherein the Ottoman imperial capital is depicted as a doomed locus. Indeed, built at an inauspicious time, the city suffered repeatedly from plagues, wars, and earthquakes throughout its ill-fated, disaster-prone history.[11]

Contra Yerasimos, Kaptein emphasizes the timeless and interchangeable nature of the eschatological materials in Aḥmed Bī-cān's writings. Thus, he objects not only to the "apocalyptification" of

Bī-cān and his oeuvre but also, more generally, to the view that Ottoman intellectual and religious traditions were influenced by the resurgence of an apocalyptic mood around the middle of the fifteenth century.[12] Kaptein's criticisms regarding Aḥmed Bī-cān's presumed apocalyptic mindset notwithstanding, Flemming and Fleischer convincingly argue that a surge in millenarian, messianic, and apocalyptic expectations occurred during the sixteenth century, particularly during the reign of Süleymān I. Whereas Flemming focuses largely on the eschatological treatise *Cāmiʿü'l-meknūnāt* (The Compendium of Hidden Things), penned in 1529 by a judge named Mevlānā ʿĪsā (fl. 1530s), Fleischer analyzes varied Ottoman expressions of millenarianism, messianism, and apocalypticism against a background dominated by two grand, interrelated processes of the Süleymānic era: the development of Ottoman imperial ideology and interimperial competition among the Habsburg, Ottoman, and Safavid polities.[13]

The analysis in this chapter benefits from the pioneering work of Flemming and Fleischer, whose arguments about the formation of imperial ideology in the Süleymānic age are also relevant to discussions of the textual iconography of Selīm, as the creation of Selīm's posthumous historiographical representation as a divinely ordained monarch began during the forty-six-year reign of Süleymān I. Whereas both scholars are equally focused on Süleymān, however, this chapter places Selīm at the forefront, demonstrating that he was imagined, above all, as a monarch with pretensions to universal sovereignty who ruled by sacred mandate. The analysis that follows also emphasizes that the creation of Selīm's royal representation was not an isolated Ottoman phenomenon but a process that emanated from the larger political-cultural landscape of an interconnected early modern Eurasia.

In an effort to trace the development of Selīm's textual iconography as a monarch who ruled by divine decree, this chapter briefly explores this sultan's self-identification in official documents—such as royal decrees, legal codes, and diplomatic correspondence—as well as references in historiography produced during his reign. Ottoman authors' retrospective attribution to Selīm of claims to preeminence in Islamdom, universal sovereignty, and sacred kingship is examined through an analysis of historical accounts in which Selīm is referred to as "Master of the Auspicious Conjunction" (*ṣāḥib-ḳırān*), "Shadow of God" (*ẓıll-Allāh*), "Succored by God" (*mu'ayyad min Allāh*), "Renewer of Religion" (*müceddid*), "Caliph" (*ḫalīfe*), "Messiah" (*mehdī*), "Messiah of the Last Age" (*mehdī-yi āḫir-i zamān*), "Divine Force" (*ḳudret-i ilāhī*), and "Alexandrine World Conqueror" (*Ẕū'l-ḳarneyn*, lit. "Possessor of the Two Horns"). A careful scrutiny of these texts demonstrates that otherworldy signs of Selīm's legitimacy were propagated in the form of dream narratives and geomantic prognostications (*reml*) before, during, and well after his reign. Over time, references to Selīm's divine mandate and to the sacrality of his sultanate became so ubiquitous that he was portrayed as a saintly figure whose "miracles" included receiving messages from invisible otherworldly saints (*ricāl-i ġayb*), foretelling the future, and accurately interpreting dreams.

Unlike sixteenth-century Mughal and Safavid rulers, Selīm did not assume the trappings of sainthood, although others bestowed such qualities on him—in large part, after his death.[14] There is no definitive contemporaneous textual evidence that "Selīm, and his court, participated in the process of fitting Ottoman sovereignty to a messianic model using the imagery of the *ṭarīḳat* religious-military brotherhood."[15] Thus, this chapter aims to demonstrate that the messianic, millenarian, and apocalyptic pretensions attributed to Selīm are largely constructs of the post-Selīmian era, as they are found exclusively in works composed during and after the reign of his son, Süleymān I (r. 1520–1566). Last but not least, this chapter highlights the impact of that particular historical milieu on the posthumous representation of Selīm by demonstrating that his claims to preeminence in Islamdom and to universal sovereignty as the invincible conqueror (*ṣāḥib-ḳırān*) were indubitably informed by the intellectual, ideological, and religious currents of the time and were expressed—especially after Ottoman victories against the Safavids (1514) and Mamluks (1516, 1517)—with a predominantly Muslim audience inhabiting the newly conquered Arab lands and the Safavid domains in mind. Finally, the analysis in this chapter reveals that all of the elements in Selīm's composite royal image reflect the religious and ideological currents prevalent in the Mediterranean basin and across Eurasia in the sixteenth century, once again demonstrating the intricate interconnectedness of these geocultural zones, of which the Ottoman realm was an integral part.

Sovereignty and Otherworldly Signs of Legitimacy

Early modern Ottomans considered sovereignty a privilege bestowed on members of the House of ʿOs̱mān by divine decree. In accordance with Turco-Mongolian political traditions of Central Asian origin, which attributed sovereignty to a sacred source of authority and a ruler's own personal fortune (*ḳut*), all male members of the House of ʿOs̱mān were assumed to possess innate charisma and personal fortune. As bearers of the hereditary and divine right to rule, all were thus theoretically eligible, and equally legitimate, for the sultanate.[16] Despite the presumption of normative legitimacy for the sultanate of any and all male members of the Ottoman dynasty, at any given time only one individual was assumed to be the recipient of the divine mandate to rule the entire imperial realm. More often than not, royal pretenders battled to determine the ultimate beneficiary of divine grace. Although the outcomes of such succession struggles were deemed the expression of divine will, no one was privy to the mysteries of God's mind. This does not mean that early modern Ottomans ever stopped looking for otherworldly signs in hopes of unveiling a divine verdict in advance. Similar to their medieval European counterparts, who, according to Marc Bloch, were "constantly and almost morbidly attentive to all manner of signs, dreams, or hallucinations,"[17] Ottoman rulers, statesmen, authors, and commoners sought—and reportedly found—clues pertaining to the legitimacy of Selīm's sultanate in the realm of dreams and geomantic prognostication.

Dreaming Selīm

"The veridical dream is one forty-sixth of prophecy," the Prophet Muḥammad is reported to have stated.[18] Due to this prophetic endorsement of oneiric data, there exists a considerable literature on dreams, dream narratives, and dream interpretation in medieval and early modern Islamic societies.[19] The widely held belief that dreams were a means of accessing genuine transcendental information from the other world, coupled with the idea that they were a manifestation of communication between the dreamer and a supernatural power, accorded an immense symbolic significance to these human experiences.[20] In the medieval Islamic context, dreams reflected the rivalries among different theological-legal schools (*madhhab*) and were used to legitimize the superiority of a particular school of thought over others through comparisons of the varied ways in which the jurists after whom the schools were named were represented in dream visions.[21] As Leah Kinberg has demonstrated, dreams not only served their legitimizing function in exactly the same manner as prophetic traditions (*ḥadīth*) but were even used to evaluate the reliability of *ḥadīth* transmitters as well as the authenticity of the contents of *ḥadīths*.[22]

The cognitive and explanatory power of dreams does not appear to have constituted an epistemological problem for the dreamers or their audiences. In fact, the firm grip oneiromancy has held on Islamic societies throughout the ages is indicated by countless historical accounts that refer to dream visions as proof of the validity of diverse religious, political, or philosophical standpoints. Not unlike historiography, dreams were intimately related to contemporary politico-ideological debates. Widely regarded as premonitions of future events, they carried special authority in political and religious spheres. As Roy Mottahedeh has argued, some dream narratives could be interpreted as embodying a contract of sovereignty between a ruler (the dreamer) and God (the sacred origin of the dream).[23] Although Mottahedeh's conjecture is based on examples from medieval Islamic history, his observation that a "dream of sovereignty" was considered the harbinger of imminent rulership is relevant for Ottoman historiography as well; for instance, the narrative of ʿOs̱mān Beg's "dream of sovereignty," found in the chronicle of ʿĀşıḳpaşazāde and in almost all Ottoman chronicles after the late fifteenth century, is a telling specimen.[24]

Presaging the sovereignty and success of members of the House of ʿOs̱mān was not the only function of dream narratives in Ottoman historical writing. Remarkably versatile as a discourse, dreams served other purposes too. In biographical dictionaries composed in the fluid political context of the late sixteenth and the early seventeenth centuries, for example, the career choices of several members of the Ottoman *ʿulemāʾ* were explained with reference to their dreams.[25] Evidence from personal miscellany collections (*mecmūʿa*) recorded by sixteenth-century bureaucrats indicates that "ordinary," educated Ottomans attributed immense value to their dreams for prognosticating the course of their private and professional lives.[26] References in early Ottoman chronicles to the conversion dream of the progenitor of the Mīḫāloğlu lineage of frontier lords, wherein the Prophet Muḥammad appears to "Mikhalis the Beardless" (*Köse Mīḫāl*) and directs him to join ʿOs̱mān Beg, have been interpreted as giving prophetic sanction to the Mīḫāloğlu family's leadership in *ġazā* and placing them in a privileged position vis-à-vis the House of ʿOs̱mān.[27] For Murād III (r. 1574–1595), dreams also constituted a means of self-fashioning, through which this sixteenth-century Ottoman sultan depicted himself as a sanctified mystic who rose through the states of sainthood along the Sufi path.[28]

Selīm also featured prominently, as both subject and object, in several dream narratives recorded in contemporaneous petitions addressed to his court and in Ottoman chronicles penned after his death. These dream accounts were intended for different audiences—ranging from the sultan himself to the entirety of the Ottoman reading public—and articulate a variety of politico-ideological viewpoints, personal opinions, and demands. In some cases, the celestial message of the dream is conveyed in a straightforward, often literal, fashion by a commanding figure, such as a sheikh, sultan, caliph, or the Prophet himself, who addresses the dreamer directly. In others, the message is cloaked in complex, and at times seemingly opaque, symbols that required interpretation by an expert.[29] Some of these accounts are quite similar to ʿĀşıḳpaşazāde's narrative of ʿOs̱mān Beg's "dream of sovereignty" in that they portray Selīm as the beneficiary of divine sanction and prognosticate, however vaguely, his empire's universal rule;[30] others are extremely limited in scope and express the personal demands of their authors. Taken together, they serve a common purpose: to reaffirm the legitimacy of Selīm's sultanate through a wide variety of references to the divinely preordained nature of his kingship.

If numerous petitions preserved in the Topkapı Palace Museum Archives are any indication, some of Selīm's subjects informed the sultan of their auspicious dreams not only as a testament to his legitimacy but also in the hope of receiving rewards. Some of these petitioners specified the reward they sought; in the case of a certain ʿAlī of Köstendil (Kyustendil, Bulgaria), the specific desideratum was a stallion:

> I, your poor slave, prayed to God night and day and wished for a stallion for the love of the Messenger [i.e., Prophet Muḥammad]. In my dream (*vāḳıʿamda*), you, my illustrious Pādişāh, appeared suddenly and said "For the love of the Messenger, His Excellency ʿAlī [b. Abī Ṭālib], and Seydī Ġāzī, I shall give you the stallion you requested from God." May it be known to my illustrious sultan that I bought a horse on credit in order to accompany my illustrious sultan to Kefe, and I went with him [to Kefe]. I suffered many winters and cold weathers. When I returned with my illustrious sultan, the creditor took my horse from me [and] I remained barefooted. My saddle remained with a stranger. I have not a single asper (*aḳçe*) or coin (*pūl*) left. I sold all my clothes and weapons, and spent up [all the money]. Now, I am left naked and barefoot. I have been walking barefooted for a month now. I wish from my illustrious sultan that he bestows his grace and kindness [upon me] and not leave his poor slave destitute, barefoot, and naked. The everlasting decree belongs to my Pādişāh.[31]

On the one hand, ʿAlī's petition is quite ordinary; it is one among many sent to Selīm by his supporters in the aftermath of his accession to the Ottoman throne, requesting the rewards that had been promised in return for their military service during the succession struggle.[32] On the other hand, it is a rare document in that its author justifies his demand in part by relaying a dream vision in which Selīm miraculously appears and personally promises to fulfill the petitioner's wishes "for the love of" a saintly and heroic triumvirate in early Islamic history. The first is none other than the Prophet Muḥammad himself. The second figure, ʿAlī b. Abī Ṭālib (d. 661), is the Prophet's cousin and son-in-law as well as the fourth of the "Rightly Guided Caliphs" (*al-Khulafāʾ al-rāshidūn*). In Islamicate historiography, ʿAlī is also remembered as wielding his double-edged sword, known as Dhūlfiqār,[33] displaying exceptional bravery on the battlefield for the early Muslim community and thereby earning the epithet "Lion of God" (*Asadullāh*). The third, "Seydī Ġāzī," is almost certainly Seyyid Baṭṭāl Ġāzī, a descendant of the Prophet—hence his honorific, *sayyid*—and a legendary Muslim warrior who, according to medieval Arabic sources, was martyred during an Umayyad expedition against Byzantium in the first quarter of the eighth century. Seyyid Ġāzī was also celebrated in religious-heroic frontier narratives composed in late medieval Anatolia. In addition to being the principal protagonist of the anonymous *Baṭṭālnāme*, he featured prominently in the anonymous *Dānişmendnāme*, an epic narrative about the eponymous founder of the Danishmendid dynasty, Melik Dānişmend Ġāzī (d. 1104).[34] The fact that Seyyid Ġāzī is portrayed as a great warrior "to whom all *ġāzī*s are servants" in the versified *Ḫıżırnāme* (Vita of Khidr) of Meḥmed Çelebi further attests to the resilience of his legacy as a foremost warrior of faith (*ġāzī*) among the Muslim inhabitants of Anatolia in the late fifteenth century.[35]

The veracity of Köstendilli ʿAlī's dream is a moot issue. One can imagine a perfectly plausible reason why the petitioner constructed this particular dream—most likely to receive the stallion he desperately needed. But if the cautionary prophetic traditions (*ḥadīth*) concerning dreams and dream interpretation are any indication, one can imagine equally logical reasons for any believer not to prevaricate.[36] Regardless of whether ʿAlī's dream was genuine or fake, the fact that his petition was preserved in the Ottoman imperial archives indicates that it was taken seriously. Although this reception was largely due to the recognition of dreams as a transcendental source of guidance and a reliable means of communication with the other world, there is little doubt that the appearance of Selīm and the allusions to the Prophet Muḥammad, ʿAlī b. Abī Ṭālib, and Seyyid Baṭṭāl Ġāzī in Köstendilli ʿAlī's vision served to elevate the status of both the dreamer and the dream.[37]

We do not know whether references to these four individuals—who personified unquestionable piety and military distinction—helped ʿAlī receive his stallion. What we do know is that ʿAlī's petition reminded Selīm of the battle for succession he had waged against his father and brothers. This rivalry was also the subject of dream visions. An undated petition—penned by a certain Mūsā Ḳalfa and addressed to Selīm—includes one such dream narrative, which, like most dream accounts, includes both literal and symbolic elements:

> We were settled in Sivas when, in the realm of the unseen, the following vision occurred (*vāḳiʿ oldı*) . . . a group of wise men gathered in this place . . . and collected the bones of the deceased and exhumed Sulṭān Meḥmed [II]—May God the Exalted's mercy be increased!—in one place. They set up a balance in-between. They say "Bring Ḳorḳud Sulṭān" and place the bones of the late Sulṭān Meḥmed on one scale of the balance and place Ḳorḳud Sulṭān on the other scale. [Ḳorḳud Sulṭān] did not lift the bones of the deceased. They took him away. This time they brought Sulṭān Aḥmed and placed him on one of the scales. Various doubts arose as some thought that he lifted [Meḥmed II's bones] and some thought that he did not. They placed him on the scale once again and he did not lift the bones. After that, when they brought Pādişāh Sulṭān Selīm—May God perpetuate his Caliphate!—and placed him on one scale of the balance, he lifted the bones of Sulṭān Meḥmed in such a way

> that the bones rose to the air. The Prophet [Muḥammad]—Prayers and Peace be upon Him—spoke thus "What did you do?" They said "Except for Pādişāh Sulṭān Selīm, no one proved heavy enough." The Prophet said "Glory be to God!" . . . [Those gathered] uttered prayers and rubbed their hands on their face.[38]

Despite the fact that Mūsā Ḳalfa's dream straddles the blurry line between the literal and the allegorical, its meaning is unambiguous: when compared to his brothers Aḥmed and Ḳorḳud, Selīm emerges as superior. In historiographical terms, the significance of this particular dream vision stretches beyond proving Selīm's ascendency vis-à-vis the other pretenders to the Ottoman throne. To begin with, the fact that all three candidates for Bāyezīd II's throne are—literally—weighed against Meḥmed II (r. 1444–1446 and 1451–1481) indicates that, at the time of Selīm's accession, Meḥmed "the Conqueror" was still the yardstick against which future Ottoman sultans were measured.[39] That Selīm's weight "lifted the bones of Meḥmed II in such a way that the bones rose to the air" further suggests that the former was superior even to the latter, the archetypal Ottoman sultan. Last but not least, the sudden appearance of the Prophet Muḥammad highlights the divine origin of the vision and confirms its auspiciousness in accordance with an oft-quoted prophetic tradition (*ḥadīth*): "He who sees me in a dream sees me in reality, because Satan does not impersonate me."[40] In addition to elevating the status of both the dreamer and the dreamed, the appearance of the Prophet and his endorsement of Selīm's sultanate also seals, once and for all, Selīm's superiority vis-à-vis other claimants to the Ottoman throne.

Selīm's ascendance to power and his subsequent dominance over his enemies constitute the subject matter of several other dream narratives included in petitions addressed to him. The undated petition composed by a certain Seyyid Kemāl provides a case in point:

> I, your slave, fell asleep after performing the necessary prayers and had a dream of a man who entered my house and said "Tonight I am a guest and you become my father in this world and the next."

> I said: "My Sultan, what do they call you?" He said: "They call me Sultan Selīm. By the grace of God, I am given the throne and I am walking toward the throne. The person in the tent across is His Excellency ʿAlī. By the grace of God, I was told [by ʿAlī] 'He who does not submit to you, you should destroy.'" I, the one who prays for you, said: "My illustrious sultan, since the throne is given to my sultan by the grace of God, I, your slave, too, would request a seal from my sultan." When I said that, my sultan offered a seal and two rings. After that the wall split open and a white-bearded old man with a tray filled with bread in his hand said to my sultan "By the grace of God, it is given to you" and placed the tray in front of my sultan. And my sultan accepted and took one bread, cut it, gave one half to me and the other to that old man. And that old man said "We entrusted you to God" and went away. I woke up as soon as the morning call to prayer was recited. I performed ablutions and prayed. Two months after that, on a Friday night, I saw [in a dream] my sultan sitting at an elevated spot on a plain at ease as his heart desires, while a dragon pounces on my sultan. I, the one who prays for you, shouted and said "Oh, my illustrious sultan, you are unaware that a dragon is attacking you!" Because of my shouting, my sultan stopped, pulled a dagger, grabbed the lower jaw of the dragon with his left hand saying "O, God!" and attacked [the dragon]. The clamor "O, Muḥammad!" came from the dagger. My sultan cut off the middle head of the dragon. Holding three of the dragon's heads under his feet and three in his hand, my sultan cut [the dragon's middle head] in half and left one part on one side and the other part on the other, and said "Now go, the accursed one, so that the Muslims are saved from your wickedness, and those who see you, see our majesty!" I woke up at that hour. When the present event transpired, I communicated it to my sultan. I swear . . . that there is no doubt or suspicion in this occurence.[41]

Seyyid Kemāl's petition is an unusual document. Written by a learned man who claims to be a descendant of the Prophet Muḥammad, it begins with a short poem in praise of Selīm and includes not one but two dream visions in which several historical and supernatural protagonists appear, including Seyyid Kemāl, Selīm, ʿAlī b. Abī Ṭālib, an unidentified saintly figure ("a white-bearded old man"), and a seven-headed dragon. The appearance of both Selīm and ʿAlī b. Abī Ṭālib—as well as the latter's endorsement of the former—are also mentioned in other petitions penned by Selīm's subjects.[42] Seyyid Kemāl's depiction of Selīm—as an epic hero of superhuman strength defeating a supernatural creature—is unusual, however. The portrayal of Selīm as a dragon slayer serves to associate his royal deeds with the heroic labors of numerous champions of Eurasian mythologies.[43] Considering that Ottoman sultans often evoked the names of legendary Persian champions from Firdawsī's *Shāhnāma* (Book of Kings), the parallel between Selīm and Rustam, whose "Seven Labors" (*Haft Khān*) included the killing of the "White Demon" (*dīv-e sefīd*), is certainly noteworthy.[44] Of particular significance, moreover, is the striking resemblance between Selīm and ʿAlī b. Abī Ṭālib, whose miraculous feats—possibly modeled after those of the legendary Rustam—included the slaying of demons and dragons.[45]

Whereas ʿAlī b. Abī Ṭālib's appearance in Seyyid Kemāl's first dream vision creates a legitimizing link between the Ottoman sultan and the first Shīʿite Imām, the attack leveled at Selīm by the seven-headed dragon epitomizes anxieties prevalent at the beginning of the sixteenth century regarding the safeguarding of Ottoman subjects. Considering that this was a time when the politico-religious ideology of the Safavid state under Shāh Ismāʿīl not only challenged the foundations of Ottoman legitimacy but also threatened the unity of the Ottoman lands in eastern Anatolia, the portrayal of Selīm as a successful warrior defeating the dragon undoubtedly accorded the Ottoman monarch immense legitimacy as the protector of the (Sunnī) Muslim community. Seen in this light, Seyyid Kemāl's self-fashioning as the individual who alerts Selīm at the critical moment of the dragon's attack confers on him the role of vigilant servant of the sultan.[46]

Whereas Seyyid Kemāl's dream vision predated Selīm's accession to the Ottoman throne, several others were recorded thereafter.

Noteworthy in this regard is an undated petition that augured Selīm's victories against the rulers of Arab lands and of Persia:

> In the world of dreams (*ʿālem-i rüʾyā*) it became manifest that His Excellency, the Pādişāh, set out prosperously to hunt and mounted a sublime horse. The son of Emīr Beg was on his right side with two falcons in his hand, and there were many people in front of, and next to, the Pādişāh, looking for prey. However, the Pādişāh was looking toward the east, watching for prey. I, too, was standing on the eastern side. Suddenly a quail emerged from my left and went away. None of the hunters noticed. After that, two male peacocks with big tails emerged from the shrubbery, escaped toward the east, and flew into the air the height of two minarets. His Excellency, the Pādişāh, saw them and released several goshawks. [The goshawks] caught up with [the peacocks] separately, exhausted them, turned them around, caused them to fall to the ground, and caught them both. And I grabbed the tail of one of them. In the large book of dream interpretation of the great Ibn Sīrīn: "It is said that if a peacock appears in the dream of a king in the direction of Persia, then the sultan will be with his possessions and grace as well as his servants and retinue." The righteous ones (*ṣuleḥā*) interpreted this dream thus: Soon our Pādişāh will catch the rulers of the Arab and Persian realms and reign over their lands. God the Compassionate willing.[47]

The concluding section of this petition includes a straightforward interpretation of the symbolic elements of its author's allegorical dream. Whereas the appearance of saintly, heroic protagonists of Islamic history, such as the Prophet Muḥammad, ʿAlī b. Abī Ṭālib, Seyyid Baṭṭāl Ġāzī, and Meḥmed II, served to authenticate the divine origins of previously mentioned dream visions, the validity (and trustworthiness) of this anonymous petitioner's prediction—of Selīm's victories against rival Muslim rulers—is emphasized through references to the authority of the renowned Muslim oneirocritic Ibn Sīrīn (d. 728) and an unidentified group of "the righteous ones" (*ṣuleḥā*).[48]

Before moving on to a discussion of dream narratives featuring Selīm in later Ottoman historiography, it should be noted that the appearance of celebrated figures of Islamicate history and the mention of trusted oneirocritics were not the only ways in which the divinely ordained nature of Selīm's sultanate was emphasized through references to his future victories communicated via dream visions. Judging by the presence of his personal seal on the pages of a manuscript entitled *Kāmilü'l-taʿbīr* (Complete Book of Dream Interpretation), Selīm deemed his own dreams to be of prognosticative significance.[49] Various other divinatory practices served the same purpose.[50] Divination books (*fālnāma*) were composed for rulers seeking divine guidance before or during military campaigns, and several Ottoman sultans turned to a variety of occult sciences and divinatory practices in hopes of predicting the outcome of their political and military struggles, both within and beyond the imperial borders.[51] Renowned Ottoman historian Muṣṭafā ʿĀlī's (d. 1600) statement that Selīm's conquest of Egypt was foretold by *fāl-i Qurʾān* indicates that divination by the interpretation of words and letters in the Qurʾān was used as a predictive practice during the reign of Selīm.[52] Ottoman monarchs extended their patronage to occult scientists who not only were allies in their domestic and interimperial contests for sanctified power but also were supportive of their claims to divinely sanctioned political legitimacy.[53] Petitions penned by astrologers (*müneccim*) seeking employment at Selīm's court suggest that the drastic increase in the number of astrologers on palace payroll during the reign of Bāyezīd II (r. 1481–1512) likely continued during Selīm's sultanate.[54] Last but not least, the prevalence of the prognosticative practice of geomancy (*reml*) is confirmed by documents preserved in the Topkapı Palace Museum Archives. One of these documents, including an undated geomantic reading (*reml*) by an unidentified geomancer (*remmāl*), provides auspicious and affirmative answers to three critical questions apparently raised during the first year of Selīm's reign: "Will [Selīm] defeat Sulṭān Aḥmed?," "If [Selīm] attacks Rhodes, will he conquer it?," and "Will [Selīm] defeat Shāh Ismāʿīl?"[55] These queries not only highlight the sultan's domestic military-political priorities but also reveal the constitutive elements of his grand strategy in the arena of interimperial competition.

Selīm did not live long enough to conquer Rhodes. He proved victorious, however, against his two most formidable enemies—his rival brother Aḥmed at home and the Safavid ruler Shāh Ismāʿīl abroad—before proceeding to conquer the Mamluk dominions. Numerous dream narratives recorded in Ottoman historiography long after Selīm's death suggest that the conquest of Arab lands was accomplished thanks to divine assistance. The account of chief white eunuch (*ḳapu aġası*) Ḥasan Agha's (d. ca. 1520) dream vision offers one such narrative. Included in the fourth anecdote (*ḥikāyet*) of Ḫoca Saʿdeddīn Efendi's (d. 1599) *Selīmnāme*, this account underscores not only the notion that Selīm descended from a saintly lineage but also the suggestion that he enjoyed the support of the Prophet Muḥammad and the "Rightly Guided Caliphs":

> I saw last night in my dream (*vāḳıʿa*) that they knocked quickly and hastily on this very door at the threshold of which we are sitting. I proceeded saying "What is it?" I saw that the door was opened a little such that the outside could be seen but no person could fit through. I looked and saw that the outer harem was filled with turbaned, Arab-looking, luminous individuals, with flags in their hands, standing armed and in excellent condition. And four luminous individuals were standing at the entrance of the door. They each had a banner in their hands. The white banner of the Pādişāh was in the hand of the one who had knocked on the door. He said to me "Do you know why we have come?" And I said "Go ahead [and tell me]." He said "The individuals you see are the Companions of God's Messenger—Prayers and Peace of God be upon Him. The Messenger of God sent us and [he sent] his greetings to Selīm Ḫān. And [the Prophet] said '[Selīm] should get up and come over, as the superintendency of the Two Holy Cities is granted to him.' And these four individuals you see are The Eminently Truthful One [Abu Bakr], ʿOmar [The Distinguisher between Right and Wrong],

> ʿOs̱mān [The Possessor of Two Lights]. I, the one who speaks with you, am ʿAlī, son of Abū Ṭālib. Go, tell Selīm Ḫān." And they disappeared from my view. I was overcome by fear and fainted. Drowning in sweat, I remained lying down unconscious until the morning. . . . And [Selīm] said, curbing his own passion, "Do we not tell you that we have not set out in any direction without being ordered? Our forefathers and ancestors had a share in sainthood (*velāyet*). They had miracles (*kerāmet*). We alone did not take after them." Thereafter he set about to realize his idea about the Arab expedition.[56]

The manifest content of this dream narrative portrays Selīm as the beneficiary of divine grace and depicts his actions as sanctioned by God. Moreover, Saʿdeddīn Efendi's emphasis on Selīm's saintly status is not conveyed merely by the mention of the Prophet Muḥammad, the presence of the four "Rightly Guided Caliphs," and Selīm's explicit statement concerning the saintly attributes of his ancestors and their miracles; rather, the anecdote concerning Ḥasan Agha's dream is preceded by a depiction of Selīm as a sultan who was in the habit of asking his men about their dreams of the previous night. As the Prophet Muḥammad is reported to have questioned his companions each morning about whether they dreamt during the night, the reference to Selīm's interest in his court's dreams is clearly intended as a narrative link between the Prophet and this Ottoman sultan.[57] The literal and symbolic elements of Ḥasan Agha's dream thus not only sanction Selīm's conquests as the result of a compact with the divine but also endow Selīm with prophet-like qualities.

Saʿdeddīn Efendi's *Selīmnāme* is not the only historical narrative highlighting Selīm's association with the Prophet Muḥammad. Whereas Saʿdeddīn's account of Ḥasan Agha's dream verifies the prophetic endorsement of Selīm's actions in a circuitous fashion, through a statement of the Prophet as reported by ʿAlī b. Abī Ṭālib, renowned seventeenth-century Ottoman traveler Evliyā Çelebi (d. after 1682) confirms the prophetic protection Selīm enjoyed rather directly, through two sets of dream narratives in which the Messenger of God acts as a principal protagonist. In both cases, Evliyā employs a narrative strategy in which the validity of a dream is corraborated by references to a reciprocal dream. In the first vision, the Prophet appears to the Mamluk ruler Ṭūmānbāy (r. 1516–1517). Commanding Ṭūmānbāy to go to Selīm, the Prophet not only tells the Mamluk ruler that he will be killed by the Ottoman conqueror but also reveals that Selīm himself will soon die. In a reciprocal dream, Selīm is ordered by the Prophet to execute Ṭūmānbāy and attend his funeral before being informed that he, too, will die after returning to Istanbul.[58]

The second set of dream visions concerns a failed attempt to assassinate Selīm.[59] On the authority of Selīm's gentleman-in-waiting (*muṣāḥib*) Ḥalīmī Çelebi, Evliyā reports that one night, when the royal guards were asleep, a Circassian warrior named Kertbāy (*Çerkez Ġāzī Kertbāy*) entered Selīm's chambers but fled in fear when the sultan awoke. When Selīm unleashed his wrath and threatened to execute the guards on duty, they asked for forgiveness and told him that earlier that night the Prophet Muḥammad had appeared to them and said:

> I am the Prophet. Selīm and I have a covenant (*ʿahd*). He serves me; and I serve him. He and his descendants are under my protection until the end of time. Have peace of mind and rest. If anything happens, do not worry, I will warn Selīm in his dream (*menām*).

Having listened to his men's account of their miraculous encounter with the Prophet, Selīm responded that the Messenger of God had indeed alerted him in his dream:

> O, Selīm! I commanded your servants to rest easy. Do not be vexed. Be prepared, someone is coming to kill you. But do not be afraid, you will not be harmed. Get up!

That the sultan's life was saved by the Prophet is confirmed by the unsuccessful assassin as well. According to Evliyā Çelebi's report of the conversation between Kertbāy and Selīm after the former's capture, when Kertbāy asked the Prophet Muḥammad for permission to kill the Ottoman monarch, the Prophet responded:

> God's will is such that fortune (*devlet*) turned its face away from the Circassians and toward the House of ʿOs̱mān. Verily, Selīm is under my protection. Do not harm him. [If] you go [to kill Selīm], I will warn Selīm.

The moral of Evliyā Çelebi's gripping narrative is rather unambigious: the Prophet Muḥammad was Selīm's steadfast guardian. By weaving three separate appearances of the Prophet into one story, Evliyā emphasizes that Selīm was not only a divinely sanctioned monarch with prophet-like qualities but also a sultan eternally graced by the spiritual presence and protection of the Prophet himself.

Foretelling a Conqueror

Among the recipients of signs from the world of the unseen auguring victory for Selīm were saintly figures, some of whom the sultan may have met on his way to Egypt.[60] For example, Evliyā Çelebi relates a local tradition from ʿAyntāb (Gaziantep, Turkey): a certain Dülük Baba, "a great master of the Melāmī-Bektāşī conviction" (*Melāmiyyūn Bektāşīyāndan bir ulu sulṭānmış*), miraculously prophesied the conquest of Egypt, told Selīm that he would become "the overlord of Mecca and Medina" (*Mekke Medīne ṣāḥibi*), and requested that the Ottoman ruler build him a convent (*tekke*). When Ottoman armies took Cairo on the date predicted by Dülük Baba, Selīm decided to fulfill the saint's wishes, so he returned to ʿAyntāb and built a lofty shrine over his grave.[61] Local lore in ʿAyntāb includes similar tales about a dervish sheikh from the village of Sam (*Sām Şeyḫi*) who not only predicted the conquest of Egypt but also facilitated it through his miracles, which caused panic and disarray among the Mamluk ranks and thereby paved the way for the Ottoman victory at Marj Dabik.[62]

As Leslie Peirce has observed, hagiography was a ubiquitous strategy for narrating the past, as "legends of local saints helped domesticate the cataclysmic events surrounding conquest and redress the balance of power in favor of the local."[63] There is no doubt that these hagiographic traditions indeed served an important function in the "vernacular mythology" of ʿAyntāb. At critical junctures in the history of a place, these narratives addressed local concerns pertaining to continuity and security. Frequent references to royal patronage of shrines dedicated to Sufis, saints, and sheikhs suggest that Ottoman sultans, including Selīm I, regarded these clairvoyant, miracle-working spiritual leaders as vehicles of political legitimation. This would explain not only why Evliyā Çelebi credited Selīm for the construction of a grand shrine for Dülük Baba but also why Selīm entrusted the village of Sam as a pious endowment (*vaḳıf*) to its local saint and his descendants.[64]

Loyal subjects and servants of the Ottoman sultan were not alone in foretelling Selīm's conquests. In this regard, it is noteworthy that Selīm focused his architectural patronage on commemorative monuments celebrating his victories in Syria and Egypt. The shrine of the prophet David in Marj Dabik, the mosque complex adjacent to the tomb of the great thirteenth-century mystic Ibn ʿArabī (d. 1240) in Damascus, and the dervish convent constructed for the Ḫalvetī sheikh İbrāhīm Gülşenī (d. 1534) in Cairo were thanks offerings for these figures' spiritual aid and miraculous predictions, which augured and thereby facilitated the Ottoman conquest of Arab lands.[65] Selīm is reported to have prayed at the tomb of David before the decisive battle at Marj Dabik, which brought greater Syria under Ottoman control—hence the attribution of the Ottoman victory to the transcendental support of this prophet.[66] Similarly, the domed mausoleum and mosque complex that Selīm erected for Ibn ʿArabī were memorials of gratitude to the "greatest master" (*al-shaikh al-akbar*), who miraculously predicted the Ottoman conquest of Syria as well as "the final conquest of Egypt and the emergence of the Ottoman House as rulers of the last, universal empire that would precede the end of time."[67] Finally, Selīm expressed his gratitude to İbrāhīm Gülşenī, who foretold the Ottoman victory at Ridaniyya, by ordering the construction of a convent in 1519, which was completed during the early years of the reign of his son, Süleymān.[68]

Judging by the construction of these monumental commemorative structures in Arab lands, Selīm bargained for—and reportedly received—spiritual aid from prophets, sheikhs, and saints, whose convents or burial places dotted the newly conquered territories. In this regard, it is highly significant that on at least seven occasions he and his immediate entourage split from the Ottoman army to visit the holy sites on their itinerary or pay their respects to local sheikhs.[69] This spiritual-political negotiation was not always a smooth process, however. In fact, there exist hagiographic traditions suggesting otherwise. One such reference hails from the local lore of ʿAyntāb, according to which Selīm suffered from constipation for three days after a certain Mevlānā Maḥmūd, a descendant of the previously mentioned "Sheikh of Sam," cursed him. We are told that, through prayer, Mevlānā Maḥmūd relieved the Ottoman monarch's three-day-long ordeal only when Selīm apologized and kissed the sheikh's hand.[70] This particular episode is similar to numerous other hagiographic stories in that it "helped bridge the tension between conquest and local autonomy." Here, the memory of the protective role of Sufi saints during the Ottoman conquest not only served to highlight the cultural continuity in, and security of, the Empire's new territories but also helped "redress the balance of power in favor of the local." This memory did so by identifying the limits of an Ottoman conqueror's dominion vis-à-vis a humble (yet saintly) servant of God and by highlighting royal acknowledgement of the supremacy of a local figure with spiritual and thaumaturgical authority.[71]

Even more significantly, in the first half of the sixteenth century members of the Ottoman religious establishment (*ʿulemāʾ*) debated whether some of the Sufi saints associated with Selīm were to be deemed inside or outside the normative boundaries of Sunnī Islam. For example, Çivizāde Muḥyiddīn Meḥmed Efendi (d. 1547), who served Süleymān I as chief jurisconsult (*şeyḫü'l-islām*), issued legal opinions (*fetvā*) against the teachings of both Ibn ʿArabī and İbrāhīm

Gülşenī—an act that led to his dismissal from office in 1542.[72] Although Ibn ʿArabī became the patron saint of the House of ʿOs̱mān in the aftermath of Selīm's conquests of Syria and Egypt,[73] and the orthodoxy of both Ibn ʿArabī and İbrāhīm Gülşenī was later confirmed by none other than Süleymān's renowned chief jurisconsult, Ebu'ssuʿūd Efendi (d. 1574),[74] it is noteworthy that Selīm participated in the reciprocal process of patronizing these controversial Sufi saints at the time of his conquest of the Arab lands.

Undoubtedly, Selīm's was a political endeavor, and it was certainly recognized as such. The fact that the destruction of the dome of Ibn ʿArabī's newly constructed mosque counted among Janbirdī al-Ghazālī's (d. 1521) first acts of rebellion against Süleymān in 1520 provides proof that this particular fruit of Selīm's architectural patronage was considered evidence of an unwelcome association between the House of ʿOs̱mān and the Sufi sheikh.[75] It would seem that by making his mark on the "sacred geography" of the newly conquered domains, Selīm established ties with the local communities residing in these territories.[76] Furthermore, by attending to and communicating with holy men of various stature, both living and dead, he participated in a saintly association, blurring the line between the patron and the saint. Ottoman authors who composed treatises on the extraordinary "signs" attending Selīm's conquest of Syria and Egypt thus contributed to the portrayal of Selīm as a divinely ordained conqueror whose victories were foretold by saintly figures, heavenly omens, and independent prognostications.[77]

Selīm's Historiographical Afterlife as Caliph and Servitor of the Two Sacred Cities

Ottoman imperial titulature not only reflected the politico-ideological ambitions of Ottoman sultans but also indicated the manner in which these monarchs prioritized one dimension of their royal identity over others. Meḥmed II (r. 1444–1446 and 1451–1481), whose reign corresponded to a key period in the transformation of the Ottoman polity from a frontier state to an imperial entity, considered himself the "greatest *ġāzī*," the leader of subjects and servants united by the ideology of holy war (*ġazā*). His successor, Bāyezīd II (r. 1481–1512), emphasized the Ottomans' preeminence in Islamdom as the "most honorable of sultans" (*eşref-i selāṭīn*). It was not until Süleymān I (r. 1520–1566) that Ottoman sultans laid claim to the "Supreme Caliphate" (*khilāfatu'l-kubrā*).[78]

The institution of the caliphate has been a potent source of normative legitimacy in Islamic political discourse since the moment of its inception in 632, when Abū Bakr (d. 634) became *khalīfat rasūl Allāh* (Successor to God's Messenger) as the new head of the Muslim community on the death of the Prophet Muḥammad. When the assassination of ʿAlī b. Abī Ṭālib (d. 661) brought the era of the "Rightly Guided Caliphs" to an end, first the Umayyads (661–750) and then the Abbasids (750–1258) assumed the title *khalīfat Allāh* (Caliph of God) in an attempt to establish the legitimacy of their dynastic caliphates by claiming to be appointed by God.[79] Although recognition by the caliph constituted a fundamental source of legitimacy for Muslim monarchs in this era, after the turn of the eleventh century one Muslim sultan after another announced his autonomy from caliphal authority. Rather than legitimizing themselves by seeking the recognition of the caliph in Baghdad, these rulers emphasized the divine source of their own sovereignty by referring to themselves as the "Shadow of God" (*ẓıll-Allāh*).[80]

By the time the Ottomans rose to prominence, the prestige of the caliphate as a source of nominal legitimacy had already declined considerably. In fact, the title *khalīfat Allāh* (Caliph of God), which appeared as early as 1421 on the title page of a royal calendar (*taḳvīm*) presented to Meḥmed I (r. 1413–1421),[81] was not used in a defined juristic sense or as a political claim before the early 1540s, when chief jurisconsult (*şeyḫü'l-islām*) Ebū'ssuʿūd Efendi (d. 1574) described Süleymān I as the "Caliph of the Messenger of the Lord of the Worlds . . . Possessor of the Supreme Imāmate . . . Inheritor of the Great Caliphate" in the Law Code of Buda (*Ḳānūnnāme-i Budin*).[82]

The Süleymānic age was indeed a period when the "Ottoman caliphate" was a subject of debate for religious scholars (*ʿulemāʾ*).[83] Whereas Ebū'ssuʿūd Efendi appears to have taken Süleymān's caliphate for granted, other Ottoman authors still considered establishing a juristic basis for such assertions to be necessary.[84] In fact, it was none other than Süleymān's erudite grand vizier and brother-in-law, Luṭfī Pasha (d. 1563), who paved the legal path for Ottoman claims to the caliphate. In 1554, Luṭfī Pasha composed a treatise entitled *Khalāṣ al-umma fī maʿrifat al-aʾimma* (The Salvation of the Islamic Community through Knowledge of the Imāms), in which he rejected the view—commonly held in Sunnī jurisprudence—that the caliph was required to be of Qurayshī or Hāshimī descent.[85] Defining the caliph as "he who commands to the good and prohibits the evil," Luṭfī Pasha argued:

> If the conditions mentioned above are combined in one person—to wit, conquest, power of compulsion, maintenance of the Faith with justice, command to the good and prohibition of evil, and the general headship—then he is a Sultan who has a just claim to the application of the names of Imām and Khalīfa and Wālī and Amīr, without contradiction.[86]

Luṭfī Pasha's principal argument was that any de facto ruler—provided he was just and maintained the ordinances of the faith—was in fact the caliph in his domains. There is no doubt that the grand vizier had a more specific agenda, however: "to hint indirectly at a more universal Caliphate for the Ottoman Sultan."[87]

Selīm was well aware of the legitimizing power of the caliphate. In fact, despite the absence of any official transfer of the institution of the caliphate to the monarchs of the House of ʿOs̱mān, Selīm transferred the person of the caliph to Istanbul and imitated the Mamluk practice of receiving authorization from him, thus enhancing his claim to normative legitimacy. His agenda nevertheless differed from that of Luṭfī Pasha. There is no concrete evidence, for example, that Selīm even considered assuming the title on conquering Cairo, where the last Abbasid caliph, al-Mutawakkil III (d. 1543), lived in the custody of Mamluk rulers.[88] Furthermore, Selīm laid no claim to the caliphate in the letter of conquest (*fetḫnāme*) he wrote to his son Süleymān or in his diplomatic correspondence with other Muslim monarchs immediately following the annexation of Syria and Egypt.[89]

Selīm's refrain was not universally shared. Narrative evidence of this fact—although admittedly rare—can be found in Luṭfī Pasha's dynastic history *Tevārīḫ-i āl-i ʿOs̱mān* (Chronicles of the House of ʿOs̱mān), which includes two congratulatory letters reportedly sent to the Ottoman sultan by "Transoxianian religious scholars" (*Māverāʾü'n-nehr ʿulemāʾsından*) after his victory at Çaldıran.[90] In these versified—and quite possibly apocryphal—letters, Selīm is hailed as "Second Alexander" (*İskender-i s̱ānī*), "Messiah of the End of Time" (*mehdī-yi āḫir-i zamān*), and "Divine Omnipotence" (*ḳudret-i ilāhī*).[91] More significantly for discussions of the Ottoman caliphate, Selīm is also dubbed "Shāh on the Throne of the Caliphate" (*ḫilāfet-serīrüñ şāhı*)[92] and "Caliph of God and of the Prophet Muḥammad" (*Khodā-rā o Muḥammad-rā khalīfa*).[93]

The earliest references to Selīm as caliph are included in the chronicle of Luṭfī Pasha, who was an active participant in debates about Ottoman claims to the caliphate during the later years of the reign of Selīm's son and successor, Süleymān. Especially after the mid-sixteenth century, when Ottoman sovereignty was defined and legitimized with reference to Islamic juristic traditions, Ottoman religious scholars, jurisconsults, and statesmen were eager to enhance their masters' legitimacy by adding the caliphate to the list of imperial titles. Seen in this light, Luṭfī Pasha's retrospective attribution of the caliphate to Selīm, through letters of dubious authenticity, should be seen as an extension of the author's preoccupation with the "Ottoman caliphate" at a time of intense interimperial rivalry. Ottoman sultans and their learned servants competed with their Muslim counterparts not only on the battlefield but also in the arena of political theology, over the championship of "true Islam."

Although Selīm refrained from assuming the caliphate, he appears to have embraced his identity as "Shadow of God" (*ẓıll-Allāh*) rather easily.[94] More significantly, he appropriated another title as soon as he conquered Egypt, at which time he declared himself "Servitor of the Two Sacred Cities" (*ḫādimü'l-ḥarameyn*). We do not know whether he was indeed so moved that he prostrated in thanks (*secde-i şükr*) when his new title was recited during Friday prayers in Cairo in 1517, as Evliyā Çelebi claimed around the middle of the seventeenth century.[95] What we do know is that Selīm and his successors embraced this title enthusiastically, and his status as the first Ottoman monarch to rightfully claim the moniker "Servitor of the Two Sacred Cities" was an important factor in Luṭfī Pasha's decision to laud Selīm's superiority by stating in the early 1550s that he was

> the most honorable one among sultans in intelligence and comprehension as well as in justice and benevolence, the Master of the Auspicious Conjunction (*ṣāḥib-ḳırān*) who reached the happiness of becoming the Servitor of the Two Sacred Cities (*ḫādimü'l-ḥarameyn*) and attained the status of the Prince of Egypt (*ʿazīz-i Mıṣr*).[96]

Writing several decades later, Muṣṭafā ʿĀlī expressed the same view even more forcefully in *Nuṣḥatü's-selāṭīn* (Counsel for Sultans, 1581), noting that Selīm "raised the honor of the Empire higher than under his great ancestors, and adding the noble title of 'Servant of the Two Sacred Cities' to his illustrious Friday sermon he surpassed all the other sultans in rank."[97]

Narrative evidence suggests that the Ottoman sultans' unrivalled status as protectors of holy sanctuaries enthralled not only the Muslim subjects of the Empire but also the rulers of contemporaneous Muslim polities. In his chronicle covering the greater part of Aḥmed I's (r. 1603–1617) reign, *Zübdetü't-tevārīḫ* (Quintessence of Histories, 1614), Muṣṭafā Ṣāfī (d. 1616) recorded a putative conversation between the Safavid ruler Shāh ʿAbbās (r. 1588–1629) and the renowned Ottoman religious scholar Cerrāḥzāde Mevlānā Muḥammed

(d. 1615).[98] On the authority of Cerrāḥzāde, Muṣṭafā Ṣāfī reports the following statement by Shāh ʿAbbās:

> This sultan [that is, Aḥmed I], who is the Shadow of God by virtue of being the Governor of Two Sacred Cities (*vālī-i ḥarameyn olmaḳ ile ẓıll-Allāhdur*), cannot be compared to other sultans of the House of ʿOs̱mān. His character (*meşreb*) is that of Selīm, and his attitude and sect (*meslek-ü-mez̲heb*) is exactly the same as Selīm's. Therefore, I am neither safe nor am I sure that he will not soon attack the Safavid domains (*dārü'l-mülk-i ʿAcem*).[99]

Muṣṭafā Ṣāfī's rendering of this exchange is significant for several reasons. First and foremost, it indicates that Shāh ʿAbbās acknowledged Aḥmed I's privileged status as "Shadow of God" by virtue of his rule over Mecca and Medina. Taken together with Cerrāḥzāde's reference to Aḥmed I as "Sultan of the Two Sacred Cities" (*sulṭānü'l-ḥarameyn*) earlier in the chronicle, there is no doubt that Muṣṭafā Ṣāfī intentionally prioritized the political dimension of the Ottoman monarch's authority over the holy sanctuaries—as governor (*vālī*) and sultan rather than servitor (*ḫādim*). It is equally significant that Shāh ʿAbbās reportedly praised Aḥmed I by comparing him to Selīm while simultaneously expressing his concern about an Ottoman expedition into Safavid territories. The Shāh's emphatic declaration therefore offers proof that the prestige of controlling Mecca and Medina buttressed Ottoman claims of preeminence in Islamdom that were recognized by competing political actors. The account also reveals that Ottoman authors imagined Selīm's memory as haunting rival Muslim monarchs well into the seventeenth century.

Selīm as Renewer of the Faith

Ottoman authors of the sixteenth and seventeenth centuries remembered Selīm as much more than *ḫalīfe* or *ḫādimü'l-ḥarameyn*, and one of the principal pillars on which his memory rested was his identification as renewer of the Islamic faith. The concept of a divinely sanctioned renewer had its origins in a prophetic tradition (*ḥadīth*) according to which "God will send to the community [of Muslims] at the turn of each century [of the Islamic calendar] someone who will renew its religion."[100] Whereas renewers usually hailed from the circles of religious scholars and mystics, honorific titles such as "Renewer of the Faith" (*müceddid*) and "Reviver of Religion" (*muḥyī al-dīn*) were also conferred on pious Muslim rulers.[101] In fact, some of the Muslim monarchs who actively espoused and maintained Sunnī doctrinal orthodoxy—by reviving prophetic customs (*iḥyā al-sunnā*) and eradicating heretical innovations (*bidʿa*)—were praised by their contemporaries as renewers of Islam.[102]

Sixteenth-century Ottoman chroniclers eulogized the House of ʿOs̱mān as an unblemished dynasty divinely preordained to rule the Islamicate world. For this reason, some of them also argued that certain Ottoman sultans were in fact divinely sanctioned renewers of the faith. Luṭfī Pasha, for example, claimed that the House of ʿOs̱mān was one of only two Muslim dynasties since the days of the "Rightly Guided Caliphs" to demonstrate "untainted faith" (*ʿaḳīdeleri pāḳ*).[103] Writing in the early 1590s, renowned chief jurisconsult and chronicler Saʿdeddīn Efendi (d. 1599) went even further, interpreting a Qurʾānic verse as a presage of Ottoman domination: "Soon God will produce a people whom He will love as they will love Him, humble towards the believers, mighty against the rejecters, fighting in the way of God." In the preface to his dynastic history *Tācü't-tevārīḫ* (Crown of Histories), Saʿdeddīn remarked that this divinely sanctioned "people" represented none other than the House of ʿOs̱mān.[104]

Whereas Saʿdeddīn cites God, Luṭfī Pasha quotes the Prophet to make a related argument. In his well-known historical work *Tevārīḫ-i āl-i ʿOs̱mān*, Luṭfī Pasha relates the previously mentioned prophetic tradition (*ḥadīth*) regarding renewers of the faith. He then identifies Selīm as the most distinguished *müceddid* produced by the House of ʿOs̱mān—the other two being ʿOs̱mān Beg (r. ?–1324?) and Meḥmed I (r. 1413–1421).[105] Luṭfī Pasha's classification of Ottoman renewers is neither arbitrary nor simply an accident of chronology. Based on the authority of two prophetic traditions, he first establishes the duration of each historical "era" (*ḳarn*) as one hundred years and then names a *müceddid* for each century of the Islamic calendar.[106] He argues that ʿOs̱mān Beg deserved the title as the eponymous founder of the Ottoman dynasty and as the leader who revived Islam in the face of the onslaught of "infidel Mongols" (*kāfir Moġollar*) at the turn of the eighth century of the Hijri calendar. He also notes that Meḥmed I earned the designation of *müceddid* at the beginning of the ninth century, having strengthened the Muslim community (*ehl-i İslām*), which had been weakened by Tīmūr's (r. 1370–1405) defeat of Bāyezīd I (r. 1389–1402) at the Battle of Ankara.[107] Nevertheless, Luṭfī Pasha claims that the most prominent Ottoman *müceddid* was Selīm, who "renewed the Islamic faith and revived the tradition of the Messenger of God" (*dīn-i İslāmı yeñileyüb sünnet-i Resūlullāhı iḥyā eylemişdür*). In fact, Selīm is the only *müceddid* whose status the author confirms "independently," via the aforementioned letters by Sunnī scholars from Transoxiana whose "content indicates (*delālet*) and bears witness (*şehādet*) that Sultan Selīm Ḫān revived (*iḥyā*) and renewed (*tecdīd*) the Islamic faith."[108]

Luṭfī Pasha's identification of Selīm as the *müceddid* par excellence stands out on several counts. To begin with, Luṭfī Pasha is probably the only prominent Ottoman man of letters who praises Selīm specifically as "Renewer of the Faith."[109] This may well be the result of his personal preference of Selīm over Süleymān, despite the fact that the latter not only lived during the same century as the former but also, auspiciously, was born at its very turn.[110] More importantly, Luṭfī Pasha's reasoning that Selīm restored Sunnī Islam by defeating the "faithless and sectless" (*bī-dīn mez̲hebsiz*) Shāh Ismāʿīl (r. 1501–1524) indicates that learned members of the Ottoman ruling elite perceived Safavid political power and Twelver Shīʿī theology as existential (and heretical) threats directed against both the Ottoman polity and Sunnī Islam.[111] The fact that Selīm himself characterized his earlier expeditions against Shāh Ismāʿīl as military enterprises organized for the sake of "protecting Islam" (*İslāmuñ ṣıyāneti içün*) confirms that this perception was a foundational element of the Ottoman grand strategy formulated within the context of sixteenth-century interimperial competition for politico-sectarian supremacy in Islamdom.[112]

Selīm as Messiah and Master of the Auspicious Conjunction

Luṭfī Pasha may have been alone in his identification of Selīm as *müceddid*. He figures, however, among a great number of sixteenth- and seventeenth-century Ottoman men of letters who contributed to the creation of Selīm's messianic image as an invincible world conqueror. In fact, Luṭfī Pasha's references to Selīm as "Lord of the Age" (*server-i devrān*),[113] "Messiah of the End of Time" (*mehdī-yi āḫir-i zamān*),[114] and "Master of the Auspicious Conjunction" (*ṣāḥib-ḳırān*)[115] comprise but a small subset of allusions to the millennial, messianic, and even apocalyptic significance attributed to this monarch in sixteenth-century Ottoman historiography.

Selīm owed his historiographical stature as a mythical, if not quasi-eschatological, figure to his achievements as a warrior-sultan. The fact that Selīm's was one of five or six swords girded on Ottoman sultans after their accession to the throne constitutes symbolic proof of his standing as one of the foremost conquerors in the history of Islam.[116] There is also ample narrative evidence to indicate that Selīm's military achievements constituted a principal point of comparison for Ottoman chroniclers and poets. That is why the renowned chronicler Selānikī praised Meḥmed III's victory at Mezőkeresztes in 1596 by stating that it was much more significant than Ottoman successes at Çaldıran or Mohács.[117] Similarly, when seventeenth-century poet Nefʿī (d. 1635) eulogized Murād IV (r. 1623–1640), he highlighted this *ġāzī*-sultan's extraordinary military feats by stating that they would bring joy to Selīm's soul.[118] Whereas authors like chief jurisconsult and chronicler Kemālpaşazāde Aḥmed (d. 1534) stressed Selīm's superior qualities as a swordsman,[119] others, including Sāʾī Muṣṭafā Çelebi (d. 1595), dubbed him, metaphorically, "Sword of the House of ʿOs̱mān" (*seyf-i Āl-i ʿOs̱mān*), "Sword of Holy War" (*ġazā ḳılıcı*), and "Sword of Islam" (*seyfü'l-İslām*).[120] By virtue of being the "Conqueror of Arab lands and Persia" (*fātīḥ-i memālik-i ʿArab-ü-ʿAcem*), he was also hailed as "foremost *ṣāḥib-ḳırān*" (*server-i ṣāḥib-ḳırān*), "universal *ṣāḥib-ḳırān*" (*ṣāḥib-ḳırān-ı ʿālem*), and "*ṣāḥib-ḳırān* of the age" (*ṣāḥib-ḳırān-ı ʿaṣrī*).[121] Yet, Selīm's standing as a potential world conqueror was established most specifically in Muṣṭafā ʿĀlī's (d. 1600) historical magnum opus *Künhü'l-aḫbār* (Essence of History). In the beginning of the fourth volume, ʿĀlī examines the political terminology used by sixteenth-century Muslim sovereigns and classifies these rulers with reference to two overarching designations: *muʾayyad min ʿind Allāh* and *ṣāḥib-ḳırān*. Whereas the first term signified a ruler who was never defeated on the battlefield, the second denoted a world conqueror whose advent was indicated astrologically.[122] ʿĀlī considered Selīm to be one of the three undefeated Ottoman sultans "Succored by God," the others being Meḥmed II (r. 1444–1446 and 1451–1481) and Süleymān I (r. 1520–1566).[123] The House of ʿOs̱mān produced no *ṣāḥib-ḳırān*, as none of its members "overwhelmed the rulers of the inhabited world in the East and the West like Alexander [the Great], Genghis [Khan], and Tīmūr."[124] Muṣṭafā ʿĀlī claimed, however, that Selīm had come closest to attaining that status and "would surely have become *ṣāḥib-ḳırān*, had he been blessed with long life" (*muʿammer olmuş olsa yaʿlemu'llāh ṣāḥib-ḳırān olurdı*).[125]

In their attribution of the status of *ṣāḥib-ḳırān* to members of the House of ʿOs̱mān, numerous other Ottoman authors were not as persnickety as Muṣṭafā ʿĀlī. Cornell Fleischer has noted that "in the second half of the sixteenth century, *ṣāḥib-ḳırān* became an increasingly standard, and to that extent 'debased,' element of formal sovereign titulature [but] was still remembered as signifying the most absolute and universal sovereignty."[126] That the universalist connotations of the term were remembered does not mean that *ṣāḥib-ḳırān* was always used in a strictly technical sense, however. In fact, there is no doubt that ʿĀlī meant this designation in a more general, laudatory sense when he accorded it to Murād III (r. 1574–1595), arguably the most sedentary of all Ottoman monarchs and a sultan who never set foot on a battlefield.[127] Poetic servants of several Ottoman rulers also used the term in couplets addressed to their masters. Renowned panegyrist Aḥmed Pasha of Bursa (d. 1497), for example, praised Meḥmed II as both *ġāzī* and *ṣāḥib-ḳırān*, noting that the conquest of Constantinople transformed "the abode of ignorance of disbelief to a realm filled with knowledge."[128] Meḥmed III (r. 1595–1603) was similarly hailed as *ṣāḥib-ḳırān* by members of his retinue who witnessed the victory of the imperial armies in the Egri expedition of 1596.[129] The term was even applied to Prince Aḥmed, Selīm's brother and archrival, who never acceded to the Ottoman throne.[130]

The fact that such Ottoman writers as Luṭfī Pasha often used the honorific *ṣāḥib-ḳırān* for Selīm in a literal rather than allegorical sense was the result of two interrelated factors. The first was historical: the extraordinary pace and extent of Selīm's conquests, which inevitably led to the question of what he could have achieved had he lived longer. The second was historiographical, related to the era in which the foundations of Selīm's textual iconography were laid. Because the formative phase of the creation of Selīm's memory corresponded to the reigns of his immediate successors, the analysis below will focus primarily on the historiographical formulation of imperial ideology and royal iconography in the Süleymanic age, which provided Ottoman men of letters with the imagery and vocabulary they used to portray Selīm as a divinely invested messianic conqueror.

Imagining Selīm in the Age of Süleymān and Beyond

As this survey of historiographical references indicates, Ottoman authors used terms such as *ḫalīfe*, *müceddid*, *ṣāḥib-ḳırān*, and *mehdī* in a variety of ways. Whether these titles were meant in a literal, juristic sense or in an allegorical and laudatory panegyric way depended on the historical context within which Ottoman bureaucrats and men of letters composed chancellery documents, imperial codes of law, poems, chronicles, and advice treatises. Judging by the textual iconography deployed in the prologue to the Law Code of Niğbolu (*Ḳānūnnāme-i Nigbolu*, 1517), Selīm and his chancellors were certainly informed by the religious and ideological currents of their time when they articulated a political theology that assigned Selīm the status of a divinely ordained warrior-king battling for universal sovereignty. Similarly, when Selīm's subjects and servants communicated dreams and prognostications (*reml*) to their sultan and master through petitions addressed to the imperial court, they employed a combination of imagery and vocabulary that circulated in Ottoman learned society at the beginning of the sixteenth century. Although some of this imagery and vocabulary carried messianic, millenarian, or apocalyptic overtones, there is no concrete textual evidence that Selīm himself expressed such pretensions.[131] On the contrary, a careful scrutiny of the aggregate of references to Selīm as *müceddid*, *ṣāḥib-ḳırān*, or *mehdī* indicates that the attribution of messianic, millenarian, and apocalyptic pretensions to this monarch is a retrospective phenomenon of the Süleymānic age, not one of the Selīmian era. In fact, in sixteenth- and seventeenth-century Ottoman historiography, this triad of honorific titles was most often used for Süleymān I, both in a literal-juristic and allegorical-panegyric sense.

There is narrative evidence to suggest that Selīm himself may have seen in his son the potential to become a universal monarch. Luṭfī Pasha alludes to an encounter that purportedly took place in the aftermath of the Egyptian expedition, when Süleymān welcomed his father in Thrace. Impressed by Süleymān's physiognomic attributes (*boyun ve şekl-ü-şemālin begenüb*), Luṭfī Pasha tells his readers, Selīm predicted that his son would become a universal ruler (*olıser ṣāḥib-ḳırān ender cihān*).[132] Such predictions were recorded in later historiography as well. In the tenth book of his *Seyāḥatnāme*, seventeenth-century traveler Evliyā Çelebi relates a tradition involving two priests, a Portuguese named Kolon and a Spaniard named Padre, who suddenly appeared in Bāyezīd II's camp during the siege of Akkirman, in 1484, and miraculously predicted the exact moments when the Kili and Akkirman fortresses were to be conquered. When granted an audience with the sultan, they also prophesied that his son, Selīm, would rule Mecca and Medina, and his grandson, Süleymān, would conquer *Ḳızıl Elma* (Red—or Golden—Apple), a city symbolizing the ultimate goal of Turco-Muslim conquests.[133]

In the sixteenth-century Ottoman context, *Ḳızıl Elma* generally referred to Vienna or Rome, neither of which Süleymān conquered.[134] He was, however, praised as a world conqueror during much of his reign and was remembered as such after his death. This was an era when the Ottomans locked horns with their Safavid and Habsburg archrivals.[135] Süleymān and Charles V (r. 1519–1556) had not yet settled their adversarial claims of universal sovereignty (*daʿvā-i ṣāḥib-ḳırānī*), and Shāh Ṭahmāsb (r. 1524–1576) was not definitively subdued. This was also a conjuncture ripe for the emergence of a Messiah as well as of the positive popular reception of messianic claims. The memory of Shāh Ismāʿīl's (r. 1501–1524) messianic message was still alive.[136] In fact, at the beginning of the sixteenth century, Ismāʿīl's Ḳızılbaş adherents in Ottoman Anatolia regarded him as the divinely invested Imām and long-awaited Mehdī.[137] When Ḳızılbaş sheikhs, such as Şāhḳulu (1511) and Celāl of Bozok (1519), rebelled against the Ottoman establishment, they claimed to be either the representative (*ḫalīfe*) of Shāh Ismāʿīl or the Mehdī themselves.[138] The impact of these popular revolts on the Ottoman social order was so devastating that some "said that this sedition of the End Time is a sign of the Day of Resurrection," hinting at the presence of eschatological anxieties in Ottoman society already during the first quarter of the sixteenth century.[139]

In these uncertain times, Süleymān appears to have attempted to publicize his imperial image—as *müceddid*, *ṣāḥib-ḳırān*, and/or *mehdī*—and to influence "public opinion" through sheikhs, poets, prophetic authors, astrologers, and geomancers, all of whose writings emphasized his messianic identity and eschatological significance.[140] Respected spiritual figures, including the Bayrāmī-Melāmī sheikh Pīr ʿAlī of Aksaray (d. 1528), may have considered Süleymān to be Mehdī.[141] Yaḥyā Beg (d. 1582), renowned poet of the later Süleymānic age, was also among the learned men who praised their master as messianic emperor and universal monarch.[142] As Barbara Flemming and Cornell Fleischer have demonstrated, when an Ottoman author such as the "mystically-minded magistrate" Mevlānā ʿĪsā (fl. 1530s) referred to Süleymān as *ṣāḥib-ḳırān*, he quite possibly understood the term literally, denoting the universal monarch who would inaugurate the dominion of the single true religion that was to coincide with the great celestial conjunction of Jupiter and Saturn.[143] Unsurprisingly, Mevlānā ʿĪsā was also convinced that Süleymān was either the Messiah (*mehdī*) or his conquering forerunner (*serʿasker*).[144] Strikingly similar ideas were undoubtedly expressed at the imperial palace, which was the locus of what Fleischer aptly labels "a court-based Süleymānic 'cult.'"[145] Perhaps the most intriguing courtier in this regard appears to have been a certain Ḥaydar, Süleymān's geomancer (*remmāl*), whose prognostications identified the Ottoman monarch as the divinely designated eschatological emperor who combined temporal dominion (as *ṣāḥib-ḳırān*) with spiritual sovereignty (as *ṣāḥib-zamān*).[146]

As one would expect, explicit conferral on Süleymān of universal temporal and spiritual authority was a principal dimension of the politico-ideological agenda of several works composed in the versatile literary epic *Shāhnāma* genre. Whereas a certain Levhī (fl. 1529) depicts Süleymān as the just *ṣāḥib-ḳırān*, accompanied by invisible otherworldly saints (*ricāl-i ġayb*), Ḫākī (fl. 1556) emphasizes the divinely appointed sultan's legitimate claim to universal sovereignty. In S̱enāʾī's (fl. 1540) *Süleymānnāme* (Book of Süleymān), the Ottoman monarch is identified as "Master of the Auspicious Conjunction and Messiah of the End of Time" (*ṣāḥib-ḳırān ve mehdī-yi āḫir-i zamān*).[147] That these references were included in works penned in a genre of writing that was most suitable to highlighting the military achievements of a mythical or historical protagonist indicates that the creation of Süleymān's textual image as a divinely ordained and messianic world conqueror was directly influenced, even necessitated, by the interimperial competition among the Ottoman, Habsburg, and Safavid polities in the sixteenth century.[148]

The textual and visual iconography of post-Süleymānic sultans of the early modern era was constructed in a similar fashion by Ottoman dynasts and their learned servants in a cultural milieu influenced by apocalyptic anxieties and messianic sentiments that were, at least to some degree, triggered by the approach of the Muslim millennium in

1591–1592.[149] The mystically inclined Murād III's (r. 1574–1595) decision to commission a six-volume illustrated biography of the Prophet Muḥammad, entitled *Siyer-i Nebī* (Life of the Prophet), has been regarded as part of the sultan's broader agenda aimed at being remembered as the "Renewer of the Faith" (*müceddid*) of the tenth century of the Islamic calendar.[150] A devoted disciple of the Ḫalvetī sheikh Şücāʿ (also Şücāʿ Dede, d. 1588), Murād III apparently sent descriptions of his dreams to his spiritual guide.[151] In these visions, Murād III fashions himself as the divinely ordained sultan who rises through various stations of sainthood to become the "Pole of Poles" (*ḳuṭb al-aḳṭāb*), the apogee of the saintly hierarchy in Islamic mysticism.[152] Furthermore, as a sultan who acceded to the throne toward the end of the Islamic millennium, Murād III appears to have envisioned himself as the long-awaited Messiah who would rule the world before the End of Time.[153]

Judging by the (self-)fashioning of Süleymān I and Murād III as divinely invested, saintly, and messianic monarchs of an ever-approaching apocalypse, learned Ottomans were not immune to the millenarian conjecture that operated throughout sixteenth-century Eurasia. Such currents influenced and shaped the textual and visual iconography associated with many an early modern monarch.[154] In fact, around the turn of the Islamic millennium, implicit or explicit claims to Mehdī-hood appear to have become an epigenetic attribute of members of the House of ʿOs̱mān.

One of the most striking illustrated manuscripts in which the Ottoman sultan is promoted as a messianic ruler was produced during the reign of Murād III's son and heir, Meḥmed III (r. 1595–1603). The work in question is an Ottoman-Turkish translation of the esoteric and prognosticative compendium of apocalyptic texts by the Ḥurūfī mystic ʿAbd al-Raḥmān al-Bisṭāmī (d. 1454), entitled *Miftāḥ al-jafr al-jāmiʿ* (Key to Comprehensive Esoteric Knowledge).[155] A renowned expert in the prophetic traditions (*ḥadīth*) and a scholar of occult sciences and divination, al-Bisṭāmī is remembered primarily as a specialist in "the science of letters and divine names" (*ʿilm al-ḥurūf wa'l-asmāʾ*), which assigned mystical and prognosticative significance to the letters of the alphabet and their combinations.[156] The work known as *Tercüme-i miftāḥ-ı cifrü'l-cāmiʿ* is an expanded translation of al-Bisṭāmī's original text by Şerīf b. Seyyid Muḥammed (also Şerīfī, fl. 1597). It was commissioned by Meḥmed III via his chief white eunuch Ġażanfer Agha (d. 1603), a prominent patron of the arts and an active promoter of a new imperial image for this Ottoman sultan, whom he desired to be seen as the messianic ruler assigned to the last ruling dynasty on earth.[157] The fact that the Messiah in *Tercüme* is referred to as "Imām Meḥmed Mehdī" and that there is a significant resemblance between visual depictions of the Mehdī in this work and portrayals of Meḥmed III in contemporary illustrated manuscripts constitutes an implicit yet powerful link between the ruling sultan and the Messiah who will appear at the End of Time.[158]

The historiographical significance of *Tercüme-i miftāḥ-ı cifrü'l-cāmiʿ* is not limited to the identification of the House of ʿO̱smān as a messianic dynasty. As an influential prognosticative work that focuses on the signs of the end of the world, *Tercüme* contextualizes the entire Ottoman dynasty within an apocalyptic framework. Only two Ottoman sultans are depicted more than once, however; whereas Meḥmed II owes his multiple appearances to the apocalyptic significance attributed to his conquest of Constantinople, the recurrence of Selīm I is due to his unprecedented military accomplishments against Mamluk and Safavid rulers. As a warrior-sultan who established the Ottomans' incontrovertible supremacy in the sixteenth-century Islamic world, Selīm was not only identified as a messianic redeemer but also inserted into an eschatological account of the end of the world as a monarch who could have established the dominion of the one true religion.[159]

The persistence of textual and visual portrayals of Selīm as a messianic figure in Ottoman historiography is also intricately related to one of the most fascinating aspects of manuscript production: networks of literary-artistic patronage. In the case of *Tercüme-i miftāḥ-ı cifrü'l-cāmiʿ*, the starting point is Ġażanfer Agha, Meḥmed III's chief white eunuch. Ġażanfer was not merely the sultan's faithful agent who joined his master in patronage activities; he was also a wealthy and influential patron who sponsored the building of an exquisite madrasa complex at a prominent location close to both the imperial palace and the main ceremonial avenue (*Dīvānyolu*).[160] Furthermore, he was a learned employer of scholars turned madrasa professors. In addition to serving as a hub for Ġażanfer Agha's patronage activities, through which the chief white eunuch actively participated in the Empire's intellectual life, this madrasa enabled him to cultivate relationships with prominent political figures. The fact that several scholars whom Ġażanfer sponsored as professors were protégés of Ḫoca Saʿdeddīn Efendi (d. 1599) highlights the intimate intellectual-political relationship between the chief white eunuch and one of the leading figures in Ottoman politics during the last quarter of the sixteenth century.[161]

The fact that Muṣṭafā ʿĀlī considered Saʿdeddīn one of the four foundational pillars of Murād III's reign attests to the exceptional influence of this scholar-statesman at the imperial court.[162] Saʿdeddīn owed his political influence, at least initially, to his position as tutor to Prince Murād. The prince later acceded to the throne as Murād III, hence Saʿdeddīn's title, *Ḫāce-i Sulṭānī* ("Instructor of the Sultan"), which he retained during the reign of Meḥmed III. After serving Murād III, first as royal tutor and later as trusted advisor, Saʿdeddīn continued to exert political influence as chief jurisconsult (*şeyḫü'l-islām*) during the reign of Meḥmed III. He also contributed to the Ottoman historical tradition as the author of *Tācü't-tevārīḫ* (Crown of Histories).

Saʿdeddīn's historiographical significance in terms of the creation of Selīm's posthumous image is due to the fact that he authored a *Selīmnāme*, which, as highlighted in Chapter 3, was a remarkably popular work composed with multiple audiences and a wide readership in mind. Unlike other *Selīmnāmes*, which provide a chronological literary-historical account of Selīm's military accomplishments, Saʿdeddīn's unique hagiographic composition is structured thematically rather than diachronically, consisting of a preface (*muḳaddime*) and twelve anecdotes (*ḥikāyet*). The composite image of Selīm that emerges is of a sultan whose birth, rule, and conquests were accompanied by supernatural signs. To give just a few examples, reporting on the authority of Kemālpaşazāde, Saʿdeddīn depicts Selīm's birth as foretold by a "miracle-working dervish" (*dervīş-i ṣāḥib-kerāmet*) who augured that this newborn member of the House of ʿOs̱mān would defeat as many prominent rulers (*ṣāḥib-serīr*) as the number of moles (*beñ, ḫāl*) on his body.[163] Saʿdeddīn's Selīm is also a friend of dervishes (*pādişāh-ı dervīş-dost*).[164] He visits the sheikhs of this world and communicates with the saints of the other (*ricāl-i ġayb*).[165] He delves into the realm of meditation (*murāḳabe ʿālemi*) and predicts his own death as well as the executions of his statesmen.[166] He is credited as well with veritable dreams that would come to fruition exactly as predicted.[167] Thus, based on "evidence" from the realm of dreams, Saʿdeddīn portrays Selīm as a monarch who receives divine blessings through otherworldly saints, the "Rightly Guided Caliphs," and the Prophet Muḥammad.[168]

Yet the most unambiguous statement identifying Selīm as a divinely chosen messianic redeemer is found in the preface of Saʿdeddīn Efendi's *Selīmnāme*. In this preface, Saʿdeddīn expresses praise that, every hundred years, God graces one of his esteemed slaves not only by designating him worthy of being His "Shadow on Earth" (*her ʿaṣrda bir ʿabd-i maḳbūlini sezāvār-ı ẓılliyet idüb*) but also by bestowing on him the "exalted crown of the sultanate" (*tāc-ı ba-ibtihāc-ı salṭanat*) and "the robe of honor of the caliphate" (*ḫilʿat-ı ḫilāfet*). The explicit mention of Selīm's dual qualifications as sultan and caliph highlights his unquestionable prestige and stature as the foremost Muslim monarch, setting him apart from the rulers of other Islamicate polities. As for Saʿdeddīn Efendi's mention of the centennial appearance of God's shadow on earth, it is nothing if not an implicit recognition of Selīm as "Renewer of the Faith" (*müceddid*). Saʿdeddīn's *Selīmnāme* thus not only contributed to Selīm's posthumous sanctification in Ottoman historiography but also definitively sealed his identity as a divinely ordained, saintly, and messianic monarch in Ottoman collective memory.[169]

Conclusion

"THE PAST IS NEVER DEAD. It's not even past," wrote William Faulkner.[1] For early modern Ottomans, memories of Selīm were neither dead nor part of a long-forgotten past but rather were an integral component of an "eternal present," constructed at numerous historical junctures by literate men and women of diverse sociocultural backgrounds with disparate—and at times conflicting—political and ideological viewpoints.[2]

These memories were by no means uniform. Writing in the Süleymānic age, Mevlānā ʿĪsā (fl. 1530s) recalled Selīm's reign as an era of peace, when "the sheep and the wolf strolled together without fighting [and] the mouse placed its head on the paw of the cat."[3] Yet the same era evoked painful memories for a "servant girl" (*ḳul ḳızı*) from the provincial town of Bergama, whose petitions are preserved in the imperial archives at Topkapı Palace. In these petitions, the writer explains that she was commissioned by Selīm to travel alone from town to town, with valuable goods in her possession, to test the orderly nature of Ottoman society (*niẓām-ı ʿālem*). She laments that she was assaulted, robbed, and molested by several men on a number of occasions. She states that during one of these instances an attacker knocked out one of her teeth. She complains that these acts of violence were so brutal that she suffered a miscarriage. Last but not least, she expresses grief that local authorities honored neither the sultanic writ nor the royal servant who accompanied her. Instead, they mocked her. More significantly, they mocked Selīm's authority as embodied in his imperial prescript.[4]

As these two accounts demonstrate, Ottoman authors who remembered Selīm and his reign did so in their own, subjective "eternal present." Their acts of memory-making did not necessarily belong to different historical periods. In fact, both Mevlānā ʿĪsā and the "servant girl" wrote within a decade of Selīm's death, suggesting that the variance in their memories resulted from factors other than chronology.[5] There is no doubt that each author's "eternal present"—and, by extension, memory—was shaped by his or her individual experiences, expectations, and agendas. In turn, the genres in which Ottoman writers recorded these memories influenced the collective memory of future generations of Ottoman readers. Whereas Mevlānā ʿĪsā included his recollection of the state of affairs during Selīm's reign in a versified historical-eschatological treatise, the "servant girl" recorded her painful personal experiences in a petition addressed to Selīm's son, Süleymān. Whereas Mevlānā ʿĪsā remembered Selīm's sultanate as an era of justice that ushered in the Süleymānic age, the *ḳul ḳızı* of Bergama recalled the pain she endured for Selīm's experiment. Whereas Mevlānā ʿĪsā employed literary tropes—replete with sheep and wolves, cats and mice—to emphasize the enduring peace, the "servant girl" narrated with brutal honesty the blow that knocked out her tooth and the beating that caused her to suffer a miscarriage. Finally, Mevlānā ʿĪsā's goal was to highlight the undisturbed natural order of things during the Selīmian era, as a prelude to the Süleymānic age, whereas that of the *ḳul ḳızı* was simply to plead for justice and compensation. Ultimately, the memory of Selīm's reign constructed by Mevlānā ʿĪsā was one of a dominion-wide peace established by an all-powerful and just monarch, whereas the recollection fashioned by the "servant girl" portrayed a sultan whose authority and justice barely stretched beyond the imperial capital.

"The Past," Nancy Partner wryly notes, "is like memorably maligned Oakland: when you're there, there is no there there."[6] The analysis throughout this study has been grounded by two interdependent conceptual anchors: that there is a "there there," and that all extant textual evidence is to be perceived as reflections of past phenomena, constructed, albeit to varying degrees, in the imaginations of the men and women who authored those texts. Specifically, the first, permanent anchor is Selīm himself, who was patently "there." The second anchor, constantly relocating, is the memory, or rather memories, of Selīm, which remained "in permanent evolution, open to the dialectic of remembering and forgetting, unconscious of its successive deformations, vulnerable to manipulation and appropriation, susceptible to being long dormant and periodically revived."[7] The texts composed by Mevlānā ᶜĪsā and the *ḳul ḳızı* of Bergama should be considered reminders of the fruitful interdependence between past phenomena and their reflections in historical record. On their own, and for a variety of reasons, these memories offer an incomplete and thus inaccurate image of a sultan and his sultanate. Together, however, they provide a multifaceted, nuanced depiction of Selīm and his reign while simultaneously reminding us of the irrefutable historical embeddedness and malleability of all textual representations.

To the extent that it explores Selīm's place in the ongoing work of Ottoman historians' reconstructive imagination, this study is also indebted conceptually to Jan Assmann, who distinguishes between the past itself and the past as it is remembered, referring to the former as "history" while labeling the latter "mnemohistory." In his discussion of the "Mosaic distinction," Assmann reminds his readers that although the Egyptian pharaoh Akhenaten (r. ca. 1353–1335 BCE) was the first historical figure to institute a monotheistic religion, it was the memory of Moses as a monotheistic prophet that lived on. Whereas Akhenaten's religion generated no tradition, the distinction between true and false in religion is attributed to Moses—despite the fact that there "are no traces of his earthly existence outside the tradition." Thus, Assmann concludes, "Moses is a figure of memory but not of history, while Akhenaten is a figure of history but not of memory."[8]

Selīm is a figure of both history and memory. In acknowledgment of this duality, this study has attempted to analyze the rise to the sultanate of the historical Selīm in light of the historiographical traditions that constructed his varied mnemohistorical imaginings. This approach required simultaneous forays into "history" as well as "mnemohistory," mutually constitutive fields of inquiry that inform and enrich one another, ultimately yielding a richly textured composite image of this controversial Ottoman monarch.

Specifically, the analysis of Selīm's controversial ascendance to the throne was based on separate but interrelated explorations in history and historiography, undertaken through the concurrent examination of contemporaneous archival documents and later historical narratives. Each of the authors who composed these texts was "there," writing from the perspective of his or her "eternal present." Chronologically, all archival documents pertaining to Selīm's rise to power were produced as the succession struggle between him and his dynastic rivals unfolded, whereas almost all historical narratives addressing this critical episode were composed subsequently, over the course of the sixteenth and seventeenth centuries. These texts were significantly different in terms of their rhetorical style and form as well. Although primary sources like imperial decrees, official correspondence, petitions, and even spy reports, penned mostly in Ottoman Turkish, were not devoid of varying degrees of literary elegance and formalism, they certainly did not measure up to the chronicles, treatises, and panegyric works composed in the sophisticated and highly ornate medium of one of the three major literary languages of the Empire. Yet the most significant difference between these two types of text pertains to their authors' vantage points and agendas.

Whether Ottoman or European, the great majority of historical texts are center-oriented, focusing either on the events that transpired in the Ottoman imperial capital or on the manner in which affairs in the provinces influenced political processes in Istanbul. Unlike the sultan- and Istanbul-centered narratives of most Ottoman chronicles, however, royal decrees, official correspondence between the imperial capital and the provinces, and spy reports penned by the sultan's agents residing in the periphery provide invaluable glimpses into the constantly shifting power dynamics between the sultan and various politico-military factions. Thus, whereas chronicles of the Ottoman tradition address historical developments from the vantage point of the imperial center, archival documentation also alludes to the power holders located in the periphery—most notably to lineages of frontier lords (*uc begleri*). As a result, the analysis of contemporaneous archival sources related to Selīm's struggle for the throne set against the textual representations of that struggle in later historiography produces a complex, sophisticated, and nuanced narrative. This revisionist analysis suggests, first and foremost, that the Ottoman political process was less state-centered and more multifocal than previously imagined and that it was marked by constant negotiation between the sultan and various power holders located in both the imperial center and the periphery. Additionally, this narrative indicates that the Ottoman polity never was a patrimonial empire, in which all political power emanated from the sultan.

Whereas the analysis of the historical Selīm's rise to the Ottoman throne benefited from the productive tension between contemporaneous archival sources and later historiography, Selīm's varied imaginings in Ottoman collective memory stemmed from the equally productive interdependence of various genres of historical writing. This mnemohistorical analysis considered dynastic chronicles of the Ottoman tradition, *Shāhnāma*-style literary-historical narratives of Selīm's reign (*Selīmnāme*), and the impressive corpus of political treatises commonly called "advice literature" (*naṣīḥatnāme*) as separate but interrelated discursive fields, all of which contributed to the formation of Selīm's posthumous textual iconography by generating particular strands of memory. Whereas narratives of the *Selīmnāme* genre aimed at, and succeeded in, rehabilitating Selīm's image as a legitimate monarch, literary-political treatises composed in the *naṣīḥatnāme* genre portrayed him as the quintessential sultan of an Ottoman "golden age" that never was. These genres of historical writing also informed and influenced each other. In fact, taken together, the traditional chronicles of the Ottoman dynasty, *Shāhnāma*-style narratives of Selīm's sultanate, and advice treatises constituted a triple helical structure that culminated in the narrative imagination of Selīm along a chronological axis that stretched between the last years of his reign and the middle of the seventeenth century.

The period of Selīm's reign and the next few decades thereafter was a particularly transformative one for the Ottoman enterprise, an era marked by the emergence in Ottoman learned circles of a historical consciousness of "decline" coupled with the prevalence of millenarian and messianic sentiments and apocalyptic expectations. Throughout this period, the Ottomans inhabited the competitive world of early modern empire building, flanked by two prominent imperial entities with rival political theologies. Within the larger context of early modern Eurasia, the sixteenth century in particular was also a time when the contours of a truly Ottoman imperial ideology were formulated in sharp contradistinction to its Habsburg and Safavid counterparts.

Because the "reworking of the past is most pronounced in periods of dramatic social transformation," it is no wonder that the most significant reworking of memories of Selīm occurred during this period.[9] Thanks to this revisionist process of memory-making, Selīm was no longer remembered as a wrathful, insubordinate, and patricidal prince but rather as a legitimately appointed and divinely invested sultan. He also was imagined as a quintessential monarch ruling an equally idealized empire supported by justice, *ḳānūn*-consciousness, and meritocratic principles. The genres of literary and historical writing that contributed to an overarching image of Selīm as a legitimate, idealized, and divinely ordained sultan were mobilized in the labor of constructing the Ottoman imperial polity as well. It was thus thanks to the productive and ever-evolving interplay between history and mnemohistory that an early modern empire and its emperor were crafted both in fact and in memory, a process that continues unabated to the present day.

Notes

Introduction

1. Most Ottoman sources refer to Selīm's fatal ailment as *şīr-pençe*, a malignant form of carbuncle. Other possible causes of Selīm's death include the plague, lung cancer, and phagedenic ulcer (*ākile, yenirce*). For sources on Selīm's cause of death, see Tansel, *Yavuz Sultan Selim*, 247n38.

2. Anonymous, *Tevārīḫ* (TSMK R.1100), 89b: "babasıyla uġraşduġı yirde dār-ı fenādan dār-ı beḳāya rıḥlet eyledi."

3. See, for example, Şükrī, *Selīmnāme* (BM Or.1039), 29b; and Hezārfen Ḥüseyin, *Tenḳīḥ* (TSMK R.1180), 122b.

4. See, for example, Ṣolaḳzāde, *Tārīḫ* (TSMK B.199), 244b–245a: "merḥūm ve maġfūruñ devrinde vezīr nāmında olanlar ayına varmadın ḳatl olunmaġın āʿyān-ı devlet biri birine bed-duʿā itseler bolay ki Sulṭān Selīme vezīr olasın dirler idi. Ḥattā şāʿirüñ birisi bu beyti ol eyyāmda söylemişdir . . . Raḳībüñ ölmesine çāre yoḳdur / Vezīr ola meger Sulṭān Selīme." During his reign of eight years, Selīm had six grand viziers; he ordered the execution of three.

5. For examples of the violence Selīm inflicted on those around him—including, but not limited to, Hersekzāde Aḥmed Pasha (d. 1516), Dūḳaginzāde Aḥmed Pasha (d. 1514), Pīrī Meḥmed Pasha (d. 1523), İskender Pasha (d. 1515), Tācīzāde Caʿfer Çelebi (d. 1515), Muṣṭafā Pasha (d. 1513), and Yūnus Pasha (d. 1517)—see Ḥaydar, *Rūznāme*, 464, 467, 476, 492. For other references on this subject, see also Chapters 3 and 4.

6. Anonymous, *Tārīḫ* (TSMK R.1099), 117b.

7. Although *Ġāzī* and *Ḫüdāvendigār* were standard elements in Ottoman dynastic titulature, the former was used specifically as an epithet for the earliest leaders of the Ottoman enterprise, ʿO̱smān Beg (r. ?–1324?) and Orḫān Beg (r. 1324? –1362), whereas the latter was generally reserved for Murād I (r. 1362–1389). Due to his expansionist policies and his swiftness on the battlefield, Bāyezīd I (r. 1389–1402) was remembered as *Yıldırım*. As the Ottoman ruler who captured Constantinople in 1453, Meḥmed II (r. 1444–1446 and 1451–1481) was dubbed *Fātiḥ* or *Ebū'l-fetḥ*, whereas Bāyezīd II's personal piety and policy of restoring the status of arable lands previously confiscated by his father appear to have earned him the nicknames *Velī* and *Ṣofu*.

8. Although over time *yāvuz* also acquired alternative meanings with positive connotations (e.g., "efficient," "excellent," "resolute," "indefatigable," etc.), in fifteenth- and sixteenth-century dictionaries and collections of proverbs the term appears to have carried exclusively inauspicious overtones (e.g., "stern," "evil," "ferocious," "violent," "nasty," "bad," and "inclement"). For numerous examples, see Aksoy and Dilçin (eds.), *Tanıklarıyla Tarama Sözlüğü*, vol. 6, 4418–33; and Onat, "'Yavuz' ve Bununla İlgili Bazı Kelimelerimizin Arap Diline Geçmiş Şekilleri." Although T. E. Colebrooke noted that "this cultivated savage better deserved the name *Yáwuz*, a Turkish word meaning cruel or inflexible, applied to him by his subjects," there is no textual evidence that this epithet was indeed used during Selīm's lifetime. See Colebrooke, "On the Proper Names of the Mohammadans," 231.

9. See, for example, Tansel, *Yavuz Sultan Selim*; Uğur, *Yavuz Sultan Selim*; and Öztuna, *Yavuz Sultan Selim*.

10. Most of these appellations are posthumously acquired. The earliest mention of *Ḳānūnī* as Süleymān I's epithet, for example, appears to date to the early eighteenth century. See Kafadar, "The Myth of the Golden Age," 41n7.

11. Anonymous, *Ḳavānīn-i yeñiçeriyān*, 155/108b. Judging by the author's mention of the suppression of the Celālī uprisings (3/1b), the work must have been composed after 1609. The second earliest reference is in a reform treatise penned in 1633 by an Ottoman statesman. See ʿAzīz Efendi, *Ḳānūnnāme-i Sulṭānī*, 132/73a.

12. The work in question was copied by a certain Yūsuf Saʿdī in 1264/1847. Anonymous, *Ḥikāyet-i ẓuhūr-ı āl-i ʿOs̱mān* (SK Fatih 4206), 68/75a: "çāre nedür o oġlān öyle yāvuz oldı."

13. For a detailed study of Selīm I's reign, see Tansel, *Yavuz Sultan Selim*; and Emecen, *Zamanın İskenderi, Şarkın Fatihi*. For a concise account, see Finkel, *Osman's Dream*, 102–14.

14. Ottoman sources refer to popular traditions that allude to Selīm's decree that the royal treasury (*ḫazīne-i hümāyūn*) be sealed with his seal (*mühr*) unless one of his descendants succeeded in filling it with more gold. That the custom of sealing the royal treasury with Selīm's seal was sustained until the collapse of the Ottoman Empire attests to Selīm's unique achievement in accumulating treasures. On this tradition, see Uzunçarşılı, *Osmanlı Devletinin Saray Teşkilâtı*, 79, 319; and Necipoğlu, *Architecture, Ceremonial, and Power*, 134, 285n46.

15. Luṭfī, *Tevārīḫ*, 243: "Sulṭān Selīm bu dünyānuñ zaḥmetin çeküb ve ḫār-u-ḫāşākın giderüb bāġ-u-būstān eyledi ve Sulṭān Süleymān zaḥmetsiz ve meşaḳḳatsiz ol bāġ-u-būstānuñ yemişlerin taṣarruf idüb mütenāvil eyledi." Writing in the seventeenth century, Ottoman chronicler İbrāhīm Peçevī (d. 1649)

emphasized another advantage of the manner in which Süleymān acceded to the throne by stating that "there is no doubt or dispute that [Süleymān's] non-committing of unlawful bloodshed of anyone innocent at the time of his enthronement, due to the fact that [other] heirs to the throne and majesty were deceased, indicates that he would prosper not only in this world, but in the other world as well [eṣnā-yı cülūs-ı hümāyūnlarında tezāhüm-i vereṣe-i cāh-ü-celāl iḥtimālından bir bī-günāhuñ ḫūn-ı nā-ḥaḳına girilmedigi dünyāları gibi āḫiretleri daḫī maʿmūr olmasına dāl idügi maḥall-i iştibāh-ü-cidāl degildür]." Peçevī, *Tārīḫ* (1283), vol. 1, 3.

16. İsmail Hâmi Danişmend, *İzahlı Osmanlı Tarihi Kronolojisi*, vol. 2, 5. Based on this narrative tradition, Anthony Dolphin Alderson mentions Princes ʿAbdullāh, Maḥmūd, and Murād as those executed but gives a date of execution (November 20, 1514) that was *after* the Battle of Çaldıran (August 23, 1514). See Alderson, *The Structure of the Ottoman Dynasty*. For a critical evaluation of the accuracy of Alderson's data, see Peirce, *The Imperial Harem*, 307n143.

17. Translation by Leslie Peirce. For a discussion of the question of succession as one of Süleymān's major preoccupations and for an analysis and the translation of the relevant section of Postel's account, entitled *De la République des Turcs*, see Peirce, *The Imperial Harem*, 84–86 and 230, respectively.

18. Guistinian, *Alla Porta Ottomana*, 48. For a discussion of the internal dynastic policies followed by Selīm, see Peirce, *The Imperial Harem*, 84–86.

19. Among others, see Veinstein, ed., *Soliman le magnifique et son temps*; and İnalcık and Kafadar, eds., *Süleymân the Second and His Time*.

20. For the clearest expression of this argument, see Şahin, *Empire and Power in the Reign of Süleyman*, 23–28. See also Buzov, "The Lawgiver and His Lawmakers," 19–26. It has been recently argued that "as Selīm's military campaigns and conquests laid the foundations of a nascent empire, the Ottoman state translated the empire's changing cultural, geographic, and demographic structure into a new imperial outlook." Emiralioğlu, *Geographical Knowledge and Imperial Culture in the Early Modern Ottoman Empire*, 21.

21. I borrow the phrase "political theology" from Ernst H. Kantorowicz's pioneering work, *The King's Two Bodies: A Study in Mediaeval Political Theology*.

22. Given the material constraints of the time, Selīm's military achievements—particularly his launch of three full-scale expeditions within three years—were certainly noteworthy. For the technological, financial, physical/environmental, and motivational limitations on Ottoman warfare during the early modern era, see Murphey, *Ottoman Warfare*, 13–34.

23. For various sources on the strength of the Ottoman and Safavid armies on the battlefield at Çaldıran, see Tekindağ, "Yeni Kaynak ve Vesikaların Işığı Altında

Yavuz Sultan Selim'in İran Seferi," 65–66; Bacqué-Grammont, *Les Ottomans, les Safavides et leurs voisins*, 49; and *İA*, s.v. "Çaldıran Muharebesi" (M. T. Gökbilgin). Safavid sources not only refer to the Ottomans' "relentless arms beyond what the imagination can picture, or the pen describe" but also highlight the Ottoman musketeers' remarkable competence, noting that "they have such skill and power in firing their guns that they can hit the indivisible atom a mile away." See Ḥasan Rūmlū, *Aḥsanu't-tawārīkh*, trans. Charles Norman Seddon, vol. 2, 68. Another contemporary Persian historian, Ghiyās al-Dīn Muḥammad Ḥusaynī, known as Khwandamīr (d. 1534), emphasized the Ottomans' military superiority by stating that "Sultan Selīm's forces were as innumerable as the motions of the celestial spheres, and they fought with all their might with their cannons and matchlocks, firing five to six thousand matchlocks at a time and obscuring the heavens with smoke." See Khwandamīr, *Tārīkh-i ḥabīb al-siyar*, trans. W. M. Thackston, 605–6. On the organization of the Safavid army under Shāh Ismāʿīl, see Floor, *Safavid Government Institutions*, 128–33.

24. Contemporary sources mention that at Marj Dabik the Ottoman army deployed three hundred—according to some sources, eight hundred—cannons and twenty thousand janissary musketeers against Qānṣūh al-Ghawrī (r. 1501–1516), whose army had none of either; at Ridaniyya, Ṭūmānbāy (r. 1516–1517) countered the Ottomans with two hundred cannons. For sources on the relative military power of the Ottomans and Mamluks at Marj Dabik and Ridaniyya, see Tansel, *Yavuz Sultan Selim*, 137–41 and 164–69, respectively. On the extent to which the Mamluks made use of gunpowder technologies in the last decades of their rule, see Ayalon, *Gunpowder and Firearms in the Mamluk Kingdom*, especially 46–133.

25. For a discussion of the Ottoman-Safavid conflict during the reign of Selīm I, see Allouche, *The Origins and the Development of the Ottoman-Safavid Conflict*, 104–30; and Bacqué-Grammont, *Les Ottomans, les Safavides et leurs voisins*, 50–274.

26. On Ottoman-Mamluk relations prior to Selīm I's reign, see Cihan Yüksel Muslu, *The Ottomans and the Mamluks*. On the Ottoman conquest of Egypt and Syria and the consolidation of Ottoman power in Mamluk lands, see Lellouch, *Les Ottomans en Égypte*, especially 1–36. For the impact of the Ottoman conquest on the political, social, and cultural history of Egypt, see the articles in Lellouch and Michel, *Conquête ottomane de l'Égypte*.

27. It has been claimed that Selīm, had he lived long enough, would have created an Islamic world empire extending to the Indian Ocean. See Asrar, *Kanunî Sultan Süleyman Devrinde Osmanlı Devletinin Dinî Siyaseti ve İslam Âlemi*, 44–59.

28. Kemālpaşazāde relates that the Sunnī religious scholars invited by Selīm to the imperial council gave legal opinions in support of a campaign against the Ḳızılbaş. See Kemālpaşazāde, *Tevārīḫ*, vol. 9, 127a/96.

29. For the texts and facsimiles of these legal opinions, see Tekindağ, "Yeni Kaynak ve Vesikaların Işığı Altında Yavuz Sultan Selim'in İran Seferi." For an analysis of the legal opinions sanctioning war against the Safavids, see Üstün, "Heresy and Legitimacy in the Ottoman Empire in the Sixteenth Century," 35–59. Here we need to note Richard Cooper Repp's important observation that neither Ṣarugürz's nor Kemālpaşazāde's "statement should perhaps be termed a fetva since both are explicitly aimed at Shāh Ismāʿīl and are not cast in the traditional impersonal form; but both may be essays based originally on fetvas." For a succinct discussion of the religious opinions that established the legality of war against the Safavids and the Mamluks, see Repp, *The Müfti of Istanbul*, 212–21. On the life and works of Kemālpaşazāde, see Saraç, *Şeyhülislam Kemal Paşazade*; Uğur, *Kemal Paşa-zade İbn-Kemal*. It is noteworthy that Selīm repeated these arguments in his letters of victory (*fetḥnāme*) addressed to numerous Muslim rulers, commanders, and notables in the Crimea, Kurdistan, and Central Asia. See Ferīdūn Beg, ed., *Münşeʾātü's-selāṭīn*, 1:386–96.

30. Ottoman sources relate that Selīm ordered the recording of the names of the Anatolian Ḳızılbaş in registers (*defter*) before proceeding to massacre more than forty thousand of them by the sword. Ostensibly he did this to guard the Ottoman army's rear from potential Ḳızılbaş harassment while heading toward the Safavid realm. For the relevant section in İdrīs-i Bidlīsī's *Salīmshāhnāma*, see Tekindağ, "Yeni Kaynak ve Vesikaların Işığı Altında Yavuz Sultan Selim'in İran Seferi," 56.

31. Bacqué-Grammont, *Les Ottomans, les Safavides et leurs voisins*, 274.

32. Tekindağ, "Yeni Kaynak ve Vesikaların Işığı Altında Yavuz Sultan Selim'in İran Seferi," 55.

33. See *EI*[2], s.v. "Harb" (M. Khadduri).

34. Bacqué-Grammont, *Les Ottomans, les Safavides et leurs voisins*, 195–97.

35. ʿĀlī, *Künhü'l-aḥbār*, vol. 2, 1164. Although explicitly directed against the Safavids and their Anatolian supporters, a similar position had already been articulated by Mevlānā Nūreddīn Ḥamza Ṣarugürz: "According to the prescripts of the holy law . . . we give an opinion according to which [the Ḳızılbaş whose chief is Ismāʿīl of Ardabil] are unbelievers and heretics. Any who sympathize with them and accept their false religion or assist them are also unbelievers and heretics. It is a necessity and a divine obligation that they be massacred and their communities dispersed." For the text of this legal opinion, see Tekindağ, "Yeni Kaynak ve Vesikaların Işığı Altında Yavuz Sultan Selim'in İran Seferi," 54–55. For an analysis of the politico-religious context of Ottoman *fetvās* against the Safavids and the Mamluks, see Finkel, *Osman's Dream*, 104–10 (Finkel's translation of the relevant section from Ṣarugürz's opinion is on page 104). On the authorship of this religious opinion, see Repp, *The Müfti of Istanbul*, 212–21.

36. Rhoads Murphey notes that "for a variety of reasons and most particularly because of the costs involved . . . the Ottomans could manage such full-scale mobilizations for war in the East only once or twice per century. [Murād IV's] record-breaking feat of mounting back-to-back sultanic campaigns in 1635 and 1638 was so exceptional as to inspire the construction of matching commemorative pavilions in the Topkapi Palace compound in Istanbul." Similarly, Selīm's successive military achievements on the eastern front were also exceptions to the rule. For an assessment of Ottoman military manpower and military spending in the early modern era, see Murphey, *Ottoman Warfare*, 35–63, quotation from page 6.

37. For the origins and development of the *tīmār* system and its foundational role in the Ottoman military-administrative structure, see *EI*[2], s.v. "Tīmār" (H. İnalcık).

38. For the impact of the rise of the Safavids on various Anatolian communities, see Sohrweide, "Der Sieg der Safaviden in Persien und Seine Rückwirkungen auf die Shiiten Anatoliens im 16. Jahrhundert," 138–64; Yıldırım, "Turkomans between Two Empires," 245–415; and Sümer, *Safevî Devletinin Kuruluşu ve Gelişmesinde Anadolu Türklerinin Rolü*. On the prominent role played by disgruntled timariots in the popular uprisings in Anatolia, see Tekindağ, "Şah Kulu Baba Tekeli İsyanı" (1967), 35–36; and Uluçay, "Yavuz Sultan Selim Nasıl Padişah Oldu?" (1953), especially 61–67.

39. Meḥmed II's centralizing policies included the transformation into military fiefs (*tīmār*) of privately owned lands (*mülk*) and lands that belonged to pious endowments (*vaḳıf*). See Babinger, *Mehmed the Conqueror and His Time*, 447; and Beldiceanu, "Recherches sur la réforme foncière de Mehmed II." Fifteenth-century historian Ṭursun Beg states that Meḥmed II confiscated more than one thousand villages or estates and converted them to military prebends. See Ṭursun Beg, *Tārīḫ-i ebū'l-fetḥ* (Tulum edition, 197; İnalcık and Murphey edition, 169a). Earlier in the text, the number of confiscated estates is given as "twenty thousand" (Tulum edition, 22; İnalcık and Murphey edition, 18a).

40. Selīm mandated the timariots to attend military campaigns in person instead of sending proxies to fight in their place. See Beldiceanu-Steinherr and Bacqué-Grammont, "A propos de quelques causes de malaises sociaux en Anatolie Centrale," 76–78.

41. Beldiceanu-Steinherr and Bacqué-Grammont, "A propos de quelques causes de malaises sociaux en Anatolie Centrale," 77.

42. Halil İnalcık notes that Selīm recognized "*mülkiyyet* or freehold rights on their *yurdluḳ* land, and *odjaḳlıḳ*, *ḥukūmet* or internal autonomy to the nine Kurdish *sandjaḳ-beys*" in the province of Amed (Diyarbakır). See *EI*[2], s.v. "Tīmār" (H. İnalcık).

43. Based on the work of Beldiceanu-Steinherr and Bacqué-Grammont, Finkel also argues that "land rights which had been formerly been heritable were now bestowed at the whim of the sultan." For a succinct evaluation of how Selīm's strategies extended the Ottomans' sphere of influence in eastern and southeastern Anatolia, see Finkel, *Osman's Dream*, 106–7.

44. Hence Heath Lowry's legitimate statement: "the question of who conquered whom is debatable." See Lowry, *The Nature of the Early Ottoman State*, 96.

45. Şahin, *Empire and Power in the Reign of Süleyman*, 28.

46. On İbrāhīm Pasha's mission to Egypt, see Turan, "The Sultan's Favorite," 223–33; Şahin, *Empire and Power in the Reign of Süleyman*, 53–59; and Lellouch, *Les Ottomans en Égypte*, 62–66.

47. Tansel, *Yavuz Sultan Selim*, 205. On the fiscal administration of the Empire in the aftermath of Selīm's conquests, which required increases both in the number of financial offices and the number of officers and secretaries employed in the management of imperial revenue sources, see Aydın and Günalan, *XV-XVI. Yüzyıllarda Osmanlı Maliyesi ve Defter Sistemi*, 23–29; and Darling, *Revenue-Raising and Legitimacy*, 51–57.

48. Tansel, *Yavuz Sultan Selim*, 196.

49. On the financial and administrative institutions through which the Ottomans ruled Egypt, see Shaw, *The Financial and Administrative Organization and Development of Ottoman Egypt*; Winter, *Egyptian Society under Ottoman Rule*; and Hathaway, *The Arab Lands under Ottoman Rule*.

50. Prominent statesman and historian Celālzāde Muṣṭafā (d. 1567) entered Ottoman service in 1516. For an analysis of his life and work, see Şahin, *Empire and Power in the Reign of Süleyman*. Religious scholar, historian, and chief jurisconsult (*şeyḫü'l-islām*) Kemālpaşazāde (d. 1534) and grand vizier Pīrī Meḥmed Pasha (d. 1523) rose to prominence during Selīm's reign and continued to serve his son Süleymān. Luṭfī Pasha (d. 1563) not only served Selīm and Süleymān in various capacities but also composed a chronicle (*Tevārīḫ-i āl-i ʿOṣmān*) and a work of advice (*Āṣafnāme*) during the reign of the latter, after he briefly held the grand vizierate.

51. See, for example, Şükrī, *Selīmnāme*, 12a–17b; and İsḥaḳ, *Selīmnāme*, 10a–12b. The term *Ḳızılbaş* (lit. "Red-Head") is derived from the distinctive crimson hat worn by the disciples of the Safavid sheikhs. The twelve gores of the hat symbolized the "Twelve Imāms" of Ithnā ʿAsharī Shīʿism. For the origins, varied meanings, and historical significance of the term, see *EI²*, s.v. "Ḳızıl-bāsh" (R. M. Savory). Savory also explains that "the *ḳızıl-bāsh*, as the *murīds* of the Safawid *shaykhs*, owed implicit obedience to their leader in his capacity as their *murshid-i kāmil* ('supreme spiritual director'). After the establishment of the Safawid state,

the Safawid *shāhs* transferred this *pīr-murīdī* relationship from the religious to the political plane, since they were now not only their followers' *murshid-i kāmil* but their king (*pādishāh*) as well."

52. There is no indication that Selīm claimed the title caliph (*ḫalīfe*), which could have aided him in legitimizing his claim to sovereignty over the entire Islamic world.

53. This claim rested on a genealogy that traced the Safavid lineage back to the seventh imam, Mūsā al-Kāẓim (d. 799). For biographical and historical information on Shāh Ismāʿīl, see, for example, Newman, *Safavid Iran*, 13–25.

54. On the question of confessionalization within the early modern Ottoman context, see Krstić, *Contested Conversions to Islam*.

55. For a brief account of the historical development of this concept to denote the Muslim body politic, see Lewis, *The Political Language of Islam*, 32.

56. See Hess, "The Ottoman Conquest of Egypt (1517) and the Beginning of the Sixteenth-Century World War." On the involvement of the Safavids and several European polities in this competition, see Bacqué-Grammont, *Les Ottomans, les Safavides et leurs voisins*, 128–45.

57. See Casale, *The Ottoman Age of Exploration*, 25–33. On the impact of Selīm's international policies on the competition between the Ottomans and the Portuguese over control of the Red Sea and the Indian Ocean, see also Mazzaoui, "Global Policies of Sultan Selim."

58. For the Persian prologue to the Law Code of Niğbolu, composed in 1517, see BOA, Maliyeden Müdevver 11, 1b. For a discussion of the political, religious, and ideological significance of these terms, see Fleischer, "The Lawgiver as Messiah"; and Fleischer, *Bureaucrat and Intellectual in the Ottoman Empire*, 279–83. On the origins of the term *ṣāḥib-ḳırān* and its significance in the early modern Ottoman context, see Chann, "Lord of the Auspicious Conjunction."

59. Fleischer, "The Lawgiver as Messiah," 162–63. The expression *muʾayyad min Allāh* is more commonly rendered as *muʾayyad min ʿind Allāh*. For a discussion of late-sixteenth-century historian Muṣṭafā ʿAlī's use of this designation, see Fleischer, *Bureaucrat and Intellectual in the Ottoman Empire*, 279–81.

60. As long as one does not count the crushing defeat he suffered (against his father Bayezīd II at the Battle of Çorlu in the summer of 1511) while still a prince.

61. On the pre-Islamic origins and early uses of the term *ṣāḥib-ḳırān*, see Chann, "Lord of the Auspicious Conjunction," 93–96.

62. Maria Subtelny explains that Tīmūr adopted the honorific title *ṣāḥib-ḳırān* "as if to underscore the cosmic dimensions of his own perceived universalist mission." See Subtelny, *Timurids in Transition*, 11, 12.

63. Fleischer, "The Lawgiver as Messiah," 163.

64. On this point, see Buzov, "The Lawgiver and His Lawmakers," 19–23.

65. For a discussion of the Mediterranean and the larger Eurasian context, see, respectively, Parker, "The Place of Tudor England in the Messianic Vision of Phillip II of Spain"; and Subrahmanyam, "Connected Histories." For discussions of political theologies in the early modern Iranian and Mughal contexts, see Babayan, *Mystics, Monarchs, and Messiahs*; Babayan, "The Cosmological Order of Things in Early Modern Safavid Iran"; and Moin, *The Millennial Sovereign*, respectively. On Selīm's "cognizance of the religious and ideological currents washing the eastern Mediterranean" in the sixteenth century, see Fleischer, "The Lawgiver as Messiah," 162–64.

66. Fletcher uses "interconnection . . . to denote historical phenomena in which there is contact linking two or more societies, as, for example, the spread of an idea, institution, or religion, or the carrying on of a significant amount of trade between societies," whereas "horizontal continuity . . . denotes an economic, social, or cultural historical phenomenon experienced by two or more societies between which there is not necessarily any communication." See Fletcher, "Integrative History," 37.

67. Fletcher, "Integrative History," 47. Having represented a loosely connected philosophical, spiritual, and cultural landscape—at least since what Karl Jaspers referred to as the "Axial Age" (*Achsenzeit*)—Eurasia was transformed into a thoroughly connected economic, political, and cultural zone from the last quarter of the fifteenth century onward. Jaspers identifies this axis of history "in the spiritual process that occurred between 800 and 200 BC." See Jaspers, *Vom Ursprung und Ziel der Geschichte*, 1. For an articulation of the argument that Eurasia had constituted an interconnected entity since the Bronze Age, see Goody, *The Eurasian Miracle*, especially 41–93; and Bentley, *Old World Encounters*.

68. For the most recent articulation of this argument, see Şahin, *Empire and Power in the Reign of Süleyman*, 6–11. For a similar analysis of Southeast Asia as part of the larger early modern Eurasian context, see Lieberman, *Strange Parallels*, especially 66–84.

69. Kunt and Woodhead, *Süleyman the Magnificent and His Age;* Aksan and Goffman, *The Early Modern Ottomans;* Goffman, *The Ottoman Empire and Early Modern Europe;* Krstić, *Contested Conversions to Islam;* Darling, "Political Change and Political Discourse in the Early Modern Mediterranean World"; and Tezcan, *The Second Ottoman Empire.* For a critique of the term "early modern" as "hopelessly Eurocentric," see Goldstone, "The Problem of the 'Early Modern' World," especially 277. In the field of Ottoman history, "early modern" has nevertheless proven to be a useful chronological bracket to delineate the historical period

between roughly the mid-fifteenth and the mid-nineteenth centuries (or parts thereof). In her article "Locating the Ottomans among Early Modern Empires," Virginia Aksan uses the term "early modern" variably to refer to the 1600–1800 period.

70. Kafadar, "The Ottomans and Europe," especially 615–25. For Kafadar's discussion of the "shared discourse" and "shared rhythms" of the Ottoman and European worlds, see pages 620–23. Victor Lieberman identifies common trends throughout Eurasia in the early modern era, including but not limited to "territorial consolidation; firearms-aided intensification of warfare; more expansive, routinized administrative systems; growing commercialization; . . . wider popular literacy, along with a novel proliferation of vernacular texts; more vigorous dissemination of standard dialects and cultural symbols; and an unprecedented intersection between specifically local culture and state power." See the introduction to Lieberman, *Beyond Binary Histories;* the quotation is from page 14.

71. For this argument, see Şahin, *Empire and Power in the Reign of Süleyman*, especially 6–11. Şahin argues that the Ottoman experience constituted a "hinge" that connected Eurasia's eastern and western parts. His historical-geographical framework serves as an immediate model for this study.

72. For Marshall G. S. Hodgson's world-civilizational approach to Islamic history and the beguiling "gunpowder-empire hypothesis" he articulated with William H. McNeill, see Hodgson, *The Venture of Islam*, vol. 3: *The Gunpowder Empires and Modern Times.* See also Streusand, *Islamic Gunpowder Empires.*

73. See, for example, Dale, *The Muslim Empires of the Ottomans, Safavids, and Mughals*; Kunt, "The Later Muslim Empires"; and Ali, "Political Structures of the Islamic Orient."

74. Berktay, "Three Empires and the Societies They Governed." Even the utilization of a Marxian theoretical framework that generally ascribes modal idiosyncrasies to "Asian" military-agrarian regimes does not exclude the possibility of a comparison of the Ottomans with non-Islamic polities. See Berktay, "The Feudalism Debate."

75. See Subrahmanyam, "A Tale of Three Empires"; and Subrahmanyam, "The Fate of Empires."

76. On cultural exchanges across early modern Eurasia, including ideas on universal monarchy as well as millenarian and messianic expectations, see Subrahmanyam, "Connected Histories"; and Subrahmanyam, "Turning the Stones Over."

77. For a discussion of Ottoman succession practices and the significance of unigeniture within that context, see Kafadar, *Between Two Worlds*, 120, 136–38. Whether the practice of fratricide was indeed codified by Meḥmed II in his

ḳānūnnāme or was included in the code of laws at a time after his reign is a matter of scholarly debate. See, for example, Dilger, *Untersuchungen zur Geschichte des Osmanischen Hofzeremoniells*. Colin Imber argues that the relevant legal clause may have been added to the *ḳānūnnāme* in the sixteenth century "by either Selīm I or Meḥmed III, to justify their own manner of succession." See Imber, *The Ottoman Empire, 1300–1650*, 109.

78. For issues related to Ottoman succession, see İnalcık, "Osmanlılar'da Saltanat Verâseti Usûlü"; Alderson, *The Structure of the Ottoman Dynasty*, 4–16; Peirce, *The Imperial Harem*, 15–25, 79–86, 99–103; and Fletcher, "Turco-Mongolian Monarchic Tradition in the Ottoman Empire."

79. In the Ottoman context, "fratricide" was not understood in the strict literal sense of the term but was used more generally to refer to the killing of any male member(s) of the dynastic family. This was a pattern established with ʿOs̱mān Beg's murder of his uncle Dündar, which constituted a critical and decisive moment for Ottoman succession practices. See Kafadar, "ʿOs̱mān Beg and his Uncle"; and Alderson, *The Structure of the Ottoman Dynasty*, 5. For a scholarly analysis of the civil war between the sons of Bāyezīd I, see Kastritsis, *The Sons of Bayezid*. For the internecine strife between Süleymān I's princes, see Turan, *Kanuni Süleyman Dönemi Taht Kavgaları*. Leslie Peirce refers to the mode of Ottoman succession also as "open succession." See Peirce, *The Imperial Harem*, 25.

80. On the historiographical controversy surrounding Bāyezīd II's death, see Tekindağ, "Bayezid'in Ölümü Meselesi." For a discussion of varied textual representations of this event in *Selīmnāme* literature, see Çıpa, "The Centrality of the Periphery," 113–16.

81. See, for example, Allouche, *The Origins and the Development of the Ottoman-Safavid Conflict*; Bacqué-Grammont, *Les Ottomans, les Safavides et leurs voisins*; Lellouch, *Les Ottomans en Égypte*; Hathaway, *The Arab Lands under Ottoman Rule*, especially 35–58; and Shaw, *The Financial and Administrative Organization and Development of Ottoman Egypt*, especially 12–50.

82. The only study focusing exclusively on Selīm's rise to power is Çağatay Uluçay's lengthy article in three parts, published between 1953 and 1955. Uluçay's emphasis on the decisive role played by the janissaries in bringing Selīm to power has determined the tenor of the general assumptions made by later scholars of Ottoman history. See Uluçay, "Yavuz Sultan Selim Nasıl Padişah Oldu?" Chapters in other scholarly works treat Selīm's succession struggle as the last phase of his father's reign. These include but are not limited to Fisher, *The Foreign Relations of Turkey*, 95–104 (based exclusively on Venetian sources); and Tansel, *Sultan II. Bâyezit'in Siyasî Hayatı*, 258–306.

83. As a case in point, the uncritical appropriation of "Yāvuz" as Selīm's epithet in modern Turkish scholarship ignores the inauspicious connotations the term carried during Selīm's own lifetime.

84. Originally formulated by the right-wing nationalist Intellectuals' Hearths (*Aydınlar Ocakları*) in the 1970s, the doctrine of the "Turkish-Islamic Synthesis" became a principal tenet of the Turkish Republic's official ideology after the 1980 coup and aided the rise of a Sunnī-sectarian variant of political Islam in Turkey. See Eligür, *The Mobilization of Political Islam in Turkey*. For a critique of the current state of Ottoman historical studies, see Berktay, "The Search for the Peasant in Western and Turkish History/Historiography."

85. For the most recent proponent of this view, see Emecen, *Zamanın İskenderi, Şarkın Fatihi*. Although the title of Emecen's monograph, "Alexander of the Age, Conqueror of the East," is reminiscent of the eulogizing language of Ottoman chroniclers, the nationalistic—even chauvinistic—sentiment of the work hints at the privileged place Selīm continues to occupy in modern Turkish popular historical consciousness and the rhetoric of Turkish political Islam.

86. Uluçay, "Yavuz Sultan Selim Nasıl Padişah Oldu?"; Tekindağ, "Bayezid'in Ölümü Meselesi"; Tekindağ, "Yeni Kaynak ve Vesikaların Işığı Altında Yavuz Sultan Selim'in İran Seferi"; Tekindağ, "Şah Kulu Baba Tekeli İsyanı"; Uluçay, "Bayazıd II.'in Ailesi"; and Tansel, *Sultan II. Bâyezit'in Siyasî Hayatı*, 258–310. The fact that the Turkish government's announcement, on May 29, 2013, of the name of the third Bosphorus bridge as "Yavuz Sultan Selim" was among the principal grievances voiced by those who participated in the Gezi Park protests of 2013, the largest popular resistance movement in the history of the Republic of Turkey, is indicative of the controversial place Selīm occupies in Turkish popular memory. While those with a Turkish-nationalist, Sunnī-Islamist, or neo-Ottomanist mindset remember Selīm fondly as the sultan who confirmed the Ottomans' claim to supremacy in Islamdom, members of the disenfranchised ʿAlevī minority consider him the personification of "annihilationist policies against the ʿAlevīs" and refer to him as "the executioner of ʿAlevīs."

87. See, for example, Tekindağ, "Selim-nâmeler"; and Uğur, *The Reign of Sultan Selīm I in the Light of the Selīm-nāme Literature*. Uğur's ambitious title misinforms its readers, as the work provides an account of the reign of Selīm I through one *Selīmnāme* only, without analyzing the divergences between different accounts or assessing the credibility of various inconsistent statements.

88. Here I take my cue from Peter Burke's pioneering work on the role played by literary and visual representations in shaping the royal images of Charles V (Holy Roman Emperor, r. 1500–1558) and Louis XIV (King of France and Navarre, r. 1643–1715) for a contemporary audience as well as for posterity.

On myth-making and mythification, see Burke, "Presenting and Re-presenting Charles V," 425.

89. Assmann, *Moses the Egyptian*, 8–9. In his study of the historiography of the deposition and subsequent assassination of ʿOs̱mān II (r. 1618–1622), Gabriel Piterberg deploys a similar approach and focuses on the formation of varied narratives of that dramatic episode in Ottoman history. See Piterberg, *An Ottoman Tragedy*. For a critical review of Piterberg's study, see Hagen, "Review of *An Ottoman Tragedy*."

90. Burke, *The Fabrication of Louis XIV*; and Burke, "Presenting and Re-presenting Charles V."

91. Burke, "Presenting and Re-presenting Charles V," 393. Acknowledging that "memory operates under the pressure of challenges and alternatives," Natalie Zemon Davis and Randolph Starn similarly juxtapose "memory" and "counter-memory." See Davis and Starn, "Introduction," 2.

92. Burke, *The Fabrication of Louis XIV*, 1.

93. On myth-making and mythification, see Burke, "Presenting and Re-presenting Charles V," 425.

94. On mnemohistory and its functions, see Assmann, *Moses the Egyptian*, 8–17.

95. Assmann, *Moses the Egyptian*, 14. The textual representation of key personae in Islamicate history writing has been the subject of numerous studies. On the historiographical deconstruction/reconstruction of the Prophet Muḥammad's wife ʿĀʾisha and the Abbasid caliphs, for example, see, respectively, Spellberg, *Politics, Gender, and the Islamic Past*; and El-Hibri, *Reinterpreting Islamic Historiography*.

96. I do not share Nora's cynical view that history "is perpetually suspicious of memory, and its true mission is to suppress and destroy it" or that its "goal and ambition is not to exalt but to annihilate what has in reality taken place." See Nora, "Between Memory and History," 8–9.

97. Halil Berktay identifies "nationalism, state-fetishism, [and] document-fetishism" as the three most pertinent problems afflicting modern Turkish scholarship in the field of Ottoman historical studies. See Berktay, "The Search for the Peasant in Western and Turkish History/Historiography."

98. See especially Spiegel, "History, Historicism, and the Social Logic of the Text"; and Spiegel, "Towards a Theory of the Middle Ground." For Ankersmit's discussion of "the *juste milieu*," see, in particular, "The Linguistic Turn: Literary Theory and Historical Theory," in *Historical Representation*, 29–74. For an exemplary utilization of the approach articulated by Spiegel and Ankersmit as an interpretive framework for sixteenth-century Ottoman historiography, see Şahin, "Imperialism, Bureaucratic Consciousness, and the Historian's Craft."

99. Spiegel, "History, Historicism, and the Social Logic of the Text."
100. Kastritsis, *The Sons of Bayezid*; and Turan, *Kanuni Süleyman Dönemi Taht Kavgaları*.

1. Politics of Succession

1. Muradiye is a quiet neighborhood in Bursa, the first Ottoman capital. Named after the Complex (*külliye*) of Murād II (r. 1421–1444, 1446–1451), it is also the location of twelve royal mausolea (*türbe*) belonging to numerous members of the Ottoman dynastic family, several of whom were executed as a result of brutal succession struggles, including those executed by Selīm's orders. Muradiye is the final resting place of Selīm's rival brother Aḥmed and his nephews Mūsā, Orḫān, and Emīr. Selīm's other rival brother, Ḳorḳud, is buried also in Bursa, in the mausoleum of Orḫān Beg. Prominent novelist Ahmet Hamdi Tanpınar (d. 1962) poignantly referred to the site as "the bitter fruit of patience," undoubtedly with these historical events in mind.

2. Tezcan, "The Politics of Early Modern Ottoman Historiography," 186.

3. For an examination of the various expressions of this potential for conflict within the context of Ottoman ceremonies of the "girding of the sword" (*ḳılıç ḳuşanma*), see Kafadar, "Eyüp'te Kılıç Kuşanma Törenleri."

4. As a rule of succession, seniority was codified in the Constitution (*Ḳānūn-ı esāsī*) of 1876. For issues related to Ottoman succession, see İnalcık, "Osmanlılar'da Saltanat Verâseti Usûlü"; Alderson, *The Structure of the Ottoman Dynasty*, 4–16; Peirce, *The Imperial Harem*, 15–25, 79–86, 99–103; and Fletcher, "Turco-Mongolian Monarchic Tradition in the Ottoman Empire." On the changing role of the Ottoman dynasty as symbolized by what Baki Tezcan calls the consolidation of "the rule of seniority" in the later seventeenth century, see Tezcan, "The Politics of Early Modern Ottoman Historiography," 184–97. It is noteworthy that not even age is mentioned as a relevant factor for rulership in Meḥmed II's *Ḳānūnnāme*.

5. Alderson, *The Structure of the Ottoman Dynasty*, 5.

6. See, for example, Peirce, *The Imperial Harem*, 96.

7. According to Halil İnalcık, the Ottomans' eschewal of restrictive traditions that would assign rulership to a specific member of the dynasty was based on the same principle upheld by Turkish states from time immemorial. On this particular argument and on the concept of *ḳut* and its utilization by Turco-Mongol dynasties, see İnalcık, "Osmanlılar'da Saltanat Verâseti Usûlü," 73–82.

8. As Muslim rulers of an Islamicate polity, the Ottomans also were heirs to the Islamic political tradition and theory, which considered both the body

politic and sovereign power to be ordained by God. See Lewis, *Political Language of Islam*, Chapter 2, especially 25–26.

9. On the meaning of *dawla* and its political use in early Islamic history, see Lewis, *The Political Language of Islam*, Chapter 2, especially 35–37. For Ottoman use of the concept of *devlet*, see Tezcan, *The Second Ottoman Empire*, 60–61; Tezcan, "The Politics of Early Modern Ottoman Historiography," 186–87; and Kastritsis, *The Sons of Bayezid*, 200–203.

10. On the Ottoman practice of unigeniture, see Kafadar, *Between Two Worlds*, 120, 136–38.

11. Despite their potentially devastating effects, succession wars also served to reaffirm the unity of the Ottoman imperial realm and to reinforce the dynastic sovereignty of the House of ʿOs̱mān. Other early modern Islamicate polities operated within similar parameters. For striking parallels between Ottoman and Mughal struggles of succession as exemplified by the conflict between the sons of the Mughal emperor Shāh Jahān (r. 1628–1658), see Richards, *The Mughal Empire*, 151–64. I am grateful to Douglas Howard for this reference.

12. See *Ḳānūnnāme-i āl-i ʿOs̱mān*, 18: "ve her kimesneye evlādumdan salṭanat müyesser ola ḳarındaşların niẓām-ı ʿālem içün ḳatl itmek münāsibdür eks̱er-i ʿulemā dah̯ī tecvīz itmişdür." Based on Konrad Dilger's demonstration that the *Ḳānūnnāme* "contains material which patently belongs to a period after the reign of Mehmed II," Colin Imber argues that "this clause is, in all probability, a sixteenth century addition to the 'Law Book,' by either Selim I or Mehmed III, to justify their own manner of accession, and represents an attempt to combat popular revulsion at what had happened" (although Dilger mentions Murād III's accession rather than that of Meḥmed III). See Dilger, *Untersuchungen zur Geschichte des osmanischen Hofzeremoniells*, 14–34; and Imber, *The Ottoman Empire, 1300–1650*, 109, 332. I find Dilger's argument—that the text of the Vienna manuscript is a modified version of the original *Ḳānūnnāme*—convincing. In light of Meḥmed II's centralist policies aimed at preventing the fragmentation of the imperial realm, however, I do not agree with the assumption that the particular clause addressing fratricide was a later addition to justify the succession of later sultans, especially as some of Meḥmed II's own actions were in need of justification; for example, immediately after his accession, Meḥmed II ordered the execution of his one-year-old brother, Aḥmed. For Meḥmed's execution of his brother, see Neşrī, *Kitāb-ı cihānnümā*, vol. 2, 683. For a detailed discussion of the "fratricide clause" and the most recent argument for its authenticity, see, respectively, Özcan, "Fâtih'in Teşkilât Kanunnâmesi ve Nizam-ı Alem İçin Kardeş Katli Meselesi"; and *Ḳānūnnāme-i āl-i ʿOs̱mān*, xxiii-xxxiv. For a general discussion of Ottoman fratricide, see Akman, *Osmanlı Devletinde Kardeş Katli*. On the notion

of the Ottoman "world order," see Hagen, "Legitimacy and World Order," especially 55–57. Hagen emphasizes that the term *niẓām-ı ʿālem* "stands for theoretical concepts which follow historically contingent sociopolitical dynamics."

13. In the Ottoman context, "fratricide" was not understood in the strict literal sense of the term but more generally, to refer to the killing of any male member(s) of the dynastic family.

14. For a discussion of the public outcry bemoaning the practice of fratricide by Murād III and Meḥmed III, see Peirce, *The Imperial Harem*, 101–3. Even after Meḥmed II's legalization of the practice, dynastic fratricide remained controversial well into the beginning of the nineteenth century. For a complete list of Ottoman fratricides, see Alderson, *The Structure of the Ottoman Dynasty*, 30–31.

15. Peirce, *The Imperial Harem*, 25. Peirce refers to the mode of Ottoman succession also as "open succession."

16. For Fletcher's definition of this "central element in the dynamics of Turkish, Mongolian, and Manchurian politics" at the tribal level, see Fletcher, "The Mongols," 17. For a discussion of tanistry as it applies to the Ottoman case, see Fletcher, "Turco-Mongolian Monarchic Tradition in the Ottoman Empire."

17. On enthronement by seniority, see Tezcan, *The Second Ottoman Empire*, 72–78.

18. For the meaning and historical significance of this expression, see Tezcan, *The Second Ottoman Empire*, 60–61; Tezcan, "The Politics of Early Modern Ottoman Historiography," 186–87; and Aksoy and Dilçin, eds., *Tanıklarıyla Tarama Sözlüğü*, vol. 5, 3434.

19. İnalcık, "Osmanlılar'da Saltanat Verâseti Usûlü," 73.

20. İnalcık, "Osmanlılar'da Saltanat Verâseti Usûlü," 94.

21. Ottoman documents from the Topkapı Palace Museum Archives (Topkapı Sarayı Müzesi Arşivi, TSMA) are listed according to their catalogue numbers; "D" denotes a register (*defter*) and "E" stands for a single document (*evrak*). Venetian documents are listed chronologically and consist of *relazioni*, ambassadorial reports delivered to the Senate. They were collected in summary fashion by Marino Sanuto (d. 1536) and published under the title *I Diarii di Marino Sanuto* (58 vols.) between 1879 and 1903.

22. For the dates of death of Bāyezīd II's sons, see Alderson, *The Structure of the Ottoman Dynasty*, table 28: ʿAbdullāh (d. 1483), Maḥmūd (d. 1507), Meḥmed (d. 1507), ʿAlemşāh (d. 1510), Şehinşāh (d. 1511).

23. For a discussion of Ottomans' strict adherence to unigeniture as the principle of succession, see Kafadar, *Between Two Worlds*, Chapter 3, particularly 120–21, 136–38. For Meḥmed II's definitive statement concerning fratricide in his code of law, see *Ḳānūnnāme-i āl-i ʿOs̱mān*, 18.

24. For the internecine strife between Ottoman princes during the civil war of 1402–1413, see Kastritsis, *The Sons of Bayezid*.

25. For the location of all cities and the approximate borders of provinces mentioned in this chapter, see maps 25 (Anatolia), 26 (Rumelia), and 30 (Black Sea) in Pitcher, *An Historical Geography of the Ottoman Empire*.

26. See imperial decree dated May 1503, TSMA E.6536.

27. Uluçay, "Yavuz Sultan Selim Nasıl Padişah Oldu?," (1953), 59. See also Ṣolaḳzāde, *Tārīḫ* (TSMK E.H.1416), 21b.

28. Saʿdeddīn, *Tācü't-tevārīḫ*, vol. 2, 168.

29. On Ḳorḳud's stay in Egypt, see Uzunçarşılı, "IIinci Bayezid'in Oğullarından Sultan Korkut," 549–58. On his reception at the Mamluk court, see Ibn Iyās, *Badāʾiʿ al-zuhūr*, vol. 4, 157. Ḳorḳud's failure was probably due to a letter of warning sent to the Mamluk court by Bāyezīd II. See Marin de Molin's *relazione* (5 January 1510), summarized in Sanuto, *I Diarii*, vol. 9, 27.

30. For a detailed analysis of the treatise Ḳorḳud sent to Bāyezīd II in an attempt to justify his actions, see al-Tikriti, "The Ḥajj as Justifiable Self-Exile." Also see Uluçay, "Yavuz Sultan Selim Nasıl Padişah Oldu?," (1953), 59; and Marin de Molin's *relazione* (10 August 1510), summarized in Sanuto, *I Diarii*, vol. 10, 76.

31. See Ḳorḳud's letter to Bāyezīd II, TSMA E.2597.

32. See Ḳorḳud's letter to his sister, TSMA E.5587.

33. According to Venetian sources, Ḳorḳud was transferred to Manisa by Bāyezīd II, which, given the circumstances, is extremely unlikely. See Nicolò Zustignan's *relazione* (28 August 1510), summarized in Sanuto, *I Diarii*, vol. 11, 418. In an attempt to depict Ḳorḳud as an apolitical figure, Kemālpaşazāde states that the reason for the prince's departure from his gubernatorial seat was the "animal-like" and unruly population of his province. See Kemālpaşazāde, *Tevārīḫ*, vol. 8 (1985), 42.

34. Aḥmed even suggested that he be appointed commander of imperial forces to punish his brother Ḳorḳud. See Saʿdeddīn, *Tācü't-tevārīḫ*, vol. 2, 169. For Selīm's request, see his petition to Bāyezīd II, TSMA E.5970.

35. Saʿdeddīn, *Tācü't-tevārīḫ*, vol. 2, 136.

36. See Kemālpaşazāde, *Tevārīḫ*, vol. 8 (1985), 33.

37. For alternative dates suggested for Selīm I's appointment to the governorship of Trabzon, see Uluçay, "Yavuz Sultan Selim Nasıl Padişah Oldu?," (1953), 74n28.

38. "Methōnē" and "Korōnē" in Greek; "Modon" and "Coron" in Venetian vernacular. Ṣolaḳzāde, *Tārīḫ* (TSMK B.199), 180a; Nişāncızāde, *Mirʾāt*, 112b.

39. Kemālpaşazāde, *Tevārīḫ*, vol. 8 (1997), 234.

40. Kemālpaşazāde, *Tevārīḫ*, vol. 8 (1997), 251; and Ṣolaḳzāde, *Tārīḫ* (TSMK B.199), 182a.

41. Saʿdeddīn, *Tācü't-tevārīḫ*, vol. 2, 130; and ʿĀlī, *Künhü'l-aḫbār*, vol. 2, 909.

42. Bāyezīd II appears to have followed a general policy of nonconfrontation whenever possible. For a dispatch reprimanding lords of the marches (*uc begleri*) for initiating skirmishes along the Balkan frontiers, see TSMA E.5898.

43. See Leonardo Bembo's *relazione* (25 June 1505), summarized in Sanuto, *I Diarii*, vol. 6, 212; see also Antonio Marzello's *relazione* (25 September 1505), summarized in Sanuto, *I Diarii*, vol. 6, 221–22, 240.

44. Ṣolaḳzāde, *Tārīḫ* (TSMK B.199), 184b; and Kemālpaşazāde, *Tevārīḫ*, vol. 8 (1997), 259–60.

45. See Andrea Foscolo's *relazioni* (6, 13 August 1508), summarized in Sanuto, *I Diarii*, vol. 7, 631.

46. See Andrea Foscolo's *relazione* (1 August 1508), summarized in Sanuto, *I Diarii*, vol. 7, 636–37.

47. See Andrea de Cividal's letter to Nicolò Venier (15 July 1510), summarized in Sanuto, *I Diarii*, vol. 11, 477; see also Nicolò Zustignan's *relazione* (5 December 1510), summarized in Sanuto, *I Diarii*, vol. 11, 809–10. That Bāyezīd followed a nonconfrontational diplomatic strategy vis-à-vis the Safavids does not mean that the direction of his foreign policy was determined by a proclivity to avoid military confrontations at all costs. For a discussion of Ottoman-Mamluk relations during the reign of Bāyezīd II and of his military campaigns against the Mamluks, see Yüksel Muslu, *The Ottomans and the Mamluks*, 134–55.

48. See Kemālpaşazāde, *Tevārīḫ*, vol. 8 (1985), 39–40.

49. Selīm was also ordered to give up some of the land he had conquered through his effective raids into the Safavid realm. See Selīm's petition to Bāyezīd II, TSMA E.5970.

50. Nişāncızāde, *Mirʾāt*, 114a; and Kemālpaşazāde, *Tevārīḫ*, vol. 8 (1985), 32.

51. See Kemālpaşazāde, *Tevārīḫ*, vol. 8 (1985), 40. For a similar report, see Celālzāde, *Meʾāṣir*, 45a.

52. Celālzāde, *Meʾāṣir*, 55b.

53. Ṣolaḳzāde, *Tārīḫ* (TSMK B.199), 185b.

54. See Ṣolaḳzāde, *Tārīḫ* (TSMK E.H.1416), 24a. See also Selīm's letter to Bāyezīd II, TSMA E.6185.

55. See Kemālpaşazāde, *Tevārīḫ*, vol. 8 (1985), 33; and Saʿdeddīn, *Tācü't-tevārīḫ*, vol. 2, 136.

56. For Selīm's petition requesting the provinces of Şebinkarahisar and Bolu for his son Süleymān, see TSMA E.5970; and Saʿdeddīn, *Tācü't-tevārīḫ*, vol. 2, 135–36.

57. Selīm had expressed his dissatisfaction with the economic backwardness and unhealthy climate of Trabzon in a petition to his father already in 1510 and asked to be transferred to a Rumelian province. See TSMA E.543. See also Saʿdeddīn, *Tācü't-Tevārīḫ*, vol. 2, 140.

58. Ṣolaḳzāde, *Tārīḫ* (TSMK B.199), 185a; Nişāncızāde, *Mir'āt*, 114a.
59. Anonymous, *Tārīḫ* (TSMK R.1099), 110b; and Sa'deddīn, *Tācü't-tevārīḫ*, vol. 2, 141.
60. Ṣolaḳzāde, *Tārīḫ* (TSMK E.H.1416), 24a, 185b; and Kemālpaşazāde, *Tevārīḫ*, vol. 8 (1985), 41.
61. See Lodovico Valdrim's *relazione* (31 May 1510), summarized in Sanuto, *I Diarii*, vol. 10, 669.
62. Ṣolaḳzāde, *Tārīḫ* (TSMK E.H.1416), 23b.
63. See Selīm's letter to the imperial court, TSMA E.6185. See also Ṣolaḳzāde, *Tārīḫ* (TSMK B.199), 186a; and Nişāncızāde, *Mir'āt*, 114a.
64. See Mevlānā Nūreddīn's letter to Bāyezīd II, TSMA E.6322.
65. See report of correspondence between Bāyezīd II and Mengli Girāy, TSMA E.6382.
66. For the report by Bālī Beg, the son of Yaḥyā Pasha, stating that the addition to Selīm's forces of one thousand Kazakh soldiers sent by the Crimean Khan increased his military strength significantly, see TSMA E.3703.
67. See the report by a certain Bālī to the imperial court, TSMA E.6329. See also Ḥadīdī, *Tevārīḫ*, 363; and Andrea Foscolo's letter to Piero Foscolo (24 June 1511), summarized in Sanuto, *I Diarii*, vol. 12, 511.
68. On the unfolding of the negotiation process, see Nūreddīn Ṣarugürz's letter to Bāyezīd II, TSMA E.5490. See also the report of correspondence between Bāyezīd II and Menglī Girāy, TSMA E.6382; and Selīm's letter to the imperial court requesting the province of Silistre, TSMA E.6185.
69. Uluçay and Tansel disagree on the exact location of the landing of Selīm and his troops and refer to Kili and Akkirman, respectively. The reference to Akkirman in the lists of Selīm's supporters in Rumelia, however, makes the latter the probable place of disembarkment. See Uluçay, "Yavuz Sultan Selim Nasıl Padişah Oldu?," (1953), 83; Tansel, *Sultan II. Bâyezit'in Siyasî Hayatı*, 274; TSMA D.5374; and TSMA D.7603.
70. For the date of Selīm's departure from Ahyolu for Kefe following the defeat his troops suffered at Çorlu, see TSMA E.6446; and Ṣolaḳzāde, *Tārīḫ* (TSMK B.199), 189a.
71. See TSMA D.7603; and TSMA D.5374.
72. See the report by a certain Meḥmed to the imperial court, TSMA E.8917.
73. See the report by a certain Bālī to the imperial court, TSMA E.6329.
74. See the letter by janissaries supporting Selīm, TSMA E.8001.
75. See the report by a certain Bālī to the imperial court, TSMA E.6329. See also Ḥadīdī, *Tevārīḫ*, 363; Nicolò Zustignan's *relazione* (18 June 1511), summarized in Sanuto, *I Diarii*, vol. 12, 299; and Andrea Foscolo's letter to Piero Foscolo (24 June 1511), summarized in Sanuto, *I Diarii*, vol. 12, 511.

76. See Bālī Beg's report to the imperial court, TSMA E.3703. See also Anonymous, *Chronikon*, 104: "[Selīm] arranged a pact with the Tatar lord . . . gathered armies of Turks and Tatars, horsemen and foot soldiers . . . gathered a large army with the aid he received."

77. For examples of petitions addressed to Selīm by his supporters, see TSMA E.6062; TSMA E.6081; TSMA E.6211; TSMA E.6619; TSMA E.6623; TSMA E.7054; TSMA E.7294; TSMA E.7634; TSMA E.8093; TSMA E.8150; TSMA E.9969; TSMA E.10013; and TSMA E.10030.

78. See Bālī Beg's report to the imperial court, TSMA E.3703.

79. For Selīm's request of Silistre, see his letters to the imperial court, TSMA E.5443, and TSMA E.6815; see also Andrea Foscolo's (13 May 1511) and Lodovico Valdrim's (27 May - 3 June 1511) *relazioni*, summarized in Sanuto, *I Diarii*, vol. 12, 244–45, and vol. 12, 273, respectively.

80. See Selīm's letter to the imperial court, TSMA E.5443.

81. See Selīm's letter to the imperial court, TSMA E.6815.

82. Ṣolaḳzāde, *Tārīḫ* (TSMK B.199), 186b.

83. ʿĀlī, *Künhü'l-aḫbār*, vol. 2, 939.

84. Kemālpaşazāde, *Tevārīḫ*, vol. 8 (1985), 51.

85. Saʿdeddīn, *Tācü't-tevārīḫ*, vol. 2, 152. Muṣṭafā ʿĀlī states that the appended areas were Izvornik (Zvornik, Varna, Bulgaria) and Alacahisar. See ʿĀlī, *Künhü'l-aḫbār*, vol. 2, 940. See also Nişāncızāde, *Mir'āt*, 114a.

86. See Saʿdeddīn, *Tācü't-tevārīḫ*, vol. 2, 153; and ʿĀlī, *Künhü'l-aḫbār*, vol. 2, 941.

87. See Aḥmed's letter to the grand vizier, TSMA E.6043: "egerçi üç sancaḳdur ammā maʿnāda bir Rūmili külliyen tevcīh olunub hemān umūr-ı salṭanatdan bir ḫuṭbe ve bir sikke ḳalmışdur . . . elbet ben daḫī ṭariḳ-i ʿiṣyāna yüriyüb varub Brusada oturub cemīʿ-i ḫāṣları bi'l-cümle deñüzden berüsini żabṭ idüb Anāṭolıdan Rūmilüñe bir eḥad geçürmezem baña muṭīʿ olmayanlaruñ evlerin ṭalanlatub kendüleri evlādı ve ensābıyle ḳatl itdirürün vebāli bāʿīs̱ olanlaruñ ẕimmetinde ola."

88. See Anonymous, *Chronikon*, 104: "[Selīm] had received word from the two pashas, his father's viziers, not to turn back but to maintain his strength." See also Kemālpaşazāde, *Tevārīḫ*, vol. 8 (1985), 51–52.

89. Kemālpaşazāde, *Tevārīḫ*, vol. 8 (1985), 52. See also Nişāncızāde, *Mir'āt*, 114b.

90. Saʿdeddīn, *Tācü't-tevārīḫ*, vol. 2, 154. Bāyezīd II may have also promised the booty from his last campaign in order to expedite Selīm's departure for Semendire. See Anonymous, *Chronikon*, 104.

91. Saʿdeddīn, *Tācü't-tevārīḫ*, vol. 2, 156. See also Selīm's letter to Bāyezīd II, TSMA E.12276: "devletlü ḫüdāvendigār ḥażretleri Rūmili livālarından Semendire livāsını bu bendesine ṣadaḳa idüb aḳın itmekiçün icāzet buyurulduḳda baʿżı

akıncılardan kimesneler cem' itmek ṣadedinde iken ba'żı ṣubaşılar ve sipāhīler cem' olunub Zağra Eskisinde sākin olunub."

92. Ṣolaḳzāde, *Tārīḫ* (TSMK E.H.1416), 25b. See also Andrea Foscolo's letter to Piero Foscolo (24 June 1511), summarized in Sanuto, *I Diarii*, vol. 12, 511–12.

93. For a list of unqualified and ineligible persons who received prebends at the expense of provincial cavalrymen hailing from old Turco-Muslim families, see the spy report to the imperial court, TSMA E.6187. See also Tekindağ, "Şah Kulu Baba Tekeli İsyanı" (1967), 35–36. For a discussion of the criticisms leveled against the strategy of assigning high offices only to those members of the Ottoman military ruling elite of *devşirme* origin (*ḳul ṭā'ifesi*), see Chapter 2.

94. Uzunçarşılı, *Osmanlı Tarihi*, vol. 2, 230.

95. Tansel, *Sultan II. Bâyezit'in Siyasî Hayatı*, 248.

96. For the spy report composed by a certain Pīr Aḥmed, explaining Şāhḳulu's connections with the Balkan provinces, see TSMA E. 6636.

97. 'Ālī, *Künhü'l-aḫbār*, vol. 2, 933–34.

98. See the letter sent by the judge of Antalya to Ḳorḳud (dated 30 March 1511), TSMA E.632.

99. See the spy reports to the imperial court, TSMA E.6187 and TSMA E.5035: "memleket ḫālīdür . . . furṣat bizimdür . . . gelüñ cemī'-i memleketi żabṭ idelüm." See also Ṣolaḳzāde, *Tārīḫ* (TSMK B.199), 187a–187b; and Kemālpaşazāde, *Tevārīḫ*, vol. 8 (1985), 42–43.

100. See TSMA E.632: "Allāh budur ve peyġamber budur."

101. See Prince 'Os̱mān's report (dated 16 April 1511), TSMA E.2829: "mehdīlik da'vāsın ider"; and TSMA E.6187.

102. See Ḳaragöz Pasha's letter, TSMA E.77; see also the letter sent to Ḳorḳud by his *defterdār*, TSMA E.6321; TSMA E.5035; and TSMA E.6187.

103. See the spy report to the imperial court, TSMA E.5035.

104. See the spy report to the imperial court, TSMA E.5035. See also the letter by the kadi of Antalya to Ḳorḳud, TSMA E.632; Prince 'Os̱mān's report to the imperial court, TSMA E.2829; and the report of a spy to the imperial court, TSMA E.6187.

105. See TSMA E.6187; TSMA E.2829; TSMA E.5035; TSMA E.6321; and TSMA E.77. See also Kemālpaşazāde, *Tevārīḫ*, vol. 8 (1985), 44–45.

106. See TSMA E.5035; see also Nicolò Zustignan's *relazione* (2–5 May 1511), summarized in Sanuto, *I Diarii*, vol. 12, 199; and Andrea Foscolo's letters to Piero Foscolo (18, 24 June, and 27 August 1511), summarized in Sanuto, *I Diarii*, vol. 12, 507–12, and vol. 13, 114–17, respectively.

107. See the letter sent by Aḥmed, the judge of Bursa, to the commander of janissaries (dated 3 May 1511), TSMA E.5451.

108. See a certain Yūsuf's report, TSMA E.5877. See also Yıldırım, "An Ottoman Prince Wearing a Qizilbash *Tāj*."

109. See Ḥaydar Pasha's letter to Bāyezīd II, TSMA E.5590. These reports suggest that Prince Murād adhered to the Ḳızılbaş movement while Şehinşāh at least contemplated an alliance with Şāhḳulu.

110. Andrea Foscolo's letter to Piero Foscolo (18 June 1511), summarized in Sanuto, *I Diarii*, vol. 12, 507–10; Anonymous, *Tevārīḫ* (Azamat edition), 132; and Nişāncızāde, *Mirʾāt*, 114b.

111. ʿAlī Pasha's troops included "four thousand soldiers of the *ḳapuḳulı* regiments and four thousand janissaries" (dört biñ miḳdārı bölük ḫalḳı ve dört biñ yeñiçeri). Saʿdeddīn, *Tācü't-tevārīḫ*, vol. 2, 167–70; Ṣolaḳzāde, *Tārīḫ* (TSMK B.199), 190a; İsḥaḳ, *Selīmnāme*, 35a–35b.

112. Ṣolaḳzāde, *Tārīḫ* (TSMK B.199), 190a; Nişāncızāde, *Mirʾāt*, 115a; and Kemālpaşazāde, *Tevārīḫ*, vol. 8 (1985), 49.

113. Kemālpaşazāde, *Tevārīḫ*, vol. 8 (1985), 46–47; Saʿdeddīn, *Tācü't-tevārīḫ*, vol. 2, 176; and Andrea Foscolo's letter to Piero Foscolo (27 August 1511), summarized in Sanuto, *I Diarii*, vol. 13, 114–17. See also Aḥmed's letter to the commanders, TSMA E.2667.

114. See Aḥmed's letter to the commanders, TSMA E.3062; an agent's report to the imperial court, TSMA E.6352; TSMA E.3062; and TSMA E.6352. See also Andrea Foscolo's letter to Piero Foscolo (27 August 1511), summarized in Sanuto, *I Diarii*, vol. 13, 114–17; Kemālpaşazāde, *Tevārīḫ*, vol. 8 (1985), 55.

115. See Aḥmed's letter to the commanders, TSMA E.3062. See also Ḥasan Rūmlū, *Aḥsanu't-tawārīkh*, vol. 2, 57.

116. See Ḥācī Muṣṭafā's letter to the imperial court, TSMA E.6664; and Aḥmed's letter to commanders, TSMA E.3062. See also Andrea Foscolo's letter to Piero Foscolo (27 August 1511), summarized in Sanuto, *I Diarii*, vol. 13, 114–17; Ṣolaḳzāde, *Tārīḫ* (TSMK B.199), 191a; and Nişāncızāde, *Mirʾāt*, 115a.

117. Only a few sources distribute the responsibility equally among the three Ottoman princes and blame their lack of cooperation for the devastation caused by the Şāhḳulu rebellion. See Anonymous, *Tevārīḫ* (Azamat edition), 132: "sancaḳ begleri biribirileriyle uzlaşamayub muḳāvemet idemediler."

118. Uluçay, "Yavuz Sultan Selim Nasıl Padişah Oldu?," (1953), 56.

119. On Prince Murād's involvement in the Ḳızılbaş movement, see Yıldırım, "An Ottoman Prince Wearing a Qizilbash *Tāj*." See a certain Yūsuf's report, TSMA E.5877; and Nicolò Zustignan's *relazione* (24 April 1512), summarized in Sanuto, *I Diarii*, vol. 14, 246; see also Andrea Foscolo's letter to Piero Foscolo (28 March 1512), summarized in Sanuto, *I Diarii*, vol. 14, 292.

120. Saʿdeddīn, *Tācü't-tevārīḫ*, vol. 2, 176.

121. Ṣolaḳzāde, *Tārīḫ* (TSMK E.H.1416), 27b.
122. Ṣolaḳzāde, *Tārīḫ* (TSMK E.H.1416), 29a–29b; Nişāncızāde, *Mir'āt*, 116a; and Ḥadīdī, *Tevārīḫ*, 358, 361.
123. Ṣolaḳzāde, *Tārīḫ* (TSMK E.H.1416), 29b; and Kemālpaşazāde, *Tevārīḫ*, vol. 8 (1985), 59–60.
124. Saʿdeddīn, *Tācü't-tevārīḫ*, vol. 2, 157; and Kemālpaşazāde, *Tevārīḫ*, vol. 8 (1985), 56.
125. Ṣolaḳzāde, *Tārīḫ* (TSMK E.H.1416), 26a; and Menavino, "Della vita et legge Turchesca," 51b. See also Selīm's letter to Bāyezīd II, TSMA E.12276.
126. Ṣolaḳzāde, *Tārīḫ* (TSMK E.H.1416), 25b.
127. Saʿdeddīn, *Tācü't-tevārīḫ*, vol. 2, 157–58.
128. Ṣolaḳzāde, *Tārīḫ* (TSMK E.H.1416), 26a.
129. Ottoman sources refer to the location of the battle between Selīm's and Bāyezīd II's troops as Uğraş, Karışdıran, or Çukurçayır. For the sake of consistency, this book will use the name Çorlu. Çorlu is located in Ottoman Thrace, between Edirne and Istanbul. The distance between Çorlu and Istanbul (roughly 120 kilometers) could be covered by the vanguard of the imperial army in approximately six days. For the approximate speed at which Ottoman armies moved in the sixteenth and seventeenth centuries, see Murphey, *Ottoman Warfare*, 65–83.
130. Ṣolaḳzāde, *Tārīḫ* (TSMK E.H.1416), 26b.
131. The narrative flow of the account of several anonymous chroniclers certainly suggests that Selīm intentionally went after his father. See Anonymous, *Tevārīḫ* (Azamat edition), 134; Anonymous, *Tevārīḫ* (Öztürk edition), 141; and Anonymous, *Tārīḫ* (TSMK R.1101), 100b.
132. ʿĀlī, *Künhü'l-aḫbār*, vol. 2, 945; and Ṣolaḳzāde, *Tārīḫ* (TSMK B.199), 188b: "ṭoplara daḫī ateş virilüb."
133. Ṣolaḳzāde, *Tārīḫ* (TSMK E.H.1416), 26a–26b: "benüm etmegim yiyüb müstaḳīm ḳulum olan cenge yürüsün diyüb istimālet virince"; and Anonymous, *Tārīḫ* (TSMK R.1099), 111a: "anda olan dilāverān-ı Rūma ceng içün pādişāh ṭarafından fermān olduġı demde."
134. Kemālpaşazāde, *Tevārīḫ*, vol. 8 (1985), 56–57.
135. Anonymous, *Chronikon*, 105: "Selīm's army had suffered as many as 32,000 casualties; Bāyezīd's amounted to 700."
136. Saʿdeddīn, *Tācü't-tevārīḫ*, vol. 2, 160; Ṣolaḳzāde, *Tārīḫ* (TSMK E.H.1416), 26b; and Kemālpaşazāde, *Tevārīḫ*, vol. 8 (1985), 58. See also a certain Ḳara Ḥüseyin Agha's letter to Selīm I, TSMA E.10161.
137. See Bālī Beg's letter to Bāyezīd II, TSMA E.3703.
138. See Ḳara Ḥüseyin Agha's letter to Selīm, TSMA E.10161.

139. Anonymous, *Tārīḫ* (TSMK R.1099), 111a–111b; and Anonymous, *Tārīḫ* (TSMK R.1101), 101a.

140. According to an anonymous seventeenth-century Greek chronicle, Selīm did marry one of the Khan's daughters. See Anonymous, *Chronikon*, 104.

141. Saʿdeddīn, *Tācü't-tevārīḫ*, vol. 2, 160; and Nişāncızāde, *Mirʾāt*, 114a. Ṣolaḳzāde relates the same account on the authority of Bālī Pasha. Ṣolaḳzāde, *Tārīḫ* (TSMK B.199), 189b: "Ḫān dikmesi olmaġı nice iḫtiyār idelüm."

142. See Selīm's letter to Bāyezīd II, TSMA E.12276.

143. Tansel, *Sultan II. Bâyezit'in Siyasî Hayatı*, 295.

144. On Bāyezīd II's permission allowing Selīm to rule his Rumelian provinces through his representatives, see the letter by a certain Ḥācī to Selīm, TSMA E.7967.

145. Tansel, *Sultan II. Bâyezit'in Siyasî Hayatı*, 287–88; and Uluçay, "Yavuz Sultan Selim Nasıl Padişah Oldu?," (1954), 117–18. See Aḥmed's letters asking for permission to come to Istanbul and to be appointed commander in chief in charge of troops he insisted be sent against his brother Selīm, TSMA E.6043; and TSMA E.2667. For a desperate letter of concern regarding Aḥmed's rebellious attitude, see Ḳāsım Pasha's letter to Bāyezīd II, TSMA E.5447.

146. Saʿdeddīn, *Tācü't-tevārīḫ*, vol. 2, 183.

147. The Ottoman-Turkish term *erkān-ı devlet* ("pillars of the state"), used in the strictest sense, included the grand vizier (*ṣadrāʿẓam*), chief military judge (*ḳāḍīʿasker*), financial commissary-general (*defterdār*), and chief chancellor (*nişāncı*). Ṣolaḳzāde, *Tārīḫ* (TSMK B.199), 192b.

148. Saʿdeddīn, *Tācü't-tevārīḫ*, vol. 2, 183–87; and Ṣolaḳzāde, *Tārīḫ* (TSMK B.199), 192b.

149. Ṣolaḳzāde, *Tārīḫ* (TSMK B.199), 192b. See also Andrea Foscolo's letter to Piero Foscolo (18, 24 June 1511), summarized in Sanuto, *I Diarii*, vol. 12, 509, 511.

150. Ṣolaḳzāde, *Tārīḫ* (TSMK B.199), 193a: "serīr-i salṭanata sezāvār Sulṭān Selīm-i nāmdārdur biz andan ġayrısını ḳabūl itmeziz ve anuñ iṭāʿati rāhından özge rāha gitmezüz"; Nişāncızāde, *Mirʾāt*, 116a; and Anonymous, *Tārīḫ* (TSMK R.1099), 111b.

151. See Nihālī Çelebi's letter to Ḥalīmī Çelebi, TSMA E.3197: "yeñiçeri aġzında üstüḫān ṭutar üstüḫān virelüm." The recipient of the letter was Selīm's tutor during his princely governorate in Trabzon.

152. See Nihālī Çelebi's letter to Ḥalīmī Çelebi, TSMA E.3197. See also Kemālpaşazāde, *Tevārīḫ*, vol. 8 (1985), 59–60.

153. Anonymous, *Tārīḫ* (TSMK R.1099), 111b.

154. Mīrim Çelebi (Maḥmūd b. Meḥmed) was a prominent mathematician and astronomer who served Bāyezīd II as his teacher and later as military judge of

Anatolia (*Anaṭolı ḳāḍīʿaskeri*). I would like to thank Ahmet Tunç Şen for reminding me that Mīrim Çelebi was also Bāyezid's astrologer and confidant. Āḫī Çelebi (Meḥmed Efendi) was Bāyezīd II's and later Selīm I's physician (*hekīmbaşı*). During the succession struggle, both figures remained loyal to their patron Bāyezīd II and thus were considered members of the pro-Aḥmed faction. See Meḥmed Süreyyā, *Sicill*, vol. 4, 310, and vol. 4, 109–10, respectively. Unless otherwise specified, all references are to the original edition (1890–1893) of this work.

155. See Nihālī Çelebi's letter to Ḥalīmī Çelebi, TSMA E.3197.

156. See Nihālī Çelebi's letter to Ḥalīmī Çelebi, TSMA E.3197. According to a Venetian source, what prevented Aḥmed from crossing to Istanbul was the fact that the Ottoman admiral (*ḳapudān*) who controlled the Bosphorus with his fleet was a supporter of Selīm. See Andrea Foscolo's letters to Piero Foscolo (24 June, 26 September 1511), summarized in Sanuto, *I Diarii*, vol. 12, 511, and vol. 13, 222, respectively; Saʿdeddīn, *Tācü't-tevārīḫ*, vol. 2, 191; Ṣolaḳzāde, *Tārīḫ* (TSMK B.199), 193a; and Nişāncızāde, *Mirʾāt*, 116a.

157. See Aḥmed's letter to Turġudoğlu Mūsā Beg (dated 3 November 1511), TSMA E.2667; and Aḥmed's decree (dated end of December 1511), appointing a certain Şeyʾillāhoğlu to the governorship of Nigde, TSMA E.2667.

158. Kemālpaşazāde, *Tevārīḫ*, vol. 8 (1985), 61.

159. See Ṣolaḳzāde, *Tārīḫ* (TSMK B.199), 193b–194a; Nişāncızāde, *Mirʾāt*, 116b; Anonymous, *Tevārīḫ* (Azamat edition), 134; Anonymous, *Tārīḫ* (TSMK R.1099), 111b–112a; Anonymous, *Tevārīḫ* (TSMK R.1100), 81b; and Anonymous, *Tārīḫ* (TSMK R.1101), 101b.

160. See TSMA E.2667: "sen ʿamelden ḳaldın bize pādişāh gerek öyle olsa biz daḫī Selīm Begi pādişāh eyledük"; Ṣolaḳzāde, *Tārīḫ* (TSMK B.199), 195a; and Anonymous, *Tārīḫ* (TSMK R.1099), 112b.

161. See a certain Yūsuf's letter to Selīm, TSMA E.7072.

162. See Bāyezīd II's letter to Selīm (dated end of March 1512), TSMA E.6185.

163. See Ferhād Agha's letter to Selīm, TSMA E.8312.

164. See Ferhād Agha's letter to Selīm, TSMA E.8312: "bu bendeñüz oğlanlaruñ içinden çıḳarsam şehri ḫarāba virürler gice ve gündüz şehri muḥāfaẓa iderüz şöyle ki bir laḥẓa aralarından ġāyib olam be-ġāyet yaramazdururlar."

165. See the letter written by Ḥasan Pasha, the governor-general of Rumelia, to Selīm, TSMA E.6420; and an anonymous letter possibly written to Selīm, TSMA E.4744: "nuḳūd cinsinden üç ḳaṭar deve yüki ṣanduḳlar . . . ḳul ṭāʾifesine iʿṭā eylemek içün yigirmi biñ filurimüz vardur." See also Anonymous, *Tevārīḫ* (Azamat edition), 134; and Ṣolaḳzāde, *Tārīḫ* (TSMK B.199), 194b.

166. See anonymous letter addressed to Defterdār Ḥasan Beg, TSMA E.6577; see also Nicolò Zustignan's *relazione* (2 April 1512), summarized in Sanuto, *I Diarii*,

vol. 14, 216. Kemālpaşazāde, *Tevārīḫ*, vol. 8 (1985), 62–63; Ṣolaḳzāde, *Tārīḫ* (TSMK B.199), 194b–195a; Anonymous, *Tārīḫ* (TSMK R.1099), 112a; Saʿdeddīn, *Tācü't-tevārīḫ*, vol. 2, 198; and Nişāncızāde, *Mir'āt*, 116b.

167. For the effectiveness of the propaganda efforts of Selīm's supporters among the janissary troops, see Ḥācī Meḥmed's letter to İskender Agha, TSMA E.8327; Anonymous, *Tevārīḫ* (Azamat edition), 134; and Anonymous, *Tevārīḫ* (TSMK R.1100), 81b.

168. Some sources claim that Selīm I became sultan one day later. See, for example, Ṣolaḳzāde, *Tārīḫ* (TSMK B.199), 199a.

169. Some chronicles from the later Ottoman period do not even question how the process of abdication took place and imply that the succession of Selīm I was devoid of any struggles. See, for example, Kemālpaşazāde, *Tevārīḫ*, vol. 8 (1985), 64; Edrenevī, *Nuḫbetü't-tevārīḫ*, 55a; Meḥmed Cemīl, *Muḫtaṣar ve manẓūm tārīḫ-i ʿOs̱mānī*, 44a; and Rıżā, *Manẓūme-i şāhān*, 2b.

170. Saʿdeddīn, *Tācü't-tevārīḫ*, vol. 2, 200–203; and Nişāncızāde, *Mir'āt*, 116b.

171. Muṣṭafā Cenābī provides the account of a lengthy argument between Selīm and Bāyezīd II that supposedly took place when the former arrived at the imperial capital. According to this account, Selīm criticized his father because of his ineffectiveness in dealing with the international threat posed by the Safavids and the Mamluks. See Cenābī, *Dürr-i meknūn*, 233b.

172. See, for example, Yūsuf, *Tārīḫ*, 266: "Sulṭān Selīm Ḫān Istanbula gelüb . . . cebren taḫta cülūs idüb." Similarly, popular sixteenth-century poet Ṭālibī marked Selīm's accession with a chronogram that read, "Selīm became the sultan in the world by virtue of the sword" (*pādişāh oldı cihānda seyf ile Sulṭān Selīm*). Ṭālibī, as quoted in Tansel, *Yavuz Sultan Selim*, 1n2.

173. Muḥyīüddīn Meḥmed Çelebi as quoted in Tansel, *Sultan II. Bâyezit'in Siyasî Hayatı*, 301; and ʿĀlī, *Künhü'l-aḫbār*, vol. 2, 249.

174. See ʿĀlī, *Künhü'l-aḫbār*, vol. 2, 950–51; Anonymous, *Tevārīḫ* (Azamat edition), 134; Anonymous, *Tevārīḫ* (Öztürk edition), 142; Anonymous, *Tārīḫ* (TSMK R.1099), 112b; Anonymous, *Tevārīḫ* (TSMK R.1100), 82a; and Anonymous, *Tārīḫ* (TSMK R.1101), 102a–102b.

175. ʿĀlī, *Künhü'l-aḫbār*, vol. 2, 951.

176. Anonymous, *Tevārīḫ* (Azamat edition), 134–35; Ṣolaḳzāde, *Tārīḫ* (TSMK B.199), 196a; and Nişāncızāde, *Mir'āt*, 116b–117a; see also Nicolò Zustignan's *relazione* (24 April 1512), summarized in Sanuto, *I Diarii*, vol. 14, 245.

177. Cenābī, *Dürr-i meknūn*, 233b; and Hezārfen Ḥüseyin, *Tenḳīḥ*, 122a.

178. For Meḥmed II's canonization of fratricide, see *Ḳānūnnāme-i āl-i ʿOs̱mān*, 18. This is probably why Hezārfen Ḥüseyin refers to Selīm I's attacks on, and subsequent execution of, his rival brothers Aḥmed and Ḳorḳud as acts of obligation (*żārūrī*). See Hezārfen Ḥüseyin, *Tenḳīḥ*, 123b.

179. Cenābī, *Dürr-i meknūn*, 234a; and Hezārfen Ḥüseyin, *Tenḳīḥ*, 122b.

180. Saʿdeddīn, *Tācü't-tevārīḫ*, vol. 2, 205; Anonymous, *Tevārīḫ* (Azamat edition), 135; Anonymous, *Tevārīḫ* (Öztürk edition), 142–43; Anonymous, *Tārīḫ* (TSMK R.1099), 113a; Anonymous, *Tevārīḫ* (TSMK R.1100), 82b; Anonymous, *Tārīḫ* (TSMK R.1101), 103a; and Ṣolaḳzāde, *Tārīḫ* (TSMK B.199), 197b.

181. Yūsuf, *Tārīḫ*, 266: "cebren taḫta cülūs idüb babası Bāyezīd Ḫānı Edreneye gönderüb." See also Anonymous, *Chronikon*, 107.

182. Saʿdeddīn, *Tācü't-tevārīḫ*, vol. 2, 205; and Ṣolaḳzāde, *Tārīḫ* (TSMK B.199), 197b.

183. For a discussion of the historiographical debate on this issue, see Tekindağ, "Bayezid'in Ölümü Meselesi."

184. There is archival evidence indicating that rumors about Selīm's involvement in his father's death circulated in the immediate aftermath of Bāyezīd II's passing. For the reference to Prince Aḥmed's letter to Qānṣūh al-Ghawrī (r. 1501–1516) to that effect, see Uzunçarşılı, "Memlûk Sultanları Yanına İltica Etmiş Olan Osmanlı Hanedanına Mensub Şehzadeler," 531.

185. İsmail Hami Danişmend insightfully observes that the silence of Ottoman sources concerning the circumstances of Bāyezīd II's death was politically motivated. See Danişmend, *İzahlı Osmanlı Tarihi Kronolojisi*, vol. 2, 2: "In any case, one can surmise that the rumor of poisoning was sounder than that of a [natural] death and [that] some Ottoman sources remained politically silent. [Her halde bu zehir rivayetinin ecel rivayetinden daha kuvvetli olduğu ve bâzı Osmanlı menbâlarının bu meselede siyaseten sükût ettikleri anlaşılmaktadır.]"

186. See, among others, Anonymous, *Tārīḫ* (TSMK R.1101), 103a.

187. Uğur, *Yavuz Sultan Selim*, 36.

188. Tansel, *Sultan II. Bâyezit'in Siyasî Hayatı*, 308–10.

189. See Aḥmed's letters to the commander of Biga (dated beginning of June 1512), TSMA E.5876, in which he is referred to as "the sultan of sultans of the age" (*sulṭān-ı selāṭīn-i zamān pādişāhımız Sulṭān Aḥmed Ḫān*). See the petition of Sulṭān Mūsā, the governor of Kastamonu (dated 17 May 1512), TSMA E.2667, complaining about these demands and asking for instructions. See also Kemālpaşazāde, *Tevārīḫ*, vol. 9, 69.

190. See the petition of Eflāṭūnzāde, the kadi of Brusa (dated 15 June 1512), TSMA E.5452; see also the report sent by Şükrī-i Bidlīsī to Selīm, TSMA E.7052. For references to these nomadic groups, including Varsaḳ and Ṭurġud, see Kemālpaşazāde, *Tevārīḫ*, vol. 9, 69–70. It is noteworthy that Ḍulḳadiroġlu and Ramażānoġlu were Mamluk vassals.

191. See the report sent by a certain Mīrʿalem Muṣṭafā to Selīm, TSMA E.6376; the report sent by court-taster Sinān to Selīm, TSMA E.6333; and TSMA E.6376. Tācüddīn Beg was later appointed by Aḥmed as the governor-general of Karaman. See also Anonymous, *Tevārīḫ* (Azamat edition), 136.

192. See TSMA E.5452; and the reports sent to Selīm by a certain Ḥācī Meḥmed (TSMA E.6376), by a certain İlyās (TSMA E.6205), and by Ṭūr ʿAlī Beg (TSMA E.6631).

193. Anonymous, *Münşeʾāt* (NK 4316), 413b. The same suggestion—most probably a remnant of the Turco-Mongol tradition of dividing the realm between a deceased ruler's descendants—had been made earlier by Meḥmed II's son Prince Cem (d. 1495). On the development of the Ottoman practice of unigeniture, see Kafadar, *Between Two Worlds*, 136–38.

194. Ṣolaḳzāde, *Tārīḫ* (TSMK B.199), 200a.

195. Whereas the commanders from Karaman insisted on going east to the Safavids, Reyḥānoğlu and Mıdıḳoğlu expressed their preference for the Mamluk realm. See the report sent by Şükrī-i Bidlīsī to Selīm, TSMA E.7052.

196. For the transliterated text of a letter by Aḥmed, see Uluçay, "Yavuz Sultan Selim Nasıl Padişah Oldu?," (1954), 240–41. For the section left out by Uluçay but that significantly mentions the province of Karaman, see Tansel, *Yavuz Sultan Selim*, 10n57. For Selīm's letter to Aḥmed expressing the former's implicit refusal of the latter's demands, see TSMA E.12277.

197. Saʿdeddīn, *Tācü't-tevārīḫ*, vol. 2, 229; Anonymous, *Tevārīḫ* (Azamat edition), 136; Anonymous, *Tārīḫ* (TSMK R.1099), 114b; Anonymous, *Tevārīḫ* (TSMK R.1100), 83b; Anonymous, *Tārīḫ* (TSMK R.1101), 104a; Anonymous, *Chronikon*, 110; and Ṣolaḳzāde, *Tārīḫ* (TSMK B.199), 201a.

198. See İdrīs-i Bidlīsī, *Salīmshāhnāma* (BM Add. 24960), 62b–63a.

199. See Selīm I's decree (dated beginning of May 1512), TSMA E.6577; and Ḳorḳud's letter to Selīm, TSMA E.5882. For Ḳorḳud's statement that he delayed the dispersal of his troops as an act of caution against a possible attack by Aḥmed, see his letters to Selīm, TSMA E.5882 and TSMA E.9659.

200. In addition to Meḥmed II's "law of fratricide," Selīm now could claim that Ḳorḳud's acts constituted treason. Saʿdeddīn, *Tācü't-tevārīḫ*, vol. 2, 231; ʿĀlī, *Künhü'l-aḫbār*, vol. 2, 1063–65; and Ṣolaḳzāde, *Tārīḫ* (TSMK B.199), 201b–203a.

201. See Aḥmed's letter to defterdār Muṣliḥüddīn (dated end of November 1512), TSMA E.2667.

202. See the petition sent by ʿAlī and Şāh Velī to Selīm, TSMA E.6118. See also Ṣolaḳzāde, *Tārīḫ* (TSMK B.199), 204a; Anonymous, *Tārīḫ* (TSMK R.1099), 116a; Anonymous, *Tevārīḫ* (TSMK R.1100), 84a; and Kemālpaşazāde, *Tevārīḫ*, vol. 9, 81.

203. See the letter sent by Aḥmed Beg, the governor of Sinop, TSMA E.6193.

204. İsmail Hami Danişmend cites Aḥmed Tevhīd Bey's reference to a historical tradition that suggests that Selīm did not feel absolutely secure until he ordered the execution of three of Prince Aḥmed's four remaining sons (Princes Murād, Maḥmūd, and ʿAbdullāh) on November 20, 1514. Danişmend also notes that the

princes may have been executed during the reign of Süleymān I. See Danişmend, *İzahlı Osmanlı Tarihi Kronolojisi*, vol. 2, 5. On the authority of none other than Muṣṭafā ʿĀlī, İsmail Hakkı Uzunçarşılı notes that Selīm also had a bastard son, Üveys (d. 1547), who later became governor-general of Yemen but somehow escaped the same fate. See Uzunçarşılı, *Osmanlı Tarihi*, vol. 2, 395–96n2.

205. Anonymous, *Tārīḫ* (TSMK R.1099), 110a.

206. Anonymous, *Tevārīḫ* (Azamat edition), 133; Anonymous, *Tevārīḫ* (TSMK R.1100), 80a; and Ṣolaḳzāde, *Tārīḫ* (TSMK B.199), 188a.

207. Nişāncızāde, *Mirʾāt*, 114a. See also Anonymous, *Chronikon*, 104.

2. Politics of Factions

1. Busbecq, "Turkish Letter I," 104–5.

2. Gritti, *Relazione a Bajezid II*, 23–24. I would like to express my gratitude to Giancarlo Casale for his translation of this passage.

3. Titian's painting is in the Samuel H. Kress Collection at the National Gallery of Art, Washington, DC.

4. On Gritti's life, see Da Mosto, *I Dogi di Venezia*, 290–308. On Gritti's *relazione*, see Libby, "Venetian Views of the Ottoman Empire from the Peace of 1503 to the War of Cyprus," 104–6.

5. Gritti, *Relazione a Bajezid II*, 9–43.

6. For the correspondence between Andrea Gritti and Hersekzāde Aḥmed Pasha, see Heller, "Venedische Quellen zur Lebensgeschichte des Ahmed Paša Hersekoghlu."

7. Written more than a century later, an anonymous seventeenth-century Greek chronicle provides a brief but remarkably similar account: "[Selīm] was the youngest son and was loved by janissaries and all the people because of his generosity to them and his eagerness for war and because he did not approve of the peace with the foreigners. His brother Aḥmed only cared for eating, drinking, and sleeping in Kastamonia. Ḳorḳud had applied himself to literature and displayed no other concerns." See Anonymous, *Chronikon*, 104.

8. See Andrea Foscolo's letter to Piero Foscolo (28 March 1512), summarized in Sanuto, *I Diarii*, vol. 14, 293: "loro son quelli che domina e signorizano el paexe. . . . "

9. Fisher, *The Foreign Relations of Turkey*, 97.

10. Uluçay, "Yavuz Sultan Selim Nasıl Padişah Oldu?," (1953), 57–58.

11. Tansel, *Sultan II. Bâyezit'in Siyasî Hayatı*, 258, 259, 261.

12. Fisher, Uluçay, and Tansel consistently mention grand vizier Ḫādım ʿAlī Pasha (d. 1511), Muṣṭafā Pasha (d. 1513), military judge (*ḳāḍīʿasker*) Müʾeyyedzāde

ʿAbdürraḥmān Efendi (d. 1516), governor-general (*emīrü'l-ümerā*) Ḥasan Pasha (d. 1514), and chancellor (*nişāncı*) Tācīzāde Caʿfer Çelebi (d. 1515) as members of the pro-Aḥmed faction.

13. Imber, *The Ottoman Empire, 1300–1650*, 319–20; and Tezcan, *The Second Ottoman Empire*, 191–93.

14. Although the presence of factions at the imperial court has been noted by several scholars, the relationship between the imperial center and military-political factions in the provinces have been rarely discussed. Notable studies focusing on the factions at the Ottoman court include Peirce, *The Imperial Harem*; Kunt, "Turks in the Ottoman Imperial Palace"; Börekçi, "Factions and Favorites at the Courts of Sultan Ahmed I (r. 1603–1617) and His Immediate Predecessors"; Hathaway, *Beshir Agha*; and Fetvacı, *Picturing History at the Ottoman Court*.

15. Cemal Kafadar emphasizes the contractual nature of the janissaries' allegiance to a particular ruler and examines the process by which the janissaries adopted the role of sultan-makers. See Kafadar, "Janissaries and Other Riffraff of Ottoman İstanbul," especially 129–34.

16. See Cenābī, *Dürr-i meknūn*, 234a. See also Selānikī, *Tārīḫ*, vol. 1, 49. For an analysis of this episode, see Kunt, "Sultan, Dynasty and State," 222–25. On Ottoman accession practices and the participation of the janissary corps in accession ceremonies, see Vatin and Veinstein, *Le Sérail ébranlé*, 259–351, especially 281–86.

17. Anonymous, *Tārīḫ* (TSMK R.1099), 113b–114a; Anonymous, *Tevārīḫ* (TSMK R.1100), 83a; Anonymous, *Tārīḫ* (TSMK R.1101), 103b; and Anonymous, *Tevārīḫ* (Azamat edition), 135. Several Ottoman chroniclers also relate that the janissaries attempted a similar, though tamer, show of force vis-à-vis Meḥmed II by flanking the sultan and demanding royal gifts (*iḥsān*) on the occasion of the successful completion of a military expedition against the Karaman emirate. Meḥmed's response was also more subdued in comparison to his grandson's: the janissary officers responsible were punished by beating (*let urub*). See, for example, [Oxford] Anonymous (or "pseudo-Rūhī"), 447; and Neşrī, *Kitāb-ı cihānnümā*, vol. 2, 687.

18. The first salary register (*mevācib defteri*) of Selīm I's reign lists the names of 2,234 members of the sultanic retinue, 396 of whom are further identified by their associations with various members of the Ottoman *ʿaskerī* class, including several members of the dynastic family. For a detailed analysis of this register, see Çıpa, "The Centrality of the Periphery," Chapter 5.

19. Although the case of Bāyezīd I (r. 1389–1402), who was still alive during the early phase of the internecine strife between his sons, was a remarkable exception, one should not forget that at the time he was as incapacitated as a dead

sultan. Having been captured by Tīmūr (r. 1370–1405) at the Battle of Ankara in 1402, Bāyezīd died in captivity in 1403.

20. Fisher, *The Foreign Relations of Turkey*, 12n22, 95. Fisher's claim is based on the early sixteenth-century accounts of Theodoro Spandugino and Donado Da Lezze. For information on Bāyezīd II's children, including eight sons, see Alderson, *The Structure of the Ottoman Dynasty*, table 28.

21. For the dates of death of Bāyezīd II's sons, see Alderson, *The Structure of the Ottoman Dynasty*, table 28: ʿAbdullāh (d. 1483), Maḥmūd (d. 1507), Meḥemmed (d. 1507), ʿAlemşāh (d. 1510), and Şehinşāh (d. 1511).

22. Anonymous, *Tārīḫ* (TSMK R.1099), 109a–110a.

23. Celālzāde, *Meʾāṣir*, 49b–53a.

24. Celālzāde, *Meʾāṣir*, 29a: "Bāyezīdīler"; 81a: "Sulṭān Aḥmedī olan paşalar." Anonymous, *Tevārīḫ* (Azamat edition), 134: "Sulṭān Aḥmedlü ekābir, . . . Sulṭān Aḥmedlü"; Anonymous, *Tevārīḫ* (TSMK R.1100), 81a: "Sulṭān Aḥmedlüler"; and Anonymous, *Tārīḫ* (TSMK R.1101), 101a: "Sulṭān Aḥmedlü daḫī kibārdan baʿżı kimseler, . . . Sulṭān Aḥmed tevābiʿleridi."

25. To the best of my knowledge, the term "Selīmlü," referring to events during the succession struggle, appears in only two petitions penned by Selīm's supporters in the immediate aftermath of his accession. See E.10158-19 and E.10158-36. The only possible exception among Ottoman historical accounts in which Selīm's name is mentioned as descriptive of a political faction is Şükrī-i Bidlīsī's versified *Selīmnāme*. The author of the critical edition of this work renders the direct-speech self-designation of members of one janissary faction as *Selīmīlerdenüz* ("we belong to the *Selīmī* faction"); see *Selīmnāme* (1997), 101. But in another manuscript of the work the same statement is awkwardly spelled *Selīmlerdenüz* ("we belong to the *Selīm* faction"); see Şükrī, *Selīmnāme*, 40a.

26. İsḥaḳ, *Selīmnāme*, 17a.

27. İsḥaḳ, *Selīmnāme*, 17a.

28. Gritti, *Relazione a Bajezid II*, 23–24.

29. Celālzāde, *Meʾāṣir*, 27a–27b.

30. Gritti, *Relazione a Bajezid II*, 23.

31. İsḥaḳ, *Selīmnāme*, 11b.

32. Ṣolaḳzāde, *Tārīḫ* (TSMK E.H.1416), 21b; ʿĀlī, *Künhü'l-aḫbār*, 189b/911; Uluçay, "Yavuz Sultan Selim Nasıl Padişah Oldu?," (1953), 59; and Ṣolaḳzāde, *Tārīḫ* (TSMK B.199), 182b.

33. Kemālpaşazāde, *Tevārīḫ*, vol. 8 (1985), 40.

34. İsḥaḳ, *Selīmnāme*, 29a–29b, 34a; ʿĀlī, *Künhü'l-aḫbār*, vol. 2, 943; and Saʿdeddīn, *Tācü't-tevārīḫ*, vol. 2, 167. See also Andrea Foscolo's letter to Piero Foscolo (24 June 1511), summarized in Sanuto, *I Diarii*, vol. 12, 510–12.

35. Ṣolaḳzāde, *Tārīḫ* (TSMK B.199), 193a; Nişāncızāde, *Mirʾāt*, 116a; and Anonymous, *Tevārīḫ* (Öztürk edition), 141. A letter Aḥmed sent to Hersekoğlu Aḥmed Pasha, then grand vizier, indicates that the latter was a member of the pro-Aḥmed faction. See Uzunçarşılı, "Şehzade Selim'in Babasına Muhalefet Ederek Muharebe Ettiği Sırada Amasya Valisi Şehzade Ahmed'in Vezir-i Âzama Mektubu." For the confirmation of this point by a Venetian source, see Andrea Foscolo's letter to the Venetian government (18 June 1509), summarized in Sanuto, *I Diarii*, vol. 9, 12.

36. Several anonymous chroniclers refer to these figures as "Sulṭān Aḥmedlü ekābir" or "Sulṭān Aḥmed tevābiʿleridi" ("the grandees belonging to Aḥmed's faction" or "subjects of Aḥmed") and include Yūnus Pasha. See Anonymous, *Tevārīḫ* (Azamat edition), 134; Anonymous, *Tevārīḫ* (TSMK R.1100), 81a; and Anonymous, *Tārīḫ* (TSMK R.1101), 101a. See also Ṣolaḳzāde, *Tārīḫ* (TSMK E.H.1416), 29a: "cümleden vezīr-i āʿẓam Hersekoğlu Aḥmed Paşanuñ ve Muṣṭafā Paşanuñ ve mīrmīrān Ḥasan Paşanuñ ve ḳāḍīʿasker Müʾeyyedzādenüñ ve nişāncı Tācīzāde Caʿfer Çelebinüñ evlerin başub. . . . " For a discussion of the expression *tābiʿ* (pl. *tevābiʿ*) and its various meanings, see Hathaway, *The Politics of Households*, 21–24. See also Abou-El-Haj, "The Ottoman Vezir and Paşa Households."

37. Muṣṭafā Pasha was executed by royal decree, along with the remaining Ottoman princes who could pose a threat to Selīm's sultanate. See Saʿdeddīn, *Tācü't-tevārīḫ*, vol. 2, 229; Ṣolaḳzāde, *Tārīḫ* (TSMK E.H.1416), 34b; Anonymous, *Tevārīḫ* (Azamat edition), 136; Anonymous, *Tārīḫ* (TSMK R.1099), 114b; Anonymous, *Tevārīḫ* (TSMK R.1100), 83b; Anonymous, *Tārīḫ* (TSMK R.1101), 104a; Anonymous, *Chronikon*, 110; Ṣolaḳzāde, *Tārīḫ* (TSMK B.199), 201a; and Ḥadīdī, *Tevārīḫ*, 378–79. Moreover, Ḥasan Pasha died in 1511, before Selīm ascended to the Ottoman throne. See Meḥmed Süreyyā, *Sicill*, vol. 2, 119.

38. Meḥmed Süreyyā, *Sicill*, vol. 3, 310.

39. Meḥmed Süreyyā, *Sicill*, vol. 2, 68–69.

40. For example, Caʿfer Çelebi was executed following the escalation of political tensions with Selīm I in 1515. See Celālzāde, *Meʾāsir*, 102b–103a.

41. Hersekoğlu Aḥmed Pasha and Yūnus Pasha held the office of grand vizier until 1514 and 1517, respectively. Yūnus Pasha's later execution appears to have been unrelated to any support given to Aḥmed during the succession struggle. For a detailed account of Hersekoğlu Aḥmed Pasha's life and career, see Lowry, *Hersekzâde Ahmed Paşa*; Reindl, *Männer um Bāyezīd*, 129–46; and Reindl, "Some Notes on Hersekzade Ahmed Pasha, His Family and His Books." Leslie Peirce interprets Hersekoğlu Aḥmed Pasha's appointment to the grand vizierate by Selīm I as an indication that the former was not a member of "an overtly partisan faction—or at least not an effective one," despite the fact that he was Prince Aḥmed's brother-in-law. See Peirce, *The Imperial Harem*, 78.

42. See Nihālī Çelebi's letter to Ḥalīmī Çelebi, TSMA E.3197: "elbet Mü'eyyedoğlu ve Muṣṭafā Paşa ve Ḥasan Paşa ve Nişāncı ve Mīrim ve Āḫī Çelebi şehrden gitmek gerekdir ve Sulṭān Aḥmed daḫī ḳanden geldiyse andan gitmek gerekdir illā fesādı min baʿd görürsüz didiler."

43. On the lives and careers of Mīrim Çelebi and Āḫī Çelebi, see Meḥmed Süreyyā, *Sicill*, vol. 4, 310, and vol. 4, 109–10, respectively.

44. Anonymous, *Tevārīḫ* (Azamat edition), 136; and TSMA E.6376. The report sent by court-taster Sinān to Selīm I mentions commanders hailing from Taşili, Karaman, and Bulgar; see TSMA E.6333.

45. Anonymous, *Tārīḫ* (TSMK R.1099), 115b.

46. Kemālpaşazāde, *Tevārīḫ*, vol. 9, 69–70.

47. See the petition of Eflāṭūnzāde, the kadi of Brusa (dated 15 June 1512), TSMA E.5452; see also the report sent by Şükrī-i Bidlīsī's to Selīm I, TSMA E.7052.

48. See the report sent by a certain Mīrʿalem Muṣṭafā to Selīm I, TSMA E.6376.

49. Later assigned to the office of the governor-general of Karaman, Tāceddīn Beg was ordered by Aḥmed to gather troops in the Anatolian provinces as well. See the *fermān* sent to Mūsā Beg by Aḥmed, TSMA E.3057.

50. For references to these soldiers in archival sources, see Uluçay, "Yavuz Sultan Selim Nasıl Padişah Oldu?," (1954), 132–34. References in narrative sources include but are not limited to Anonymous, *Tevārīḫ* (TSMK R.1100), 84a: "Yevmlüler"; and Anonymous, *Tārīḫ* (TSMK R.1099), 115b: "Yevmlü ṭā'ifesi." Muṣṭafā ʿĀlī points to the Anatolian origins of this terminology (*Anaṭolı ıṣṭılāḥı*). For the relevant reference in *Künhü'l-aḫbār*, see Turan, *Kanunî'nin Oğlu Şehzâde Bayezid Vakʿası*, 87n11.

51. The same strategy was used later by Süleymān I's son Bāyezīd against his rival brother Selīm. See Turan, *Kanunî'nin Oğlu Şehzâde Bayezid Vakʿası*, 87–88, 99–100; and Cezar, *Osmanlı Tarihinde Levendler*, 30–40. For a discussion of the circumstances in which Muslim-born *reʿāyā* could attain *ʿaskerī* status, see Káldy-Nagy, "The 'Strangers' (*Ecnebiler*) in the 16th Century Ottoman Military Organization," especially 167–68.

52. See TSMA E.6333: "andan ṣoñra yanında olan Ḳaramānīler ḫüdāvendigāruñ veft olduġunı işidüb soġudılar."

53. Although Aḥmed ultimately stayed in Anatolia, three of his sons escaped to Cairo. See Uzunçarşılı, "Memlûk Sultanları Yanına İltica Etmiş Olan Osmanlı Hanedanına Mensub Şehzadeler," 530–35.

54. Whereas the commanders from Karaman insisted on going east to the Safavids, Reyḥānoğlu and Mıdıḳoğlu expressed their preference for the Mamluk realm. See the report sent by Şükrī-i Bidlīsī to Selīm I, TSMA E.7052.

55. Ṣolaḳzāde, *Tārīḫ* (TSMK E.H.1416), 3a, 30a; and Ṣolaḳzāde, *Tārīḫ* (TSMK B.199), 194a.

56. Saʿdeddīn, *Tācü't-tevārīḫ*, vol. 2, 197; Ṣolaḳzāde, *Tārīḫ* (TSMK B.199), 195a; Nişāncızāde, *Mirʾāt*, 116b; and Ṣolaḳzāde, *Tārīḫ* (TSMK E.H.1416), 30b.

57. Ṣolaḳzāde, *Tārīḫ* (TSMK B.199), 194a; and Ṣolaḳzāde, *Tārīḫ* (TSMK E.H.1416), 30a.

58. Saʿdeddīn, *Tācü't-tevārīḫ*, vol. 2, 168; and Ṣolaḳzāde, *Tārīḫ* (TSMK B.199), 183a. See also Andrea Foscolo's letter to the Venetian government (18 June 1509), summarized in Sanuto, *I Diarii*, vol. 9, 12.

59. For other Ottoman princes who sought asylum in the Mamluk realm, see Uzunçarşılı, "Memlûk Sultanları Yanına İltica Etmiş Olan Osmanlı Hanedanına Mensub Şehzadeler." On Prince Cem's asylum in Mamluks lands, see Yüksel Muslu, *The Ottomans and the Mamluks*, 136–39.

60. For examinations of the work in question, see al-Tikriti, "Şehzade Korkud," 186–234; and Fleischer, "From Şeyhzade Korkud to Mustafa Âli."

61. For the content and analysis of this autobiographical work, entitled *Wasīlat al-aḥbāb biiʿjāz taʾlīf walad ḥarrakahu'l-shawq ilā'l arḍ al-Ḥijāz* (The Means of the Beloved for Authorization Composed by a Son Whom Desire Has Driven to the Land of the Ḥijāz), see al-Tikriti, "The Ḥajj as Justifiable Self-Exile." Kemālpaşazāde defends Ḳorḳud by arguing that his sole purpose was to perform the pilgrimage. See Kemālpaşazāde, *Tevārīḫ*, vol. 8 (1985), 34–35.

62. Al-Tikriti, "The Ḥajj as Justifiable Self-Exile," 138.

63. Ṣolaḳzāde, *Tārīḫ* (TSMK B.199), 182b; ʿĀlī, *Künhü'l-aḫbār*, vol. 2, 911; and Uluçay, "Yavuz Sultan Selim Nasıl Padişah Oldu?," (1953), 59.

64. Al-Tikriti refers to this vaguely, as "a mutual assistance understanding of some sort." See al-Tikriti, "The Ḥajj as Justifiable Self-Exile," 138.

65. See Marin de Molin's letter to the Venetian government (5 January 1510), summarized in Sanuto, *I Diarii*, vol. 9, 27.

66. See the undated letter summarized in Sanuto, *I Diarii*, vol. 9, 126; Marin de Molin's letter to the Venetian government (10 August 1510), summarized in Sanuto, *I Diarii*, vol. 11, 76; and Uluçay, "Yavuz Sultan Selim Nasıl Padişah Oldu?," (1953), 59.

67. Ṣolaḳzāde, *Tārīḫ* (TSMK B.199), 183b.

68. See Ḳorḳud's letter to Bāyezīd II, TSMA E.2597. For the facsimile, transliteration, and an English translation of this letter, see al-Tikriti, "Şehzade Korkud," 334–41.

69. In an attempt to depict Ḳorḳud as an apolitical figure, Kemālpaşazāde states that the reason for the prince's departure from his gubernatorial seat was the "animal-like" and unruly population of his province. See Kemālpaşazāde, *Tevārīḫ*, vol. 8 (1985), 41–42.

70. Probably with *Daʿwat* in mind, Kemālpaşazāde states that by the time Ḳorḳud traveled to Egypt, he had already given up worldly concerns and

forfeited his right to the sultanate. See Kemālpaşazāde, *Tevārīḫ*, vol. 8 (1985), 34–35.

71. See, for example, Saʿdeddīn, *Tācü't-tevārīḫ*, vol. 2, 197; and Ṣolaḳzāde, *Tārīḫ* (TSMK E.H.1416), 30b.

72. See Ferhād Agha's letter to Şehzāde Selīm, TSMA E.8312.

73. See the letter written by Ḥasan Pasha, governor-general of Rūmili, to Selīm, TSMA E.6420. See also the anonymous letter addressed to Mevlānā Efendi, TSMA E.4744; Ṣolaḳzāde, *Tārīḫ* (TSMK B.199), 194b; Anonymous, *Tevārīḫ* (Azamat edition), 134; and Nişāncızāde, *Mirʾāt*, 116b. For the facsimile, transliteration, and an English translation of the anonymous letter, see al-Tikriti, "Şehzade Korkud," 342–47.

74. See the anonymous letter addressed to Mevlānā Efendi, TSMA E.4744: "nuḳūd cinsinden üç ḳaṭar deve yüki ṣanduḳlar . . . ḳul ṭāʾifesine iʿṭā eylemek içün yigirmi biñ filurimüz vardur."

75. Saʿdeddīn, *Tācü't-tevārīḫ*, vol. 2, 198; Ṣolaḳzāde, *Tārīḫ* (TSMK B.199), 195a; and Nişāncızāde, *Mirʾāt*, 116b.

76. See Tansel, *Sultan II. Bâyezit'in Siyasî Hayatı*, 289–306; Uluçay, "Yavuz Sultan Selim Nasıl Padişah Oldu?," (1954), 120–27; Fisher, *The Foreign Relations of Turkey*, 100–102; and Öztuna, *Yavuz Sultan Selim*, 38–41.

77. A small sample of letters sent to Selīm by his agents includes TSMA E.3147; TSMA E.5591; TSMA E.5839; TSMA E.6663; TSMA E.7086; TSMA E.8318; and TSMA E.8758.

78. For the narrative of events immediately preceding Selīm's face-off with his father, see Ṣolaḳzāde, *Tārīḫ* (TSMK E.H.1416), 26a: "āsitānede olan aḥbāb ṭarafından peyderpey ḫaberler gelür idi ki bervech-i istiʿcāl ile gelüb yetişesiz taḫt-ı devlet size müteraḳḳıbdır diyü."

79. See Mevlānā ʿĪsā, *Cāmiʿü'l-meknūnāt*, 78a: "Paşalardan yine hem geldi ḫaber / Tīz iriş kim taḫt senüñdür didiler." Barbara Flemming states that date of composition of Mevlāna ʿĪsā's work is sometime between 1529 and 1535. See Flemming, "Der *Ǧāmiʿ ül-Meknūnāt*," 84.

80. Saʿdeddīn, *Selīmnāme*, 603; and Celālzāde, *Meʾāṣir*, 90b, 101b–102a.

81. See the report sent by Şükrī-i Bidlīsī to Selīm, TSMA E.7052. There is strong evidence that Aḥmed's son Murād (d. 1513?) tried to persuade his father to enter an alliance with Safavid ruler Shāh Ismāʿīl. See Yıldırım, "An Ottoman Prince Wearing a Qizilbash *Tāj*," 105–9.

82. Saʿdeddīn, *Tācü't-tevārīḫ*, vol. 2, 168; and Ṣolaḳzāde, *Tārīḫ* (TSMK B.199), 183a. See Andrea Foscolo's letter to the Venetian government (18 June 1509), summarized in Sanuto, *I Diarii*, vol. 9, 12. On the reception of Ḳorḳud at the Mamluk court, see Ibn Iyās, *Badāʾiʿ al-zuhūr*, vol. 4, 157. For an analysis of Ḳorḳud's "tenuous position as a royal guest, refugee, and diplomatic pawn," see Yüksel Muslu, *The Ottomans and the Mamluks*, 168–71.

83. See, for example, Anonymous, *Tevārīḫ* (Azamat edition); Anonymous, *Tevārīḫ* (TSMK R.1100); Anonymous, *Tārīḫ* (TSMK R.1101); Edāʾī, *Shāhnāma*; Keşfī, *Selīmnāme*; and Sucūdī, *Selīmnāme*.

84. See, for example, Saʿdeddīn, *Selīmnāme*, 605; and Ṣolaḳzāde, *Tārīḫ* (TSMK B.199), 189b–190a. But Ogier Ghislain de Busbecq, Habsburg ambassador to the Porte, confidently refers to the Crimean Khan as Selīm's "father-in-law." See Busbecq, "Turkish Letter I," 108.

85. Saʿdeddīn, *Tācü't-tevārīḫ*, vol. 2, 160; and Nişāncızāde, *Mirʾāt*, 114a. Ṣolaḳzāde relates the same account on the authority of Bālī Pasha: "Ḫān dikmesi olmağı nice iḫtiyār idelüm" (*Tārīḫ* [TSMK B.199], 189b). Taking the accounts of Celālzāde Muṣṭafā and Saʿdeddīn at face value, Ahmet Uğur argues that Selīm's refusal of the Khan's offer proves that he was a "unique statesman." See Uğur, "Yavuz Sultan Selim ile Kırım Hanı Mengli Giray ve Oğlu Muhammed Giray Arasında Geçen İki Konuşma," 357.

86. Despite the relatively Mongol/Tatar-friendly attitude discernible in some of the earliest Ottoman historical narratives, representations of Tatars in later Ottoman historiography are generally quite negative, and the word Tatar is commonly followed by rhyming descriptives with negative meanings or connotations, such as "shameless" (*bī-ʿār*), "wicked" (*bed-kirdār*), and so on. For a discussion of the manner in which Ottomans' relationship with the Mongols is reflected in fourteenth-century historiography, see Tezcan, "The Memory of the Mongols in Early Ottoman Historiography." In sixteenth-century historical narratives, Tatars are generally depicted as unruly and rebellious; see, for example, Luṭfī, *Āṣafnāme* (Uğur edition), 251 (*ṭāġī ṭāʾifedür*). The fact that the Crimea had been on the itinerary of several anti-establishment figures in earlier periods of Ottoman history may have contributed to the chroniclers' reluctance. For the case of Sheikh Bedreddīn b. İsrāʿīl (d. 1416)—who, following the suggestion of İsfendiyāroġlu, intended to reach Rumelia via the Crimea—see, for example, Ḫalīl b. İsmāʿīl, *Menāḳıb-ı Şeyḫ Bedreddīn*, 45a; and Yücel, "Candar-oğlu Çelebi İsfendiyar Bey," 168.

87. See Mevlānā Ṣarugürz's report of the correspondence between Bāyezīd II and Mengli Girāy, TSMA E.6382: "pādişāh-ı gerdūñ-penāhuñ muḫliṣ bendesiyin . . . pādişāh rıżāsına muḫalif emre rıżām yoḳdur şöyle bilesiz."

88. See, for example, the report by Bālī Beg, the son of Yaḥyā Pasha, TSMA E.3703.

89. See the report by a certain Bālī to the imperial court, TSMA E.6329; Ḥadīdī, *Tevārīḫ*, 363; and Andrea Foscolo's letter to Piero Foscolo (24 June 1511), summarized in Sanuto, *I Diarii*, vol. 12, 511.

90. Anonymous, *Chronikon*, 104. Elizabeth Zachariadou has demonstrated that this early seventeenth-century chronicle was based on the mid-sixteenth-century account of the Italian man of letters Francesco Sansovino (d. 1586). See

Zachariadou, *To Chroniko ton Tourkon soultanon*. Another anonymous sixteenth-century Greek chronicle provides a similar account. See Anonymous, *Ekthesis Chronike*, 109: "[Selīm] led an army composed of the Scythians of the Han and his men from his own Porte, as well as some other unattached individuals, and marched by land with his troops . . ."

91. According to this source, Selīm also married one of the Khan's daughters. See Anonymous, *Chronikon*, 104.

92. Celālzāde, *Meʾās̱ir*, 61a: "mālikāne taṣarruf idüñ."

93. Celālzāde, *Meʾās̱ir*, 62a: "pādişāhlar memleket alurlar kimesneye memleket virmezler."

94. Celālzāde, *Meʾās̱ir*, 63a.

95. The alliance between Selīm and Mengli Girāy continued after the former's accession. In fact, there exists archival evidence that the Khan continued to advise Selīm on military strategies against his rival brother Aḥmed. See TSMA E.7084-8. At the final battle with Aḥmed, Selīm's army included troops commanded by Mengli Girāy's son, Saʿādet Girāy. See, for example, Şükrī, *Selīmnāme* (Argunşah edition), 131.

96. For a discussion of princely governorates, see Alderson, *The Structure of the Ottoman Dynasty*, 17–24.

97. See Selīm's petition to Bāyezīd II, TSMA E.543. See also Saʿdeddīn, *Tācü't-tevārīḫ*, vol. 2, 140.

98. See Selīm's letter to the imperial court, TSMA E.6185.

99. Lodovico Valdrim's letter to the Venetian government (31 May 1510), summarized in Sanuto, *I Diarii*, vol. 10, 669.

100. See the report by a certain Bālī to the imperial court, TSMA E.6329. Ottoman chroniclers mention a wide range of figures, between twenty and sixty thousand. See Ṣolaḳzāde, *Tārīḫ* (TSMK B.199), 187b: close to twenty to thirty thousand; Nişāncızāde, *Mirʾāt*, 115b: thirty thousand; Anonymous, *Chronikon*, 104: forty thousand; ʿĀlī, *Künhü'l-aḫbār*, vol. 2, 943: forty to fifty thousand; Celālzāde, *Meʾās̱ir*, 27b: fifty thousand; and Mevlāna ʿĪsā, *Cāmiʿü'l-meknūnāt*, 77b: fifty to sixty thousand.

101. İsḥaḳ, *Selīmnāme*, 39a: "Sulṭān Aḥmedüñ pādişāh olmasına anlaruñ ḥüsn-i ḳabūlı müteʿalliḳ ola"; 70b: "çün ol emrüñ ḥuṣūle mevṣūl olması dükeli Rūmili beglerinüñ ḳabūlüne mevḳūf idi"; and 88b–89a.

102. İsḥaḳ, *Selīmnāme*, 73a, 74a.

103. İsḥaḳ, *Selīmnāme*, 82b–83a.

104. İsḥaḳ, *Selīmnāme*, 112b.

105. Celālzāde, *Meʾās̱ir*, 26a.

106. Celālzāde, *Meʾās̱ir*, 28a–28b: "külliyen Rūmili beglerini ve sipāh-ı ẓafer-penāhı cümle ḳāpūya getirdüb."

107. Celālzāde, *Me'āṣir*, 77a: "cümle Rūmilinüñ sipahsālarları."

108. Ṣolaḳzāde, *Tārīḫ* (TSMK E.H.1416), 24b: "Rūmili begleri min-ba'd cenge rıżā virmeyüb mabeynüñ muṣāleḥesini ricā eylediler"; and Ṣolaḳzāde, *Tārīḫ* (TSMK B.199), 186b.

109. Kemālpaşazāde, *Tevārīḫ*, vol. 8 (1985), 49: "Rūmilüñde olan sancaḳ begleri."

110. See Ḳara Ḥüseyin Agha's letter to Selīm, TSMA E.10161.

111. See Şeyḫoğlu ʿAlī's letter to Selīm, TSMA E.129.

112. See a certain Bālī's letter to Bāyezīd II, TSMA E.3703: "Şehzāde Sulṭān Selīme varan Ḥasan Beg ve begzādelere ve sūbāşılara ve dūvıcalara ve aḳıncılara ve sāyir aġāvāta . . . Ḳāsım ve . . . Rüstem ve Baltaoğlu Pīrī ve . . . Ḥasan ve sūbāşılardan Pīrī bendeñüz ve bir nice sipāhīler ve Ḳırḳoğlu ʿĪsā ḳulınuz gemiye girüb şehzāde ḥażretleri ile bile gitmek tedārikünde iken." For the list of Selīm's supporters who joined the prince in Akkirman, see TSMA D.7603; and TSMA D.5374.

113. For a list of Ottoman titles and their changing meanings over time, see Bayerle, *Pashas, Begs, and Effendis*.

114. The term *dūvıca* appears in a variety of forms both in contemporary Ottoman sources and in modern scholarly studies, most commonly as "*ṭovica*." In her authoritative analysis of the subject, Irène Beldiceanu-Steinherr refers to these soldiers as "*ṭoviǧe*" and states that they were fief-holding "deputy chiefs" (*sous-chefs*) of raiders. See Beldiceanu-Steinherr, "En Marge d'un Acte Concernant le Penǧyek et les Aqınǧı," 32–34. See also Deny, "Osmanlı Ancien *Tovija*." For references to *aḳıncı* officers who, as late as 1571, possessed land grants (rendered by Barkan as "*çiftliklü tviçe*") in Ottoman registers of important affairs (*mühimme defteri*), see Barkan, "Osmanlı İmparatorluğunda Bir İskân ve Kolonizasyon Metodu Olarak Sürgünler" (1951–1952), 73–74. For a brief but comprehensive discussion of the duties of these soldiers in the Ottoman army, see Kiprovska, "The Military Organization of the *Akıncı*s in Ottoman Rumelia," 67–68. In *Tarama Sözlüğü*, it is rendered as *tovuça/tovuca*, described as "a type of volunteer soldier" and used as a synonym for "raider" (*aḳıncı*). See Aksoy and Dilçin, eds., *Tanıklarıyla Tarama Sözlüğü*, vol. 5, 3832. Abdülkadir Özcan spells it *toyca* or *taviçe*. See *DİA*, s.v. "Akıncı" (A. Özcan). Mehmet Zeki Pakalın renders the term as *taviç* or *tavice* and claims that these were "native Christian raiders" (*yerli Hıristiyan akıncılar*). See Pakalın, *Osmanlı Tarih Deyimleri ve Terimleri Sözlüğü*, vol. 1, 36–40. İsmail Hakkı Uzunçarşılı, who uses *tavıca*, states that these were officers responsible for the summoning of rank-and-file raiders. See *İA*, s.v. "Akıncı" (İ. H. Uzunçarşılı). On the *aḳıncı* organization and its role in the westward expansion of the Ottoman realm, see *EI²*, s.v. "Aḳındjı" (A. Decei); and Arslan, "Erken Osmanlı Dönemi (1299–1453)'nde Akıncılar ve Akıncı Beyleri." Ottoman sources referring to this group of soldiers include but are not limited to Ḫalīl b. İsmāʿīl,

Menāḳıb-ı Şeyḫ Bedreddīn, 48a: *duvıcalar*; ʿĀşıḳpaşazāde, *Menāḳıb* (Giese edition), 82: *ṭavcılar*; and Yūsuf, *Tārīḫ*, 102: *ṭuvcılar*.

115. Perhaps the best depiction of the economic dependence of the *aḳıncı* on raiding expeditions can be found in Giovanni Maria Angiolello's eyewitness account of Meḥmed II's campaign of 1473 against Uzun Ḥasan (r. 1453–1478): "Besides the five columns we have mentioned, there was also another of the Aganzi, who are not paid, except by the booty which they may gain in guerilla warfare. These men do not encamp with the rest of the army, but go traversing, pillaging, and wasting the country of the enemy on every side, and yet keep up a great and excellent discipline among themselves, both in the division of the plunder and in the execution of all their enterprises. In this division were thirty thousand men, remarkably well mounted." Angiolello, "A Short Narrative of the Life and Acts of the King Ussun Cassano," 80–81. There is evidence to suggest, however, that, at least in some cases, *aḳıncı* troops received advance payment to cover their campaign expenses. For the facsimile, transliteration, and translation of Meḥmed II's order (dated 1472) regarding the conscription of raiders to that effect, see Lowry, *The Nature of the Early Ottoman State*, 53–54.

116. See Selīm's letter to Bāyezīd II, TSMA E.12276: "devletlü ḫüdāvendigār ḥażretleri Rūmili livālarından Semendire livāsını bu bendesine ṣadaḳa idüb aḳın itmekiçün icāzet buyurulduḳda baʿżı aḳıncılardan kimesneler cemʿ itmek ṣadedinde iken baʿżı ṣubaşılar ve sipāhīler cemʿ olunub Zağra Eskisinde sākin olunub."

117. Spy reports composed by Bāyezīd II's agents, as well as petitions sent by Selīm's supporters to him after he successfully deposed his father, indicate the extent of the military support he enjoyed in Rumelia. See, among others, TSMA E.6062; TSMA E.6081; TSMA E.6211; TSMA E.6619; TSMA E.6623; TSMA E.7054; TSMA E.7294; TSMA E.7634; TSMA E.8093; TSMA E.8150; TSMA E.9969; TSMA E.10013; and TSMA E.10030.

118. Celālzāde, *Meʾāṣir*, 54b: "Anāṭolıdan ve Rūm ve Ḳaramāndan gelen bahādırlaruñ āʿyān ve dilāverlerinden baʿżıları."

119. Celālzāde, *Meʾāṣir*, 54b–55a: "Atam āsitānesinde olan bī-hünerler ṭarrārlar māl-ü-menāle ṭamaʿakārlar hedāyā-vü-pīşkeşleri maʿbūd idinürler ṭaparlar belāya mübtelālardır ecdād-ı ʿiẓāmım devirlerinden berü āsitānemize ḫıẕmet idegelen merdümzādeleri ve yarār ve güzīde pehlevān ve nāmdār yigitleri ilerü getürmekden el çeküb dayimā terbiyet-ü-iḥsānları ḳul ṭāʾifesine münḥaṣır olub ḳuldan ġayrıya manṣıb virmedikleri içün vilāyet-ü-memleketimiz ḫalḳınūñ yarārları Ḳızılbāş ṭāʾifesine meyl eyleyüb ol āsitāne ile buluşmak üzre olmuşlardır deyü işitdüm Gürcīye aḳın itmegi ol ecilden iḫtiyār idüb sizi getürmekden murādım bu idi benüm naẓar-ı ferḫunde-eṣerüm sizüñ ṭāʾifeñüzedür dedelerimiz

zemānlarından berü bize naṣīḥatler ol vechiledir ki āsitānemizde aṣıl ḳulumuz yolumuza ṣadāḳat üzre cān-ü-bāş oynayub bize yoldāşlıḳ ve ḫıẕmet idenlerdir ʿālī manṣıblar ve yarār dirlikler anlaruñdır ḥaḳḳ sübḥānehu ve teʿālā ben ḳulına devlet erzānī iderse benüm naẓar-ı ʿāṭıfet-eṣerüm merdümzādeleredir ḥüsn-i iltifātım yarār ve güzīde ḳılıç uran pehlevānlaradır ḳullarumıza ne minnet anlar ḫāliṣ bendelerdür içlerinde Müslümān ve ehl-i inṣāf pāk-iʿtiḳād dīndār fażāyil-şiʿār olanları ilerü çekmek gerek yoḥsa ḳuldur deyü bī-hünerleri (*sic.*) ḫasīs ve denīlere iʿtibār idüb yarāmazı ādem itmek pādişāhlıḳ ʿalāmeti degildür merdümzādelerden yüz çevirmek revā olmaz inşāʾallāhu teʿālā ben bu niyyet üzre ber-ḳarārım."

120. Whereas the anti-*ḳul* sentiments in the late fifteenth and the early sixteenth centuries reflected a nostalgic yearning to return to the "good old days" when the *ġāzī* ethos reigned supreme, criticisms leveled at the *ḳul* in later periods concerned—primarily although not exclusively—what was perceived as a restrictive policy to appoint to high office only bureaucrats and statesmen of *devşirme* origin. As several such criticisms will be discussed in detail in Chapter 4, noted here as examples are Ḥasan Kāfī's (d. 1616) statements concerning the widespread chaos caused by the royal servants (*ḫünkār ḳulı*) during the last decade of the sixteenth century, Veysī's (d. 1628) rendering of Aḥmed I's complaint regarding the unruly attitude of the royal *ḳul*, and prince Ḳorḳud's (d. 1513) protest against the janissaries' insubordination. See Ḥasan Kāfī, *Uṣūl al-ḥikam*, 275; and Veysī, *Ḫābnāme*, 83. For an examination of Ḳorḳud's complaints, see Fleischer, "From Şeyhzade Korkud to Mustafa Âli," 71.

121. To render the meaning of "champion" or "hero," Celālzāde uses *bahādır*, *yigit*, and *pehlevān* interchangeably.

122. To the best of my knowledge, Mevlānā ʿĪsā is the only other Ottoman author who mentioned this term within the context of Selīm's bid for the throne. See *Cāmiʿü'l-meknūnāt*, 75b. Feridun Emecen, probably confusing the term *merd-i tīmār* (also *tīmār eri*, which meant *tīmār*-holder) with the term *merdümzāde*, states that *merdümzāde*s were *tīmār*-holders; he ignores, however, not only that Celālzāde makes no mention of the latter but also that Selīm's target audience included militarily active men of diverse backgrounds, possibly including but definitely not limited to timariots. Emecen, *Zamanın İskenderi, Şarkın Fatihi*, 38–39.

123. The term is a compound noun (*merdüm-zāde*). The second part of the compound (*-zāde*) means "son of." The exact meaning of the first part is difficult to capture. In its original Persian form (*mardum*), *merdüm* meant "a (polite, civilized, worthy) man," while in its Ottoman-Turkish rendering, the primary meaning of the term appears to be more literal, namely "man," "person," or

"human being." In a salary register (*mevācib defteri*) prepared in the beginning of Selīm's reign, for example, the phrase "man of" (*merdüm-i*, also *m.* in shorthand) is used to identify individual members of the royal retinue at the imperial palace by their association to specific members of the military ruling elite. See TSMA D. 2921-1. For the significance of this register within the context of Selīm's bid for the sultanate, see Çıpa, "The Centrality of the Periphery," Chapter 4. It is also possible that the opacity of such terms was intentional. For a discussion of similarly and perhaps deliberately vague terms, such as *Rūm oġlānı* and *evlād-ı ʿArab*, see Hathaway, "The *Evlâd-i ʿArab* ('Sons of the Arabs') in Ottoman Egypt."

124. In a petition addressed to the vizier at his father's court, Ḳorḳud referred to himself as *kişizāde* in order to emphasize his noble, dynastic descent. For a discussion of this letter and its historical context, see Uluçay, "Yavuz Sultan Selim Nasıl Padişah Oldu?," (1953), 58–61. For the facsimile, transliteration, and an English translation of this letter, see al-Tikriti, "Şehzade Korkud," 334–41. Al-Tikriti renders the term as "nobility." Luṭfī Pasha argues for the promotion to high office of sons of viziers (*vezīrzāde*), provided they were meritorious. See Luṭfī, *Āṣafnāme* (Uğur edition), 253.

125. All three references to *merdümzāde*s are either preceded or followed by the mention of *ḳul*s, and Selīm's praise for the former is always coupled with criticism of the latter.

126. Celālzāde, *Meʾās̱ir*, 48b: "Sulṭān Bāyezīd Ḫān zamānına gelince . . . ʿatabe-yi ʿulyā-yı ʿOs̱māniyyede ʿādet ve ḳānūn cümle-yi şāhān-ı ʿālī-şānuñ ḳapuları mesdūd olmāyub mekşūf olub . . . erkān-ı devlet ve āʿyān-ı salṭanatları ol zemānenüñ merdümzādeleri kemāl-i maʿarif-ü-feżāyil ile maʿmūr āzādeleri olub ḥaḳīḳaten müslümānlar pāk iʿtiḳādlar nisbet-ü-taʿaṣṣubdan ʿārī ḥaḳḳ-şināslar merḥamet-istināslar ṣāliḥ-ü-mütedeyyinler olurlardı . . . bu evṣāf ile maʿmūr ve mevṣūf olmāyınca kimesne pādişāha vezīr olmazdı merdümzāde aṣīl olmayub lakin ʿatabe-yi ʿulyālarında beslenüb ādāb-ü-taʿlīm ile mürebbā feżayil-ü-maʿarif ile maʿmūr ve muʿallā olmuş bendelerden kimesne irişürse ki vezārete tamām müsteḥaḳḳ ve lāyıḳ ola aña daḫī ol maḳām-ı muʿallāyı ʿināyet iderlerdi."

127. On elite households, see Abou-El-Haj, "The Ottoman Vezir and Paşa Households"; Hathaway, *The Politics of Households*; and Toledano, *Slavery and Abolition in the Ottoman Middle East*, especially 20–53.

128. For a discussion of what Tijana Krstić calls "one-upmanship in religion" as an important facet of Ottoman political life in the sixteenth century, see Krstić, "Conversion and Converts to Islam in Ottoman Historiography of the Fifteenth and Sixteenth Centuries," 70–71. On the significance of the ethnic and

geographical origins of members of the Ottoman ruling elite as a source of sociopolitical cohesion, see Kunt, "Ethnic-Regional (*Cins*) Solidarity."

129. Celālzāde, *Meʾāsir*, 53b: "ʿatabe-yi ʿulyāda olan mutaṣarrıfān-ı salṭanat ve mübāşirān-i umūr-ı ḫilāfetüñ naẓar-ı kīmyā-eserleri cümle ḳul tāyifesine olub ḥaseb-ü-neseb ṣāḥibleri olan merdümzādeler ve ocāḳ erleri derecāt-ı ʿulyāda olan menāṣıbdan maḥrūm ḳalub ḫāssa tīmār etmegi yarāra virilmeyüb bī-aṣl-ü-bī-ḥamiyyet denīlere ḫasīs-ü-cehl-küster küştenīlere maʿrifden ḫālī-vü-ʿārī hedāyā-nisār-ü-irtişā-şiʿār nādānlara muḫanneslere tevcīh olunmaġla dilāverler ilerü gelmekden meʾyūs olub cümle ḫavāṭıra ıżṭırāb gelüb."

130. For Mevlānā ʿĪsā and his oeuvre, see Flemming, "Der *Ǧāmiʿ ül-Meknūnāt*"; and Flemming, "Ṣāḥib-Ḳırān und Mahdī." Flemming states that *Cāmiʿü'l-meknūnāt* must have been composed sometime between 1529 and 1535 ("Der *Ǧāmiʿ ül-Meknūnāt*," 84).

131. See *Cāmiʿü'l-meknūnāt*, 75b: "Kande merdümzāde var aña varur"; 76a: "Rūm ilinde ḳande bir yarar yigit / Vār-ise yānına vardı ki işit" and "Geldi ḫāna Rūm ilinüñ begleri."

132. A rare glimpse is provided by a certain Bālī's aforementioned letter to Bāyezīd II, TSMA E. 3703.

133. The document in question is in the Topkapı Palace Museum Archives and is registered under the catalog number TSMA D.5374. Another document, TSMA D.7603, which is seemingly identical at first glance, must be an earlier draft of TSMA D.5374. For a discussion of the interrelationship between these two versions, see Çıpa, "The Centrality of the Periphery," 44–51.

134. The names of thirty-six military commanders are listed in accordance with the order in which they appear in TSMA D.5374. The first numerical entry in the parenthetical note after each name indicates the total amount of money allocated to that particular individual; the second numerical entry refers to the amount spent. Although there is no indication in either document as to the monetary unit implied, asper (*akçe*) is most probable. The names and figures in brackets reflect the record in TSMA D.7603, an earlier draft of TSMA D.5374. The names of Üveys Beg's son Meḥmed Beg, Gümlioğlu Muṣṭafā Beg, Yaʿḳūb the Physician's son Maḥmūd, and Üveys voyvoda of Malḳoçoğlu do not appear in TSMA D.7603. The military commanders who came with Selīm from Kefe (*Kefeden bile gelenler*) included Maḥmūd [Meḥmed] Beg, son of İlaldı Sulṭān (100,000/71,300); Gümlioğlu İskender Beg (30,000/19,100); Ḳarlıoğlu İskender Beg (30,000/17,721); Muṣṭafā Beg, son of Dāvud Beg (40,000/25,810); Meḥmed [Muḥammed], son of the governor of Eġriboz (45,000/32,000); ʿAlī, son of the governor of Eġriboz (27,000/16,000); Muṣṭafā Beg, son of Ḳāsım Beg (50,000/20,000); and Muḥammed Beg of Mora (35,000/22,800). The military commanders who joined Selīm

from Akkirman onward (*Akkirmandan berü istikbāle gelenler*) included Meḥmed [Muḥammed] Beg, son of Yaḥyā Pasha (unspecified/142,426); Astaneşoğlu ʿAlī Beg (40,000/28,726); İḫtimānoğlu Ḳāsım Beg (55,000/34,000); İḫtimānoğlu Meḥmed [Muḥammed] (26,000/15,850); Ḫalīl Beg, son of Şādī Beg (47,000/39,100); Meḥemmed Beg, brother of Dilsüz (40,000/29,334); İdrīs Beg, son of 'Ömer Beg (40,000/26,858); İsfendiyāroğlu Celīl Çelebī (86,000/68,510) [70,000/52,000]; Aḥmed Çelebī, son of Rüstem Beg (40,000/31,300); Rüstem Beg, relative (*ḫışm*) of Yaḥyā Pasha (30,000/21,000); Ḳāsım Beg of Güvere (30,000/22,200); Ḥaydar Beg, son of Ḳoca Dāvud Pasha (65,000/51,800); Ḳızḳapanoğlu Ḥüseyin Beg (40,000/32,490); İnaloğlu Meḥmed Beg (25,000/15,000) [25,000/16,400]; Melik Arslan, son of İbrāhīm Beg (30,000/20,000); Mūsā Beg, son of Alp Arslan (40,000/30,853) [40,000/30,000]; Meḥmed Beg, son of the brother of Ḳoca Dāvud Pasha (28,000/23,000); Minnetoğlu Ḳazġān Beg (unspecified/42,074); Pīrī Beg, son of Çengī Ḫıżır Beg (27,000/21,560); Bālī Beg, son of Dāye Ḫātūn (30,000/24,600); Ḫıżır Beg, son of Ṭuraḫān Beg (20,000/15,000); Baltaoğlu Pīrī Beg (40,000/27,304); Bālī Beg, son of İskender Beg (70,000/56,500); Meḥmed Beg, son of Üveys Beg (25,000/17,200); Gümlioğlu Muṣṭafā Beg (25,000/14,240); soldier (*sipāh*) of Cerrāḥ voyvoda (18,000/13,000); Maḥmūd, son of Yaʿḳūb the Physician (*Hekīm*) (18,000/13,000); and Üveys voyvoda of Malḳoçoğlu (25,000/19,000).

135. As I have undertaken a detailed prosopographical investigation elsewhere, the current discussion will be limited to an analysis of that investigation's results. See Çıpa, "The Centrality of the Periphery," Chapter 4.

136. These exceptions are İlaldı Sulṭān's son Maḥmūd [Meḥmed] Beg, Ḳāsım Beg of Güvere, and İnaloğlu Meḥmed Beg. İlaldı Sulṭān was one of Bāyezīd II's daughters (and therefore Selīm's sister), and she sent a congratulatory letter to Selīm on his accession. Selīm appears to have reciprocated with a generous allocation of salary and allowances to one of İlaldı Sulṭān's daughters. See Uluçay, "Bayazıd II.'in Ailesi," 122. One can safely assume that the descriptive "Güvereli" ("of Güvere") in the name of Ḳāsım Beg refers to a toponym, with at least two possibly matching locations near the eastern Mediterranean coast of Asia Minor, one in the province of İçel and the other in Antakya; both were immediately outside the borders of the Ottoman Empire at the time. While one was situated in the area under the control of the Emirate of Ramażān, a vassal state of the Ottomans ruled by one of the petty Anatolian dynasties, the other was part of the lands under Mamluk control. The name of a certain İnaloğlu İbrāhīm, the leader of a local petty dynasty with a power base around Tokad, is mentioned along with several Turcoman leaders with whom Bāyezīd I's son Meḥmed I fought to reestablish Ottoman supremacy in Anatolia after the Battle of Ankara in 1402. Although the İnaloğlus are significant in their own right due

to their opposition to the re-Ottomanization of Anatolia, one of their members, İnaloğlu Meḥmed Beg, seems to be particularly important within the context of Selīm's struggle for the Ottoman throne. More than a century after İnaloğlu İbrāhīm Beg is mentioned as a Turcoman *beg* unsuccessfully fighting Meḥmed I's attempts at recentralization, references to an İnaloğlu Meḥmed Beg place him among the supporters of a prince opposing the central authority of his father, Bāyezīd II. See Neşrī, *Kitāb-ı cihānnümā*, vol. 1, 387; and Imber, *The Ottoman Empire, 1300–1481*, 64.

137. For example, a certain Meḥmed Beg is identified as "sibling of Dilsüz." In all likelihood, the descriptive "Dilsüz" refers to an unidentified deaf-mute individual employed at the Ottoman Palace, probably as guard, attendant, or messenger. This tentative identification hints at a probable connection between two brothers who served two different members of the Ottoman dynasty: one employed within the confines of the imperial palace, serving the sultan, the other active on the battlefield following a dissident prince. On deaf-mutes in Ottoman imperial service, see *EI*[2], s.v. "Dilsiz" (B. Lewis). Another such figure, Bālī Beg, identified as "son of Dāye Ḫātūn," was probably Selīm's son Süleymān's wet-nurse, who commissioned a mosque in the Mahmudpaşa district of Istanbul (1530/1531) and was buried in Eyüb. See Meḥmed Süreyyā, *Sicill*, vol. 2, 326. A certain Maḥmūd, who is identified as "son of Yaʿḳūb the Physician (*Hekīm*)," was the son, or possibly the grandson, of Hekīm Yaʿḳūb Pasha (d. 1484), a palace physician of Jewish descent who rose to prominence during the reign of Meḥmed II. On the career of Yaʿḳūb Pasha, see Lewis, "The Privilege Granted by Meḥmed II to His Physician"; and Uzunçarşılı, *Osmanlı Tarihi*, vol. 2, 523. Ḳızḳapanoğlu Ḥüseyin Beg appears to have been more directly related to Selīm than were other commanders mentioned in the list, as he was most probably the son of Selīm's tutor (*lala*), Ḳızḳapanoğlu Meḥmed Beg.

138. For example, Meḥmed [Muḥammed] and ʿAlī are identified individually as "son of the governor of Eġriboz" (Evvoia/Euobea, Greece).

139. For example, Ḥaydar Beg and Meḥmed Beg are identified as "son of Ḳoca Dāvud Pasha" and "son of the brother of Ḳoca Dāvud Pasha," respectively. For Ḳoca Dāvud Pasha's (d. 1498) career, see Reindl, *Männer um Bāyezīd*, 162–76.

140. Originally a Slavic term denoting the first in command of a military unit, *voivod* (or *voivode*) later came to refer to the governor of a province, similar to the Ottoman-Turkish term *sancaḳbegi*. Although also used as part of the official designation of sovereign princes in Moldavia and Wallachia, the Ottoman rendering of the term seems to have been used generally to refer to commanders in charge of their own troops of raiders in the Balkans. For the various meanings of the term, see Bayerle, *Pashas, Begs, and Effendis*. Taken together with references

to various *akıncı* commanders as *voyvoda* in other Ottoman sources, the list's mention of "Cerrāḥ voyvoda" and "Üveys voyvoda" establishes these figures as frontier lords active as commanders of troops of raiders. For references to a "Ḥasan voyvoda" active as *akıncı* commander in 1498, see Uzunçarşılı, *Osmanlı Tarihi*, vol. 2, 185; for references to a "Yūnus voyvoda" in charge of *akıncı* troops in 1480, see Imber, *The Ottoman Empire, 1300–1481*, 246.

141. See Kastritsis, *The Sons of Bayezid.*

142. ʿĀşıḳpaşazāde's *Menāḳıb* is among the earliest historical accounts that refer to the second Minnet Beg. In the seventy-sixth chapter of ʿĀşıḳpaşazāde's account, which relates the aftermath of Meḥmed I's conquest of Samsun, Minnet Beg is depicted as the leader of a significant group of Tatars who chose to stay in İskilib (modern İskilip, Çorum) after Tīmūr's victory at the Battle of Ankara. According to ʿĀşıḳpaşazāde, Meḥmed I was surprised to learn that not all Tatars departed from Anatolia with Tīmūr. Discontented with the fact that these Tatars did not join his military campaigns even though they were settled within the borders of the Ottoman realm, Meḥmed called for Minnet Beg and ordered their exile (*sürüb*) to Ḳonuşḥiṣārı near Filibe (modern Plovdiv, Bulgaria) in Rumelia. See ʿĀşıḳpaşazāde, *Menāḳıb* (Yavuz and Saraç edition), 425–26. See also Neşrī, *Kitāb-ı cihānnümā*, vol. 2, 543. For a discussion of the transfer of Minnet Beg's Tatars to Rumelia, see Boykov, "In Search of Vanished Ottoman Monuments in the Balkans," 48–49.

143. ʿĀşıḳpaşazāde portrays Minnet Beg and his followers as a destitute bunch and bluntly dismisses the designation of *ġāzī* (which at least some of his contemporaries used for Minnet Beg), referring instead to the Tatar leader simply as *akın begi* (commander of raiders). But the role that Minnet Beg's son Meḥmed Beg played in the development of the Tatars' new settlements in Ḳonuşḥiṣārı is appreciated by several Ottoman chroniclers. See ʿĀşıḳpaşazāde, *Menāḳıb* (Yavuz and Saraç edition), 425–26; Neşrī, *Kitāb-ı cihānnümā*, vol. 2, 543; and Yūsuf, *Tārīḫ*, 95. A certain "Minnetzāde" is mentioned among the prominent commanders who joined Murād II at the Battle of Varna in 1444, whereas a "Minnetoğlu Meḥmed Beg" is referred to as the governor who collected the revenue of Serbia (*Lāz İli*) and was granted the governorship of Bosna in 1463. See Yūsuf, *Tārīḫ*, 153, 163; Neşrī, *Kitāb-ı cihānnümā*, vol. 2, 767; and Uzunçarşılı, *Osmanlı Tarihi*, vol. 2, 82–83. On Minnet Beg's descendants and their relationship with the Ottoman administration, see Boykov, "In Search of Vanished Ottoman Monuments in the Balkans," especially 59–60.

144. İsfendiyār Beg was the son of Bāyezīd Beg (d. 1385), ruler of the principality of Cāndār. For the history of the Cāndāroğlu emirate, see Yücel, *Anadolu Beylikleri Hakkında Araştırmalar*, vol. 1, 53–181. Following the crushing defeat

the Ottoman army suffered at the Battle of Ankara, İsfendiyār Beg first joined Meḥmed Beg, the ruler of the principality of Menteşe, in accepting the overlordship of Tīmūr and then gained control of former lands of the Cāndāroğlu principality, including Kastamonu. During the interregnum period he became known as a key supporter first of ʿĪsā (d. 1408) and then of Mūsā (d. 1413), who, using the Balkans as their power base, contested Meḥmed Çelebi's claim to the Ottoman throne. Even after Meḥmed I reunified the Ottoman realm in 1413, İsfendiyār Beg continued to challenge the sultan's authority and sided with Sheikh Bedreddīn b. İsrāʾīl (d. 1416), former chief military judge of Mūsā and leader of probably the most important, albeit failed, revolutionary movement in Ottoman history. Despite effective marriage alliances between the two families, relations between the Ottoman rulers and the emirs of İsfendiyār were colored by their open struggle to gain direct control of regions along the Black Sea coast during the reigns of Murād II and Meḥmed II. Yet even the tensest periods seem to have been punctuated by episodes of peaceful negotiation and mutual acts of generosity. Especially noteworthy in this context is Meḥmed II's grant of Filibe to İsmāʿīl Beg of İsfendiyār, not only because it temporarily eased the tensions between the two dynasties but also because it provided a power base in the Balkans for later generations of emirs. See Yücel, "Candar-oğlu Çelebi İsfendiyar Bey"; Uzunçarşılı, *Osmanlı Tarihi*, vol. 1, 85, 88; Çıpa, "Contextualizing Şeyḫ Bedreddīn"; and Ḫalīl b. İsmāʿīl, *Menāḳıb-ı Şeyḫ Bedreddīn*, 44a–45a. For a detailed analysis of İsfendiyāroğlu İsmāʿīl Beg's architectural patronage and governorship of Filibe, see Boykov, "Anatolian *Emir* in Rumelia." For İsmāʿīl Beg's architectural patronage in Kastamonu, see Çetin, *Candaroğlu Yurdunda Bey İmaretleri*, 61–96. For information in Ottoman cadastral registers on the pious endowments of the İsfendiyāroğlu family, see Gökbilgin, *XV. ve XVI. Asırlarda Edirne ve Paşa Livası*, 328–30. İsmāʿīl Beg's titulature, as recorded in the dedicatory inscriptions of his buildings and his endowment deeds, rivals Ottoman claims to preeminence in the Muslim world. In these İsmāʿīl Beg is referred to as "the great sultan (*as-sulṭānu'l-muʿaẓẓam*)" and the "great sultan and emperor [and] master of the Arab and Persian realms (*as-sulṭān wa'l-khāḳānu'l-ʿaẓīm mawlātu'l-mulūku'l-ʿarab wa'l-ʿacam*)." For İsmāʿīl Beg's titles in dedicatory inscriptions in Kastamonu and his endowment deeds, see Yücel, *Anadolu Beylikleri Hakkında Araştırmalar*, vol. 1, 173–75 and 113n366, respectively.

145. These commanders were Gümlioğlu İskender Beg, Gümlioğlu Muṣṭafā Beg, Ḳarlıoğlu İskender Beg, İḫtimānoğlu Ḳāsım Beg, İḫtimānoğlu Meḥmed, Üveys voyvoda of Malḳoçoğlu, Ṭuraḫān Beg's son Ḫızır Beg, Malḳoçoğlu Yaḥyā Pasha's son Meḥmed Beg, and Yaḥyā Pasha's relative (*ḫışm*) Rüstem Beg. Whereas a certain Muṣṭafā Beg, son of Ḳāsım Beg, mentioned in the list was most probably a

member of the İḫtimānoğlu family, Muḥammed Beg of Mora and ʿÖmer Beg's son İdrīs Beg may have descended from the lineage of the Ṭuraḫānoğlu. For a discussion regarding the identities of the last three figures, see Çıpa, "The Centrality of the Periphery," 181–83, 190–91.

146. Originally Malkovič, i.e., Markovič. On this family's origins, members, and their roles as military leaders and office-holders, see Babinger, "Beiträge zur Geschichte des Geschlechtes der Malkoč-oghlu's"; Başar, "Malkoçoğulları"; and Zlatar, "O Malkočima," 105–14. On the Malḳoçoğlus' architectural patronage, see *DİA*, s.v. "Malkoç Bey Camii" (S. Eyice); *DİA*, s.v. "Malkoçoğlu Türbesi" (S. Eyice); and Gero, "Neuere Angaben zur Geschichte der türkischen Architektur in Ungarn," 191–209.

147. Meḥmed Süreyyā, *Sicill*, vol. 4, 94.

148. For the careers of ʿAlī and ʿAlī Ṭur, see Meḥmed Süreyyā, *Sicill*, vol. 3, 495. For references to Malḳoçoğlu Bālī Pasha as governor of Semendire in 1476, and his participation in raids into Wallachia in 1480, see Imber, *The Ottoman Empire, 1300–1481*, 228; and Meḥmed Süreyyā, *Sicill*, vol. 2, 3.

149. Uruç, *Tevārīḫ* (Öztürk edition), 179.

150. Malḳoçoğlu Ṭur ʿAlī Beg's death is recorded in a register prepared in the immediate aftermath of the Battle of Çaldıran. See BOA, Maliyeden Müdevver 7, 85a. I would like to thank Mariya Kiprovska for this reference. See also Ṣolaḳzāde, *Tārīḫ* (TSMK B.199), 200a.

151. See TSMA D.5374.

152. On the career of Yaḥyā Pasha, see Reindl, *Männer um Bāyezīd*, 336–45. On his marriage into the sultan's family, see Uluçay, "Bayazıd II.'in Ailesi," 118.

153. On Meḥmed Pasha's life, career, and architectural patronage, see Fotić, "Yahyapaşa-oğlu Mehmed Pasha's *Evkaf* in Belgrade."

154. Although the exact amount allocated to Meḥmed Beg is not specified, the list indicates that he spent a total of 142,426 *aḳçes*, suggesting that his actual allotment was much larger. The second-largest sum allocated to a commander mentioned in the list is 100,000 *aḳçes* (for Maḥmūd Beg, son of İlaldı Sulṭān), and the third largest is 86,000 *aḳçes* (for İsfendiyāroğlu Celīl Çelebi).

155. Laonikos Chalkokondyles (d. ca. 1490) refers to the earliest representative of this family as "Koumouli." See Kurat, *Die türkische Prosopographie bei Laonikos Chalkokandyles*, 56; and Anonymous, *Ġazavāt-ı Sulṭān Murād*, 105n36. In modern scholarship, the name of this family is rendered in various forms. Faik Reşit Unat and Mehmed A. Köymen, the editors of Neşrī's *Kitāb-ı cihānnümā*, render the name as "Gümlüoğlu"; Efdal Sevinçli, the editor of Yūsuf b. ʿAbdullāh's history, as "Gümlü oglı"; Nuri Akbayar, the editor of Meḥmed Süreyyā's *Sicill*, as "Kümlüoğlu"; Kemal Yavuz and M. A. Yekta Saraç, the editors of ʿĀşıḳpaşazāde's *Menāḳıb*, as "Kömlüoglı"; and Colin Imber as "Kümelioğlu."

156. On this curious episode in Ottoman history, see Melville-Jones, "Three Mustafas (1402–1430)"; ʿĀşıḳpaşazāde, *Menāḳıb* (Yavuz and Saraç edition), 434; and Neşrī, *Kitāb-ı cihānnümā*, vol. 2, 561. This rebellion is noteworthy in that it reveals that the Rumelian supporters of both Muṣṭafā and Selīm belonged to the same sociopolitical stratum.

157. Yūsuf, *Tārīḫ*, 111.

158. Even as he prepared for his campaigns of 1443–1444, Murād II appears to have remembered how easily the frontier lords switched sides. See Anonymous, *Ġazavāt-ı Sulṭān Murād*, 13.

159. For probably the earliest extant source on the endowments (*vaḳıf*) and freehold properties (*mülk*) of the Gümlioğlu family in Zağra Eskisi (Stara Zagora, Bulgaria), dated 1489, see BOA, Tahrir Defteri 26, 50–53. For an eighteenth-century record of the endowment deed, see Vakıflar Genel Müdürlüğü Arşivi, Vakfiye Defteri 734, f. 77, no. 49. For references to archival documentation regarding grants of freehold properties and endowments to specific members of the family, such as Ṣālṭıḳ, İskender, and Paşa Yigit, see Gökbilgin, *XV. ve XVI. Asırlarda Edirne ve Paşa Livası*, 229–31. For a brief study of the endowments of the Gümlioğlu family, see Pala, "Rumeli'de Bir Akıncı Ailesi: Gümlüoğulları ve Vakıfları." Unfortunately, Pala simply repeats the information provided by earlier scholars, such as M. Tayyib Gökbilgin and Halil İnalcık, and confuses the identities of two commanders by the name Paşa Yigit; his article is useful, however, as a point of departure, as it provides a short but updated bibliography on this family of frontier lords.

160. See Anonymous, *Ġazavāt-ı Sulṭān Murād*, 41, 105n36; and Imber, *The Ottoman Empire, 1300–1481*, 130.

161. Gümlioğlu Muṣṭafā Beg's death is recorded in a register prepared in the immediate aftermath of the Battle of Çaldıran. See BOA, Maliyeden Müdevver 7, 84b. I would like to thank Mariya Kiprovska and Grigor Boykov for this reference.

162. For a brief discussion of the relevant section of the register dated 925/1519, see Gökbilgin, *XV. ve XVI. Asırlarda Edirne ve Paşa Livası*, 229. Another register mentioning Gümlioğlu İskender Beg is dated 1530. See BOA, Tahrir Defteri 370, ff. 2, 65, 73–74.

163. Carlo Tocco was count of Cephalonia and despot of Ioannina (Ott. Yanya) and Arta (Ott. Narda) in Epirus; his descendants continued to hold the empty title Despot of Epirus well into the seventeenth century. On the history of the Tocco family, see Zachariadou, "Les Tocco," 11–22; and Uzunçarşılı, *Osmanlı Tarihi*, vol. 1, 411. An anonymous fifteenth-century chronicle on the Tocco family was published by Giuseppe Schirò; see *Cronaca dei Tocco di Cefalonia: Prolegomeni, Testo Critico e Traduzione*.

164. According to Franz Babinger, the term "Ḳarlı-ili" was used not to refer to Carlo Tocco's dominion in Epirus but to part of Macedonia (the area around Prilep, Monastir/Bitolja, Štip) ruled by Marko Kraljevič (d. 1395). The original usage, therefore, was not *Ḳārlı-ili* (after *Carlo*) but *Ḳral-ili* (after *Kraljevič*). See Babinger, *Beiträge zur Frühgeschichte der Türkenherrschaft in Rumelien*, 74n36. For the history of the region, see Babinger, "Beiträge zur Geschichte von Qarly-Eli." For an overview of the province of Ḳarlı-ili in the Ottoman period, see *DİA*, s.v. "Karlı-ili" (M. Kiel); and *EI*², s.v. "Karlı-īli, also Karlo-īli" (V. L. Ménage). Neşrī attests to the strategic importance of this region by referring to its fortresses as "the lock of the province of Morea" (*Mora vilāyetinüñ kilīdidür*). See Neşrī, *Kitāb-ı cihānnümā*, vol. 2, 733.

165. Imber, *The Ottoman Empire, 1300–1481*, 71, 96, 111.

166. Neşrī refers to the family's area of influence in the late 1450s, whereas Uruç b. ʿĀdil mentions a certain Ḳarlıoğlu as one of Bayezīd II's frontier lords around 1498. See Neşrī, *Kitāb-ı cihānnümā*, vol. 2, 735; and Uruç, *Tevārīḫ* (Öztürk edition), 179.

167. For a discussion of the identity of ʿAlī b. Ḳarlı (or Ḳarlıoğlu ʿAlī Beg) and his role in the foundation and development of the town of Karlovo, see Boykov, "Karlızâde ʿAli Bey." The original endowment deed has not survived. For the text of a nineteenth-century copy of the deed and its Bulgarian translation by Boris Nedkov, see Todorov and Nedkov (eds.), *Fontes Turcici Historiae Bulgaricae*, vol. 2, 480–97.

168. A cadastral register dated 1478–1479 includes evidence that Ḳarlıoğlu ʿAlī Beg was granted a prebend (*tīmār*) in the province of Thessaloniki during the reign of Meḥmed II. See BOA, Tahrir Defteri 7, 276–78: "Tīmār-ı ʿAlī Beg veled-i Ḳarlı (prebend of ʿAlī Beg, son of Ḳarlı)." Another register, dated 1516, indicates that ʿAlī Beg's landed estates in Karlova were granted private property (*mülk*) status during the reign of Bāyezīd II. See BOA, Tahrir Defteri 77, 835. I am grateful to Grigor Boykov for allowing me access to the digital copies of these cadastral registers. For the transliteration and a Russian translation of Murād IV's decree (*fermān*) dated 1632, see Galabov, "Turetskie dokumentiy po istorii goroda Karlovo," 168–72.

169. For the text, English translation, and a photograph of this inscription, see Boykov, "Karlızâde ʿAli Bey," 248, 263.

170. For the office of the princely tutor (*lala*) and his duties, see *EI*², s.v. "Lālā" (C. E. Bosworth); and Uzunçarşılı, *Osmanlı Devletinin Saray Teşkilâtı*, 123–25, 128.

171. Şikārī, *Ḳaramānnāme*, 243. For a discussion of the identity of Frenk ʿAlī Beg, see Boykov, "Karlızâde ʿAli Bey," 249–51. For the authoritative sources on the succession struggle between Bāyezīd and Cem, see Vatin, *Sultan Djem*.

172. For evidence of Bāyezīd II's grant of private property (*mülk*) status to ʿAlī Beg's estates in Karlova, see BOA, Tahrir Defteri 77, 835.

173. See Boykov, "Karlızâde ʿAli Bey," 252–53.

174. For references to prebends (*tīmār*) in Manastır (Bitola, Macedonia) granted in 1519–1520 to Ḳāsım and Aḥmed, the sons of a certain Ḳarlıoğlu Sinān Beg, see BOA, Tahrir Defteri 73, 290–303.

175. For information about this mosque complex, which the renowned seventeenth-century traveler Evliyā Çelebi referred to as "Ḳarluzāde," see Evliyā Çelebi, *Seyāḥatnāme*, vol. 5, 297; Evliyā Çelebi, *Seyāḥatnāme*, vol. 5, 556; Kumbaracı-Bogojeviç, *Üsküp'te Osmanlı Mimarî Eserleri*, 184–88; and *DİA*, s.v. "Karlı-ili Beyi Mehmed Bey Külliyesi" (M. Özer). For archival evidence concerning Ḳarlıoğlu Meḥmed Beg's service to the Ottoman state as governor (*sancaḳ begi*) of Vulçitrin (Vučitrn, Kosovo) in 1514, see BOA, Maliyeden Müdevver 7, 111b. In another register he is mentioned as the deputy administrator (*ketḫüdā*) of the province of Rumelia in 1503; see IAK, Muallim Cevdet, O.71, 9a. One of Meḥmed Beg's companions (*merdüm*) is specifically mentioned as "İskender m. Meḥmed Beg b. Ḳarlı"; he is among members of the mounted regiment of "sword-bearers" (*silāḥdār*) at Selīm's court in the earliest salary register (*mevācib defteri*) of his reign. See TSMA D.2921-1, 11a.

176. Uluçay, "Bayazıd II.'in Ailesi," 118.

177. Although Dāvud Pasha's son Muṣṭafā Pasha, Yaḥyā Pasha, Ḳarlıoğlu Meḥmed Beg, and Hersekzāde Aḥmed Pasha were married to Bāyezīd II's daughters, other members of these prominent families supported Selīm's bid for the sultanate. Malḳoçoğlu ʿAlī Beg's marriage to Prince Ḳorḳud's daughter also did not preclude the military assistance Selīm received from other members of this noble family of frontier lords. For a complete list of Bāyezīd II's sons-in-law, see Uluçay, "Bayazıd II.'in Ailesi," 117–24.

178. For a transliteration of the undated document (TSMA D.9772) and a discussion of its content and probable date of composition (ca. 1526), see Barkan, "H. 933–934 (M. 1527–1528) Malî Yılına Ait Bir Bütçe Örneği," 303–7. Ḳarlıoğlu İskender Beg is mentioned as the commander of "müsellemān-ı Ḳırḳkilīsā" on page 304.

179. For a recent study on the Ṭuraḫānoğlu family and their relations with the Ottoman dynasty, see Stavrides, "Alternative Dynasties."

180. The two "wings" of the troops of Rumelian raiders, the "left wing" and the "right wing," were referred to as "Ṭurḫānlu" and "Mīḫāllu," respectively. See Káldy-Nagy, "The First Centuries of the Ottoman Military Organization," 178; and Imber, *The Ottoman Empire, 1300–1650*, 260–65. For the geographical distribution of districts from which raiders were recruited for the respective "wings," see Kiprovska, "The Military Organization of the *Akıncıs* in Ottoman Rumelia," 80–81.

181. Stavrides, "Alternative Dynasties"; L. Kayapınar, "Teselya Bölgesinin Fatihi Turahan Bey Ailesi ve XV.–XVI. Yüzyıllardaki Hayır Kurumları"; L. Kayapınar, "The Charitable Foundations of the Family of Turahan Bey"; Başar, "Turahanoğulları," 47–50;

182. For the Ṭuraḫānoğlu family's architectural patronage, see Kiel, "Das türkische Thessalien," 109–96; Halaçoğlu, "Teselya Yenişehiri ve Türk Eserleri Hakkında Bir Araştırma," 89–99; Özer, "Edirne-Uzunköprü-Kırkkavak Köyü Gazi Turhan Bey Külliyesi," 367–88; and L. Kayapınar, "Teselya Bölgesinin Fatihi Turahan Bey Ailesi ve XV.-XVI. Yüzyıllardaki Hayır Kurumları," 183–95. On their military service to the Ottoman enterprise, see, for example, Uzunçarşılı, *Osmanlı Tarihi*, vol. 2, 21, 24–28, 71, 76, 99, 100–102, 112, 114–15, 121–22.

183. Babinger's statement about Ḥasan Beg's career is based on Meḥmed Süreyyā. Babinger even refers to a certain Fāʾiḳ Pasha, a late descendant of Ṭuraḫān Beg who was executed in 1643 because of his extortions as governor of Rumelia. See *EI*², s.v. "Turakhān Beg" (F. Babinger).

184. A budgetary register prepared during the early years of Süleymān I's reign mentions Ṭuraḫānoğlu İdrīs Beg as "İdrīs Beg, son of ʿÖmer Beg (ʿÖmer Beg oğlu İdrīs Beg)," the governor of Rūm-ḳalʿa near Aleppo. See Barkan, "H. 933–934 (M. 1527–1528) Malî Yılına Ait Bir Bütçe Örneği," 306. It is possible that one additional Ṭuraḫānoğlu joined forces with Selīm. The list of Selīm's supporters also includes a certain "Muḥammed Beg of Morea." Although the toponymic designation of Morea as the origin of this commander immediately evokes the name of the Ṭuraḫānoğlu family (and the name of a certain "Meḥmed Beg" indeed comes up among the sons of Ṭuraḫān Beg), it is difficult to ascertain whether he was alive during Selīm's struggle for the throne. No definitive conclusion can be reached at this point, but it is not impossible that "Muḥammed Beg of Morea" was in fact "Meḥmed Beg, son of Ṭuraḫān Beg." Meḥmed Süreyyā states that Ṭuraḫānoğlu Meḥmed Beg went missing after 1480. See Meḥmed Süreyyā, *Sicill*, vol. 3, 254.

185. See Káldy-Nagy, "The First Centuries of the Ottoman Military Organization," 178; and Imber, *The Ottoman Empire, 1300–1650*, 264.

186. For the history of the Mīḫāloğlu family composed by a later descendant, see Nüzhet Paşa, *Aḥvāl-i Ġāzī Mīḫāl*. For informative but unfortunately somewhat outdated studies of this distinguished family, see Trifonov, "Tarih ve Rivâyetlerde Mihalbey Oğulları"; Gökçek, "Köse Mihal Oğulları"; Başar, "Mihaloğulları"; and Sümer, "Osman Gazi'nin Silah Arkadaşlarından Mihal Gazi." For the most recent studies, including updated information and analysis, see Sabev, "The Legend of Köse Mihal"; Sabev, "Osmanlıların Balkanları Fethi ve İdaresinde Mihaloğulları Ailesi"; and Kiprovska, "Byzantine Renegade and Holy Warrior."

187. Ḥarmanḳaya, modern Harmanköy, is situated near Bilecik, Turkey. See ʿĀşıḳpaşazāde, *Menāḳıb* (Yavuz and Saraç edition), 331–34. On debates concerning the location of Ḥarmanḳaya, see Gazimihal, "Harmankaya Nerededir?"; Erdem, "Harmancık - Harmankaya"; Gazimihal, "Harmankaya Nerededir III"; Gazimihal, "Harmancık ve Mihaloğulları I"; Gazimihal, "Harmancık ve Mihaloğulları II"; and Gazimihal, "Rumeli Mihaloğulları ve Harmankaya." On the Mīḫāloġlus' estates near Ḥarmanḳaya, see Gazimihal, "İstanbul Muhasaralarında Mihâloğulları."

188. On the raiding expeditions led by members of this family, see Levend, *Ġazavāt-nāmeler*, 187–96.

189. For the most up-to-date discussion of the prebends and properties granted to the Mīḫāloġlus, see Kiprovska, "Shaping the Ottoman Borderland," especially 192–207.

190. Like other noble families of frontier lords, the Mīḫāloġlus contributed to the development of the Rumelian provinces through architectural patronage. See, for example, Kiprovska, "The Mihaloğlu Family"; Eyice, "Sofya Yakınında İhtiman'da Gaazî Mihaloğlu Mahmud Bey İmâret-Câmii"; *DİA*, s.v. "Gazi Mihaloğlu Mahmud Bey Camii" (S. Eyice); A. Kayapınar, "Kuzey Bulgaristan'da Gazi Mihaloğulları Vakıfları"; Kazancıgil, "Gazi Mihal İmareti"; and Özer, "Edirne'de Mihaloğulları'nın İmar Faaliyetleri." The deed of Mīḫāloġlu Maḥmūd Beg's endowment in İḫtimān was renewed by Selīm I. See Öz, "Topkapı Sarayı Müzesinde Yemen Fatihi Sinan Paşa Arşivi," 174. On the development of the two, or possibly three, branches of the family, see Sabev, "Osmanlıların Balkanları Fethi ve İdaresinde Mihaloğulları Ailesi"; and Kiprovska, "Shaping the Ottoman Borderland."

191. See Enverī, *Düstūrnāme*, 36. On the history of the town of İḫtimān, see *DİA*, s.v. "İhtiman" (M. Kiel); and Kiprovska, "Shaping the Ottoman Borderland," 198–202. See also Babinger, *Beiträge zur Frühgeschichte der Türkenherrschaft in Rumelien*, 72n28.

192. Possibly a third member of this family was among Selīm's supporters: Muṣṭafā Beg, son of Ḳāsım Beg, who is mentioned within the context of the Moldavian campaign of 1498 as one of the fellow commanders of Malḳoçoġlu Bālī Beg (d. 1514), a renowned frontier lord and the governor of Silistre. See Uruç, *Tevārīḫ* (Öztürk edition), 179. Uruç Beg refers to Bālī Beg as governor (*sancaḳbegi*) of Aḳkirman.

193. On Mīḫāloġlus' military service during the Moldavian campaign, see Uruç, *Tevārīḫ* (Öztürk edition), 179. On their role during the Hungarian expedition, see Uzunçarşılı, *Osmanlı Tarihi*, vol. 2, 334–36. On Ḳāsım Beg's raids near Segedin and Temeşvar, see Uzunçarşılı, *Osmanlı Tarihi*, vol. 2, 573. A budgetary register prepared during the early years of Süleymān I's reign refers to Ḳāsım Beg as

"İḫtimānlı Ḳāsım," the governor of Ḥumṣ (Homs, Syria). See Barkan, "H. 933–934 (M. 1527–1528) Malî Yılına Ait Bir Bütçe Örneği," 306.

194. Uzunçarşılı, *Osmanlı Tarihi*, vol. 2, 262, 471, 573.

195. Equally noteworthy is the absence of members of the Evrenosoğlu lineage among Selīm's supporters.

196. Anonymous, *Chronikon*, 59–60. For an analysis of the significance of this dream for the centralization policies of Ottoman rulers, see Kafadar, *Between Two Worlds*, 151–54; Lowry, *The Nature of the Early Ottoman State*, 139–43; and Yürekli, *Architecture and Hagiography in the Ottoman Empire*, 131–33. That Murād II doubted the loyalty of the Rumelian frontier lords is confirmed by Ottoman sources as well. For an anonymous account relating Murād's painful memory of certain lords of the marches betraying his uncle, Mūsā, see Anonymous, *Ġazavāt-ı Sulṭān Murād*, 13.

197. Kafadar, *Between Two Worlds*, 151–54. Similar concerns had been expressed by Murād II's great-grandfather, Murād I (r. 1362–1389). For his letter to Evrenos Beg, warning the frontier lord against pride resulting from extensive conquests, see Ferīdūn Beg, ed., *Münşeʾātü's-selāṭīn*, vol. 1, 87–89.

198. On the varied dimensions of Meḥmed II's "imperial project," see Kafadar, *Between Two Worlds*, 96–97, 151–54. On the notion of *ġazā* and *ġāzī*-hood, see Tekin, "Türk Dünyasında Gazâ ve Cihâd Kavramları Üzerine Düşünceler"; and Emecen, "Gazaya Dair."

199. The earliest known recruitment register of raiders (*aḳıncı defteri*) is dated 1472. For an analysis of this register and Meḥmed II's centralization policies, see Kiprovska, "The Military Organization of the *Akıncıs* in Ottoman Rumelia." The incorporation of independent groups of soldiers ruled by their hereditary chiefs into the military was a strategy of centralization used by earlier Ottoman rulers as well. For the registration of Tatar warriors formerly under the command of Aḳṭāv into the Ottoman cavalry (*sipāhī*), see Barkan, "Osmanlı İmparatorluğunda Bir İskân ve Kolonizasyon Metodu Olarak Sürgünler" (III), 211–13.

200. İnalcık, "Periods in Ottoman History," 48. For examples of freehold grants of conquered regions to their conquerors during the reigns of Murād I and Bāyezīd I, see Aktepe, "XIV. ve XV. Asırlarda Rumeli'nin Türkler Tarafından İskânına Dair," 308–12. For cases when conquerors of a region became its de facto rulers, see ʿĀşıḳpaşazāde, *Menāḳıb* (Yavuz and Saraç edition), 382, 390. Families of frontier lords established power bases and were granted freehold properties in the areas they conquered. The Mīḫāloġlus' strongholds, for example, were located near Bīlecik, Edirne, and later İḫtimān and Pilevne (Pleven, Bulgaria); the Malḳoçoġlus' in Niğbolu (Nikopol, Bulgaria), Silistre (Silistra, Bulgaria), and Çirmen (Ormenio, Greece); the Evrenosoġlus' in Yeñice-i Vārdār (Giannitsa,

Greece), Sīroz (Serres, Greece), Selānīk (Thessaloniki, Greece), Gümülcine (Komotini, Greece), and Loutra; and the Ṭuraḫānoğlus'in Yeñişehr and Tırḥāla (Trikala, Greece). See Arslan, "Erken Osmanlı Dönemi (1299–1453)'nde Akıncılar ve Akıncı Beyleri," 217; and Lowry, *The Shaping of the Ottoman Balkans*.

201. The appointment of members of prominent families to provinces as far away as possible from their power bases had been an integral part of Ottoman policy as early as the reign of Murād II, who appointed princes of Anatolian tributary dynasties to governorates in Rumelia. For appointments of members of the Ḳaramānoğlu and Cāndāroğlu families to Rumelian provinces, see Alderson, *The Structure of the Ottoman Dynasty*, 20n1. Similarly, members of frontier families with strongholds in Rumelia were assigned to the Arab provinces during the reign of Süleymān I. For references in a budgetary register to Ṭuraḫānoğlu İdrīs Beg as the governor of Rūm-ḳalʿa (near Aleppo) and İḫtimānoğlu Ḳāsım Beg as the governor of Ḥumṣ (Homs, Syria), see Barkan, "H. 933–934 (M. 1527–1528) Malî Yılına Ait Bir Bütçe Örneği," 306. For a discussion of the extraordinarily quick succession of gubernatorial offices held by members of the Mīḫāloğlu, Malḳoçoğlu, and Evrenosoğlu families, see Kiprovska, "The Military Organization of the *Akıncıs* in Ottoman Rumelia," 30–35; and Kiprovska, "The Mihaloğlu Family," 214–15. Earlier Ottoman rulers used exile in a similar fashion against any potential threat to their own sovereignty. See Barkan, "Osmanlı İmparatorluğunda Bir İskân ve Kolonizasyon Metodu Olarak Sürgünler" (III), 214, 222–24.

202. For cases of confiscation involving the estates of the Malḳoçoğlu and Ṭuraḫānoğlu families, see Gökbilgin, *XV. ve XVI. Asırlarda Edirne ve Paşa Livası*, 276, 340–41. Machiel Kiel claims that the estates of the Mīḫāloğlu family were also confiscated by Meḥmed II; see *DİA*, s.v. "İhtiman" (M. Kiel). Confiscation of landed estates and their transformation into military fiefs was a controversial yet prevalent practice for military-agrarian polities in both the medieval and the early modern eras. A revealing case in point is the confiscation of ecclesiastical properties by the Frankish ruler Charles Martel (r. 718–741).

203. Kiprovska, "The Military Organization of the *Akıncıs* in Ottoman Rumelia," iv.

204. Probably based on Koçi Beg's (d. ca. 1650) *Risāle* written in 1631, Halil İnalcık states that by the end of the first quarter of the seventeenth century the *aḳıncı* organization was considerably weakened and that in 1034/1625 "there were only two or three thousand left." See İnalcık, "The Rise of the Ottoman Empire," 33; and Koçi Beg, *Risāle*, 53/222.

205. Yürekli, *Architecture and Hagiography in the Ottoman Empire*, 131.

206. Daniele Barbarigo, *Relazione dell'Imperio Ottomano*, 19. For a discussion of the significance of Barbarigo's account within the mid-sixteenth-century Ottoman context, see Yürekli, *Architecture and Hagiography in the Ottoman Empire*, 131–33. I

am not aware of any concrete evidence that supports Yürekli's assumption that "Yaḥyālı" and "Malḳoçoğlu" are one and the same. The translation of the relevant section of Barbarigo's *relazione* is cited as it appears in Yürekli's study and includes the author's explanatory notes. For the sake of consistency, the names of the noble lineages are transliterated in accordance with the format followed throughout this book.

207. Ḳızıl Aḥmedli refers to the branch of the İsfendiyāroğlu family that descended from the eponymous İsfendiyār Beg's brother. See Yücel, *Anadolu Beylikleri Hakkında Araştırmalar*, vol. 1, 117–23.

208. Cemal Kafadar uses the term "minidynasty" for the Mīḫāloğlu family; see Kafadar, *Between Two Worlds*, 26.

209. One of these poets was Ḥayretī (d. 1535), almost certainly an Abdāl of Rūm or Işıḳ, who hailed from the Rumelian town of Vardar Yenicesi (Giannitsa, Greece). Some of Hayretī's patrons were members of the Yaḥyālı, Mīḫāloğlu, and Ṭuraḫānoğlu families of frontier lords. Ḥayretī's famous couplets include: "Ne Süleymāna esīrüz ne Selīmüñ ḳulıyuz / Kimse bilmez bizi bir şāh-ı kerīmüñ ḳulıyuz" (We are neither Süleymān's slave nor Selīm's servant / No one knows us, we are the servant of an honorable king). The ambiguous reference to "an honorable king" most probably refers to ʿAlī b. Abī Ṭālib (d. 661) or a Rumelian Abdāl whom Ḥayretī accepted as his spiritual guide. The couplet is cited in ʿĀlī, *Künhü'l-aḫbār (Tezkire)*, 208. For biographical information on Ḥayretī and examples of his poetry, see also ʿĀşıḳ Çelebi, *Meşāʿirü'ş-şuʿarā*, vol. 2, 639–43. On the Abdāls of Rūm, see Karamustafa, *God's Unruly Friends*, 70–78. I am grateful to Ahmet T. Karamustafa for his help with the interpretation of Ḥayretī's couplet.

210. For an analysis of the development of two Bektashi shrines through the patronage of several families of frontier lords, see Yürekli, *Architecture and Hagiography in the Ottoman Empire*.

211. For the manner in which prominent Rumelian commanders sealed Meḥmed I's (r. 1413–1421) victory over his rival brother Mūsā (d. 1413) at the end of the period of civil war (1402–1413) after the Battle of Ankara, see, for example, Neşrī, *Kitāb-ı cihānnümā*, vol. 2, 486–516. On the role played by frontier lords of the Balkan provinces—including Ṭuraḫān Beg and Gümlioğlu—in determining the outcome of the rebellion of Muṣṭafā Çelebi, the eldest son of Bāyezīd I (r. 1389–1402), who had been taken hostage by Tīmūr in 1402, see Melville-Jones, "Three Mustafas"; and Yūsuf, *Tārīḫ*, 111.

Part 2 Introduction

1. Silāḥdār Meḥmed Aġa, *Nuṣretnāme*, 218b: "şefḳatlü pādişāhımız ḥażretleri başçādırda ḳara ot tenāvül buyururken ʿaceb müverrih bizim ḳara ot yidügimizi

daḫī tārīḫe yazar mı buyurduḳda bu ʿabd-ı aḥḳarları kemāl-i ādab şerm-i ḥicāb ile muṭlaḳ ḫünkārımın bu laṭīfeden murād-ı hümāyūnları ancaḳ yazsun dimekdir deyü cevāb virüb ḳayd olunub."

2. Rifaʾat Abou-El-Haj's final verdict is that Muṣṭafā II suffered from "injured primary narcissism." See Abou-El-Haj, "The Narcissism of Mustafa II," 120, 124.

3. See Kafadar, "Self and Others," 136; for a similar approach, see Hagen, "Dreaming ʿOs̱māns," 102.

4. Silāḥdār Meḥmed Aġa, Nuṣretnāme, 217a, 230b. For a detailed discussion of the "obvious," "symbolic," and "underlying" meanings of these episodes, see Abou-El-Haj, "The Narcissism of Mustafa II."

5. Abou-El-Haj, "The Narcissism of Mustafa II," 120.

6. On the creation of the post of the official chronicler (vaḳʿanüvīs) at the end of the seventeenth century, see Thomas, *A Study of Naima*; and İA, s.v. "Vekāyinüvis" (B. Kütükoğlu).

7. On the question of the work's patronage, see Fodor, "Aḥmedī's Dāsitān as a Source of Early Ottoman History," 41–43; and Aḥmedī, Tevārīḫ, xiii.

8. On early Ottoman historiography, see Ménage, "The Beginnings of Ottoman Historiography"; and İnalcık, "The Rise of Ottoman Historiography." For a recent critique of İnalcık's state-centered approach to historiographical production during Bāyezīd II's reign, see Mengüç, "Histories of Bayezid I, Historians of Bayezid II."

9. İnalcık, "The Rise of Ottoman Historiography," 164–67.

10. İpşirli, "Ottoman Historiography," 526. Judging by scholarly statements about various periods of Ottoman history, "historiographical explosions" were common phenomena. Robert Mantran finds one during the reign of Süleymān I, whereas Cornell Fleischer states that "the reign of Murād III witnessed something of an historiographical explosion." See Mantran, "L'historiographie ottomane à l'époque de Soliman le Magnifique," 26–29; and Fleischer, *Bureaucrat and Intellectual in the Ottoman Empire*, 242.

11. İnalcık, "The Rise of Ottoman Historiography," 165–66. For similar interpretations, see Kafadar, *Between Two Worlds*, 97; and Piterberg, *An Ottoman Tragedy*, 36.

12. The *Anonymous Chronicles* are comprehensive histories of the Ottoman dynasty written in simple language. They incorporate textual information from "Royal Calendars" (taḳvīm); popular Turkish "religio-heroic literature" (menāḳıbnāme), including accounts of the heroic deeds of frontier warriors (ġazavātnāme), folktales, mythical stories, and popular poetry; and accounts of anonymous narrators (rāvī) from various walks of life, probably including soldiers, common people, and local notables. On the sources of the *Anonymous*

Chronicles, see Ménage, "A Survey of the Early Ottoman Histories," 183–202, 365–400. On the "religio-heroic literature" and its origins, see İnalcık, "The Rise of Ottoman Historiography," 156–57.

13. Mengüç, "Histories of Bayezid I, Historians of Bayezid II," 373. Similarly but more generally, "rather than construing historiographers and other literati as the mouthpieces of a unified central power promulgating a unity of 'faith and state' (*din ve devlet*)," Gottfried Hagen pleads "for a perspective that takes them seriously as independent participants in a discourse *within* the central power." See Hagen, "Legitimacy and World Order," 57. Italics as they appear in the original.

14. Similarly, Bidlīsī explains that he composed his work "in a style favored by the distinguished as well as by ordinary people." For translations of the relevant fragments of the *sebeb-i teʾlīf* sections of these works, see İnalcık, "The Rise of Ottoman Historiography," 165 (Rūḥī, Neşrī), 166 (Kemālpaşazāde, İdrīs-i Bidlīsī).

15. Kafadar, *Between Two Worlds*, 91.

16. For a discussion of the political and ideological ramifications of Rūḥī's references to Ottoman monarchs as *eşref-i selāṭīn*, see İnalcık, "The Rise of Ottoman Historiography," 165, 166. For earlier works that treat the history of the Ottomans as an addition to universal history and a continuation of Islamic history and that portray Ottoman rulers as warriors of faith, see, for example, Aḥmedī, *Tevārīḫ*; Şükrullāh, *Behçetü't-tevārīḫ*; and Enverī, *Düstūrnāme*. For a succinct discussion of these early works, see Ménage, "The Beginnings of Ottoman Historiography."

17. For an analysis rejecting the evolutionary view of early Ottoman historiography, see Kafadar, *Between Two Worlds*, in particular the section titled "The Chronicles of the House of Osman and Their Flavor: Onion or Garlic?," 90–117; the quotations here are from pages 97 and 98.

18. Over time, the complex process of the legitimation of the Ottoman enterprise culminated in the creation of what Colin Imber has called "the Ottoman dynastic myth." See Imber, "The Ottoman Dynastic Myth." See also Imber, "Frozen Legitimacy." On the related notion of "Ottoman exceptionalism" as expressed in the writings of sixteenth-century Ottoman authors, see Hagen and Menchinger, "Ottoman Historical Thought," 100–101.

19. On the post of *şehnāmeci* and an analysis of the *şehnāmeci*s' textual production as "a form of official historiography in the Ottoman Empire which predates that of the *vaḳʿanüvīs*," see Woodhead, "An Experiment in Official Historiography"; the text quoted here is from page 170. Abdülkadir Özcan labeled this historiography "semi-official" (*yarı resmî bir ekol*); see Özcan, "Kanuni Sultan Süleyman Devri Tarih Yazıcılığı ve Literatürü," 148. Sinem Eryılmaz disagrees

with Woodhead and argues that the post was actually established during the tenure of Seyyid Loḳmān (1569–1596). See Eryılmaz, "The Shehnamecis of Sultan Süleymān," 9. Emine Fetvacı challenges Woodhead's assumption about the "permanent" nature of the post by highlighting the occasional nature of *şehnāmeci* Seyyid Loḳmān's work while simultaneously emphasizing that his position was "as much an administrative as a creative one"; see Fetvacı, "The Office of Ottoman Court Historian." For analyses of some of the major works in this historiographical corpus, see Kangal, *The Sultan's Portrait*; and Bağcı et al., *Ottoman Painting*.

20. On this point, see İnalcık, "The Rise of Ottoman Historiography," 156–57. Yaḫşı Faḳīh's account did not survive in its original form but can be found in a version embedded in ʿĀşıḳpaşazāde's (d. 1484) *Menāḳıb-ü-tevārīḫ-i āl-i ʿOsmān*.

21. For an analysis of these early sources and their textual interrelations, see Kafadar, *Between Two Worlds*, Chapter 2, especially 90–105. See also İnalcık, "The Rise of Ottoman Historiography"; Ménage, "The Beginnings of Ottoman Historiography"; and Ménage, "A Survey of the Early Ottoman Histories," especially 19–31.

22. On Aḥmedī's versified historical narrative, see Aḥmedī, *Tevārīḫ*, i-xix. See also Bağcı, *Minyatürlü Ahmedî İskendernameleri*; and Bağcı et al., *Ottoman Painting*, 28–35.

23. On these genres, see Levend, *Ġazavāt-Nāmeler*, which includes the complete text of Sūzī Çelebi's versified *Ġazavātnāme-i Mīḫāloġlu ʿAlī Beg*. For an anonymous prose narrative of Murād II's (r. 1421–1444 and 1446–1451) military exploits between 1443–1444, see Anonymous, *Ġazavāt-ı Sulṭān Murād*.

24. Mertol Tulum gives the date of composition of this work as 1490–1495. See Ṭursun Beg, *Tārīḫ-i ebū'l-fetḥ* (Tulum edition), xxiv. Franz Babinger identifies an earlier work by a certain Ḳıvāmī (fl. 1488), titled *Fetḥnāme-i Sulṭān Meḥmed* (Book of Conquest of Sultan Meḥmed), and states that it was completed in 1488. See Babinger, *Mehmed the Conqueror and His Time*, 470. Babinger also published a facsimile of Ḳıvāmī's work, with an introduction, as *Fetihnâme-i Sultan Mehmed*.

25. See Woodhead, "An Experiment in Official Historiography," 158–59; and Fetvacı, *Picturing History at the Ottoman Court*, 15–20. Kathryn Babayan emphasizes that "the Shāhnāme with its wide circulation came to organize a worldview for its listeners—a particularly Persianate sense of time and being," a sense the Ottomans appear to have shared. See Babayan, *Mystics, Monarchs, and Messiahs*, 26. On the adoption of venerable Persian imperial symbols and regal vocabulary (e.g., *Shāhanshāh*) for Ottoman monarchs, see Yıldız, "Ottoman Historical Writing in Persian," 500.

26. Köprülü, "Türkler'de Halk Hikâyeciliğine Âit Bâzı Maddeler: Meddahlar"; and *EI*², s.v. "Maddāḥ" (P. N. Boratav). For a discussion of large-scale paintings shown by narrators to their audiences during the reading of stories, including

tales from the *Shāhnāma*, see Atasoy, "Illustrations Prepared for Display during Shahname Recitations"; and Mahir, "A Group of 17th Century Paintings Used for Picture Recitation." As examples of Anatolian-Turkish religious-heroic literature, see Ebū'l-ḫayr-i Rūmī, *Ṣaltuḳnāme*; Anonymous, *Dānişmendnāme*; and Anonymous, *Baṭṭālnāme*. For the *Ḥamzanāme* cycle in the Turkish context, see Sezen, *Halk Edebiyatında Hamzanâmeler*. On storytelling and popular preaching within the larger context of Islamicate societies, see Berkey, *Popular Preaching and Religious Authority in the Medieval Islamic Near East*.

27. İnalcık, "The Rise of Ottoman Historiography," 162–63.

28. Fetvacı, *Picturing History at the Ottoman Court*, 26.

29. On *Shāhnāma* manuscripts in Ottoman repositories and on the work's translation into Turkish, see Uluç, "The *Shahnama* of Firdausi in the Lands of Rum"; and Tanındı, "The Illustration of the *Shahnama* and the Art of the Book in Ottoman Turkey." This is not to suggest that the popularity *Shāhnāma* enjoyed was limited to the Ottoman court. In fact, the earliest versified Turkish translation of the full text of Firdawsī's masterpiece was completed in 1511 for the Mamluk ruler Qānṣūh al-Ghawrī (r. 1501–1516). Possibly taken as war booty by Selīm I, it is currently preserved in the Topkapı Palace Museum Library. On early Turkish translations of *Shāhnāma*, see Schmidt, "The Reception of Firdausi's *Shahnama* among the Ottomans," 128–32. Because Ottoman historiography constitutes the principal focus of this study, my remarks here are limited to the Turcophone Ottoman context.

30. For the reception of the *Shāhnāma* in lands neighboring Iran, see articles in Melville and Van den Berg, *Shahnama Studies II*, Part II.

31. Robert Hillenbrand notes that two-thirds of all illustrations in the *Shāhnāma* of Shāh Tahmāsb (r. 1524–1576) focused on the epic feud between the Iranians and Turanians. On the centrality of this rivalry in the *Shāhnāma*, see Hillenbrand, "The Iconography of the Shah-namah-yi Shahi."

32. Here I do not mean to suggest that sixteenth-century Ottomans identified themselves essentially as Turkish. If this were so, the fact that the *Shāhnāma* portray the Turanians as losers would have rendered the original narrative difficult for the Ottomans to enjoy, and the Ottomans would not have adopted the royal epithets of the legendary Iranian kings. There is also no reason to assume that the Safavids considered themselves absolutely removed from the Turanians, at least not linguistically. In fact, as Edward G. Browne noted, it is "a remarkable fact that while Sulṭān Selīm and Shāh Ismāʿīl both possessed poetic talents, the former wrote almost exclusively in Persian, and the latter, under the pen-name of Khaṭāʾī, almost exclusively in Turkish." See Browne, *A History of Persian Literature in Modern Times*, 12. On Shāh Ismāʿīl's poetry, see Minorsky, "The Poetry of Shāh Ismāʿīl I."

33. On these points, see Schmidt, "The Reception of Firdausi's *Shahnama* among the Ottomans," 121; and Fetvacı, *Picturing History at the Ottoman Court*, 15. See also Tanındı, "The Illustration of the *Shahnama* and the Art of the Book in Ottoman Turkey"; and Uluç, "The *Shahnama* of Firdausi in the Lands of Rum." The proliferation of the Ottoman variant of the popular genre of literary-political writing commonly referred to as "mirror for princes" or "advice literature" is discussed in Chapter 4.

34. Woodhead, "An Experiment in Official Historiography," 158–59. See also Woodhead, "Reading Ottoman *Şehnames*," 67–70.

35. Woodhead, "An Experiment in Official Historiography," 159; İnalcık, "The Rise of Ottoman Historiography," 163; and Muʿālī. *Ḫünkārnāme*.

36. Although Şehdī's *şehnāme*-style account of *Tevārīḫ-i mülūk-i āl-i ʿOs̱mān* in Persian has not survived, both the poet and his work are mentioned in ʿĀşıḳ Çelebi's (d. 1572) biographical dictionary of poets. See ʿĀşıḳ Çelebi, *Meşāʿirü'ş-şuʿarā*, vol. 3, 1451.

37. Laṭīfī, as quoted in İnalcık, "The Rise of Ottoman Historiography," 163.

38. Translation, with minor modifications, as quoted in Raby, "A Sultan of Paradox," 8. The original poem by an anonymous author is in *Risāletü'l-leṭā'if ve ḥikāyātü'l-Ḥācı Ṣabrī*. It is quoted by Süheyl Ünver as "Gel dilersen şāh eşiginde olasın muḥterem / Yā Yahūd ol gel bu mülke yā Frenk ol yā ʿAcem / Ādını ḳo Ḳābīlī vü Habīlī vü Ḥāmidī / Żūrzīlikten ġāfil olma maʿrifetten urma dem." See Ünver, *İstanbul Üniversitesi Tarihine Başlangıç*, 248.

39. In this context, Halil İnalcık refers to "Qivāmī's *Fetḥnāme* on the Conqueror's *ghazās*, Kemāl's *Selāṭīnnāme*, a general history of the Ottomans, the *Quṭbnāme* by Firdevsī on the naval expedition for Mytilene, and the *ghazavātnāme* by Ṣafayī on the exploits of Kemāl Re'īs." See İnalcık, "The Rise of Ottoman Historiography," 163.

40. On the events that led to these treaties and their significance, see Şahin, *Empire and Power in the Reign of Süleyman*, 109–36.

41. On this point, see Fleischer, "The Lawgiver as Messiah," 172; and Emiralioğlu, *Geographical Knowledge and Imperial Culture in the Early Modern Ottoman Empire*, 27–45, especially 43–44.

42. For contemporary elegies that decry Prince Muṣṭafā's execution and criticize Süleymān, see Çavuşoğlu, "Şehzâde Mustafa Mersiyeleri." See also Turan, *Kanuni Süleyman Dönemi Taht Kavgaları*, 159–62 (elegy by Ṭaşlıcalı Yaḥyā, d. 1582), 163–65 (elegy by Sāmī, fl. 1550s).

43. Fleischer, "The Lawgiver as Messiah," 172.

44. On the works composed by court historiographers, their contents, and their varied functions, see Woodhead, "An Experiment in Official Historiography";

and Woodhead, "Reading Ottoman *Şehnames*." For ʿĀrif's career and Ottoman *shāhnāmas* composed during the reign of Süleymān, see Eryılmaz, "The Shehnamecis of Sultan Süleymān"; and Eryılmaz, "From Adam to Süleyman." For an analysis of the sociopolitical context within which Ottoman *shāhnāmas* were composed, see Tezcan, "The Politics of Early Modern Ottoman Historiography."

45. See Woodhead, "Reading Ottoman *Şehnames*," 79; and Schmidt, *Pure Water for Thirsty Muslims*, 42, 64.

46. Necipoğlu, "A Ḳānūn for the State, a Canon for the Arts," 212. Italics mine.

47. For a people-centered analysis of the formation of the Ottoman imperial household between ca. 1470 and ca. 1670, see Murphey, *Exploring Ottoman Sovereignty*, 141–74. Murphey's calculations demonstrate that the total number of individuals comprising the imperial household increased from 3,365 to 9,022 between ca. 1520 and ca. 1670. The quotation here is from page 142.

48. Fetvacı, *Picturing History at the Ottoman Court*, 25.

49. For discussions on "contemporary readings" of *şehnāme* works and on the circulation of these books at the imperial palace by various segments of the Ottoman court, see Woodhead, "Reading Ottoman *Şehnames*," 70–76; Fetvacı, *Picturing History at the Ottoman Court*, 29–57; Eryılmaz, "The Shehnamecis of Sultan Süleymān," especially 1–11; and Necipoğlu, "A Ḳānūn for the State, a Canon for the Arts."

50. Even some of these manuscripts (e.g., *Zübdetü't-tevārīḫ* and *Şemāʿilnāme*) were produced in multiple copies. See Necipoğlu, "Word and Image."

51. As an example, Woodhead mentions the sixty-nine craftsmen who received remuneration for the production of a volume of Loḳmān's *Hünernāme*. See Woodhead, "Reading Ottoman *Şehnames*," 75. On the evolution of networks of artistic patronage at the Ottoman imperial court during the sixteenth century and on the various groups of artists, see Fetvacı, *Picturing History at the Ottoman Court*, especially 59–100.

52. On the production process of Seyyid Loḳmān's *Şāhnāme-i Selīm Ḫān*, see Fetvacı, "The Production of the Şehnāme-i Selīm Ḫān." On the sultan's membership in a "vetting committee," which included the grand vizier, the chief jurisconsult, and other leading religious scholars, see Woodhead, "Reading Ottoman *Şehnames*," 71.

53. For the careers and works of Süleymān I's two historiographers, see Eryılmaz, "The Shehnamecis of Sultan Süleymān." On ʿĀrifī's *Shāhnāma*, see also Eryılmaz, "From Adam to Süleyman."

54. Eryılmaz, "The Shehnamecis of Sultan Süleymān," 4.

55. See Fetvacı, *Picturing History at the Ottoman Court*, especially 158–75; and Tezcan, "The Politics of Early Modern Ottoman Historiography," 171–80.

56. Baki Tezcan notes that the Imperial Scroll "lacks a proper ending but seems to have been updated until 1596." See Tezcan, "The Politics of Early Modern Ottoman Historiography," 173. Sinem Eryılmaz argues that the first composer of the document was not ʿĀrifī but Eflāṭūn. See Eryılmaz, "The Shehnamecis of Sultan Süleymān," 252–56. On Seyyid Loḳmān and his career, see Kütükoğlu, "Şehnâmeci Lokman."

57. On the *Ṭomār-ı Hümāyūn*, its content, and its political message, see Eryılmaz, "The Shehnamecis of Sultan Süleymān," 129–61; and Eryılmaz, "From Adam to Süleyman," 114–15.

58. On the relationship between these two works, see Fetvacı, *Picturing History at the Ottoman Court*, 174–75. See also Renda, "New Light on the Painters of the Zubdet al-Tawarikh."

59. Fetvacı, *Picturing History at the Ottoman Court*, 175.

60. For a critical contemporary account of Murād III policies, see Selānikī, *Tārīḫ*, vol. 1, 427–32. On Murād's absolutist policies and their critics, see Tezcan, "The Politics of Early Modern Ottoman Historiography," 171–80.

61. The three copies presented to the sultan, the grand vizier, and the chief black eunuch were illustrated. Ḫoca Saʿdeddīn's copy, titled *Mücmelü'ṭ-ṭomār* (Summary of the Scroll), was in abridged form and not illustrated. See Fetvacı, *Picturing History at the Ottoman Court*, 138, 296n18.

62. Tezcan, "The Politics of Early Modern Ottoman Historiography," 183.

63. On the circulation of copies of *Zübdetü't-tevārīḫ*, see Tezcan, "The Politics of Early Modern Ottoman Historiography," 175n16.

64. The only exception seems to be the prominent Ottoman bureaucrat and litterateur Muṣṭafā ʿĀlī. See Woodhead, "Reading Ottoman *Şehnames*," 79; and Schmidt, *Pure Water for Thirsty Muslims*, 42, 64.

65. Tezcan, "The Politics of Early Modern Ottoman Historiography," 170. In a more nuanced argument, Fleischer similarly notes that, ultimately, "the experiment failed, in large measure because dynastic control of the imperial image was successfully challenged by the elite that Süleymān created. . . . Indeed, by the late sixteenth century there developed a tension over the control of historiographical territory between a dynast that sought to monopolize control of the imperial image, and a literate elite that saw itself as the proper guardian and articulator of the Ottoman historical experience; the post of *şehnāmeci* died out in the early seventeenth century, but historical writing did not." See Fleischer, "The Lawgiver as Messiah," 172.

66. Woodhead, "Reading Ottoman *Şehnames*," 79.

67. Woodhead, "Reading Ottoman *Şehnames*," 80.

68. Woodhead, "Reading Ottoman *Şehnames*," 79. Woodhead compares the "six personal gifts and sixteen requirements of rule of the Ottoman dynasty"

listed in Muṣṭafā ʿĀlī's work of advice titled *Nuṣḥatü's-selāṭīn* (Counsel for Sultans, 1581) with the twenty "admirable qualities of the dynasty from the court historiographer's—and supposedly the sultan's—point of view" highlighted in royal *şehnāmeci* Ṭaʿlīḳīzāde's *Şemāʾilnāme* (Book of Dispositions, 1579).

69. Woodhead, "Reading Ottoman *Şehnames*," 79–80.

70. Woodhead, "An Experiment in Official Historiography," 181–82.

71. Fetvacı, *Picturing History at the Ottoman Court*, 282. See also Fetvacı, "Enriched Narratives and Empowered Images in Seventeenth-Century Ottoman Manuscripts."

72. Fetvacı, "Enriched Narratives and Empowered Images in Seventeenth-Century Ottoman Manuscripts," 243–44.

73. Among the notable exceptions were Meḥmed III (r. 1595–1603), who led his armies in the Egri (Hun. Eger; Ger. Erlau) expedition of 1596, ʿOs̱mān II (r. 1618–1622), who campaigned against Poland in 1621, and Murād IV (r. 1623–1640), who mounted two sultanic campaigns against the Safavids, in 1635 and 1638. On "*ġāzī*-sultans" in Islamic history, see Anooshahr, *The Ghazi Sultans and the Frontiers of Islam*.

74. For typical expressions of this sentiment, see, among others, Uzunçarşılı, *Osmanlı Tarihi*, vol. 3, Part 1, 114–26, especially 119–20; Uzunçarşılı, *Osmanlı Devletinin Saray Teşkilâtı*, 70; Parry, "The Successors of Sulaimān," 107–8; and Shaw, *History of the Ottoman Empire and Modern Turkey*, vol. 1, 170. For a critical analysis of this view in modern scholarship, see Peirce, *The Imperial Harem*, 153–85, especially 168–77; and Karateke, "'On the Tranquillity and Repose of the Sultan,'" especially 122–28. A brief survey of Ottoman *naṣīḥatnāme* literature and a critical discussion of the "decline paradigm" in late Ottoman historiography and modern scholarship can be found in Chapter 4.

75. For a discussion of various factors that contributed to the development of "the sedentary sultanate," see Peirce, *The Imperial Harem*, 168–77. For a discussion of the development of the controversy surrounding the sultan's participation in military campaigns after the late sixteenth century, see Karateke, "On the Tranquillity and Repose of the Sultan."

76. For a discussion of the technological and cost-related constraints on, as well as of the physical, environmental, and motivational limits of, Ottoman warfare in the early modern period, see Murphey, *Ottoman Warfare*, 13–34. Murphey refers to the combination of these many factors as the "immutable context."

77. On the procedural relationship between the sultan and his grand vizier, see Fodor, "Sultan, Imperial Council, Grand Vizier"; Uzunçarşılı, *Osmanlı Devletinin Merkez ve Bahriye Teşkilâtı*, 132–36; and Faroqhi, "Das Grosswesir-telḫīṣ."

78. Karateke, "On the Tranquillity and Repose of the Sultan," 122.

79. For the vizierate and its centrality in Ottoman governance, especially during and after the reign of Süleymān I, see Yılmaz, "The Sultan and the Sultanate," 274–383.

80. According to the historian Selānikī (d. 1600), Murād was afraid that the janissaries would depose him if he left the palace compound. See Selānikī, *Tārīḫ*, vol. 2, 445. For a critical evaluation of Murād III by the contemporary historian Muṣṭafā ʿĀlī, see Fleischer, *Bureaucrat and Intellectual in the Ottoman Empire*, 293–307.

81. In her article exploring the influence of European models on an Ottoman imperial portrait book titled *Ḳıyāfetü'l-insāniyye fī şemāʾilü'l-ʿOs̱māniyye* (Human Physiognomy and the Disposition of the Ottomans), Emine Fetvacı convincingly argues that the work in question was "a response to a particularly Ottoman problem," namely, how to praise an Ottoman monarch who, unlike his predecessors, was exceptionally sedentary and secluded. See Fetvacı, "From Print to Trace," 244.

82. One of the best descriptions of this new type of sultan in seclusion is provided by the Ottoman historian Muṣṭafā ʿĀlī, who noted that "[the sultans of] this praise-worthy dynasty . . . reside all by themselves in a palace like unique jewels in the depths of the oyster-shell, and totally sever all relations with relatives and dependents." See ʿĀlī, cited in Woodhead, "Murad III and the Historians," 85.

83. For an analysis of this shift in emphasis, see Fetvacı, "From Print to Trace." Christine Woodhead makes a similar point and states that these works "portray the ultimate Ottoman dynastic myth, that of power through unassailable virtue and magnificence." See Woodhead, "Reading Ottoman *Şehnames*," 78. Genealogy was one of the principal pillars of what Colin Imber calls "the Ottoman dynastic myth." On the Ottoman emphasis on genealogy, see Imber, "The Ottoman Dynastic Myth"; and Flemming, "Political Genealogies in the Sixteenth Century." On the theory of sultanate as divine grace, see Yılmaz, "The Sultan and the Sultanate," 220–73. On the multiple images of Ottoman sultans reflecting the changing nature of the Ottoman sultanate, see Fetvacı, *Picturing History at the Ottoman Court*, 267–82.

84. Paradoxically, the most number of *Şehnāme*s were produced for Murād III, arguably the most sedentary of all Ottoman monarchs. The royal image created for Murād, of course, was equally sedentary, whereas the military spotlight was reserved for his viziers.

85. Karateke notes that Selīm spent 1,323 days away from Istanbul and Süleymān 3,721, corresponding to 45.1 and 22.1 percent of their respective reigns. For the dates and durations of Selīm's and Süleymān's campaigns, see Karateke, "On the Tranquillity and Repose of the Sultan," 119.

86. See Naʿīmā, *Tārīḫ*, vol. 2, 401. Naʿīmā uses this phrase to highlight the mobility of Aḥmed I (r. 1603–1617) by likening him to Selīm: "Sulṭān Aḥmed ḥażretleri cedd-i büzürg-vārları Sulṭān Selīm-i ḳadīm gibi ḳalīlü'l-ḳarār olmağın." For a discussion of the military mobility of Selīm I and his son Süleymān I, see Karateke, "On the Tranquillity and Repose of the Sultan," especially 118–19.

87. Assmann, *Moses the Egyptian*, 14.

88. Nora, "Between Memory and History," 8.

3. Selīm, the Legitimate Ruler

1. Lane-Poole, *The Story of Turkey*, 152: "When Selīm I had deposed his father Bāyezīd, who did not long survive his humiliation, he resolved that the trouble and anxiety of another Prince Jem should not disturb his own reign. His father had had eight sons, of whom two, besides himself, were still alive, and, including grandsons, there were no less than eleven dangerous persons to be made away with. 'Selīm the Grim,' as the Turks still call him, did not shrink from the task; he delighted in blood. . . . "

2. See Ḥaydar, *Rūznāme*, 464, 467, 476, 492. Ḥaydar Çelebi also relates that Selīm calmly sat and watched as four hundred Mamluk soldiers were decapitated outside his royal tent (*Rūznāme*, 486). Most of these episodes are repeated by other chroniclers as well. On the anecdote about Selīm hitting Muṣṭafā Pasha with a bow, see, for example, ʿĀlī, *Künhü'l-aḫbār*, vol. 2, 1206.

3. Anonymous, *Tārīḫ* (TSMK R.1099), 117b.

4. During his reign of eight years, Selīm had six grand viziers; he ordered the execution of Ḳoca Muṣṭafā Pasha (d. 1512), Dūḳagīnzāde Aḥmed Pasha (d. 1515), and Yūnus Pasha (d. 1517). Ḫādım Sinān Pasha (d. 1517) was killed on the battlefield at Ridaniyya, and Hersekzāde Aḥmed Pasha (d. 1517) died of natural causes near Aleppo after the Egyptian expedition.

5. On the lives and oeuvres of Celālzāde Muṣṭafā and Muṣṭafā ʿĀlī, see Şahin, *Empire and Power in the Reign of Süleyman*; and Fleischer, *Bureaucrat and Intellectual in the Ottoman Empire*, respectively. On Celālzāde, see also Uzunçarşılı, "Onaltıncı Asır Ortalarında Yaşamış Olan İki Büyük Şahsiyet," 391–422. On Persian epistolary historical writing and its impact on Ottoman historiographical output, see Yıldız, "Ottoman Historical Writing in Persian, 1400–1600," 480–99.

6. ʿĀlī, *Künhü'l-aḫbār*, vol. 2, 1205–06: "Merḥūm Pīrī Paşa vezāret ṣadrında dāʾimā bī-ḳarīne ve yektā ḳalub vezīr nāmına olanlar ayına varmadan siyāsetle nā-būd olmağın Sulṭān Selīm merḥūmun zamān-ı salṭanatları bir dereceye varmış idi ki devletlü birbirine bed-duʿā itdükde 'bolay ki Sulṭān Selīme vezīr olasın' dirlerdi ve vekālet ṣadrına gelenler vaṣiyyet-nāmelerini ḳoynunda

getirüb her ʿarża girüb çıḳdıḳca yeniden dünyāya gelmiş gibi meserret-i ʿarża ḳılurdı. Menḳūldür ki Pīrī Paşa bir gün ol şāh-ı memālik-güşāya söylemiş 'en son bir bahāne ile beni de öldüreceksen hemān bir gün evvel ḫalās itsen münāsib idi' diyüb ḫavfini beyān eylemiş şehriyār-ı cihān vāfir gülmüşler 'benim daḫī bu maʿnā murādım ve seni bī-cān ve ḫāke yeksān itmek muḳtażā-yı fūādımdır, lākin yerüni tutar bir ādem bulunmaz ve ḫızmet-i vezāreti kemāyenbaġī edā ider kimse idügi taḥḳīḳ olunmaz. Yoḳsa seni murāda vāṣıl itmek emr-i sehldir' dimiş laṭīfe ve kināye ile." With minor modifications, several later Ottoman chroniclers mention the same episodes; one seventeenth-century chronicler even provides a versified couplet referring to the statesmen's curse. See Ṣolaḳzāde, *Tārīḫ* (TSMK B.199), 244b–245a: "merḥūm ve maġfūruñ devrinde vezīr nāmında olanlar ayına varmadın ḳatl olunmaġın āʿyān-ı devlet biri birine bed-duʿā itseler 'bolay ki Sulṭān Selīme vezīr olasın' dirler idi. Ḥattā şāʿirüñ birisi bu beyti ol eyyāmda söylemişdir . . . Raḳībüñ ölmesine çāre yoḳdur / Vezīr ola meger Sulṭān Selīme."

7. For Meḥmed II's definitive statement concerning fratricide in his code of law, see *Ḳānūnnāme-i āl-i ʿOs̱mān*, 18. For a discussion of the public outcry bemoaning the practice of fratricide by Murād III and Meḥmed III, see Peirce, *The Imperial Harem*, 101–3. For a complete list of Ottoman fratricides, see Alderson, *The Structure of the Ottoman Dynasty*, 30–31.

8. The nephews Selīm executed on December 16, 1512, were Prince Maḥmūd's sons Mūsā, Orḫān, and Emīr; Prince ʿĀlemşāh's son ʿOs̱mān; and Prince Şehinşāh's son Meḥmed. On May 14, 1513, Selīm ordered the executions of Prince Aḥmed's son ʿOs̱mān and Prince Murād's son Muṣṭafā.

9. See Uluçay, "Yavuz Sultan Selim Nasıl Padişah Oldu?," (1953), 197–98. Selīm's acts of benevolence (*iḥsān*) and distribution of alms (*ṣadaḳa*) in Bursa are recorded in the city's court registers (*sicill*). See Kepecioğlu, "Bursa'da Şer'î Mahkeme Sicillerinden ve Muhtelif Arşiv Kayıtlarından Toplanan Tarihi Bilgiler ve Vesikalar," 410–11.

10. Uzunçarşılı, "IIinci Bayezid'in Oğullarından Sultan Korkut," 589; and al-Tikriti, "Şehzade Korkud," 310.

11. Ṣolaḳzāde, *Tārīḫ* (TSMK B.199), 204b: "Rivāyet olınur ki Sinān Aġa şehzāde-i merḥūmuñ izālesi içün ḥużūrına varıcaḳ Sulṭān Aḥmedüñ meger barmāġında Rūm ḫarācına muʿādil bir ḫātemi var imiş çıḳarub ol gevher-i girān-behāyı Sinān Aġaya teslīm eyleyüb bundan özge pādişāha lāyıḳ nesnemiz yoḳdur iḥsān idüb maʿżur ṭutsunlar dimiş sābıḳü'l-ẕikr Sinān Aġadan menḳūldır ki ol ḫātem-i bī-mis̱āl pādişāh-ı bā-iḳbāl ḥażretlerine vāṣıl olıcak kendülere bükyā ʿārıż olub bī-iḫtiyār destmālin mübārek yüzlerine ṭutub girye-ü-zār eyledi. Beyt: Ḫüdā virmek gerekdir tāc-ü-taḫtı / Virir mi meyve bāġıñ her duraḫtı."

12. Şolaḳzāde, *Tārīḫ* (TSMK B.199), 204a: "niẓām-ı ʿālem içün ḳavāʿid-i āl-i ʿOsmān . . . üzere ḳaydı görüldi."

13. Cited in Uğur, *İbn-i Kemal*, 94: "bu ḳānūnı ḳoyanlar dünyāda ve ʿuḳbāda raḥmet-i Ḥaḳḳdan baʿīd olsun."

14. Al-Tikriti, "Şehzade Korkud," 310.

15. It is safe to assume that Ottoman chroniclers were familiar with the historiographical currents of the early Islamic era. Their chronicles include various renderings of the succession struggle between the Abbasid caliph Hārūn al-Rashīd's (r. 786–809) sons Muḥammad al-Amīn (r. 809–813) and ʿAbdallāh al-Maʾmūn (r. 813–833). Some of these accounts relate that al-Maʾmūn felt great sorrow and wept when his brother's severed head was brought to him. I would like to thank Jane Hathaway for pointing out that the weeping of a victorious dynast after a civil war that resulted in the execution of his rival brother(s) is probably a literary trope dating back to this particular event. On the representations of the civil war between al-Amīn and al-Maʾmūn in Islamic historiography, see El-Hibri, *Reinterpreting Islamic Historiography*, especially 59–94. References to al-Maʾmūn's weeping are on pages 67–68.

16. Şükrī, *Selīmnāme*, 18b: "Bilmedi mi şāh-ı baḥr-u-ber meni / Onları men sevmezem onlar meni."

17. Menavino, "Della vita et legge Turchesca," 60.

18. Spandounes, *Petit traicté de l'origine des Turcz*, 331; for his Greco-Italian origins and biography, see xxxviii–xliii.

19. Da Lezze, *Historia Turchesca*, 272. On Menavino, Angiolello, Spanduguino, and Da Lezze as sources of information for Ottoman history, see Fisher, *The Foreign Relations of Turkey*, 110.

20. Hierosolimitano, *Domenico's Istanbul*, 4.

21. Knolles, *The Generall Historie of the Turkes*, 495. Here Knolles most probably refers to Süleymān I's physician Moses Hamon, one of whose sons, Joseph Hamon, served Selīm II (r. 1566–1574) as royal physician. On Jewish physicians at the Ottoman court, see Galanté, *Médecins juifs au service de la Turquie*. On the relationships of various editions of Knolles's work to their seventeenth-century context, see Woodhead, "The History of an Historie." Combining the information he culled from various sources, Michel Baudier (d. 1645) recorded the name of the Jewish physician as Ustarabin or Hamen. See Baudier, *Inventaire de l'histoire generale des Turcz*, 172–73. In his addendum to Laonikos Chalkokondyles's (d. ca. 1490) history titled *Continuation de l'histoire des Turcs*, Artus Thomas (Sieur d'Embry, d. after 1614) provides a similar account. For the relevant sections of these works, see Tekindağ, "Bayezid'in Ölümü Meselesi,"15 (Thomas), 16 (Baudier).

22. Şehabettin Tekindağ interprets Hezārfen Ḥüseyin's statement in *Tenḳīḥü't-tevārīḫ* (IUK.2396, 175b), that Bāyezīd "drank the sherbet of martyrdom" (*şerbet-i şehādet nūş itmekle*), as a reference to murder. See Tekindağ, "Bayezid'in Ölümü Meselesi," 13. Another manuscript of the same work includes a similar expression, that Bāyezīd "embarked on the journey to eternity by way of martyrdom" (*şehādetle sefer-i āḫirete teveccüh buyurub*). See Hezārfen Ḥüseyin, *Tenḳīḥ*, 122b.

23. Şükrī, *Selīmnāme*, 29b; and Hezārfen Ḥüseyin, *Tenḳīḥ*, 123a–127b, with the reference to Bāyezīd's martyrdom (*şehādet*) on folio 122b.

24. Zeynep Tarım Ertuğ states that the honor of martyrdom was also ascribed to Süleymān I after his death. See Ertuğ, *XVI. Yüzyıl Osmanlı Devleti'nde Cülûs ve Cenaze Törenleri*, 90. This was probably due to the fact that Süleymān died in Szigetvár, while campaigning in Hungary. Selīm was called as a martyr as well—even though he died of an infected boil. See Keşfī, *Selīmnāme*, 9a.

25. See, among others, Anonymous, *Tārīḫ* (TSMK R.1101), 103a: "nā-ḥaḳ yire ḳān dökmeyesin."

26. Keşfī, *Selīmnāme*, 19a–19b: "bir vaḳt-i ṣabāḥ şehriyār . . . keẟret-i ṣafrādan gül-ruḫsārı nīlüfer gibi zerd olub ṣoldı . . . ser-ü-bālāsına bīd gibi raʿşe düşüb ve ḥarāret-i ġarīziyyeden cismi yanub ṭutuşub ve lebinde ẕerratdan betḫāleler belürdi ve devār-ı devrāndan ve sudāʿ-ı gerdiş-gerdāndan dimāġı muḫtell olub delürdi."

27. The relevant section in Cenābī's work is quoted in Tekindağ, "Bayezid'in Ölümü Meselesi," 14n54. For a German translation of the relevant section and its analysis, see Heeren-Sarka, *Sultan Bāyezīd II. (1481–1512) in der Chronik des Muṣṭafā Genābī*, 79–84.

28. Tekindağ also mentions a history in Persian wherein the phrase "some say [that he] was poisoned" referred to Bāyezīd's death. For references to these works, see Tekindağ, "Bayezid'in Ölümü Meselesi," 14.

29. By the second half of the sixteenth century, a highly sophisticated form of Ottoman Turkish had emerged as the preferred language of composition for dynastic histories, while Arabic was marginalized. Celālzāde Muṣṭafā (d. 1567) and Muṣṭafā ʿĀlī (d. 1600) composed their works in this refined form of Ottoman Turkish. For their careers and oeuvres, see Şahin, *Empire and Power in the Reign of Süleyman*; and Fleischer, *Bureaucrat and Intellectual in the Ottoman Empire*, respectively.

30. See Evliyā, *Seyāḥatnāme*, vol. 1, 68: "baʿżılar mesmūmen merḥūm olurken"; and Peçevī, *Tārīḫ* (1283), vol. 1, 430: "babası Sulṭān Bāyezīdi daḫī tesmīm idüb."

31. Al-Tikriti, "Şehzade Korkud," 329.

32. On the Ottoman civil war that erupted after the Battle of Ankara in 1402, see Kastritsis, *The Sons of Bayezid*.

33. For the range of meanings of *yāvuz*, see Aksoy and Dilçin, eds., *Tanıklarıyla Tarama Sözlüğü*, vol. 6, 4418–33; and Onat, "'Yavuz' ve Bununla İlgili Bazı Kelimelerimizin Arap Diline Geçmiş Şekilleri."

34. Although this chapter focuses on the manner in which Selīm is depicted in Ottoman historiography, there exists a corpus of historical narratives on Selīm penned in Arabic by chroniclers living in the former Mamluk lands. Some of these chroniclers witnessed the Ottoman conquest of Egypt and the fall of the Mamluk Empire. On the "cross-fertilization between central and provincial literary compositions, and between works in Turkish and Arabic," see Hathaway, *The Arab Lands under Ottoman Rule*, 133–37. On the memory of Selīm in Egyptian chronicles, see Hathaway, *A Tale of Two Factions*, 123–33.

35. Despite addressing the reign of one of the most paradigmatic Ottoman sultans, *Selīmnāme*s have not received the scholarly attention they deserve. Franz Babinger was the first to provide comprehensive information on *Selīmnāme*s and their authors. See Babinger, *Die Geschichtsschreiber der Osmanen und ihre Werke*, 45–49, 50–51, 51–52, 53, 54–55, 60–61, 61–63, 95–97, 98, 102–3, 123–26. Despite its apparent need for a thorough update, Şehabettin Tekindağ's article-length study remains the single most important reference for the study of *Selīmnāme*s to date, not only because of Tekindağ's meticulous critical use of earlier studies by Babinger, Ateş, and Levend but also because it provides the most comprehensive list of *Selīmnāme* writers and *Selīmnāme* manuscripts. See Tekindağ, "Selim-nâmeler." The most recent study with an exclusive focus on *Selīmnāme*s was published by Ahmet Uğur under a promising but misleading title. Although a welcome contribution to the field of Ottoman studies as the first publication of the "supplementary" section of Book Eight (on Bāyezīd II's reign) and the full text of Book Nine (on Selīm I's reign) of Kemālpaşazāde's (d. 1534) history of the Ottoman dynasty, Uğur's work fails to fulfill the promise its title implies: it does not cover the whole reign of Selīm I but only the period between 1509 and 1514; it does not make use of all known *Selīmnāme*s but focuses on the eight that Uğur probably considered particularly important; and, most significantly, it does not acknowledge, let alone analyze, the similarities and divergences among various narratives penned by different authors in different periods. See Uğur, *The Reign of Sultan Selīm I*; see also Celia Kerslake's "Review." Since the publication of Uğur's study, scholarship on *Selīmnāme*s has taken the form of modern Turkish transliterations of sections from, or full texts of, individual manuscripts prepared for graduate degrees in Turkish universities. Although a few of these theses and dissertations have been developed into critical editions within the last two decades, most remain unpublished and therefore out of reach for most scholars of Ottoman history and historiography.

36. İdrīs-i Bidlīsī's work was collated and completed as *Salīmshāhnāma* by his son Ebū'l-fażl Meḥmed (d. 1579).

37. Although most of these works are referred to simply as *Selīmnāmes*, they are also known under other titles. They are listed here under their alternative titles and in chronological order with respect to their dates of composition. Less-known *Selīmnāmes* referred to by Babinger, Levend, and Tekindağ include the following works, of which no extant manuscripts are known: Senāʾī's *Selīmnāme*, Ḥayātī's *Şāhnāme*, Şuhūdī's *Şāhnāme*, ʿĀrifī's (Fetḥullāh ʿĀrif Çelebi, d. 1562) *Selīmnāme*, Derūnī's *Muḥārebāt-ı Selīm-i evvel bā Şāh İsmāʿīl ü Ġavrī* (The Battles of Selīm I with Shāh Ismāʿīl and [Qānṣūh al-]Ghawrī), and Seyyid Meḥemmed b. Seyyid ʿAlī-i İznīḳī's *Selīmnāme*. For further information on these works, see the relevant sections in Babinger, *Die Geschichtsschreiber der Osmanen und ihre Werke*; Levend, *Ġazavāt-nāmeler*; and Tekindağ, "Selim-nâmeler."

38. Kafadar, "A Rome of One's Own," 11. On the relationship between the emergence of a "Rūmī" identity among members of the Ottoman ruling elite and its impact on Ottoman cultural production, see also Fetvacı, *Picturing History at the Ottoman Court*, especially 6–7, 25–26.

39. Al-Laḫmī's *al-Durr al-musān fī sīrat al-muẓaffar Salīm Khān* was written in Arabic.

40. It is noteworthy that three of these five works were closely interrelated: the accounts of ʿAzmīzāde Muṣṭafā and Cevrī İbrāhīm Çelebi were re-versified versions of Şükrī-i Bidlīsī's *Selīmnāme*.

41. "High literary Ottoman historical prose developed at the hands of scribes of the chancellery among whose duties was to compose stylistically elaborate diplomatic letters and documents. This epistolary or chancellery style (*enshāʾ*) was shaped by the balance and cadence of rhymed phrasing (*sajʾ*), and distinguished by its elevated diction achieved through ample use of verse, Qorʾanic quotation, figurative language, rhetorical embellishment, esoteric references, and obscure vocabulary choices." See Yıldız, "Ottoman Historical Writing in Persian," 481. On Ottoman epistolary style, see *EI*[2], s.v. "Inshāʾ" (H. R. Roemer).

42. Whereas Ahmet Ateş highlighted the literary qualities of these works, Agâh Sırrı Levend focused on their historical aspects and maintained that these historical narratives should be considered part of a larger body of such narratives generally referred to as *ġazavātnāme* literature, or chronicles of raids and conquests. See Ateş, "Selim-nâmeler"; and Levend, *Ġazavāt-nāmeler*, especially 22–38.

43. Kerslake, "The *Selīm-nāme* of Celāl-zāde Muṣṭafā Çelebi as a Historical Source," 51.

44. Hathaway, *A Tale of Two Factions*, 126.

45. See Kerslake, "The *Selīm-nāme* of Celāl-zāde Muṣṭafā Çelebi as a Historical Source."

46. For studies noting the impact of language of composition, form of language (i.e., prose versus verse), and linguistic registers on several sixteenth- and seventeenth-century Ottoman historical texts, see, for example, Piterberg, *An Ottoman Tragedy*, especially 50–68; Kappert, *Geschichte Sultan Süleymān Ḳānūnīs von 1520 bis 1557*, 36–40; and Şahin, "Imperialism, Bureaucratic Consciousness, and the Historian's Craft," especially 41–42.

47. This chronological spectrum is limited to the early modern Ottoman era and thus necessarily ignores narratives one may call "modern *Selīmnāmes*," composed by late-Ottoman and early-Republican authors like Nāmıḳ Kemāl (d. 1888) and Yahya Kemal Beyatlı (d. 1958). See Nāmıḳ Kemāl, "Yāvuz Sulṭān Selīm"; and Beyatlı, "Selimnâme." For a detailed literary discussion of Beyatlı's work, see Banarlı, *Şiir ve Edebiyat Sohbetleri*, 172–99. There are also numerous scholarly works eulogizing Selīm that could easily fit into this category. See Uğur, *Yavuz Sultan Selim*; Öztuna, *Yavuz Sultan Selim*; and Emecen, *Zamanın İskenderi, Şarkın Fatihi*. This may be due to the fact that Selīm's reign, in the words of one Turkish historian, "was a period of great and heroic achievement which was flattering to national pride." See Uğur, *The Reign of Sultan Selīm I*, 4.

48. Feridun Emecen's blanket statement implying that *Selīmnāmes* were mostly the product of Selīm's reign and Ahmet Uğur's hypothesis that most of these works were composed during the reign of Süleymān I are equally flawed. See Emecen, *Zamanın İskenderi, Şarkın Fatihi*, 26; and Uğur, *The Reign of Sultan Selīm I*, 11.

49. İsḥaḳ Çelebi does not mention Selīm's campaigns against the Safavids or the Mamluks. This omission strongly suggests that the work was composed in the immediate aftermath of Selīm's accession in 1512 and before the Çaldıran expedition of 1514. See Tekindağ, "Selim-nâmeler," 201.

50. İdrīs-i Bidlīsī states that he composed his *Selīmnāme* on Selīm's verbal order. Selīm appears to have been the intended audience of the *Selīmnāmes* by İsḥaḳ Çelebi, Edāʾī, Sucūdī, and al-Laḫmī.

51. Selīm appears to have verbally commissioned İdrīs-i Bidlīsī to compose his *Salīmshāhnāma*. See İdrīs, *Salīmshāhnāma* (Kırlangıç edition), 61.

52. In the introductory section of *Selīmnāme*, Bidlīsī states that his narrative is based on his personal observations as well as information provided by his patrons Şehsüvāroğlu ʿAlī Beg (1521 version) and Ḳoçi b. Ḫalīl Beg (1524 version). See Şükrī, *Selīmnāme*, 8b–9b.

53. On Cevrī's life and works, see Ayan, *Cevrî*.

54. This tumultuous period is analyzed in Tezcan, *The Second Ottoman Empire*; and Piterberg, *An Ottoman Tragedy*.

55. ʿOs̱mān II, who campaigned against Poland in 1621, was one of the three post-Süleymānic sultans to lead his armies in person. The others were Meḥmed III (r. 1595–1603) and Murād IV (r. 1623–1640).

56. Ṭūġī Çelebi, *İbretnümā*, 503.

57. Süleymān's penultimate campaign was against the Safavids and culminated in the Amasya Settlement of 1555. For the dynastic strife that marked the later years of Süleymān's reign, see Turan, *Kanuni Süleyman Dönemi Taht Kavgaları*. See also Uluçay, "Selim-Bâyezid Mücadelesi"; Uzunçarşılı, "Şehzade Bayezid'in Amasya'dan Babası Kanunî Sultan Süleyman'a Göndermiş Olduğu Ariza"; and Uzunçarşılı, "İran Şahına İltica Etmiş Olan Şehzade Bayezid'in Teslimi."

58. For an excellent analysis contextualizing Celālzāde's *Meʾās̱ir* in the later years of Süleymān I's reign, see Şahin, *Empire and Power in the Reign of Süleyman*, 178–85.

59. Woodhead, "An Experiment in Official Historiography," 172.

60. Woodhead, "Reading Ottoman *Şehnames*," 69. Previously, I had followed Woodhead uncritically and stated incorrectly that the "Selīmnāme literature" was "*initiated* and supported by Süleymān I." Italics added for the present work, to highlight my error. See Çıpa, "The Centrality of the Periphery," 4.

61. Ebū'l-fażl Meḥmed also notes that his father composed the previous version of the work on receiving a verbal order from Selīm I. İdrīs, *Salīmshāhnāma* (Kırlangıç edition), 61–62.

62. Şükrī-i Bidlīsī (d. after 1530) presented his *Selīmnāme* to Süleymān in 1530 and was awarded 15,000 silver aspers (*aḳçe*). See Şükrī, *Selīmnāme* (Argunşah edition), 7; see also Tekindağ, "Selim-nâmeler," 215.

63. On İbrāhīm Pasha's involvement in the arts, see Necipoğlu, "Süleyman the Magnificent and the Representation of Power in the Context of Ottoman-Hapsburg Rivalry." For an argument that two illustrated manuscripts of the work were intended for the sultan and his grand vizier, see Bağcı et al., *Ottoman Painting*, 62–63.

64. *Selīmnāmes* written by Keşfī (d. 1524), Şīrī (d. after 1545?), and Saʿdī b. ʿAbdü'l-müteʿāl are addressed to Süleymān, but whether they were presented to him is not known.

65. See Tekindağ, "Selim-nâmeler," 201. On İsḥaḳ Çelebi's life and works as portrayed in a sixteenth-century Ottoman biographical dictionary, see ʿĀşıḳ Çelebi, *Meşāʿirü'ş-şuʿarā*, vol. 1, 328–41.

66. See Tekindağ, "Selim-nâmeler," 218–19; and Edāʾī, *Salīmnāma*, 12b–13a. During the reign of Süleymān I, Fenārīzāde Meḥmed Şāh Çelebi served as chief military judge of both Anatolia and Rumelia (1522–1523). On the identity of Edāʾī's patron and his loyal service to both Selīm and Süleymān, see Yıldız,

"Ottoman Historical Writing in Persian," 465; and Repp, *The Müfti of Istanbul*, 233, 263–68.

67. On Pīrī Meḥmed Pasha, see Meḥmed Süreyyā, *Sicill*, vol. 2, 43.

68. See Tekindağ, "Selim-nâmeler," 216.

69. Celālzāde, *Meʾās̱ir*, 94b.

70. See Meḥmed Ṭāhir, *ʿOs̱mānlı Müʾellifleri*, vol. 3, 122.

71. Şīrī, *Tārīḫ-i feth-i Mıṣr*, 221a: "hemān taḫtidi aḳṣā-yı murādı." On Hersekzāde Aḥmed Pasha's biography and his career in Ottoman service, see Reindl, *Männer um Bāyezīd*, 129–46. On the identity of Şīrī, see ʿĀşıḳ Çelebi, *Meşāʿirü'ş-şuʿarā*, vol. 3, 1463.

72. Keşfī, *Selīmnāme*, 19a–20b.

73. On the history of the Emirate of Dulkadir and the political relations between the Ottoman sultans and Dulkadirid emirs, see Yinanç, *Dulkadir Beyliği*, 34–105.

74. See Bacqué-Grammont, *Les Ottomans, les Safavides et leurs voisins*, 189–93; and *EI²*, s.v. "Dhu'l-Ḳadr" (J. H. Mordtmann and V. L. Ménage).

75. For an account of Janbirdī al-Ghazālī's rebellion, see Yurdaydın, *Kanunî'nin Cülûsu ve İlk Seferleri*, 7–14; and Bakhit, *The Ottoman Province of Damascus*, 19–34. On the fate of Şehsüvāroğlu ʿAlī Beg and the annexation of the Turcoman principality of Dulkadir, see Yinanç, *Dulkadir Beyliği*, 80–105; and Uzunçarşılı, *Osmanlı Tarihi*, vol. 2, 309–10.

76. According to Muṣṭafā ʿĀlī, Şükrī was Şehsüvāroğlu ʿAlī Beg's tutor (*ḫāce*). See ʿĀlī, *Künhü'l-aḫbār (Teẕkire)*, 234. For the significance of Aḥmedī's work as the earliest extant text of Ottoman history, see the introduction to Part 2. See also Aḥmedī, *Tevārīḫ*, xiii-xv.

77. Şükrī, *Selīmnāme*, 8b–9b. On the patronage of the work, see also Bağcı et al., *Ottoman Painting*, 62–63.

78. Although Şükrī-i Bidlīsī states that he destroyed the early version of the versified text, a manuscript of that text is located in Österreichische Nationalbibliothek, Vienna. See Flügel, *Die arabischen, persischen, türkischen Handschriften*, no. 1007.

79. Şükrī, *Selīmnāme*, 8b. Ḳoçi Beg noted that his ancestors served three Ottoman sultans, Bāyezīd I (r. 1389–1402), Murād II (r. 1421–1444 and 1446–1451), and Meḥmed II (r. 1444–1446 and 1451–1481).

80. Süleymān I received his father's visual representation as well. On the two illustrated manuscripts that were intended for Süleymān and his grand vizier İbrāhīm Pasha, see Bağcı et al., *Ottoman Painting*, 62–63. The illustrated presentation copy of the work was kept in the Imperial Treasury and is now part of the Topkapı Palace Museum Library collections (TSMK Hazine 1597–1598).

81. See Çerkesler Kātibi Yūsuf, *Selīmnāme*, 2a–2b: "ʿavāmm[-u-]nās daḫī anuñ nes̱rinden ḥaẓẓ alalar." See also Tekindağ, "Selim-nâmeler," 229.

82. Kātib Çelebi, *Kashf al-ẓunūn*, vol. 1, 267. The multiple audiences Saʿdeddīn had in mind—which most likely included Meḥmed III—will be discussed later.

83. On the impact of İsḥaḳ Çelebi's *Selīmnāme* on Saʿdüddīn's *Tācü't-tevārīḫ*, see Parmaksızoğlu, "Üsküplü İshak Çelebi ve Selimnâmesi," 132–34.

84. Edāʾī, *Shāhnāma*, 13a.

85. Celālzāde, *Meʾās̱ir*, 24a.

86. Celālzāde, *Meʾās̱ir*, 33a (*Kemāl Paşa*), 34a (*Edāʾī*), 119b (*Mevlānā İdrīs*).

87. Saʿdeddīn, *Selīmnāme*, 619.

88. Saʿdeddīn, *Selīmnāme*, 603.

89. See, for example, Saʿdeddīn, *Tācü't-tevārīḫ*, vol. 2, 160; and Ṣolaḳzāde, *Tārīḫ* (TSMK E.H.1416), 189a.

90. Celālzāde, *Meʾās̱ir*, 29a.

91. Celālzāde, *Meʾās̱ir*, 101b–102a.

92. Celālzāde, *Meʾās̱ir*, 102b–103a.

93. Edāʾī, *Shāhnāma*, 23b–24a.

94. Keşfī, *Selīmnāme*, 17b–18a: "emr-i rabbānī ve taḳdīr-i ilāhī birle." For a discussion of Ottoman advice literature with specific emphasis on the representation of Selīm therein, see Chapter 4.

95. Emine Fetvacı describes *mülemmaʿ* as "a trilingual form consisting of Arabic, Persian, and Ottoman Turkish, the three components of the Ottoman court language" and as a "more floriated version of Ottoman Turkish." See Fetvacı, *Picturing History at the Ottoman Court*, 31–32. Gülru Necipoğlu notes that this linguistic form was "a sign of distinction that would separate the ruling elite from the common people." See Necipoğlu, *Architecture, Ceremonial, and Power*, 115. A late seventeenth-century description of *mülemmaʿ* is provided by Albert Bobovi (later ʿAlī Ufḳī, d. 1675). See Bobovi, *Description du Serail du Grand Seigneur* (Fisher and Fisher edition), 78: "[*mülemmaʿ*] is written in an ornate way and is the combination of Turkish, Arabic and Persian words. It is used as much in prose as in verse, and is very elegant and filled with beautiful and rich thoughts."

96. Whereas Ḳāḍīzāde's exclusive focus is the Egyptian campaigns, al-Laḫmī also mentions Selīm's victories against the Safavid "heretics" (*mülḥid*).

97. The accounts of İdrīs-i Bidlīsī, Edāʾī, Keşfī, Şükrī-i Bidlīsī (and, following him, Çerkesler Kātibi Yūsuf, ʿAzmīzāde Muṣṭafā, and Cevrī İbrāhīm Çelebi), Muḥyī, Celālzāde, and Şīrī fall into this category.

98. Sucūdī's account begins with a lengthy address Selīm reportedly gave immediately after his accession. See Sucūdī, *Selīmnāme*, 3b–6a.

99. For a partial comparison of the contents of several *Selīmnāme*s related to these themes, see Uğur, *The Reign of Sultan Selīm I*, 146–275.

100. Eight *Selīmnāme*s with extant manuscripts are excluded from the analysis provided below. Whereas the accounts of ʿAlī b. Muḥammad al-Laḫmī and Kebir b. Üveys Ḳāḍīzāde are omitted because they focus exclusively on Selīm I's expeditions against the Safavids and the Mamluks, the works penned by Çerkesler Kātibi Yūsuf, ʿAzmīzāde Muṣṭafā, and Cevrī İbrāhīm Çelebi are excluded because they are abridged versions of Şükrī-i Bidlīsī's *Selīmnāme.* Muḥyī's account and the two anonymous *Selīmnāme*s mentioned earlier were unavailable for consultation.

101. See Sucūdī, *Selīmnāme,* 3a: "ṣaded-i münāzaʿa ve muḫālefetde ve daʿvā-yı salṭanat-ü-ḫilāfetde olanları müddet-i yesīre içinde vech-i vecīh ve aḥsen-i ṭarīḳ-i birle külliyen refʿ-ü-defʿeyledi." Unless otherwise specified, all references to Sucūdī's *Selīmnāme* are to this manuscript.

102. For a detailed account of the unfolding of events during Selīm's rise to the sultanate, see Chapter 1.

103. The author is most frequently referred to as İsḥaḳ Çelebi but is also called "Ḳılıççızāde" ("son of the sword-maker," after his father's profession) or "Üsküblü" ("of Skopje," after his place of origin). On his life, works, and poetry, see ʿĀşıḳ Çelebi, *Meşāʿirü'ş-şuʿarā,* vol. 1, 328–41; Parmaksızoğlu, "Üsküplü İshak Çelebi ve Selimnâmesi," 123–34; and Tekindağ, "Selim-nâmeler," 200–202.

104. The other two figures were Nihālī Caʿfer Çelebi of Bursa and Ḳāżī Bozan, judges of Galata and Mihalıç, respectively. See ʿĀşıḳ Çelebi, *Meşāʿirü'ş-şuʿarā,* vol. 1, 328–31. See also Parmaksızoğlu, "Üsküplü İshak Çelebi ve Selimnâmesi," 124–25.

105. Parmaksızoğlu, "Üsküplü İshak Çelebi ve Selimnâmesi," 131. In the introduction to his *Selīmnāme,* İsḥaḳ Çelebi complains about the undue respect paid to undeserving members of the literary elite during the reign of Bāyezīd, which resulted in his choice of voluntary isolation. Given the neglect that he claims he suffered, it is not surprising that İsḥaḳ applauds Selīm I's succession as a welcome development. See İsḥaḳ, *Selīmnāme* (TSMK R. 1276), 3a–4a. Unless otherwise specified, all references to İsḥaḳ's *Selīmnāme* are to this particular manuscript.

106. İsḥaḳ, *Selīmnāme,* 10a–12a.

107. İsḥaḳ, *Selīmnāme,* 12a.

108. İsḥaḳ, *Selīmnāme,* 15a.

109. The Crimean Khanate was an Ottoman protectorate in 1475.

110. Despite covering the succession struggle in some detail, Keşfī and Edāʾī do not mention the collaboration between Selīm and the Crimean Khan. Similarly, Şīrī notes Selīm's arrival at Kefe but does not mention the Crimean Khan. İdrīs-i Bidlīsī does not refer to Selīm's contact with Menglī Girāy but creates a vague narrative link between Selīm's demand of the *sancaḳ* of Kefe for his son and his later request of an audience with Bāyezīd II. See İdrīs, *Salīmshāhnāma,* 52b.

111. On the date of composition of Saʿdī's work, see Saʿdī, *Selīmnāme* (Speiser edition), 8; and Babinger, *Die Geschichtsschreiber der Osmanen und ihre Werke*, 60.

112. On Saʿdī's identity, see Saʿdī, *Selīmnāme* (Speiser edition), 8; Babinger, *Die Geschichtsschreiber der Osmanen und ihre Werke*, 60; and Tekindağ, "Selimnâmeler," 217.

113. For a critical discussion of the draft of a letter that survived in a register of important affairs (*mühimme defteri*), which states that "more than 50–60,000 soldiers from among the enemy-hunting and windstorm-quick Tatars" were sent in the time of Süleymān, see Ivanics, "The Military Co-operation of the Crimean Khanate with the Ottoman Empire," 283–84.

114. According to Saʿdī, these were the *sancaḳ*s of Sivriḥiṣār and Bolu. See Saʿdī, *Selīmnāme* (TSMK R.1277), 18b. Unless otherwise specified, all references to Saʿdī's *Selīmnāme* are to this particular manuscript.

115. Saʿdī, *Selīmnāme*, 19a–19b.

116. Saʿdī, *Selīmnāme*, 20b: "[Menglī Girāy'ın] mülk-i mevrūs̱ı rahgüzārlarında olmağın aña dāḫil olmayınca Rūmili vilāyetinde olan memālik-i maḥrūse-i ʿOs̱mānī duḫūlına mecāl olmaz."

117. Saʿdī, *Selīmnāme*, 21a–22b.

118. Celālzāde, *Meʾās̱ir*, 58a.

119. Celālzāde, *Meʾās̱ir*, 59b: "uḫuvvet-i ṣādıḳa üzere olub."

120. For a discussion of the relevant section of this letter, see Ivanics, "The Military Co-operation of the Crimean Khanate with the Ottoman Empire," 276.

121. Celālzāde, *Meʾās̱ir*, 61a: "mālikāne taṣarruf idüñ."

122. Celālzāde, *Meʾās̱ir*, 62a: "pādişāhlar memleket alurlar kimesneye memleket virmezler."

123. It is likely that the "complete mistrust" that, according to Halil İnalcık, existed between Selīm and Muḥammed Girāy dates back to this incident. See İnalcık, "Power Relationships between Russia, the Crimea and the Ottoman Empire as Reflected in Titulature," 186.

124. Celālzāde, *Meʾās̱ir*, 63a.

125. The collaboration between Saʿādet Girāy and Selīm was enhanced by the marriage alliance between the former and one of the daughters of the latter. See Alderson, *The Structure of the Ottoman Dynasty*, 88.

126. Şükrī, *Selīmnāme*, 21b: "hem varam paşalar eṭvārın görem . . . devlet erkānıyla olam hemnişīn . . . ola kim refʿ ola benden kibr-ü-kīn."

127. Şükrī, *Selīmnāme*, 22b–23a.

128. Şükrī, *Selīmnāme*, 23a: "mendaḫī bir bendeyem fī külli bāb."

129. Saʿdeddīn, *Selīmnāme*, 604: "inhizāmdan ve vüzerā-vü-ümerānuñ Sulṭān Aḥmed cānibine meylinden ġam çekmeñ . . . Tatar leşkerin size ḳoşayam . . . ḳuvvet-i ḳāhire ile mülk-i mevrūs̱uñuza mālik oluñ."

130. Saʿdeddīn, *Selīmnāme*, 605.

131. Contrary to Saʿdeddīn's claim, according to an anonymous seventeenth-century Greek chronicle, Selīm did marry one of the Khan's daughters. See Anonymous, *Chronikon*, 104. It is possible that Selīm was the Khan's son-in-law by virtue of being married to the latter's daughter Ayşe, who was also the widow of his brother Meḥmed (d. 1507). See, for example, Alderson, *The Structure of the Ottoman Dynasty*, 88; and *EI*^{2}, s.v. "Mengli Girāy" (B. Kellner-Heinkele).

132. Saʿdeddīn, *Selīmnāme*, 604: "Biz mülk ṭamaʿında olsaḳ daḫī nişānde-i Ḫān olmaġı nice iḫtiyār eylerüz? Ve ol salṭanatdan ne ḥaẓẓ olınur? Bā-ḫuṣūṣ ābā-vü-ecdādumuz fetḥ itdügi memālik-i maḥrūseyi pāmāl-i süyul-mis̱āl Tātār itmek ve Tātār-ı yaġmā-kār ayaġın memleketümüze açmak ḫaṭā idügi ẓāhir mi degildür? Salṭanat maṭlūb olsa daḫī bunsuz bile bi-ʿavnillāh müyesserdür. Tātār imdādına ḥācet yoḳ."

133. It is noteworthy that Ottoman authors writing in the late medieval and early modern eras used the term "Tatar" to refer to "Mongols" too, and they appear to have expressed similar views about various other polities ruled by the descendants of the Mongol ruler Genghis Khan (r. 1206–1227). For a discussion of the gradual omission of the memory of the Mongols from Ottoman historiography from the fifteenth century onward, see Tezcan, "The Memory of the Mongols in Early Ottoman Historiography."

134. Saʿdeddīn, *Selīmnāme*, 603.

135. See Saʿdeddīn, *Selīmnāme*, especially anecdotes 1, 3, 4, 5, 6.

136. Among the rare—and unfortunately cursory—examinations of readership in the early modern Ottoman context are Neumann, "Üç Tarz-ı Mütalaa"; and Değirmenci, "Bir Kitabı Kaç Kişi Okur?" The reading habits of two eighteenth-century eunuchs, however, were studied by Jane Hathaway. See Hathaway, *Beshir Agha*; and Hathaway, "The Wealth and Influence of an Exiled Ottoman Eunuch in Egypt."

137. Nevīzāde ʿAṭāʾī, as quoted in Fetvacı, *Picturing History at the Ottoman Court*, 43.

138. These points were mentioned by none other than Muṣṭafā ʿĀlī, a contemporary of Meḥmed III. See Fleischer, *Bureaucrat and Intellectual in the Ottoman Empire*, 179–80. Unlike his son, Murād III was well-versed in Persian. On Murād III's and Meḥmed III's language skills and reading preferences, see Fetvacı, *Picturing History at the Ottoman Court*, 43–46 and 46–48, respectively. For Meḥmed III's command to the court historiographer that he compose his works in Ottoman Turkish and not in Persian, see Woodhead, "Murad III and the Historians," 98n26.

139. See Fetvacı, *Picturing History at the Ottoman Court*, 47, 289n98, 289n100. I am grateful to my dear friend and colleague Emine Fetvacı for generously sharing

with me her archival notes from registers recording the lists of books lent to readers at the Ottoman imperial palace.

140. On the participation of prominent members of the Ottoman ruling elite (chief jurisconsult, the military judges of Anatolia and Rumelia, etc.) in a consultation (*meşveret*) session arranged by Meḥmed III's grand vizier to advise the sultan to participate in military campaigns personally, see Selānikī, *Tārīḫ*, vol. 2, 548–49.

141. The other statesman was the grand vizier Sinān Pasha (d. 1596). See Selānikī, *Tārīḫ*, vol. 2, 548–49. Ottoman chroniclers like İbrāhīm Peçevī and Muṣṭafā Naʿīmā narrate that Saʿdeddīn convinced Meḥmed III to put on the Holy Mantle of the Prophet (*ḫırḳa-i şerīf*) and thereby miraculously secured the Ottoman victory. See Peirce, *The Imperial Harem*, 171, 324n77.

142. The fact that Selānikī argued that the victory at Egri was more significant than Ottoman successes at Çaldıran and Mohács indicates that Selīm's military triumphs indeed constituted a principal point of comparison for Ottoman chroniclers. See Selānikī, *Tārīḫ*, vol. 2, 647.

143. Kortepeter, *Ottoman Imperialism during the Reformation*, 151.

144. This historical context has been studied by Carl Max Kortepeter. See Kortepeter, *Ottoman Imperialism during the Reformation*, 146–52.

145. For a survey of political and military relations between the Ottomans and the Crimean Tatars, see, for example, Kortepeter, *Ottoman Imperialism during the Reformation*; İnalcık, "Power Relationships between Russia, the Crimea and the Ottoman Empire as Reflected in Titulature"; Ivanics, "The Military Co-operation of the Crimean Khanate with the Ottoman Empire"; and Królikowska, "Sovereignty and Subordination in Crimean-Ottoman Relations."

146. Others who played an important role in the factional politics at the Ottoman court at this time included but were not limited to Ṣafiye Sulṭān (d. 1605, favorite wife of the late Murād III and the mother of Meḥmed III), Ġazanfer Aġa (d. 1603, chief white eunuch and overseer of palace affairs), and Çiġālazāde Sinān Pasha (d. 1605, a protégé of Saʿdeddīn Efendi and Ġazanfer Agha). It is noteworthy that it was Çiġālazāde Sinān Pasha who, after having been recently appointed to the grand vizierate himself, appointed Feth Girāy to the Khanate.

147. Given the Genghisid—and therefore superior—genealogy of the Crimean Khan, this was a sensitive issue. For fifteenth-century attempts by Ottoman authors to create a noble Turkish pedigree superior to that of dynasties neighboring the Ottoman realm, see Imber, "The Ottoman Dynastic Myth," especially 16–22.

148. The only exception is Şīrī, who states that, before reaching Edirne, Selīm ordered the gathering of a great army in order to fight against the Ḳızılbaş. As

mentioned earlier, the fact that Şīrī was the son of a prominent member of the pro-Aḥmed faction is significant. See Şīrī, *Tārīḫ-i fetḥ-i Mıṣr*, 221a: "buyurdı cemᶜ ola bir ulu leşker."

149. Saᶜdī, *Selīmnāme*, 31b.

150. Celālzāde, *Meʾāṡir*, 26a.

151. İdrīs, *Salīmshāhnāma*, 52b, 53b.

152. Şükrī, *Selīmnāme*, 30a: "bir çeri cemᶜ itdi merd-i dūr-bīn kim melāyik gökde itdi āferīn."

153. Edāʾī and Keşfī fall into the first group of authors and ignore the Battle of Çorlu altogether.

154. Sucūdī, *Selīmnāme*, 2a.

155. Sucūdī, *Selīmnāme*, 2b.

156. İsḥaḳ, *Selīmnāme*, 41b–42b.

157. İsḥaḳ, *Selīmnāme*, 43a.

158. İdrīs, *Salīmshāhnāma*, 53b–54b; Saᶜdī, *Selīmnāme*, 32b–35a; and Şīrī, *Tārīḫ-i fetḥ-i Mıṣr*, 224a.

159. Şükrī, *Selīmnāme*, 31a–31b.

160. Celālzāde, *Meʾāṡir*, 30b.

161. Celālzāde, *Meʾāṡir*, 25a.

162. Celālzāde, *Meʾāṡir*, 27b. The author later gives this number as thirty thousand (78a). Similarly, Şīrī notes that "Selīm's heart did not agree to waging war." See Şīrī, *Tārīḫ-i fetḥ-i Mıṣr*, 223b: "velī yoḳ idi dilden cenge āheng."

163. Celālzāde, *Meʾāṡir*, 26a–26b.

164. Celālzāde, *Meʾāṡir*, 27b: "ṭālib-i salṭanatdur"; 28a: "murād-ı salṭanat itdügine iştibāh yoḳdur."

165. Celālzāde, *Meʾāṡir*, 28a: "külliyen Rūmili beglerini ve sipāh-ı ẓafer-penāhı cümle ḳapuya getirdüb."

166. Celālzāde, *Meʾāṡir*, 28b–29a.

167. Celālzāde, *Meʾāṡir*, 29a: "Sulṭān Selīm maġlūb olub kaçdı."

168. Celālzāde, *Meʾāṡir*, 29b.

169. Celālzāde, *Meʾāṡir*, 78a–78b. Earlier in his narrative, the author gives this number as fifty thousand (27b).

170. Celālzāde, *Meʾāṡir*, 78b.

171. Celālzāde, *Meʾāṡir*, 79a: "selāṭīn-i Āᶜcām neslinden."

172. For a discussion of Celālzāde's years in Ottoman service during the reign of Selīm I, see Şahin, *Empire and Power in the Reign of Süleyman*, 15–33.

173. For a discussion of Prince Muṣṭafā's rebellion, his execution, and its repercussions, see Turan, *Kanuni Süleyman Dönemi Taht Kavgaları*, 22–43.

174. For a discussion of Prince Bāyezīd's rebellion and his execution, see Turan, *Kanuni Süleyman Dönemi Taht Kavgaları*, 50–136.

175. For an excellent analysis contextualizing Celālzāde's *Meʾāṣir* in the later years of Süleymān I's reign, see Şahin, *Empire and Power in the Reign of Süleyman*, 178–85.

176. Saʿdeddīn, *Selīmnāme*, 605.

177. Not all *Selīmnāmes* cover the episode of Selīm's succession in detail. Saʿdeddīn, for example, does not address the topic at all, whereas Sucūdī's account includes only a vague statement that Selīm rose to the sultanate in the "soundest way" (*ṭarīḳ-i eslem birle*). See Sucūdī, *Selīmnāme*, 2b.

178. İsḥaḳ, *Selīmnāme*, 91a.

179. İsḥaḳ, *Selīmnāme*, 90a.

180. İsḥaḳ, *Selīmnāme*, 99b.

181. İsḥaḳ, *Selīmnāme*, 111b–112a.

182. Keşfī, *Selīmnāme*, 14a: "kātib-i ecel ʿömrin ṭomarın dürmiş."

183. Keşfī, *Selīmnāme*, 14a–14b: "bīşe-i şecāʿatinden bir şīr-i ner getüre."

184. Keşfī, *Selīmnāme*, 14b–16b: "sizler dāḫī ne dirsiz."

185. Keşfī, *Selīmnāme*, 17a: "velīʿahd-ı sulṭānī ve ḳāyim-i maḳām-ı ḫāḳānī . . . serīr-i salṭanātı ve tedbīr-i memleketi birle teslīm."

186. İdrīs, *Salīmshāhnāma*, 55a–55b.

187. Şükrī, *Selīmnāme*, 32a–33b.

188. Şükrī, *Selīmnāme*, 40a–40b.

189. Edāʾī, *Shāhnāma*, 15b–16b.

190. Edāʾī, *Shāhnāma*, 17a.

191. Edāʾī, *Shāhnāma*, 17b–18a.

192. Edāʾī, *Shāhnāma*, 18b: "gurūhī az arkān-e ʿālī-maḳām."

193. Edāʾī, *Shāhnāma*, 19a: "Sulṭān Salīm ast shāh-e jehān."

194. Edāʾī, *Shāhnāma*, 19a–20a.

195. Edāʾī, *Shāhnāma*, 20a.

196. Edāʾī, *Shāhnāma*, 21b.

197. Edāʾī, *Shāhnāma*, 23a–23b. Selīm is referred to as the "head of society" (*sar-e ancuman*).

198. Celālzāde, *Meʾāṣīr*, 83a.

199. Celālzāde, *Meʾāṣīr*, 83a.

200. Celālzāde, *Meʾāṣīr*, 83a–83b.

201. Celālzāde, *Meʾāṣīr*, 84a.

202. Celālzāde, *Meʾāṣīr*, 85a.

203. Celālzāde, *Meʾāṣīr*, 85b.

204. Celālzāde, *Meʾās̱ir*, 86a: "tabīʿatları sipāhī-meşreb olmayub."
205. Celālzāde, *Meʾās̱ir*, 89a.
206. Celālzāde, *Meʾās̱ir*, 89b: "baʿżı mütekellim dilāverler ve söz ehli hünerverler . . . ḳullaruñ ser-ʿasker olduġuñuza rıżā virmezler . . . serīr-i salṭanat himmet olunursa fermān-berüz."
207. Celālzāde, *Meʾās̱ir*, 90a: "mādām ki dāʾire-yi ṣıḥḥatdeyim kimesneye salṭanat virmezem."
208. Celālzāde, *Meʾās̱ir*, 90a.
209. Saʿdī, *Selīmnāme*, 36a: "Yularḳaṣdı Sinānı öldürmek ḳaṣdın itdiler."
210. Şīrī, *Tārīḫ-i fetḥ-i Mıṣr*, 225a: "Günāhım bilürem Ḫānum kerem ḳıl / Suçum ʿafv eyle Sulṭānum kerem ḳıl. . . . Rıża gösterdi buyurdı taḫtı ol dem."
211. İsḥaḳ, *Selīmnāme*, 121a.
212. İdrīs, *Salīmshāhnāma*, 60a; Edāʾī, *Shāhnāma*, 26a–26b; Saʿdī, *Selīmnāme*, 49b–50b; Şükrī, *Selīmnāme*, 43a; Celālzāde, *Meʾās̱ir*, 91b; and Şīrī, *Tārīḫ-i fetḥ-i Mıṣr*, 225b–226a.
213. Keşfī, *Selīmnāme*, 19a–20b.
214. For contemporaneous and modern references to the discussion of Bāyezīd II's death, see Tekindağ, "Bayezid'in Ölümü Meselesi."
215. Saʿdeddīn's *Selīmnāme* does not include an account of this episode.
216. Keşfī, *Selīmnāme*, 28a: "münāzaʿat ve muḥālefet ḳılanlaruñ kārlaruña itmām ve rüzgārlaruña encām virüb."
217. Sucūdī, *Selīmnāme*, 3a: "basṭ-ı ḳavānīn-i maʿdelet-i sulṭānī ve neşr-i āyīn-i nıṣfet-i ʿOs̱mānī idüb ṣaded-i münāzaʿa ve muḫālefetde ve daʿvā-yı salṭanat-ü-ḫilāfetde olanları müddet-i yesīre içinde vech-i vecīh ve aḥsen-i ṭarīḳ birle külliyen refʿ-ü-defʿ eyledi."
218. Edāʾī, *Shāhnāma*, 24b.
219. Şīrī, *Tārīḫ-i fetḥ-i Mıṣr*, 230b.
220. In addition to Aḥmed and Ḳorḳud, Celālzāde lists Selīm's nephews Muḥammed, ʿOs̱mān, Mūsā, Orḫān, and Emīrḫān among the princes executed in Bursa. Whereas Şükrī-i Bidlīsī does not mention Emīrḫān, İdrīs-i Bidlīsī adds the name of Prince Muṣṭafā to this list. See Celālzāde, *Meʾās̱ir*, 100a–100b; İdrīs, *Salīmshāhnāma*, 61b; and Şükrī, *Selīmnāme*, 51a. Saʿdī does not mention the names of executed princes.
221. İdrīs, *Salīmshāhnāma*, 62a; Şükrī, *Selīmnāme*, 51a; and Celālzāde, *Meʾās̱ir*, 100a–100b. See also the section relating Selīm's expeditions against Ḳorḳud and Aḥmed in Saʿdī, *Selīmnāme*, 56a–61a; and Şīrī, *Tārīḫ-i fetḥ-i Mıṣr*, 230b: "bir fitne ḳopmaya cihānda."
222. İdrīs, *Salīmshāhnāma*, 61b.

4. Selīm, the Idealized Ruler

1. From *Kitāb al-maḥāsin wa'l-aḍdād*, as quoted by Franz Rosenthal, *Complaint and Hope*, vii.

2. TSMA E.3192.

3. Selâhattin Tansel considered ʿAlī Ḫalīfe "a zealot but a great patriot." See Tansel, *Yavuz Sultan Selim*, 29.

4. For an analysis of Ḳorḳud's *Daʿwat*, see Fleischer, "From Şeyhzade Korkud to Mustafa Âli"; and al-Tikriti, "Şehzade Korkud," Chapter 5. For the significance of Ḳorḳud's scholarly works within their historical context, see al-Tikriti, "The Ḥajj as Justifiable Self-Exile"; and al-Tikriti, "Şehzade Korkud."

5. Al-Tikriti, "Şehzade Korkud," 672.

6. See TSMA E.6185/11 and E.6185/2, respectively. A *ḳānūnnāme* that Selīm sent to his son Süleymān for the "chastisement of wicked ones and the punishment of thieves" in the latter's province is also indicative of the former's emphasis on the establishment of law and order throughout the Ottoman realm. For the text of the *ḳānūnnāme* and a brief discussion of its historical significance, see Karal, "Yavuz Sultan Selim'in Oğlu Şehzade Süleyman'a Manisa Sancağını İdare Etmesi İçin Gönderdiği Siyasetnâme."

7. Some of Ḳorḳud's other writings were known to Ottoman intellectuals. According to Cornell Fleischer, the prominent Ottoman historian and bureaucrat Muṣṭafā ʿĀlī (d. 1600) "and others were apparently familiar with a collection, now lost, of the *fatwās* of the jurist-prince." See Fleischer, "From Şeyhzade Korkud to Mustafa Âli," 73.

8. Fleischer, "From Şeyhzade Korkud to Mustafa Âli," 72.

9. See Howard, "Ottoman Historiography and the Literature of 'Decline,'" 54.

10. See Fodor, "State and Society, Crisis and Reform," 217–18.

11. See Fleischer, "From Şeyhzade Korkud to Mustafa Âli," 67.

12. Baki Tezcan refers to these works also as "political tracts." See Tezcan, *The Second Ottoman Empire*, 51, 96.

13. Abou-El-Haj, "The Expression of Ottoman Political Culture in the Literature of Advice to Princes."

14. See Howard, "Genre and Myth in the Ottoman Advice for Kings Literature."

15. See ʿĀlī, *Nuṣḥatü's-selāṭīn*, vol. 2, 115/254.

16. In addition to referring to Ottoman monarchs as *Shāhanshāh*, *pādishāh*, etc., Ottoman authors also highlight the affinity between Ottoman sultans and the mythical heroes of the Persian *Shāhnāma* tradition. For a discussion of Süleymān I's endowment deed (*vaḳfiyye*) as a document indicating the extent of Persian influence on Ottoman regal vocabulary and self-identification, see

Yıldız, "Ottoman Historical Writing in Persian," 500. The endowment deed was transliterated and published with facsimile by Kemâl Edîb Kürkçüoğlu in *Süleymaniye Vakfiyesi.*

17. For a detailed and annotated list of works composing the advice literature throughout Islamic history, with particular emphasis on the Ottoman experience, see Levend, "Siyaset-nameler"; and Uğur, *Osmanlı Siyâset-nâmeleri.*

18. For a careful analysis problematizing the term *decline*, see Kafadar, "The Myth of the Golden Age." For the uncritical usage of the term *decline*, see Lewis, "Ottoman Observers of Ottoman Decline"; and Lewis, "Some Reflections on the Decline of the Ottoman Empire."

19. For discussions of the significance of this genre in the Safavid context, see Lambton, "Quis Custodiet Custodes." For the Mughal context, see Sajida Sultana Alvi's introduction to her edition of Muḥammad Bāqir Najm-i Sānī's (d. 1637) advice treatise, published as *Advice on the Art of Governance: Mauʿiẓah-i Jahāngīrī of Muḥammad Bāqir Najm-i Sānī.* With seventeenth-century Spain in mind, Peter Burke points to reform proposals called *arbitristas* as a parallel to the Ottoman "memoranda to the sultan." Burke's statement that European addresses to princes should not be written off "as empty or servile" is relevant for Ottoman works of advice as well. Although Burke refers to these addresses as "a form of prince-management," it would be more accurate in the Ottoman context to consider them a form of sultan management. See Burke, "Concepts of the 'Golden Age' in the Renaissance," 159–60, 162.

20. On the evolution of the concept of "the circle of justice" throughout the history of the Middle East and within the early modern Ottoman context, see Darling, *A History of Social Justice and Political Power in the Middle East*, especially 127–54.

21. From *Aḫlaḳ-ı ʿAlāʾī*, as quoted by Cornell Fleischer, "Royal Authority, Dynastic Cyclism, and 'Ibn Khaldûnism,'" 201. Composed in 1082, Kay-Kāʾūs ibn Iskandar's *Ḳābūsnāma* appears to have served Ḳınālızāde ʿAlī Çelebi as a model. In a chapter titled "Rules for the Vizierate," Kay-Kāʾūs ibn Iskandar suggests how the harmonious coexistence between the ruler and the ruled can be achieved: "Make it your constant endeavor to improve cultivation and to govern well; for, understand this truth, good government is secured by armed troops, armed troops are maintained with gold, gold is acquired through cultivation and cultivation sustained through payment of what is due to the peasantry by just dealing and fairness. Be just and equitable, therefore." See Kay-Kāʾūs ibn Iskandar, *Ḳābūsnāma*, 213.

22. See Tezcan, "Ethics as Domain to Discuss the Political," 110.

23. The analysis below focuses primarily, though not exclusively, on works of advice in which Selīm I is mentioned explicitly. Although a definitive monograph

on the subject is still wanting, there are numerous studies, some of them excellent, that survey various aspects of the Ottoman advice literature. See, for example, Levend, "Siyaset-nameler"; Uğur, *Osmanlı Siyâset-nâmeleri*; Kafadar, "The Myth of the Golden Age"; Lewis, "Ottoman Observers of Ottoman Decline"; Lewis, "Some Reflections on the Decline of the Ottoman Empire"; Fodor, "State and Society, Crisis and Reform"; Sariyannis, "The Princely Virtues as Presented in Ottoman Political and Moral Literature"; and Sariyannis, "Ottoman Critics of Society and State." Two recent articles by Douglas A. Howard that highlight the literary aspects of the genre represent the most notable contributions to the scholarly literature on the subject. See Howard, "Genre and Myth in the Ottoman Advice for Kings Literature"; and Howard, "Ottoman Historiography and the Literature of 'Decline.'"

24. Luṭfī, *Āṣafnāme*, 245: "ʿasker az gerek uz gerek . . . ʿulūfeli onbeş bin ʿasker çok ʿaskerdür. Hiç eksilmeyüb sāl-be-sāl onbeş bin ādeme mevācib yetişdürmek pehlevānlıḳdur."

25. See Ḥasan Kāfī, *Uṣūl al-ḥikam*, especially 267–75. Military expeditions led by the sultan were rare occurences in the post-Süleymānic era. Meḥmed III's Egri expedition of 1596, ʿOs̱mān II's (r. 1618–1622) campaign against Poland in 1621, and Murād IV's (r. 1623–1640) sultanic campaigns against the Safavids in 1635 and 1638 were among the notable exceptions.

26. Ḥasan Kāfī, *Uṣūl al-ḥikam*, 275. The author also states that this was the reason why "God Almighty sent enemies to attack the [Empire's] Rumelian frontiers."

27. On the "periodical levy of Christian children for training to fill the ranks of the Janissaries and to occupy posts in the Palace service and in the administration," see *EI*², s.v. "Devshirme" (V. L. Ménage); and ʿĀlī, *Nuṣḥatü's-selāṭīn*, vol. 2, 30/148. ʿĀlī continued to state that the method of *devşirme* "was only adopted in the past out of need as a means to increase the number of Muslims."

28. Luṭfī, *Āṣafnāme*, 245: "vezīr-i ḳul ṭāʾifesine müdebbir ve żābıṭ kimesneleri aġa . . . itmek gerekdür."

29. Veysī, *Ḫābnāme*, 46. For an analysis of Veysī's work as a representation of "declinist sensibilities" within the context of early modern Ottoman political consciousness, see Şen, "A Mirror for Princes, a Fiction for Readers," especially 46–48.

30. This traumatic episode and its representation in later Ottoman historiography have been studied by Gabriel Piterberg. See Piterberg, *An Ottoman Tragedy*. A contemporary author narrates ʿOs̱mān II's deposition and subsequent execution by the janissaries and notes that "such cruelty did not occur" (*bu cefālar olmadı*) even at the time of Selīm's forcible deposition of his father, Bāyezīd II. See Tūġī Çelebi, *İbretnümā*, 503.

31. On the requirements of the grand vizierate, see Luṭfī, *Āṣafnāme*, 244–48. Luṭfī Pasha argues that the upward mobility of the tax-paying subjects of the Empire could lead to decreasing imperial revenues and comments that it is imperative that the state not only prevent the *reʿāyā* from rising into the ranks of the *ʿaskerī* but also send subject peasants back to their provinces, even if they deserted their lands because of oppression. See Luṭfī, *Āṣafnāme*, 248, 251.

32. On this point, see Fodor, "State and Society, Crisis and Reform."

33. ʿĀlī, *Nuṣḥatü's-selāṭīn*, vol. 2, 41/164.

34. Rifaʾat Ali similarly notes that "the complaints about corruption and decline, moral and otherwise, that are found in the language of the *nasihatname* writers should be understood in relation to the authors' support or opposition to the social, economic, or cultural experiments that were transforming Ottoman society in these decades." See Abou-El-Haj, "The Expression of Ottoman Political Culture in the Literature of Advice to Princes," 286.

35. See Luṭfī, *Āṣafnāme*, 244: "maġlūb-i nisā olmayub anlaruñ mekrinden emīn olmaḳ içün ṣadāret-i ʿuẓmādan fāriġ olub." Although Luṭfī Pasha's cryptic remarks in the introductory section of *Āṣafnāme* suggest that he retired from the grand vizierate voluntarily, Ottoman chroniclers provide details of the curious circumstances that led to his dismissal. These authors relate that a disagreement between Luṭfī Pasha and his wife Şāh Sulṭān (d. 1572) over the pasha's brutal punishment of a prostitute turned violent, that Luṭfī Pasha beat Şāh Sulṭān, and that the latter requested a divorce. When Süleymān granted his sister's wishes, Luṭfī Pasha's marriage ended—and so did his grand vizierate. For a discussion of this episode as well as references to Ottoman authors who mention it, see Peirce, *The Imperial Harem*, 201–2, 329n62.

36. See Veysī, *Ḫābnāme*, 76; and Ḥasan Kāfī, *Uṣūl al-ḥikam*, 268: "ʿulemāʾdan ḥīle ve ḫıyānet vāḳiʿ olmaz." On the identities of these figures, see Veysī, *Ḫābnāme*, 12–13; and Ḥasan Kāfī, *Uṣūl al-ḥikam*, 239–41, respectively.

37. On Muṣṭafā ʿĀlī's life and oeuvre, see Fleischer, *Bureaucrat and Intellectual in the Ottoman Empire*, especially 201–31.

38. Anonymous, *Ḳavānīn-i yeñiçeriyān*, 16a.

39. See Howard, "Genre and Myth in the Ottoman Advice for Kings Literature," 151; and Fodor, "State and Society, Crisis and Reform," 218n2.

40. For an identification of the Süleymānic era as the pinnacle of Ottoman history, see Fodor, "State and Society, Crisis and Reform," 223; and İnalcık, "Sultan Süleymân," 100–103. For a sophisticated approach, see Fleischer, "From Şeyhzade Korkud to Mustafa Âli"; and Kafadar, "The Myth of the Golden Age."

41. Fleischer, "From Şeyhzade Korkud to Mustafa Âli," 71.

42. Fleischer, "From Şeyhzade Korkud to Mustafa Âli," 74.

43. Kafadar, "The Myth of the Golden Age," 40. Veysī's *Ḫābnāme*, in which even the time of the Prophet Muḥammad is not granted immunity from corruption and devastation, is an Ottoman narrative confirming Kafadar. External and rather implicit confirmation of Kafadar's view comes from Peter Burke, who states that "European writers traditionally took the idea of a golden age much more seriously than their counterparts in other cultures." See Burke, "Concepts of the 'Golden Age' in the Renaissance," 162.

44. See Fleischer, "From Şeyhzade Korkud to Mustafa Âli," 67: "[Ottoman *naṣīḥatnāme* writers] usually define administrative and social ideals by depicting the present as a period of decline from a 'classical' (or, more properly, classicized) standard assumed to have been in effect during a 'Golden Age.'"

45. Kafadar observes that "the topos of 'the good old days when Ottoman classical traditions and laws held sway' is not devoid of historicity." See Kafadar, "The Myth of the Golden Age," 38.

46. Kafadar, "The Myth of the Golden Age," 38–39; and Fleischer, "From Şeyhzade Korkud to Mustafa Âli," 67. Italics mine.

47. See Ḥasan Kāfī el-Aḳḥiṣārī's (d. 1616) *Uṣūl al-ḥikam fī niẓām al-ʿālam* (Principles of Wisdom Pertaining to the Order of the World, written in 1596); Üveys b. Meḥmed Veysī's (d. 1628) *Ḫābnāme* (Book of Dreams, written in 1608); Kātib Çelebi's (d. 1657) *Düstūrü'l-ʿamel li-ışlāḥü'l-ḫalel* (The Rule of Action for the Rectification of Defects, written in 1653); and Ṣarı Meḥmed Pasha's (d. 1717) *Neṣāʾiḥü'l-vüzerā ve'l-ümerā* (Counsel for Viziers and Governors, written around 1703).

48. *Book of Asaph*, written after 1553.

49. *Counsel for Sultans*, written in 1581.

50. *Treatise*, written in 1631.

51. *Code of Sultanic Laws* by ʿAzīz Efendi, written in 1633.

52. *A Memorandum on the Laws of the House of ʿOs̱mān*, written around 1675.

53. *Amulet of Rulers*, written around 1580.

54. *Laws of the Janissaries*, written during the reign of Aḥmed I, sometime between 1609 and 1617.

55. *The Pleasant Book*, written around 1620.

56. *The Book on the Proper Course for Muslims and the Benefits for Believers*, written around 1637–1640.

57. Despite the statement of Tayfun Toroser, the editor of the work, that *Ḳavānīn-i yeñiçeriyān* may have been composed either between May and December 1606 or between 1606 and 1617, the anonymous author's vague statement about the annihilation of the "Celālīs who rebelled in Anatolia" in the introductory section suggests a date of composition after 1609 or 1610. See Anonymous, *Ḳavānīn-i yeñiçeriyān*, xi–xiii, 1b.

58. Anonymous, *Ḳavānīn-i yeñiçeriyān*, 32a. The folio numbers given here refer to the manuscript (Veliyüddin Efendi 1973) published as a facsimile by Tayfun Toroser.

59. Danişmend, *İzahlı Osmanlı Tarihi Kronolojisi*, vol. 2, 5.

60. ʿĀlī, *Nuṣḥatü's-selāṭīn*, vol. 1, 51/142.

61. Luṭfī Pasha served Selīm in various capacities, ultimately as governor-general of Anatolia. A critical edition of the work was published by Rudolf Tschudi under the title *Das Aṣafnâme des Luṭfî Pascha*. The references given here, however, are to a later edition by Ahmet Uğur. See Luṭfī, *Āṣafnāme*, 254.

62. See Ṭaşköprīzāde, *Al-Şaḳā'iḳ al-nuʿmāniyya fī ʿulamā al-dawlat al-ʿOs̱māniyya*, 305, 306.

63. Süleymān lifted his father's ban on silk trade with the Safavid realm and returned the confiscated goods to the merchants immediately after he acceded to the throne. Süleymān also freed members of six hundred families that his father had deported from Egypt after 1517 and punished several high-ranking members of the military ruling elite for the injustices they had inflicted on Ottoman subjects. For a discussion of Ottoman historians' coverage of the acts of justice and equity that established Süleymān's image as a just monarch, see Woodhead, "Perspectives on Süleyman," especially 164–67. For a contemporary account, see Celālzāde Muṣṭafā, *Ṭabaḳātü'l-memālik ve derecātü'l-mesālik*, 27a–27b.

64. Anonymous, *Ḥırzü'l-mülūk*, 193: "kendü muḳteżāsı üzre ḥażż-ı nefs içün Müslümānları ẓulmen ḳatl itmek [. . .] bir cüz'ī günāh içün bir nice ḳullarıñuzuñ ḳatline fermān."

65. Anonymous, *Ḳavānīn-i yeñiçeriyān*, 12a.

66. Koçi Beg, *Risāle*, 61/63. References to *Risāle-i Koçi Beg* are based on the 2007 edition of the work by Seda Çakmakcıoğlu. The first page number refers to the editor's simplified modern Turkish translation, and the second refers to the page numbers of the facsimile provided at the end of that edition.

67. Anonymous, *Ḥırzü'l-mülūk*, 179: "ne ġażūb ve ne ḥalīm [. . .] belki ġażab cānibine māyil olmaları dīn-ü-devlete enfaʿ olmaḳ fehm olunur." A similar point is made by Muṣṭafā ʿĀlī: "Although statesmen are a necessity and viziers are important and indispensable, the most important thing is to employ wise ones and to strictly check on their irregular actions in order to assure their fear and awe of the king's anger and their effort and attention to carry out the orders in conformity with the divine law." See ʿĀlī, *Nuṣḥatü's-selāṭīn*, vol. 1, 40/125.

68. Anonymous, *Ḥırzü'l-mülūk*, 175. See also Howard, "Genre and Myth in the Ottoman Advice for Kings Literature," 151.

69. Anonymous, *Kitāb-ı müstetāb*, 18–19. According to the anonymous author of *Ḳavānīn-i yeñiçeriyān*, Selīm also hit Pīrī Meḥmed Pasha on the head numerous times with a bow (*kebāde*) when the latter questioned the appropriateness of the

former's decision to enlist some of the youth in the Trabzon region as *devşirme*. See Anonymous, *Ḳavānīn-i yeñiçeriyān*, 13a.

70. The fact that *Āṣafnāme* is mentioned in later works of advice suggests that Luṭfī Pasha's concerns and criticisms resonated with other *naṣīḥatnāme* authors as well. *Āṣafnāme* is reproduced in its entirety by Hezārfen Ḥüseyin in *Telḫīṣü'l-beyān*. For a brief summary of the major points raised in *Āṣafnāme*, see Fodor, "State and Society, Crisis and Reform," 223–24; and Lewis, "Ottoman Observers of Ottoman Decline," 71–74.

71. Luṭfī, *Āṣafnāme*, 244–45.

72. Luṭfī, *Āṣafnāme*, 247.

73. See, for example, Hezārfen Ḥüseyin, *Telḫīṣ*, 86.

74. See Hezārfen Ḥüseyin, *Telḫīṣ*, 183. The same point was made in Celālzāde, *Meʾā̱sir*, 23b.

75. Fleischer, *Bureaucrat and Intellectual in the Ottoman Empire*, 192.

76. For an alternative wording of the same distinction (i.e., "general legislation" versus "usage based on precedent"), see Fleischer, *Bureaucrat and Intellectual in the Ottoman Empire*, 212.

77. Fleischer, *Bureaucrat and Intellectual in the Ottoman Empire*, 100. For Luṭfī Pasha's life and the significance of his oeuvre, see *EI*[2], s.v. "Luṭfī Pasha" (C. H. Imber); and *İA*, s.v. "Lutfi Paşa" (M. T. Gökbilgin).

78. For a general discussion of "*ḳānūn*-consciousness," see Fleischer, *Bureaucrat and Intellectual in the Ottoman Empire*, 191–97.

79. The notion of "*ḳānūn*-mindedness" has been identified by Cemal Kafadar as one of "at least two distinct and often rival attitudes within the decline-and-reform discourse of the post-Süleymānic age" and is used by that author in a more restricted sense, as an allusion to the viewpoint of Ottoman reformists who envisioned "an exemplary Ottoman order, with a mature political-legal-social paradigm, located in a classical age stretching from Meḥmed the Conqueror to Süleymān the Lawgiver." Juxtaposed with proponents of the other, *selefī* ("fundamentalist") strand of reformist thought, who regarded the time of the Prophet Muḥammad and his companions as the only "golden age" in Islamic history and proposed a more *sharīʿa*-oriented reform agenda, *ḳānūn*-minded intellectuals, by and large, argued for the revival of what they selectively perceived as Ottoman tradition. See Kafadar, "The Myth of the Golden Age," 42–44.

80. Luṭfī, *Āṣafnāme*, 243; quoted in Lewis, "Ottoman Observers of Ottoman Decline," 71. On the "prophetic voice" assumed by Ottoman authors of advice works as a standard trope, see Howard, "Genre and Myth in the Ottoman Advice for Kings Literature," 149–50.

81. To name a couple: the abuses associated with the imperial courier service (*barīd*, *ulāḳ*) and pervasive bribery (*rüşvet*). The unusual length of the discussion

in the chronicle on the history and significance of the oppression caused by the imperial courier service (*ulāḳ ẓulmü*) suggests that Luṭfī Pasha considered this problem particularly troubling. See Luṭfī, *Tevārīḫ*, 283–91. For an analysis of Ḳorḳud's *Daʿwat*, see Fleischer, "From Şeyhzade Korkud to Mustafa Âli"; and al-Tikriti, "Şehzade Korkud," Chapter 5. For a discussion of ʿAlī Ḫalīfe's petition addressed to Selīm in the immediate aftermath of the latter's accession to the throne, see Tansel, *Yavuz Sultan Selim*, 20–30.

82. For a brief summary of the problems observed and remedies suggested in *Āṣafnāme*, see Lewis, "Ottoman Observers of Ottoman Decline," 71–74; and Fodor, "State and Society, Crisis and Reform," 223–24.

83. Luṭfī Pasha specifically compliments Selīm for respecting legal precepts that required camels to be given to various high-ranking officials during a military expedition and that expected Ottoman sultans on campaign to bequeath janissaries and horsemen six days' provisions. See Luṭfī, *Āṣafnāme*, 248–49.

84. For his life, his works, and his significance as an Ottoman historian of the sixteenth century, see Fleischer, *Bureaucrat and Intellectual in the Ottoman Empire.* In his meticulous analysis of political viewpoints regarding Ottoman royal authority and its limits that were prevalent in learned circles in the late sixteenth and seventeenth centuries, Baki Tezcan identifies two distinct political positions ("constitutionalist" and "absolutist") and refers to Muṣṭafā ʿĀlī as one of the "most eloquent defenders" of the "constitutionalist case." See Tezcan, *The Second Ottoman Empire*, 55.

85. ʿĀlī, *Nuṣḥatü's-selāṭīn*, vol. 1, 37/119–20. With the exception of minor modifications to ensure consistency in spelling and transliteration throughout this work, translations of excerpts from *Nuṣḥatü's-selāṭīn* are quoted as they appear in Andreas Tietze's edition of *Muṣṭafā ʿĀlī's Counsel for Sultans of 1581.*

86. ʿĀlī, *Nuṣḥatü's-selāṭīn*, vol. 1, 40/125: "ḫilāf-ı ḳavānīn ẓuhūr iden iḫtilāl-i mevfūr."

87. For the author's emphasis on the centrality of "the laws of the House of ʿOs̱mān," see ʿĀlī, *Nuṣḥatü's-selāṭīn*, vol. 2, 113/252. For a discussion of the symbolic and practical significance of *ḳānūn* for Ottoman bureaucrats in the later sixteenth century in general and for ʿĀlī in particular, see Fleischer, *Bureaucrat and Intellectual in the Ottoman Empire*, 191–213.

88. ʿĀlī, *Nuṣḥatü's-selāṭīn*, vol. 1, 50/140.

89. Anonymous, *Ḥırzü'l-mülūk*, 175: "ḳānūn-ı ʿOs̱mānīye muḫālifdir dimeyüb."

90. Anonymous, *Ḥırzü'l-mülūk*, 175: "selāṭīn-i ʿiẓām ne iderlese ḳānūn olur."

91. For a discussion of the varied interpretations of law in the late sixteenth-century Ottoman context, see Tezcan, *The Second Ottoman Empire*, Chapter 2, especially 48–59.

92. See Anonymous, *Ḳavānīn-i yeñiçeriyān*, 1b. The work is also the principal source utilized by İsmail Hakkı Uzunçarşılı, whose two-volume *Osmanlı Devleti Teşkilâtından Kapukulu Ocakları* is the definitive scholarly study of the slave-servants (*ḳul*) of Ottoman sultans and the janissary corps.

93. Anonymous, *Ḳavānīn-i yeñiçeriyān*, 25a–26b.

94. Anonymous, *Ḳavānīn-i yeñiçeriyān*, 25b: "itdim ḳānūn oldı."

95. For a detailed discussion of varying contemporary Ottoman interpretations regarding the limits of the royal prerogative and the political positions, see Tezcan, *The Second Ottoman Empire*, Chapter 2.

96. Murād III's absolutist agenda appears to have marked him specifically as a target for *ḳānūn*-conscious *naṣīḥatnāme* authors. For a discussion of Murād III's absolutist policies and the contemporary criticisms of these policies voiced by Ottoman intellectuals, see Tezcan, *The Second Ottoman Empire*, 97–108 and 55–59, respectively.

97. Anonymous, *Ḳavānīn-i yeñiçeriyān*, 108b–109a. To the best of my knowledge, this anonymous treatise is the first literary-historical narrative that refers to Selīm I as "Yāvuz."

98. Luṭfī, *Āṣafnāme*, 244–45.

99. Based on the limited information in *Ḥırzü'l-mülūk* on the identity of its anonymous author, Yaşar Yücel argues that he must have been a learned holder of a fief (*dirlik*). See Yücel, *Osmanlı Devlet Teşkilâtına Dair Kaynaklar*, Part III, 147–48. On Pīrī Meḥmed Pasha's career path, see Anonymous, *Ḥırzü'l-mülūk*, 180.

100. See, for example, ʿĀlī, *Nuṣḥatü's-selāṭīn*, vol. 1, 67/165.

101. ʿĀlī, *Nuṣḥatü's-selāṭīn*, vol. 1, 51/142. ʿĀlī emphasizes repeatedly the necessity of making administrative and bureaucratic career paths accessible to all deserving individuals, even those without training at the imperial palace. See, for example, *Nuṣḥatü's-selāṭīn*, vol. 1, 25/101: "As long as qualification is not sought for, as long as educated men are not given employment and high standing under the excuse that they had not been trained in the Imperial Palace, it will be necessary that the happiness-vested person that is the sultan be laden with sin, and that the awe-inspiring person, the 'illustrious vizier' (by name only!), be the protector of the low-class people, the promoter of the scum."

102. As the sentiments of a bureaucrat hailing from a freeborn Muslim background, Muṣṭafā ʿĀlī's views were akin to those regarding *merdümzādes* expressed by Celālzāde Muṣṭafā. See the discussion on the *merdümzāde* in Chapter 2.

103. For a discussion of the changes in Ottoman career paths between the late fifteenth and the late sixteenth centuries, see Fleischer, *Bureaucrat and Intellectual in the Ottoman Empire*, 200–213. For an analysis of the increasing

institutionalization and the rise of a bureaucratic consciousness during the Süleymānic era, see Şahin, *Empire and Power in the Reign of Süleyman*, Chapter 7. A parallel transformation in the provincial administration between the mid-sixteenth and mid-seventeenth centuries is explored in Kunt, *The Sultan's Servants.*

104. For a discussion of contemporary Ottoman reactions to this process (and a critique of Murād III's absolutist policies voiced by none other than Muṣṭafā ʿĀlī), see Tezcan, *The Second Ottoman Empire*, 58. Tezcan characterizes this development by referring to the closely interrelated processes of "proto-democratization" and "*civilization*" of the Ottoman imperial polity. See Tezcan, *The Second Ottoman Empire*, 10, 77, 198, and 10, 76, 197, respectively.

105. As mentioned earlier, both Cornell Fleischer and Cemal Kafadar argue that Ottoman historians and *naṣīḥatnāme* authors regarded either Meḥmed II or Süleymān I or both as sultans of an Ottoman "classical age." See Kafadar, "The Myth of the Golden Age," 38–39; and Fleischer, "From Şeyhzade Korkud to Mustafa Âli," 67.

106. ʿĀlī, *Nuṣḥatü's-selāṭīn*, vol. 2, 37/157–58.

107. ʿĀlī, *Nuṣḥatü's-selāṭīn*, vol. 2, 39/160. I would like to thank Jane Hathaway for reminding me that Muṣṭafā ʿĀlī wrote at a time when the merchants he detested were playing an increasingly active role in international trade in the eastern Mediterranean. For a study focusing on a prominent merchant active in Cairo during the last quarter of the sixteenth century and the first quarter of the seventeenth, see Hanna, *Making Big Money in 1600*. On Ottoman merchant communities active in Egypt in the early sixteenth century, see Casale, *The Ottoman Age of Exploration*, 26–29.

108. ʿĀlī, *Nuṣḥatü's-selāṭīn*, vol. 1, 52/142: "Furthermore, the eminent companions of this mighty and august King were the late Tācīzāde Caʿfer Çelebi and Mevlānā Āḫī, and his skillful physician, pleasant friend, a store[house] of expertise, and possessor of high qualities, Mevlānā Aḫī. [Therefore] his illustrious circle was distinguished by learned conversations, his noble gatherings were always embellished by fine anecdotes concerning history, and the world was in good order, breezes of justice were blowing, and the rose-bed of justice and benignity was flourishing in every respect."

109. ʿĀlī, *Nuṣḥatü's-selāṭīn*, vol. 1, 52/142–43.

110. ʿĀlī, *Nuṣḥatü's-selāṭīn*, vol. 1, 52/143–44.

111. ʿĀlī, *Nuṣḥatü's-selāṭīn*, vol. 1, 53/144. It is noteworthy that Muṣṭafā ʿĀlī penned his *Nuṣḥat* during the reign of Murād III, whom he criticized for surrounding himself with boon companions and thereby allowing palace dwarves, court jesters, and mutes to exert undue political influence. On the unofficial figures at Murād III's court and Meḥmed III's decision to remove them from the

palace after his accession to the throne, see Fetvacı, *Picturing History at the Ottoman Court*, 84, 289n83, and 289n84.

112. ʿĀlī, *Nuṣḥatü's-selāṭīn*, vol. 1, 75–76/175–76.

113. Anonymous, *Ḥırzü'l-mülūk*, 175.

114. Anonymous, *Ḥırzü'l-mülūk*, 175. The anonymous author of the work must have considered Selīm's iron-fisted attitude significant, as he repeats the same point a few pages later (*Ḥırzü'l-mülūk*, 180).

115. The appointment of finance minister (*defterdār*) Pīrī Meḥmed Pasha to the grand vizierate constituted one such break. See Anonymous, *Ḥırzü'l-mülūk*, 175, 180.

116. Anonymous, *Ḥırzü'l-mülūk*, 179.

117. Luṭfī, *Āṣafnāme*, 247.

118. In a similar fashion, Celālzāde Muṣṭafā expressed his concern with the direction of the state of affairs during the last years of Süleymān's reign and implicitly criticized the aging sultan by depicting Selīm as an ideal sultan, and his reign as an ideal era, in *Selīmnāme*. For an analysis of the *Selīmnāme* as a reassessment anchored in the historical context within which it was penned, see Şahin, *Empire and Power in the Reign of Süleyman*, 178–85.

119. Luṭfī, *Āṣafnāme*, 251.

120. Luṭfī, *Āṣafnāme*, 251–52.

121. Luṭfī, *Āṣafnāme*, 250. For a more general statement about the situation Süleymān inherited from Selīm, see Luṭfī, *Tevārīḫ*, 243: "Selīm suffered greatly to remove the thorns and sticks (*ḫār-u-ḫāşāk*) of this world to turn it into a vineyard and garden (*bāġ-u-būstān*) and Sultan Süleymān received the fruits of that vineyard and garden without difficulty and hardship." Writing several decades later, Muṣṭafā ʿĀlī placed a similar emphasis on the importance of maintaining a healthy balance between revenues and expenditures. In fact, he went one step further and mentioned it as one of the six gifts (*mevhibe*) "of special Divine favor" enjoyed by the Ottoman dynasty. For ʿĀlī's discussion of the six divine favors that set the Ottomans apart from all other noble houses, see ʿĀlī, *Nuṣḥatü's-selāṭīn*, vol. 1, 38–39/122–23.

122. Luṭfī, *Āṣafnāme*, 250.

123. Luṭfī, *Āṣafnāme*, 249. Writing in 1675, Hezārfen Ḥüseyin expressed a similar view. See *Telḫīṣ*, 183: "In fairness, among the felicitous sovereigns [who were the] descendants of ʿOs̱mān, whose abode is heaven, there is no other sultan of exalted reputation resembling the aforementioned Sulṭān Selīm Ḫān."

124. Despite the fact that *Tevārīḫ* is not part of the *naṣīḥatnāme* genre, here it will be briefly analyzed to illustrate Luṭfī Pasha's general attitude toward Selīm's exceptional standing among all other Ottoman rulers.

125. Luṭfī, *Tevārīḫ*, 211.

126. Luṭfī Pasha mentions ʿO̱smān Beg and Meḥmed I (r. 1413–1421) as the other two Ottoman renewers of religion. See Luṭfī, *Tevārīḫ*, 147–53.

127. Guenée, *States and Rulers in Late Medieval Europe*, 69.

128. For a discussion of decline-consciousness among Ottoman intellectuals in the sixteenth century and thereafter, see Kafadar, "The Question of Ottoman Decline"; and Kafadar, "The Myth of the Golden Age." On the changes that occurred in the social composition of historians and *naṣīḥatnāme* authors between the sixteenth and seventeenth centuries, see Hagen, "Afterword: Ottoman Understandings of the World in the Seventeenth Century," 252–55.

129. As a case in point, the reform treatise that Koçi Beg composed in 1631 for Murād IV (r. 1623–1640) includes a chapter addressing the "disturbances" (*iḫtilāl*) during the reign of Süleymān I. In this context, the sultan's decision not to attend the proceedings of the imperial council; his appointment of İbrāhīm Pasha (d. 1536) to the grand vizierate, contrary to established traditions; and the decision of his next grand vizier, Rüstem Pasha, to initiate tax-farming on royal domains are all mentioned as factors leading to the deterioration of the imperial order. See Koçi Beg, *Risāle*, 81–82/96–99.

5. Selīm, the Divinely Ordained Ruler

1. Ibn Iyās, *Badāʾiʿ al-zuhūr* (Salmon edition), 91. On the diplomatic correspondence between Selīm I and Mamluk rulers, see Yüksel Muslu, *The Ottomans and the Mamluks*, 176–80; and Kerslake, "The Correspondence between Selīm I and Ḳānṣūh al-Ġawrī."

2. See BOA, Maliyeden Müdevver 11 (*Sancaḳ-ı Nigbolu Mufaṣṣal Defteri*), 1b. On the late-sixteenth-century historian Muṣṭafā ʿAlī's discussion of this designation (in its more common rendering as *muʾayyad min ʿind Allāh*), see Fleischer, *Bureaucrat and Intellectual in the Ottoman Empire*, 279–81.

3. On the imperial ambitions and universalist claims of the Habsburg and Ottoman polities within the sixteenth-century Eurasian context, see Ágoston, "Information, Ideology, and Limits of Imperial Policy," especially 97–99.

4. I borrow this term from Sanjay Subrahmanyam. See Subrahmanyam, "Connected Histories." On the interconnectivity of cultural zones across Eurasia, see also Fletcher, "Integrative History."

5. Subrahmanyam, "Connected Histories," 748. See also Subrahmanyam, "Turning the Stones Over."

6. On the life and religious views of the popular puritanical preacher and prophet Girolamo Savonarola (d. 1498), see Weinstein, *Savonarola and Florence*.

On Yazıcıoğlu Aḥmed Bī-cān (d. after 1465) and his cosmographical work *Dürr-i meknūn* (The Hidden Pearl), see Kaptein, *Apocalypse and the Antichrist Dajjal in Islam*. On the intellectual cosmos of the uneducated but surprisingly well-read miller Domenico Scandella ("Mennochio," d. 1599), see Ginzburg, *The Cheese and the Worms*. On the personal and political ramifications of Lucrecia de León's (d. after 1595) prophetic visions and mystical predictions, see Kagan, *Lucrecia's Dreams*.

7. For a discussion of these themes, see Babayan, *Mystics, Monarchs, and Messiahs*; Babayan, "The Waning of the Qizilbash"; and Babayan, "The Cosmological Order of Things in Early Modern Safavid Iran."

8. See Babayan, "The Cosmological Order of Things in Early Modern Safavid Iran," 248; and Moin, *The Millennial Sovereign*, 1.

9. In particular, see Flemming, "Der *Ǧāmiʿ ül-Meknūnāt*"; Flemming, "Ṣāḥib-Ḳırān und Mahdī"; Yerasimos, *La fondation de Constantinople et de Sainte-Sophie dans les traditions turques*; Fleischer, "Ancient Wisdom and New Sciences"; Fleischer, "Mahdi and Millennium"; Fleischer, "Shadows of Shadows"; Fleischer, "Seer to the Sultan"; Fleischer, "The Lawgiver as Messiah"; Kaptein, *Apocalypse and the Antichrist Dajjal in Islam*; and Şahin, "Constantinople and the End Time." On the resurgence of these themes during the reign of Murād III (r. 1574–1595), see Felek, "(Re)creating Image and Identity"; and Fetvacı, *Picturing History at the Ottoman Court*, 245–49.

10. On the apocalyptic significance of Constantinople and its conquest by the Ottomans, see Yerasimos, *La fondation de Constantinople et de Sainte-Sophie dans les traditions turques*; and Şahin, "Constantinople and the End Time." See also the articles in Yerasimos and Lellouch, eds., *Les traditions apocalyptiques au tournant de la chute de Constantinople*.

11. Aḥmed Bī-cān, *Dürr-i meknūn*, 457–58. On the place of Constantinople and its conquest in Aḥmed Bī-cān's apocalypticism, see Şahin, "Constantinople and the End Time," 339–50; and Yerasimos, *La fondation de Constantinople et de Sainte-Sophie dans les traditions turques*, 69. On the prevalence of apocalyptic speculations among the Ottomans at the time of the conquest of Constantinople, see Emecen, *İstanbul'un Fethi Olayı ve Meseleleri*, Chapter 3, especially 62–65. For a discussion of Aḥmed Bī-cān's mental universe, see Kaptein, *Apocalypse and the Antichrist Dajjal in Islam*. On portrayals of the Istanbul earthquake of 1509 in Ottoman historiography, see Çıpa, "The Lesser Day of Resurrection."

12. Kaptein, *Apocalypse and the Antichrist Dajjal in Islam*, 138.

13. See Flemming, "Der *Ǧāmiʿ ül-Meknūnāt*"; Flemming, "Ṣāḥib-Ḳırān und Mahdī"; Fleischer, "Ancient Wisdom and New Sciences"; Fleischer, "Mahdi and Millennium"; Fleischer, "Shadows of Shadows"; Fleischer, "Seer to the Sultan"; and Fleischer, "The Lawgiver as Messiah."

14. Possibly to emphasize the sultan's humility, Saʿdeddīn reports that Selīm specifically denied such a claim. See Saʿdeddīn, *Selīmnāme*, 609: "Our forefathers and ancestors had a share in sainthood (*velāyet*). They had miracles (*kerāmet*). We alone did not take after them."

15. Based on a unique reference in Luṭfī Pasha's *Chronicle*, Cornell Fleischer argues that Selīm attempted to cultivate the image of a spiritual leader of a brotherhood of Ottoman statesmen. Luṭfī reports that when Selīm announced his decision to march against the Safavid ruler Shāh Ismāʿīl (r. 1501–1524), he addressed his viziers as his "devoted disciples" (*benim cān-ü-göñülden mürīdlerim*). That Selīm referred to his ministers and commanders as his spiritual followers (*mürīd*) is significant, especially because the same term was applied to Ḳızılbaş adherents of Ismāʿīl, who was both the political head of the Safavid state and the spiritual leader of the Safavid order. Contemporary narrative evidence suggests that Ḳızılbaş notables who participated in the Şāhḳulu rebellion of 1511 expressed respect for their spiritual leader by prostrating in front of him (*uluları ve reʾīsleri Şāh Ismāʿīle secde itdiler*) when they arrived in Tabriz. Considering that Luṭfī Pasha composed his chronicle more than three decades after Selīm's death, I am inclined to regard this reference as a reflection of the sentiments of the Süleymānic era rather than of the realities of Selīm's reign. See Luṭfī, *Tevārīḫ*, 198; Anonymous, *Tevārīḫ* (Azamat edition), 133; and Fleischer, "The Lawgiver as Messiah," 164.

16. For a discussion of Ottoman succession practices, see Chapter 1. See also İnalcık, "Osmanlılar'da Saltanat Verâseti Usûlü," 73–82; and Peirce, *The Imperial Harem*, 96.

17. Bloch, *Feudal Society*, vol. 1, 73.

18. For a detailed list of variants of this prophetic tradition, see Kister, "The Interpretation of Dreams," 71n20. On the acknowledgement of dreams as part of prophecy, see also Von Grunebaum, "The Cultural Function of the Dream as Illustrated by Classical Islam," 7n2. That this Islamic tradition is part of a larger cluster of Near Eastern religious/cultural traditions is suggested by a remarkably similar statement found in the Babylonian Talmud: "A dream is one sixtieth of prophecy" (*Berakhot* 57b).

19. Various aspects of dreams and their historical significance in Islamic societies are discussed in several of the articles in Von Grunebaum and Caillois, *The Dream and Human Societies*; see also Lory, *Le rêve et ses interprétations en Islam*. For a detailed list of studies on this subject, see Kinberg, "Interaction between This World and the Afterworld in Early Islamic Tradition," 295n50. For a general overview of the functions of dreams in the Islamic context, see Green, "The Religious and Cultural Roles of Dreams and Visions in Islam." For a medieval Muslim intellectual's outlook on the significance of dreams and their interpretation in Islamicate societies, see Ibn Khaldūn, *Muqaddimah*, vol. 3, 103–10.

20. Kinberg, "Interaction between This World and the Afterworld in Early Islamic Tradition." On the communicative, pragmatic, and evidentiary features of dreams in Islamic Sufi tradition and the Sufi claim of "having access to a persisting suprasensible and suprapersonal knowledge through the medium of dreams and dreaming," see Ohlander, "Behind the Veil of the Unseen."

21. Kinberg, "The Legitimization of the *Madhāhib* through Dreams."

22. Kinberg, "Literal Dreams and Prophetic *Ḥadīṯ*s in Classical Islam"; and Kinberg, "Dreams as a Means to Evaluate Ḥadith."

23. Mottahedeh, *Loyalty and Leadership in an Early Islamic Society*, 69–70.

24. ʿĀşıḳpaşazāde, *Menāḳıb* (Yavuz and Saraç edition), 325–27. For analyses of this particular dream, see Kafadar, *Between Two Worlds*, 29–30, 132–33; and Hagen, "Dreaming ʿOs̱māns." For the analysis of a similar dream narrative attributed to Muḥammad al-Qā'im, the founder of the Saʿdī dynasty of Morocco, and its impact on the consolidation of the dynasty's political power and legitimacy, see Yahya, *Morocco in the Sixteenth Century*, 5–6. For a historiographical case study of dreams presaging the future preeminence of the Safavid dynasty, see Quinn, "The Dreams of Shaykh Safi al-Din and Safavid Historical Writing."

25. Niyazioğlu, "The Very Special Dead and a Seventeenth-Century Ottoman Poet."

26. See Fleischer, "Secretaries' Dreams."

27. See Uruç, *Tevārīḫ* (Öztürk edition), 12; and Imber, "Ideals and Legitimation in Early Ottoman History," 142–43.

28. For the content of Murād III's (r. 1574–1595) "dream book" and the role of dreams in his royal self-fashioning, see Felek, *Kitābü'l-Menāmāt*; and Felek, "(Re) creating Image and Identity," respectively.

29. In classical oneirocriticism, the first type of dream is classified as theorematic (or literal) and the second as allegorical (or symbolic). On this distinction (as made in the pre-Byzantine *oneirocriticon* of Artemidorus), see Oberhelman, *Dreambooks in Byzantium*, 22.

30. TSMA E.9970: "I saw a dream concerning my sultan. Last year, on the fifteenth day of the month of Safer, before Friday prayer [I dreamt of a] white-bearded man of medium height, wearing a muslin and green-colored clothes. In front of my sultan, a silver candle on a tray. However, this tray and candle are made of silver and gold. Gathered around this tray were white roses made of a white substance, sprouting continuously. The big ruby of the candle is very high. The candle burns day and night and its flame touches every land. Now, in the current month of Safer on a Friday night I saw the exact same dream I saw previously and the situation is described and communicated to my sultan. The everlasting decree belongs to my sultan. İdrīs, the weakest of slaves." At the risk

of assuming the role of the oneirocritic, I would argue that the symbolism of the candle's flame that "touches every land" in this petition serves the same universalist purpose as ʿĀşıḳpaşazāde's reference to the tree that sprouts from ʿOs̱mān Beg's navel and whose shade encompasses the whole world.

31. TSMA E.10158-34.

32. For examples of petitions addressed to Selīm by his supporters, see TSMA E.6062; TSMA E.6081; TSMA E.6211; TSMA E.6619; TSMA E.6623; TSMA E.7054; TSMA E.7294; TSMA E.7634; TSMA E.8093; TSMA E.8150; TSMA E.9969; TSMA E.10013; and TSMA E.10030.

33. On the Ottomans' use of the Dhūlfiqār motif as a protective charm, military emblem, and symbol of justice and legitimate authority, see Yürekli, "*Dhu'l-faqār* and the Ottomans." On the Dhūlfiqār tradition within the context of Ottoman Egypt, see Hathaway, "The Iconography of the Sword Zülfikâr in the Ottoman World."

34. On Anatolian-Turkish religious-heroic narratives and the anonymous *Baṭṭālnāme*, which was "one of the earliest prose works of Islamic Turkish literature in Anatolia," see Anonymous, *Baṭṭālnāme*, 1–25. See also Anonymous, *Dānişmendnāme*. On medieval Anatolian frontier narratives, see Kafadar, *Between Two Worlds*, 62–90.

35. Legendary accounts of Seyyid Baṭṭāl Ġāzī and the architectural transformation of his shrine through the patronage of the families of frontier lords situated in the Balkan provinces of the Ottoman realm are expertly studied by Zeynep Yürekli. On the portrayal of Seyyid Ġāzī in popular hagiographies in late medieval Anatolia, see Yürekli, *Architecture and Hagiography in the Ottoman Empire*, especially 4–5 (for references to Seyyid Ġāzī in Meḥmed Çelebi b. Pīr Meḥmed Hoyī's *Ḫıżırnāme*, a versified work about the prophet-saint Khidr, written in 1475–1476) and 51–56 (for the legends of Seyyid Ġāzī and the "discovery" of his shrine).

36. According to a popular prophetic tradition, "He who lies about his dream will be ordered [at the Day of Judgement] to join two barley corns and will be put on burning coal." For references to this tradition, see Kister, "The Interpretation of Dreams," 74n28. For a "dream-warning pair," see Kinberg, "Literal Dreams and Prophetic *Ḥadīṯs* in Classical Islam," 286n19 ("He who lies about his dream will have to tie a knot in a small barley corn on the Day of Judgement"), and 287n20 ("He who lies about dreams deliberately will have to join a barley corn on the Day of Judgement").

37. In addition to the Prophet Muḥammad and the "Rightly Guided Caliphs," any of the Prophet's companions (*ṣaḥābah*) are also commonly used to exalt the figure discussed. See Kinberg, "The Legitimization of the *Madhāhib* through Dreams," 50.

38. TSMA E.10592.

39. Halil İnalcık argues that the imperial legal, institutional, and political structure perfected by Süleymān "the Magnificent" was established by Meḥmed II. See İnalcık, "Sultan Süleymân"; and İnalcık, "State, Sovereignty and Law." For a discussion of the ways in which Meḥmed II served as a point of reference for advice authors, see Chapter 4.

40. For references to this prophetic tradition as well as to the Shīʿī outlook on this subject, see Kister, "The Interpretation of Dreams," 73n27; and Kinberg, "Literal Dreams and Prophetic *Ḥadīṯ*s in Classical Islam," 285n16. On historical controversies surrounding this issue, see Goldziher, "The Appearance of the Prophet in Dreams."

41. TSMA E.6113.

42. In addition to the previously mentioned petitions, see, for example, TSMA E.10158-22: "The sultan ordered me, his slave: 'Invite His Excellency ʿAlī.' So, I invited him. A lion-faced person came. However, when he arrived, the sultan had [already] gone inside. I said [to ʿAlī]: 'Go ahead, go in.' [ʿAlī] said: 'May [Selīm] be at ease now.' We sat at a place, he uttered some words and said: 'This disagreement is not surprising, it happened in my time, as well, when I was caliph.' I told His Excellency every day that it is not strange, it is auspicious."

43. Altınkaynak, "Analysis of the Dragon Killing Scene in the Mythology of the Peoples of Eurasia."

44. In his official correspondence, Selīm likened himself to King Solomon in status, claimed to possess Alexander the Great's seal, and stated that he was "surrounded by an aura of victory like Ferīdūn," the Iranian mythic hero. See Ferīdūn Beg, ed., *Münşeʾātü's-selāṭīn*, vol. 1, 382–83. On Ferīdūn, see *Encyclopaedia Iranica*, s.v. "Ferēdūn" (A. Tafazzoli). On the seventh and last of the challenges that Rustam faced, see Clinton and Simpson, "How Rustam Killed White Div."

45. See, for example, Muḥammad b. Ḥusāmuddīn Ibn Ḥusām's (d. 1470) *Khāwarānnāma* (Book of Eastern Exploits).

46. It should be noted here that the figure of the seven-headed "Beast of the Apocalypse," a prominent symbol in Christian apocalyptic traditions, narratives, and illustrations, appears to have migrated into Islamic apocalyptical thought. In Islamic paintings, including those from the Ottoman tradition, it often represented the growling mouth of Hell. Thus, Selīm's victory over the seven-headed dragon in Seyyid Kemāl's dream can be interpreted alternatively as an apocalyptical portrayal of the Messiah, victorious over Hell. On the seven-headed dragon *figura* in famed Christian visionary Joachim of Fiore's (d. 1202) *Liber Figurarum* (Book of Figures), the earliest surviving version of which contains "the earliest

depiction of the Prophet of Islam created in a Christian context and intended for Christian consumption," see Coffey, "Unleashing the Dragon," especially 67–135. On representations of dragon figures within the context of medieval Islamicate societies, see Berlekamp, *Wonder, Image and Cosmos in Medieval Islam*, 77–85.

47. TSMA E.10158-10. The statement attributed to the renowned Muslim oneirocritic Ibn Sīrīn (d. 728) is rendered in Persian.

48. For an English translation of Ibn Sīrīn's magnum opus on the interpretation of dreams, titled *Tafsīr al-aḥlām al-kabīr* (Great Book of Dream Interpretation), see Sanioura, *Interpretation of Dreams*.

49. See Birnbaum, "Superstitious Tough Guy?" I would like to thank Professor Birnbaum for generously sharing his article prior to its publication.

50. The authoritative work on Islamic divination is Toufic Fahd's *La divination arabe*. On divinatory practices in Islamic cultures in general, see Francis, "Magic and Divination in the Medieval Islamic Middle East"; Savage-Smith, "Magic and Islam"; and Gruber, "Divination." On Qurʾānic prognostication in particular, see Gruber, "The 'Restored' Shīʿī *muṣḥaf* as Divine Guide?" On geomantic prognostication, see Savage-Smith and Smith, "Islamic Geomancy and a Thirteenth-Century Divinatory Device."

51. For examples, see Gruber, "Divination," 210.

52. ʿĀlī, *Künhü'l-aḥbār*, vol. 2, 1181–83. On Ottoman bibliomancy, see Schmidt, "Hāfız and Other Persian Authors in Ottoman Bibliomancy," especially 65–66 and 71–72.

53. I would like to thank Ahmet Tunç Şen for generously sharing his findings with me and for allowing me to cite his paper here. See Şen, "Astrology at the Early Modern Ottoman Court."

54. Whereas the palace payroll registers during the last years of Meḥmed II's reign include the name of only one astrologer, evidence from registers compiled during the reign of Bāyezīd II indicates that this number rose to five or six, depending on the year. These figures do not include astrologers who enjoyed royal patronage but were not identified in official salary registers. See Şen, "Astrology at the Early Modern Ottoman Court." For a self-identified astrologer's petition seeking employment at Selīm's court, see TSMA E.10158-38.

55. TSMA E.6673.

56. Saʿdeddīn, *Selīmnāme*, 608–9.

57. For a list of references to the Prophet Muḥammad inquiring of his companions about their dreams, see Kinberg, "Literal Dreams and Prophetic *Ḥadīṯs* in Classical Islam," 284n15; and Fahd, "The Dream in Medieval Islamic Society," 356n16.

58. Evliyā, *Seyāḥatnāme*, vol. 10, 69. Evliyā notes that Selīm died 1,463 days after he returned from Egypt to Istanbul, a fact he "confirms" by alphanumerically computing the value of the letters in the Prophet's reference to "Ġāzī Selīm."

59. For the tripartite narrative of this episode, see Evliyā, *Seyāḥatnāme*, vol. 10, 70–71.

60. According to Evliyā Çelebi, whereas Emīr Sulṭān (d. 1430) of Bursa had predicted Selīm's conquest of Egypt from beyond the grave, Nāṣır-ı Ṭarsūsī of Damascus communicated his prediction directly to the Ottoman sultan. See Evliyā, *Seyāḥatnāme*, vol. 10, 63 and vol. 10, 66, respectively.

61. Evliyā, *Seyāḥatnāme*, vol. 9, 181. On popular hagiographic traditions about Dülük Baba within the context of the "sacred geography" of ʿAyntāb, see Peirce, *Morality Tales*, 46–49. See also Güzelbey, *Gaziantep Evliyaları*, 22–26.

62. On the "Sheikh of Sam" and the miracles he performed with dry grapevine cuttings that he offered to Selīm and his soldiers, see Güzelbey, *Gaziantep Evliyaları*, 54–58; and Peirce, *Morality Tales*, 47–48.

63. Peirce, *Morality Tales*, 47.

64. See Peirce, *Morality Tales*, 48, 398n95, and 398n96.

65. On Selīm's architectural patronage, see Necipoğlu, *The Age of Sinan*, 60–63, 222–24.

66. See Necipoğlu, *The Age of Sinan*, 61, 523n87.

67. See Fleischer, "Shadows of Shadows," 56. Fleischer also highlights Selīm's "search for and restoration of the tomb of Ibn ʿArabī on his entrance into Damascus [as] a reference to the prophecy apparently drawn from [the probably pseudoepigraphic work attributed to Ibn ʿArabī titled *al-Shajarah al-nuʿmāniyya fī al-dawla al-ʿUthmāniyya* (The Crimson Tree on Ottoman Glory)] to the effect that 'when S(elīm) enters SH(ām), the tomb of Muḥyiddīn will appear.'" See Fleischer, "Seer to the Sultan," 295. On Ibn ʿArabī, see *EI²*, s.v. "Ibn al-ʿArabī" (A. Ateş). Selīm's subjugation of eastern Anatolia and Iran was most probably also regarded as confirmation of the prediction found in a work attributed to Ibn ʿArabī, titled *Djafr al-Imām ʿAlī b. Abī Ṭālib* (Divination of Imām ʿAlī b. Abī Ṭālib). See Schmidt, *Pure Water for Thirsty Muslims*, 126; and *EI²*, s.v. "Djafr" (T. Fahd).

68. See Necipoğlu, *The Age of Sinan*, 60–63.

69. The tombs of prophets David, Isaac, and Joseph, the birthplace of the prophet Abraham, and numerous sacred sites in the city of Jerusalem were among the places Selīm visited. See, for example, Celālzāde, *Meʾāṣir* (Uğur and Çuhadar edition), 187, 190, 194–95; and Ercan, *Kudüs Ermeni Patrikhanesi*, 9–14. Visual depictions of Selīm's visits to sacred sites and spiritual leaders are included in an illuminated copy of Saʿdeddīn Efendi's dynastic history. See Saʿdeddīn,

Tācü't-tevārīḫ (BNF Supplément turc 524), 173a (Selīm with Sheikh Muḥammad Badakhshī, d. 1517), and 183b (Selīm in Jerusalem).

70. See Güzelbey, *Gaziantep Evliyaları*, 57; see also Peirce, *Morality Tales*, 398n94. Although Güzelbey states that Selīm was cursed by Mevlānā Maḥmūd, Peirce notes that it was the "Sheikh of Sam" who caused Selīm's royal discomfort. For the narrative of a more damning premonitory curse, by which Sheikh Gümüşlüoğlu Meḥmed supposedly caused Selīm's death, see ʿĀlī, *Künhü'l-aḥbār*, vol. 2, 1194–98.

71. Peirce, *Morality Tales*, 47.

72. Çivizāde's legal opinions also targeted Mevlānā Celāleddīn-i Rūmī, the founder of the Mevlevī order. See Necipoğlu, *The Age of Sinan*, 63. Victor L. Ménage notes that the real reason for Çivizāde's dismissal was his hostility toward mysticism (*taṣavvuf*). See *EI²*, s.v. "Čiwi-Zāde" (V. L. Ménage).

73. See Fleischer, "Shadows of Shadows," 57.

74. See Necipoğlu, *The Age of Sinan*, 63. See also Repp, *The Müfti of Istanbul*, 250–52.

75. See Masters, *The Arabs of the Ottoman Empire*, 117.

76. I borrow this term from Yasser Tabbaa. See Tabbaa, *Constructions of Power and Piety in Medieval Aleppo*, 25.

77. One of these treatises was penned by the prominent chronicler and chief jurisconsult Kemālpaşazāde (d. 1534). See Fleischer, "Seer to the Sultan," 295.

78. Flemming, "Public Opinion under Sultan Süleymân," 49. On the use of caliphal titles by Ottoman monarchs, see Imber, "Süleymân as Caliph of the Muslims," 179.

79. On the history of the office of the caliphate, see *EI²*, s.v. "Khalīfā" (D. Sourdel). On Umayyad and Abbasid conceptions of the caliphate, see Crone and Hinds, *God's Caliph*.

80. Lambton, "Quis Custodiet Custodes," 127.

81. See Atsız, *Osmanlı Tarihine Ait Takvimler*, 9. D. Sourdel notes that Murād I (r. 1362–1389) called himself "chosen *khalīfa* of the Creator" and "shadow of God on the earth," whereas Bāyezīd I (r. 1389–1402) applied to himself the Qurʾānic verse "we have made of you a representative (*khalīfa*) on the earth." See *EI²*, s.v. "Khalīfā" (D. Sourdel). For several other early cases of the use of caliphal titles by Ottoman monarchs as "elements in literary panegyric," see Imber, "Süleymân as Caliph of the Muslims," 179.

82. In the *ḳānūnnāme*, Süleymān is hailed as *khalīfat rasūlu'l-rabbu'l-ʿālamīn . . . ḥāʾizu'l-imāmatu'l-ʿuẓmā . . . vārithu'l-khilāfatu'l-kubrā*. See Barkan, *XV ve XVIıncı Asırlarda Osmanlı İmparatorluğunda Ziraî Ekonominin Hukukî ve Malî Esasları*, vol. 1, 296. Ebū'ssuʿūd Efendi used the same description for Selīm II

(r. 1566–1574) in the law code of Skopje and Thessaloniki in 1574. For a discussion of Ebū'ssuʿūd's formulation of the Ottoman claim to the caliphate, see Imber, "Süleymân as Caliph of the Muslims." On Ottomans' claim to the caliphate, see also Karateke, "Legitimizing the Ottoman Sultanate," 25–31.

83. See Yılmaz, "The Sultan and the Sultanate," 176–91.

84. As Colin Imber accurately pointed out, Ebū'ssuʿūd Efendi never formulated a definitive theory of the Ottoman caliphate. Thus, "when Ebū'ssuʿūd died in 1574, the theory of the Ottoman caliphate died with him." See Imber, "Ideals and Legitimation in Early Ottoman History," 154.

85. According to an oft-quoted tradition (*ḥadīth*), the Prophet Muḥammad stated that "the imāms are of [the tribe of] Quraysh (*al-aʾimma min Quraysh*)," making descent from the prophetic line a precondition for the caliphate and thereby disqualifying the Ottomans due to their Turkic descent.

86. Luṭfī, as quoted in Gibb, "Luṭfī Paşa on the Ottoman Caliphate," 290.

87. Gibb, "Luṭfī Paşa on the Ottoman Caliphate," 295n1.

88. See Asrar, "The Myth about the Transfer of the Caliphate to the Ottomans."

89. Ferīdūn Beg, ed., *Münşeʾātü's-selāṭīn*, vol. 1, 427–30 (letter to Prince Süleymān), and 430 ff. On this point, see Karateke, "Legitimizing the Ottoman Sultanate," 26.

90. Luṭfī, *Tevārīḫ*, 149–53. These letters, one in Chagatay Turkish, the other in Persian, are also included in the prominent chief clerk (*münşī*) and chief chancellor (*nişāncı*) Ferīdūn Aḥmed Beg's (d. 1583) *Münşeʾātü's-selāṭīn* (Correspondence of Sultans, 1575), vol. 1, 416–18. There are, however, variances between Luṭfī Pasha's and Ferīdūn Beg's versions.

91. For an interpretation of these references as suggestive of an "apocalyptic interpretive mode" and a messianic model of sovereignty with respect to Selīm's military accomplishments, see Fleischer, "The Lawgiver as Messiah," especially 163–64. Whereas Fleischer acknowledges that the Transoxianian letters "may of course be Luṭfī's own creation," Imber considers them "spurious." See Fleischer, "The Lawgiver as Messiah," 176n23; and Imber, "Ideals and Legitimation in Early Ottoman History," 149, 150. If authentic, these letters also substantiate Sanjay Subrahmanyam's arguments regarding the early modern processes of elite circulation and flow of millenarian, messianic, and apocalyptic ideas and concepts across political boundaries. See Subrahmanyam, "Connected Histories," especially 745–59.

92. For this reference in the letter composed in Chagatay Turkish, see Luṭfī, *Tevārīḫ*, 149.

93. For this reference in the letter composed in Persian, see Luṭfī, *Tevārīḫ*, 152.

94. See, for example, Şükrī, *Selīmnāme*, 64b: "Since they recite my name as Shadow of God (*çün ki ẓıll-Allāh oḳurlar adumı*)"; and Luṭfī, *Tevārīḫ*, 199: "Since

they gave us the honorific titles Shadow of God and Sultan of the Muslim community" (*çün ki bize ẓıll-Allāh ve Sulṭān-ı ehl-i İslām deyü laḳab ḳomuşlardır*)." See also Şīrī, *Tārīḫ-i fetḥ-i Mıṣr*, 247b.

95. See Evliyā, *Seyāḥatnāme*, vol. 10, 69. According to other chroniclers, this event took place in Aleppo. For alternative renderings of this anecdote, see Tansel, *Yavuz Sultan Selim*, 216.

96. Luṭfī, *Āṣafnāme*, 249.

97. ʿĀlī, *Nuṣḥatü's-selāṭīn*, vol. 1, 51/142.

98. Cerrāḥzāde Mevlānā Muḥammed was captured in Nakhchivan by Safavid forces and lived briefly in captivity at the court of Shāh ʿAbbās. See Meḥmed Süreyyā, *Sicill*, vol. 4, 125.

99. Muṣṭafā Ṣāfī, *Zübdetü't-tevārīḫ*, vol. 1, 171.

100. On this prophetic tradition as transmitted by prominent *ḥadīth* collector Abū Dāwūd (d. 889), see Landau-Tasseron, "The 'Cyclical Reform.'"

101. For examples, see *EI*², s.v. "Mudjaddid" (E. van Donzel); and Landau-Tasseron, "The 'Cyclical Reform.'"

102. A case in point was Tīmūr's (r. 1370–1405) son and eventual successor Shāhrukh (r. 1409–1447). See Subtelny, "The Sunni Revival under Shāh-Rukh and Its Promoters"; and Subtelny and Khalidov, "The Curriculum of Islamic Higher Learning in Timurid Iran in the Light of the Sunni Revival under Shah-Rukh."

103. The other being the Seljukids, whom the author considers the Ottomans' "spiritual guides and exemplars (*mürşid ve pīşvā*)." See Luṭfī, *Tevārīḫ*, 144.

104. Qurʾān 5:54. See Saʿdeddīn, *Tācü't-tevārīḫ*, vol. 1, 13.

105. On the use of the canonical texts of Islam (i.e., the Qurʾān and the six principal collections of prophetic tradition) to legitimize Ottoman rule, see Imber, "Ideals and Legitimation in Early Ottoman History," 150–51.

106. For Luṭfī Pasha's discussion of the length of a *ḳarn*, see Luṭfī, *Tevārīḫ*, 145.

107. Luṭfī, *Tevārīḫ*, 147. The reunification of the Ottoman realm was such a significant achievement that some of Meḥmed I's contemporaries praised him as Messiah (*mehdī*). See ʿAbdü'lvāsiʿ Çelebi, *Ḫalīlnāme*, 255–56. For an analysis and translation of the relevant sections of ʿAbdü'lvāsiʿ Çelebi's (fl. ca. 1414) versified work, see Kastritsis, *The Sons of Bayezid*, 217–20, 221–22, 229; and Kastritsis, "The Historical Epic *Aḥvāl-i Sulṭān Meḥemmed*," 8.

108. Luṭfī, *Tevārīḫ*, 153.

109. As Jane Hathaway has pointed out, the only reference that comes close—but not close enough—is in Celālzāde Ṣāliḥ Çelebi's (d. 1565) *Tārīḫ-i Mıṣr-ı cedīd* (New History of Egypt). Here, Selīm is praised as "renewer of the laws" (*müceddid-i ḳānūnlar*) after defeating the Mamluks, "presumably referring to the imposition of sultanic law in Egypt." See Hathaway, *A Tale of Two Factions*, 126–27.

110. For a comparative analysis of Ottoman works of advice (*naṣīḥatnāme*) in which Selīm is portrayed as a monarch superior to other sultans of the House of ʿOs̱mān, see the section titled "Selīm as Yardstick" in Chapter 4. Süleymān is hailed as a *müceddid* in numerous other Ottoman sources. See, for example, Mevlānā ʿĪsā, *Cāmiʿü'l-meknūnāt*, as referenced in Fleischer, "The Lawgiver as Messiah," 165; and Evliyā, *Seyāḥatnāme*, vol. 10, 62.

111. Luṭfī, *Tevārīḫ*, 148.

112. Selīm expressed this view in a letter addressed to his father, Bāyezīd II, during his princely governorship in Trabzon. See TSMA E.5970. For a facsimile of this document, see Tansel, *Sultan II. Bâyezit'in Siyasî Hayatı*, 260–61.

113. Luṭfī, *Tevārīḫ*, 211.

114. Luṭfī, *Tevārīḫ*, 149.

115. Luṭfī, *Āṣafnāme*, 249.

116. The other swords mentioned in Ottoman sources include those belonging to the Prophet Muḥammad, the "rightly guided" caliphs ʿUmar (r. 634–644) and ʿUthmān (r. 644–656), Khālid b. al-Walīd (a prominent Arab commander of the early Islamic era dubbed *Sayf Allāh*, or "Sword of God," d. 642), and ʿOs̱mān Beg. On Ottoman ceremonies of the "Girding of the Sword" (*taḳlīd-i seyf* or *ḳılıç kuşanma*), see Alderson, *The Structure of the Ottoman Dynasty*, 41–42; Uzunçarşılı, *Osmanlı Devletinin Saray Teşkilâtı*, 189–200; and Kafadar, "Eyüp'te Kılıç Kuşanma Törenleri."

117. Selānikī, *Tārīḫ*, vol. 2, 647.

118. Nefʿī, as quoted in Cunbur, "Anadolu Gazileri ve Edebiyatımız," 796: "Bir ġazā itdün ki hiç itmiş degül bir pādişāh / İşidüb olsa nola Sulṭān Selīmüñ rūḥı şād."

119. See Kemālpaşazāde, *Tevārīḫ*, vol. 8 (1985), 28–29.

120. See Sāʾī Muṣṭafā, *Tez̲kiretü'l-bünyān*, 121; and Sāʾī Muṣṭafā, *Tez̲kiretü'l-ebniye*, 173, 179.

121. See, for example, Anonymous, *Tevārīḫ* (Azamat edition), 137; Kemālpaşazāde, *Tevārīḫ*, vol. 8 (1985), 28; Sāʾī Muṣṭafā, *Tez̲kiretü'l-bünyān*, 121; and Sucūdī, *Selīmnāme*, 2a.

122. ʿĀlī, *Künhü'l-aḫbār*, vol. 1, 27–29. For an analysis of Muṣṭafā ʿĀlī's classification, see Fleischer, *Bureaucrat and Intellectual in the Ottoman Empire*, 279–80. See also Fleischer, "The Lawgiver as Messiah," 162–63.

123. Selīm, of course, was defeated at least once by his father, Bāyezīd II, at Çorlu. For Muṣṭafā ʿĀlī's defensive account as to why that setback should not be regarded as a defeat, see ʿĀlī, *Künhü'l-aḫbār*, vol. 1, 28.

124. Allusions to Tīmūr as *ṣāḥib-ḳırān* are included in earlier Ottoman chronicles as well. See, for example, ʿĀşıḳpaşazāde, *Menāḳıb* (Yavuz and Saraç edition),

407. For Germiyānoğlu's reference to Tīmūr as *ṣāḥib-ḳırān*, see Neşrī, *Kitāb-ı cihānnümā*, vol. 1, 343. In the same textual context, Ottoman ruler Bāyezīd I (r. 1389–1402) was called a "tyrant" (*ʿOs̱mānoğlu bir ẓālim kişidür*).

125. ʿĀlī, *Künhü'l-aḫbār*, vol. 1, 27–28.

126. Fleischer, "The Lawgiver as Messiah," 163.

127. On this point, see Schmidt, *Pure Water for Thirsty Muslims*, 179.

128. Aḥmed Pasha, as quoted in Cunbur, "Anadolu Gazileri ve Edebiyatımız," 792: "Ġāzī-i ṣāḥib-ḳırān oldur ki devrinde ānuñ / Küfr dārü'l-cehli şimdi ʿilm şehristānıdur."

129. For poems composed by master of the horse (*mīrāḫūr*), Dervīş Agha, and a member of the cavalry corps (*sipāhī*), Emīnī Çelebi, see Selānikī, *Tārīḫ*, vol. 2, 642–43.

130. For the reference to Aḥmed as "the justest and most illustrious sultan and the greatest *ṣāḥib-ḳırān*, sultan, son of sultan" in an Arabic-language medical treatise dated 1501, see ʿAbdurraḥmān b. Abī Yūsuf el-Ḥāfıẓ el-Müneccim, *Jawharu'l-ḥıfẓı'ṣ-ṣıḥḥa wa ʿilācu'l-marżā* (The Jewel for Preserving Health and the Medicine for the Diseased Ones), SK Ayasofya 3635, 4a. I would like to thank Walter Lorenz for bringing this treatise to my attention.

131. Cornell Fleischer seems to suggest otherwise. For his discussion of an "evocative form of testimony to Selīm's apocalyptic pretensions," found in Luṭfī Pasha's chronicle, see Fleischer, "The Lawgiver as Messiah," 163.

132. Luṭfī, *Tevārīḫ*, 241. For references in Muṣṭafā ʿĀlī's *Künhü'l-aḫbār* to the popular "science" of physiognomy and Selīm's application of physiognomic principles to the selection of state officials, see Schmidt, *Pure Water for Thirsty Muslims*, 116–17, 302.

133. Evliyā, *Seyāḥatnāme*, vol. 10, 284.

134. On the *Ḳızıl Elma* motif and the identification of Constantinople, Budapest, Vienna, and Rome as the ultimate goals of Ottoman conquest, see *EI²*, s.v. "Ḳızıl Elma" (P. N. Boratav); Fodor, "Ungarn und Wien in der Osmanischen Eroberungsideologie," 67–69; and Fodor, "The View of the Turk in Hungary," 92–103. On Evliyā Çelebi's references to a total of six cities as *Ḳızıl Elma*, see Dankoff, *An Ottoman Mentality*, 105n63.

135. See Elliott, "Ottoman-Habsburg Rivalry." On Mevlānā ʿĪsā's representation of the rivalry between the Ottoman sultan and the Habsburg emperor, see Flemming, "Public Opinion under Sultan Süleymân," 52–53. On the contemporary portrayal of Charles V as the universal ruler of an impending "golden age," see Burke, "Concepts of the 'Golden Age' in the Renaissance," 160–61. On the Ottoman-Safavid competition over legitimacy in Islamdom, see Dressler, "Inventing Orthodoxy."

136. Several Ottoman authors noted Shāh Ismāʿīl's claim to universal spiritual sovereignty as the Messiah. See, for example, Luṭfī, *Tevārīḫ*, 148: "mehdī-yi ṣāḥib-zamānem dir idi." On Safavid propaganda (*daʿwa*) and its dissemination among the Turcoman tribes of Anatolia, southern Caucasus, and Azerbaijan, see *Encyclopaedia Iranica*, s.v. "Esmāʿīl I Ṣafawī" (R. M. Savory). On Shāh Ismāʿīl's claims to divine kingship and its reception in European sources, see Brummett, "The Myth of Shah Ismail Safavi." On the ideological and sociopolitical background of "revolutionary" and "mystical" messianic movements in sixteenth-century Anatolia, see Ocak, "XVI. Yüzyıl Osmanlı Anadolu'sunda Mesiyanik Hareketlerinin Bir Tahlil Denemesi." On Ismāʿīl's "mahdist claim" and its consequences in the Safavid realm and beyond, see Arjomand, "The Rise of Shah Esmāʿil as a Mahdist Revolution," 45–57.

137. See Glassen, "Schah Ismāʿīl, ein Mahdī der anatolischen Turkmenen?"

138. On Şāhḳulu's claim, see Prince ʿOs̱mān's report (dated 16 April 1511), TSMA E.2829: "mehdīlik daʿvāsın ider"; and TSMA E.6187. On Celāl's claim, see Şükrī, *Selīmnāme*, 184a, 185a. Similar claims appear to have been made by leaders of earlier popular revolts. According to an anonymous chronicler, Sheikh Bedreddīn of Simavna (or his agent, Börklüce Muṣṭafā) noted, "They call me Mahdi King" (*baña melik mehdī dirler*). See Anonymous, *Tevārīḫ* (Azamat edition), 58.

139. Şükrī, *Selīmnāme*, 184b: "dediler bu fitne-i āḫir-zamān / bir ʿalāmetdür ḳıyāmetden hemān."

140. Flemming uses the term "public opinion" in the sense of "opinion publicly held and expressed." See Flemming, "Public Opinion under Sultan Süleymân," 49.

141. See Flemming, "Public Opinion under Sultan Süleymân," 57. Flemming refers to an anecdote mentioned in Gölpınarlı, *Melâmîlik ve Melâmîler*, 43–44. According to Gölpınarlı's rendering of a conversation between the sultan and the sheikh, Pīr ʿAlī reportedly addressed Süleymān, stating, "my Pādişāh, now to outward appearance you are the Mehdī."

142. For Yaḥyā Beg's references to the sultan as "Messiah [and] the Master of the Auspicious Conjunction" (*mehdī-i ṣāḥib-ḳırān*), "Messiah of the Age and the Solomon of the Time" (*mehdī-i devrān Süleymān-ı zamān*), "Messiah of the Distinguished Religion [i.e., Islam]" (*mehdī-i dīn-i güzīn*), and "Messiah of the Age" (*mehdī-i devr*), see Yaḥyā Beg, *Dīvān*, 28, 29, 41, 181. For the poet's reference to Süleymān as universal *ṣāḥib-ḳırān* (*ʿālemüñ ṣāḥib-ḳırānı*), see Yaḥyā Beg, *Dīvān*, 188–89.

143. See Fleischer, "The Lawgiver as Messiah," especially 164–67; and Flemming, "Ṣāḥib-Ḳırān und Mahdī," especially 52–53. Mevlānā ʿĪsā's *Cāmiʿü'l-meknūnāt* survived in three recensions dated 1529, 1533, and 1543. See Flemming, "Public Opinion under Sultan Süleymân," 51.

144. Fleischer, "The Lawgiver as Messiah," 165. Barbara Flemming mentions chief paladin (*server*). See Flemming, "Public Opinion under Sultan Süleymân," 53.

145. Fleischer, "Seer to the Sultan," 296.

146. The contribution of Ḥaydar-ı Remmāl to the articulation of "a new ideology that presented the sultan as the Last World Emperor, Saint of Saints, and Messiah" during the reign of Süleymān I has been masterfully studied by Cornell Fleischer. See Fleischer, "Seer to the Sultan," especially 295–99; Fleischer, "The Lawgiver as Messiah," 169–71; Fleischer, "Shadows of Shadows," 58–62; and Fleischer, "Ancient Wisdom and New Sciences," 240–42. The intimate involvement of Ḥaydar in palace politics is indicated by a geomantic reading (*reml*) included in a denunciative letter about Süleymān's grand vizier Rüstem Pasha (d. 1561) that was presented to the sultan after the controversial execution of Prince Muṣṭafā (d. 1553). This letter, which Fleischer considers "very likely" the work of Ḥaydar, is published in Gökbilgin, "Rüstem Paşa ve Hakkındaki İthamlar," 38–43.

147. For a discussion of the contents and politico-ideological agendas of Levhī's *Cihādnāme-i Sulṭān Süleymān* (*Book of Holy War of Sulṭān Süleymān*) as well as of H̱ākī's and Senāʾī's works titled *Süleymānnāme* (*Book of Süleymān*), see Fleischer, "The Lawgiver as Messiah," 168–69.

148. Levhī penned his work immediately after the first siege of Vienna, whereas H̱ākī was a participant in Süleymān's final campaign against the Safavids, which culminated with the 1555 Treaty of Amasya. Considering that the siege of Vienna failed and the eastern campaign of 1553–1555 led to the acknowledgment of the stalemate between the Ottomans and their eastern neighbors, these texts can be evaluated as literary-historical works aimed at the creation of a favorable image for Süleymān—as a world conqueror successful against both of his principal rivals—at the imperial court. On the development during the later part of Süleymān's reign of a "more sober view" of the sultan as the protector of Sunnī beliefs against the Safavid "heretics" rather than as Messiah, see Faroqhi, "Presenting the Sultan's Power, Glory and Piety," 59; and Necipoğlu, "The Süleymaniye Complex in Istanbul," especially the section on inscriptions.

149. The fact that several Ottoman authors either began writing their historical works in the Hijri year 1000 or narrated the events beginning with that date has been interpreted as signifying "a new beginning worthy of celebrating" for Ottoman intellectuals who may have anticipated the End of Time. For a critical discussion of this argument as well as of the emergence of a new perspective on history around the turn of the seventeenth century, see Tezcan, "The Politics of Early Modern Ottoman Historiography," 188–90. For a superb discussion of the impact of the approach of the millennium on the historical consciousness of

a late-sixteenth-century statesman and historian, see Fleischer, *Bureaucrat and Intellectual in the Ottoman Empire*, 109–42. On the interrelation between millenarian thought and millenarian expectations in Islamicate societies, see Hodgson, "A Note on the Millennium in Islam."

150. Fetvacı, *Picturing History at the Ottoman Court*, 43.

151. Murād's dream accounts are included in letters addressed to his sheikh. These letters were compiled under the title *Kitābü'l-menāmāt* (Book of Dreams) by the imperial master of the horse (*mīrāḫūr*) Nūḥ Agha, possibly on the orders of the sultan. They were published in Felek, *Kitābü'l-Menāmāt*. Correspondence between disciples and sheikhs, including dream accounts, appears to have been common practice. For the dream register of a certain Asiye Ḫātūn, a female follower of a Sufi sheikh, recorded in the seventeenth-century, see Kafadar, *Rüya Mektupları*.

152. See Felek, "(Re)creating Image and Identity," especially 256–62. On the interrelated concepts *ḳuṭb* and *ḳuṭb al-aḳṭāb*, see *EI*[2], s.v. "al-Ḳuṭb" (F. de Jong).

153. Felek notes that "although Murād is never named as the awaited Mehdī, he is implicitly portrayed as a messianic figure" in his *Kitābü'l-menāmāt*. See Felek, "(Re)creating Image and Identity," especially 263.

154. On the prevalence of this millenarian conjuncture in early modern Eurasia, see Subrahmanyam, "Turning the Stones Over"; and Subrahmanyam, "Connected Histories," especially 745–59.

155. Pointing out the popularity of *Miftāḥ*, Cornell Fleischer states that copies of the work "seem to have circulated freely throughout the sixteenth century" at the Ottoman court. See Fleischer, "The Lawgiver as Messiah," 170, 177n47.

156. On the significance of al-Bisṭāmī and his works within the context of the development of Ottoman historical consciousness, see Fleischer, "Seer to the Sultan," especially 292–95; Fleischer, "Shadows of Shadows," 55–56; and Fleischer, "Ancient Wisdom and New Sciences," especially 232–36. On the "science of letters," see *EI*[2], s.v. "Ḥurūf" (T. Fahd).

157. On the prominent role of Ġażanfer Agha in the commissioning of this work and the creation of a new royal image for his master, see Fetvacı, *Picturing History at the Ottoman Court*, Chapter 6, especially 243–49.

158. See Fetvacı, *Picturing History at the Ottoman Court*, 246. I would like to thank Emine Fetvacı for her invaluable guidance in evaluating this visual evidence. On the apocalyptic visual iconography deployed in *Tercüme-i miftāḥ-ı cifrü'l-cāmiᶜ*, see Yaman, "Osmanlı Resim Sanatında Kıyamet Alametleri."

159. See Artan, "Arts and Architecture," 413–15.

160. See Necipoğlu, *The Age of Sinan*, 508–9.

161. The list of poets and scholars who were Saᶜdeddīn's students before becoming Ġażanfer Agha's employees includes, most notably, Şerīfī, the translator

of *Miftāḥ al-jafr al-jāmiʿ*. On the relationship between Saʿdeddīn and Ġażanfer and its ramifications in the cultural, intellectual, and political sphere, see Fetvacı, *Picturing History at the Ottoman Court*, 253–58.

162. The other pillars were the chief white eunuch Ġażanfer Agha and two royal companions (*muṣāḥib*), Şemsī Aḥmed Pasha (d. 1580) and Meḥmed Pasha ("Doġancı," d. 1589). See Schmidt, *Pure Water for Thirsty Muslims*, 123.

163. Saʿdeddīn, *Selīmnāme*, 619.

164. Saʿdeddīn, *Selīmnāme*, 613.

165. Saʿdeddīn, *Selīmnāme*, 613 and 610, respectively.

166. Saʿdeddīn, *Selīmnāme*, 603 and 618, respectively.

167. Saʿdeddīn, *Selīmnāme*, 614.

168. Saʿdeddīn, *Selīmnāme*, 608–9. On the objective evidentiary significance of the "realm of images" in medieval Islamic mysticism and history, see Rahman, "Dream, Imagination, and *ʿĀlam al-mithāl*."

169. Saʿdeddīn, *Selīmnāme*, 602.

Conclusion

1. Faulkner, *Requiem for a Nun*, 92.

2. For the definition of memory as "a perpetually actual phenomenon, a bond tying us to the eternal present," see Nora, "Between Memory and History," 8.

3. Mevlānā ʿĪsā, as quoted in Flemming, "Der *Ǧāmiʿ ül-Meknūnāt*," 87: "ḳoyun ḳurd ile yürür yoḳ savaşı / kedi pāyına mūşek ḳodı başı."

4. The texts and translations of both petitions (TSMA E. 8542/1 and TSMA E. 8542/2) were published with a commentary in Fleischer, "Of Gender and Servitude." The Ottoman-Turkish texts, however, were published with errors by the editors. I would like to express my sincere gratitude to Cornell Fleischer for allowing me to consult the correct rendering of these petitions, which he presented at the faculty seminar on Texts and Manuscripts of the Islamic World at Indiana University, Bloomington, on April 5, 2006.

5. Whereas Mevlānā ʿĪsā penned the earliest version of his treatise *Cāmiʿü'l-meknūnāt* (The Compendium of Hidden Things) in 1529, the *ḳul ḳızı* composed her petitions in 1520–1521. On the dates of the three recensions of this work, see Flemming, "Public Opinion under Sultan Süleymân," 51. On the dates of the petitions by the "servant girl," see Fleischer, "Of Gender and Servitude," 143.

6. Partner, "Making Up Lost Time," 95.

7. Nora, "Between Memory and History," 8.

8. Assmann, *Moses the Egyptian*, 2.

9. Susan E. Alcock, as quoted in Van Dam, *Remembering Constantine at the Milvian Bridge*, 9.

Bibliography

Institutional Abbreviations

BDK	Beyazıt Devlet Kütüphanesi
BM	The British Museum
BNF	Bibliothèque Nationale de France
BOA	Başbakanlık Osmanlı Arşivi (Prime Ministry Ottoman Archives)
İAK	İstanbul Atatürk Kütüphanesi (Istanbul Atatürk Library)
İÜK	İstanbul Üniversitesi Kütüphanesi (Istanbul University Library)
NK	Nuruosmaniye Kütüphanesi (Nuruosmaniye Library)
SK	Süleymaniye Kütüphanesi (Süleymaniye Library)
TSMA	Topkapı Sarayı Müzesi Arşivi (Topkapı Palace Museum Archives)
TSMK	Topkapı Sarayı Müzesi Kütüphanesi (Topkapı Palace Museum Library)

Abbreviations of Journals and Encyclopaedias

AÜİFD	*Ankara Üniversitesi İlâhiyat Fakültesi Dergisi*
AÜSBFD	*Ankara Üniversitesi Siyasal Bilgiler Fakültesi Dergisi*
BSOAS	*Bulletin of the School of Oriental and African Studies*
BTTD	*Belgelerle Türk Tarihi Dergisi*
DİA	*Türkiye Diyanet Vakfı İslâm Ansiklopedisi*
EI[2]	*The Encyclopaedia of Islam*, 2nd ed.
EÜİFD	*Erciyes Üniversitesi İlâhiyat Fakültesi Dergisi*
İA	*İslâm Ansiklopedisi*
JESHO	*Journal of the Economic and Social History of the Orient*
JNES	*Journal of Near Eastern Studies*
JOS	*Journal of Ottoman Studies*
TD	*İstanbul Üniversitesi Edebiyat Fakültesi Tarih Dergisi*
TED	*İstanbul Üniversitesi Edebiyat Fakültesi Tarih Enstitüsü Dergisi*

TSAB	*Turkish Studies Association Bulletin*
ZDMG	*Zeitschrift der Deutschen Morgenländischen Gesellschaft*

Archival Documents

Ottoman Documents: Topkapı Palace Museum Archives

Ottoman documents from the Topkapı Palace Museum Archives (Topkapı Sarayı Müzesi Arşivi, TSMA) are listed according to their catalogue numbers; "D" denotes a register (*defter*) and "E" stands for a single document (*evrak*).

D. 2921-1	Salary register (*mevācib defteri*) of members of the royal retinue at the imperial palace
D.5374	List of commanders who accompanied Selīm from Kefe and Akkirman onward
D.7603	Draft of D.5374
E.77	Ḳaragöz Pasha's letter to the imperial court
E.129	Şeyḫoğlu ʿAlī's letter to Selīm
E.543	Selīm's petition to Bāyezīd II
E.632	Letter by the kadi of Antalya to Ḳorḳud
E.2597	Ḳorḳud's letter to Bāyezīd II
E.2667	Aḥmed's letters to commanders; petition of Mūsā, the governor of Kastamonu; Aḥmed's letter to defterdār Muṣliḥeddīn
E.2829	Prince ʿOs̱mān's report to the imperial court
E.3057	Aḥmed's letter to Mūsā Beg
E.3062	Aḥmed's letter to commanders
E.3192	ʿAlī b. ʿAbdülkerīm Ḫalīfe's petition to Selīm I
E.3197	Nihālī Çelebi's letter to Ḥalīmī Çelebi
E.3703	Bālī Beg's report to Bāyezīd II
E.4744	Anonymous letter addressed to Mevlānā Efendi
E.5035	Spy report to the imperial court
E.5443	Selīm's letter to the imperial court
E.5447	Ḳāsım Pasha's letter to Bāyezīd II
E.5451	Letter sent by Aḥmed, the kadi of Bursa, to the janissary commander
E.5452	Petition of Eflāṭūnzāde, the kadi of Bursa, to the imperial court
E.5490	Nūreddīn Ṣarugürz's letter to Bāyezīd II
E.5587	Ḳorḳud's letter to his sister

E.5590 Ḥaydar Pasha's letter to Bāyezīd II
E.5679 Ḳorḳud's petition to Bāyezīd II
E.5876 Aḥmed's letter to the commander of Biga
E.5877 A certain Yūsuf's report to the imperial court
E.5882 Ḳorḳud's letter to Selīm
E.5898 Bāyezīd II's letter to Rumelian commanders
E.5970 Selīm's petition to Bāyezīd II
E.6043 Aḥmed's letter to Bāyezīd II
E.6062 Petition to Selīm by a supporter
E.6081 Petition to Selīm by a supporter
E.6113 Petition to Selīm by Seyyid Kemāl
E.6118 Petition by ʿAlī and Şāh Velī to Selīm
E.6185 Selīm's letter to Bāyezīd II and the latter's response
E.6186 A certain Ḥācī's letter to Selīm
E.6187 Spy report to the imperial court
E.6193 Letter by Aḥmed Beg, the governor of Sinop, to the imperial court
E.6205 Report by a certain İlyās to Selīm
E.6211 Petition to Selīm by a supporter
E.6321 Letter sent to Ḳorḳud by his *defterdār*
E.6322 Nūreddīn Ṣarugürz's letter to Bāyezīd II
E.6329 Report by a certain Bālī to the imperial court
E.6333 Report by court-taster Sinān to Selīm
E.6352 An agent's report to the imperial court
E.6376 Report by a certain Mīrʿalem Muṣṭafā to Selīm; report sent by a certain Ḥācī Meḥmed to Selīm
E.6382 Report of correspondence between Bāyezīd II and Mengli Girāy
E.6420 Letter by Ḥasan Pasha to Selīm
E.6536 Bāyezīd II's decree
E.6577 Selīm I's decree
E.6619 Petition to Selīm by a supporter
E.6623 Petition to Selīm by a supporter
E.6631 Report by Ṭūr ʿAlī Beg to Selīm
E.6636 Pīr Aḥmed's report to Bāyezīd II
E.6664 Ḥācī Muṣṭafā's letter to the imperial court
E.6673 Geomantic reading (*reml*) prepared for Selīm
E.6815 Selīm's letter to the imperial court
E.7052 Report by Şükrī-i Bidlīsī to Selīm
E.7054 Petition to Selīm by a supporter

E.7072	A certain Yūsuf's letter to Selīm
E.7294	Petition to Selīm by a supporter
E.7634	Petition to Selīm by a supporter
E.7967	Letter by a certain Ḥācī to Selīm
E.8001	Letter by janissaries supporting Selīm
E.8093	Petition to Selīm by a supporter
E.8150	Petition to Selīm by a supporter
E.8312	Ferhād Agha's letter to Selīm
E.8327	Ḥācī Meḥmed's letter to İskender Agha
E.8917	Report by a certain Meḥmed to the imperial court
E.9659	Ḳorḳud's letter to Selīm
E.9969	Petition to Selīm by a supporter
E.9970	Petition to Selīm by İdrīs
E.10013	Petition to Selīm by a supporter
E.10030	Petition to Selīm by a supporter
E.10158-10	Petition to Selīm by a supporter
E.10158-19	Petition to Selīm by a supporter
E.10158-22	Petition to Selīm by a supporter
E.10158-34	Petition to Selīm by ʿAlī of Köstendil
E.10158-36	Petition to Selīm by a supporter
E.10158-38	Petition to Selīm by an anonymous astrologer
E.10161	Ḳara Ḥüseyin Agha's letter to Selīm
E.10592	Petition to Selīm by Mūsā Ḳalfa
E.12276	Selīm's letter to Bāyezīd II
E.12277	Selīm's letter to Aḥmed

Ottoman Documents: Prime Ministry Ottoman Archives

BOA, Maliyeden Müdevver 7

BOA, Maliyeden Müdevver 11

BOA, Tahrir Defteri 7

BOA, Tahrir Defteri 26

BOA, Tahrir Defteri 73

BOA, Tahrir Defteri 77

BOA, Tahrir Defteri 370

Venetian Documents

Venetian documents are listed chronologically and consist of *relazioni*, ambassadorial reports delivered to the Senate. They were collected in summary fashion by Marino Sanuto (d. 1536) and published under the title *I Diarii di Marino Sanuto* (58 vols.) between 1879 and 1903. References to *relazioni* include the name of the author of each report and the date of the report followed by the volume and page numbers in *I Diarii*.

Leonardo Bembo (25 June 1505), 6, 212
Antonio Marzello (25 September 1505), 6, 240
Andrea Foscolo (1 August 1508), 7, 636
Andrea Foscolo (6, 13 August 1508), 7, 631
Andrea Foscolo (18 June 1509), 9, 12
Marin de Molin (5 January 1510), 9, 27
Andrea Foscolo (21 May 1510), 10, 667
Lodovico Valdrim (31 May 1510), 10, 668–69
Andrea de Cividal's letter to Nicolò Venier (15 July 1510), 11, 477
Marin de Molin (10 August 1510), 10, 76
Nicolò Zustignan (28 August 1510), 11, 418
Nicolò Zustignan (5 December 1510), 11, 809–10
Nicolò Zustignan (2–5 May 1511), 12, 199
Andrea Foscolo (13 May 1511), 12, 244–45
Lodovico Valdrim (27 May–3 June 1511), 12, 273
Nicolò Zustignan (18 June 1511)
Andrea Foscolo's letter to Piero Foscolo (18 June 1511), 12, 507–10
Andrea Foscolo's letter to Piero Foscolo (24 June 1511), 12, 510–12
Nicolò Zustignan (26 June 1511), 12, 299
Andrea Foscolo's letter to Piero Foscolo (27 August 1511), 13, 114–17
Andrea Foscolo's letter to Piero Foscolo (26 September 1511), 13, 220–22
Andrea Foscolo's letter to Nicolò Zustignan (29 January 1512), 13, 520–21
Andrea Foscolo's letter to Piero Foscolo (28 March 1512), 14, 291–93
Nicolò Zustignan (2 April 1512), 14, 216
Nicolò Zustignan (24 April 1512), 14, 245–46
Nicolò Zustignan (11 June 1512), 14, 483–84.

Sources

ʿAbdü'lvāsiʿ Çelebi. *Ḫalīlnāme*. Edited and transliterated by Ayhan Güldaş. Ankara: Kültür Bakanlığı, 1996.

ʿAbdurraḥmān b. Abī Yūsuf el-Ḥāfıẓ el-Müneccim. *Jawharu'l-ḥıfẓı'ṣ-ṣıḥḥa wa ʿilācu'l-marżā*. SK Ayasofya 3635.

Aḥmed Bī-cān [Yazıcıoğlu]. *Dürr-i meknūn*. Critical edition and commentary by Laban Kaptein. Asch: privately published, 2007.

Aḥmedī [Tāceddīn İbrāhīm b. Ḫıżır]. *Tevārīḫ-i mülūk-i āl-i ʿOs̱mān ve ġazv-ı īşān bā-küffār*. Edited by Kemal Silay. Cambridge, MA: Harvard University, Department of Near Eastern Languages and Civilizations, 2004.

Al-Laḫmī [Abu al-Ḥasan ʿAlī ibn Muḥammad]. *Al-Durr al-musān fī sīrat al-muẓaffar Salīm Khān*. Edited by Hans Ernest. Cairo: ʿĪsā al-Bābī al-Ḥalabī, 1962.

Angiolello, Giovanni Maria. "A Short Narrative of the Life and Acts of the King Ussun Cassano." In *A Narrative of Italian Travels in Persia in the Fifteenth and Sixteenth Centuries*, edited and translated by Charles Grey, 73–138. London: The Hakluyt Society, 1873.

Anonymous. *Baṭṭālnāme*. Edited and translated by Yorgos Dedes. Cambridge, MA: Harvard University, Department of Near Eastern Languages and Civilizations, 1996.

Anonymous. *Chronikon peri ton Tourkon soultanon*. Translated and annotated by Marios Philippides. In *Byzantium, Europe, and the Ottoman Sultans, 1373–1513: An Anonymous Greek Chronicle of the Seventeenth Century (Codex Barberinus Graecus 111)*. New Rochelle, NY: Aristide D. Caratzas, 1990.

Anonymous. *Dānişmendnāme*. Critical edition by Necati Demir. Cambridge, MA: Harvard University, Department of Near Eastern Languages and Civilizations, 2002.

Anonymous. *De fatti illustri di Selim Imperator de Turchi*. In *Dell'historia universale dell'origine et imperio de Turchi*, edited by Francesco Sansovino. Venice, 1564.

Anonymous. [*Ekthesis Chronike*]. Translated and annotated by Marios Philippides. In *Emperors, Patriarchs and Sultans of Constantinople, 1373–1513: An Anonymous Greek Chronicle of the Sixteenth Century*. Brookline, MA: Hellenic College Press, 1986.

Anonymous. *Ġazavāt-ı Sulṭān Murād b. Meḥemmed Ḫān*. Edited and transliterated by Halil İnalcık and Mevlûd Oğuz. In *Gazavât-ı Sultân Murâd b. Mehemmed Hân: İzladi ve Varna Savaşları (1443–1444) Üzerinde Anonim* Gazavâtnâme. Ankara: Türk Tarih Kurumu Basımevi, 1978.

Anonymous. *Ḥikāyet-i ẓuhūr-ı āl-i ʿOs̱mān*. Transliterated by Sebahattin Köklü. In "Anonim Tevârîh-i Âl-i Osmân: Hikâyet-i Zuhûr-ı Âl-i Osmân [Transkripsiyon, İnceleme, Dizin]." Master's thesis, Marmara University, 2004. SK Fatih 4206.

Anonymous. *Ḥırzü'l-mülūk*. Edited and transliterated by Yaşar Yücel. In *Osmanlı Devlet Teşkilâtına Dair Kaynaklar*, Part III. Ankara: Türk Tarih Kurumu Basımevi, 1988.

Anonymous. *Ḳavānīn-i yeñiçeriyān*. Edited and transliterated by Tayfun Toroser. In *Kavanin-i Yeniçeriyan: Yeniçeri Kanunları*. Istanbul: Türkiye İş Bankası Kültür Yayınları, 2011.

Anonymous. *Kitāb meṣāliḥü'l-Müslimīn ve menāfiʿü'l-müʾminīn*. Edited and transliterated by Yaşar Yücel. In *Osmanlı Devlet Teşkilâtına Dair Kaynaklar*, Part II. Ankara: Türk Tarih Kurumu Basımevi, 1988.

Anonymous. *Kitāb-ı müstetāb*. Edited and transliterated by Yaşar Yücel. In *Osmanlı Devlet Teşkilâtına Dair Kaynaklar*, Part I. Ankara: Türk Tarih Kurumu Basımevi, 1988.

Anonymous. *Münşeʾāt*. NK 4316.

Anonymous. *Tārīḫ-i āl-i ʿOs̱mān*. TSMK Revan 1099.

Anonymous. *Tārīḫ-i āl-i ʿOs̱mān*. TSMK Revan 1101.

Anonymous. *Tevārīḫ-i āl-i ʿOs̱mān*. TSMK Revan 1100.

Anonymous. *Tevārīḫ-i āl-i ʿOs̱mān*. Transliterated by Nihat Azamat. In *Anonim Tevârîh-i Al-i Osman--F. Giese Neşri*. Istanbul: Marmara Üniversitesi Edebiyat Fakültesi Basımevi, 1992.

Anonymous. *Tevārīḫ-i āl-i ʿOs̱mān*. Transliterated by Necdet Öztürk. In *Anonim Osmanlı Kroniği, 1299–1512*. Istanbul: Türk Dünyası Araştırmaları Vakfı, 2000.

[Oxford] Anonymous. Oxford University, Bodleian Library, Marsh 313. Transliterated and published with facsimile by H. E. Cengiz and Y. Yücel as "Rûhî Târîhi." In *Belgeler* 14–18 (1989–1992): 359–472.

ʿĀşıḳ Çelebi. *Meşāʿirü'ş-şuʿarā*. Edited and transliterated by Filiz Kılıç. 3 vols. Istanbul: İstanbul Araştırmaları Enstitüsü, 2010.

ʿĀşıḳpaşazāde [Dervīş Aḥmed]. *Menāḳıb-ü-tevārīḫ-i āl-i ʿOs̱mān*. (1) Edited and transliterated by Kemal Yavuz and M. A. Yekta Saraç. In *Aşık Paşazade: Osmanoğulları'nın Tarihi*, 319–586. Istanbul: K Kitaplığı, 2003. (2) Edited and transliterated by Nihal Atsız. In *Osmanlı Tarihleri*,

91–254. Istanbul: Türkiye Basımevi, 1949. (3) Edited by Friedrich Giese. In *Die Altosmanische Chronik des ʿĀšıkpašazāde*. Leipzig: O. Harrassowitz, 1929. (4) Edited by ʿAlī Bey. In *Tevārīḫ-i Āl-i ʿOs̱mān'dan ʿĀşıḳpaşazāde Tārīḫi*. Istanbul: Maṭbaʿa-i ʿĀmire, 1332/1914.

ʿAzīz Efendi. *Ḳānūnnāme-i Sulṭānī li ʿAzīz Efendi*. Edited, transliterated, and translated by Rhoads Murphey. In *Aziz Efendi's Book of Sultanic Laws and Regulations: An Agenda for Reform by a Seventeenth-Century Ottoman Statesman*. Cambridge, MA: Harvard University, 1985.

Barbarigo, Daniele. *Relazione dell'Imperio Ottomano*. Serie 3, vol. 2 of *Relazioni degli Ambasciatori Veneti al Senato*, edited by Eugenio Albèri, 1–59. Florence: Società Editrice Fiorentina, 1844.

Baudier, Michel. *Inventaire de l'histoire generale des Turcz*. Paris: Sebastien Chappelet, 1617.

Bobovi, Albert. *Description du Serail du Grand Seigneur par M. Girardin, ambassadeur de France à la Porte*. BNF Fr. Nouv. Mss. 4997. Translated by C. G. Fisher and A. Fisher. In "Topkapı Sarayı in the Mid-Seventeenth Century: Bobovi's Description." *Archivum Ottomanicum* 10 (1985): 5–81.

Busbecq, Ogier Ghislain de. "Turkish Letter I." In *The Life and Letters of Ogier Ghiselin de Busbecq*, translated by Charles Thornton Forster and F. H. Blackburne Daniell, vol. 1, 75–173. London: C. K. Paul, 1881.

Celālzāde Muṣṭafā. *Meʾās̱ir-i Selīm Ḫānī* (or *Selīmnāme*). (1) BM Add. 7848. (2) Edited and transliterated by Ahmet Uğur and Mustafa Çuhadar. In *Selim-nâme*. Ankara: Kültür Bakanlığı, 1990.

——. *Ṭabaḳātü'l-memālik ve derecātü'l-mesālik*. In *Geschichte Sultan Süleymān Ḳānūnīs von 1520 bis 1557, oder, Ṭabaḳātü'l-Memālik ve Derecātü'l-Mesālik / von Celālzāde Muṣṭafā genannt Ḳoca Nişāncı*, edited by Petra Kappert. Wiesbaden: Steiner, 1981.

Cenābī [Muṣṭafā]. *Dürr-i meknūn ve sırr-ı maṣūn*. TSMK Revan 1136. Turkish translation of *Tārīḫ-i Cenābī*.

Da Lezze, Donado. *Historia Turchesca (1300–1514)*. Edited by I. Ursu. Bucharest: Carol Göbl, 1909.

Ebū'l-ḫayr-i Rūmī. *Ṣaltuḳnāme*. Facsimile edition by Fahir İz. Cambridge, MA: Harvard University Printing Office, 1974–84.

Edāʾī [Mollā Meḥemmed]. *Shāhnāmā-ye Salīm Ḫānī* (or *Salīmnāma*). (1) İÜK FY 835. (2) Edited and translated by Abdüsselam Bilgen. In "Adāʾī-yi Şīrāzī ve Selīm-nāmesi." PhD diss., Ankara University, 1987. (3) Edited and translated by Abdüsselam Bilgen. In *Adāʾī-yi Şīrāzī ve Selim-nāmesi*. Ankara: Türk Tarih Kurumu, 2007.

Edrenevī [Meḥmed b. Meḥmed]. *Nuḫbetü't-tevārīḫ*. TSMK Hazine 1368.
Enverī. *Düstūrnāme*. Edited and transliterated by Necdet Öztürk. Istanbul: Kitabevi, 2003.
Evliyā Çelebi [Meḥmed Ẓıllī b. Dervīş]. *Seyāḥatnāme*. Edited and transliterated by Robert Dankoff, Seyit Ali Kahraman, Yücel Dağlı, et al. In *Evliyâ Çelebi Seyahatnâmesi*. 10 vols. Istanbul: Yapı Kredi Yayınları, 1999–2006.
Ferīdūn Beg, Aḥmed, ed. *Münşe'ātü's-selāṭīn*. 2 vols. Istanbul, 1265–74/1848–58.
Gritti, Andrea. *Relazione a Bajezid II*. Serie 3, vol. 3 of *Relazioni degli Ambasciatori Veneti al Senato*, edited by Eugenio Albèri, 1–43. Florence: Società Editrice Fiorentina, 1855.
Guistinian, Antonio. *Alla Porta Ottomana*. Serie 3, vol. 3, of *Relazioni degli Ambasciatori Veneti al Senato*, edited by Eugenio Albèri, 45–50. Florence: Società Editrice Fiorentina, 1855.
Ḥadīdī. *Tevārīḫ-i āl-i ʿOs̱mān*. Edited and transliterated by Necdet Öztürk. In *Tevârih-i Al-i Osman (1299–1523)*. Istanbul: Marmara Üniversitesi Edebiyat Fakültesi Basımevi, 1991.
Ḫalīl b. İsmāʿīl [b. Şeyḫ Bedreddīn Maḥmūd]. *Menāḳıb-ı Şeyḫ Bedreddīn b. İsrā'īl*. İAK Muallim Cevdet K.157.
Ḥasan Kāfī [el-Aḳḥiṣārī]. *Uṣūl al-ḥikam fī niẓām al-ʿālam*. Edited and transliterated by Mehmet İpşirli. In "Hasan Kâfî el-Akhisarî ve Devlet Düzenine Ait Eseri *Usûlü'l-Hikem fî Nizâmi'l-Âlem*." *TED* 10–11 (1979–1980): 239–78.
Ḥasan Rūmlū. *Aḥsanu't-tawārīkh*. Edited and translated by C. N. Seddon. In *A Chronicle of the Early Ṣafawīs Being the Aḥsanu't-Tawārīkh of Ḥasan-i Rūmlū*. 2 vols. Baroda: Oriental Institute, 1931–34.
Ḥaydar Çelebi. *Rūznāme*. In *Münşe'ātü's-selāṭīn*, edited by Aḥmed Ferīdūn Beg, vol. 1, 458–500. Istanbul, 1274/1858.
Hezārfen Ḥüseyin. *Telḫīṣü'l-beyān fī ḳavānīn-i āl-i ʿOs̱mān*. Edited and transliterated by Sevim İlgürel. Ankara: Türk Tarih Kurumu, 1998.
——. *Tenḳīḥ-i tevārīḫ-i mülūk*. TSMK Revan 1180.
Hierosolimitano, Domenico. *Domenico's Istanbul*. Translated with an introduction and commentary by Michael Austin. Edited by Geoffrey Lewis. Warminster: E. J. W. Gibb Memorial Trust, 2001.
Ibn Ḥusām, Muḥammad b. Ḥusāmuddīn. *Khāwarānnāma*. Translated by Muhammad Savoji as *Khavaran Nameh: A Masterpiece of Iranian Literature and Painting (15th c.)*. Tehran: Ministry of Culture and Islamic Guidance & Cultural Heritage Organization, 2002.

Ibn Iyās [Muḥammad b. Aḥmad]. *Badāʾiʿ al-zuhūr fī waqāʾiʿ al-duhūr.* (1) Edited by Muḥammad Muṣṭafā. 9 vols. Wiesbaden and Cairo: Franz Steiner, 1960–92. (2) Edited and translated by W. H. Salmon as *An Account of the Ottoman Conquest of Egypt in the Year A.H. 922/A.D. 1516, Translated from the Third Volume of the Arabic Chronicle of Muhammed ibn Ahmed Ibn Iyas, an Eyewitness of the Scenes He Describes.* London: Royal Asiatic Society, 1921.

Ibn Khaldūn. *Muqaddimah.* Edited and translated by Franz Rosenthal as *The Muqaddimah: An Introduction to History.* 3 vols. New York: Pantheon Books, 1958.

Ibn Sīrīn [Abū Bakr Muḥammad]. *Tafsīr al-aḥlām al-kabīr.* Edited and translated by Rania Mounir Sanioura as *Interpretation of Dreams.* Beirut: Dar al-Kutub al-Ilmiyah, 2007.

İdrīs-i Bidlīsī. *Salīmshāhnāma.* Collated and completed by his son Ebū'l-fażl Meḥmed. (1) BM Add. 24960. (2) Edited and translated by Hicabi Kırlangıç. In *İdrîs-i Bidlîsî: Selim Şah-nâme.* Ankara: Kültür Bakanlığı, 2001.

İsḥaḳ Çelebi. *Selīmnāme.* (1) TSMK Revan 1276. (2) Edited and transliterated by Burhan Keskin. In "Selîm-nâme (İshâk b. İbrâhîm)." Master's thesis, Ege University, 1998.

Ḳāḍīzāde [Kebir b. Üveys]. *Selīmnāme (Ġazavāt-ı Sulṭān Selīm).* Selim Ağa Library 825.

Ḳānūnnāme-i āl-i ʿOs̱mān. Edited and transliterated by Abdülkadir Özcan. In *Fatih Sultan Mehmed: Kânunnâme-i Âl-i Osman (Tahlil ve Karşılaştırmalı Metin).* Istanbul: Kitabevi, 2003.

Kātib Çelebi [Ḥācī Ḫalīfe Muṣṭafā b. ʿAbdullāh]. *Düstūrü'l-ʿamel li-ıṣlāḥü'l-ḫalel.* Istanbul, 1864.

——. *Kashf al-ẓunūn ʿan asāmī al-kutūb wa al-funūn.* Edited and translated by Rüştü Balcı as *Keşfü'z-zunûn: An Esâmi'l-Kütübi ve'l-Fünûn (Kitapların ve İlimlerin İsimlerinden Şüphelerin Giderilmesi).* Istanbul: Tarih Vakfı Yurt Yayınları, 2007.

Kay-Kāʾūs ibn Iskandar. *Ḳābūsnāma.* Translated by Reuben Levy as *A Mirror for Princes: The Qābūs Nāma by Kai Kāūs ibn Iskandar, Prince of Gurgān.* New York: E. P. Dutton, 1951.

Kemāl. *Selāṭīnnāme.* Edited and transliterated by Necdet Öztürk. In *Selâtîn-nâme (1299–1490).* Ankara: Türk Tarih Kurumu, 2001.

Kemālpaşazāde [Aḥmed]. *Tevārīḫ-i āl-i ʿOs̱mān.* Vol. 4. Edited and transliterated by Koji Imazawa. Ankara: Türk Tarih Kurumu, 2000. (1)

Vol. 8. Edited and transliterated by Ahmet Uğur. Ankara: Türk Tarih Kurumu, 1997. (2) Concluding section. Edited and transliterated by Ahmet Uğur. In *The Reign of Sultan Selīm I in the Light of the Selīm-nāme Literature*, 28–64. Berlin: K. Schwarz, 1985. (3) Vol. 9. Edited and transliterated by Ahmet Uğur. In *The Reign of Sultan Selīm I in the Light of the Selīm-nāme Literature*, 65–128. Berlin: K. Schwarz, 1985. (4) Vol. 10. Edited and transliterated by Şefaettin Severcan. Ankara: Türk Tarih Kurumu, 1996.

Keşfī [Meḥmed Çelebi]. *Selīmnāme* (also known as *Tārīḫ-i Sulṭān Selīm Ḫān* or *Bāġ-ı firdevs-i ġuzāt ve ravża-yı ehl-i cihād*). (1) SK Esad Efendi 2147. (2) Edited and transliterated by Abdurrahman Sağırlı. In "Keşfî Mehmed Çelebi: Selim-nâme veya Bağ-ı Firdevs-i Guzat ve Ravza-i Ehl-i Cihâd." Master's thesis, Istanbul University, 1993.

Khwandamīr [Ghiyās al-Dīn Muḥammad Ḥusaynī]. *Tārīkh-i ḥabīb al-siyar.* Edited and translated by W. M. Thackston. In *Habibu's-Siyar, Tome Three: The Reign of the Mongol and the Turk.* Cambridge, MA: Harvard University, Department of Near Eastern Languages and Civilizations, 1994.

Ḳıvāmī. *Fetḥnāme-i Sulṭān Meḥmed.* (1) Edited, transliterated, and published with modern Turkish translation by Ceyhun Vedat Uygur as *Kıvâmî: Fetihnâme*, 32–609. Istanbul: Yapı Kredi Yayınları, 2007. (2) Facsimile published with an introduction by Franz Babinger as *Fetihnâme-i Sultan Mehmed.* Istanbul: Maarif Basımevi, 1955.

Knolles, Richard. *The Generall Historie of the Turkes.* London: Adam Islip, 1603.

Koçi Beg. *Risāle-i Koçi Beg.* Edited by Seda Çakmakcıoğlu. In *Koçi Bey Risaleleri.* Istanbul: Kabalcı Yayınevi, 2008.

Luṭfī Paşa. *Āṣafnāme.* (1) Edited and translated into German by Rudolf Tschudi. In *Das Aṣafnâme des Luṭfî Pascha.* Berlin: Mayer and Müller, 1910. (2) Edited and transliterated by Ahmet Uğur. In *İslam İlimleri Enstitüsü Dergisi* 4 (1980): 243–58.

——. *Tevārīḫ-i āl-i ʿOs̱mān.* Edited and transliterated by Kayhan Atik. In *Lütfi Paşa ve Tevârih-i Âl-i Osman.* Ankara: Kültür Bakanlığı, 2001.

Meḥmed Cemīl. *Muḫtaṣar ve manẓūm tārīḫ-i ʿOs̱mānī.* TSMK Mehmed Reşad 576.

Meḥmed Paşa [Ḳaramānī]. *Tawārīkh al-salātīn al-ʿUthmāniyya.* Edited and translated to Turkish by İbrahim Hakkı Konyalı as "Osmanlı Sultanları Tarihi." In *Osmanlı Tarihleri*, edited by Nihal Atsız, 323–69. Istanbul: Türkiye Yayınevi, 1947.

Meḥmed Paşa [Ṣarı]. *Neṣāʾiḥü'l-vüzerā ve'l-ümerā*. Edited and translated by Walter Livingston Wright. In *Ottoman Statecraft: The Book of Counsel for Vezirs and Governors (Naṣāʾiḥ ül-vüzera ve'l-ümera) of Sarı Meḥmed Pasha, the Defterdār*. Princeton: Princeton University Press, 1935.

Menavino, Giovanni Antonio. "Della vita et legge Turchesca." In *Dell'historia universale dell'origine et imperio de Turchi*, edited by Francesco Sansovino. Venice, 1564.

Mevlānā ʿĪsā. *Cāmiʿü'l-meknūnāt*. Leiden University Library, Or. 1448.

Muʿālī. *Ḫünkārnāme*. Edited and published by Robert Anhegger. In "Muʿālī'nin Hünkārnāmesi." *TD* 1, no. 1 (1949): 145–66.

Muḥammad Bāqir Najm-i Sānī. *Advice on the Art of Governance: An Indo-Islamic Mirror for Princes: Mauʿiẓah-i Jahāngīrī of Muḥammad Bāqir Najm-i Sānī*. Edited by Sajida Sultana Alvi. Albany: State University of New York Press, 1989.

Muṣṭafā ʿĀlī. *Künhü'l-aḫbār*. Kayseri Raşid Efendi Library 901 and 920. Edited by Ahmet Uğur, Ahmet Gül, Mustafa Çuhadar, and İbrahim Hakkı Çuhadar. 2 vols. Kayseri: Erciyes Üniversitesi Yayınları, 1997.

———. *Künhü'l-aḫbār (Teẕkire)*. Edited and transliterated by Mustafa İsen. In *Künhü'l-ahbâr'ın Tezkire Kısmı*. Ankara: Atatürk Kültür Merkezi, 1994.

———. *Nuṣḥatü's-selāṭīn*. Edited and translated by Andreas Tietze. In *Muṣṭafā ʿĀlī's Counsel for Sultans of 1581*. 2 vols. Vienna: Verlag der Österreichischen Akademie der Wissenschaften, 1979–82.

Muṣṭafā Naʿīmā. *Tārīḫ-i Naʿīmā*. Edited and transliterated by Mehmet İpşirli. 2 vols. Ankara: Türk Tarih Kurumu, 2007.

Muṣṭafā Ṣāfī. *Zübdetü't-tevārīḫ*. Edited and transliterated by İbrahim Hakkı Çuhadar. In *Mustafa Sâfî'nin Zübdetü't-Tevârîh'i*. 2 vols. Ankara: Türk Tarih Kurumu, 2003.

Neşrī [Mevlānā Meḥemmed]. *Kitāb-ı cihānnümā*. Edited and transliterated by Faik Reşit Unat and Mehmed A. Köymen. In *Kitâb-ı Cihan-nümâ: Neşrî Tarihi*. 3rd ed. 2 vols. Ankara: Türk Tarih Kurumu, 1995.

Nişāncızāde [Meḥmed b. Aḥmed]. *Mirʾāt-ı kāʾināt*. TSMK Revan 1135.

Peçevī İbrāhīm. *Tārīḫ-i Peçevī*. (1) 2 vols. Istanbul: Maṭbaʿa-i ʿĀmire, 1283/1866–1867. (2) Edited, simplified, and annotated by Bekir Sıtkı Baykal. In *Peçevi Tarihi*. 2 vols. Ankara: Kültür Bakanlığı Yayınları, 1992.

Ramażānzāde [or Küçük Nişāncı] Meḥmed Paşa. *Tārīḫ-i Ramażānzāde* (or *Tārīḫ-i Küçük Nişāncı*). TSMK Revan 1128.

Rıżā [Şeyḫzāde Aḥmed Ağaoğlu]. *Manẓūme-i şāhān*. TSMK Yeni Yazmalar 732.

Saʿdeddīn [Ḫoca Efendi]. *Selīmnāme*. (1) In *Tācü't-Tevārīḫ*, vol. 2, 602–19. [Istanbul]: Ṭabʿḫāne-i ʿĀmire, 1280/1863. (2) SK Esad Efendi 2147.

——. *Tācü't-tevārīḫ*. (1) BNF Supplément turc 524. (2) 2 vols. [Istanbul]: Ṭabʿḫāne-i ʿĀmire, 1279–80/1862–63.

Saʿdī b. ʿAbdü'l-Müteʿāl. *Selīmnāme*. (1) TSMK Revan 1277. (2) Edited and translated into German by Marie Thérèse Speiser. In *Das Selimname des Saʿdī b. ʿAbd ül-Müteʿāl*. Zurich: Dissertationdruckerei AG. Gebr. Leeman, 1946.

Sāʾī Muṣṭafā Çelebi. *Teẕkiretü'l-bünyān*. Edited and transliterated by Hayati Develi. In *Yapılar Kitabı: Tezkiretü'l-Bünyan ve Tezkiretü'l-Ebniye (Mimar Sinan'ın Anıları)*, 115–69. Istanbul: K Kitaplığı, 2003.

——. *Teẕkiretü'l-ebniye*. Edited and transliterated by Hayati Develi. In *Yapılar Kitabı: Tezkiretü'l-Bünyan ve Tezkiretü'l-Ebniye (Mimar Sinan'ın Anıları)*, 173–95. Istanbul: K Kitaplığı, 2003.

Sanioura, Rania Mounir, ed. and trans. *Interpretation of Dreams*. Beirut: Dar al-Kutub al-Ilmiyah, 2007.

Sanuto, Marino. *I Diarii*. Edited by Nicolo Barozzi et al. 58 vols. Venice: F. Visentini, 1879–1903.

Schirò, Giuseppe, ed. *Cronaca dei Tocco di Cefalonia: Prolegomeni, Testo Critico e Traduzione*. Rome: Accademia Nazionale dei Lincei, 1975.

Selānikī [Muṣṭafā Efendi]. *Tārīḫ-i Selānikī*. Edited and transliterated by Mehmed İpşirli. In *Tarih-i Selânikî*. 2 vols. Istanbul: İstanbul Üniversitesi Edebiyat Fakültesi Basımevi, 1989.

Şikārī [Aḥmed]. *Ḳaramānnāme*. Edited and transliterated by Metin Sözen and Necdet Sakaoğlu. In *Karamannâme: Zamanın Kahramanı Karamanîler'in Tarihi*. Istanbul: Karaman Valiliği, 2005.

Silāḥdār Meḥmed Aġa. *Nuṣretnāme*. (1) BDK Veliyüddin 2369. (2) Edited and transliterated by İsmet Parmaksızoğlu. In *Nusretnâme*. 2 vols. Istanbul: Milli Eğitim Basımevi, 1962–69.

Şīrī [ʿAlī]. *Tārīḫ-i fetḥ-i Mısr*. TSMK Emanet Hazinesi 1433/II, 218b–267b.

Ṣolaḳzāde [Meḥemmed Hemdemī Çelebi]. *Tārīḫ-i āl-i ʿOs̱mān* (or *Ṣolāḳzāde Tārīḫi*). (1) TSMK Bağdat 199. (2) Under the title *Sulṭān Bāyezīd-i s̱ānī ve Sulṭān Selīm-i evvel faṣılları*. TSMK Emanet Hazinesi 1416. (3) Edited and translated by Vahid Çabuk. In *Solak-zâde Tarihi*. 2 vols. Ankara: Kültür Bakanlığı, 1989.

Spandounes, Theodore. *On the Origin of the Ottoman Emperors.* Edited and translated by Donald M. Nicol. Cambridge, UK: Cambridge University Press, 1997.

———. *Petit traicté de l'origine des Turcz.* Translated and annotated by Charles Schefer. Paris: Ernest Leroux, 1896.

Sucūdī Çelebi. *Selīmnāme.* (1) TSMK Revan 1284. (2) Edited and transliterated by İbrahim Hakkı Çuhadar. In "Sucûdî'nin Selim-nâmesi." Master's thesis, Erciyes University, 1988.

Şükrī-i Bidlīsī. *Selīmnāme.* (1) BM Or. 1039. (2) Edited and transliterated by Mustafa Argunşah. In *Selîm-nâme.* Kayseri: Erciyes Üniversitesi Yayınları, 1997.

Şükrullāh. *Behçetü't-tevārīḫ.* Translated by Nihal Atsız. In *Osmanlı Tarihleri,* edited by Nihal Atsız, 37–76. Istanbul: Türkiye Yayınevi, 1947.

Sūzī Çelebi. *Ġazavātnāme-i Mīḫāloġlu ʿAlī Beg.* In *Ġazavāt-Nāmeler ve Mihaloğlu Ali Bey'in Ġazavāt-nāmesi,* edited and transliterated by Agâh Sırr Levend, 228–358. Ankara: Türk Tarih Kurumu, 2000.

Ṭaşköprīzāde, Aḥmed. *Al-Şaḳāʾiḳ al-nuʿmāniyya fī ʿulamā al-dawlat al-ʿOs̱māniyya.* Translated by Mecdī Efendi. In *Ḥadāʾiḳu'ş-şaḳāʾiḳ,* edited by Abdülkadir Özcan. Istanbul: Çağrı Yayınları, 1989.

Ṭūġī Çelebi [Ḥüseyin bin Sefer]. *İbretnümā* (also called *Tārīḫ-i Ṭūġī*). Edited and transliterated by Mithat Sertoğlu as *Tugî Tarihi.* In *Belleten* 11 (1947): 489–514.

Ṭursun Beg. *Tārīḫ-i ebū'l-fetḥ.* (1) Facsimile edition and summary English translation by Halil Inalcık and Rhoads Murphey. In *The History of Mehmed the Conqueror.* Minneapolis and Chicago: Bibliotheca Islamica, 1978. (2) Edited and transliterated by Mertol Tulum. In *Târîh-i Ebü'l-Feth.* Istanbul: Baha Matbaası, 1977.

Uruç b. ʿĀdil. *Tevārīḫ-i āl-i ʿOs̱mān.* (1) Edited by Franz Babinger. In *Die frühosmanischen Jahrbücher des Urudsch: Nach den Handschriften zu Oxford und Cambridge erstmals herausgegeben und eingeleitet.* Hanover: H. Lafaire, 1925. (2) Edited and translated by Richard F. Kreutel. In *Der Fromme Sultan Bayezid: Die Geschichte seiner Herrschaft (1481–1512) nach den altosmanischen Chroniken des Oruc und des Anonymus Hanivaldanus.* Graz: Verlag Styria, 1978. (3) Edited and transliterated by Necdet Öztürk. In *Oruç Beğ Tarihi.* Istanbul: Çamlıca, 2007.

Veysī [Üveys b. Meḥmed]. *Ḫābnāme.* Edited and transliterated by Mustafa Altun. In *Hâb-nâme-i Veysî.* Istanbul: MVT Yayıncılık, 2011.

Yaḥyā Beg. *Dīvān*. Edited and transliterated by Mehmed Çavuşoğlu. In *Dîvan: Tenkidli Basım*. Istanbul: Edebiyat Fakültesi Matbaası, 1977.
Yūsuf [Çerkesler Kātibi]. *Selīmnāme*. TSMK Hazine 1422.
Yūsuf b. ʿAbdullāh. *Tārīḫ-i āl-i ʿOsmān*. Edited and transliterated by Efdal Sevinçli. In *Bizans Söylenceleriyle Osmanlı Tarihi: Târîh-i âl-i Osmân*. Izmir: Eylül Yayınları, 1997.

Studies

Abou-El-Haj, Rifaʾat Ali. "The Expression of Ottoman Political Culture in the Literature of Advice to Princes (Nasihatnameler) Sixteenth to Twentieth Centuries." In *Sociology in the Rubric of Social Science*, edited by R. K. Bhattacharya and Asok K. Ghosh, 282–92. Calcutta: Ministry of Human Resource Development, Department of Culture, Government of India, 1995.
——. "The Narcissism of Mustafa II (1695–1703): A Psychohistorical Study." *Studia Islamica* 40 (1974): 115–31.
——. "The Ottoman Vezir and Paşa Households, 1683–1703: A Preliminary Report." *Journal of the American Oriental Society* 94, no. 4 (1974): 438–47.
——. "Power and Social Order: The Uses of the *Kanun*." In *The Ottoman City and its Parts: Urban Structure and Social Order*, edited by Irene A. Bierman, Rifaʾat Abou-El-Haj, and Donald Preziosi, 77–99. New Rochelle, NY: Aristide D. Caratzas, 1991.
Ágoston, Gábor. "Information, Ideology, and Limits of Imperial Policy: Ottoman Grand Strategy in the Context of Ottoman Habsburg Rivalry." In *The Early Modern Ottomans: Remapping the Empire*, edited by Virginia H. Aksan and Daniel Goffman, 75–103. Cambridge, UK: Cambridge University Press, 2007.
Akman, Mehmet. *Osmanlı Devletinde Kardeş Katli*. Istanbul: Eren, 1997.
Aksan, Virginia H. "Locating the Ottomans among Early Modern Empires." *Journal of Early Modern History* 3, no. 2 (1999): 103–34.
Aksan, Virginia H., and Daniel Goffman, eds. *The Early Modern Ottomans: Remapping the Empire*. Cambridge, UK: Cambridge University Press, 2007.
Aksoy, Ömer Asım, and Dehri Dilçin, eds. *XIII. Yüzyıldan Beri Türkiye Türkçesiyle Yazılmış Kitaplardan Toplanan Tanıklarıyla Tarama Sözlüğü*. 8 vols. Ankara: Türk Dil Kurumu, 1963–77.

Aktepe, M. Münir. "XIV. ve XV. Asırlarda Rumeli'nin Türkler Tarafından İskânına Dair." *Türkiyat Mecmuası* 10 (1953): 299–312.

Alderson, Anthony Dolphin. *The Structure of the Ottoman Dynasty*. Oxford, UK: Clarendon Press, 1956.

Ali, M. Athar. "Political Structures of the Islamic Orient in the Sixteenth and Seventeenth Centuries." In *Mughal India: Studies in Polity, Ideas, Society, and Culture*, 94–105. Delhi: Oxford University Press, 2006.

Allouche, Adel. *The Origins and the Development of the Ottoman-Safavid Conflict (906–962/1500–1555)*. Berlin: K. Schwarz Verlag, 1983.

Altınkaynak, Erdoğan. "Analysis of the Dragon Killing Scene in the Mythology of the Peoples of Eurasia." *Karadeniz* 19 (2013): 125–32.

Anhegger, Robert. "Hezarfen Hüseyin Efendi'nin Osmanlı Devlet Teşkilâtına Dair Mülâhazaları." *Türkiyat Mecmuası* 10 (1953): 365–93.

Ankersmit, Frank N. *Historical Representation*. Stanford: Stanford University Press, 2001.

Anooshahr, Ali. *The Ghazi Sultans and the Frontiers of Islam: A Comparative Study of the Later Medieval and Early Modern Periods*. London: Routledge, 2009.

Arjomand, Said Amir. "The Rise of Shah Esmāʿil as a Mahdist Revolution." *Studies on Persianate Societies* 3 (2005): 44–65.

Arslan, H. Çetin. "Erken Osmanlı Dönemi (1299–1453)'nde Akıncılar ve Akıncı Beyleri." In *Osmanlı*, edited by Güler Eren, vol. 1, 217–25. Ankara: Yeni Türkiye Yayınları, 1999.

Artan, Tülay. "Arts and Architecture." In *The Later Ottoman Empire, 1603–1839*, edited by Suraiya Faroqhi, 408–80. Vol. 3 of *Cambridge History of Turkey*. Cambridge, UK: Cambridge University Press, 2006.

Asrar, N. Ahmad. *Kanunî Sultan Süleyman Devrinde Osmanlı Devletinin Dinî Siyaseti ve İslam Âlemi*. Istanbul: Büyük Kitaplık, 1972.

———. "The Myth about the Transfer of the Caliphate to the Ottomans." *Journal of the Regional Cultural Institute* 5, nos. 2–3 (1972): 111–20.

Assmann, Jan. *Moses the Egyptian: The Memory of Egypt in Western Monotheism*. Cambridge, MA: Harvard University Press, 1997.

Atasoy, Nurhan. "Illustrations Prepared for Display during Shahname Recitations." In *The Memorial Volume of the 5th International Congress of Iranian Art and Archaeology, Tehran, Isfahan, Shiraz, 11th–18th April 1968*, edited by A. Tajvidi and M. Y. Kiani, vol. 2, 262–72. Tehran: Ministry of Culture and Arts, 1972.

Ateş, Ahmet. "Selim-nâmeler." PhD diss., Istanbul University, 1938.

Atsız, Nihal. *Osmanlı Tarihine Ait Takvimler I: 824, 835 ve 843 Tarihli Takvimler.* Istanbul: Küçükaydın Matbaası, 1961.
Ayalon, David. *Gunpowder and Firearms in the Mamluk Kingdom: A Challenge to a Mediaeval Society.* London: Vallentine, Mitchell, 1956.
Ayan, Hüseyin. *Cevrî: Hayâtı, Edebî Kişiliği, Eserleri ve Divanının Tenkidli Metni.* Erzurum: Atatürk Üniversitesi Basımevi, 1981.
Aydın, Bilgin, and Rıfat Günalan. *XV-XVI. Yüzyıllarda Osmanlı Maliyesi ve Defter Sistemi.* Istanbul: Yeditepe, 2008.
Babayan, Kathryn. "The Cosmological Order of Things in Early Modern Safavid Iran." In *Falnama: The Book of Omens*, edited by Massumeh Farhad and Serpil Bağcı, 245–55. London: Thames and Hudson, 2009.
——. *Mystics, Monarchs, and Messiahs: Cultural Landscapes of Early Modern Iran.* Cambridge, MA: Harvard University Press, 2002.
——. "The Waning of the Qizilbash: The Temporal and the Spiritual in Seventeenth-Century Iran." PhD diss., Princeton University, 1993.
Babinger, Franz. *Beiträge zur Frühgeschichte der Türkenherrschaft in Rumelien (14.-15. Jahrhundert).* Brünn: R. M. Rohrer, 1944.
——. "Beiträge zur Geschichte des Geschlechtes der Malkoč-oghlu's." In *Aufsätze und Abhandlungen zur Geschichte Südeuropas und der Levante*, vol. 1, 355–69. Munich: Südosteuropa-Verlagsgesellschaft, 1962.
——. "Beiträge zur Geschichte von Qarly-Eli vornehmlich aus osmanischen Quellen." In *Aufsätze und Abhandlungen zur Geschichte Südosteuropas und der Levante*, vol. 1, 370–77. Munich: Südosteuropa-Verlagsgesellschaft, 1962.
——. *Die Geschichtsschreiber der Osmanen und ihre Werke.* Leipzig: O. Harrassowitz, 1927.
——. *Mehmed the Conqueror and His Time.* Edited by William C. Hickman. Translated by Ralph Manheim. Princeton: Princeton University Press, 1978. Revised edition of *Mehmed der Eroberer und seine Zeit.* Munich: F. Bruckmann, 1953.
Bacqué-Grammont, Jean-Louis. *Les Ottomans, les Safavides et leurs voisins (1514–1524).* Istanbul: Nederlands Historisch-Archaeologisch Instituut te Istanbul, 1987.
Bağcı, Serpil. *Minyatürlü Ahmedî İskendernameleri: İkonografik Bir Deneme.* PhD diss., Hacettepe University, 1989.
Bağcı, Serpil, Filiz Çağman, Günsel Renda, and Zeren Tanındı. *Ottoman Painting.* Ankara: Ministry of Culture and Tourism, 2010.
Bakhit, Muhammad Adnan. *The Ottoman Province of Damascus in the Sixteenth Century.* Beirut: Librairie du Liban, 1982.

Banarlı, Nihad Sâmi. *Şiir ve Edebiyat Sohbetleri*. Istanbul: Kubbealtı Neşriyâtı, 1982.

Barkan, Ömer Lütfi. "H. 933–934 (M. 1527–1528) Malî Yılına Ait Bir Bütçe Örneği." *İstanbul Üniversitesi İktisat Fakültesi Mecmuası* 15, nos. 1–4 (1953–54): 251–329.

——. "Osmanlı İmparatorluğunda Bir İskân ve Kolonizasyon Metodu Olarak Sürgünler." *İstanbul Üniversitesi İktisat Fakültesi Mecmuası* 11 (1949–50): 524–69; 13 (1951–52): 56–78; 15 (1953–54): 209–37.

——. *XV ve XVIıncı Asırlarda Osmanlı İmparatorluğunda Ziraî Ekonominin Hukukî ve Malî Esasları*. Vol. 1: *Kanunlar*. Istanbul: Bürhaneddin Erenler Matbaası, 1945.

Başar, Fahamettin. "Osmanlı Devleti'nin Kuruluş Döneminde Hizmeti Görülen Akıncı Aileleri: Malkoçoğulları." *Türk Dünyası Tarih Dergisi* 6, no. 66 (1992): 47–50.

——. "Osmanlı Devleti'nin Kuruluş Döneminde Hizmeti Görülen Akıncı Aileleri: Mihaloğulları." *Türk Dünyası Tarih Dergisi* 6, no. 63 (1992): 20–26.

——. "Osmanlı Devleti'nin Kuruluş Döneminde Hizmeti Görülen Akıncı Aileleri: Turahanoğulları." *Türk Dünyası Tarih Dergisi* 6, no. 65 (1992): 47–50.

Bayerle, Gustav. *Pashas, Begs, and Effendis: A Historical Dictionary of Titles and Terms in the Ottoman Empire*. Istanbul: The Isis Press, 1997.

Beldiceanu, Nicoara. *Le timar dans l'État ottoman (début XIVe-début XVIe siècle)*. Wiesbaden: Otto Harrassowitz, 1980.

——. "Recherches sur la réforme foncière de Mehmed II." *Acta Historica* 4 (1965): 27–39.

Beldiceanu-Steinherr, Irène. "En marge d'un acte concernant le penğyek et les aqınğı." *Revue des Etudes Islamiques* 37 (1969): 21–47.

Beldiceanu-Steinherr, Irène, and Jean-Louis Bacqué-Grammont. "A propos de quelques causes de malaises sociaux en Anatolie Centrale." *Archivum Ottomanicum* 7 (1982): 71–115.

Bentley, Jerry H. *Old World Encounters: Cross-Cultural Contacts and Exchanges in Pre-Modern Times*. Oxford, UK: Oxford University Press, 1993.

Berkey, Jonathan P. *Popular Preaching and Religious Authority in the Medieval Islamic Near East*. Seattle: University of Washington Press, 2001.

Berktay, Halil. "The Feudalism Debate: The Turkish End—Is Tax-vs.-Rent Necessarily the Product and Sign of a Modal Difference?" *Journal of Peasant Studies* 14, no. 3 (1987): 291–333.

——. "The Search for the Peasant in Western and Turkish History/Historiography." *Journal of Peasant Studies* 18, nos. 3–4 (1991): 109–84.

——. "Three Empires and the Societies They Governed: Iran, India, and the Ottoman Empire." In *New Approaches to State and Peasant in Ottoman History*, edited by Halil Berktay and Suraiya Faroqhi, 242–63. London: Frank Cass, 1992.

Berlekamp, Persis. *Wonder, Image and Cosmos in Medieval Islam*. New Haven, CT: Yale University Press, 2011.

Beyatlı, Yahya Kemal. "Selimnâme." In *Eski Şiirin Rüzgârıyle*, 5–20. Istanbul: Baha Matbaası, 1962.

Birnbaum, Eleazar. "Superstitious Tough Guy? Yavuz Sultan Selīm and Dream Interpretation." In *Turkish Language, Literature, and History: Travelers' Tales, Sultans, and Scholars since the Eighth Century*, edited by Bill Hickman and Gary Leiser, 46–52. London: Routledge, 2016.

Bloch, Marc. *Feudal Society*. Translated by L. A. Manyon. 2 vols. Chicago: University of Chicago Press, 1968.

Börekçi, Günhan. "Factions and Favorites at the Courts of Sultan Ahmed I (r. 1603–17) and His Immediate Predecessors." PhD diss., The Ohio State University, 2010.

Boykov, Grigor. "Anatolian *Emir* in Rumelia: İsfendiyaroğlu İsmail Bey's Architectural Patronage and Governorship of Filibe (1460s–1470s)." *Bulgarian Historical Review* 1–2 (2013): 137–47.

——. "In Search of Vanished Ottoman Monuments in the Balkans: Minnetoğlu Mehmed Beg's Complex in Konuş Hisarı." In *Monuments, Patrons, Contexts: Papers on Ottoman Europe Presented to Machiel Kiel*, edited by Maximilian Hartmuth and Ayşe Dilsiz, 47–68. Leiden: Nederlands Instituut voor het Nabije Oosten, 2010.

——. "Karlızâde ʿAli Bey: An Ottoman Dignitary's Pious Endowment and the Emergence of the Town of Karlova in Central Bulgaria." *Journal of Turkish Studies* 39 (2013): 247–67. (Special Issue: *Defterology: Festschrift in Honor of Heath Lowry*, edited by Selim S. Kuru and Baki Tezcan. Cambridge: Harvard University, Department of Near Eastern Languages and Civilizations, 2013.)

Browne, Edward Granville. *A History of Persian Literature in Modern Times, A.D. 1500–1924*. Cambridge, UK: [Cambridge] University Press, 1930.

Brummett, Palmira. "The Myth of Shah Ismail Safavi: Political Rhetoric and "Divine' Kingship." In *Medieval Christian Perceptions of Islam:*

A Book of Essays, edited by John Victor Tolan, 331–59. London: Garland Publishing, 1996.
Burke, Peter. "Concepts of the 'Golden Age' in the Renaissance." In *Süleyman the Magnificent and His Age: The Ottoman Empire in the Early Modern World*, edited by Metin Kunt and Christine Woodhead, 154–63. London and New York: Longman, 1995.
———. *The Fabrication of Louis XIV*. London: Yale University Press, 1992.
———. "Presenting and Re-presenting Charles V." In *Charles V 1500–1558 and His Time*, edited by Hugo Soly, 393–475. Antwerp: Mercatorfonds, 1999.
Buzov, Snjezana. "The Lawgiver and His Lawmakers: The Role of Legal Discourse in the Change of Ottoman Imperial Culture." PhD diss., University of Chicago, 2005.
Casale, Giancarlo. *The Ottoman Age of Exploration*. Oxford, UK: Oxford University Press, 2010.
Çavuşoğlu, Mehmed. "Şehzâde Mustafa Mersiyeleri." *TED* 12 (1981–82): 641–86.
Çetin, Halil. *Candaroğlu Yurdunda Bey İmaretleri*. Çankırı: Çankırı Belediyesi Yayınları, 2013.
Cezar, Mustafa. *Osmanlı Tarihinde Levendler*. Istanbul: Çelikcilt Matbaası, 1965.
Chann, Naindeep Singh. "Lord of the Auspicious Conjunction: Origins of the *Ṣāḥib-Qirān*." *Iran and the Caucasus* 13 (2009): 93–110.
Çıpa, H. Erdem. "The Centrality of the Periphery: The Rise to Power of Selīm I, 1487–1512." PhD diss., Harvard University, 2007.
———. "Contextualizing Şeyḫ Bedreddīn: Notes on Ḫalīl b. İsmāʿīl's *Menāḳıb-ı Şeyḫ Bedreddīn b. İsrāʾīl*." In *Şinasi Tekin'in Anısına: Uygurlardan Osmanlıya*, 285–95. Istanbul: Simurg, 2005.
———. "'The Lesser Day of Resurrection': Ottoman Interpretations of the Istanbul Earthquake of 1509." In *Catastrophes and the Apocalyptic in the Middle Ages and the Renaissance*, edited by Jaime R. Lara. Tempe and Turnhout: Arizona Center for Medieval and Renaissance Studies and Brepols Press, 2017.
Clinton, Jerome W., and Marianna S. Simpson. "How Rustam Killed White Div: An Interdisciplinary Inquiry." *Iranian Studies* 39, no. 2 (2006): 171–97.
Coffey, Heather M. "Unleashing the Dragon: Picturing the Prophet Muhammad in Joachim of Fiore's *Liber Figurarum*." PhD diss., Indiana University, 2012.

Colebrooke, T. E. "On the Proper Names of the Mohammadans." *Journal of the Royal Asiatic Society of Great Britain and Ireland (New Series)* 11, no. 2 (1879): 171–237.

Crone, Patricia, and Martin Hinds. *God's Caliph: Religious Authority in the First Centuries of Islam*. Cambridge, UK: Cambridge University Press, 1986.

Cunbur, Müjgan. "Anadolu Gazileri ve Edebiyatımız." *Erdem: Atatürk Kültür Dil ve Tarih Yüksek Kurumu Atatürk Kültür Merkezi Dergisi* 3, no. 9 (1987): 777–807.

Dale, Stephen F. *The Muslim Empires of the Ottomans, Safavids, and Mughals*. Cambridge, UK: Cambridge University Press, 2010.

Da Mosto, Andrea. *I Dogi di Venezia*. Milano: A. Martello, 1966.

Danişmend, İsmail Hâmi. *İzahlı Osmanlı Tarihi Kronolojisi*. 5 vols. Istanbul: Türkiye Yayınevi, 1947.

Dankoff, Robert. *An Ottoman Mentality: The World of Evliya Çelebi*. Leiden: Brill, 2004.

Darling, Linda T. *A History of Social Justice and Political Power in the Middle East: The Circle of Justice from Mesopotamia to Globalization*. London: Routledge, 2013.

———. "Political Change and Political Discourse in the Early Modern Mediterranean World." *The Journal of Interdisciplinary History* 38, no. 4 (2008): 505–31.

———. *Revenue-Raising and Legitimacy: Tax Collection and Finance Administration in the Ottoman Empire, 1560–1660*. Leiden: Brill, 1996.

Davis, Natalie Zemon, and Randolph Starn. "Introduction." *Representations* 26 (Special Issue: *Memory and Counter-Memory*, 1989): 1–6.

Değirmenci, Tülün. "Bir Kitabı Kaç Kişi Okur? Osmanlı'da Okurlar ve Okuma Biçimleri Üzerine Bazı Gözlemler." *Tarih ve Toplum: Yeni Yaklaşımlar* 13 (2011): 7–43.

Deny, Jean. "Osmanlı Ancien *Tovija (Dovija)*." *Journal Asiatique* 221 (1932): 160–61.

Dilger, Konrad. *Untersuchungen zur Geschichte des Osmanischen Hofzeremoniells im 15. und 16. Jahrhundert*. Munich: Trofenik, 1967.

Dressler, Markus. "Inventing Orthodoxy: Competing Claims for Authority and Legitimacy in the Ottoman-Safavid Conflict." In *Legitimizing the Order: The Ottoman Rhetoric of State Power*, edited by Hakan Karateke and Maurus Reinkowski, 151–73. Leiden: Brill, 2005.

El-Hibri, Tayeb. *Reinterpreting Islamic Historiography: Hārūn al-Rashīd and the Narrative of the ʿAbbāsid Caliphate*. Cambridge, UK: Cambridge University Press, 1999.

Eligür, Banu. *The Mobilization of Political Islam in Turkey*. New York: Cambridge University Press, 2010.

Elliott, John. "Ottoman-Habsburg Rivalry: The European Perspective." In *Süleymân the Second and His Time*, edited by Halil Inalcık and Cemal Kafadar, 153–62. Istanbul: Isis Press, 1993.

Emecen, Feridun M. "Gazaya Dair: XIV. Yüzyıl Kaynakları Arasında Bir Gezinti." In *Prof. Dr. Hakkı Dursun Yıldız Armağanı*, edited by Mustafa Çetin Varlık, 191–97. Ankara: Türk Tarih Kurumu, 1995.

——. *İstanbul'un Fethi Olayı ve Meseleleri*. Istanbul: Kitabevi, 2003.

——. *Zamanın İskenderi, Şarkın Fatihi: Yavuz Sultan Selim*. Istanbul: Yitik Hazine Yayınları, 2010.

Emiralioğlu, Pınar. *Geographical Knowledge and Imperial Culture in the Early Modern Ottoman Empire*. Farnham, UK: Ashgate, 2014.

Ercan, Yavuz. *Kudüs Ermeni Patrikhanesi*. Ankara: Türk Tarih Kurumu, 1988.

Erdem, Mehmet. "Harmancık--Harmankaya." *Uludağ* 75 (1946): 14–16.

Ertuğ, Zeynep Tarım. *XVI. Yüzyıl Osmanlı Devleti'nde Cülûs ve Cenaze Törenleri*. Ankara: T. C. Kültür Bakanlığı, 1999.

Eryılmaz, Fatma Sinem. "From Adam to Süleyman: Visual Representations of Authority in ʿĀrif's *Shāhnāma-yi Āl-i ʿOsmān*." In *Writing History at the Ottoman Court: Editing the Past, Fashioning the Future*, edited by H. Erdem Çıpa and Emine Fetvacı, 100–28. Bloomington: Indiana University Press, 2013.

——. "The Shehnamecis of Sultan Süleymān: ʿĀrif and Eflatun and Their Dynastic Project." PhD diss., University of Chicago, 2010.

Eyice, Semavi. "Sofya Yakınında İhtiman'da Gaazî Mihaloğlu Mahmud Bey İmâret-Câmii." *Kubbealtı Akademi Mecmuası* 2 (1975): 49–61.

Fahd, Toufic. *La divination arabe: Études religieuses, sociologiques et folkloriques sur le milieu natif de l'Islam*. Leiden: Brill, 1966.

——. "The Dream in Medieval Islamic Society." In *The Dream and Human Societies*, edited by G. E. von Grunebaum and Roger Caillois, 351–63. Berkeley: University of California Press, 1966.

Faroqhi, Suraiya. "Das Grosswesir-telḫīṣ: Eine aktenkundliche Studie." *Der Islam* 45 (1969): 96–116.

——. "Presenting the Sultan's Power, Glory and Piety: A Comparative Perspective." In *Another Mirror for Princes: The Public Image of the Ottoman Sultans and its Reception*, 53–85. Istanbul: Isis Press, 2008.

Faulkner, William. *Requiem for a Nun*. New York: Random House, 1951.

Felek, Özgen, ed. *Kitābü'l-Menāmāt: Sultan III. Murad'ın Rüya Mektupları*. Istanbul: Tarih Vakfı Yurt Yayınları, 2014.

——. "(Re)creating Image and Identity: Dreams and Visions as a Means of Murād III's Self-Fashioning." In *Dreams and Visions in Islamic Societies*, edited by Özgen Felek and Alexander Knysh, 249–71. Albany: State University of New York Press, 2012.

Fetvacı, Emine. "Enriched Narratives and Empowered Images in Seventeenth-Century Ottoman Manuscripts." *Ars Orientalis* 40 (2011): 243–66.

——. "From Print to Trace: An Ottoman Imperial Portrait Book and Its Western European Models." *Art Bulletin* 95, no. 2 (2013): 243–68.

——. "The Office of Ottoman Court Historian." In *Studies on Istanbul and Beyond: The Freely Papers*, edited by Robert Ousterhout, vol. 1, 7–21. Philadelphia: The University of Pennsylvania Museum of Archaeology and Anthropology, 2007.

——. *Picturing History at the Ottoman Court*. Bloomington: Indiana University Press, 2013.

——. "The Production of the Şehnāme-i Selīm Ḫān." *Muqarnas* 26 (2009): 263–315.

Finkel, Caroline. *Osman's Dream: The Story of the Ottoman Empire, 1300–1923*. New York: Basic Books, 2006.

Fisher, Sydney Nettleton. *The Foreign Relations of Turkey, 1481–1512*. Urbana: University of Illinois Press, 1948.

Fleischer, Cornell. "Ancient Wisdom and New Sciences: Prophecies at the Ottoman Court in the Fifteenth and Early Sixteenth Centuries." In *Falnama: The Book of Omens*, edited by Massumeh Farhad and Serpil Bağcı, 231–43. London: Thames & Hudson, 2009.

——. *Bureaucrat and Intellectual in the Ottoman Empire: The Historian Mustafa Âli (1541–1600)*. Princeton: Princeton University Press, 1986.

——. "From Şeyhzade Korkud to Mustafa Âli: Cultural Origins of the Ottoman *Nasihatname*." In *Third Congress on the Social and Economic History of Turkey*, edited by Heath W. Lowry and Ralph S. Hattox, 67–77. Istanbul: The Isis Press, 1990.

———. "The Lawgiver as Messiah: The Making of the Imperial Image in the Reign of Süleyman." In *Soliman le Magnifique et son temps*, edited by Gilles Veinstein, 159–77. Paris: La Documentation Française, 1992.

———. "Mahdi and Millennium: Messianic Dimensions in the Development of Ottoman Imperial Ideology." In *Philosophy, Science and Institutions.* Vol. 3 of *The Great Ottoman-Turkish Civilisation*, edited by Kemal Çiçek, vol. 3: 42–54. Ankara: Yeni Türkiye Yayınları, 2000.

———. "Of Gender and Servitude, ca. 1520: Two Petitions of the Kul Kızı of Bergama to Sultan Süleyman." In *Mélanges en l'Honneur du Prof. Dr. Suraiya Faroqhi*, edited by Abdeljelil Temimi, 143–51. Tunis: Fondation Temimi pour la Recherche Scientifique et l'Information, 2009.

———. "Royal Authority, Dynastic Cyclism, and 'Ibn Khaldûnism' in Sixteenth-Century Ottoman Letters." *Journal of Asian and African Studies* 18, nos. 3–4 (1983): 198–220.

———. "Secretaries' Dreams: Augury and Angst in Ottoman Scribal Service." In *Armağan: Festschrift für Andreas Tietze*, edited by Ingeborg Baldauf and Suraiya Faroqhi, 77–88. Prag: Enigma Corporation, 1994.

———. "Seer to the Sultan: Haydar-i Remmal and Sultan Süleyman." In *Cultural Horizons: A Festschrift in Honor of Talat S. Halman*, edited by Jane L. Warner, 290–99. Syracuse, NY: Syracuse University Press, 2001.

———. "Shadows of Shadows: Prophecy in Politics in 1530s Istanbul." *International Journal of Turkish Studies* 13, nos. 1–2 (2007): 51–62.

Flemming, Barbara. "Der *Ǧāmiʿ ül-Meknūnāt*: Eine Quelle ʿĀlīs aus der Zeit Sultan Süleymāns." In *Studien zur Geschichte und Kultur des Vorderen Orients: Festschrift für Bertold Spuler zum Siebzigsten Geburtstag*, edited by Hans R. Roemer and Albrecht Noth, 79–92. Leiden: Brill, 1981.

———. "Political Genealogies in the Sixteenth Century." *Osmanlı Araştırmaları* 7–8 (1988): 123–37.

———. "Public Opinion under Sultan Süleymân." In *Süleymân the Second and His Time*, edited by Halil İnalcık and Cemal Kafadar, 49–57. Istanbul: The Isis Press, 1993.

———. "Ṣāḥib-Ḳırān und Mahdī: Türkische Endzeiterwartungen im ersten Jahrzehnt der Regierung Süleymāns." In *Between the Danube and the Caucasus*, edited by György Kara, 43–62. Budapest: Akadémiai Kiadó, 1987.

Fletcher, Joseph. "Integrative History: Parallels and Interconnections in the Early Modern Period, 1500–1800." *Journal of Turkish Studies* 9 (1985): 37–57.

——. "The Mongols: Ecological and Social Perspectives." *Harvard Journal of Asiatic Studies* 46, no. 1 (1986): 11–50.

——. "Turco-Mongolian Monarchic Tradition in the Ottoman Empire." *Harvard Ukrainian Studies* 3–4, no. 1 (1979–80): 236–51.

Floor, Willem. *Safavid Government Institutions*. Costa Mesa: Mazda Publishers, 2001.

Flügel, Gustav. *Die arabischen, persischen, türkischen Handschriften der kaiserlichen und königlichen Hofbibliothek zu Wien*. Vienna: Drück und Verlag der K. K. Hof- und Staatsdruckerei, 1865.

Fodor, Pál. "Aḥmedī's Dāsitān as a Source of Early Ottoman History." *Acta Orientalia Academiae Scientiarum Hungaricae* 38, nos. 1–2 (1984): 41–54.

——. "State and Society, Crisis and Reform, in 15th–17th Century Ottoman Mirror for Princes." *Acta Orientalia Academiae Scientiarum Hungaricae* 40, nos. 2–3 (1986): 217–40.

——. "Sultan, Imperial Council, Grand Vizier: Changes in the Ottoman Ruling Elite and the Formation of the Grand Vizieral *Telḫīṣ*." *Acta Orientalia Academiae Scientiarum Hungaricae* 47, nos. 1–2 (1994): 67–85.

——. "Ungarn und Wien in der Osmanischen Eroberungsideologie (im Spiegel der *Târîḫ-i Beç Ḳralı*–17. Jahrhundert)." In *In Quest of the Golden Apple: Imperial Ideology, Politics, and Military Administration in the Ottoman Empire*, 45–69. Istanbul: Isis Press, 2000.

——. "The View of the Turk in Hungary: The Apocalyptic Tradition and the Legend of the Red Apple in Ottoman Hungarian Context." In *In Quest of the Golden Apple: Imperial Ideology, Politics, and Military Administration in the Ottoman Empire*, 71–103. Istanbul: Isis Press, 2000.

Fotić, Alexandar. "Yahyapaşa-oğlu Mehmed Pasha's *Evkaf* in Belgrade." *Acta Orientalia Academiae Scientiarum Hungaricae* 54, no. 4 (2001): 437–52.

Francis, Edgar W. "Magic and Divination in the Medieval Islamic Middle East." *History Compass* 9, no. 8 (2011): 622–33.

Galabov, Galab. "Turetskie dokumentiy po istorii goroda Karlovo." In *Vostochniye istochniki po istorii narodov Yugo-vostochnoy i Tsentralnoy Evropiy*, edited by Anna Stepanovna, 162–85. Moscow: Nauka, 1964.

Galanté, Abraham. *Médecins juifs au service de la Turquie*. Istanbul: Babok, 1938.

Gazimihal, Mahmut Ragıp. "Harmankaya Nerededir?" *Uludağ: Bursa Halkevi Dergisi* 72–73 (1945): 1–4.

——. "Harmankaya Nerededir III: Kitabe, Türbe ve Rivayetler." *Uludağ: Bursa Halkevi Dergisi* 77 (1946): 1–7.

——. "Harmancık ve Mihaloğulları I." *Uludağ: Bursa Halkevi Dergisi* 78 (1946): 9–13.

——. "Harmancık ve Mihaloğulları II." *Uludağ: Bursa Halkevi Dergisi* 79 (1946): 4–10.

——. "İstanbul Muhasaralarında Mihâloğulları ve Fatih Devrine Ait Bir Vakıf Defterine Göre Harmankaya Mâlikânesi." *Vakıflar Dergisi* 4 (1957): 125–38.

——. "Rumeli Mihaloğulları ve Harmankaya." *Uludağ: Bursa Halkevi Dergisi* 81 (1947): 21–26.

Gero, Gyozo. "Neuere Angaben zur Geschichte der türkischen Architektur in Ungarn: Die Malkotsch Bey Dschami in Siklós." *Materialia Turcica* 7, no. 8 (1981–82): 191–209.

Gibb, Hamilton. "Luṭfī Paşa on the Ottoman Caliphate." *Oriens* 15 (1962): 287–95.

Ginzburg, Carlo. *The Cheese and the Worms: The Cosmos of a Sixteenth-Century Miller.* Translated by John Tedeschi and Anne Tedeschi. Baltimore: Johns Hopkins University Press, 1980.

Glassen, Erika. "Schah Ismāʿīl, ein Mahdī der anatolischen Turkmenen?" *ZDMG* 121, no. 1 (1971): 61–69.

Goffman, Daniel. *The Ottoman Empire and Early Modern Europe.* Cambridge, UK, and New York: Cambridge University Press, 2002.

Gökbilgin, M. Tayyib. "Rüstem Paşa ve Hakkındaki İthamlar." *TD* 8, nos. 11–12 (1955): 11–50.

——. *XV. ve XVI. Asırlarda Edirne ve Paşa Livası: Vakıflar-Mülkler-Mukataalar.* 2nd ed. Istanbul: İşaret Yayınları, 2007.

Gökçek, Yaşar. "Köse Mihal Oğulları." Bachelor's thesis, Istanbul University, 1950.

Goldstone, Jack A. "The Problem of the 'Early Modern' World." *Journal of the Economic and Social History of the Orient* 41, no. 3 (1998): 249–84.

Goldziher, Ignác. "The Appearance of the Prophet in Dreams." *Journal of the Royal Asiatic Society of Great Britain and Ireland* (1912): 503–6.

Gölpınarlı, Abdülbaki. *Melâmîlik ve Melâmîler.* Istanbul: Devlet Matbaası, 1931.

Goody, Jack. *The Eurasian Miracle.* Cambridge, MA: Polity, 2009.

Green, Nile. "The Religious and Cultural Roles of Dreams and Visions in Islam." *Journal of the Royal Asiatic Society* 13, no. 3 (2003): 287–313.

Gruber, Christiane Jacqueline. "Divination." In *Medieval Islamic Civilization: An Encyclopedia*, edited by Josef W. Meri, 209–11. New York: Routledge, 2006.

——. "The 'Restored' Shīʿī *muṣḥaf* as Divine Guide? The Practice of *fāl-i Qur'ān* in the Ṣafavid Period." *Journal of Qur'anic Studies* 13, no. 2 (2011): 29–55.

Guenée, Bernard. *States and Rulers in Late Medieval Europe*. Oxford: B. Blackwell, 1985.

Güzelbey, Cemil Cahit. *Gaziantep Evliyaları*. Gaziantep: Güneş Matbaası, 1964.

Hagen, Gottfried. "Afterword: Ottoman Understandings of the World in the Seventeenth Century." In *An Ottoman Mentality: The World of Evliya Çelebi*, edited by Robert Dankoff, 215–56. Leiden: Brill, 2004.

——. "Dreaming ʿOsmāns: Of History and Meaning." In *Dreams and Visions in Islamic Societies*, edited by Özgen Felek and Alexander Knysh, 99–122. Albany: State University of New York Press, 2012.

——. "Legitimacy and World Order." In *Legitimizing the Order: The Ottoman Rhetoric of State Power*, edited by Hakan Karateke and Maurus Reinkowski, 55–83. Leiden: Brill, 2005.

——. "Review of *An Ottoman Tragedy: History and Historiography at Play* (by Gabriel Piterberg)." H-Turk (https://networks.h-net.org/h-turk) (April 2006).

Hagen, Gottfried, and Ethan M. Menchinger. "Ottoman Historical Thought." In *A Companion to Global Historical Thought*, edited by Prasenjit Duara, Viren Murthy, and Andrew Sartori, 92–106. Chichester, UK: Wiley Blackwell, 2014.

Halaçoğlu, Yusuf. "Teselya Yenişehiri ve Türk Eserleri Hakkında Bir Araştırma." *Güneydoğu Avrupa Araştırmaları Dergisi* 2–3 (1973–74): 89–99.

Hanna, Nelly. *Making Big Money in 1600: The Life and Times of Ismaʿil Abu Taqiyya, Egyptian Merchant*. Syracuse: Syracuse University Press, 1998.

Hathaway, Jane. *The Arab Lands under Ottoman Rule, 1516-1800*. With contributions by Karl K. Barbir. London: Pearson Longman, 2008.

——. *Beshir Agha: Chief Eunuch of the Ottoman Imperial Harem*. Oxford: Oneworld, 2005.

——. "The *Evlâd-i ʿArab* ('Sons of the Arabs') in Ottoman Egypt: A Rereading." In *Frontiers of Ottoman Studies*, edited by Colin Imber and Keiko Kiyotaki, vol. 1, 203–16. London: I. B. Tauris, 2005.

——. "The Iconography of the Sword Zülfikâr in the Ottoman World (with Special Reference to Egypt)." *International Congress on Learning and Education in the Ottoman World, Istanbul, 12-15 April, 1999*, edited by Ali Çaksu, 365–75. Istanbul: IRCICA, 2001.

——. *The Politics of Households in Ottoman Egypt: The Rise of the Qazdağlıs.* Cambridge, UK: Cambridge University Press, 1997.

——. *A Tale of Two Factions: Myth, Memory, and Identity in Ottoman Egypt and Yemen.* Albany: State University of New York Press, 2003.

——. "The Wealth and Influence of an Exiled Ottoman Eunuch in Egypt: The Waqf Inventory of Abbas Agha." *JESHO* 37, no. 4 (1994): 293–317.

Heeren-Sarka, Ctirad. *Sultan Bāyezīd II. (1481-1512) in der Chronik des Muṣṭafā Ğenābī.* München: R. Trofenik, 1980.

Heller, Erdmute. "Venedische Quellen zur Lebensgeschichte des Ahmed Paša Hersekoghlu." PhD diss., Ludwig-Maximilians Universität München, 1961.

Hess, Andrew C. "The Ottoman Conquest of Egypt (1517) and the Beginning of the Sixteenth-Century World War." *International Journal of Middle East Studies* 4, no. 1 (1973): 55–76.

Hillenbrand, Robert. "The Iconography of the Shah-namah-yi Shahi." In *Safavid Persia: The History and Politics of an Islamic Society*, edited by Charles Melville, 53–78. London: I. B. Tauris, 1996.

Hodgson, Marshall G. S. *The Gunpowder Empires and Modern Times.* Vol. 3 of *The Venture of Islam: Conscience and History in a World Civilization.* Chicago: The University of Chicago Press, 1974.

——. "A Note on the Millennium in Islam." In *Millennial Dreams in Action: Essays in Comparative Study*, edited by Sylvia L. Thrupp, 218–19. The Hague: Mouton, 1962.

Howard, Douglas A. "Genre and Myth in the Ottoman Advice for Kings Literature." In *The Early Modern Ottomans: Remapping the Empire*, edited by Virginia H. Aksan and Daniel Goffman, 137–66. Cambridge, UK: Cambridge University Press, 2007.

——. "Ottoman Historiography and the Literature of 'Decline' of the Sixteenth and Seventeenth Centuries." *Journal of Asian History* 22, no. 1 (1988): 52–77.

Imber, Colin. "Frozen Legitimacy." In *Legitimizing the Order: The Ottoman Rhetoric of State Power*, edited by Hakan Karateke and Maurus Reinkowski, 99–107. Leiden: Brill, 2005.

——. "Ideals and Legitimation in Early Ottoman History." In *Süleyman the Magnificent and His Age: The Ottoman Empire in the Early Modern World*, edited by Metin Kunt and Christine Woodhead, 138–53. London and New York: Longman, 1995.

———. "The Ottoman Dynastic Myth." *Turcica* 19 (1987): 7–27.
———. *The Ottoman Empire, 1300–1481*. Istanbul: Isis Press, 1990.
———. *The Ottoman Empire, 1300-1650: The Structure of Power*. New York: Palgrave Macmillan, 2002.
———. "Süleymân as Caliph of the Muslims: Formulation of Ottoman Dynastic Ideology." In *Soliman le Magnifique et son temps*, edited by Gilles Veinstein, 179–84. Paris: La Documentation Française, 1992.
İnalcık, Halil. "Adâletnâmeler." *Belgeler* 2, nos. 3–4 (1965): 49–145.
———. "Osmanlılar'da Saltanat Verâseti Usûlü ve Türk Hakimiyet Telâkkisiyle İlgisi." *AÜSBFD* 14, no. 1 (1959): 69–94.
———. "Periods in Ottoman History: State, Society, Economy." In *Ottoman Civilization*, edited by Halil İnalcık and Günsel Renda, vol. 1, 31–239. Ankara: Republic of Turkey, Ministry of Culture, 2003.
———. "Power Relationships between Russia, the Crimea and the Ottoman Empire as Reflected in Titulature." In *Turco-Tatar Past, Soviet Present: Studies Presented to Alexandre Bennigsen*, edited by Ch. Lemercier-Quelquejay, G. Veinstein, and S. E. Wimbush, 175–211. Paris: Éditions Peeters, 1986.
———. "The Rise of the Ottoman Empire." In *A History of the Ottoman Empire to 1730*, edited by M. A. Cook, 10–53. Cambridge, UK: Cambridge University Press, 1976.
———. "The Rise of Ottoman Historiography." In *Historians of the Middle East*, edited by Bernard Lewis and P. M. Holt, 152–67. London: Oxford University Press, 1962.
———. "State, Sovereignty and Law during the Reign of Süleymân." In *Süleymân the Second and His Time*, edited by Halil Inalcık and Cemal Kafadar, 59–92. Istanbul: Isis Press, 1993.
———. "Sultan Süleymân: The Man and the Statesman." In *Soliman le Magnifique et son temps*, edited by Gilles Veinstein, 89–103. Paris: La Documentation Française, 1992.
İnalcık, Halil, and Cemal Kafadar, eds. *Süleymân the Second and his Time*. Istanbul: The Isis Press, 1993.
İpşirli, Mehmet. "Ottoman Historiography." In *Culture and Learning in Islam*. Vol. 5 of *The Different Aspects of Islamic Culture*, edited by Ekmeleddin İhsanoğlu, 525–37. Paris: UNESCO, 2003.
Ivanics, Mária. "The Military Co-operation of the Crimean Khanate with the Ottoman Empire in the Sixteenth and Seventeenth Centuries."

In *The European Tributary States of the Ottoman Empire in the Sixteenth and Seventeenth Centuries*, edited by Gabor Karman and Lovro Kunčević, 275–99. Leiden: Brill, 2013.

Jaspers, Karl. *Vom Ursprung und Ziel der Geschichte*. Zurich: Artemis-Verlag, 1949.

Kafadar, Cemal. *Between Two Worlds: The Construction of the Ottoman State*. Berkeley: University of California Press, 1995.

———. "Eyüp'te Kılıç Kuşanma Törenleri." In *Eyüp: Dün/Bugün*, edited by Tülay Artan, 50–61. Istanbul: Tarih Vakfı Yurt Yayınları, 1994.

———. "Janissaries and Other Riffraff of Ottoman İstanbul: Rebels Without a Cause?" *International Journal of Turkish Studies* 13, nos. 1–2 (2007): 113–34.

———. "The Myth of the Golden Age: Ottoman Historical Consciousness in the Post-Süleymânic Era." In *Süleymân the Second and His Time*, edited by Halil İnalcık and Cemal Kafadar, 37–48. Istanbul: Isis Press, 1993.

———. "ʿOs̱mān Beg and His Uncle: Murder in the Family?" In *Studies in Ottoman History in Honour of Professor V. L. Ménage*, edited by Colin Heywood and Colin Imber, 157–63. Istanbul: Isis Press, 1994.

———. "The Ottomans and Europe." In *Structures and Assertions*. Vol. 1 of *Handbook of European History, 1400–1600: Late Middle Ages, Renaissance, and Reformation*, edited by Thomas A. Brady, Heiko A. Oberman, and James D. Tracy, 589–635. Brill: Leiden, 1994.

———. "The Question of Ottoman Decline." *Harvard Middle Eastern and Islamic Review* 4, nos. 1–2 (1997–98): 30–75.

———. "A Rome of One's Own: Reflections on Cultural Geography and Identity in the Lands of Rum." *Muqarnas* 24 (2007): 7–25.

———. *Rüya Mektupları: Asiye Hatun*. Istanbul: Oğlak Yayıncılık, 1994.

———. "Self and Others: The Diary of a Dervish in Seventeenth Century Istanbul and First-Person Narratives in Ottoman Literature." *Studia Islamica* 69 (1989): 121–50.

Kagan, Richard L. *Lucrecia's Dreams: Politics and Prophecy in Sixteenth-Century Spain*. Berkeley: University of California Press, 1990.

Káldy-Nagy, Gyula. "The First Centuries of the Ottoman Military Organization." *Acta Orientalia Academiae Scientiarum Hungaricae* 31, no. 2 (1977): 147–83.

———. "The 'Strangers' (*Ecnebiler*) in the 16th Century Ottoman Military Organization." In *Between the Danube and the Caucasus*, edited by György Kara, 165–69. Budapest: Akadémiai Kiadó, 1987.

Kangal, Selmin (ed.). *The Sultan's Portrait: Picturing the House of Osman.* Istanbul: İşbank, 2000.
Kantorowicz, Ernst H. *The King's Two Bodies: A Study in Mediaeval Political Theology.* Princeton: Princeton University Press, 1957.
Kaptein, Laban. *Apocalypse and the Antichrist Dajjal in Islam: Ahmed Bijan's Eschatology Revisited.* Asch, 2011.
Karal, Enver Ziya. "Yavuz Sultan Selim'in Oğlu Şehzade Süleyman'a Manisa Sancağını İdare Etmesi İçin Gönderdiği Siyasetnâme." *Belleten* 6, nos. 21–22 (1942): 37–44.
Karamustafa, Ahmet T. *God's Unruly Friends: Dervish Groups in the Islamic Later Middle Period, 1200–1500.* Oxford, UK: Oneworld, 2006.
Karateke, Hakan. "Legitimizing the Ottoman Sultanate: A Framework for Historical Analysis." In *Legitimizing the Order: The Ottoman Rhetoric of State Power,* edited by Hakan Karateke and Maurus Reinkowski, 13–52. Leiden: Brill, 2005.
———. "'On the Tranquillity and Repose of the Sultan': The Construction of a *Topos.*" In *The Ottoman World,* edited by Christine Woodhead, 116–29. New York: Routledge, 2011.
Kastritsis, Dimitris J. "The Historical Epic *Aḥvāl-i Sulṭān Meḥemmed* (The Tales of Sultan Mehmed) in the Context of Early Ottoman Historiography." In *Writing History at the Ottoman Court: Editing the Past, Fashioning the Future,* edited by H. Erdem Çıpa and Emine Fetvacı, 1–22. Bloomington: Indiana University Press, 2013.
———. *The Sons of Bayezid: Empire Building and Representation in the Ottoman Civil War of 1402–13.* Leiden: Brill, 2007.
Kayapınar, Ayşe. "Kuzey Bulgaristan'da Gazi Mihaloğulları Vakıfları (XV ve XVI. Yüzyıl)." *Abant İzzet Baysal Üniversitesi Sosyal Bilimler Enstitüsü Dergisi* 10 (2005): 169–81.
Kayapınar, Levent. "The Charitable Foundations of the Family of Turahan Bey Who Conquered Thessaly Region in Greece in the 15th–16th Centuries." In *Proceedings of the Second International Symposium on Islamic Civilisation in the Balkans (Tirana, Albania, 4–7 December 2003),* 149–62. Istanbul: IRCICA, 2006.
———. "Teselya Bölgesinin Fatihi Turahan Bey Ailesi ve XV.–XVI. Yüzyıllardaki Hayır Kurumları." *Abant İzzet Baysal Üniversitesi Sosyal Bilimler Enstitüsü Dergisi* 10 (2005): 183–95.
Kazancıgil, Ratip. "Gazi Mihal İmareti: Orta İmaret." In *Edirne İmaretleri,* 27–32. Istanbul: Türk Kütüphaneciler Derneği Edirne Şubesi Yayınları, 1991.

Kepecioğlu, Kamil. "Bursa'da Şer'î Mahkeme Sicillerinden ve Muhtelif Arşiv Kayıtlarından Toplanan Tarihi Bilgiler ve Vesikalar." *Vakıflar Dergisi* 2 (1942): 405–17.

Kerslake, Celia. "The Correspondence between Selīm I and Ḳānṣūh al-Ğawrī." *Revue de Philologie Orientale* 10 (1980): 219–34.

———. "A Critical Edition and Translation of the Introductory Sections and the First Thirteen Chapters of the Selimname of Celalzade Mustafa Çelebi." PhD diss., University of Oxford, 1975.

———. "Review of *The Reign of Sultan Selīm in the Light of the Selīm-nāme Literature* (by Ahmet Uğur)." *BSOAS* 51, no. 2 (1988): 346–48.

———. "The *Selīm-nāme* of Celāl-zāde Muṣṭafā Çelebi as a Historical Source." *Turcica* 9, nos. 2–10 (1978): 39–51.

Kiel, Machiel. "Das türkische Thessalien: Etabliertes Geschichtsbild versus Osmanische Quellen." In *Die Kultur Griechenlands in Mittelalter und Neuzeit*, edited by Reinhard Lauer and Peter Schreiner, 109–96. Göttingen: Vandenhoeck & Ruprecht, 1996.

Kinberg, Leah. "Dreams as a Means to Evaluate Ḥadith." *Jerusalem Studies in Arabic and Islam* 23 (1999): 79–99.

———. "Interaction between This World and the Afterworld in Early Islamic Tradition." *Oriens* 29–30 (1986): 285–308.

———. "The Legitimization of the *Madhāhib* through Dreams." *Arabica* 32, no. 1 (1985): 47–79.

———. "Literal Dreams and Prophetic *Ḥadīṯs* in Classical Islam—A Comparison of Two Ways of Legitimation." *Der Islam* 70, no. 2 (1993): 279–300.

Kiprovska, Mariya. "Byzantine Renegade and Holy Warrior: Reassessing the Character of Köse Mihal, a Hero of the Byzantino-Ottoman Borderland." *Journal of Turkish Studies* 40 (2013): 245–69. (Special Issue: *Defterology: Festschrift in Honor of Heath Lowry*, edited by Selim S. Kuru and Baki Tezcan. Cambridge: Harvard University, Department of Near Eastern Languages and Civilizations, 2013.)

———. "The Mihaloğlu Family: *Gazi* Warriors and Patrons of Dervish Hospices." *Osmanlı Araştırmaları* 32 (2008): 193–222.

———. "The Military Organization of the *Akıncıs* in Ottoman Rumelia." Master's thesis, Bilkent University, 2004.

———. "Shaping the Ottoman Borderland: The Architectural Patronage of the Frontier Lords from the Mihaloğlu Family." In *Bordering Early Modern Europe*, edited by Ivan Parvev, Maria Baramova, and Grigor Boykov, 185–220. Wiesbaden: Harrassowitz Verlag, 2015.

Kister, M. J. "The Interpretation of Dreams: An Unknown Manuscript of Ibn Qutayba's *ʿIbārat al-Ruʾyā*." *Israel Oriental Studies* 4 (1974): 67–103.

Köprülü, M. Fuat. "Türkler'de Halk Hikâyeciliğine Âit Bâzı Maddeler: Meddahlar." In *Edebiyat Araştırmaları*, 361–412. Ankara: Türk Tarih Kurumu Basımevi, 1966.

Kortepeter, Carl Max. *Ottoman Imperialism during the Reformation: Europe and the Caucasus*. New York: New York University Press, 1972.

Królikowska, Natalia. "Sovereignty and Subordination in Crimean-Ottoman Relations (Sixteenth–Eighteenth Centuries)." In *The European Tributary States of the Ottoman Empire in the Sixteenth and Seventeenth Centuries*, edited by Gabor Karman and Lovro Kunčević, 43–65. Leiden: Brill, 2013.

Krstić, Tijana. *Contested Conversions to Islam: Narratives of Religious Change in the Early Modern Ottoman Empire*. Stanford: Stanford University Press, 2011.

——. "Conversion and Converts to Islam in Ottoman Historiography of the Fifteenth and Sixteenth Centuries." In *Writing History at the Ottoman Court: Editing the Past, Fashioning the Future*, edited by H. Erdem Çıpa and Emine Fetvacı, 58–79. Bloomington: Indiana University Press, 2013.

Kumbaracı-Bogojeviç, Lidiya. *Üsküp'te Osmanlı Mimarî Eserleri*. Istanbul: Enka, 2008.

Kunt, İ. Metin. "Ethnic-Regional (*Cins*) Solidarity in the Seventeenth-Century Ottoman Establishment." *International Journal of Middle East Studies* 5, no. 3 (1974): 233–39.

——. "The Later Muslim Empires: Ottomans, Safavids, Mughals." In *Islam: The Religious and Political Life of a World Community*, edited by Marjorie Kelly, 113–36. New York: Praeger, 1984.

——. "Sultan, Dynasty and State in the Ottoman Empire: Political Institutions in the Sixteenth Century." *The Medieval History Journal* 6, no. 2 (2003): 217–30.

——. *The Sultan's Servants: The Transformation of Ottoman Provincial Government, 1550–1650*. New York: Columbia University Press, 1983.

——. "Turks in the Ottoman Imperial Palace." In *Royal Courts in Dynastic States and Empires*, edited by Jeroen Duindam, Tülay Artan, and Metin Kunt, 289–312. Boston: Brill, 2011.

Kunt, İ. Metin, and Christine Woodhead, eds. *Süleyman the Magnificent and His Age: The Ottoman Empire in the Early Modern World*. London and New York: Longman, 1995.

Kurat, Akdes Nimet. *Die türkische Prosopographie bei Laonikos Chalkokandyles.* Hamburg: Neimann & Moschinski, 1933.

Kürkçüoğlu, Kemâl Edîb, ed. *Süleymaniye Vakfiyesi*. Ankara: Vakıflar Umum Müdürlüğü, 1962.

Kütükoğlu, Bekir. "Şehnâmeci Lokman." In *Prof. Dr. Bekir Kütükoğlu'na Armağan*, 39–48. Istanbul: Edebiyat Fakültesi Basımevi, 1991.

Lambton, Ann K. S. "Quis Custodiet Custodes: Some Reflections on the Persian Theory of Government." *Studia Islamica* 5 (1956): 125–48; 6 (1956): 125–46.

Landau-Tasseron, Ella. "The 'Cyclical Reform': A Study of the *Mujaddid* Tradition." *Studia Islamica* 70 (1989): 79–117.

Lane-Poole, Stanley. *The Story of Turkey*. New York: G. P. Putnam's Sons, 1897.

Lellouch, Benjamin. *Les Ottomans en Égypte: Historiens et conquérants au XVIe siècle*. Paris: Peeters, 2006.

Lellouch, Benjamin, and Nicolas Michel, eds. *Conquête ottomane de l'Égypte (1517): Arrière-plan, Impact, Échos*. Leiden: Brill, 2013.

Levend, Agâh Sırrı. *Ġazavāt-nāmeler ve Mihaloğlu Ali Bey'in Ġazavāt-nāmesi*. Ankara: Türk Tarih Kurumu, 1956.

——. "Siyaset-nameler." *Türk Dili Araştırmaları Yıllığı: Belleten* (1963): 167–94.

Lewis, Bernard. "Ottoman Observers of Ottoman Decline." *Islamic Studies* 1, no. 1 (1962): 71–87.

——. *The Political Language of Islam*. Chicago: The University of Chicago Press, 1988.

——. "The Privilege Granted by Meḥmed II to His Physician." *BSOAS* 14, no. 3 (1952): 550–63.

——. "Some Reflections on the Decline of the Ottoman Empire." *Studia Islamica Studies* 9 (1958): 111–27.

Lewis, G. L. "The Utility of Ottoman Fetḥnāmes." In *Historians of the Middle East*, edited by Bernard Lewis and P. M. Holt, 192–96. London: Oxford University Press, 1962.

Libby, Lester J. "Venetian Views of the Ottoman Empire from the Peace of 1503 to the War of Cyprus." *Sixteenth Century Journal* 9, no. 4 (1978): 103–26.

Lieberman, Victor, ed. *Beyond Binary Histories: Re-Imagining Eurasia to c. 1830*. Ann Arbor: University of Michigan Press, 1999.

——. *Strange Parallels: Southeast Asia in Global Context, c. 800–1830*. 2 vols. New York: Cambridge University Press, 2003.

Lory, Pierre. *Le rêve et ses interprétations en Islam*. Paris: Albin Michel, 2003.

Lowry, Heath W. *Hersekzâde Ahmed Paşa: An Ottoman Statesman's Career & Pious Endowments*. Istanbul: Bahçeşehir University Press, 2011.

———. *The Nature of the Early Ottoman State*. Albany: State University of New York Press, 2003.

———. *The Shaping of the Ottoman Balkans, 1350–1550: The Conquest, Settlement & Infrastructural Development of Northern Greece*. Istanbul: Bahçeşehir University Press, 2008.

Mahir, Banu. "A Group of 17th Century Paintings Used for Picture Recitation." In *Turkish Art: 10th International Congress of Turkish Art, Geneva, 17-23 September, 1995*, 443–55. Geneva: Max van Berchem Foundation, 1999.

Mantran, Robert. "L'historiographie ottomane à l'époque de Soliman le Magnifique." In *Soliman le Magnifique et son temps*, edited by Gilles Veinstein, 25–32. Paris: La Documentation Française, 1992.

Masters, Bruce. *The Arabs of the Ottoman Empire, 1516–1918: A Social and Cultural History*. Cambridge, UK: Cambridge University Press, 2013.

Mazzaoui, Michel M. "Global Policies of Sultan Selim, 1512–1520." In *Essays on Islamic Civilization Presented to Niyazi Berkes*, edited by Donald P. Little, 224–43. Leiden: Brill, 1976.

Meḥmed Süreyyā. *Sicill-i ʿOs̱mānī*. (1) 4 vols. Istanbul: Maṭbaʿa-i ʿĀmire, 1308–11/1890–93. (2) 6 vols. Edited and transliterated by Nuri Akbayar. In *Sicill-i Osmanî: Osmanlı Ünlüleri*. Istanbul: Tarih Vakfı Yurt Yayınları, 1996.

Meḥmed Ṭāhir [Bursalı]. *ʿOs̱mānlı Müʾellifleri*. 3 vols. Istanbul: Maṭbaʿa-yı ʿĀmire, 1333–43/1914–25.

Melville, Charles, and Van den Berg, Gabrielle, eds. *Shahnama Studies II: The Reception of Firdausi's* Shahnama. Leiden: Brill, 2012.

Melville-Jones, John R. "Three Mustafas (1402–1430)." *Annuario. Istituto Romeno di cultura e ricerca umanistica* 5 (2004): 255–76.

Ménage, Victor L. "The Beginnings of Ottoman Historiography." In *Historians of the Middle East*, edited by Bernard Lewis and P. M. Holt, 168–79. London: Oxford University Press, 1962.

———. "A Survey of the Early Ottoman Histories, with Studies on Their Textual Problems and Their Sources." PhD diss., University of London, 1961.

Mengüç, Murat Cem. "Histories of Bayezid I, Historians of Bayezid II: Rethinking Late Fifteenth-Century Ottoman Historiography." *BSOAS* 76, no. 3 (2013): 373–89.

Minorsky, Vladimir. "The Poetry of Shāh Ismāʿīl I." *BSOAS* 10, no. 4 (1942): 1005–53.

Moin, A. Azfar. *The Millennial Sovereign: Sacred Kingship and Sainthood in Islam*. New York: Columbia University Press, 2012.

Mottahedeh, Roy P. *Loyalty and Leadership in an Early Islamic Society*. Princeton: Princeton University Press, 1980.

Murphey, Rhoads. *Exploring Ottoman Sovereignty: Tradition, Image and Practice in the Ottoman Imperial Household, 1400-1800*. London: Hambledon Continuum, 2008.

——. *Ottoman Warfare, 1500-1700*. New Brunswick, NJ: Rutgers University Press, 1999.

Nāmıḳ Kemāl. "Yāvuz Sulṭān Selīm." In *Evrāk-ı Perīşān*. Modern Turkish edition by İskender Pala as *Namık Kemal'in Tarihî Biyografileri*, 117–54. Ankara: Türk Tarih Kurumu Basımevi, 1989.

Necipoğlu, Gülru. *The Age of Sinan: Architectural Culture in the Ottoman Empire*. London: Reaktion, 2005.

——. *Architecture, Ceremonial, and Power: The Topkapı Palace in the Fifteenth and Sixteenth Centuries*. Cambridge, MA: MIT Press, 1991.

——. "A Ḳānūn for the State, a Canon for the Arts: Conceptualizing the Classical Synthesis of Ottoman Art and Architecture." In *Soliman le Magnifique et son temps*, edited by Gilles Veinstein, 195–216. Paris: La Documentation Française, 1992.

——. "The Süleymaniye Complex in Istanbul: An Interpretation." *Muqarnas* 3 (1985): 92–117.

——. "Süleyman the Magnificent and the Representation of Power in the Context of Ottoman-Hapsburg Rivalry." *Art Bulletin* 71, no. 3 (1989): 401–27.

——. "Word and Image: The Serial Portraits of Ottoman Sultans in Comparative Perspective." In *The Sultan's Portrait: Picturing the House of Osman*, edited by Selmin Kangal, 22–61. Istanbul: İşbank, 2000.

Neumann, Christoph. "Üç Tarz-ı Mütalaa: Yeniçağ Osmanlı Dünyası'nda Kitap Yazmak ve Okumak." *Tarih ve Toplum Yeni Yaklaşımlar* 1 (2005): 51–76.

Newman, Andrew J. *Safavid Iran: Rebirth of a Persian Empire*. London: I. B. Tauris, 2009.

Niyazioğlu, Aslı. "The Very Special Dead and a Seventeenth-Century Ottoman Poet: Nevʾīzāde ʿAṭāʾī's Reasons for Composing his *Meṡnevīs*." *Archivum Ottomanicum* 25 (2008): 221–32.

Nora, Pierre. "Between Memory and History: *Les Lieux de Mémoire.*" *Representations* 26 (Special Issue: Memory and Counter-Memory, 1989): 7–24.

Nüzhet Paşa. *Aḥvāl-i Ġāzī Mīḫāl*. Dersaʿādet [Istanbul]: Yovānākī Panāyoṭīdīs Maṭbaʿası, 1315/1896–97.

Oberhelman, Steven M. *Dreambooks in Byzantium: Six Oneirocritica in Translation*. Aldershot: Ashgate, 2008.

Ocak, Ahmet Yaşar. "XVI. Yüzyıl Osmanlı Anadolu'sunda Mesiyanik Hareketlerinin Bir Tahlil Denemesi." In *V. Milletlerarası Türkiye Sosyal ve İktisat Tarihi Kongresi: Tebliğler*, 817–25. Ankara: Türk Tarih Kurumu, 1990.

Ohlander, Erik S. "Behind the Veil of the Unseen: Dreams and Dreaming in the Classical and Medieval Sufi Tradition." In *Dreams and Visions in Islamic Societies*, edited by Özgen Felek and Alexander Knysh, 199–213. Albany: State University of New York Press, 2012.

Onat, Naim Hazım. "'Yavuz' ve Bununla İlgili Bazı Kelimelerimizin Arap Diline Geçmiş Şekilleri." *Belleten* 17 (1953): 123–48.

Öz, Tahsin. "Topkapı Sarayı Müzesinde Yemen Fatihi Sinan Paşa Arşivi." *Belleten* 10 (1946): 171–93.

Özcan, Abdülkadir. "Fâtih'in Teşkilât Kanunnâmesi ve Nizam-ı Alem İçin Kardeş Katli Meselesi." *TD* 33 (1980–81): 7–56.

———. "Kanuni Sultan Süleyman Devri Tarih Yazıcılığı ve Literatürü." In *Prof. Dr. Mübahat S. Kütükoğlu'na Armağan*, edited by Zeynep Tarım Ertuğ, 113–546. Istanbul: İstanbul Üniversitesi Yayınları, 2006.

Özer, Mustafa. "Edirne'de Mihaloğulları'nın İmar Faaliyetleri ve Bu Aileye Ait Mezar Taşlarının Değerlendirilmesi." In *1. Edirne Kültür Araştırmaları Sempozyumu Bildirileri (23-25 Ekim 2003)*, edited by Levent Doğan, 311–46. Istanbul: Edirne Valiliği, 2003.

———. "Edirne-Uzunköprü-Kırkkavak Köyü Gazi Turhan Bey Külliyesi." In *Sanatta Anadolu-Asya İlişkileri*, edited by Turgay Yazar, 367–88. Ankara: Hacettepe Üniversitesi Yayınları, 2006.

Öztuna, Yılmaz. *Yavuz Sultan Selim*. Istanbul: Babıali Kültür Yayıncılığı, 2006.

Pakalın, Mehmet Zeki. *Osmanlı Tarih Deyimleri ve Terimleri Sözlüğü*. 3 vols. Istanbul: Milli Eğitim Basımevi, 1946.

Pala, Ayhan. "Rumeli'de Bir Akıncı Ailesi: Gümlüoğulları ve Vakıfları." *Hacı Bektaş Veli Dergisi* 43 (2007): 137–44.

Parker, Geoffrey. "The Place of Tudor England in the Messianic Vision of Phillip II of Spain." *Transactions of the Royal Historical Society* 12 (2002): 167–221.

Parmaksızoğlu, İsmet. "Üsküplü İshak Çelebi ve Selimnâmesi." *TD* 5–6 (1953): 123–34.

Parry, V. J. "The Successors of Sulaimān, 1566–1617." In *A History of the Ottoman Empire to 1730: Chapters from the Cambridge History of Islam and the New Cambridge Modern History*, edited by M. A. Cook, 103–32. Cambridge, UK: Cambridge University Press, 1976.

Partner, Nancy. "Making Up Lost Time: Writing on the Writing of History." *Speculum* 61, no. 1 (1986): 90–117.

Peirce, Leslie P. *The Imperial Harem: Women and Sovereignty in the Ottoman Empire*. Oxford: Oxford University Press, 1993.

———. *Morality Tales: Law and Gender in the Ottoman Court of Aintab*. Berkeley: University of California Press, 2003.

Pitcher, Donald Edgar. *An Historical Geography of the Ottoman Empire*. Leiden: Brill, 1972.

Piterberg, Gabriel. *An Ottoman Tragedy: History and Historiography at Play*. Berkeley: University of California Press, 2003.

Quinn, Sholeh A. "The Dreams of Shaykh Safi al-Din and Safavid Historical Writing." *Iranian Studies* 29, nos. 1–2 (1996): 127–47.

Raby, Julian. "A Sultan of Paradox: Mehmed the Conqueror as a Patron of the Arts." *Oxford Art Journal* 5, no. 1 (1982): 3–8.

Rahman, Fazlur. "Dream, Imagination, and *ʿĀlam al-mithāl*." In *The Dream and Human Societies*, edited by G. E. von Grunebaum and Roger Caillois, 409–19. Berkeley: University of California Press, 1966.

Reindl, Hedda. *Männer um Bāyezīd: Eine Prosopographische Studie über die Epoche Sultan Bāyezīds II. (1481–1512)*. Berlin: K. Schwarz, 1983.

———. "Some Notes on Hersekzade Ahmed Pasha, His Family and His Books." *Journal of Turkish Studies* 40 (2013): 315–26. (Special Issue: *Defterology: Festschrift in Honor of Heath Lowry*, edited by Selim S. Kuru and Baki Tezcan. Cambridge, MA: Harvard University, Department of Near Eastern Languages and Civilizations, 2013.)

Renda, Günsel. "New Light on the Painters of the Zubdet al-Tawarikh in the Museum of Turkish and Islamic Art in Istanbul." In *Fourth International Congress of Turkish Art, Aix-en-Provence, 10–15 September, 1971*, 183–200. Aix-en-Provence: Éditions de l'Université de Provence, 1976.

Repp, Richard Cooper. *The Müfti of Istanbul: A Study in the Development of the Ottoman Learned Hierarchy*. London: Ithaca Press, 1986.

Richards, John F. *The Mughal Empire*. Cambridge, UK: Cambridge University Press, 1993.

Rosenthal, Franz. *"Sweeter than Hope": Complaint and Hope in Medieval Islam*. Leiden: Brill, 1983.

Sabev, Orlin. "The Legend of Köse Mihal. Additional Notes." *Turcica* 34 (2002): 241–52.

———. "Osmanlıların Balkanları Fethi ve İdaresinde Mihaloğulları Ailesi (XIV.–XIX. Yüzyıllar): Mülkler, Vakıflar, Hizmetler." *Osmanlı Tarihi Araştırma ve Uygulama Merkezi Dergisi (OTAM)* 33 (2013): 229–44.

Şahin, İ. Kaya. "Constantinople and the End Time: The Ottoman Conquest as a Portent of the Last Hour." *Journal of Early Modern History* 14 (2010): 317–54.

———. *Empire and Power in the Reign of Süleyman: Narrating the Sixteenth-Century Ottoman World*. New York: Cambridge University Press, 2013.

———. "Imperialism, Bureaucratic Consciousness, and the Historian's Craft: A Reading of Celālzāde Muṣṭafā's *Ṭabaḳātü'l-Memālik ve Derecātü'l-Mesālik*." In *Writing History at the Ottoman Court: Editing the Past, Fashioning the Future*, edited by H. Erdem Çıpa and Emine Fetvacı, 39–57. Bloomington: Indiana University Press, 2013.

Saraç, Yekta. *Şeyhülislam Kemal Paşazade: Hayatı, Şahsiyeti, Eserleri ve Bazı Şiirleri*. Istanbul: Risale, 1995.

Sariyannis, Marinos. "Ottoman Critics of Society and State, Fifteenth to Early Eighteenth Centuries: Toward a Corpus for the Study of Ottoman Political Thought." *Archivum Ottomanicum* 25 (2008): 127–50.

———. "The Princely Virtues as Presented in Ottoman Political and Moral Literature." *Turcica* 43 (2011): 121–44.

Savage-Smith, Emilie. "Magic and Islam." In *Magic and Science, Tools and Magic*, edited by Francis Romeril F. Maddison et al., part I, 59–71. London/Oxford: Azimuth Editions/Oxford University Press, 1997.

Savage-Smith, Emilie, and Marion B. Smith. "Islamic Geomancy and a Thirteenth-Century Divinatory Device: Another Look." In *Magic and Divination in Early Islam*, edited by E. Savage-Smith, 211–76. Aldershot: Ashgate Variorum, 2004.

Schmidt, Jan. "Hāfız and Other Persian Authors in Ottoman Bibliomancy: The Extraordinary Case of Kefevī Hüseyn Efendi's *Rāznāme* (Late Sixteenth Century)." *Persica* 21 (2006–2007): 63–74.

———. *Pure Water for Thirsty Muslims: A Study of Muṣṭafā ʿĀlī of Gallipoli's* Künhü l-Aḫbār. Leiden: Het Oosters Instituut, 1991.

———. "The Reception of Firdausi's *Shahnama* among the Ottomans." In *Shahnama Studies II: The Reception of Firdausi's* Shahnama, edited by

Charles Melville and Gabrielle van den Berg, 121–39. Leiden: Brill, 2012.

Şen, Ahmet Tunç. "Astrology at the Early Modern Ottoman Court: A New Look at the Scientific Writings of Mīrim Çelebi." Paper presented at the annual meeting of the Renaissance Society of America, Berlin, March 2015.

——. "A Mirror for Princes, a Fiction for Readers: The *Habnâme* of Veysī and Dream Narratives in Ottoman Turkish Literature." *Journal of Turkish Literature* 8 (2011): 417–65.

Sezen, Lütfi. *Halk Edebiyatında Hamzanâmeler*. Ankara: Kültür Bakanlığı, 1991.

Shaw, Stanford J. *Empire of the Gazis: The Rise and Decline of the Ottoman Empire, 1280–1808*. Vol. 1 of *History of the Ottoman Empire and Modern Turkey*. Cambridge: Cambridge University Press, 1976.

——. *The Financial and Administrative Organization and Development of Ottoman Egypt, 1517–1798*. Princeton: Princeton University Press, 1962.

Sohrweide, Hanna. "Der Sieg der Safaviden in Persien und Seine Rückwirkungen auf die Shiiten Anatoliens im 16. Jahrhundert." *Der Islam* 41 (1965): 95–223.

Spellberg, Denise A. *Politics, Gender, and the Islamic Past: The Legacy of ʿA'isha bint Abi Bakr*. New York: Columbia University Press, 1994.

Spiegel, Gabrielle. "History, Historicism, and the Social Logic of the Text." In *The Past as Text: The Theory and Practice of Medieval Historiography*, 3–28. London: The Johns Hopkins University Press, 1997.

——. "Towards a Theory of the Middle Ground." In *The Past as Text: The Theory and Practice of Medieval Historiography*, 44–56. London: The Johns Hopkins University Press, 1997.

Stavrides, Theoharis. "Alternative Dynasties: The Turahanids and the Ottomans in the Fifteenth Century." *Journal of Turkish Studies* 36 (2011): 145–71.

Streusand, Douglas E. *Islamic Gunpowder Empires: Ottomans, Safavids, and Mughals*. Boulder: Westview Press, 2010.

Subrahmanyam, Sanjay. "Connected Histories: Notes Towards a Reconfiguration of Early Modern Eurasia." *Modern Asian Studies* 31, no. 3 (1997): 735–62.

——. "The Fate of Empires: Rethinking Mughals, Ottomans and Habsburgs." In *Shared Histories of Modernity: China, India, and the*

Ottoman Empire, edited by Huri İslamoğlu and Peter C. Perdue, 74–108. Delhi and London: Routledge, 2009.
——. "A Tale of Three Empires: Mughals, Ottomans, and Habsburgs in Comparative Context." *Common Knowledge* 12, no. 1 (2006): 66–92.
——. "Turning the Stones Over: Sixteenth-Century Millenarianism from the Tagus to the Ganges." *The Indian Economic and Social History Review* 45, no. 2 (2003): 129–61.
Subtelny, Maria Eva. "The Sunni Revival under Shāh-Rukh and Its Promoters: A Study of the Connection between Ideology and Higher Learning in Timurid Iran." In *Proceedings of the 27th Meeting of Haneda Memorial Hall Symposium on Central Asia and Iran, August 30, 1993*, 14–22. Kyoto: Institute of Inner Asian Studies, 1993.
——. *Timurids in Transition: Turko-Persian Politics and Acculturation in Medieval Iran*. Leiden: Brill, 2007.
Subtelny, Maria Eva, and Anas B. Khalidov. "The Curriculum of Islamic Higher Learning in Timurid Iran in the Light of the Sunni Revival under Shah-Rukh." *Journal of the American Oriental Society* 115, no. 2 (1995): 210–36.
Sümer, Faruk. "Osman Gazi'nin Silah Arkadaşlarından Mihal Gazi." *Türk Dünyası Tarih Dergisi* 50 (1991): 3–8.
——. *Safevî Devletinin Kuruluşu ve Gelişmesinde Anadolu Türklerinin Rolü*. Ankara: Türk Tarih Kurumu, 1992.
Tabbaa, Yasser. *Constructions of Power and Piety in Medieval Aleppo*. University Park: Pennsylvania State University Press, 1997.
Tanındı, Zeren. "The Illustration of the *Shahnama* and the Art of the Book in Ottoman Turkey." In *Shahnama Studies II: The Reception of Firdausi's* Shahnama, edited by Charles Melville and Gabrielle van den Berg, 141–58. Leiden: Brill, 2012.
Tansel, Selâhattin. *Sultan II. Bâyezit'in Siyasî Hayatı*. Istanbul: Milli Eğitim Basımevi, 1966.
——. *Yavuz Sultan Selim*. Ankara: Milli Eğitim Basımevi, 1969.
Tekin, Şinasi. "Türk Dünyasında Gazâ ve Cihâd Kavramları Üzerine Düşünceler." *Tarih ve Toplum* 109 (1993): 9–18; 110 (1993): 73–80.
Tekindağ, Şehabettin. "Bayezid'in Ölümü Meselesi." *TD* 24 (1970): 1–23.
——. "Korkud Çelebi ile İlgili İki Belge." *BTTD* 17 (1969): 36–42.
——. "Şah Kulu Baba Tekeli İsyanı." *BTTD* 3 (1967): 34–39; 4 (1968): 54–59.
——. "Selim-nâmeler." *TED* 1 (1970): 197–230.

——. "Yeni Kaynak ve Vesikaların Işığı Altında Yavuz Sultan Selim'in İran Seferi." *TD* 22 (1967): 49–76.

Tezcan, Baki. "Ethics as Domain to Discuss the Political: Kınalızâde Ali Fendi's *Ahlâk-ı Alâî*." In *Proceedings of the International Congress on Learning and Education in the Ottoman World, Istanbul, 12–15 April 1999*, edited by Ali Çaksu, 109–20. Istanbul: IRCICA, 2001.

——. "The Memory of the Mongols in Early Ottoman Historiography." In *Writing History at the Ottoman Court: Editing the Past, Fashioning the Future*, edited by H. Erdem Çıpa and Emine Fetvacı, 23–38. Bloomington: Indiana University Press, 2013.

——. "The Politics of Early Modern Ottoman Historiography." In *The Early Modern Ottomans: Remapping the Empire*, edited by Virginia H. Aksan and Daniel Goffman, 167–98. Cambridge, UK: Cambridge University Press, 2007.

——. *The Second Ottoman Empire: Political and Social Transformation in the Early Modern World*. New York: Cambridge University Press, 2010.

Thomas, Lewis V. *A Study of Naima*. Edited by Norman Itzkowitz. New York: New York University Press, 1972.

al-Tikriti, Nabil. "The Ḥajj as Justifiable Self-Exile: Şehzade Korkud's *Wasīlat al-aḥbāb* (915–916/1509–1510)." *Al-Masāq* 17, no. 1 (2005): 125–46.

——. "Şehzade Korkud (ca. 1468–1513) and the Articulation of Early 16th Century Ottoman Religious Identity." PhD diss., The University of Chicago, 2004.

Todorov, Nikolai, and Boris Nedkov, eds. *Fontes Turcici Historiae Bulgaricae*. Vol. 2. Sofia: Bulgarian Academy of Sciences, 1966.

Toledano, Ehud R. *Slavery and Abolition in the Ottoman Middle East*. Seattle: University of Washington Press, 1998.

Trifonov, Yordan. "Tarih ve Rivâyetlerde Mihalbey Oğulları." *Ülkü* (January 1941): 390–98; (February 1941): 533–41.

Turan, Ebru. "The Sultan's Favorite: Ibrahim Pasha and the Making of the Ottoman Universal Sovereignty in the Reign of Sultan Süleyman (1516–1526)." PhD diss., The University of Chicago, 2007.

Turan, Şerafettin. *Kanuni Süleyman Dönemi Taht Kavgaları*. Istanbul: Bilgi Yayınevi, 1997. Revised second edition of *Kanunî'nin Oğlu Şehzâde Bayezid Vak'ası*. Ankara: Türk Tarih Kurumu Basımevi, 1961.

——. "Şehzade Bayezid'in Babası Kanunî Sultan Süleyman'a Gönderdiği Mektuplar." *Tarih Vesikaları Dergisi* 1, no. 16 (1955): 118–27.

Tveritinova, Anna, ed. *Vostochniye istochniki po istorii narodov Yugo-vostochnoy i Tsentralnoy Evropiy*. Moscow: Nauka, 1964.

Uğur, Ahmet. "Celal-zade Mustafa ve Selim-nâmesi." *AÜİFD* 26 (1983): 407–25.

——. *İbn-i Kemal*. Izmir: Kültür ve Turizm Bakanlığı Yayınları, 1987.

——. *Kemal Paşa-zade İbn-Kemal*. Ankara: Milli Eğitim Basımevi, 1996.

——. "Kemal Paşa-zade ve Şah İsmail (Safavîler)." *EÜİFD* 4 (1987): 13–27.

——. *Osmanlı Siyâset-nâmeleri*. Kayseri: Kültür ve Sanat Yayınları, 1987.

——. *The Reign of Sultan Selīm I in the Light of the Selīm-nāme Literature*. Berlin: K. Schwarz, 1985.

——. "Selim-nâmeler." *AÜİFD* 22 (1978): 367–79.

——. "Şükri-i Bitlisi ve Selim-nâmesi." *AÜİFD* 25 (1981): 325–47.

——. *Yavuz Sultan Selim*. Kayseri: Erciyes Üniversitesi Sosyal Bilimler Fakültesi, 1992.

——. "Yavuz Sultan Selim ile Kırım Hanı Mengli Giray ve Oğlu Muhammed Giray Arasında Geçen İki Konuşma." *AÜİFD* 21 (1976): 357–61.

Uluç, Lâle. "The *Shahnama* of Firdausi in the Lands of Rum." In *Shahnama Studies II: The Reception of Firdausi's* Shahnama, edited by Charles Melville and Gabrielle van den Berg, 159–80. Leiden: Brill, 2012.

Uluçay, Çağatay. "Bayazıd II.'in Ailesi." *TD* 14 (1959): 105–24.

——. "Selim-Bâyezid Mücadelesi." *Tarih Vesikaları* 1, no. 3 (1961): 374–87.

——. "Yavuz Sultan Selim Nasıl Padişah Oldu?" *TD* 9 (1953): 53–90; 10 (1954): 117–42; 11–12 (1955): 185–200.

Ünver, Süheyl. *İstanbul Üniversitesi Tarihine Başlangıç: Fatih, Külliyesi ve Zamanı İlim Hayatı*. Istanbul: İstanbul Üniversitesi Yayınları, 1946.

Üstün, İsmail Safa. "Heresy and Legitimacy in the Ottoman Empire in the Sixteenth Century." PhD diss., University of Manchester, 1991.

Uzunçarşılı, İsmail Hakkı. "Babasından Sonra Saltanatı Elde Etmek İçin Kardeşi Selim'le Çatışan Şehzade Bayezid'in Amasya'dan Babası Kanunî Sultan Süleyman'a Göndermiş Olduğu Ariza." *Belleten* 96 (1960): 597–600.

——. "IIinci Bayezid'in Oğullarından Sultan Korkut." *Belleten* 120 (1966): 539–601.

——. "İran Şahına İltica Etmiş Olan Şehzade Bayezid'in Teslimi İçin Sultan Süleyman ve Oğlu Selim Taraflarından Şaha Gönderilen Altınlar ve Kıymetli Hediyeler." *Belleten* 96 (1960): 103–10.

——. "Onaltıncı Asır Ortalarında Yaşamış Olan İki Büyük Şahsiyet: Tosyalı Celâl Zâde Mustafa ve Salih Çelebiler." *Belleten* 87 (1958): 391–441.

———. "Onbeşinci Yüzyılın İlk Yarısiyle Onaltıncı Yüzyılın Başlarında Memlûk Sultanları Yanına İltica Etmiş Olan Osmanlı Hanedanına Mensub Şehzadeler." *Belleten* 68 (1953): 519–35.

———. *Osmanlı Devletinin Merkez ve Bahriye Teşkilâtı*. 3rd ed. Ankara: Türk Tarih Kurumu, 1988.

———. *Osmanlı Devletinin Saray Teşkilâtı*. 3rd ed. Ankara: Türk Tarih Kurumu, 1988.

———. *Osmanlı Devleti Teşkilâtından Kapukulu Ocakları: Acemi Ocağı ve Yeniçeri Ocağı*. Vol. 1. 3rd ed. Ankara: Türk Tarih Kurumu, 1988.

———. *Osmanlı Devleti Teşkilâtından Kapukulu Ocakları: Cebeci, Topcu, Top Arabacıları, Humbaracı, Lâğımcı Ocakları ve Kapukulu Süvarileri*. Vol. 2. 3rd ed. Ankara: Türk Tarih Kurumu, 1988.

———. *Osmanlı Tarihi*. (1) Vol. 1. 8th ed. Ankara: Türk Tarih Kurumu, 2003. (2) Vol. 2. 8th ed. Ankara: Türk Tarih Kurumu, 1998. (3) Part 1. Vol. 3. 4th ed. Ankara: Türk Tarih Kurumu, 1988.

———. "Şehzade Selim'in Babasına Muhalefet Ederek Muharebe Ettiği Sırada Amasya Valisi Şehzade Ahmed'in Vezir-i Âzama Mektubu." *Belleten* 96 (1960): 595–96.

Van Dam, Raymond. *Remembering Constantine at the Milvian Bridge*. New York: Cambridge University Press, 2011.

Vatin, Nicolas. *Sultan Djem: Un prince ottoman dans l'Europe du XVe siècle d'après deux sources contemporaines: Vâḳıʿât-ı Sulṭân Cem, Œuvres de Guillaume Caoursin*. Ankara: Türk Tarih Kurumu, 1997.

Vatin, Nicolas, and Gilles Veinstein. *Le Sérail ébranlé: Essai sur les morts, dépositions et avènements des sultans ottomans (XIVᵉ–XIXᵉ siècle)*. Paris: Fayard, 2003.

Veinstein, Gilles, ed. *Soliman le Magnifique et son temps*. Paris: La Documentation Française, 1992.

Von Grunebaum, G. E. "The Cultural Function of the Dream as Illustrated by Classical Islam." In *The Dream and Human Societies*, edited by G. E. von Grunebaum and Roger Caillois, 3–21. Berkeley: University of California Press, 1966.

Von Grunebaum, G. E., and Roger Caillois, eds. *The Dream and Human Societies*. Berkeley: University of California Press, 1966.

Weinstein, Donald. *Savonarola and Florence: Prophecy and Patriotism and the Renaissance*. Princeton: Princeton University Press, 1970.

Winter, Michael. *Egyptian Society under Ottoman Rule, 1517–1798*. London: Routledge, 1992.

Woodhead, Christine. "An Experiment in Official Historiography: The Post of Şehnāmeci in the Ottoman Empire, c. 1555–1605." *Wiener Zeitschrift für die Kunde des Morgenlandes* 75 (1983): 157–82.

——. "The History of an Historie: Richard Knolles' *Generall Historie of the Turkes*, 1603–1700." In "Barbara Flemming Armağanı II," ed. Jan Schmidt. Special issue, *Journal of Turkish Studies* 26, no. 1 (2002): 349–57.

——. "Murad III and the Historians: Representations of Ottoman Imperial Authority in Late 16th-Century Historiography." In *Legitimizing the Order: The Ottoman Rhetoric of State Power*, edited by Hakan Karateke and Maurus Reinkowski, 85–98. Leiden: Brill, 2005.

——. "Perspectives on Süleyman." In *Süleyman the Magnificent and His Age: The Ottoman Empire in the Early Modern World*, edited by Metin Kunt and Christine Woodhead, 164–90. London and New York: Longman, 1995.

——. "Reading Ottoman *Şehnames*: Official Historiography in the Late Sixteenth Century." *Studia Islamica* 104–5 (2007): 67–80.

Yahya, Dahiru. *Morocco in the Sixteenth Century: Problems and Patterns in African Foreign Policy*. Harlow: Longman, 1981.

Yaman, Bahattin. "Osmanlı Resim Sanatında Kıyamet Alametleri: Tercüme-i Cifru'l-Câmi ve Tasvirli Nüshaları." PhD diss., Hacettepe University, 2002.

Yerasimos, Stéphane. *La fondation de Constantinople et de Sainte-Sophie dans les traditions turques: légendes d'Empire*. Paris: Librairie d'Amérique et d'Orient J. Maisonneuve, 1990.

Yerasimos, Stéphane, and Benjamin Lellouch, eds. *Les traditions apocalyptiques au tournant de la chute de Constantinople: Actes de la Table Ronde d'Istanbul, 13–14 avril 1996*. Paris: L'Harmattan, 1999.

Yıldırım, Rıza. "An Ottoman Prince Wearing a Qizilbash *Tāj*: The Enigmatic Career of Sultan Murad and Qizilbash Affairs in Ottoman Domestic Politics, 1510–1513." *Turcica* 43 (2011): 91–119.

——. "Turkomans between Two Empires: The Origins of the Qizilbash Identity in Anatolia (1447–1514)." PhD diss., Bilkent University, 2008.

Yıldız, Sara Nur. "Ottoman Historical Writing in Persian, 1400–1600." In *Persian Historiography*. Vol. 10 of *A History of Persian Literature*, edited by Ehsan Yarshater and Charles Melville, 436–502. London: I. B. Tauris, 2012.

Yılmaz, Hüseyin. "The Sultan and the Sultanate: Envisioning Rulership in the Age of Süleyman the Lawgiver (1520–1566)." PhD diss., Harvard University, 2005.

Yinanç, Refet. *Dulkadir Beyliği*. Ankara: Türk Tarih Kurumu Basımevi, 1989.
Yücel, Yaşar. *Anadolu Beylikleri Hakkında Araştırmalar*. 2 vols. Ankara: Türk Tarih Kurumu, 1991.
———. "Candar-oğlu Çelebi İsfendiyar Bey, 1392–1439." *Tarih Araştırmaları Dergisi* 2, no. 2–3 (1964): 157–74.
Yüksel Muslu, Cihan. *The Ottomans and the Mamluks: Imperial Diplomacy and Warfare in the Islamic World*. London: I. B. Tauris, 2014.
Yurdaydın, Hüseyin Gazi. *Kanunî'nin Cülûsu ve İlk Seferleri*. Ankara: Türk Tarih Kurumu Basımevi, 1961.
Yürekli, Zeynep. *Architecture and Hagiography in the Ottoman Empire: The Politics of Bektashi Shrines in the Classical Age*. Farnham, UK: Ashgate, 2012.
———. "*Dhu'l-faqār* and the Ottomans." In *People of the Prophet's House: Artistic and Ritual Expressions of Shiʿi Islam*, edited by Fahmida Suleman, 163–72. London: Azimuth Editions in association with The Institute of Ismaili Studies and the British Museum, 2015.
Zachariadou, Elizabeth A. *To Chroniko ton Tourkon Soultanon (tou Barberinou Hellen, Kodika 111) kai to Italiko tou Protypo* [The Chronicle about the Turkish Sultans (of Codex Barberinus Graecus 111) and Its Italian Prototype]. Thessalonica: Demosieumata tes Hetaireias Makedonikon Spoudon, 1960.
———. "Les Tocco: Seigneurs, Vassaux, Otages, Renegats." *Ankara Üniversitesi Güneydoğu Avrupa Çalışmaları Uygulama ve Araştırma Merkezi Dergisi* 1, no. 1 (2012): 11–22.
Zlatar, Behija. "O Malkočima." *Prilozi* 26 (1976): 105–14.

Index

ʿAbbās I, 237–38
Abbasids, 234, 236
ʿAbd al-Raḥmān al-Bisṭāmī: *Miftāḥ al-jafr al-jāmiʿ*, 247–48
Abou-El-Haj, Rifaʾat, 111–12
Abū Bakr (caliph), 227, 234
Āḫī Çelebi (Meḥmed Efendi), 53, 74
Aḥmed (son of Bāyezīd II), 18, 32, 45, 52, 56, 58–59, 76–77, 79, 80, 94, 135–36, 139, 154, 158, 173–74, 179, 221–22, 226–27, 243; as described by Andrea Gritti, 62–63; execution of, 60, 134–35, 147, 173; and gubernatorial appointments, 34, 37–38; and Ḫādım ʿAlī Pasha, 33, 46–48, 72; as heir apparent, 38, 42, 44, 48, 55, 63, 64, 70–71, 78, 83–84, 158; and Şāhḳulu rebellion, 46–48, 83, 170, 171; sons of, 34, 37–38, 45, 47, 53, 60, 74, 134; supporters of (pro-Aḥmed faction), 36–38, 46, 50–52, 65, 68–75, 77–78, 83, 148, 151–52, 159, 166, 169–73
Aḥmed Beg, 99
Aḥmed I, 126, 184, 188, 198, 237–38
Aḥmed Pasha, 79
Aḥmed Pasha of Bursa, 242–43
Aḥmed Şikārī, 97
Aḥmedī: *İskendernāme*, 113, 117, 149; *Tevārīḫ-i mülūk-i āl-i ʿOs̱mān ve ġazv-ı īşān bā-küffār*, 117
Ahyolu, 50–51, 166
Akhenaten, 253
aḳıncı (raider), 84–85, 92–95, 98–107
Akkirman, 38, 39–40, 81, 82, 84, 91, 94, 113, 159, 244
ʿAlāʾ al-dawla, 148
Alacahisar, 41
ʿAlāʾeddīn (son of Prince Aḥmed), 53, 58, 74; and gubernatorial appointments, 34
Alanya, 59
Alderson, Anthony Dolphin, 29
ʿAlemşāh (son of Bāyezīd II): execution of son, 59
Alexander the Great, 204, 207, 210, 242
ʿAlī b. ʿAbdülkerīm Ḫalīfe, 176–78, 180, 196; confidence in Selīm, 178
ʿAlī b. Abī Ṭālib (caliph), 219–21, 223–24, 225, 228, 234
ʿAlī of Köstendil, 219–21
Amasya, 34, 47, 59, 62, 121
Anatolia, 1, 3, 5–8, 11, 16, 33–37, 39, 42–46, 53, 58–59, 64, 69, 73–75, 81–82, 85, 91–93, 104, 118–19, 148–49, 156–57, 166, 171–73, 178, 180, 183, 188, 192, 220, 224, 245
Ankara, 44; Battle of, 33, 93, 94, 96, 240
Ankersmit, Frank, 22
Anonymous Chronicles, 113
Antalya, 45, 48, 77
apocalypticism, 12, 23, 131, 212–15, 241, 244, 246–48, 256
ʿĀrifī (also Fetḥullāh Çelebi or ʿĀrif), 122; *Shāhnāma-ye āl-e ʿOs̱mān*, 123–24; *Ṭomār-ı hümāyūn*, 124
Asaph, 184

ʿĀşıḳpaşazāde, 95, 218, 219
Assmann, Jan, 17, 20, 253
Aydın, 34, 77
ʿAyntāb, 230–31, 232
ʿAzīz Efendi: *Ḳānūnnāme-i Sulṭānī li ʿAzīz Efendi*, 187
ʿAzmīzāde Muṣṭafā: *Selīmnāme*, 141–42, 144

Babayan, Kathryn, 212–13
Baghdad, 128, 234
Bālī Beg, 80
Bālī Pasha, 79, 94, 151, 168
Balkans, 7, 19, 24, 33, 38–41, 44, 48–49, 56, 64, 66, 81–83, 85, 92–94, 96, 99–100, 104–5, 156–57, 166
Baltaoğlu Pīrī, 84
Barbarigo, Daniele, 104–5
Baṭṭālnāme, 118, 220
Bavaria, 94
Bāyezīd (son of Süleymān I), 121, 145, 167–68
Bāyezīd I, 94–96, 139, 240; sons of, 30, 82, 95
Bāyezīd II, 3, 10, 30–35, 40–42, 48–51, 62–67, 74–77, 79, 82–84, 89–90, 94–98, 103, 106, 107, 151–54, 156–58, 164, 166–68, 178, 180, 196, 222, 226, 234, 244; abdication of, 55–56, 78, 83, 169–72; criticism of, 37, 70, 71, 85–88, 165, 177; death of, 2, 15, 18, 31, 56–58, 75, 136–40, 148, 155, 169, 173; as described by Ottoman chroniclers, 38, 55–57, 70, 71, 137–40, 173; deposition of by Selīm I, 1–2, 60, 136, 144, 164; and Mengli Girāy, 39, 79–80, 158; and Andrea Gritti, 63; and Shāh Ismāʿīl, 35–36; patronage of historians, 113–16; and pro-Selīm janissaries, 53–54, 56, 57, 69, 78; and the Şāhḳulu rebellion, 43, 44, 45, 46, 72, 83
Bedreddīn (Sheikh), 82
Belgrade, 100
Bergama, 33, 251–53
Bolu, 34
Boratav, Pertev Naili, 118
Bosnia, 41, 100
Bulgaria, 100
Burdur, 45
Burke, Peter, 19–20
Bursa, 58, 59, 60, 134, 243
Byzantium, 220

Çaldıran, 6, 132, 148, 153; Battle of, 3, 5, 94–95, 129, 143, 153, 190–91, 236, 241
Cāmiʿü'l-meknūnāt, 90
Carlo Tocco, 96
Carlo Tocco II, 96
Celāl of Bozok, 245
Celālī uprisings, 188
Celālzāde Muṣṭafā Çelebi (Ḳoca Nişāncı), 13, 37, 79, 83, 133, 201; *Me'āṡir-i Selīm Ḫānī*, 80–81, 83–91, 141–42, 144–45, 147, 150–52, 154, 158–60, 163–68, 170–74, 201–2
Cem (also Cem Sulṭān, son of Meḥmed II), 76, 97–98, 115, 139
Cerrāḥzāde Mevlānā Muḥammed, 237–38
Cevrī İbrāhīm Çelebi: *Selīmnāme*, 141–42
Charles V, 19–20, 121, 245
Circassian, 38, 229, 230
Çirmen, 42
Çivizāde Muḥyiddīn Meḥmed Efendi, 232–33
Constantinople, 66, 100–102, 213, 243, 248. *See also* Istanbul.

Corfu, 128
Çorlu, Battle of, 40, 43, 48–51, 60, 67, 81, 83, 84, 151, 152, 155, 159; in Ottoman chronicles, 49, 163–68, 172
Çorum, 34
Crimea/Crimean, 18, 37–40, 50–51, 61, 79–83, 155, 157–60, 162–63, 172

Damascus, 231
Danishmendid dynasty, 220
Dānişmendnāme, 118, 220
Danube River, 41, 164
Deve Kemāl Agha, 51
devlet (fortune), 30–31, 172, 230
devlet ṣınaşmak (mutual testing of fortune), 31
devşirme, 87, 89, 92, 179, 183–85, 188, 196, 198, 201
Dhūlfiqār, 220
Dimetoka, 31–32, 56, 57, 136, 138
dreams, 101–2, 111–12, 161, 184, 212, 215, 216, 217–30
Dūḳaginzāde Aḥmed Pasha, 132
Dulkadir, 3, 5, 35, 148–49
Ḏulḳadiroğlu, 58, 74
Dülük Baba, 230–31

Ebū'l-fażl Meḥmed: *Salīmshāhnāma*, 144–46
Ebu'ssuᶜūd Efendi, 233–35
Edirne, 41, 42, 49, 56, 83–84, 100, 164, 177
Eflāṭūn, 122; *Ṭomār-ı hümāyūn*, 124
Egri campaign, 162, 183, 243
Egypt, 1, 3, 5–6, 8–11, 15, 33, 39, 47, 76, 79, 141, 148, 166, 191, 203, 206, 210–11, 226, 230–31, 233, 236–37, 244, 253
Emecen, Feridun, 58
Emīr (son of Prince Maḥmūd), 59
Enverī: *Düstūrnāme*, 100
Ertuġrul, 117
Eryılmaz, Sinem, 123
Erzincan, 36
Eskişehir, 58
eşref-i selāṭīn (most honorable of sultans), 115, 234
Eurasia, 12–16, 23, 25, 131, 181, 211–14, 216, 224, 247, 256
Evliyā Çelebi, 139, 155, 228–31, 233, 237; *Seyāḥatnāme*, 244
Evrenos Beg, 95, 102
Evrenosoġlu family, 102, 104

fāl-i Qur'ān (divination by the Qur'ān), 226
fālnāma (divination book), 226
Fenārīzāde Meḥmed Şāh Çelebi, 147
Ferdinand I, 121
Ferhād Agha, 54, 77
Ferhād Beg, 50
Ferhād Pasha, 79, 151, 168
Fetḥ Girāy, 162
fetḥnāme (treatise of conquest), 117, 236
Fetvacı, Emine, 118, 126
Filibe, 44
Firdawsī: *Shāhnāma*, 116–20, 127–29, 130, 141–43, 153–55, 181, 224, 246, 255
Fisher, Sydney Nettleton, 64–65
Fleischer, Cornell, 11, 122, 186–87, 195, 213–14, 242, 245–46
Flemming, Barbara, 213–14, 245
Fletcher, Joseph, 12–13, 31
Fodor, Pál, 185
Forêt, Jean de la, 4
Foscolo, Andrea, 64
fratricide, 14, 15, 30, 33, 56, 59–60, 78, 134–35, 139, 155, 173–75, 179–80
Fürstenspiegel genre, 23

ġazā (holy war), 164, 218, 234
Ġażanfer Agha, 248–49
ġazavātnāme (campaign narrative), 117, 118, 153
ġāzī (warrior of faith), 1, 102–3, 114–15, 117, 127, 220, 234, 241, 243
Ġāzī Girāy II, 162
Genghis Khan, 242
Georgia/Georgians, 1, 9, 36–37, 85–87, 154, 156
al-Ghazālī: *Kitāb naṣīḥat al-mulūk*, 181
Gritti, Andrea, 62–64, 67
Gümlioğlu family, 93, 95–96, 101, 107
Gümlioğlu İskender Beg, 95–96
Gümlioğlu Muṣṭafā Beg, 95
Gümlioğlu Ṣāltıḳ Beg, 96

Habsburgs, 5, 10, 13, 23, 25, 121, 131, 162, 209, 211–12, 214, 245–46, 256
Ḫādım ʿAlī Pasha, 51, 72, 170; and Aḥmed, 33, 72; and Bāyezīd II, 72; and Ḳorḳud, 33, 72, 76; and Şāhḳulu rebellion, 45–46, 47, 48, 72; and Selīm, 72
Ḫādım Sinān Pasha, 148
Ḫākī, 246
Ḥalīmī Çelebi, 229
Hamid, 33
Ḥamzanāme, 118
Ḥarmanḳaya, 99
Ḥasan Agha, 227–28
Ḥasan Cān b. Ḥāfıẓ Muḥammed İṣfahānī, 151, 168
Ḥasan Ḫalīfe, 43–44
Ḥasan Kāfī el-Aḳḥiṣārī, 183, 185
Ḥasan Pasha, 41, 52, 72
ḥaseb (personal merit), 90
Hathaway, Jane, 142
Ḥaydar (geomancer for Süleymān I), 246
Ḥaydar (Sheikh), 44
Ḥaydar Çelebi: *Rūznāme*, 132–33
Hemdem Pasha, 133
Hersekzāde Aḥmed Pasha, 52, 62, 64, 69, 73, 132, 136, 148, 172
Hezārfen Ḥüseyin Efendi: *Telḫīṣü'l-beyān fī ḳavānīn-i āl-i ʿOs̱mān*, 187, 194, 195; *Tenḳīḥü't-tevārīḫ*, 137
Hierosolimitano, Domenico, 136
Ḥırzü'l-mülūk, 187, 190, 197, 198, 200, 204–5
Holy Roman Empire, 19, 121
House of ʿOs̱mān, 2, 3, 12, 29, 30, 59, 68, 87, 102, 104–6, 113–17, 122, 124, 133, 135, 137, 140, 144, 149–50, 174–75, 182, 186, 193–94, 196, 199, 202, 207, 210, 216, 218, 230, 233, 235–36, 238–39, 241–42, 247–48, 250
Howard, Douglas, 185
Hünernāme, 129
Hungary, 68, 96, 100, 121, 128, 164

Ibn ʿArabī, 231, 232–33
Ibn Sīrīn, 225
İbrāhīm I, 191
İbrāhīm Gülşenī, 231–33
İbrāhīm Pasha, 8, 146, 205–6
İdrīs-i Bidlīsī, 59, 113–14, 116, 150; *Hasht bihisht*, 114; *Salīmshāhnāma*, 140, 142, 144, 150; *Selīmnāme*, 143, 154, 157, 163–65, 169–70, 173–74
İḫtimān, 100
İḫtimānoğlu family, 100
İḫtimānoğlu Ḳāsım Beg, 100
İḫtimānoğlu Meḥmed Beg, 100
İnalcık, Halil, 29, 31, 113, 118, 120
inşāʾ (epistolary prose), 133, 142, 153
İsfendiyār, 104
İsfendiyār Beg, 93

İsfendiyāroğlu Celīl Çelebi, 93
İsḥaḳ b. İbrāhīm (also İsḥaḳ Çelebi): *İsḥaḳnāme*, 140; *Selīmnāme*, 83, 143, 146, 150, 153, 154, 155–57, 163, 164, 165, 169, 173
İskender Çelebi, 206
İskender Pasha, 132
Ismāʿīl I (also Shāh Ismāʿīl), 4–7, 10, 35, 43–44, 46–47, 53, 55, 148, 155, 178, 211, 224, 226–27, 240, 245
Istanbul, 17–18, 24, 33–34, 38, 42, 44, 46, 49, 51–54, 56–57, 63–64, 66–67, 72, 74, 77, 79, 81–84, 96, 103, 106, 120, 128, 132, 136, 138, 148, 151, 153, 166, 170–71, 177, 203, 229, 235, 254
Izmit, 60

Janbirdī al-Ghazālī, 148–49, 233
janissaries, 2, 6, 24, 47, 48, 52–57, 59, 63, 65–69, 75, 77–78, 81, 90, 106, 134, 144, 149, 166, 170–72, 174, 179, 183–86, 188, 190–91, 198–99, 209; rebellion of, 64, 72–74, 169, 172
Jerusalem, 11

Kafadar, Cemal, 13–14, 30, 111, 115, 141, 186–87
Kāmilü'l-taʿbīr, 226
ḳānūn (dynastic law), 186, 188, 193, 195–98, 256
Ḳānūnnāme-i Nigbolu, 11, 210–11, 243
Kaptein, Laban, 213–14
Ḳaragöz Pasha, 45
Ḳara Ḥüseyin Agha, 84
Karaman, 53, 58–59, 74, 85, 171
Ḳaramānī Meḥmed Pasha: *Tawārīkh al-salāṭīn al-ʿUthmāniyya*, 114
Ḳaraoğlu Aḥmed Beg, 58, 74
Ḳarlı-ili, 96
Ḳarlıoğlu ʿAlī Beg, 97–98
Ḳarlıoğlu family, 93, 96–98, 101, 107
Ḳarlıoğlu İskender Beg, 97–98
Ḳarlıoğlu Meḥmed Beg, 98
Karlova, 97
Kāshifī: *Ghazānāma-yi Rūm*, 120
Ḳāsım, 84
Ḳāsım Çelebi, 52
Ḳāsım Pasha, 57, 79, 151
Kastritsis, Dimitris, 24
Kātib Çelebi, 150
Ḳavānīn-i yeñiçeriyān, 187, 188–90, 198–200, 209
Kay-Kāʾūs ibn Iskandar: *Ḳābūsnāma*, 181
Kayumars, 119
Kebir b. Üveys Ḳāḍīzāde: *Ġazāvāt-e Sulṭān Salīm*, 140, 142–43, 146–47, 153–54
Kefe, 34, 37–39, 44, 49–51, 81, 83, 91, 98, 156–59, 166, 219
Kemālpaşazāde (also İbn Kemāl), 6, 35, 36, 77, 113–14, 116, 150, 241, 250
Kerslake, Celia, 142
Kertbāy (Çerkez Ġāzī), 229–30
Keşfī (Meḥmed Çelebi): *Tārīḫ-i Sulṭān Selīm Ḫān*, 138, 141, 143, 147–48, 152, 154, 157, 163–64, 169, 173–74
al-Khulafāʾ al-rāshidūn (Rightly Guided Caliphs), 161, 220, 227, 234, 239, 250
Kili, 38, 40, 82, 113, 244
Ḳınālızāde ʿAlī Çelebi: *Aḫlaḳ-ı ʿalāʾī*, 182
Kiprovska, Mariya, 103
Ḳırḳkilīsā, 98
ḳıṣṣaḫān (story-reader), 118
Kitāb-ı müstetāb, 187, 191-93, 195
Kitāb meṣāliḥü'l-Müslimīn ve menāfiʿü'l-müʾminīn, 187
Kitāb-ı tevārīḫ-i Sulṭān Selīm, 161

Ḳıyāfetü'l-insāniyye fī şemā'ilü'l-'Os̱māniyye, 129
Ḳızıl Aḥmedli, 104
Ḳızılbaş, 10, 16, 86–87, 245. *See also* Şāhḳulu rebellion.
Ḳızıl Elma, 244–45
Knolles, Richard, 136–37
Koçi Beg, 191; *Risāle*, 187
Ḳoçi b. Ḫalīl Beg (governor), 149
Kolon, 244
Konya, 53
Köprülü, Mehmet Fuat, 118
Ḳorḳud, 18, 32, 44–45, 48, 53–54, 56, 59–60, 67, 70, 72, 139, 154, 170–71, 196, 221–22; *Da'wat al-nafs al-ṭāliḥa ilā al-a'māl al-ṣāliḥa*, 76, 178–80, 186; as described by Andrea Gritti, 62–63; and Egypt, 39, 47, 75–77, 79; execution of, 60, 78, 134–35, 173–74; and gubernatorial appointments, 33–35; and Ḫādım 'Alī Pasha, 33; and janissaries, 54, 75, 77–78, 171; and Qānṣūh al-Ghawrī, 33, 75–77; supporters of (pro-Ḳorḳud faction), 64–65, 75–78
Koron, 35
ḳul (slave-servant of the sultan), 86, 88–90
Kurds, 7
ḳut (personal fortune), 30, 216
Kütahya, 45, 200

al-Laḫmī, 'Alī b. Muḥammad: *al-Durru'l-mus̱ān fī sīratu'l-muẓaffar Selīm Ḫān*, 140, 143, 153, 154
Laṭīfī, 120
Levhī, 246
Lezze, Donado da, 136
Louis XIV, 19–20
Luṭfī Pasha, 3, 183–84, 189, 195, 197, 200, 209, 239, 241, 244; *Āṣafnāme*, 185, 187, 193–96, 205–6; *Khalāṣ al-umma fī ma'rifat al-a'imma*, 235; *Tevārīḫ-i āl-i 'Os̱mān*, 3–4, 193, 206–7, 236, 239–40

Maḥmūd (son of Bāyezīd II), 59
Maḥmūd Beg, 84
Malḳoç Muṣṭafā Beg, 94, 102
Malḳoçoğlu 'Alī Beg, 94
Malḳoçoğlu Bālī Beg, 94
Malḳoçoğlu family, 93–94, 101, 102, 103, 107
Malḳoçoğlu Ṭur 'Alī Beg, 94
Mamluks, 6, 7, 8, 33, 47, 59, 70, 75–77, 79, 113, 116, 132, 148–49, 210, 229–30, 235–36; defeat by Selīm I, 1, 3, 5, 10–11, 143, 147, 153–54, 207, 215–16, 227, 248
Manisa, 34, 44–45, 62, 77
Marj Dabik, 5, 10, 129, 143, 153, 230–31
Mecca, 1, 6–7, 11, 33, 230, 238, 244
meddāḥ (panegyrist), 118
Medina, 1, 6–7, 11, 230, 238, 244
Meḥmed (son of Prince Şehinşāh), 53, 59
Meḥmed Agha, 124
Meḥmed Çelebi: *Ḫızırnāme*, 220
Meḥmed I, 93, 96, 139, 234, 239–40
Meḥmed II, 3, 76, 94–97, 101, 115, 117, 141, 187, 221–22, 225, 233, 242–43, 248; and Bāyezīd II, 70; centralization strategies of, 7, 102–3, 106; and code of law, 30, 33, 134; and comparisons to Selīm in *naṣīḥatnāme* literature, 202–5; literary patronage of, 120; and patrimonialism, 66; and unigeniture, 30
Meḥmed III, 124, 126, 161–62, 183, 241, 243, 247–49; and fratricide, 30, 33
Meḥmed IV, 112, 195
Meḥmed Pasha, 94–95

Melik Dānişmend Ġāzī, 220
menāḳıb (religio-heroic literature), 116
menāḳıbnāme (religious epics), 118
Menavino, Giovanni Antonio, 136
Menemen, 77
Mengli Girāy, 39, 51, 79–81, 157–60, 162–63, 168, 172
Mengüç, Murat Cem, 113
Menteşe, 39, 58, 82
merdümzāde, 85–91
Mesīḥ Pasha, 136, 194
messianism, 10, 12, 14, 23, 25, 131, 211–16, 241–43, 244–48, 250, 256
Mevlānā ʿĪsā, 79, 245–46, 251–53; *Cāmiʿü'l-meknūnāt*, 90–91, 214
Mevlānā Maḥmūd, 232
Mevlānā Nūreddīn Ḥamza Ṣarugürz, 6, 38–39, 41
Mezö Kerésztés, 162, 241
Mıdıḳoğlu, 58
Midilli, 59
Mīḫāl Beg, 99–100, 102
Mīḫāloğlu family, 93, 99–102, 104, 107, 218
Mīḫāloġulları, 103
millennialism, 23, 131, 213, 241
Minnet Beg, 94
Minnetoğlu Ḳazġān Beg, 93
Mīrim Çelebi (Maḥmūd Efendi), 52, 74
mnemohistory, 17, 20, 253, 255, 256
Mohács, 241
Moin, Azfar, 212–13
Moldavia, 100
Mora, 41
Moravia, 94
Morea, 98
Moses, 124, 253
Moton, 35
Muʿālī: *Ḫünkārnāme*, 120
Müʾeyyedzāde ʿAbdürraḥmān Efendi, 52, 69, 73
Mughals, 13, 126, 182, 212–13, 215
Muḥammed Edāʾī: *Shāhnāma-ye Salīm Ḫānī*, 140, 142, 147, 150, 152, 154, 157, 163, 164, 170–71, 173–74
Muḥammed Girāy, 80–81, 158
Muḥyī: *Selīmnāme*, 140, 143
Muḥyīüddīn Çelebi, 55
Murād (son of Prince Aḥmed), 45, 47, 60
Murād I, 82
Murād II, 95–96, 101–2, 107, 128
Murād III, 124–26, 128–29, 136, 161–62, 185, 198, 203–4, 208, 218, 242, 247, 249; accession to throne of, 30; and commission of *Siyer-i Nebī*, 247; and fratricide, 30
Murād IV, 97, 143, 144, 191, 241
Mūsā (son of Bāyezīd I), 96
Mūsā (son of Prince Maḥmūd), 59
Mūsā Ḳalfa, 221–22
Muṣṭafā (son of Bāyezīd I), 95
Muṣṭafā (son of Murād I), 82
Muṣṭafā (son of Prince Murād), 60
Muṣṭafā (son of Süleymān I), 121, 145, 167
Muṣṭafā ʿAlī, 41, 44, 55, 122, 133–34, 183–85, 189, 204, 206, 208–9, 226, 237, 249; *Künhü'l-aḫbār*, 242; *Nuṣḥatü's-selāṭīn*, 187, 189, 197, 200–204, 237
Muṣṭafā Cenābī, 67–68; *Tārīḫ*, 138
Muṣṭafā I, 144
Muṣṭafā II, 111–12
Muṣṭafā Naʿīmā, 112–13, 129
Muṣṭafā Pasha, 52–53, 59, 73, 132
Muṣṭafā Ṣāfī: *Zübdetü't-tevārīḫ*, 237–38

al-Mutawakkil III, 235–36
naṣīḥatnāme genre, 23, 87, 127, 131, 180–207, 255; comparison of Selīm

naṣīḥatnāme genre (*continued*)
and Meḥmed II, 202, 204–5; comparison of Selīm and Süleymān I, 202, 205–7; influence of Persian works on, 181; intended audience of, 185–86, 195; milieu of authors, 184–85, 207–9; and patronage, 182, 185, 187; periods of production, 181–83; praise of Selīm, 186–202, 207–9; on Selīm as fearsome, 188–91; on Selīm and *ḳānūn*, 195–99, 208; on Selīm as meritocratic, 199–202; on Selīm and state secrets, 191–95
Nefʿī, 241
neseb (ancestral distinction), 90
Neşrī, 95, 114, 116
Niẓām al-Mulk: *Siyāsatnāma*, 181
niẓām-ı ʿālem (universal order), 30, 134–35, 174, 184, 188, 251
Noah, 124
Nora, Pierre, 21
Nūr ʿAlī Ḫalīfe, 53

Orḫān (son of Prince Maḥmūd), 59
Orḫān Beg, 99
ʿOs̱mān (son of Prince Aḥmed): and gubernatorial appointments, 34; execution of, 59, 60
ʿOs̱mān Beg, 99, 103, 218–19, 239–40
Osmancık, 34
ʿOs̱mānoġulları, 103
ʿOs̱mān II, 144, 184, 192, 195

Padre, 244
Palestine 3, 6, 11
Partner, Nancy, 252
Paşa Yigit Beg, 98
patrimonialism, 66, 69, 255
Peçevī İbrāhīm Efendi, 139
Peirce, Leslie, 230
Philip II, 212
Pīr ʿAlī of Aksaray, 245
Pīrī Meḥmed Pasha, 79, 132, 133–34, 147, 151, 191–94, 200–202, 205
Pleven, 100
Portuguese, 10–11, 76, 211–12, 244
Postel, Guillaume, 4
Prophet Muḥammad, 39, 112, 124, 147, 178, 204, 207, 217–23, 225, 227–30, 234, 239, 247, 250

Qānṣūh al-Ghawrī, 6, 155; and Ḳorḳud, 33, 75–77

Ramażānoġlu, 58, 74, 104
Reyḥānoġlu, 58, 74
Rhodes, 128, 226–27
Ridaniyya, 5, 10, 129, 143, 153, 210, 231
Rome, 245
Rūḥī, 113, 114, 116
Rumelia, 18, 35, 37–43, 44, 50–52, 54, 57, 61, 66, 69, 73, 78, 80–85, 91–95, 97–102, 104, 106–7, 147, 155, 157–58, 163–64, 166, 192
Rūmili begleri (Rumelian commanders), 82–85
Rūmili dilāverleri (Rumelian champions), 83, 164, 166
Rūmili sancaġı begleri (Rumelian governors), 83
Rüstem, 84
Rüstem Beg, 94

Saʿādet Girāy, 39, 40, 80, 158–59
Saʿdeddīn (Ḫoca Efendi), 41, 79, 124, 239, 249; *Selīmnāme*, 141, 150–51, 154, 159–63, 164, 165, 168, 227–28, 249–50; *Tācü't-tevārīḫ*, 239, 249

Saᶜdī b. ᶜAbdü'l-müteᶜāl: *Selīmnāme*, 141, 154, 157, 160, 163–64, 172, 174
Safavids, 4–8, 10, 13, 15, 23, 25, 34–37, 48, 56, 59, 64, 70, 72, 75, 79, 87, 100, 119, 121, 126, 131–32, 147, 156, 171, 182, 209, 211–15, 224, 237–38, 240, 245–46, 256; defeat by Selīm I, 1, 3, 11, 35, 143, 153, 154, 207, 216, 227, 248. *See also* Çaldıran, Battle of.
Şahin, Kaya, 13, 168
Şāhḳulu rebellion, 34–35, 43–48, 64, 72, 83, 166, 168, 170–71, 245
Sāʾī Muṣṭafā Çelebi, 241
Ṣaltuḳnāme, 118
Sam, 230–31, 232
Şarābdār Muṣṭafā Çelebi, 49, 50
Sarāc-ili, 95
Saruhan, 33
Sassanians, 119
sebeb-i teʾlīf (reason for composition), 114, 149, 167
Şebinkarahisar, 34
Şehdī, 120
Şehinşāh (son of Bāyezīd II), 45, 51, 53, 59
Şehnāme, 120–27, 141; audience for, 122–25
şehnāmeci (court historiographer), 116–27; and demise of post, 125–27
şehnāmegūy (*şehnāme* performer), 118
şehnāmeḫān (*şehnāme* reciter), 118
Şehnāme-i Türkī, 119, 246, 255
Şehsüvāroğlu, 58
Şehsüvāroğlu ᶜAlī Beg, 148–49
Selanik, 44, 96
Selānikī Muṣṭafā Efendi, 68, 241
Selīm I, 128, 154, 248; accession to throne of, 18, 23, 32, 40, 54–56, 64, 66–68, 98, 146, 152–53, 155–56, 165, 168–72, 176, 220, 222, 224; appointment as *serdār* of the imperial army, 54, 77; association with the Prophet Muḥammad, 204, 207, 222, 227–30; as *ᶜazīz-i Mıṣr* (Prince of Egypt), 206, 237; and bureaucratic consolidation, 8–9; and Crimea, 18, 37–39, 40, 51, 61, 79–82, 83, 155–63, 172; criticism of, 57, 138, 151–52, 172, 189–91; death of, 1, 2, 143; depicted as a dragon-slayer, 223–24; described by Andrea Gritti, 62–63; execution of brothers and nephews, 14, 59–60, 78, 134–36, 147, 155, 162, 173–75; execution of janissary officer and member of cavalry, 68; execution of scholars, 152; execution of sons, 4, 188–89; execution of subjects and servants, 188, 190; execution of viziers and statesmen, 2, 59, 132–34, 149, 152, 188–89, 191, 250; as *fātiḥ-i memālik-i ᶜArab-ü-ᶜAcem* (Conqueror of Arab Lands and Persia), 241; as *ġazā ḳılıcı* (Sword of Holy War), 241; called ultimate *ġāzī* (Warrior of Faith), 1; and gubernatorial appointments, 3, 18, 35, 38–39, 41–42, 48, 82, 87, 147, 154–56; as *ḫādimü'l-ḥarameyn* (Servitor of the Two Sacred Cities), 1, 10, 201, 206, 237; as *ḫalīfe* (Caliph), 215, 236–38; as *ḫilāfet-serīrüñ şāhı* (Shāh on the Throne of the Caliphate), 236; incorporation of those loyal to rivals, 68–69, 73; as *İskender-i s̱ānī* (Second Alexander), 236; and Islam, 1, 6, 9–11, 14, 154, 176, 215, 232–33, 238–41, 248, 250; and janissaries, 2, 5, 24, 52–55, 57, 59, 64, 66–69, 77–78, 106, 134, 144, 166, 169–72, 174, 190, 198–99; as *ḳānūn-*

Selīm (*continued*)
conscious in *naṣīḥatnāme* literature, 195–99, 208; as *khalīfat Allāh* (Caliph of God), 234; as *ḳudret-i ilāhī* (Divine Force), 215, 236; as *mehdī* (Messiah), 1, 215; as *mehdī-yi āḫir-i zamān* (Messiah of the Last Age), 215, 236, 241, 246; military victories of, 1, 3, 5–6, 10–11, 129, 211; as *muʾayyad min Allāh* (Succored by God), 11, 210, 215; as *müceddid* (Renewer of Religion), 1, 161, 207, 215, 238–41, 250; portrayed as mournful brother, 134–35; prologue to *Ḳānūnnāme-i Nigbolu*, 11, 210–11, 243–44; reign foretold by saints, 230–33; and Rumelia, 18, 34–35, 37–43, 50–51, 54, 61, 66, 80–85, 91–101, 106–7, 155, 157–58, 163–64, 166; and the Safavids, 1, 3–8, 10, 11, 35–37, 48, 56, 100, 143, 147, 153–54, 156, 171, 207, 211, 216, 227; as *ṣāḥib-ḳırān* (Master of the Auspicious Conjunction), 1, 11, 12, 206, 210, 215, 237, 241, 243, 244; as *ṣāḥib-ḳırān-ı ʿālem* (universal *ṣāḥib-ḳırān*), 242; as *ṣāḥib-ḳırān-ı ʿaṣrī* (*ṣāḥib-ḳırān* of the Age), 165, 242; as *server-i devrān* (Lord of the Age), 207, 241; as *server-i ṣāḥib-ḳırān* (foremost *ṣāḥib-ḳırān*), 242; as *seyf-i āl-i ʿOs̱mān* (Sword of the House of ʿOs̱mān), 241; as *seyfüʾl-İslām* (Sword of Islam), 241; supporters at his father's court, 78–79; supporters of (pro-Selīm faction), 36, 54, 78–107, 147, 151, 164, 167, 170; territorial expansion, 1, 3, 5–6, 8, 10, 14, 211; as *yāvuz* (the Grim), 2–3, 15, 140, 145, 199; as *ẓıll-Allāh* (Shadow of God), 1, 11, 210, 215, 237; as *Ẕūʾl-ḳarneyn* (Possessor of the Two Horns), 215

Selīm II, 68, 128, 145, 167–68

Selīmnāme, 22, 32, 61, 66, 70, 79, 85, 130–31, 140–43, 208, 255; adaptation of *Shāhnāma* genre, 141; authorship, 146–47; on the Battle of Çorlu, 163–68; classification as literary or historical, 142–43; criticism of Selīm within, 151–52; differences among, 153; in Ottoman Turkish, 141–42; patronage, 145–50, 167; on Selīm's collaboration with the Tatars, 155–60; on Selīm's removal of rivals, 173–75; on Selīm's rise to the throne, 153–75; textual interdependency among, 150–52; waves of production, 143–45, 163; written by supporters of Aḥmed, 148

Seljukid, 118

Seljuks, 119

Semendire, 41, 42

Senāʾī: *Süleymānnāme*, 246

Serez, 44

Şerīf b. Seyyid Muḥammed (also Şerīfī): *Tercüme-i miftāḥ-ı cifrüʾl-cāmiʿ*, 248

Severin, 95

Seyyid Baṭṭāl Ġāzī, 220–21, 225

Seyyid Emīr Ṣadreddīn Meḥmed, 146

Seyyid Kemāl, 222–24

Seyyid Loḳmān, 122, 129

Shāhnāma, 116–27. *See also* Firdawsī.

Shīʿī Islam, 6, 10, 35, 224; Twelver Shīʿism, 10, 240. *See also* Sunnī-Shīʿite rift.

Silāḥdār Meḥmed Agha: *Nuṣretnāme*, 111–12

Silistre, 39, 82
Sinān Agha, 135
Sinān Pasha, 96
Sinop, 93
Şīrī ʿAlī: *Tārīḫ-i Feth-i Mısr*, 140–43, 148, 154, 157, 165, 172–74
Sivas, 46, 221
Siyavuş Pasha, 124
Siyer-i Nebī, 247
Sofya, 44
Sokullu Meḥmed Pasha, 68
Ṣolaḳzāde (Meḥmed Hemdemī Çelebi), 38, 48, 78; *Tārīḫ-i āl-i ʿOsmān*, 134–35
Solomon (Biblical king), 184, 204
Spain, 244
Spandugino, Theodoro, 136
Spiegel, Gabrielle, 22
Şücāʿ (also Şücāʿ Dede), 247
Sucūdī, 147; *Selīmnāme*, 141, 143, 154, 164, 165, 173, 174
Şükrī-i Bidlīsī: *Fütuḥāt-ı Selīmiyye* (also *Selīmnāme*), 136, 137, 141, 142, 144, 146, 148–50, 154, 158, 159, 160, 163, 164, 165, 169–70, 173, 174
Süleymān (son of Bāyezīd I), 117
Süleymān I, 3–4, 6, 8, 31, 59, 82, 85–87, 90, 95, 98, 100, 104, 121, 127–30, 131, 137, 143, 147, 149, 151, 163, 183, 185, 187, 189–90, 193, 195–96, 202, 208–9, 214–15, 232–33, 235–36, 240, 243, 247, 252; comparisons to Selīm I in *naṣīḥatnāme* literature, 202, 205–7; death of, 68, 168; execution of sons, 121, 167; and gubernatorial appointments, 34–35, 37–38, 81, 157; as heir presumptive, 4; internecine struggle of sons, 24, 30; as *Ḳānūnī* (Lawgiver), 2, 31, 186; as "the Magnificent," 2, 5, 188; as *müceddid*, *ṣāḥib-ḳırān*, or *mehdī*, 244–46; and patrimonialism, 66; and patronage of historians, 116, 118, 121–24, 144–46, 167; reign as Ottoman "golden age," 15, 186–87, 255; as *ṣāḥib-ḳırān* (Master of the Auspicious Conjunction), 245–46; as *ṣāḥib-ḳırān ve mehdī-yi āḫir-i zamān* (*ṣāḥib-ḳırān* and Messiah of the End of Time), 246; as *ṣāḥib-zamān* ([Spiritual] Master of the Age), 246; as "Succored by God," 242
Süleymān Çelebi, 96
Sunnī Islam, 5, 6, 9–10, 14–16, 24, 47, 154, 211, 224, 232, 235, 239–40
Sunnī-Shīʿite rift, 23
Syria, 1, 3, 6, 8–9, 11, 155, 231, 233, 236
Szigetvár, 68, 128

Tabriz, 128, 151
Tāceddīn Beg, 58, 74
Tācīzāde Caʿfer Çelebi, 52, 69, 73, 132, 148, 151–52, 173
Tahmāsb I, 121, 245
tanistry, 31
Tansel, Selâhattin, 51, 58, 65
Tārīḫ-i Sulṭān Selīm Ḫān, 141
Taşili, 58
Ṭaşköprīzāde Aḥmed Efendi: *Al-Şaḳāʾiḳ al-nuʿmāniyya fī ʿulamā al-dawlat al-ʿOsmāniyya*, 189–90
Teke, 33, 35, 43–44, 59, 64
Tezcan, Baki, 124–26
Thessaly, 99
Thrace, 39, 168, 244
al-Tikriti, Nabil, 76
timariot (also *tīmārlı sipāhī*), 7, 45
Tīmūr, 11, 94, 96, 240, 242

"Timurid débâcle," 139
Ṭomār-ı hümāyūn, 124
Trabzon, 18, 35, 37–39, 48–49, 60, 82–83, 87, 147, 154–56
Transoxiana, 240
Transylvania, 100, 162
Tūġī Çelebi, 144
Ṭūmānbāy, 6, 155, 210, 229
Ṭuraḫān Beg, 95, 98–99, 102
Ṭuraḫānoġlu family, 93, 98–99, 101, 103–4, 107
Ṭuraḫānoġlu Ḥasan Beg, 99
Ṭuraḫānoġlu Ḫıżır Beg, 98–99
Ṭuraḫānoġlu İdrīs Beg, 98–99
Ṭuraḫānoġlu ʿÖmer Beg, 98–99
Turan, Şerafettin, 24
Turanians, 119
Turco-Mongolian political tradition, 29, 31, 216
Ṭurġud, 74
Ṭurġudoġlu, 58, 74
Ṭursun Beg: *Tārīḫ-i ebū'l-fetḥ*, 117

uc begi (frontier lord), 19, 93, 99, 101–6, 218, 255
Uğur, Ahmet, 58
Uluçay, Çağatay, 65
Umayyad, 220, 234
unigeniture, 14, 30–33
Uruç Beg, 94
Üsküb, 98, 99
Üsküdar, 52
"Ustarabi," 136

vaḳʿanüvīs (imperial annalist), 113, 129
Varsaḳ, 74
Venice/Venetian, 32, 49, 60–66, 104, 136
Veysī, 185; *Ḫābnāme*, 184
Vidin, 41
Vienna, 128, 245
voyvoda, 92
Vulçitrin, 98

Woodhead, Christine, 120, 125–26, 145

Yaḫşī Beg, 84
Yaḫşı Faḳīh: *Menāḳıb-ı āl-i ʿOs̱mān*, 116–17
Yaḥyā Beg, 245
Yaḥyā Pasha, 94
Yaʿḳūb Çelebi, 139
Yanya, 96
Yazıcıoğlu Aḥmed Bī-cān: *Dürr-i meknūn*, 213–14
Yenibahçe, 54–55
Yenişehir, 60, 134
Yeñīşehr-i Fenār, 99
Yerasimos, Stéphane, 213
Yularḳaṣdı Sinān Pasha, 52–53, 171–72
Yūnus Agha, 79
Yūnus Pasha, 57, 69, 73, 132–33
Yürekli, Zeynep, 104
Yūsuf (Çerkesler Kātibi): *Selīmnāme*, 141, 144, 150
Yūsuf b. ʿAbdullāh, 56

Zağra-i Atik (also Zağra Eskisi), 43, 48, 96
Zağra Yenicesi, 44
Zenbīlli ʿAlī Efendi, 190
Zübdetü't-tevārīḫ, 124–25, 129

H. ERDEM ÇIPA is Assistant Professor of Ottoman History at the University of Michigan, Ann Arbor. He is author of *Yavuz'un Kavgası: I. Selim'in Saltanat Mücadelesi* and co-editor, with Emine Fetvacı, of *Writing History at the Ottoman Court: Editing the Past, Fashioning the Future* (IUP, 2013). The primary focus of his work is the history and historiography of the Ottoman Empire, with a specific emphasis on dissident movements and succession struggles. He is also interested in issues related to the socioeconomic history of the Ottoman Empire within the larger framework of military-agrarian societies of the late Middle Ages and the early modern era.